Y0-DKO-319

Ballad of the Bible

Written By George F. Haveman

George F. Haveman (signature)

Copyright © 1992 by George F. Haveman
Library of Congress Cataloge Card Number: 91-92230
ISBN: 0-9630663-0-7

INTRODUCTION

I'm not explaining scripture
'Cause I only mean to show
There are stories in the Bible
That every one should know.

Nor do I take the credit
For the messages of these pages
Because I'm sure 'twas planned
By the Lord of all the ages.

I have no slightest hope
That this will tell it all
And that is not the plan
Nor do I feel the call.

But I'll tell just a little
Of those days of old
Of people who were timid
Of some who were so bold.

You'll meet those people here
Like some you've loved or known,
And it may seem their problems
Should long ago have flown.

But what surprised me most
And adds to their mystique,
Those who gained such fame
Were just plain folks like me.

George F. Haveman

TABLE OF CONTENTS

GENESIS

CHAPTER 1

We're told earth was shape-
less, that it had no form.
The darkness of the void
Had for eons been the norm.

Then said our God Jehovah,
"Let there now be light."
And that was the last of
Eternal night.

He separated the water
From stuff we call land.
He formed all creatures
And then He made man.

And though we were last
We were not least, for
He made us superior to
Every creature and beast.

Of the wisdom of this
I'm not always sure,
Because our use of power
Is seldom very pure.

CHAPTER 2

But every thing He did we
Are sure is for the best.
Including six days to work,
The seventh one to rest.

He placed Adam in Eden,
Then gave him a wife.
Eve was his helpmate,
Who led him to strife.

Of all the food and
Fruit that grew there,
They'd eat as they needed,
The work they would share.

Of the tree of knowledge
They must not partake.
This they were warned
Would be a fatal mistake.

CHAPTER 3

Then Satan as a serpent
Came slithering along.
And he convinced Eve
That God had been wrong.

So she ate of the fruit
And passed it around.
Then poor Adam weakened
And soon ran aground.

Now the fruit they ate
Soon wised them up some.
They noticed real quick
The wrong they had done.

Soon they were banished
From Eden their home
And cast into the world
To wander and roam.

So this is the story
Of Adam and of Eve.
If you read the Bible
For them you may grieve.

For they were just folk
Like you and like me.
They weren't very wise,
That's plain to see.

CHAPTER 4

Cain was the first born
Who came into their life,
And with brother Abel
He practiced much strife.

As they were working
In the field one day,
Cain rose up in wrath
And his brother did slay.

And so he was banished
From the land of his birth,
To be a fugitive forever
From joy on this earth.

CHAPTER 5

We have all read the gen-
eology of Adam, when it
Came to descendants those
Folks really had `em.

CHAPTER 6

Now a population explos-
ion took place on earth.
And people were involved
More in sin than in worth.

As the Lord looked down
On the world grown so bad,
He felt that by man he'd
Most certainly been had.

So He decided He must
Cleanse the earth. He'd
Destroy all those people
So sinful since birth.

There was a family who
Were running life's race,
Who did only their best
As they kept up the pace.

For they knew that God
Was mighty and just.
To be honest and true
Was an absolute must.

It was headed by Noah
Who'd raised his boys,

To trust in the Lord
Through sorrow or joy.

Sons Shem and Ham
Were two of these,
And Japheth, another,
Made a total of three.

Now God in His sorrow
Meant for Noah to live.
So these instructions
To him He would give.

It was certain that they
Must build a mighty boat
To house all the animals,
Cattle, sheep and goats.

The ark was built with
Great strength, seventy
Five feet wide, four
Hundred fifty in length.

With a door in the side
Forty-five feet high
With stalls for animals
And windows for light.

It was wide and
It was tall
In fact it was a full
Three stories in all.

It must have been a very
Imposing sight
On which they labored
From morning till night.

CHAPTER 7

With room for each pair
Of every kind of beast,
And Noah and his families
Were last but not least.

Forty days and nights
It rained upon the earth.

The ark rode on the flood
Proved worthy of the work.

CHAPTER 8

Water covered earth for a
Hundred fifty days. Folks
Who'd laughed at Noah
With their lives now paid.

Three months it took for
Mountains to reappear.
When they left the ark
It had been half a year.

CHAPTER 9

God blessed old Noah and
All of his family.
He led them from the ark
To start a family tree.

He showed them the rainbow
In its splendorous attire;
He swore not to flood again
But cleanse earth with fire!

So those folk all did
As the Lord had bid them do.
They repopulated earth
With more than just a few.

Then Noah became a farmer
And raised so many grapes;
That he became quite drunk
On the wine he'd made.

Then Ham saw his nakedness
As in his tent he lay
And tattled to his brothers
But learned it didn't pay.

For when Noah sobered up
To what his son had done,
He cursed Ham's descendants
And favored the other ones.

Old Noah lived on earth
Nine hundred-fifty years
Then finally crossed over
And left this vale of tears.

CHAPTER 10

So each family grew
Till it became a tribe
And then grew into nations
As they swiftly multiplied.

CHAPTER 11

Soon they got so arrogant
As their numbers grew,
Their brilliance was assured,
So they'd do something new.

They built a beautiful tower,
Up toward Heaven so high.
God looked down on them,
And He sadly sighed.

Because He knew they
Were headed for a fall,
So He must stop this
Before He lost them all!

So He confused them as He
Gave them many tongues;
They could not communicate
From the oldest to the young.

Now this scattered men
On the surface of the earth,
Thus they were shown by God,
They were not of royal birth.

Now we read of Abram, his
Half-sister became his wife.
Now Abram was timid and
Feared for his life.

CHAPTER 12

God appeared to him and said,
"Leave all this behind, if

You travel where I tell you,
Great fortune you will find.

As you go on your journey
I'll be there all the way,
You'll be a blessing to
Others, if you do as I say."

Now as they visited with
The kings across the land,
Abe called Sarai, "sister,"
He feared to be her man.

When a palace guard saw her
He praised her to the king.
Pharaoh put her in a harem
Gave Abram gifts and things.

God plagued Pharaoh's house
Because Sarai was there. So
Pharaoh chided Abe and said,
"You lied, that's not fair.

Now take your wife and go,
For here you may not stay.
I'll send my army too, to
Make sure you stay away."

CHAPTER 13

Abram and his nephew Lot
Went to the Negeb and Bethel.
They both were very rich
And good friends as well.

Abram journeyed north where
He'd been in days gone by
Set an altar to worship God
As he gazed toward the sky.

Now Lot was very wealthy
With cattle and servants
Too, so as time went by the
Herdsmen began to feud.

So they agreed to separate
And each would go his way.
Lot chose fertile Jordan,
But in Caanan Abe would stay.

Then God said to Abram,
"Look, as far as you can see;
All this land I'll give you,
A gift to you from me."

So Abram moved to Hebron
And built an altar there,
A place to praise Jehovah
In thankful song and prayer.

CHAPTER 14

Of course, as time went on
Great wars filled the land.
Lot was captured with goods
And servants every man.

So Abram gathered his army
And went and rescued Lot.
He soon became so famous
That he could call the shots.

In a vision in his sleep
God came to him again
And promised many wonders
Would happen to His man.

God promised him a life
Of great length and beauty.
To father great nations
Had now become his duty.

He would be successful
In all he wanted done,
And Sarai and himself
Were going to have a son.

His children would be slaves
For four hundred years. But
He'd live to a ripe old age
And die without a fear.

CHAPTER 15

Now this pair of folk
Had not borne child one.
So naturally they thought
God must be making fun.

CHAPTER 16

Of course Abram had a son
By Hagar, Sarai's maid.
But to have one legally
Would never be the same.

CHAPTER 17

Yet God had promised,
And Abe was ninety-nine.
"I'm ninety," Sarai laughed,
"My husband's past his time."

God named him "Abraham,"
For "Father of the Nations."
She was "Sarah," ("Princess,")
For a son made preparation.

CHAPTER 18

Now Sodom and Gomorrah's
Destruction was slated;
But Abraham pleaded with the
Lord whose anger was abated.

CHAPTER 19

So Lot was led away by angels
And with family urged to flee.
His wife was turned to salt
When she turned back to see!

Lot moved to the town of Zoar,
But soon in fear left there.
Back across the plain smoke
And flames still flared.

Abe had saved his nephew
Again in troubled times. Lot

Was in a cave with daughters
Who seduced him with wine.

CHAPTER 20

Now Abraham made his home
Between Kadesh and Shur.
King Abimelech heard of Sarah
And he soon sent for her.

Because once again Abraham
Who still feared for his life,
Had called Sarah "sister,"
Rather than risk her as wife.

But the king had a dream
As he slumbered one night.
God said, "Do not touch her."
Which gave him quite a fright.

Next day he summoned
   Abraham
And called him on the carpet,
Because Abraham was wrong in
Putting Sarah on the market.

And once again Abraham
Was forced to explain why,
Instead of being truthful
Had chosen to tell a lie.

Now Abe, who was a prophet,
Went to God again to press,
For relief for his friends
From a curse of barrenness.

King Abimelech could see
Abraham lived in grace.
So he made a pact with Abe
To keep him in that place.

CHAPTER 21

Then God kept his promise,
And Sarah had a son. If a

Child was ever favored
Then Isaac was the one.

Now Sarah who was jealous,
As most folks seem to be,
Made Abe send Hagar and
Son to wonder aimlessly.

Now things seemed hopeless,
She could not help herself.
She laid Ishmael under a bush
And God's angel came to help.

He showed her fresh water as
It gushed from out a well.
Ishmael grew tall and strong
As in wilderness they dwelt.

CHAPTER 22

Of course we know how Isaac
Was ordered to be sacrificed;
And how Abe passed that test
Will make us all think twice.

CHAPTER 23

In time Sarah grew old
And went to her reward.
Abe, a stranger in the land,
Was still favored by the Lord.

Then people of the land
Sold Abe the property,
Where he could bury Sarah
With silver as the fee.

CHAPTER 24

Now as Abraham grew older,
God blessed him every way.
Abe called a trusted servant
To come to him one day.

He sent him on a mission
To find his son a wife.

God led him to Rebekah
With very little strife.

Rebekah left her family
And traveled by caravan, in
The distance she saw Isaac,
Who was to be her man.

And so the two did marry
And lived on happily.
But Isaac's age was sixty
Before they had a family.

CHAPTER 25

Now Abe was old and weary
And nearing the end of life.
For he'd had another family
With Keturah, his new wife.

So he gave gifts to many sons
And sent them to the east.
He then turned back to Isaac
For his final feast.

Sadly Ishmael and Isaac
Buried Abraham one day. He
Was laid to rest in the cave
Where his beloved Sarah lay.

Ishmael grew older,
And one day he too, died.
Those he left behind often
Fought within their tribes.

So it was up to Isaac
To raise the family tree.
The problems that he had
Were quite a thing to see.

Now Rebekah suffered greatly
With the twins she carried.
And so she must have
  wondered
Why she'd ever married!

One day she asked Jehovah
Why she should be in pain.
He said her sons would vary
As the sunshine does to rain.

In time Esau became a hunter
And how he loved to roam,
While Jacob was the quiet one
Who preferred to stay at home.

Jacob was his mother's pet,
His brother was often away.
So Jacob traded some stew
For Esau's rights one day.

He'd come home so hungry
He was tired and faint,
So he traded his birthright
To Jacob, who was no saint.

Esau was the careless type
So it didn't bother him.
He must have known in time
It would cause a crimp.

CHAPTER 26

Now Isaac moved away, for
A famine gripped this land.
He thought to go to Egypt,
There to make his stand.

He stopped off in Gerar,
Ruled by a Philistine King.
Then God said, "Stay here,
I'll help in everything."

Now Isaac made the mistake
That his father had before,
Calling his wife, "sister,"
And fouling up the score.

He might have known the
Truth would surely out,
Then the King wised up
With an angry shout.

Isaac really talked then
And got in good grace.
Isaac's crops grew tall as
He got rich in that place.

The Philistines grew jealous,
Filled his wells and fussed,
And said, "Go leave this land,
You're much too rich for us."

As he camped in Beer-sheba,
God came to him one night;
So he built an altar there
To worship as he felt right.

Now King Abimelech
Wanted him to sign a pact.
Isaac had grown so powerful
The king now feared the axe.

Isaac's herds and flocks had
Multiplied and crops as well.
He had all that he could use,
And there was much to sell.

So he threw a banquet for
The king and all his friends
And all made solemn oaths
Of friendship to the end.

When the party was over, and
His friends had gone home,
They dug a brand new well
Which he named, "The Oath."

Then Esau married
A couple of Hethite maids,
And Rebekah and Isaac
Were mighty near enraged.

CHAPTER 27

Days stretched into months,
The months became long years,
Until Isaac knew in time,
That he'd not long be here.

Soon the day must come
When Isaac would retire,
So now he called in Esau
Before he could expire.

But Jacob and his mother
Got their plans arranged.
They pulled a fast one, so
Some things were changed.

Esau came for his blessing
To learn of his great loss.
Fearing his brother's rage,
Jacob soon got lost.

CHAPTER 28

So Jacob left in haste to
Visit his uncle in Haran.
He soon got weary as in
Headlong flight he ran.

His pillow was a rock that
Night as he bedded down,
And for a softer mattress
He used the solid ground.

But he was very tired, and
As he slumbered there,
He saw a golden ladder
With angels on the stairs.

God stood at the top and
Stretched forth His hand
Saying, "Jacob, I'll bless,
And give you this land.

I'll go with you always,
As you journey through life,
Protecting you from enemies
And I'll ease your strife."

Jacob awoke and promised,
That he would give a tithe

Of all that he would earn,
Throughout his future life.

CHAPTER 29

As Jacob traveled eastward
He came upon a well with
Rachel tending flocks where
Her father Laban dwelt.

So he moved a rock to let
The flocks all water. Then
He kissed sweet Rachel, who
Was his uncle's daughter.

Then Jacob stuck around
And was a useful man,
Till Laban offered him
A full employment plan.

Jacob worked for Rachel,
He labored seven years, to
Learn he'd been tricked
And was angered unto tears.

Seven years became fourteen
Just for the girl he wanted.
But he was deeply in love,
So by work was not daunted.

CHAPTER 30

Now it became a contest
Between Jacob's wives,
Each wanted many children
To brighten up their lives.

So Rachel and Leah must
Have kept him well spent,
As they kept urging him
To move from tent to tent.

And so as time went on
His family multiplied.
He had eleven sons who
Were his joy and pride.

Jacob wished to leave;
Laban wanted him to stay.
Help was badly needed
Though he'd get no pay.

Jacob was a clever man,
Not averse to subterfuge.
Thus he built his flocks
So they became quite huge.

CHAPTER 31

The truth soon would out
Because Laban was no fool.
Suspicion began to mount,
So their friendship cooled.

As tempers began to flare
Folks complained and moaned,
Jacob often remembered
Happier days back home.

So Jacob and his families
All took off in flight;
Rachel stole Laban's jewels,
She thought she had a right.

Angered, Laban catching up
Searched the camp for loot,
But all the stolen stuff
Was in her saddle boot.

CHAPTER 32

So Jacob and his household
All hit the trail again.
But Jake was still uneasy
For he'd been a tricky man.

So he sent gifts to Esau
And stayed behind in camp.
He seemed to spend the night
Wrestling with a man.

Now Jacob was tenacious
And he would not give in,

Till smitten on the hip
So hard he couldn't win.

His opponent blessed Jake
And told him not to fear.
God would still be with him
As He had for years.

Then Jacob trembled greatly
When he suddenly realized,
That it was his maker he'd
Wrestled with all night.

He named the place "Peniel,"
Meaning, "The Face of God,"
For he sincerely believed
That this was hallowed sod.

CHAPTER 33

In the distance Jacob saw
His brother Esau coming,
Now should he stay? Or
Leave that place arunning?

But Esau met him joyfully
And welcomed him back home.
His journey now was over
So he could cease to roam.

From the family of Hamor
Jacob bought a place to live.
Then built an Altar to God
Where many thanks he'd give.

CHAPTER 34

He'd had a daughter by Leah
Who was lovely to look upon.
Schechem was young and lusty,
Hamor's spoiled and only son.

So when he spotted Dinah he
Thought nothing of disgrace.
So he took and raped her
And suffered a loss of face.

Now when her brothers heard,
They were mighty angry boys.
So listening to his excuses,
They were only playing coy.

They said he could marry
Her, if she'd be his bride;
But he and all his kingdom
Must first be circumcised.

The third day after that
They were still so tender,
No man could raise a sword,
So they had no defenders.

Jacob's sons murdered them,
While helpless rendered
Taking women and possessions,
They accepted no surrender.

CHAPTER 35

Now God was still with Jacob
As he had promised to be,
And caused terror in the land
Through which they'd flee.

Toward the land of Canaan
They journeyed on and on.
And when they reached Bethel
He built an altar to God.

Then old nurse Deborah died
And was laid to rest. She
Was Rebekah's servant who
Had always done her best.

She was buried under an oak
In the valley below Bethel
Amid sadness and weeping-
For they loved her well.

Now once again Jacob
Was spoken to by God.
And so he felt for sure
Bethel was Holy sod.

So he built an altar there;
He made it out of rocks.
Then he named that place,
"Bethel, the House of God."

Then God changed his name,
It would now be, "Israel."
Because he was so faithful,
With God he would prevail.

"You will father a nation,
Descendants will be kings,
You will have your father's
Land and many other things."

Now they forged ahead as
They went toward Bethehem,
Jacob and his families, the
Women, children and men.

Rachel was expecting,
As we would say today,
But they must travel on
For the goal was far away.

Now the pain got greater
While there upon the trail,
Rachel breathed her last
As they heard a baby wail.

She named him, "Ben-Oni,"
Meaning "Son of my sorrow."
Jacob named him "Benjamin,"
"My right hand tomorrow."

It would seem that Isaac
Had waited all those days
For his beloved son Jacob
To travel back that way.

He'd lived for 180 years,
It came his time to leave.
So Esau and Jacob
Buried him and grieved.

CHAPTER 36

And now Esau moved from
The land of Canaan, be-
cause with Jake's return
They were short of land.

And as God had promised,
Their people, multiplied.
First were only families
Who then grew to tribes.

Each tribe multiplied
Till it became a clan.
And as time went on laid
Claims upon the land.

CHAPTER 37

Jacob settled in Canaan.
Here Isaac had lived before.
He had many sons who now
Would help with chores.

Joseph was his favorite son
Who now was seventeen.
He always told the truth,
The facts he'd not demean.

When his father gave him
A coat of many colors,
He became unpopular as he
Showed it to his brothers.

Then, when in dreams, his
Brothers paid obeisance,
It was to be expected they
Would feel a grievance.

Then as his brothers
Tended flocks near Shechem,
Jacob sent young Joseph
To get facts and fetch `em.

So he was Shechem bound as
He left the Hebron valley,

Only to learn his brothers
Had moved to another alley.

His brothers spied him
While he was yet far off,
But with sinister thoughts
Where they'd only scoffed.

They'd've killed him, but
Put him in a well instead.
They planned to leave him
Until he was quite dead.

As they sat down to eat
They saw a caravan,
So they pulled Joseph up
And sold him to a man.

Reuben meant to save him
When the chance arrived
But sold him as a slave
So he'd still be alive.

To Jacob it looked bad be-
cause they killed a goat
And splattered it's blood
On Joseph's beautiful coat.

By circumstantial evidence,
And they also lied,
Poor Jacob was convinced
His favorite son had died.

For they made it look
That he had fallen prey
To some vicious animal
As he was on his way.

In the meantime his new
Owners traveled far and
Sold Joseph into Egypt
To Pharaoh's palace guard.

CHAPTER 38

Meantime: back in Hebron
Judah looked around, then

Married a Canaanite girl
And moved to Chezib town.

Er, Onan and Sheilah were
The sons they had. It soon
Became quite obvious that
Er was just plain bad.

Now according to custom,
Quite common in that day,
Judah planned for a friend
To give his daughter away.

So it was cut and dried
For Tamar to marry Er.
So she took him even then
For better or for worse.

We know not what he did,
The Bible doesn't say, but
It must have been real bad
For he threw his life away.

This left Onan to inherit
His older brother's wife.
Yet in his inner mind this
Caused a certain strife,

Because the heir he sired
Would not be his own.
So he was very careful
His seed was never sown.

Of course God was angry
Because Onan's duty was
To raise up Er an heir
In that land of beauty.

So after ample time to
Do the job as sent to do,
God gave up on Onan
And did him in, too.

Now the job was Shelah's
Who was still too young.

But Judah promised Tamar
She'd get his living son.

But Judah meant his word
To never be fulfilled;
He feared his youngest
Might also end up killed.

And so as time went on
Judah ignored the fact,
Tamar still was waiting
For Shelah's promised act.

Shelah grew to manhood
And then his mother died.
Judah was now a widower
And Tamar knew he'd lied.

So Tamar stacked the deck,
Tricking Judah into doing
The thing she wanted done
Without the extra wooing.

Judah heard by others
That Tamar was expecting.
He promptly condemned her
Wasting no time checking.

But she soon proved to him
He was the only one who
Could have fathered twins,
And that they were his sons.

So Judah finally admitted
He certainly had been wrong.
But he never married Tamar
Who'd waited so very long.

CHAPTER 39

Now Joseph, while in Egypt,
Didn't really have it hard.
His owner, Captain Potiphar,
Was the king's own bodyguard.

God walked with Joseph
And blessed him everyday. So

Potiphar put him in charge
And let him have his way.

And everything he touched
Turned into gold or good;
With great love and honesty
Was just where Joseph stood.

CHAPTER 40

Joe was young and handsome
And stood tall and straight.
So it was only natural the
Girls would think him great.

Of course the boss' wife
Started giving him the eye.
But his morals offended her
So she told a whopping lie.

Potiphar heard her story,
And got mad as he could be;
Tossed Joseph into prison
And threw away the key.

Joe was kept in jail for
Quite a lengthy season,
Though his being there
Lacked in rhyme or reason.

Of course God went with him
As you might know He would
And changed Joe's bad luck
Into something good.

One day he was joined, while
He was there in prison,
By a winetaster and a baker
Who improved his condition.

They spent time together
As Joseph catered to them.
So they learned to trust him
Because he loved all men.

One day they were worried
By the dreams they'd had.

Hoping the dreams were good,
Fearing they might be bad.

So they told their dreams
As Joseph listened there.
God was still with Joe
And His wisdom shared.

So Joseph's interpretation
Proved true in three days,
One went back to work,
With life the other paid.

But as we might guess, he
Who lived and prospered,
Failed to help poor Joe;
He forgot or didn't bother.

CHAPTER 41

Two more years Joseph lived
Within the prison walls.
Then Pharaoh had bad dreams
And Joseph got a call.

The wise men of the day
Had been called to help.
No matter how they tried,
No message could they tell.

Pharaoh said to Joseph,
"I'll tell you my dream,
I've been told that you
Can tell me what it means.

Upon the fertile banks
Of the River Nile I sat;
Seven fatted cows came up
And grazed on the grass.

Then seven others, as
Scrawny as could be, came
Out of the Nile too, and
The fat ones they did eat.

Then on a stalk of grain
Seven plump heads did grow,

Joined by seven thin ones
Who quickly stole the show

Yet after it was over the
Thin cows still were thin.
The sickly heads of grain
Would never fill a bin."

So Joseph said to Pharaoh,
"It is up to God, you see.
But a message in the dream
Seems quite plain to me.

For seven years to come
Across the land will be
A great surplus and plenty,
Of everything you need.

But seven years that follow
Will go the other way;
Everything that grows
In drought will only fade.

Now it's up to you, oh king,
To find a trusty man
To store up all the surplus
In good times while you can.

So you can handle problems
When years of famine come,
For every border country
Surely will need some."

Pharaoh called his wise men
And asked if one was able
To guide the land of Egypt
And avoid barren tables.

Then he thought of Joseph
And deemed it only wise
To give to him the job
Of saving all their lives.

To Joe he gave great power,
On his finger placed a ring.

Great authority Joseph had
Next only to the king.

To Joe he gave the chariot
Of his second-in-command.
Then he chose a bride from
The beauties of the land.

So Joseph traveled Egypt
And got things all aligned
To be ahead of famine when
They came upon bad times.

So when the famine came
And living got real rough,
They had food to eat
And even sold the stuff.

So the time of plenty passed
And famine gripped the land.
As their savings dwindled,
It worried every man.

Pangs of hunger soon gnawed
At every country around,
But in granaries of Egypt
There was food to be found.

Now not only Egyptians,
But those from around about,
Soon learned to their sorrow
How it was to go without.

CHAPTER 42

Jacob, back in Canaan, soon
Felt the grip of drought.
So Joseph's brothers went
To buy the grain they sought.

Imagine their consternation,
When they journeyed there,
To be treated like thieves
Who'd stolen another's share.

Joseph threw them all in jail
And shook them up a bit.

As far as they could tell,
This might well be it.

It was three days later
When he spoke to them again.
He shook them up some more
And sent them back to Canaan.

They arrived back home to
Find they'd been tricked.
It scared them pretty bad
And poor Jacob felt sick.

CHAPTER 43

Now as time marched on
And the food ran low,
Joseph's older brothers
Decided again to go.

To Egypt they returned
With many gifts in hand,
Because of their terror,
Each and every man.

This time in Egypt, at
Joseph's palace there,
They were slow to enter
Because they were scared.

They soon decided, their
Fear had been for naught,
As the money was returned
For the grain they bought.

Then they were wined
And dined in style, as
Brother Joseph watched
And planned more guile.

CHAPTER 44

Soon after the brothers
Started the journey back,
They found Joseph's cup
Hidden in Benjamin's sack.

To the ruler's palace the
Timid brothers returned,
And for a decent alibi
You can bet they yearned.

Judah stuck his neck out
Offering himself as slave,
If Joseph would accept him,
A father's sorrow he'd save.

CHAPTER 45

Soon Joe gave up the sham
And stopped playing games.
He told them who he was
And of his climb to fame.

It was a glad reunion with
The brother they'd crossed.
Joseph knew all had gained
And no longer felt so lost.

He let them go to Canaan
To bring their father back,
With many gifts and goods
In each brother's sack.

Of course when Jacob heard,
He just could not believe.
So the brothers confessed,
And he no longer grieved.

CHAPTER 46

So Jacob, known as Israel,
Hit the trail again.
The last time, he hoped,
For an old and tired man.

And now God told him in
The middle of night. "My
Blessings are upon you,
Go die at Joseph's side."

Now travelling on the way
It must have been a sight.

Jacob sent Judah ahead to
Tell Joe they'd arrived.

Joseph rode his chariot to
Meet his beloved kin; he
Told Jacob what to say
When Pharaoh spoke to him.

CHAPTER 47

Joseph took five brothers
To plead a familys cause,
So they were given land
Where they'd be the boss.

They were able to settle
In Goshen's pasture land.
In other parts of Egypt
They hated a shepherd man.

Now as the famine spread
It covered all the land,
And as hunger does, it
Made beggars out of man.

Soon he spent his money
And there was little left.
But Joe worked for Pharaoh
And was at trading deft.

Once they spent the money,
Next came land and cattle.
Soon all that was left
Were lives as chattel.

In desperation they'd give
A fifth of all they earned,
As the price they'd pay to
Live the life they yearned.

The people were so pleased
To have come through alive,
They'd even work as slaves
And through life to strive.

Jacob lived in Egypt for
Ten more years plus seven.

He knew he'd soon be called
To his new job in Heaven.

So calling Joseph aside,
Jacob told him of his plan.
He wanted Joe to bury him
Back home in Canaan's land.

CHAPTER 48

Of course Joseph agreed to
What his father requested,
So his final resting place
Would be with his ancestors.

CHAPTER 49

The day soon arrived and
Jacob called his sons
Explaining what to expect
In the days to come.

As for Joseph's sons,
Jacob adopted them.
They were born in Egypt,
Manasseh and Ephraim.

Now he blessed them all
Telling them once again,
He wanted to be buried
Back in his home land.

Then he lay down exhausted
Upon his bed and sighed,
And before his many sons,
Breathed his last and died.

CHAPTER 50

The embalming of his body
Took fully forty days.
For seventy more, Egyptians
Mourned the parting ways.

Now they made the journey
Back to Canaan far away.

'Twas a larger caravan
Than in those early days.

They laid Jacob to rest
Beyond the Jordan River.
He'd gone back to God,
The great original Giver.

On the return to Egypt the
Brothers began to worry;
If Joe didn't forgive them,
He might make them sorry.

So they wrote a letter
And admitted their shame.
They asked his forgiveness
Offering to be his slaves.

But Joseph had no thought
To carry on the fight.
So he sincerely told them
He would treat them right.

The years went drifting by
As they've been known to do.

Old folks all grew older,
The young ones only grew.

Joseph watched his sons and
Grandsons as they played,
Till his strength was spent,
Then knew he'd had his day.

So called his people close
And told them for a fact,
They'd all return to Canaan,
God would lead them back.

Then he made them promise
When they started home,
That they would guarantee
To carry back his bones.

Then Joseph did expire
At age one hundred ten.
His life was one of beauty
As it's all been put to pen.

END OF GENESIS

EXODUS

CHAPTER 1

Israel's people multiplied
Until they filled the land.
Pharaoh noted their numbers
And decided to take a stand.

He was not the King of old
And felt no responsibility
To Joseph's kind of people
Or respected their liberty.

As they steadily multiplied,
He worried and he fumed
And bound them into slavery
As their enmity he assumed.

Those Israelis, to Egyptians,
Were now-a-days only slaves;
Backs were bowed in labor as
Their very lives they gave.

By royal decree, baby boys
Would be drowned in the Nile.
The only babe to live
Would be the girl child.

CHAPTER 2

This is the story of Moses
Who was born to Levi's tribe.
He was saved from drowning
By going for a basket ride.

He was such a beautiful baby
That his mother couldn't bear
His being thrown in the river
To suffer and perish there.

Sealing leaks with pitch
In the basket she wove,
She set the babe adrift as
His sister stayed close.

We know it happened,
As the basket floated there,
An Egyptian princess bathing
Found the babe and cared.

She looked for help to raise
Him, the babys sister came,
To offer the help of mother
And played her little game.

He grew up strong of body
And also strong of mind. And
Tho' raised by Egyptians,
Israeli's were his kind.

So when a brother was beaten
By an Egyptian overlord,
He killed him then and there
And feared greatly afterward.

Soon the deed was known,
And Moses had to leave.
His life was in jeopardy
For Pharaoh had decreed,

He was to be arrested, and
Death would be the price.
Killing an Egyptian
Was not considered wise.

So Moses cut and ran, it
Was the only thing to do.
In Midian's land he stopped
Instead of passing through.

Nearby lived a priest
With seven daughters fair,
Whom Moses chanced to meet
As he was pausing there.

He interferred with shepherds
Who made their flocks athirst,
And drew water from the wells
So their sheep watered first.

So Ruel, who was their father,
Invited Moses into their lives.
His daughter Zipporah
Would now be Moses' wife.

The first they named Gershom
Who would grow to be a man
Because Moses was a stranger
And in a foreign land.

And so the days went on
As time went slipping by.
Then Pharaoh, King of Egypt,
One day gave up and died.

The Hebrews still were slaves
As they'd been for many years.
Their backs were bending low,
Their vision blurred by tears.

Jehovah God was listening
As their cries reached Heaven.
So he would send them help
Because of promises given.

For in the days of Abraham,
Of Isaac and of Jacob,
God had promised them
The golden land of Canaan.

CHAPTER 3

Moses, a shepherd who was
Out tending sheep all day;
Saw a burning bush, which
He couldn't explain away.

So he moved up closer
To get a better look,
And what happened then
Left our hero shook.

The bush burned fiercely
But never was devoured.
And a voice from the flame
Made Moses a sudden coward.

CHAPTER 4

He, whom God had chosen to
Lead His children free,
More than once protested,
"Please don't send me."

But God accepts no failures,
It would spoil his plans,
So He soon showed Moses
How to be a better man.

He promised many miracles
For the job ahead, but
In spite of promises,
Moses was full of dread.

His staff became a snake
From which he ran in fear,
Then his hand was leprous
But in an instant cleared.

Thus God showed power to
Break King Pharaoh's will.
No matter what the problem,
He'd be with Moses still.

Then brother Aaron joined
To lead the growing nation
Out of slavery to the
Land of their salvation.

Aaron had a speaking voice
So his would be the job

Of telling all the people
About the will of God.

CHAPTER 5

So they went to Pharaoh to
Plead their cause to him,
But Pharaohs heart was hard,
So their hope was slim.

It tells us in the Bible
They argued back and forth
As Pharaoh kept them there
For all that he was worth.

He was hard of heart, and
Many times they failed to
Get their nation started
Upon the homeward trail.

We've read it in the Book
And heard it in church,
Moses performed miracles
That God caused to work.

CHAPTER 6

People listened to Moses,
But Pharaoh did them dirt.
He wanted them to stay
And do his dirty work.

CHAPTER 7

Now God kept His promise,
And showed his mighty hand.
Moses still tried to argue
He should send another man.

But God will not listen
To a man paralyzed by fear;
Because if the job gets done
Someone must get in gear.

Of course God had promised
To make Pharaoh let them go.

And by the staff of Moses
It would all be so.

Fish died in the Nile, as
The river turned to blood;
Pestilence came to Egypt,
And problems came in floods.

CHAPTER 8

Then the frogs moved in
Till there seemed no end;
As trouble piled up, surely
Pharaoh's will must bend.

Egyptians got the itch, it
Continued night and day;
They now had lice which
Apparently came to stay.

So Pharoah called Moses,
Who then went to God,
To get the siege of lice
To leave old Egypt's sod.

But Pharaoh broke his word,
And once the lice were gone,
With the misery only memory,
He sang a different song.

So the Lord sent flies
In such great quantity
To convince the King
That he must believe.

CHAPTER 9

So Egypt's cattle sickened,
For God now sent a plague
To convince King Pharaoh
That he'd had his day.

Yet he still refused to
Let them go their way, for
When all was said and done
He planned to have his say.

Moses tossed some ashes,
From the kiln toward the sky,
So the boils that they got
Caused man and beast to cry.

When the King's magicians
Tried to do their thing,
It appeared to their dismay,
Boils had sapped their zing.

Then God said to Pharoah
"Now let my people go, I
Could have killed you, if
I'd wanted to, you know.

I've done this to show
That I'm the God of all;
You'll come on bended knee
Or suffer a serious fall.

Tomorrow I'll send hail,
Like none you ever saw.
I will ruin all of Egypt
Unless you begin to thaw."

And so the hail came down
On crops, beast and man.
Wreaking terrible havoc,
Killing across the land.

Still the land of Goshen
God spared just as before.
Because Israel's people
Were chosen by the Lord.

So Pharaoh promised again
To let the people go. But
Moses calmed the storm, and
The King again said, "No."

CHAPTER 10

So the Lord said to Moses,
"Go back and try again,
We know it will not work
Pharaoh's a stubborn man.

It'll be a wonderful story
After the battle is won, to
Tell your grand children,
In days and years to come.

It should remove all doubt
That Jehovah God I am,
Because of miracles I've
Performed across the land."

Now Moses asked the king
"How long will you delay
To do Jehovah's will
And let God have his way?

If you refuse again, He'll
Send locusts to devour what
Ever escaped the storm
To prove to you his power."

Pharaoh made another offer,
The men could go their way,
But to cover all angles, the
Flocks and herds must stay.

Again the staff swung up,
So locusts filled the land,
They drifted upon the wind
As never saw by man.

Then said Pharaoh to Moses,
"I accede to what you ask;
Leave your herds and flocks,
So I know you'll come back."

Moses would never go along
With leaving their cattle,
Yet this was like declaring
An outright state of battle.

So he was ordered out in
Angered rage by Pharaoh,
And under threat of death
It behooved him now to go.

CHAPTER 11

But one last announcement
He would in anger hurl,
And 'twas enough to make
Old Pharaoh's wiskers curl.

"More disaster is your fate!
All first borns die tonight;
For you are hard of heart
And won't do what is right.

The eldest of your flocks
And of your servants too,
Will suffer identical fate
Just the same as you."

CHAPTER 12

Now to the Israelis, Moses
Made this plea; "Your door-
Posts mark with blood for
The angel of death to see.

Stand in total readiness to
Take your goods and flee,
And when the time is come
You'll get word from me.

This must be remembered
Over all the years ahead. So
Every year you'll celebrate.
Eat lamb and Kosher bread."

In both Egypt and in Goshen
Moses was a mighty man. So
The Israelis were favored
All across the land.

And so the day did come
As God had said it would,
When they prepared to travel
And leave Egypt for good.

They prepared to leave for
They'd suffered much wrong.

Hebrews and their families
Six hundred thousand strong.

But not before the King
Had lost his eldest son,
And every Egyptian family
Had each lost one.

Over four hundred years ago
Joseph brought them here.
But the years of promise
Had lost all hope and cheer.

So now God brought them out
Toward the promised land,
Wave upon wave of people,
The families of every man.

CHAPTER 13

Jehovah instructed Moses
For a passover celebration.
How it should be conducted
By the future Jewish nation.

And so our Lord led them,
They followed day and night;
A pillar of fire and smoke
Was always in their sight.

He led them indirectly
Around the great Red Sea,
To avoid the Philistines,
For he wanted no retreat.

CHAPTER 14

They had a three-day pass
To go and worship God.
But it soon was obviously
Abandonment of Egypt's sod.

So Pharaoh gave the order
To assemble every man
To go after the children
And bring them back again.

The Royal Chariot Corps was
Six hundred units strong.
With all of Pharaoh's army,
Could this chase go wrong?

The children pitched camp
Upon the shore of the sea.
Seeing the Legion coming,
There was no place to flee.

When seeing Pharaoh coming,
They feared failing health,
'Cause while in preparation
They'd stolen Egypt's wealth.

It began to appear to some
Slavery was a better way,
Than on chancing death,
Perhaps this very day.

But God was with them,
Answering Moses' prayers.
He told him what to do,
As they cowered there.

So Moses pointed his staff
Out across the mighty sea;
Parting waters made a path
For the Israelites to flee.

The people crossed over
While walking on dry land.
They gained the other shore
And never lost a man.

So the mighty army pursuing
Came rushing in from behind.
They still doubted miracles
Or perhaps lost their minds.

Between those walls of water
Every chariot, horse and man
Of Pharaoh's legions drowned
When Moses raised his hand.

Now the doubters believed
They should honor God. And
Could have trusted Moses,
Ere he ever raised his rod.

CHAPTER 15

Then Moses and the people
Sang a song unto the Lord,
He was their savior who'd
Spared them from the sword.

From Pharaoh's multitudes
They had all been saved,
The great pursuing army
Was dead beneath the waves.

Now the journey continued
As they'd planned at first,
Till a place of bitter water
Made them suffer thirst.

As the cries grew plaintive
God showed Moses a tree,
Which thrown into the water,
Made it all turn sweet.

A dozen wells of water and
Seventy palms tall and slim,
Marked the place they'd camp
At the oases called Elim.

CHAPTER 16

Wilderness they journeyed
Between Elim and Mt. Sinai,
People started to hunger
And of course began to cry.

Again God forged a rescue,
As Moses had said he'd do,
With manna for breakfast,
Quail for roast or stew.

So the people ate and
Lived from day to day.

Forty years they wandered,
Traveling the longest way.

CHAPTER 17

Many times they grumbled and
Were rescued by their God.
For even when they thirsted
He drew water from a rock.

When Moses raised his Staff
By which God changed a river,
The clear cool water gushed.
A gift from a loving giver.

Now Amalek was the leader
Of warriors in that land,
Who objected to their passing
And vowed he'd make a stand.

A call to arms was issued
By Joshua who would lead
The Hebrew men of war who
Hoped to do great deeds.

Moses stood a-top a hill as
The battle raged and waned.
If he held his staff up high
Israel's army gained.

But when his arm got tired
And the staff came down,
The battle went against them,
They started losing ground.

Aaron and Hur rolled a stone,
Upon which Moses sat,
And then held up his arms
Which kept the battle pat.

So Joshua crushed the enemy
Before the setting of the sun;
Tonight they would celebrate
The battle they had won.

CHAPTER 18

The people thought of Moses
As the judge of every one
And accepted his decisions
As if from God above.

Jethro, Moses' father-in-law,
Said the job must be divided
Among many other judges,
And so it was decided.

So Moses had more time to
Take care of other things.
He must have thought time
Fled by on slower wings.

CHAPTER 19

They camped near a mountain,
And the Lord called out; He
Told their leader, Moses,
To keep the people out.

Then he called Moses to
Scale Mount Sinai. And
When he'd gained the crest,
Jehovah would tell him why.

CHAPTER 20

The people all must serve
And give their very best!
He had rescued them, as His
People they were blessed.

Thus he told Moses, "I'm
The Lord thy God. Make no
Graven images of things
On earth or under sod.

Remember the seventh day
Is a holy day for you.
But in the other six you
Have much work to do."

For in six days He made
The Heavens and the Earth.
And then upon the seventh
He rested from His work.

Honor father and mother so
Your days will always be,
Full of life and long, in
The land God gave to thee.

Thou shalt not kill nor
Commit adultery, or steal
Or bear false witness;
Then ask for help from me.

Thy neighbor's house
Or anything he owns,
Thou shalt not covet;
Nor complain or moan.

When you begrudge what
Belongs to another man,
You've already slipped,
And won't fit God's plan.

Big rings of fire and smoke
Then came from out the hill.
And the trumpet of the Lord
Gave the people a thrill.

With fear they trembled as
They watched from far away.
Moses climbed the mountain
To hear what God would say.

CHAPTER 21

Of how to treat a servant
When old or sold or bought,
Or if a man did murder
He must die when caught.

It was an eye for an eye
And a tooth for a tooth,
As the Lord gave Moses
The word of law and truth.

Now if a man owned an ox,
And by the ox was gored,
The fate of that ox
Already was in store.

CHAPTER 22

If a man should steal,
Or even start a fire,
The full force of the law
Would surely be required.

And many such things
Were explained to him
About what must be done
To atone for sin.

In general, the theme
Of all that he was told,
Was for everyones conduct
In those days of old.

That men should obey
The only living Lord, and
Always guide their lives
By His Holy living word.

CHAPTER 23

On the witness stand
We must perjure not
And return what is found
That a neighbor's lost.

And take no gift
In the way of a bribe,
Which may make a man
Often act unwise.

Moses was told
Of feasts to be held.
To be honest with God
And all would be well.

CHAPTER 24

Moses built twelve altars
At the foot of Mt. Sinai,

A place to do worship for
Each and all the tribes.

Then he struggled upward
And climbed to the heights.
A ring of cloud and glory
Hid him from their sight.

For forty days and nights
They awaited his return;
Glory crowned the summit
As it blazed and burned.

CHAPTER 25

Moses got the word as he
Sojourned on the mount,
Those acceptable offerings,
Those that God would count.

A sacred temple He would
Have the people build; so
God could live among them,
As they obeyed His will.

The temple of the Lord of
Acacia wood should be made,
Where the ten commandments
On tablets would be laid.

With a lid of pure gold
And golden Angels there on,
With many golden rings
And also golden knobs.

CHAPTER 26

The beauty of their work
Surely was a thing to see;
The Ark of the Covenant,
A thing God meant to be.

CHAPTER 27

With many wonders that
I'm not gifted to tell
About the wondrous Ark
Where-in God would dwell.

CHAPTER 28

Aaron and his sons
Would have a special job,
They'd be high priests
And dedicated to God.

To be clothed in dignity
As they served the Lord,
With the finest linens of
Gold and jeweled cords.

On two stones of onyx
The names of each tribe,
With great care and skill
Were to be inscribed.

It would be astounding to
See the clothes they wore;
Nothing surpassed it since
Nor had it ever before.

CHAPTER 29

The order of the sacrifice
Was next thing he was told,
So that Aaron and his sons
Would have it down cold.

Aaron and his sons would
Be the priests of God
As they ministered there
And made easier Moses' job.

This way Jehovah would be
With Israel night and day,
He'd be their live-in God
As they went on their way.

CHAPTER 30

They built a special altar
Where incense they'd burn,
It would only be compounded
According to his terms.

Aaron trimmed lamps at dawn
Burning spices on the altar.
In evening it was incense,
And they must never falter.

For this would be the method
They would use to sanctify
The altar and the priests
Until the day they'd die.

Each man would pay
A ransom for his soul, and
They'd make a brazen laver,
Or really a washing bowl.

CHAPTER 31

God gave great wisdom to
Those who worked each day.
For jobs more difficult
He helped them find a way.

Now they kept the Sabbath,
No work that day they'd do;
He'd made the world in six,
The seventh He was through.

This was a covenant between
His people and their Lord,
They must worship only Him
While living by His word.

To Moses He gave the law
Written on slabs of stone
To take down the mountain
When he headed for home.

Imagine, if you can, that
Day so long ago, when Ten
Commandments did the job
Of keeping crime down low.

It must have been simple,
In this day of you and me,
We cannot know what's so
With laws to rule a galaxy.

Perhaps that's why we fail,
Our laws are made by man.
But those Ten Commandments
Were by our Lord's own hand.

CHAPTER 32

Absence makes a heart fond,
Or so at least we've heard,
But often it grows fainter
Seems to be the word.

So as Moses lived in glory
On the mountain with God,
The children down below
Were raising lots of hob.

For some had given up
Once Moses left them there;
They were no longer sure
God still lived or cared.

They'd made a golden calf
To take the place of Diety,
Around which they danced
In naked impropriety.

In anger, the Lord was ready
To wipe the earth with them;
But Moses interceded, and
God's great anger stemmed.

As Abraham had done
To save his nephew Lot,
He reasoned with his God
When temper waxed too hot.

So God agreed to save
Those who would atone, and
Moses descended the mount
With two tablets of stone.

But when he saw the revelry
He got so very mad,
That in boiling anger
He broke those Holy slabs.

Now the people of Levi
Stood beside the Lord,
And they got the order to
Put others to the sword.

Three thousand backsliders
Bit the dust that day
As they learned that idols
Their lives could not save.

Thus the Lord plagued them
When they proved untrue. So
As we would say today, "They
Boiled in their own stew."

CHAPTER 33

Now the Lord told Moses it
Was time to break up camp
And continue on the journey
Toward the promised land.

He would drive the enemy,
Before them as they'd march,
To a land of milk and honey
If to God they'd only hark.

An Angel now would lead
  them
So He wouldn't likely kill
In a sudden frenzy of anger
If they flaunted His will.

He feared to live too near
And have them so close by,
Their petty cries and sins
Made Him more than sigh.

Moses moved the tabernacle
From out the Hebrew camp.
When he went to talk to God,
People in awe would stand.

When the pillar of cloud
Came down before the door,

The Lord talked with Moses
Of wondrous things in store.

His continued presence
In their midst those days,
Moses often asked of God
When he came to pray.

Because he and his God
Were very much like friends
Who'd stick it out together
Right to the bitter end.

CHAPTER 34

Two more tablets Moses hewed
And carried up the mount.
God came close and tarried
All wrapped up in cloud.

Moses bowed upon the earth
To worship then and there
Asking God to come along
And their journey share.

God said, "Behold I agree
To do the thing you ask!
But they'll be true to me
Or be taken to task.

I will drive the enemy out
So you can have the land.
But you must not fraternize
With foreign woman or man.

All groves and altars wreck,
Their idols you must break;
If you follow in their ways
Your futures are at stake."

Forty days and forty nights
Moses was again on Sinai, so
Commandments on the stone
God once more did write.

Then Moses again descended
From that Holy place,

And the glory of the Lord
Still showed upon his face.

The people all held back
Until Moses called to them.
Then they came and listened
To what Jehovah had said.

CHAPTER 35

"You shall keep the Sabbath
And observe the Holy days,
For if you want God's help
You will do things his way.

And now we will need help
As the tabernacle we build.
It's time for volunteers
Of all you folks who will.

Cloth of silk and linen,
We need oil and incense too.
Gold and precious stones
All those things we'll use."

Now Bezaleel and Aholiab
Were the ones to do the job,
For their skills and talents
Were given them by God.

CHAPTER 36

Now many men of wisdom
Came to do the work of God.
People brought so many gifts
That Moses called a stop.

The important work continued
As they plied an art of love.
And God smiled down on them
From a pillar of cloud above.

They made a veil of scarlet
Of purple and of blue;
Many fine threads of linen
Were woven in there too.

CHAPTER 37

An overlay of gold was on
The hooks and rings,
All the staffs and staves,
And on many other things.

From acacia wood the ark was
Made, from pure gold they beat
The vessels and the spoons,
The cherubims and mercy seat.

They made a candle stick,
It surely was a thing to see.
The description is so grand
That it amazes me.

There was pure incense
And Holy anointing oil;
It was made quite perfectly,
And with much exacting toil.

CHAPTER 38

The tabernacle's furnishings
Were done with greatest skill
In order to do the job
According to Jehovah's will.

CHAPTER 39

Of blue and of purple
And of scarlet they made
Cloths for every service
Within that Holy place.

All the priestly vestments
Were made as they were told
Of the very finest cloth and
Glowing threads of gold.

Precious stones and jewels
Such as I have never seen,
It must have been so grand
As to cast a glowing sheen.

All the work was finished
On the tabernacle tent;
They polished things all up
And then for Moses, sent.

Moses examined carefully
All the work they'd done,
And he could see for sure
Just how far they'd come.

'Twas as Jehovah'd ordered
And of the very best,
So Moses gave approval,
And all the people blessed.

CHAPTER 40

To Moses spake the Lord
As He gave him work to do.
He set the tabernacle up
And all the fixtures too.

Aaron and his sons were
Sanctified as priests;
All the Lord had commanded,
Moses did all these.

A Column of smoke led by day
A pillar of fire at night,
If it covered the tabernacle
To travel was not right.

END OF EXODUS

LEVITICUS

CHAPTER 1

From the tabernacle the
Lord called out to him
To instruct the people on
Burnt offerings for sin.

So Moses gave them rules
For offerings by fire.
It must be the firstborn
And never old or tired.

If flock or fowl be given,
It should always be an
Offering made by fire and
To the Lord a savor sweet.

CHAPTER 2

If an offering is of grain
It should be ground up fine;
Do not spare your effort
Or be stingy with your time.

Olive oil and Frankincense
On the offering thou shalt
Give only the first fruits
And don't forget the salt.

CHAPTER 3

Animals from the herd shall
Be an offering of peace
Slain before the tabernacle
By he who is the priest.

CHAPTER 4

For a sacrifice of sin,
Each must give oblation,
If he be priest or ruler,
A commoner, or the nation.

CHAPTER 5

Trespass offerings were
Then brought into play.
Sacrilege or ignorance
Was no excuse those days.

CHAPTER 6

If one had lied or stolen
From a neighbor or friend,
He'd confess and pay or
Be guilty to the end.

Aaron and his sons were
To keep the altar fire.
For it must not die,
And they dare never tire.

CHAPTER 7

Sacrifice of thanksgiving,
Meat or grain or otherwise,
And portions for the priest,
As He'd told Moses on Sinai.

CHAPTER 8

Then Moses called on Aaron
And also Aaron's sons; he
Clothed and consecrated
As God had ordered done.

All offerings to the Lord
Moses made that day,
As Aaron and his sons
He did consecrate.

Seven days they stayed
Within tabernacle doors,
And they kept the charge
As given by the Lord.

CHAPTER 9

Then on the eighth day
Aaron and Moses blessed
All the people of Israel,
For they'd passed the test.

Fire burst upon the altar
Consuming offering and fat.
People, awed and shouting
Fell on their faces flat.

CHAPTER 10

Nadab and Abihu, both
Priests and Aaron's sons,
Took it upon themselves
To add to what was done.

Not as God had ordered, so
His flame burned them too,
The moral of this story,
As applies to me and you,

Always try to do His will
No matter what the case,
Nor second guess His plans
As through life we race.

CHAPTER 11

Some animals were clean,
But some of them were not.
Only some were approved
To be cooked in Hebrew pots.

That held true for fowl
And creatures of the sea.
God told through Moses
All things approved to eat.

So the people could choose
Between the bad and good,
Even as we in our day
Have ability and should.

CHAPTER 12

Childbirth in those days!
Mother was thought unclean.
Her rites of purification
Could last days or weeks.

Her duty it was to offer
A lamb in its first year,
And a pigeon or turtle dove,
To before the priest appear.

But if she could not afford
To bring a lamb with her,
Two young birds of each she
Could for offering burn.

CHAPTER 13

That day of which we speak
The "Priest" you'll guess,
Took the place of "Doctor,"
And could curse or bless.

He had the authority
To decide if anyone might
Have boils or freckles
Or maybe too much sun.

Of course some had boils,
But others would surely be
So diseased of skin, as to
Be labeled, "With leprosy."

I can only cringe and think
What it would mean to me to
Hide or call out, Unclean!
Unclean! with leprosy!

CHAPTER 14

Now when the sick got well
He must go to the priest
And surely bring offering
If he'd again be clean.

And once again the priest
With offerings must atone
For every one affected,
In this he stood alone.

He also had the job
Of teaching the difference
Of what was clean or not
And to work with reverence.

CHAPTER 15

And here we are reminded to
Often wash and keep us clean.
This is good advice from God,
And should never be
    demeaned.

An important case in point,
At least so it would seem,
Is keep from being infected
And to thus avoid disease.

CHAPTER 16

Once again Aaron was called
To intercede for the clan.
He made sacrifices to God
For the many sins of man.

The sins of all the people
Were borne by a lonely goat
Led away from camp and
Yonder forced to go.

For the "Scapegoat" as you
See was in symbolism made
To do as the name implies,
And help their sins to fade.

Once a year they would have
The feast of expiation; it
Would cover all the sins
Of their entire nation.

CHAPTER 17

No citizen or foreigner will
Make offering in the field.
You must abide by God's Law,
Nor shall you ever yield.

For the sacrifice you make
Must be done as decreed,
And at the tabernacle only
May you do this deed.

When you kill for food,
To consume the meat,
Do so reverently and
Blood you shall not eat.

CHAPTER 18

On and on we read in the
Holy Book of God, things
That may be done and
Some that should not.

Of incest we are warned,
That all forms of lust
Will only degrade, and
Hasten our return to dust.

CHAPTER 19

Again, through Moses God
Made this plea. "Now you
Must listen well, please
Harken unto me.

Due honor pay your father,
And to your mother. Love
And honor sisters and of
Course your brothers.

When you make the harvest
To fill the empty stores,
Leave some grapes or grain
To help feed the poor.

Help the sick or invalid
And of course the blind,

And when judging any man,
Make certain to find

With honesty and justice,
No matter what his class,
Whether he be rich or poor,
Or from another clan.

May you not sin for profit,
Especially if it is yours,
Be kind to everyone; keep
Your good will in store"

CHAPTER 20

Diverse laws and ordinances,
To them the Lord God gave;
Those who worshipped idols,
He surely would not save.

"You must not do as those
I've cast out of the land.
After all I banished them
Because of the sins of man."

CHAPTER 21

A priest must be pure
For he's a chief among men.
Nor shall he mourn as others
Nor his clothes shall rend.

In marriage he shall take
A wife in her virginity,
Because a widow or a harlot
Will cost him his divinity.

No man with infirmity will
Be allowed to be a priest;
No moles, or scabs or sores,
They can have none of these.

CHAPTER 22

All the laws of priests,
Concerning offerings made,
Were lengthy and exacting
Away back in those days.

CHAPTER 23

Each sabbath day was holy
Along with each of these.
Israel was expected to
Keep the times of feast.

"Passover Festival shall
Be when all are well fed.
Followed next by the Fest-
ival of unleavened bread.

Gaining the promised land,
You will soon plant roots.
Then you must celebrate the
Festival of First Fruits.

The Festival of Pentecost,
When your crops grow tall,
Will be a time to celebrate
And do no work at all.

Then in mid-September
Is a solemn time for all
At the Festival of Trumpets
Held in early fall.

The Festival of Atonement
You will next attend, so
Consider with deep sorrow
The sinful ways of men.

A Festival of Tabernacles,
The thirtieth of September,
Will last for seven days
And is one to remember.

For in this one you will
Celebrate those days of
Forty years of journey as
God led you all the way."

CHAPTER 24

Olive oil was burned in the
Tabernacle of the congreg-

ation, its fire must never
Fade from Gods creation.

Now when a man was angry
And he cursed the Lord,
He was promptly stoned, for
They believed the word

That none would be excused
When doing what was wrong.
This was the law of God
And in Israel very strong.

Their laws were very strict
But every man was equal,
And be he rich or poor
He must not practice evil.

CHAPTER 25

While Moses was on Sinai
The Lord God said to him,
"Remember, I rescued you,
You must not turn to sin.

So always keep the Sabbath,
'Tis a day of rest so dear,
And I'll also tell you now
To rest each seventh year.

Seven times you'll do so,
And then next year will be
The one to be remembered
As half a century.

Let all trumpets blow long
And loud throughout the land.
It will be a day of jubilee
For every beast and man.

In this year you shall not
Sow or the harvest reap.
Leave the crop upon the field
For the use of man and beast.

For the crop that grows
Has cost you naught,

Neither price nor labor
Or even worry of drought.

All old debts you will cancel
And slaves you'll set free
In this fiftieth year which
Will be known as Jubilee."

CHAPTER 26

"Now if you keep my law
By being obedient unto me,
You'll never live in fear
And each day will be a feast.

But if you go against me, I
Will smite you seven times,
For every time you fail
Will be a major crime.

You'll flee the enemy
Such will be your fears
That your imagination will
Even cause you tears."

CHAPTER 27

"If a man shall vow to
Dedicate his life, then he
Shall pay instead, and the
Priest shall name a price.

And everyone shall give
A tenth of all he earns.
Each shall give his tithe;
There are no other terms."

These are all commandments
God gave Moses on Sinai,
And it's not up to us to
Ask, "How come, or why?"

THE END OF LEVITICUS

NUMBERS

CHAPTER 1

Two years had passed since
Their journey had begun
With some of the strangest
Happenings under the sun.

The Red Sea had parted, so
They could walk through.
There'd been the wilderness
Which they'd traversed too.

They'd fought their battles,
And beside mountains camped,
Were given Ten
   Commandments
And worshipped a golden calf.

So I suppose it made sense,
That they do something new.
Because the Lord God wanted
A tally of those Jews.

All the healthy young men
Of twenty years or so
Would be ready to do battle
If they were told to go.

So by tribe and by family
They were to be named and
Would go down in history
To great and lasting fame.

Moses and brother Aaron
Were directing the scribes.
And with the leaders help,
Numbered all the tribes.

Over six hundred thousand
They counted there in all,
Ready for the battle, who
Would march to Israel's call.

All except the tribe of Levi,
Were inscribed upon the roll,
Their jobs henceforth to
Steer toward heaven's goal,

To shield a sinful people
From the wrath of angry God
After worshipping idols or
Other ways deserved the rod.

CHAPTER 2

Each tribe had captains, and
Of course, lieutenants too,
With each one in position
As the Lord had said to do.

I can imagine such a scene
Back in the mists of time.
What a pageant I can see
In the window of my mind.

Each tribe's banner raised,
They marched across the land.
And at evening encampment,
"Oh what a mighty band."

Great companies of soldiers
Were placed with strategy in
Relation to the Tabernacle
As each tribe should be.

Each tribe pitched tents
In a very special place
With it's own flag pole
Where tribal banners wave.

CHAPTER 3

Now with two remaining sons
Aaron was made high priest.
Anyone else presuming to be
Would surely come to grief.

The Tabernacle chores
Must all be met with pride.
So they would all be done
By Levi's tribe.

They would care for the Altar,
The drapes and coverings too,
All fencing of the courtyard
And all repair work do.

So when the census takers had
All finished up their work,
There'd be so many projects
That no one there need shirk.

CHAPTER 4

When the journeys were ended,
And the journeys began, it was
Aaron's sons and Levites
Who came first in the plan.

They entered the Tabernacle
And took down the veil
With which to cover the Ark
And make ready for the trail.

There were many things more
They would have to prepare
Before it was ready
To be taken from there.

'Twas the sons of Kohath
Of the Levite tribe
On whose muscular shoulders
The Tabernacle would ride.

But there was one little
Thing they must never forget,
To look at any item would
Bring them instant death.

The Gershonites were counted,
And the Merari's would share.
They each had their jobs
And many others would spare.

Nearly eighty-six hundred
Were chosen there
Just for transportation
And the Tabernacle's care.

CHAPTER 5

Then the Lepers were removed,
And banished from the camp;
They were not allowed to
Live beside a healthy man.

Any one who sinned
Must necessarily confess
And pay the one wronged
Plus one fifth, no less.

Also the trial of jealousy
Was instituted there.
It seems stacked against the
   woman, and
Today she'd cry, "Unfair."

CHAPTER 6

The Lord talked to Moses
Quite often those days,
About how His people
Should mind their ways.

A Nazarite, to be holy to
God in that time, ate
No grapes or raisins, or
Drank old or new wine.

He'd be surely defiled if
He got close to the dead--
Must atone by sacrifice
And by shaving his head.

His hair he'd grow long
As a sign of his vow; and
If he should slip, he'd
Lose his credits now.

His head he would shave
To start over again

And make a sin offering
Of a yearling ewe lamb.

Numerous offerings other
Than I've mentioned,
All meant for atonement,
To prove good intentions.

Then God allowed Aaron
And his sons to
Evoke His blessings
On each and every one.

"May the Lord God bless
And protect you each,
Be gracious and favor
And give you His peace."

CHAPTER 7

Each item of the Tabernacle
Was anointed and sanctified.
Then gifts were presented by
Whom the census was
  organized

In six covered wagons,
Each drawn by two oxen, and a
Wagon for every two leaders,
With an ox for each one,

Came the leaders of Israel,
The chiefs of each tribe,
For work on the Tabernacle
Where God would abide.

With much gold and silver,
Incense and things. Young
Rams, bulls, and lambs,
All for burnt offerings.

For peace offerings,
Two oxen, five rams,
Five male goats, and
Five male yearling lambs.

A male goat was brought
To offer for man's sin,
If he'd cover his chances
From without and within.

There were a dozen leaders,
Each the chief of a tribe.
Every one gave the same, so
By a dozen they multiplied.

To the tabernacle Moses went
To speak to God within. Now a
Message came from the Mercy
Seat between two cherubim.

Moses passed word along, and
Aaron lit the lamps of gold.
The lights all shone ahead,
Just as the Lord foretold.

"Now gather in the Levites
Before the Tabernacle door.
They must wash and shave;
Then show them the score.

Sprinkle them with water
And wash their clothing too.
They must bring offerings;
Two yearling bulls will do.

Let their offerings be fine
Flour with oil mixed in.
This, and one of the bulls
To be their offering for sin.

The leaders of the tribes
Shall lay hands on them and
Present them to the Lord
For they will be His men.

Thus we'll tell the world
The Lord has made a choice.
To accept the Levites in
Place of Israel's eldest boys.

For the night of passover, as
Your enemies' sons I slew,
I claimed your eldest
And of your cattle too."

From the tribes of Israel
A dozen mighty princes came
With gifts and sacrifices,
And each one gave the same.

CHAPTER 8

Levites were comissioned
To do the work of God. The
Service of the Tabernacle
Was now to be their job.

For a quarter of a century
They would do their best.
With automatic retirement
And a future life of rest.

CHAPTER 9

Now someone came to Moses,
And this question asked:
"What if I'm unclean or on
A journey, don't get back?

And wish to honor passover,
Will God take me to task?"
So Moses asked Jehovah,
"How shall I answer that?"

Then in a flash the answer
Came as they waited there.
Believers were entitled
A passover feast to share.

But for those who'd ask,
There'd be a month delay.
"They may celebrate with
Bitter herbs, I say.

You shall treat strangers
Just as you do your own

With only one ordinance
And no favoritism shown."

Cloud covered the Tabernacle,
On the very day 'twas raised.
And if they stayed in camp,
It always stayed in place.

But if the cloud moved on,
They'd break camp and go.
Wherever went the cloud,
This nation went also.

And when the sun went down
The cloud lit up like fire.
It did this forty years
And never seemed to tire.

CHAPTER 10

Two beaten silver trumpets
God had them hammer out.
'Twould be a better signal
Than all the loudest shouts.

They'd signal many things
The way the trumpets blew.
Whether to stay in camp
Or head for some place new.

It also might be used
To signal great alarm.
Or that they were safe
And free from any harm.

Thus they could signal
The orders of the day.
Whether to move out,
Or if they should stay.

And Jehovah would
    remember,
As those bugles pealed,
That these were His people
With whom He must deal.

CHAPTER 11

Now there came a time when
The people all complained.
They remembered only good
Had forgotten all the pain.

Time had dimmed the memory
Of when they were slaves.
Eating naught but manna had
Caused them quite a strain.

They dreamed of fresh fish,
Cucumbers and onions too.
Of ripe fruit and melons,
With garlic in the stew.

So Moses got the feeling
As they were crying there,
This was too much trouble,
And he had too much care.

So the Lord sent quail in
Such a great profusion, the
Very job of catching them
Must have caused confusion.

So they gorged themselves on
Meat for which they'd cried;
Many suddenly sickened,
And some even died.

CHAPTER 12

A humble man was Moses
In faith was very zealous.
Aaron and Miriam envied him;
Actually they were jealous.

They grumbled to each other,
Which was very bad, because
The Lord overheard them,
And it made him awfully mad.

He was in a cloud of anger,
Or so one might say, as

Before the Tabernacle
He confronted them one day.

Now when the Lord departed,
Miriam's skin turned white.
And Moses cried out to God
To make her right.

"She'll suffer seven days,"
The Lord then said.
"As a leper treat her, and
Out of camp she'll bed."

CHAPTER 13

The children now had come
Near the promised land.
So Moses sent some spies
From out the Hebrew band.

Forty days they spied out
The hill country up ahead.
Then reported back filled
With awe and dread.

For the land they'd scouted
Was one of milk and honey,
With crops in abundance,
Climate warm and sunny.

But they'd seen giants that
Made them feel so small,
They now lost all courage,
It made them want to crawl.

CHAPTER 14

"A land of milk, and honey,"
Caleb, and Joshua said,
"And God is always with us,
So we should move ahead."

But the people were cowed,
Fearing battles to come.
They wailed and grumbled;
To Egypt they'd have run.

The Lord was angry; He'd
Have had their heads. But
Moses pleaded with God or
They'd have surely been dead.

But God was so disgusted
By people's lack of faith,
He'd make them suffer for
The cowardly acts displayed.

"Ten times they've rebelled,
And now they'd stone my
man.
So not one of these doubters
Will see the promised land."

The Lord was so angry with
The ten who backed away,
That all were struck dead
Before Him there that day.

Next morn' the people rose,
To do His will too late.
But God and Moses did not
And left them to their fate.

Into the hills they marched
Until the foe they met, then
They stopped at Hormah, or
They might be running yet.

CHAPTER 15

Now every man was equal
According to their law. If
He erred in ignorance, it
Was thought a common flaw.

For breaking the Sabbath
No one asked if he'd atone,
They took him out of camp
And killed him with stones.

CHAPTER 16

Korah, Dathan, and Abiram,
With two hundred followers,

Moved forward in rebellion
Against those in power.

The famous brothers again
Were on the spot, but soon
Turned the tables on their
Enemies, and made it hot.

For Moses made them play
By the rules God had made.
So as they confronted him,
It was no even trade.

They were swallowed up
By the earth that day,
With the lives of families
And friends they all paid.

Then all the people fled
As they heard the screams;
They'd not expected this
In their wildest dreams.

Almost fifteen thousand more
Were consumed in sudden fire;
When once again in rebellion,
They caused their leaders ire.

CHAPTER 17

Then Moses bid them come
And bring their wooden rods,
The owners' names inscribed,
As ordered by their God.

By the buds that grew on one
They all would surely know,
He whom God had chosen
As priest to run the show.

When the results were known,
They could hardly believe.
Aaron's budded and blossomed
With ripe almonds and leaves.

So if those back biters
Began to complain again,

Moses would have the means
To silence every man.

Still the people grumbled,
As they were oft' to do. For
They were a rebellious lot
Who would complain anew.

CHAPTER 18

Again the Lord told Aaron,
The Tabernacle was his share.
And only he and his sons
Should do the service there.

The Levites would be there
To do the maintenance jobs.
They'd avoid priestly work,
Or face the wrath of God.

Levites wages would be
Taken from the tithes. But
They could own no property
So needless in this life.

A tithe Levites will give
The best for sacrifice do.
They must give their share
And accept commitment too.

CHAPTER 19

The water of separation was
Explained to Moses too.
For one touching the dead
Would be an unclean Jew.

He must sacrifice a heifer
Unblemished, red, and pure.
Then strain water through
Her ashes to perform a cure.

The cure, by special ritual,
Was the province of a priest.
It took seven days before
'Twould make one clean.

Now if a man should fail
To see the program through,
He would be excommunicated,
And his rights he'd lose.

CHAPTER 20

In the Wilderness of Zin they
Camped, Miriam expired there.
Then a lack of drinking water
Added to their cares.

Again the mob complained,
Of which they'd done a lot.
Moses, with Aaron's rod, made
Water gush from a rock.

Now they came to Edom, and
Were not allowed to pass.
Rather than fight their kin,
They turned and headed back.

Atop a mountain Aaron died;
The children camped below.
For he and Moses stole God's
Glory and made water flow.

They'd taken credit at Meriba
For a miracle of God's hand.
Thus they missed their chance
To reach the promised land.

Now when they learned
That Aaron had passed away,
They were very sorry
And grieved for thirty days.

CHAPTER 21

Local kings were alarmed, as
Israel started moving in. Who
Can count on good will? They
Thought a war they'd win.

They must not have known,
That God was Israel's King, for

Though Israel went to battle
Jehovah pulled the strings.

So the King of Arad rose up
To fight them at the border,
But God helped Israel to
Put him out of order.

After all their victories
The people cried once more.
God had heard so much
The griping made Him sore.

He sent poisonous snakes,
Which they cried about.
Now they screamed to Moses
To again come bail them out.

So once more he asked God
To tell him what to do; as
He'd done so oft' before,
God now helped him too.

So a brazen serpent he cast
And placed it upon a pole
That they could gaze upon
To make them once more
  whole.

Now the children traveled on,
So many places they camped.
Like Oboth, Iye-abarim, and
Zared Brook, as on and on
They tramped,

To cross the River Arnon and
Camp upon its banks. Then
To a well called "Beer", and
There they all gave thanks.

This was the well the leaders
Dug when to God they harked.
Among Amonites and
  Moabites,
On the border they parked.

The desert they left behind,
As they drifted through.
Mattanah, Nahaliel, Bamoth,
And the Moab Valley plateau.

Out across the desert they
Could see Mt. Pisgah there.
This trip had been so long,
Theyd've given their share.

When they asked permission
To pass through Sihon's land,
The king brought up his army,
And Israel killed every man,

Then vanquished the Amorites
And soon attended to Bashan.
King Og and sons died there,
So Israel now held more land.

CHAPTER 22

East of the River Jordan, on
The Moab plains they camped,
Just across from Jericho,
And near King Balak's land.

A mighty reputation as rough,
Tough, and mean they'd made;
So the king just wasn't ready
To give them an even break.

So he tried to bribe Balaam
To put Israel under a curse.
But that worthy individual
Appeared to be averse.

For he wanted to do only
What the Lord would say.
King Balak was determined
To have it done his way.

The king was so insistent,
Balaam journeyed there.
Now his means of travel
Was upon a donkey mare.

But the angel of the Lord
Stood upon the trail, so
The donkey shied away and
Persuasion seemed to fail.

Now Balaam beat his steed
And got her on the road.
He'd not seen the angel
And was determined to go.

Thrice he beat his mount,
Would've killed her there.
But then he saw the angel,
Amazed could only stare.

Then the angel told him
That he was being a fool.
His would-be friend Balak
Would use him as a tool.

Never curse Israelites
Who Jehovah has blessed.
Only say what God decreed;
That was greatly stressed.

He could see he was beat,
And it was surely time
That he change his plan
Lest he commit a crime.

CHAPTER 23

Now Balak was real anxious
To have things go his way,
So he listened closely to
What this man would say.

"From out the land of Aram,
The mountains of the east, I
Came to curse a people, so
King Balak would be pleased.

They're a peculiar nation,
Whom God plainly condones.
Wishing no harm to others
They prefer to live alone.

They are great in numbers
And God is on their side.
If I could have my wish,
I would die an Israelite."

Balak wasn't happy; things
Just weren't going right. If
Balaam wouldn't curse them,
It could be one tough fight.

So he tried again to get
Balaam on his side. But God
Would not allow him to
Cater to Balak's pride.

So Balaam said to him,
"Now listen to what I say;
God sees no fault in Israel
And will not say them nay.

He always keeps promises
Will not change His way. He
Finds no fault with Jacob
Stands with them every day.

He brought them out of Egypt
With miracles of great might.
He shields them from harm
And keeps them in his sight."

Then King Balak said to him,
"It certainly seems to me
If I can't get your help,
You shouldn't help the enemy.

Many sacrifices I made
And was doing all I could.
But for all my effort
It did me little good."

CHAPTER 24

Again Balak called on him
To get him on his side.
But could hardly believe his
Ears when Balaam prophesied.

"God's spirit was there as
I looked across the plains;
I could see Israel blessed
By sunshine and the rain.

I could see the future. In
Valleys would be fine homes
With plenty for everyone
And no more need to roam.

By beautiful river gardens
Abundance spreads with
Joyful peace and quiet
And not a thing to dread.

They'll live in many places;
Their kingdom will be great.
None can oppose them, nor
Can enemies afford to hate.

They'll be mighty in battle,
Their valor oft' will show.
They're favored by the Lord
And with them, He will go."

Now Balak was unhappy; this
Wasn't his best day. So
In anger and frustration
Ordered Balaam on his way.

Yet Balaam made answer as
He prophesied to him.
"I've heard Jehovah's word,
And my vision is not dim.

There will come a star from
Jacob down histories trail.
The land of Moab He'll
Smite, this ruler of Israel.

They'll destroy Seth's sons,
To possess Edom and Seir.
Many cities they'll plunder;
None can oppose them there.

Amalek is a mighty nation
But its destiny is to fall.
You Kenites live among rocks
With your backs to the wall.

Ships will come from Cyprus;
Assyria, and Eber will fall.
For this is the will of God,
And the score He shall call."

So those who'd been friends,
Went sadly on their way, for
They had disagreed but each
Had had his say.

CHAPTER 25

Moabite girls liked parties,
Worshipping a god named Baal.
Some Israelite youth did too
And their religeon failed.

Most of the nation followed
And God's anger waxed hot.
So orders came and leaders
Named to execute the lot.

Zimri, of Simeon's tribe,
Brought a girl into his tent.
Phinehas followed killing
Both, and God did now repent.

Twenty-four thousand had died
Because of what they'd done.
The price they paid was high,
And all in the name of fun.

Word soon came from God,
    "The
Midianites you'll destroy,
Before all Israel follows the
Fate of that girl and boy."

CHAPTER 26

After the years of wandering
They took a census once more.

All the doubters had died,
Who were in the tally before.

Caleb and Joshua remained,
Still steadfast and strong.
Stayed and obeyed, when
All the others went wrong.

Forty years upon the trail,
The census told the score.
Their army now would count
A few less than it had before.

CHAPTER 27

Zelophehad of Joseph's line
Wanted a share, her father
Had died in honor, and she
Wanted the status of heir.

So Moses asked Jehovah, and
Quickly the Lord agreed.
She had a reasonable claim,
And a law should read!

If a man had all daughters
With no brothers to share,
The girls should inherit,
And it would be only fair.

Now the Lord told Moses,
It was time he must die.
And Moses didn't complain
Nor did he ask why.

But he pled with God
To help find a good man
To lead Israel's nation
Toward the promised land.

So the Lord gave him orders
To put Joshua on the job.
For he was a good man
And in favor with God.

Henceforth he'd get word
Through Eleazar, the priest.

And with God's help,
All the children he'd lead.

So Moses blessed Joshua
Before those people there.
He surely needed something
For the burdens he'd bear.

CHAPTER 28

Again we are told all the
Rules for the clan:
Of offerings by fire,
Of yearling male lambs.

The burnt offerings and
Drink offerings ordained;
Of mixing flour and oil,
And offerings of grain.

Offerings on the Sabbath,
Each month the first day.
There were many others
Celebrated in similar ways.

CHAPTER 29

Offerings for vows
And those for free will.
At every offering
An animal was killed.

A lamb offered for this
And a bullock for that.
A he-goat for sin, without
Blemish, perfect, and fat.

CHAPTER 30

The leaders of the tribes
Were summoned to appear
And listen, for the Lord
Wanted them to hear.

If a man or a woman
Or a girl took a stand,

Their undying adherence
The Lord would demand.

But if the girl's father
Thought the load too great,
He could ease the problem
If he would only so state.

For a husband or father
Could cancel the vow, if
He'd only speak up and
Do it right now.

But if he said nothing in
His role as the man, the
Vow would be binding and
Certainly would stand.

On the day that he heard
He would have to decide.
For any time after that
By the word he'd abide.

Because if he was late
When he changed his mind,
The penalty was his
And he'd be in a bind.

CHAPTER 31

The Lord said to Moses,
"The Midianites banish,
They led Israel's idolatry,
For that they must vanish."

Twelve thousand warriors
They sent out to the war.
Led by brave Phinehas,
The son of Eleazar.

They marched out in force;
The trumpets all blaring.
With the Ark in the lead,
They went a warfaring.

They wiped out the enemy
To the very last man.

With kings Rekem, Zur,
Hur, Reba, even Balaam.

The women and children
They took for their own,
But faced Moses' wrath
When returning back home.

For the women were there
Who'd caused the downfall.
So Moses gave orders
To get rid of them all.

"Slay all those women
And all the boys as well.
Little girls you may keep
And raise for your selves.

Now stay out of the camp
For the next seven days
And purify your selves
In the ceremonial ways."

Then they took inventory
Of the booty they had won.
There was gold, jewelry,
And much under the sun.

Every Israelite gained at
The battles they'd had,
They had not lost a man
And that wasn't all bad.

CHAPTER 32

The land of Caanan was an
Answer to their prayers.
But on the way there they
Crossed other lands fair.

So some came to Moses
With a petition to stay.
His answer was eloquent,
This, he had to say.

"Your fathers were spies
Whom to Caanan I sent.

But returned in great fear
When they saw giant men.

Then Jehovah in anger
Said they'd never see
The fair promised land,
Its flowers and trees.

So He made us wander the
Wilderness forty years,
Death and destruction
For those who'd had fears.

Caleb and Joshua were the
Only ones who stood firm
For the Lord
And didn't want to run.

Those two had real nerve
Believing in God's might.
Surely they would win
And were ready to fight.

There are more of us now
Than in those days, so
God will be angrier if
You insist on your ways."

They quickly assured him
And all stood their ground.
They'd be first in battle
If they could build towns.

This place where they were
Was perfect to raise sheep.
And to live on this land
Their promise they'd keep.

To the east of Jordan the
Sheep folds they'd build
With walled-in cities,
If the Lord only willed.

This was insurance that
The children would be

Safe from molestation
And also from thieves.

Moses then let them
Do just as they asked,
As long as they'd abide
By all agreed-upon tasks.

Much of the land through
Which they had fought
Was now their own come
Flood, frost, or drought.

CHAPTER 33

For forty long years they
Had wandered the wilds.
It might be believed they
Were tired of the miles.

They'd trekked a sea with
Water walled on each side,
And made the far shore as
Their pursuers all died.

They'd come from Egypt
And trekked a far land
Camped in the mountains
And walked desert sands.

Some kings let them pass
As they wended their way,
But some were obstinate,
And they had said, "Nay."

Some they'd avoided
By travelling way around.
Others were stubborn,
Refusing to give ground.

That was a mistake, as
Those kings would learn,
Kingdoms were pillaged,
And looted and burned.

Aaron, their high priest
Was called to the heights

And there on the mountain
He gave up his life.

For forty long years
They'd wandered the land,
Through wind and rain
And blowing sand.

But now they were camped
On Jordan's banks, and
For the land over there
They could give thanks.

The land would be given
To all of the tribes, but
Before they could claim it
They must pay the price.

All of the idols and
The images they found
Must be broken up and
Cast to the ground.

Places in the hills of
Worship to heathen gods,
Were totally destroyed,
And put to the rod.

The home He had promised
'Twas a vast land indeed
To be given to the tribes
According to size or need.

CHAPTER 34

Long and irregular
The borders would be
Bordered on the west by
The mediterranean sea.

It touched on the Red
And one called Gallilee,
Along the river Jordan
And to the dead sea.

They circled and twisted
Went straight and turned

Encompassing great areas
That battles had earned.

Ten leaders were chosen,
Every one a good man,
To deed to each tribe
Its Share of the land.

CHAPTER 35

Levites would be given
Some cities of their own
With pastures, cattle,
And flocks and homes.

Six of those cities a
Refuge would be where
An innocent fugitive
To safety could flee.

He would be safe
As long as he stayed
Within that city
But never must stray.

However while there by
His peers he'd be tried,
And if found guilty he'd
No place to hide.

A tooth for a tooth
And an eye for an eye.
If murder was intended,
Then he surely must die.

Yet if he'd killed a man
With no intent shown,
He could safely stay
And call it his home.

He'd be safe there until
The death of the priest,
And after that happened
'Twould be safe to leave.

This was the law that
Would keep Israel pure.

God wanted it so,
And that was for sure.

He said He would live on
The land with them all;
It must be kept clean
So they could walk tall.

CHAPTER 36

An heiress must marry
Within her own tribe or
Lose all her influence,
Ownership and pride.

To marry without, she
Might move away still
Owning the property, but
Her tribe would lose say.

So a law was developed
Keeping each tribe to its
Own, so a girl owning land
Should marry near home.

END OF NUMBERS

DEUTERONOMY

CHAPTER 1

Moses asked the children,
"Do you remember long ago?
When we came to Canaan
Our fear first showed.

God promised to lead, but
People complained instead;
So in sorrow and anger He
Let them wander till death.

Caleb and Joshua were brave;
They deserve all the best.
Both are still with us
They've outlived the rest.

I tried to dissuade Israel;
I'd have led them that day.
They feared unknown
  enemies
Ignoring whatever I'd say.

Our people saw they'd sinned
So they tried to make up by
Racing headlong into battle,
But they ran out of luck.

So from the battle they ran,
And that was a day of defeat.
Without the help of the Lord,
They were assuredly beat.

I, too, will never enter the
Land we've sought so long.
For I failed to be humble
And did the Lord wrong."

CHAPTER 2

"Through the wilderness we
Returned toward the Dead Sea.
It seemed forever we'd wander,
But God instructed me.

All the years we wandered,
God led us night and day,
Keeping peace with others,
As he steered us on our way.

Thirty-eight years of journey
To the brook called Zered
Until all who'd rebelled had
Joined the number of dead.

We finally won the victories
That our God got us through.
The Lord had promised
That this was what he'd do.

The giants you feared before
Fell as grass to the fire,
As we raged across the land
And never did tire.

We captured all the cities,
The valleys and the plains.
Our enemies all vanquished,
Their possessions our gains."

CHAPTER 3

"Next we came to Bashan
King Og attacked us there;
We killed them, every one,
And their goods we shared.

Now all the Amorite lands
From the River Jordon east
Had fallen to our armies;
We no longer counted least.

King Og of Bashan was the
Last of the giant Rephaim;
His iron bed in a museum
Indicates the size of him.

Six feet wide it is and
Thirteen and a half long.
He was a mighty man
Indeed was very strong.

But our Lord is greater,
And he is on our side.
When we hunt the enemy,
He has no place to hide.

We divided a mighty land
And the spoils of war, but
I was not allowed to share;
Jehovah still was sore.

And when I begged to go He
Said, "Speak of it no more!
But go up Mt. Pisgah, and
You'll see what's in store.

I gazed across the valley,
The plains and desert sand;
But won't go over Jordan or
Live in the promised land.

God said to appoint Joshua
To lead and conquerors be,
And he is now your leader;
The end is near for me."

CHAPTER 4

"Now we are encamped in
The valley of Beth-Peor.
Here I shall teach the laws
You must obey forever more.

You are a mighty people for
Your God has smiled on you.
So do as you are taught,
And His Law do not undo.

His word wise and prudent
Will bring peace and fame.
But demands a total effort,
You'll find it is no game.

Now tell your children what
Jehovah has done for you.
And how he'll help again
If you'll only ask Him to.

Remember The Ten
  Commandments
As Horeb blew fire and
  smoke?
You did not see God up there
But heard him as He spoke.

So do not defile yourselves
By making idols of anything.

Be sure to heed his voice
With life and truth it rings.

As I have said before, the
Promised land I'll not see.
Because I belittled God,
And he did not pardon me.

So take your cue from that
And never anger him, for He
Will destroy and scatter you,
If you spend lives in sin.

He will keep his promise
And answer if you call. The
Lord your God is merciful
And wants to save you all."

CHAPTER 5

Out of the mountain
Came fire and smoke,
And from its midst
Our Lord Jehovah spoke.

"You must not use
My name in vain
When making a vow
Or stating a claim.

Six days you should work,
On the seventh rest, for
You were slaves but with
Freedom now you're blessed.

Give honor to your father
And to your mother too
And enjoy all the years
Your God has given you.

Murder and adultery
You must strictly avoid,
And the sin of falsehood
With all these are alloyed.

Never be jealous of anyone
If good fortune is his lot.

Better to be his friend
And the very best he's got.

All His laws were given you
On that memorable day.
And you would do well to
Walk along Jehovah's way.

Many feared to go close
When the mountain flared,
But I heard Jehovah's call,
So I climbed up there.

That was when He told me,
If you would obey His will,
He would give you all
Of Caanan's land to till."

CHAPTER 6

These were some things
That old Moses taught,
For he loved those people
And his waking thoughts--

Were to save them trouble
From heartbreak or sorrow,
To guarantee their future
A brighter tomorrow.

So he taught them daily
And tried to reinforce all
Of those things that had
Been taught before.

"Oh people, listen well,
Jehovah is our living Lord.
So be sure your children
Will often hear His word.

For it is very good
To do just as you're told,
And our God will keep you
Safely in His fold.

You will live in homes
You did not toil to build

And also reap the harvest
Some one else has tilled.

Remember God is jealous;
He'll not brook idolatry.
So never mimic neighbors
And do not tempted be.

Tell your sons the story;
You were Pharaoh's slaves,
And then God rescued you
How many times He saved.

Miraculous is the word for
What He brought us through.
So enjoy the promised land
And make him proud of you."

CHAPTER 7

"Seven nations destroyed
To give you Caanan's land.
So do not favor the enemy,
Kill woman, child and man.

If you are soft hearted,
And decide to save a few,
Your sons will marry them
And follow their ways too.

We are a Holy people, and
He promised long ago;
He'd bless and keep you,
Great love and honor show.

He will make you multiply,
Disease you will not know.
While he is leading, crops
Will flourish and grow.

You must burn their idols;
Their gold or jewels abhor.
All those things are snares
And horrible to the Lord."

CHAPTER 8

"For forty years He led you,
To be His children indeed.
He fed you on his manna
Fulfilled your every need.

He led us beside mountains
And across valley floors.
Our feet were not blistered
But protected by the Lord.

So walk now in His way,
Reap what you have sown.
God is here to bless you
And claim you for His own.

A land of milk and honey,
Pools and gushing springs,
Grapes, figs and olives,
And every needed thing.

When you've eaten enough,
Thank God for everything.
And for all He's given you
Let your praises ring.

When you're fat and happy
Don't take credit yourselves.
You'd have never made the
Grade without God's help."

CHAPTER 9

"Listen all Israel, while I
Tell you once again, it's
Not that you're so great
Or better than any man,

God will give you victory
Because the enemy is so bad.
Not because you are better,
For you often make Him sad.

Always you've complained
And kicked over the traces.

Only because I work so hard
Are you in His good graces.

The enemy are all fighters
Of nations greater than you;
The cities have high walls,
And the Anak Giants too.

But He hates their ways
And will help you win,
Not because you're good
But because of all their sin.

Often He'd have dumped you
But in fear I took your part
And was lucky to remind him
He'd taken you to his heart.

Egyptians would not believe
Unless He helped you through.
You were His chosen people,
God truly does love you."

CHAPTER 10

Then once again the Lord
Said,"Make tablets of stone."
The first two I had broken
And the writing was all gone.

Again I climbed the mountain,
So He gave the law once more;
It should guide you well, as
He steers toward the shore.

He had us build an ark;
Within we put those slabs.
They were for your guidance
And the only law you had.

It should be a simple thing
To please the Lord our God.
So now cleanse your hearts,
And do your christian jobs.

Remember when our ancestors
Went down to Egypt's land,

Only seventy of them then
Made up the entire caravan.

How the Lord smiled on you
And accepted you as you are;
So now you are a multitude
As countless as the stars."

CHAPTER 11

"So, listen to what I say
You elders of these tribes,
For you are all witnesses to
The miracles I'll describe.

He led you through the sea
And safely beyond the shore;
How He fed you on the
   manna
And did a great deal more.

Made your enemies powerless
Up to this very day,
And He has been your savior
In every conceivable way.

This land He is giving you
Is lush and verdant soil;
Here you may live in plenty
With a minimum of toil!

Be sure your hearts are true
And never worship other gods;
Or He'll stop the blessings,
And you'll push up the sod.

Tie a string on your finger
To remind you every day to
Tell your children of our God
And raise them up His way.

No enemy can stand up to you,
He'll be where you are. You
Will have no problems; you'll
Be feared both near and far."

CHAPTER 12

"Destroy every inhabitant
For they are a wicked people
Who would lead you all astray
And make you weak and
   feeble.

Make sacrifices in places
Which God will show to you;
Call your sons and daughters,
Your servants and Levites too.

Always share with the Levites,
For land they do not own.
And teach your children well,
For they will soon be grown."

CHAPTER 13

"Do not follow prophets
If they beckon to other gods.
Place your hand against them
And do not spare the rod.

Even your son or daughter
Or beloved wife shall draw
Execution by the community,
For this is Jehovah's law.

If one of our cities turns
And worships not our Lord,
Then make sure it is so
And put it to the sword.

Then God will be merciful
With compassion every day,
So follow His command to
Do right in all your ways."

CHAPTER 14

"The Lord has claimed you
From people of the earth,
These things now observe
Convince Him of your worth.

Unless an animal chews the
Cud and has a cloven hoof,
It will not be meat for you
You'd better stay aloof.

The Eagle, the Vulture,
And the Falcon are out,
The Osprey, the Raven,
The Seagull and Owl.

The Ostrich and mighty Hawk,
The Pelican and Cormorant,
The Stork and the Heron,
The Hoopee and the Bat.

They are birds of a feather
And are not for you to eat,
But most all the others
You may take for meat.

Insects are off limits
If equipped with wings,
But many others are okay
If you need such things.

Do not eat an animal
That has died naturally.
A foreignor or stranger
May a paying customer be.

Never boil a young goat
In its mothers milk, or
Hob-nob with heathen
Or any of their ilk.

Give a tithe every year
Of your grapes and wine,
And flocks and herds,
Keep God in your lives.

Give to the Levites, for
They lack crops or lands.
And give every third year
To welfare programs.

Levites or foreigners
From your income share.

For widows and orphans
We must also care.

So make them welcome
And share your wealth;
Jehovah will bless and
Assure your good health."

CHAPTER 15

"You will forgive your
Debtors each seventh year,
And help the poor
Whenever they appear.

Every six years, all your
Hebrew slaves you'll free
And bless them at parting
As God has blessed thee.

Now heed my command,
And you'll know no loss;
But if you complain,
It will add to your cost.

For he who complains
When helping another man,
Has spoiled his own fun
And pleasure is banned.

If a slave should prefer
To serve you all his days,
You shall pierce his ear;
And he'll be yours always.

Give the first of flocks,
And those of your herds,
The best fruit and grain;
Now please heed my words.

If there be a blemish
Or a wound or spot, then
Eat it all yourselves,
Find a better in the lot.

The blood do not eat but
Pour it out like water.

For this is the law
Of your heavenly father."

CHAPTER 16

"In the dark of the night
You left Egypt behind. So
Celebrate the journey,
Keep it ever on your mind.

A lamb or ox for sacrifice,
Unleavened bread will do,
In a place God will name,
He'll not leave that to you.

In April you will do this
And then go home. For this
Is the feast of Passover
And is no time to roam.

Use no yeast for seven days,
Then gather before the Lord.
This feast is a solemn rite,
The seventh day don't work.

A week after harvest begins
There will be another feast
Before the Lord Jehovah
To be the festival of weeks.

Your sacrifice appropriate
To gifts you've received.
Be thankful and celebrate
To God whom you believed.

Help Levites, foreigners,
Widows and orphans too. For
If you share good fortune,
He too will share with you.

Before the God of Israel,
Three times in every year,
At the festival of shelters
Each and every man appears.

Choose judges and officials
To serve cities of the land.

They'll administer justice
And be fair to every man.

Never bribe a man of wisdom
Nor make the poor man wail.
Use wise and sober decisions
For wisdom must prevail.

Never erect an image other
Than an altar to your Lord.
Don't set up an obelisk;
God even hates the word."

CHAPTER 17

"If another god is found
In a man or woman's home,
Then they must be taken
And shall then be stoned.

One witness is not enough
To cause a person to die.
There must be two or more
And very good reasons why.

They'll be first to throw
Before the people take over.
This way you'll purge evil,
But it's no field of clover.

If the people cannot decide
Which way a case should go,
Take it to the sanctuary;
Those in charge will know.

Their decision is absolute
And there'll be no reprieve.
The chief judge will decide
And no second pleas receive.

Soon all criminals will hear
Of justice swift and sure.
Few murderers will chance
Falling before your cure.

When arriving in the land
Jehovah has given to you,

You'll notice other nations
And want your own king too.

Then select a man with care,
An Israelite he must be. A
Rich man will not do, nor
One with many wives to feed.

He must not turn from God,
But study to be a priest.
He must love all justice
And walk the narrow street.

Now if he listens to God
And does not walk alone,
His sons will naturally
Succeed him to the throne."

CHAPTER 18

"Levites are His people so
Will own no property. Part
Of each sacrifice is theirs,
It is the right of a priest.

On arrival in Caanan, do not
Follow local customs there;
Fortune telling, black magic,
Wizardry, or any evil fare.

The reason I'm on your side
Is because of these things.
I'll raise up a prophet
And the truth he will bring.

You begged me on the
   mountain
When you were afraid of fire.
God confided in me then that
He'd cater to your desires.

He will raise up a prophet,
An Israelite, just like you.
And communicate through
   him
To tell you what to do.

You can always tell a prophet
By what he says to you.
For if he is not God's man,
His promises are not true."

CHAPTER 19

"One day the enemy you'll
Destroy then own his land.
Save three cities of refuge
To rescue an innocent man.

If he did not kill in anger, but
Was trapped by circumstance,
He can find a refuge, and
There he'll get the chance--

To prove that he is innocent
Of premeditated wrong, he
Won't have to run forever;
He may not be that strong.

If you follow God's Commands,
Your kingdom will double.
So you'll need more cities
For those who get in trouble.

But only protect the innocent
For the guilty ones must pay.
Purge murder or false witness
For that is the only way."

CHAPTER 20

"When you go to war and see
A greater army than your own,
Don't feel small and weak,
Or let yourselves be thrown.

For God will go before you
As He has been all your days.
A mighty champion He'll be;
Just let Him have His way.

Your officers will send you
Back home if you're afraid.

They do not want a coward; it
Would cause a battle charade.

When you march upon a city,
First offer it a truce;
And if it then refuses,
To ashes that city reduce.

If you must take that city,
Destroy everything there
Except women and children,
Cattle and booty share.

But if it does capitulate,
Then save it all intact. The
People will be servants;
They'll be slaves in fact.

This only applies to cities
That lie beyond your land.
Of those within your borders
You must let nothing stand.

You must destroy all those
Who might lead you astray.
Their absolute destruction
Is the only certain way.

Take trees for timber to
Batter down their walls.
You may eat their fruit, but
Those trees must not fall."

CHAPTER 21

"If you find a murder victim
When you arrive in that land,
But he who did the deed
Is obviously a missing man--

The elders and the judges
Of the city it is closest to, in
A wild and beautiful valley,
With rivers flowing through--

Will lead an unbroken heifer,
And her neck they'll break.

Then the priests shall come
And wash their hands and say,

Oh Lord, forgive our people
For the crime they didn't do--
Thus to take away the guilt,
So it will not rest on you.

When enemies are delivered
And among the spoils of war,
You see a beautiful girl
Whom your heart hungers for;

Shave her, pare her nails,
Change her clothing too, for
A month she'll mourn parents,
Then she'll belong to you.

But if soon you tire of her
She must be let go free. For
You've already humiliated her
And a slave she shall not be.

Now if your eldest son
Was by a wife you scorn,
And a wife you love more
Mothered your second born,

A first still gets double
As he would normally do.
This is now the law
As it applies to you.

If you have a son who is
Rebellious and drunken too
And will not be controlled
No matter what you do,

Take him to the elders
And state your case. Then
The men of that city will
With stones his life erase.

Others will hear the story
And they will toe the mark.

For that kind of penalty
Is rather cold and stark.

If a man draws a sentence
And hanging is decreed,
Cut him down that day; do
Not leave him on the tree.

It's a curse to hang upon
A tree all night thru.
So do not defile the land
Your Lord has given you."

CHAPTER 22

"Be helpful to a neighbor
Help him find lost stock.
To hide sex with clothing
Is abhorrent to your God.

Do not rob a bird's nest
And take the mother too.
Houses need a guard rail
All the way around the roof.

Between the rows of grapes
Do not sow other crops, or
Priests will harvest both.
It will be too late to stop.

A man who's guilty of rape
Of a girl not spoken for
Must pay her father a fine,
Marry her, never to divorce.

Any man shall never with
His father's widow sleep.
She was first his father's,
And this law you'll keep."

CHAPTER 23

Many rules were made which
To us seem strange. They
Were made for that day and
Were not meant to change.

The sanctuary was sacred,
Off limits to many Jews. If
You were a bastard, ten
Generations it haunted you.

If a man lost his manhood
The same applied to him.
And Ammonites or Moabites
Were never to go within.

When you came to settle
They'd try to hold you back.
With Egyptians and Edomites,
Use a different tack.

They are like brothers who
Came from Egypt with you.
Their grandchildren may go
Within the sanctuary too.

For God lives among you,
And you must be sure; the
Path on which He walks
Is absolutely pure.

If a slave escapes a master,
Don't force him to return.
Let him settle if he wishes
Where a living he may earn.

Prostitutes or homosexuals,
Neither man or woman allow.
Charge no interest on loans
For you are brothers now.

Interest you may collect
Only from a foreigner. And
Keep all the vows you've
Made before your Lord.

Walking in others vineyards,
It's okay to eat some grapes.
A basket to carry them home
You should never take.

In a neighbor's field you may
Strip some heads of grain;

But to sample with a sickle,
Your welcome may be a pain.

CHAPTER 24

A man who is newly married
Is draft exempt for a year
To live at home in peace
And no extra problems fear.

Do not take a millstone
For your neighbor's pledge.
With it he makes a living;
Without, he'd lose his edge.

Never kidnap a brother Jew
To make of him a slave; for
When the evil is purged, you
Will go to an early grave.

If you would a lender be, do
Not chase him to the house;
For he will pay his debt,
So let him bring it out.

If he is very poor and his
Cloak he offers to give,
Do not keep it over night;
He needs it just to live.

Pay your hired man
At the close of each day,
For of course he is poor
And always needs his pay.

A man who's worthy of death
Should pay for his crime.
Help the orphans and widows
And aid justice every time.

When reaping your harvest,
Leave a few sheaves
And some of the fruit
On your olive trees.

When you pick your grapes,
Be sure to leave a few, for

Migrants, widows or orphans
Often get hungry too.

Now if you do all these
And honor well your God,
He will smile and bless you
And surely spare the rod.

Remember Egypt's slavery,
How God brought you home.
So be thankful to the Lord
And from him never roam."

CHAPTER 25

"Forty lashes before a
Judge," if it was a bad
Crime, limiting the sent-
ence a custom of the time.

As he treads out grain on
The threshing floor, don't
Muzzle the ox; what he
Eats won't make you poor.

A man's name should continue
So if he dies without a son,
His brother should marry his
Widow and so beget him one.

His sister in-law then,
If he refuses to so do,
Will spit in his face after
Pulling off his shoe.

So he'll be infamous, as the
Man who lost his sandal. For
Not getting his brother a
Family caused a scandal.

Be honest and be true; God
Detests a liar and a cheat.
So stand up straight ye Jews
And walk the narrow street.

Amalek is your enemy
Whom you must destroy.

Until the deed is done,
You will know no joy."

CHAPTER 26

Give of tithes and gifts
When in the promised land.
It is from such as these
We help our fellow man.

Every third year remember
Helpless and orphans too.
Do your special tithing;
They all depend on you.

Be sure to thank God and to
Show how good you've been,
For He watches from Heaven
To note the affairs of men.

Obey all his commandments
And do as he asks of you.
For he has made you great
As he smiled upon the Jews.

CHAPTER 27

Then Moses and the elders
Gave people one more job.
After gaining Caanan to
Build a monument to God.

Using rocks off the bottom
Where River Jordon flows
To just beyond the mountain
There to pile those stones.

Faced those rocks with lime,
Wrote thereon these words:
You'll rejoice and sacrifice
And gather before the Lord.

Moses and the Levite Priests
Addressed the people there.
Laws written on the
   monument
Were for every one to share.

When they crossed over Jordan
And gained the other side,
Half climbed Mt. Gerazim; Mt,
Ebal held the other tribes.

Then the Levites stood be-
Tween the mountains to shout,
"Now listen closely Israel;
This is what it's all about.

Curses on he who makes
Or worships an Idol,
Whether made from wood
Or if its cast from metal.

Curses on him who despises
His father or his mother,
Or who moves the markers
Of his land and another's.

Cursed be an adulterer
In any way, shape or form.
Taking unfair advantage of
Others is not the norm.

Cursed is he who slays
Another or accepts a bribe.
If he doesn't keep the law,
An outcast from his tribe."

Levites extolled the law,
As God declared it then; and
The people on the mountains
In return replied, "Amen."

CHAPTER 28

Keep all the commandments,
I'm enjoining you today.
God will be with you, and
He'll make clear your way.

Blessings will be yours;
You'll excell in all you do.
He'll defeat your enemies,
As He walks along with you.

Blessings He promised, you
Must work at for his help.
For God aids those most
Who also help themselves.

But if you will not listen,
And do not do your share;
Your future will decay,
Of this, please be aware.

Curses will come upon you
No matter where you are.
The trials that befall you
Will surely leave their scar.

You'll be confused and fail
In all things you undertake.
For you cannot be successful
If you your God forsake.

You'll be defeated in battle
And scourged by much
    disease.
Heat and dust will choke you;
They're the least of these.

For God will be against you,
Without him you cannot stand.
He'll turn the enemy on you,
And you will lose your land.

You'll be slaves, imprisoned,
Till your last hope is gone,
And to call on God won't help
For you have done so wrong.

CHAPTER 29

'Twas on the plains of Moab
Moses told all these things,
How to overcome much
    trouble
They'd even unseated kings,

Had fled the army of Egypt,
And saw it put asunder. And

Back in camp lived God, who
Spoke from smoke and thunder.

"Forty years you've wandered,
Never wearing out your shoes.
Your clothes, still wearing,
It's time to pay your dues.

You could have been in
Caanan many long years ago,
But Jehovah was teaching you
Things that you should know.

Now it should be obvious from
Miracles that He's caused, He
Loved you from the beginning;
There has never been a pause.

This is a serious contract;
It means you belong to God!
You must not fail Jehovah,
Or He will apply the rod.

For if you slip and fall,
Or ignore His clear commands,
He will turn against you;
Of you, He'll wash His hands.

After all the good He's done,
He's loved you for His own.
But if you go against Him the
Course you will have blown.

Nations of the land will
Wonder what happened to you.
Your life will be a disaster,
If on you He lowers the boom.

His promises will be a waste;
Your lives will be diseased,
If you break the covenant
Lord Jehovah has decreed."

CHAPTER 30

Moses had warned them again
How serious failure would be,

But they could get back to
God if they would only see

That they must be His,
Heart and body and soul;
He must be their preference
In fact, their only goal.

Heaven and earth are witness
To how they met the need, and
Their future lives in Caanan
Depended upon their deeds.

CHAPTER 31

Now Moses was getting older,
A hundred twenty to be sure,
He could not live in Caanan,
Because he'd been impure.

He knew his hour was near,
So Joshua he appointed to
Lead, to take Israel across
The river where they would
Plant their seed.

He said they could well obey
The Commandments they'd
    been
Given, because they weren't
Hidden away in Heaven.

Then Moses wrote a song to
Remind them all tomorrow; if
They failed their God, it
Could only bring them sorrow.

The Levites were told to keep
Those laws beside the Ark.
It would be a just reminder
To make those rebels hark.

CHAPTER 32

Then Moses recited his song
For all the people to hear,

While hoping they'd remember
Through all the coming years.

Oh listen, Heaven and Earth,
Now hear ye, what I say;
How glorious is our Lord
As He smiles on us today.

He is our glorious rock,
The sunshine of our lives.
He gives us all our strength
And powers all our drives.

Others had guardian angels
To help them on their way.
But to us He came in person
To lead us night and day.

He gave us fertile fields,
Mountains and valleys wide.
We lived on milk and honey
And drifted with the tide.

If we grow fat and lazy
And forget the words of God,
If we follow idols or images,
And if we spurn the rock;

He'll soon turn the tables
And treat us as we deserve.
He'll smile at the Gentiles
And leave us in the lurch.

He'll show us His vengeance,
As he gives us our just dues.
As a nation of happy people,
He'll show us we are through.

There'll be drouth and fever
And every fatal disease,
Plus the danger of death,
From many wild beasts.

Thus the song was written
To guide all Israel's tribes,

As Moses made the point,
It would be no easy ride.

The Lord is all powerful; of
Life or death, He holds sway.
He kills or makes alive,
Wounds or heals, His way.

And again Moses warned them
To pay attention to His words.
Remember that their future
Would depend upon the Lord.

CHAPTER 33

Then Moses gave a blessing
To the people before he died.
For they were his great love
In whom he took much pride.

"God has smiled upon us from
Each mountain we've crossed.
He led us by smoke and flame
While in doubt we tossed.

He greatly loves His people,
Your lives are in His hand.
Yet you wavered in faith, as
You trekked across the land.

May all tribes of this nation
Bathe in His loving care;
From the fullness of earth
May you all in plenty share.

May the tribe of Reuben
Increase and forever live.
Levi's tribe will serve, so
Your thankful offerings give.

The tribe of Benjamin
Is deeply loved of God.
May they be richly blessed
By the best of sunkist crops.

May blessings be on Joseph,
A prince above them all.

On the multitude of Ephraim,
May many blessings fall."

Of the thousands of Manasseh,
From the tribe of Zebulun, he
Said, "Rejoice in sunshine
As life's race you run.

Sacrifice and celebrate, oh
Issachar, lovers of your
Tents. Taste the richness of
The sea, treasures God has
  sent.

With savage arm and face and
Head, God reserved good land.
It was chosen for a leader
And Gad was a leading man.

Like unto a lion cub
Is the tribe of Dan, and
Happy is Naphtali's tribe
With God's blessing unto man.

Now the tribe of Asher
Is like a favorite son. He
Bathes his feet in olive oil
And is honored by everyone.

Who can match Jerusalem's
  God?
With him lives are charmed.
He helps us in His splendor,
Holds us in his loving arms.

In safety Israel prospers in
A land of corn and wine.
Heaven's gentle rain descends,
Giving life to all our kind."

CHAPTER 34

Then Moses left the plains,
To climb Mt. Pisgahs peak.
The Lord came to him there
And again to him did speak.

Now look across the valleys
And you'll see over there,
Land I promised your fathers;
It is bountiful and fair.

'Tis the promised land, of
Course, you have come to see.
But don't cross the river, in
Death you'll stay with me."

God buried him in the valley
Quite near to Beth Peor.
No one knows just where
'Tis a secret of the Lord.

A hundred twenty years he
Lived, a prophet of great
Fame, Doing miracles in the
Wilderness and an Egyptian
Pharaoh tamed.

His eye was clear,
The voice was strong,
With a steady hand
To right the wrongs--

He beheld along the way.
With God's help he led well.
Now Joshua takes the reins;
His story we'll next tell.

**THE END OF
DEUTERONOMY**

JOSHUA

CHAPTER 1

Joshua, who'd been Moses'
  man,
Advanced to the leader's place.
With crossing of the Jordan
The next thing he would face.

"Wherever you go," God said,
"Will be part of Israel's land.
Be a strong courageous leader
For you'll be in great demand.

From the Negeb desert north
To the mountains of Lebanon,
From the Mediterranean sea,
To the westward, on and on,

Throughout Hittite land, to
The Euphrates River east.
I will never abandon you,
You may be last but not least."

The leaders, Reuben, Gad and
Manasseh, Joshua bid abide
Their earlier deal with Moses,
When land they chose this side.

Their land was east of Jordan,
Which they'd still not crossed
But had given Moses their word,
Who at that time was boss.

They'd fight in battles ahead
Being subject to their chief.
So Joshua would have courage
To count on help when in need.

CHAPTER 2

Two spies crossed the river
To assess strength in Jericoh,

Now city gates were closed,
So they'd no place to go.

But under some bales of flax
On an inn's roof that night,
Those two spies from Israel
Were kept well out of sight.

For a lady of the evening
Had hidden them away
And had sent local police
Beyond the city gates.

She set a price for the favor
As you might guess she would,
For the safety of her family
Is a thing well understood.

"We know your God is with
  you;
Our land is yours to spoil.
We cannot win this battle
No matter how we toil.

So when the battle's raging,
Do save my relatives and me."
To this they eagerly agreed,
Then she helped them flee.

So they reported to Joshua
About the adventure there
And the certainty of victory
Of which they were aware.

For the people of the city
Were all fainting hearts
And winning was just a matter
Of each man doing his part.

CHAPTER 3

At dawn they pulled stakes
And marched all that day.

Then camped on Jordan's banks
For the last stop on the way.

Next morning they started out
After briefing, once again,
For God would perform
    another
Miracle for the eyes of man.

A priest waded into the river
And stopped its mighty flow,
So across it on dry land
The Israelites could go.

So once again Jehovah,
Had shown to all the world,
How mighty is the Lord
Whose banner they'd unfurled.

While those carrying the ark
Stood there in midstream,
The children filed across
To their land of many dreams.

CHAPTER 4

There were twelve men chosen
From each tribe of the clan,
And a special job awaited
For every able-bodied man.

Each took from Jordan's bed,
A rock upon his shoulders.
On Caanan's shore they built
A monument of those boulders.

So they crossed over with
An army forty thousand strong.
Planning to take up residence
In land they'd sought so long.

In one day a nation crossed;
Again the Jordan River flowed,
As God once separated the sea
And formed a dry land road.

Then Joshua advised them all,
"Tell all children the story,
Of Jehovah, your living God
And how to share His glory."

CHAPTER 5

Now the natives of the land
Soon heard of this feat, in
Instant fear they trembled
Knowing they were beat.

According to God's command,
Joshua set one day aside,
When a generation of Jewish
Young men were circumcised.

Now while they rested so
Their wounds could heal,
They celebrated the passover
And changes in their meals.

For the manna they had eaten
Never fell to them again.
Now they fared much better
While living off the land.

As he gazed at Jericoh to
Assess their chances there, a
Stranger stood not far away,
Of whom Joshua became
    aware!

Joshua strode up close to the
Man who'd drawn his sword.
"Are you friend or foe?" he
Asked and heard these words.

"The army of the Lord,
Is under my command.
Bare your feet when standing
Here, this is Hallowed land."

Then Joshua knelt before him
And did as he was told. For
He knew God's Messenger was
Fearless, right, and bold.

CHAPTER 6

Jericho's gates were closed,
To keep Israel at bay. But
God told Joshua, "Never fear,
The battle will go your way.

Assemble your army and march
Around their walls each day.
Each priest with a ram's horn
Trumpet and do as I say."

Joshua gathered the priests
And paraded around the walls.
For six days they marched
Preparing the city to fall.

The army led the procession,
Followed by seven priests.
The ark was carried along, as
Trumpets shattered the peace.

Six days they circled and
Then again on the seventh.
Seven times they circled and
Trumpeted a blast to Heaven.

People heard trumpets and
Shouted loud as they could.
The city walls tumbled and
Fell from where they stood.

People ran over the rubble
Looting and pillaging then.
Killing cows, sheep and oxen,
Even women, children and men,

But saved the wayward woman
And her family hiding there,
As they'd promised to do, for
Home with spies she'd shared.

Outside the camp she lived,
To be accepted there in time.
Because saving Israeli spies
They did not consider a crime.

Joshua cursed the city, so no
One would rebuild it again.
God was always with Joshua,
So he became a famous man.

CHAPTER 7

Bronze, iron, silver and gold
Were many things they saved,
To put in the Lord's treasury
From the cities they razed.

But one man had slipped,
As we so often do,
And had stolen for himself
A share of the loot.

The next target after Jericoh
Was a small city named Ai;
It looked like easy picking
To the Israeli spies.

So they reported to Joshua;
It could be taken with ease.
So only three thousand men
Went marching to the east.

Their defeat was complete;
They were routed in shame,
And they suddenly realized,
God had shaded their game.

Joshua and the elders rent
Their clothes crying to God,
"Oh, why have you failed us
And dealt us such a lot?"

Then the word came down, "In
Your camp you have a thief.
Bring him quickly to justice,
And then you'll get relief."

Next morning they checked
Each tribe and clan. Thus
Every family they searched
Until they found their man.

In confessing his crime he
Said greed had done him in.
So it was decreed he'd pay
With his life for this sin.

It ended no easier for rela-
tives, sons or daughters,
Whose herds and possessions,
Were all led to slaughter.

CHAPTER 8

"Fear not, nor be discouraged,
The word came to Joshua then,
For the city of Ai is yours;
Go take it with your men."

Thirty-five thousand hiding
West of the city now waited.
Ai's King watched the valley
And by Israel was baited.

He attacked and they ran,
Just as they had before.
He took all his men in chase
And thus he lost the war.

Joshua had divided his men
So some were being pursued,
The others were in hiding
Waiting for what ensued.

Now Joshua pointed his spear
At the city they hid behind.
They set it on fire and put
Its defenders in a bind.

With no place to run, Ai's
Army suddenly turned. From
The lost city came Israelis;
Too late, a king had learned.

Twelve thousand enemies died,
Israel dealt a mighty blow.
Joshua hanged the King of Ai,
Jehovah's warning to show.

The animals and the loot, the
Israelis kept as their own.
Jehovah'd okayed the move,
And Joshua had made it
    known.

They built an alter of rocks,
To God, who'd led them here.
On stone unbroken, unhewn,
His laws again would appear.

Joshua read them all just
As Moses handed them down
To each man, woman and child
And anyone else around.

CHAPTER 9

The kings of Caanan were
Alarmed and tense with fear
Knowing what happened at Ai
Could easily happen here.

Some approached by trickery
Claiming to come from afar,
So Israel signed a treaty
And agreed not to go to war.

When the truth became known,
Israel knew they'd been had.
So three cities became slaves,
As an alternative, not bad.

CHAPTER 10

The survivors combined to
Stop this loss of their lands,
But Joshua was invincible,
His army wiped out every man.

CHAPTER 11

Many kings remained in
    Caanan
But lived much farther away,

And mobilized under King
 Hazor,
The Israeli armies to stay.

But Joshua never gave up, in
Triumph over the land he
 swept.
Moses had willed him a mission
And at fighting he was adept.

Seven years the battles raged
Just to call Caanan their own.
All the countries around about
Must have watched and
 groaned.

The territories were divided
And were blessed by the Lord.
The land at long last rested
And healed from rigors of war.

CHAPTER 12

On the east side of Jordan,
Which they had crossed over,
Was a rich golden land
Where some lived in clover.

Thirty-one kingdoms
In all they'd destroyed, as
They rampaged across Caanan
Losing not a man nor a boy.

Then the land was divided
Into parcels for each tribe.
According to its need
Or whatever betide.

CHAPTER 13

Now Joshua was growing old
With much still to do.
Compared to what was left
They had only won a few.

The land Jehovah'd promised
Stretched on and on with

Many battles yet to fight,
And of course to be won.

Many Kingdoms they
 destroyed,
And many more they would.
But every able bodied man
Must do everything he could.

The land was equally divided,
As each tribe had need.
The way it was accomplished
Was quite unique indeed.

But the Levites got no land
For God was all they'd need.
It had long been so decided
And Joshua quite agreed.

CHAPTER 14

They divided land by lottery;
Dice were often thrown,
Thus deciding for each tribe
Just what land they'd own.

Two tribes from Joseph still
Would settle east of Jordan.
They'd earlier decided that
Here they'd seek a fortune.

So they were not included in
The lottery across the river.
Levites got no land at all,
But God was theirs forever.

Then Caleb came to Joshua and
Reminded him of days gone by;
When in the hills of Hebron,
"We two, were Moses' spies."

How all others had feared
The Anakim giants there,
"But we were willing and
Into battle would've fared.

The Lord told Moses then
That this would be our land.
Then I was only forty,
Now here I wish to stand."

And so the land was given to
The man who'd shown no fear
Some forty years ago
When they had traveled here.

The local people there were
Obliged to let them settle,
For the battles they'd waged
Had often shown their mettle.

CHAPTER 15

Now Caleb was given a city,
So drove the inhabitants out
And fought against Debir, but
Those folks he couldn't rout.

So he offered the hand of
His daughter, who was fair,
To any young warrior
Who could conquer Debir.

Soon the city was razed
By Othniel, son of Kenaz,
He was Caleb's young nephew
With plenty of pizazz.

But as he led her donkey away
She made a further demand,
For her dowry was a desert
In a dry and dusty land.

But there was property near
That belonged to her father,
So she asked for it now with
Its springs of cool water.

So Caleb gave in,
As fathers usually do.
He gave her that land
So she had water too.

From the country of Ekron
With its village towns,
To the Mediterranean Sea
And all the area around,

The tribe of Judah
Waxed mighty and strong,
But in the city of Jerusalem
Something seemed to go wrong.

For in spite of their might,
As the battles waxed hot,
To abandon their city
The Jebusites would not.

And among the Israelites
They elected to stay, so
You'll find them still there
Right up to this day.

CHAPTER 16

From the River Jordan west,
East to the Mediterranean sea
Ephraim, Manasseh's half tribe
Were secure as they could be.

This was land they'd chosen,
Rolling hills and valleys deep,
Where they could graze cattle
And herd great flocks of sheep.

Joining this great territory
Was a land of equal breadth,
Which the tribe of Manasseh
Would defend until death.

Some of Manasseh's cities
Went to Ephraim too. Some
Other Caananites in Gezer
Stayed the battles through

And were not driven out but
Stayed on there as slaves,
Absorbed by Israel's ranks
They live there yet today.

74

CHAPTER 17

Two of Joseph's tribes were
Unhappy with their share. So
Joshua offered an alternative
Which he thought quite fair.

"Dispossess the Perizzites
In forest lands nearby." But
This was not their wish
And so they made reply.

"The Perizzites are mighty,
Rephaim giants are there too.
They both own iron Chariots,
Those battles we would lose."

"Take the mountain forests,"
Joshua then replied, "For
You have many people with
Sheer numbers on your side.

Drive out the Caananites
From all the valleys too.
You number in the thousands,
They can't stand up to you."

CHAPTER 18

At the tabernacle in Shiloh,
All Israel gathered there.
For there were seven tribes
Still awaiting a share.

So Joshua sent out scouts
To size up the job ahead.
This was God's promise in
The days when Moses led.

When the scouts returned to
Tell what they had found,
By a throw of sacred dice,
They apportioned ground.

CHAPTER 19

The land was divided among
Simeon, Zebulon and Dan,
Asher, Issachar, all Israel
Were granted plenty of land.

Some natives resisted and
Proved impossible to route.
Dan's tribe battled Lesham,
And finally wiped them out.

Calling it the City of Dan,
They settled there to stay.
But some cities in the area
Just continued on their way.

Joshua chose Timnath-Serah
As the city that he wanted.
God had promised his choice
Would surely be granted.

CHAPTER 20

To Joshua Jehovah spoke again.
"Now cities of refuge will be
A safe place for all, where
An accidental killer may flee.

There he can get a fair trial
And be safe until that time,
When he'll be proven innocent
Or pay society for his crime."

Now the city of Kedesh
In the hills of Galilee
And also known as Hebron
Was a place a man could flee.

Also Sheckem of Ephraim, and
Kiriath-Arba in Judah's hills,
Where one could avoid danger
If he hadn't meant to kill.

Now east of the River Jordan
And across from Jericho,
Were three other towns where
A hunted man could go.

In Reuben's wilderness land
The town of Bezer was one.

To Ramoth of Gilead, in the
Land of Gad one could run.

Then Golan in the country of
Bashan was another of those,
Where even a stranger could
Flee in his time of woe.

CHAPTER 21

Now came the Levite leaders
To consultation at Shiloh.
For God had promised Moses
Many cities long years ago.

All the Levite tribes were
Given cities and surroundings;
Also to Levite priests, who
Had come for an accounting.

Now those cities were decided
By a throw of the sacred dice,
And thus it was all settled
With gifts from many tribes.

So, as Jehovah had decreed,
The land was shared by Israel.
For he'd promised faithfully,
And the future did look well.

All that God had promised
Was there to fill their fancy.
Their enemies all were routed,
Of blessings there were many.

CHAPTER 22

Now at last the war was over
So a time of peace prevailed.
It must have seemed unusual
After all the war travail.

Then Joshua called to order
Those who'd wanted to stay
On the other side of Jordan
When they had come this way.

They'd helped brothers
To win their Holy Wars;
Now they could go back home,
Just what they'd battled for.

Joshua blessed them as they
Started upon the trail car-
rying booty with them for
In battle they'd prevailed.

Before crossing the Jordan,
They did an altar build, and
Then to their dismay, their
Relationship was chilled.

The brothers back in Caanan
Thought what they had done,
Was rebellion against God,
And so thought every one.

But they were soon convinced
That it was a work of love,
All built in thankfulness
To Jehovah God above.

So their brothers returned
And talked of war no more
And men of Reuben and Gad
Made for the eastern shore.

CHAPTER 23

In time Joshua grew feeble,
So spoke to them again.
Elders, Judges and officers,
Saying, "I'm now an old man.

Remember what God Has
done;
He vanquished all your foes
From the banks of Jordan to
The Mediterranean, as you go.

Now you know full well
That God's promise is true;

So long as you honor Him, He
Will bring blessings on you.

But if you backslide and
Let your lives fall away,
You'll lose all your gains
Up to the day that you stray.

Your home you will lose; you
Will disappear from the scene.
He'll not hear your cries
Nor listen to your screams.

My time will soon come when
I'll be called by the Lord.
So please think of me often
And live by God's word."

CHAPTER 24

Joshua talked to them often,
Of those other days, when
Abraham's father lived and
Worshipped heathen ways.

How Jehovah called Abraham
To Caanan, where they were
   now.
How Joseph was sold into
   Egypt,
How God and Moses got them
   out.

How they fled from oppression
With Pharaoh's army in trail,
But God came to their rescue
And saved them from travail.

He lead them through the sea,
When Israel cried out in fear;
And He vanquished Egypt's
Army when it came too near.

Forty years they wandered, as
Jehovah fulfilled their lives.

He was always there to rescue
Before they gave in to strife.

Enemies, He always
   vanquished
And led them safely through.
Spoils of wars were theirs,
The honor of winning too.

So love your God Jehovah; He's
Your true savior, you know,
He'll treat you as deserved,
And be with you where you go.

As for us, we will follow God
And let the whole world go by.
All of you here are witness
To His Holy word from on
high.

In those days we read about,
The world must have been a
Safer and healthier place for
Joshua lived to a hundred ten.

When Israel obeyed God's laws
They shared wondrous ways.
For He'd been their salvation
When living in fear every day.

Joseph's remains were returned
On this march God had
   wrought
To be buried with honor in the
Plot that Jacob had bought.

Then Aaron's son, Eleazar also
Succumbed to old age, and his
Body rests in Ephraim's hills,
This story ends on this page.

END OF JOSHUA

JUDGES

CHAPTER 1

Now after Joshua's death
There would come a change.
But in spite of all that,
Their faith still remained.

The campaigns continued
Much as they had before.
The inhabitants of the land
Were still involved in war.

Judah and Simeon joined
armies
And ten thousand enemies
died.
Their king escaped but was
Caught and then cried:

"Seventy kings I've conquered,
Who minus thumbs and big
toes,
Ate crumbs from my table
And contemplated their woes.

But now it is my turn as in
My defeat God has decreed.
And it is a fitting fate
That he has wished upon me."

Then taken to Jerusalem,
He lived out his days.
We're sure prone to wonder,
If he regretted his ways.

Many days the battles raged,
Some won with others a draw.
Many natives are still there
In spite of the battles lost.

The Amorites Forced Dan
To run for the hills.

Kept from the valley, they
Might be there still--

But the tribe of Joseph
Came to their relief,
So the Amorite rule
Became rather brief.

Defeated soon after,
And taken as slaves,
Although in the battle
They'd been very brave.

CHAPTER 2

Those folks who'd lived
When Joshua was there were
Replaced by those younger
Who really didn't care.

They'd seen no miracles or
Walked through the Red Sea.
They'd not eaten manna or
Known how loving God can be.

They soon failed to keep
The promises they had made
And worshipped pagan gods,
Their religion a charade.

Then God's angel came and
Sent them into tears, for
God gave up on them. They'd
Shunned Him too many years.

When they went into battle
God helped them no longer.
Their luck was all bad and
The enemy waxed stronger.

Belatedly they cried
And promised to reform.

That kind of behavior
Had always been the norm.

So God's anger softened, or
He wouldn't hold grudges;
In any case, He relented,
And instituted judges.

The judge gave relief
From political oppression,
But when he died,
They sinned with obsession.

Then God's anger heated up,
He despised them all again;
Their problems multiplied
Due to puny efforts of man.

CHAPTER 3

Five nations lived in Caanan
Who had never been defeated.
So the wilderness lessons
Would have to be repeated.

Then Israel intermarried
With nations from there
Causing much unhappiness,
And they had their share.

The King of Mesopotamia
Proved mightier than they,
So eight years they served
As his unwilling slaves.

Then Jehovah raised a judge
Whose name was Othniel; he
Won the war to set them free,
So forty years all went well.

Now their judge expired so
People committed evil again.
Then the King of Moab struck
And they were "also rans".

But Ehud was God's chosen
Who went to deliver a gift.

He slew the King of Moab
Which caused a policy shift.

The children followed Ehud
Causing ten thousand to fall.
The enemy were mighty men,
Men of valor, warriors all.

Moab was subdued that day, so
Israel relaxed eighty years.
The next Judge was Shamgar,
Who showed very little fear.

He slew six hundred enemies,
With an ox goad he did so
And delivered Israel again
Which was the way to go.

CHAPTER 4

People again fell into sin,
Soon after Ehud's death.
Nine hundred iron chariots of
The enemy caused them stress.

For twenty years they slaved
Under King Jabin's heavy hand.
When Debra was a prophetess,
And judge over Israel's land.

Now she sent for Barak,
Who a mighty soldier was,
To send him after Sisera
For whom they had no love.

Sisera, King Jabin's man,
On Israel laid the yoke.
Ten thousand Cisera men
Before Baraks army broke.

Sisera abandoned chariot
And did in panic flee.
To Jael's tent he ran,
And there he fell asleep.

Jael, a Jewish woman, now
Speeded Sisera's death.
Israel again was able
To draw an easy breath.

Barak wrecked Jabin's army,
After its leaders demise.
Thus it was, the children
Again were on the rise.

CHAPTER 5

The people sang of Debra,
She predicted Jabin's fall.
Barak was hero, conqueror
And "Commander of All."

So God helped win again
Freedom so often sought.
The army'd followed Barak
And with bravery fought.

Their future brightened,
And tomorrow looked good.
Now the nation had peace
And forty years it stood.

CHAPTER 6

Again they worshipped pagan
Gods instead. National pride
And strength were a thing
Quite dead.

Under the hand of Midian, who
Prevailed against them now,
They did much work in secret;
The question was often how?

They even hid in caves and
Dug holes in mountain walls.
Israel worked and sowed,
But the enemy harvested all.

So children often suffered,
Their yoke so heavy to bear.

The Midianites were many
And had no plans to share.

So Israel cried again
For God to help them out.
So He sent a messenger and
This came from his mouth,

"I led you out of slavery
And helped you many times.
Yet against me all too often
You committed every crime."

But in their unfaithfulness
He loved them as they were.
By now He must have known,
This often would occur.

So an angel came to Ophrah
Where Gideon while threshing
Hid. Blessing him well, he
Said to do as God would bid.

Gideon wrecked Baal's altar
And cut down the grove.
Then built an altar to God
And worshipped there also.

The enemy sought his death,
But dad stood by his side.
So enemies in anger left,
Gideon no more need hide.

Often God proved to him, He
Truly had given the order.
Gideon would be a hero who
Would save their borders.

CHAPTER 7

Gideon with a multitude,
Camped by Midians legions.
God held him back, for
Israelis in the region.

If sheer numbers won
They'd fail to credit God.

So for full attention
He increased the odds.

So those who were afraid
Were all let go home. So
Two and twenty thousand
No longer wished to roam.

But with ten thousand left
There were too many still,
So he led them to water,
And said, "Drink your fill."

Those who lapped to drink
Were three hundred strong,
Those who knelt and sipped,
It seemed had done it wrong.

Three hundred Gideon took
And headed down the valley.
Hearing Midianite voices,
They now feared to rally.

So Gideon returned to camp,
Worshipping Jehovah, prayed.
For God had proven to him
That he need not be afraid.

Three companies he formed,
Each a hundred men strong.
Each with an empty pitcher,
And trumpet to carry along.

A lamp he also gave them,
Which in pitchers they hid.
Then encircling the camp,
For fame and fortune bid.

Everyone blew a trumpet at
The hour of midnight, broke
Pitchers to show flame, the
Enemy panicked in flight.

"For the Lord, and Gideon,"
They all cried. In darkness

The enemy fought, and by
Friendly swords many died.

Many Israelis gathered, and
Pursued the Midianite host,
Slew princes Oreb and Zeeb,
Bringing the war to close.

CHAPTER 8

Men of Ephraim were angry,
Not being invited to war,
But had done much better,
So they forgot to be sore.

Gideon came to the Jordan,
And now he crossed over.
They'd travelled many miles
Through no field of clover.

All three hundred followers
Were very hungry and weak.
To the men of Succoth in
This manner did he speak.

"We are weak and hungry, so
Sustain us with some food,"
Succoth's Prince answered,
"We owe nothing to you."

At Penuel, he asked again,
The answers were the same;
So pursued the enemy 'till
He won the battle and fame.

Then at Succoth and Penuel
As he returned that way,
Made examples of everyone
Who had said him nay.

Israel asked him to rule,
To keep them from slavery.
They would willingly answer
To a man of such bravery.

But he said "No," to them,
"I'll not rule, nor my son;

Only God will be your ruler
So obey Him, every one."

With the enemies' earrings
As some booty from the war,
He made them into an ephod
That would haunt him sore.

His people worshipped it
So that it became a snare.
Gideon would much prefer
Of God they'd be aware.

Forty years of peace, and
Gideon prospered well.
Seventy sons he fathered
In the land where he dwelt.

They finally buried him
Where his father Joash lay.
Now people turned from God,
For they would rather play.

Remembered not Jehovah and
Forgot all Gideon's deeds.
Pagan idols they worshipped
Enthused by sin and greed.

CHAPTER 9

Abimelech, Gideon's son who
Was born of a concubine,
Wanted authority, to wear
The crown he was inclined.

So with maternal relatives,
Whispering in their ears,
He built up his own image
Playing on their fears.

They financed his move, so
Hiring street thugs, he
Killed off his brothers
To remove all serious bugs.

So he'd rule as he pleased,
But brother Jotham got away

And found a place to hide,
Cursing Abimelech's play.

In time, as one might know,
Shekem's men turned on him.
So fighting former allies
He was paying for his sins.

He murdered many ex-friends
To rule his inimicable way.
So all his erstwhile pals,
Wished for his last day.

He warned those in Shechem
Tricking the warriors out.
So once they left the city,
He forced them into rout.

Other townspeople noticed,
So took refuge in the fort.
So he set fire to it
And their safety did abort.

A thousand people died of
Smoke and flames that day.
So when he attacked Thebez,
He tried to win that way.

A lady cast a millstone
And struck him on the head.
It was a fatal blow and
A quicker death he plead.

His ego forbade him to die
At a lowly woman's hand, so
He hurried his demise and
Was killed by his own man.

His men all left in fright
Once Abimelech got his due.
No longer wishing to fight
As Jotham's curse came true.

CHAPTER 10

After Abimelech's Tyranny
Tola came on the scene.

A true son of Israel, his
Rule was not demeaned.

Twenty-three years of rule,
And nothing bad was said.
Not while he judged
Or even after his death.

Then Jair, a Gileadite, he
Judged them twenty and two.
He fathered thirty sons,
And his rule was smooth.

But then his time ran out;
He died and went to rest.
He left no royal records
But his rule was blest.

Then the children turned,
After other gods they ran.
So Jehovah saw their ways
And was angry once again.

So Amonites vexed them,
And Philistines did too.
Again they cried to God,
Whatever could they do?

Then He reminded them
Of many ways and times
They'd humiliated him
For no reason or rhyme.

They fell upon his mercy
And promised to reform, so
He said, "Call those other
Gods; see if they perform."

So they forsook other gods
And followed Jehovah's way.
Then soon his anger abated
And he'd not say them nay.

The children gathered at
Mizpah; there they stayed.

Amonites were at Gilead
Not very far away.

"Who will lead our forces?"
Israel's leaders asked,
"And we also need a king, a
Good man for the task."

CHAPTER 11

Jephtha, a warrior great,
Now from Gilead came.
The son of a prostitute,
So he came not with fame.

Half brothers banished him
Their dad was Gilead too.
They would disinherit him,
So he fled the land of Tob.

His followers, malcontents,
Unhappy with their lot,
Were living as bandits who
Robbed to fill the pot.

The Amonites declared war,
And Gilead needed a leader.
They now called on Jephtha,
But he was not too eager.

"You first punished me for
Crime I couldn't help, so
Now when you're in trouble
It's me to whom you yelp.

Can I actually believe you
And trust you in any thing?"
"Yes," they vowed, "we need
You now, please be our King."

Now their word they kept,
So he was crowned with pomp.
Now he sent a message to
  Ammon
Asking, "Why to war now
  come?"

The King of Ammon answered,
"From us you stole this land,
So we intend to take it back
And we're quite sure we can."

"That was three centuries
Ago," Jehpthah then replied.
"We asked for passage through,
Which your Kings denied,

So your borders we skirted,
And took the long way 'round.
Sihon we couldn't avoid, for
He never would give ground.

In Heshbon he made a stand,
And our people had to fight.
We won the battle and war,
Because God was on our side.

The other Kings we conquered
Have let us live in peace.
So why are you so different
Than any one of these?"

But Ammon's King was greedy;
He would not change his ways.
Jephthah knew he'd have to do
The thing he'd tried to stay.

He offered human sacrifice,
Yes, he even went that far!
For he must win this battle,
Or he would lose the war.

First to come and greet him
Would be the one he'd offer.
But now he'd go to war and
Put off such minor bothers.

So to the battle he went
And wiped the Ammonites out;
Because the Lord helped him,
It's where he got his clout.

Then in triumph he returned
And to Jephthah's horror,

First to run and meet him
Was his only daughter.

Most would scream and claim
This world is much too tough.
But she stood tall and fine,
And was made of better stuff.

"Do as you must," she said, "I
Need time to grieve and roam
My beloved hills, for I'll
Never marry or have a home."

Now she returned, so Jephthah
Did as he'd vowed to do. It
Is now a fashion in Israel,
Girls lament this date, too.

CHAPTER 12

Now Ephraim accused
   Jephthah
And called him lots of names.
But Jephthah didn't want to
Fight; to him it was a shame.

They insisted on a battle
Bad mouthing him no end.
It soon became obvious
They could not be friends.

So he mobilized an army
And Jordan's fords he took.
Ephraims people crossed
To be waylaid at the brook;

"Shibboleth," were made to
Say. If they tried in vain,
To sound the "H," by
The army they were slain.

Forty-two thousand died
Before peace was achieved.
Jephthah judged in Israel
Six years till deceased.

Now Ibzan was the judge,
Who came from Bethlehem,
Fathering thirty daughters
Who married outside men.

Seven years he judged as
Each son became a man, whom
He married off to girls
Who came from other clans.

For ten years Elon judged;
Of him we have no record.
He may have done well, for
History notes no discord.

Now Abdon from Pirothon,
Eight years called score,
And fathered forty sons
Who fathered thirty more.

CHAPTER 13

Israel slipped away again
And worshipped other Gods.
Philistines subdued them
And often applied the rod.

Of Daniel's tribe one day
In a city of Zorah appeared,
An Angel of the Lord, whom
The wife of Manoah cheered,

Saying, "Years you waited,
But soon you shall conceive.
It may seem strange to you,
But you surely may believe.

Drink no wine or beer and
Eat nothing not kosher. You
Will bear a mighty man who
From enemies will take over.

You must never cut his hair;
For he will be a Nazirite,
A special man of God,
Who will set things right."

She informed her husband
Of all that she'd been told.
Then Manoah prayed to God
For information of his own.

The angel soon returned, so
Manoah offered him food.
He said, "Sacrifice to God,
But food I must refuse."

He would not give his name,
So Manoah sacrificed a goat.
The angel stepped into flame
And upward he did float

Manoa and his wife believed
It was a sign from Jehovah.
For the angel had ascended,
And time of doubt was over.

One day their son was born,
And Sampson he was named.
 He
Was blessed by Jehovah and
For his strength was famed.

He often became excited to
Think of the army of Dan.
He dreamed of great warriors
And would be a mighty man.

CHAPTER 14

Now in the City of Timna,
While Sampson visited there,
He met a Philistine girl
Who was exceedingly fair.

His folks objected; he
Should marry a Jewish girl.
He couldn't forget her; she
Seemed a priceless pearl.

So they headed for Timnah,
For he'd not be denied.

On the way a Lion attacked,
At Sampson's hand he died.

He mentioned it to no one
And marriage was arranged.
Returning that wedding day,
On the lions body he gazed.

Lo and behold he noted bees
Had taken residence there.
So Sampson took some honey
To the wedding to share.

Then he threw a party as
Was the custom of the day,
Where young village men
Could party and play.

So he gave them this riddle.
During wine, music and song,
Food came out of the eater,
Sweetness from the strong.

Four days later they were
No closer to the answer,
And were getting rowdy,
Showing considerable anger.

They threatened his new bride
Till the answer she wheedled,
And then he got the feeling
He had sure been needled.

So the Spirit possessed him,
In Ashkelon he found the
Clothing he needed to pay off
Those cheating clowns.

He killed thirty Philistines
And all their clothing took,
Paid the winners of his
Riddle, and new wife forsook.

The best man at his wedding
Then married her instead. So

Sampson lived with parents,
It's where he slept and fed.

CHAPTER 15

One day when in passion's grip
Back to his wife he went, but
Her father refused him entry
And out of shape Sampson
   bent.

Her father explained to him
He'd married her off instead,
To the guy who was best man,
And Sampson really saw red.

He caught three hundred foxes
And tied their tails in pairs.
With lighted torches between
Them, he let'em out of there.

Over Phillistine fields they
Ran mid sheaves and shocks.
Creating a tremendous fire,
Which surely did raise hob.

The Philistines asked, "Who
Did this thing to us?"
And when they found out,
Made a terrible fuss.

This misfortune they blamed
On girl and father then;
Sampson swore new vengeance
And became angry again.

Many Philistines he killed
And into a cave he went, so
They sent many men into
Judah on havoc bent.

Three thousand men of Judah
After him to the cave did go.
They reasoned with him there;
Agreeing, he followed in tow.

So with new rope he was bound
And back to Lehigh was led.
The Philistines shouted with
Glee planning an early death.

Strength of God he possessed,
So broke the ropes with ease.
A donkey's jawbone he grabbed,
Many Philistines deceased.

Discarding it he said, "Heaps
On heaps with a donkey's jaw,
I've killed more Philistines
Than most folks ever saw."

Now thirst possessed him and
To Jehovah he cried. "After
This wonderful deliverance,
Must I thirst until I die?"

Water gushed from the ground,
So at the stream he was saved.
Now he named that place,"The
Spring of the man who prayed."

For twenty years he judged but
Enemies controlled the land.
Of all the judges we've read,
He was a most unusual man.

CHAPTER 16

Samson was a mighty man,
As we have oft been told.
And from his many exploits,
We know that he was bold.

Once he spent an evening
With a lady of the night;
Enemies planned to kill him
As soon as it got light.

Police planned to trap him
As he left by the city gate.
He lay abed till midnight,
And again thwarted fate.

He lifted up the gateposts,
Pulling them from the ground,
Slung them on his shoulders
And walked away from town.

He took them to a mountain
Top, so I guess that's where
They are. If the enemy trailed
Him, they didn't go that far.

Delilah, a Philistine beauty
With whom he fell in love,
To hurry his demise, would
Have moved the heavens
    above.

She tied him with bowstrings
And again with new ropes, but
He broke them all with ease
And dashed her fondest hopes.

So she teased and wheedled,
Till his secret she thought
She knew, because he told her,
"Weave my hair into your
    loom."

So while Samson slumbered
She did as he had said.
And got his hair all woven
As he slept upon the bed,

Then awoke him with a scream,
"The Philistines are here." He
Smashed her loom to splinters
As he broke into the clear.

Then he finally told her,
To God he was a Nazarite.
And if his hair were cut,
He'd be too weak to fight.

So she crooned and coddled
Him with his head on her lap.
Sampson soon quite foolishly
Relaxed and took a nap.

Then she called the barber;
All his locks were shorn.
He lost that beautiful hair
He'd had since he was born.

So a woman brought him
  down;
Weakened, he lost the fight.
Now they gouged out his eyes
And thus he lost his sight.

He was put into prison,
And forced to grind grain.
Then they brought him out
To taunt and cause him pain.

While he'd been a prisoner,
Again his hair had grown; so
God gave back his strength,
And he came into his own.

At the center of the temple
Two pillars held up the roof.
With a hand on each column,
That was where he stood.

With great muscles bulging,
To God he prayed, "Lord help
Me take these Philistines,
As I go my fated way."

Then with a mighty push
Those pillars fell down.
Three thousand Philistines
Died, as the roof crashed
To the ground.

Yes, he died there too, but
This moral should read;
He was a mighty man of God
Sent to do great deeds.

CHAPTER 17

Now Israel had no king;
There was no serious rule.

Each man did what seemed
To help him keep his cool.

In the land of Ephraim, of
Rolling hills and valleys,
Lived a man named Micah,
Whom to Jehovah rallied.

His mother saved some money,
Which Micah one day stole;
Now she got very angry and
Played the witch's role.

She cursed and swore and
Raved and screamed; but
That her son had stolen,
She Just never dreamed.

Now Micah soon repented
And then he gave it back.
So now she was so happy
That she changed her tack.

She had it changed to silver,
And on an idol had some cast.
It was a gift to God in
Thanks for days gone past.

Micah owned many idols,
An ephod and teraphim too.
And he gave them loving care;
It seemed the thing to do.

From the town of Bethlehem a
Young priest journeyed forth.
Answering Micah's question, he
Said, "A home I'm looking
  for."

So Micah invited him to stay,
Of a priest he felt in need.
So the Levite was like a son
In word and act and deed.

Micah anticipated blessings,
For God might smile on him;

And a personal priest he
Needed to keep free of sin.

CHAPTER 18

But now the tribe of Dan was
Looking for land to conquer;
They sent a party of scouts
To look the country over.

On their spying mission they
Sojourned at Micah's home.
And they decided, "This land
Is weak where we roam."

They even got a blessing
Given by Micah's priest.
They sent back word, "This
Land we'll easily defeat."

So they returned to plunder,
Marching through the hills.
Passed the home of Micah,
Where they'd ate their fill.

They stole his Teraphim and
Ephod; his priest went along.
Micah tried to stop them, but
They were much too strong.

So the conquering army went
On into the land of Ephraim
To the city of Laish and
Found it easy game.

They soon plundered the city
Slaughtering the people there.
There wasn't a guard in town;
It had been a city unaware.

They named that city, "Dan",
And set up Micah's Idols then,
And also appointed a priest,
So people could worship them.

The city was rebuilt and they
Lived there quite some time.

Micah's idols were worshipped
By the entire tribe.

CHAPTER 19

A man lived beyond the hills
Who was from Levi's tribe.
He brought a girl from Judah
To be his concubine.

She angered soon and left him
So he returned and called.
Her father asked him to stay,
And for six days he stalled.

But one eve they left, even
Though 'twas close to night.
They passed by Jerusalem,
For there he feared a fight.

So they went on to Gibe-ah,
Benjamin's tribe lived there.
They were not invited in so
Camped in the village square.

An old man offered his home
For them to spend the night.
A gang of thugs arrived, so
They might have to fight.

It had to be a fearful thing
With no sense of chivalry. He
Pushed her out the door and
Let them ply their deviltry.

He spent the night in safety
As they did their evil will.
He found her in the morning
In death cold and still.

So he tied her on a donky
And went on home to Shiloh.
He cut her in a dozen pieces
Each tribe in Israel to show.

"A terrible thing," they said
"We've never seen such crime,

So we'll do what we must do,
It certainly is high time."

CHAPTER 20

From far and near Israel came
To discipline Benjamin's tribe.
But several battles were lost,
So unto the Lord they cried.

With hopes of winning, forty-
Three thousand enemies died
And forty thousand of theirs
Who'd been the pick and pride.

Benjamin's tribe was decimated,
Everything killed and burned.
All the land was conquered;
Such havoc sin had earned.

CHAPTER 21

Leaders gathered at Mizpah
And soon regret took over.
Now they were short a tribe
They'd considered brothers.

Six hundred men were left
Of those they had plundered.
They fought Gilead, who by
Staying home had blundered.

It had been agreed before
The battle, that any one
Refusing to fight, would
Give his life as chattel.

Israel had sworn to God that
Their daughters never would
Marry a Benjamite man, but
Oaths would do no good.

Four hundred girls were left
From the Jabesh Gilead brawl.
To Benjamin's survivors, they
Decided to give them all.

At a religeous festival girls
Would come out to dance.
And so this year at Shiloh
They would get their chance.

They'd hide in the vineyards,
When girls came out to play,
Each unmarried man would
  grab
One and then be on his way.

END OF JUDGES

RUTH

CHAPTER I

When the Judges ruled,
With famine in the land,
To feed and clothe a family
Was a trial for any man.

A man named Elimelech, with
Two sons, settled there,

From Bethlehem to Moab
To find a better fare.

But he died while living
There, and his sons as well.
So now his widow, Naomi,
Thought of home in Israel.

Daughters-in-law, Ruth and
Orpah, planned to go along.

But she foresaw problems,
For things might go wrong.

Orpah, she prevailed upon
To stay here in her home.
But Ruth, the other one,
Claimed Naomi as her own.

And so the two did travel
All the way to Bethlehem.
Naomi's people were there,
So that was where they went.

Now Ruth had told Naomi,
I will go where ever you go.
I'll die where you die, and
Her actions proved it so.

They arrived in Bethlehem,
The barley harvest in sway.
Now Ruth became a gleaner,
For that was Israel's way.

CHAPTER 2

Now a wealthy relative of
Naomi's owned some fields.
Ruth worked with his workers;
It was a bounteous yield.

He arrived from the city
As she labored there, so
He asked another her name,
For he was prone to stare.

Then he spoke to her and
Invited her to stay, for he
Thought she was lovely and
Wished to see her every day.

By kindness she was touched
And managed to let him know.
He was captive to her beauty,
An inner, radiant glow.

Through the barley harvest,
She stayed and worked along.

Also the harvest of wheat,
Her heart light with song.

CHAPTER 3

Now Naomi started to plot to
Make Ruth his wife, saying
"Get all prettied up, and
You must smell real nice.

When his day is over and
With food his belly's full,
Go to the threshing floor,
Where in sleep he's lulled."

Now I'd bet, with favor
Ruth obeyed Naomi's plan,
A time honored method
For a girl to get her man.

So as Boaz slumbered by a
Pile of grain he'd threshed,
She raised the blanket at his
Feet, and there she slept.

Now as midnight neared, he
Awoke and in dismay, dis-
covered that at his feet,
A beautiful woman lay.

So she'd made her pitch, for
She wished to make him hers.
But he had another relative
Who by law was rated first.

He sent her home at daybreak,
And sent extra grain along.
Now when she told Naomi,
   they
Knew this plan wasn't wrong.

"Just be patient dear," she
Said, "he'll settle it today,
Boaz is a very good man
Who goes his own way."

CHAPTER 4

Boaz found his relative
Down at the marketplace. He
Suggested buying Naomi's
Property with a sober face.

It required he marry Ruth to
Carry on her husband's name.
The relative backed away for
This wasn't his kind of game.

Remember we read before, if a
Woman's first husband died,
Children of the next bore his
Name. To this he'd be tied.

A contract was sealed by a
Sandal being exchanged. So
Before witness it was done,
In favor of Boaz arranged.

So Boaz married Ruth, and
Of sons, they soon had one,
They proudly named him
   "Obed."
David would be his grandson.

END OF RUTH

FIRST SAMUEL

CHAPTER 1

Hanna and Peninah were both
Elkana's wives. Hannah had
No children but for the joy
Of motherhood did strive.

Each year they went to Shilo,
Sacrificed and prayed. 'Twas
A time to worship God; that's
Why the trip was made.

Elkanah gave them gifts acc-
ording to the children born.
So Peninah got the presents,
And Hannah felt forlorn.

She prayed she'd be blessed,
Her barren time would cease.
From Peninah's usual heck-
ling to finally be released.

Elkanah never understood
Why Hannah often mourned,

He already had children,
Those by Peninah, born.

One evening when at Shilo,
After dinner was done, she
Visited the tabernacle and
Prayed to the mighty one.

She promised God, if she
Could have a son to give,
He'd be the Lord's for as
Long as he should live.

Now Eli was the priest
And as he watched her pray,
He thought she was drunk
And should be driven away.

But he noted she was sober,
And that she asked for help.
Then he encouraged her
And took her side as well.

Now in due time it proved
God had answered her plea.
And she bore a baby boy
For every one to see.

So as soon as he was weaned
She gave him to the Lord,
For it had been her promise,
And she would keep her word.

CHAPTER 2

Now this was Hannah's song,
"God heard me in distress.
He thwarted all my enemies,
And I've been truly blessed.

He has solved my problem;
There is no other so great.
He knows what we have done
And how well we rate.

God is fully aware and
He will judge our needs.
He'll bring the mighty
Down and lift up the weak.

He will feed the starving,
The barren woman cure. He
Is no friend of the wicked,
He is an ally of the pure.

In his hand he holds earth,
Rules over Prince and King.
Makes or breaks and conquers
To him we owe everything."

Then they returned to Ramah,
Leaving baby Samuel behind.
He was raised for the Lord,
So he grew up tall and kind.

The sons of Eli were wicked
And did not honor the Lord.
They seduced young women
Made a mockery of His word.

They desecrated sacrifices,
Imposed their will on all.
So it was inevitable that
God would cause their fall.

So one day a prophet came,
And to Eli made a prophesy.
"You have sinned and fallen
Short, so now answer to me.

You'll be a priest no more;
Your life will be short.
You've abused your office;
Your priesthood I'll abort.

Your life will be forfeit;
In misery you shall live.
Now I turn my back on you
And help to others give.

Just to prove I mean it,
I'll take your sons away.
They both will die; this
Will happen in one day.

Your priestly days are over;
Hungry, you'll beg for food.
I'll raise up a godly priest
Who will replace you."

CHAPTER 3

Now Samuel became a prophet
While he was yet a boy.
He heard the voice of God
And answered it with joy.

He forecast word to Levi,
If God was vexed or sore.
Now as he grew older
He prophesied even more.

CHAPTER 4

Israel fought Philistines,
And a battle they had lost.

Four thousand Israelis died;
It seemed a frightful cost.

From Shilo came the ark
Hoping to improve their lot.
It shook the enemy badly,
As this news they got.

They went into panic, in
Fear of Israel's God. It
Seemed sure they'd lose; to
Fight they'd rather not.

The leaders marshalled
Them and gave a great pep
Talk. To fight much better
Or be taken at a walk.

The battle erupted and the
Enemy fought as never before.
Israel lost the battle and
Almost lost the war.

Thirty thousand of Israel died
And the ark was captured too.
Phinehas and Hophni perished;
Their debts had all come due.

Now Eli was up in years and
At ninety-eight was blind.
He was also fat and feeble,
And the news was very
   unkind.

Now when the word came that
The ark and sons he'd lost,
He fell and broke his neck;
So his life too, it cost.

Phinehas' wife was pregnant
When she got the bad news,
She went into sudden labor;
Her chances for life were few.

Now as she lay there dying
According to the story,

"Name my baby, Ichabod," she
Said, "meaning there is no
   Glory."

Now if I'd lost my family,
I'd surely be feeling low.
But I cannot help but wonder
If I could name a baby so.

CHAPTER 5

A temple in the city was the
Home of the Philistines' god.
He was of course a pagan idol,
In the city temple of Ashdod.

The ark of God was placed
In the temple facing Dagon.
Next day they came to look,
A line of curious pagans.

They found their idol god
Face down on the ground.
Before the ark it fell, as
Though it had lost a round.

Then they set him up again
As if to make it right. But
Next day found him headless;
It was a shocking sight.

In the doorway of the temple,
His head and hands lay there.
The effect was immediate; it
Gave the Philistines a scare.

Many were infected with boils
In the city and land nearby.
They'd move it elsewhere,
Or at least they'd try.

They called a council meeting
To see where to take it next.
But no matter where they took
It, it became an instant hex.

To Garth, they took it first;
Plague killed young and old.
At Ekron they tried next, but
The people stopped them cold.

So the mayors of the cities
Were all summoned once again,
But were told to go away
And try another plan.

"Send it back to Israel,"
Was what the people cried.
"Just get it out of here
Or we'll all surely die."

CHAPTER 6

For seven months in all in
Philistine land it stayed.
They wished it would leave,
Because they were afraid.

"Take it to Israel," they
Cried, "Send gifts along,
For as long as it is here
Everything goes wrong."

Each city sent gifts;
Gold, a tumor and a rat, on
A cart pulled by two fresh
Cows taken from the calves.

Now the cows wandered away
Toward Israel's border, so
The Philistines felt better,
Hoping it would be in order.

Directly to Beth-shemesh,
The cattle hauled the cart.
The Israelites saw them
And took new heart.

It stopped in a field owned
By Joshua, an Israelite.
People broke up the cart and
Used the cows for sacrifice.

Many men looked in the ark,
To see what was there.
Seventy suddenly died, so
They were plainly scared--

Cried, "Who can stand before
Jehovah? Send the Ark away."
To a nearby town they said,
"Come get it without delay."

CHAPTER 7

So the Ark was recovered
By the Kiriath-jearim men.
Twenty years Israel wept,
"Had God foresaken them?"

Samuel came to their rescue,
He said, "Return to the Lord.
Destroy Ashtaroth and Baal,
And live by Jehovah's word."

They gathered at Mizpah, and
He prayed for them there. To
Worship and fast all day,
Judging Israel was his fare.

The Philistines came while
Israel at Mizpah did tarry.
Fear was a tangible thing;
Enemy numbers were scary.

Crying to Samuel for help,
He sacrificed and prayed all
Day. God spoke like thunder;
Their enemies ran away.

Israelites sped their flight
Killing many in retreat. Some
Israeli towns they recovered;
The enemy was in defeat.

Between Mizpah and Jeshanah,
A rock called Ebenezer was
Placed. "The Stone Of Help,"
Samuel said, "To honor that
Day of God's grace."

The rest of his life, he
Rode circuit over Israel's
Lands, serving God long and
Well, a good dependable man.

CHAPTER 8

His sons were unlike Samuel,
But greedy and ethics poor.
But as fathers are, their
Fault he laid at other doors.

He made them Judges, and they
Applied vicious trickery. For
They were mean, greedy men,
Which people noted quickly.

The leaders came to Ramah and
To him their cause they pled.
And after much time in prayer,
Sadly this is what he said.

"You are asking for a king,
For you trust not God nor me.
But that's not best for you,
In time you'll surely see.

Sons he'll take for his army,
Before his chariots to run.
Others will be his slaves,
You won't think that's fun!

He'll tax your income, take
Your fields and groves.
Build his arms and chariots,
And he will bring you low.

You will shed bitter tears
As daughters he takes away.
His friends he will favor
While his bills you'll pay."

But no matter how he argued
They still were adamant.
So the Lord said, "Go ahead
Give them what they want."

CHAPTER 9

Kish was rich and famous,
His son Saul, handsome too.
Head and shoulders taller,
Though he was still a youth.

One day Kish had problems for
His donkeys had strayed. So
Saul and a servant searched
Traveling a very long way.

Thru Ephraim's hills and the
Shaalim area they searched;
Both were tired and weary
But saw no sign on earth.

They hunted high and low
Through out the land of Zuph.
Both were near their limit
And felt they'd had enough.

The servant knew a prophet
To whom they might appear. It
Was Samuel of whom he spoke
Who was a famous seer.

Now Saul was not too sure;
He feared this might be rash.
For now they had no food
And were also low on cash.

God had spoken to Samuel. So
When this young man arrived,
He knew it was the leader
Who'd save Israel from strife.

"Your donkeys were found," he
Said, "The problem is no more.
You'll be ruler of the nation,
With great things in store."

Then Saul made answer back,
"Of Benjamins tribe I am, a
Family of no importance, I'm
Surely not your man."

Samuel was not concerned. He
Made Saul the honored guest.
He dined and slept in style,
A more enjoyable quest.

In the morning as they left
Samuel gave Saul the word.
For it was time to tell him,
He was chosen by the Lord.

CHAPTER 10

Now Samuel anointed Saul
With a flask of olive oil.
And he said, "Your future
Will be as king, to toil."

He told him many signs
Would prove that this was so,
Now as they went along,
Traveling down the road--

It proved to be the truth,
All that Samuel prophesied
Happened as foretold,
For Samuel never lied.

Samuel anointed him with oil
So the spirit came upon Saul,
Who prophesied and prayed
For he had heard God's call.

Then he returned back home
And answered everything,
How he'd looked for donkeys
But not that he'd be king.

Israel gathered at Mizpah and
Samuel called a convocation
Saying, "God saved you from
Egypt and enemy nations.

Now you insist on a king, so
Appear to God by tribes and
Clans, to proclaim your king
And he will rule the land."

So Samuel presented Saul, and
They claimed him as king. Now
Many followers loved the Lord
But some thought other things.

"What, Saul a Prophet?" they
Said, "we find it hard to
Believe! We knew him before,
He'd never turn a new leaf."

They despised and detested,
But to them he gave no heed.
For he had finer thoughts
And strove for better deeds.

CHAPTER 11

Jabesh Gilead was threatened
By Ammonites at its gates,
And Israel pleaded for time
Trying to alter their fate.

A messenger came to Gibe-ah,
His news made everyone cry.
Nahash had said, at winning,
He'd blind their right eyes.

So Saul made a point in turn,
Which put Israel on his side.
Three hundred thousand men
Fought against Ammon's pride.

Three armies he led to fight.
Three thousand Judeans went;
He pulled a surprise and
Ammon's army was spent.

They wrecked Nahash's army
So nothing usefull was left.
Saul had won Israel's heart
Completely and quite deft.

They remembered the rebels
Doubting his sudden change.
And were ready right then
A death sentence to arrange.

Saul was not after revenge;
He knew God had been there.
Forgiveness was in order;
It seemed to him only fair.

Now Samuel told the people,
"Let us make Saul our king."
So they sacrificed to God
And songs made Israel ring.

CHAPTER 12

Samuel called the people
And gave them this account.
I've done my best by you all
The years I've been around.

From you I've never stolen
Nor ever told a lie;
And I'll continue so
Until the day I die.

The people all agreed
It was as he had said, for
They knew he'd been honest
All the years he'd led.

He reminded them of Moses,
Aaron, Gideon and Barak too.
Also of Jephtha and Samuel,
If important work was due.

They'd always been delivered
From enemies and self fears.
God had always forgiven them,
Though they caused Him tears.

Now they'd asked for a king,
Though a mighty one they had.
Again the Lord had listened
So they'd best not turn bad.

Because if they failed again
And turned once more to sin.
They'd surely be destroyed,
Their sins on them he'd pin.

CHAPTER 13

Battles still were fought,
Two thousand men were Saul's.
Another thousand he left
To answer Johnathan's call.

He attacked the Philistines;
At Geba victory was complete.
So called all Israeli men,
But the enemy didn't retreat.

A mighty army Israel faced,
Three thousand chariots strong.
Six thousand horsemen and
Men afoot, a fighting throng.

The enemy were so many; they
Were like sands of the sea.
Israel wished to run or hide;
Unto the hills they'd flee.

Saul stayed in Gilgal, his
Troops trembling with fear.
Samuel planned to arrive, but
Somehow failed to appear.

Saul's troops often deserted;
They'd no stomach for fight.
And everyday he waited
Only added to their fright.

Samuel finally appeared, but
Saul'd made offering to the
Lord, provoking Samuel, for
Saul had spurned God's word.

"You are a stupid man," he
Said, "taking matters in your
Hands; you'll never have a
Dynasty, or be fit to rule
  The land."

Saul and Johnathan stayed in
Fear with a dwindling band.
The Philistines camped near
While raiding Israel's land.

Israeli's were not allowed to
Own sword shield or bow.
So all were rendered helpless
And Philistines kept it so.

CHAPTER 14

The Philistines controlled
The lands where Israel dwelt.
Saul's army, an outlaw band,
Pressure from the enemy felt.

Then Johnathan felt an urge
To engage the enemy force.
He and his young bodyguard
Proceeded to sally fourth.

He felt that God was there
To back them in the fight
So climbed upon a mountain
Within the enemy's sight.

Soon challenged to battle,
They met it with zest; they
Charged into the fray, and
Twenty enemy's sent west.

The enemy suddenly panicked
Scattering and running away.
An earthquake caused more
Terror, and havoc held sway.

Saul's army added carnage.
Now erstwhile deserters, and
Hebrew slaves of the enemy,
To freedom were alerted.

So they all fell upon him
To settle old scores today.
Everyone got in his licks
As the enemy ran away.

Saul, being victory hungry,
Put a curse on any who ate.
Johnathan had tasted honey
So for him it was too late.

When told of the curse, He
Said, "Oh no, it's silly.
If we had't been so hungry
We'd have done more killing."

By evening, weary and hungry,
Most had not eaten all day.
They fell on battle spoils;
Cattle and sheep did slay.

Saul heard of their doing,
And called them to a feast.
They'd sacrifice over a fire
'Twas wrong to eat raw meat.

Saul would pursue the enemy
All through the night. But
The priest said "Let's ask
God; to march without word
  Isn't right."

All that night he waited, but
Word from Jehovah never came.
Surely someone had sinned,
So he must know who to blame.

Fault settled on Johnathon,
Under death threat he stood.
Troops wouldn't let him die,
Thinking his presence good.

I know that I may be wrong,
But I'd bet Saul was glad.
His son would now live, and
That wasn't all bad.

Now Saul sent his armies
Against all the enemy Kings.
In every battle fought, they
Heard the victory sound ring.

But Philistines continued
Like burrs in their sides.
All through Saul's lifetime
They slowed down his stride.

Young men of valor he sought,
And Samuel's warning came
   true
Saul conscripted their sons,
And taxed them heavily too.

CHAPTER 15

Now Samuel sent King Saul to
Destroy the Amalekite nation.
He said to leave the scene in
A state of total desolation.

But Saul spared the life of
Agag, who was the enemy
   king.
They kept the choice animals
And a number of other things.

Samuel was very upset, as he
Faced Saul with these facts.
Saul tried to find excuses
To minimize his acts.

Samuel took Saul's sword, and
Cut Agag in many a small
Piece. Then returned to Ramah
Solemnly nursing His grief.

As he said to Saul that day,
"You were God's chosen to
Rule, but proud and arrogant,
You behaved like a fool."

CHAPTER 16

The Lord convinced Samuel,
For Saul,
He'd mourned long enough;
God had already chosen a
Man of more kingly stuff.

Samuel feared Saul's revenge
If he anointed anyone.
Jehovah said, "Tell them all,
To sacrifice, you've come.

Now call Jesse to come along,
And one of his sons anoint."
City fathers came to meet him
Scared and bent out of joint

Feeling something was wrong.
Samuel told them all was well.
"I go to Bethlehem to sacri-
fice. Come purify yourselves."

Jesse's eldest was presented,
Samuel thought, "This is he,"
But Jehovah said, "Not him
For you do not think like me.

Because I look inside a man,
That is more than you can do.
And you can rely on me
To show the one to you."

So it was with all that came,
The Lord accepted not a one.
But then it soon came out
That Jesse had another son.

"He's the youngest," Jesse
Said, "and he's out tending
Sheep." "Send for him," said
Samuel, "when he comes we'll
   eat."

When David was presented,
A fine young man was he, of
Ruddy face and kindly eyes,
A pleasant sight to see.

Then Samuel anointed David,
And God's spirit to him came.
So everything he undertook
Became a winning game.

Saul was often tormented,
Filled with unnamed fears.
A harpist was suggested to
Lighten his day with cheer.

David was presented to him,
Talented, handsome and brave.
Saul fell under the spell of
Musical renditions he gave.

CHAPTER 17

Now the Philistines camped
Across a valley from Israel.
They had a mighty champion,
A giant, nine feet tall.

He liked to strut his stuff
Before the Hebrew lines;
It had the desired effect,
It nearly blew their minds.

Always ready to fight, he
Would go it man to man; but
When he made his challenge,
The Hebrews turned and ran.

Forty days he goaded them;
It was twice a daily thing.
Now he met a shepherd boy
Who swung a lethal sling.

David came to the scene with
Food for his older brothers.
He found them very fearful
Along with all the others.

Goliath strutted forth and
Flung his challenge again.
Those soldiers next to David
Lost their nerve and ran.

It was obvious David wanted
To challenge this big bully.
His brothers thought that he
Didn't realize fully--

The danger of his quest
And tried to send him back.
But he wasn't ready to run
And wouldn't consider that.

He knew God was with him,
He'd killed lions and bears,
So Goliath was just a bully
Who was putting on airs.

David unleashed his sling,
His aim unerring and true.
So he killed this giant
And set free the Jews.

CHAPTER 18

Jonathan, son of the king,
Soon was David's best friend.
They made a pact and vowed
Brotherhood to the end.

Jonathan gave him garments,
His girdle, sword and bow.
Now whatever either did,
The other was in the know.

Then King Saul adopted him
And kept him near his throne.
David protected the kingdom
As though it were his own.

He wore each day in dignity
And like a common man.
And everyone who knew him
Was his undying fan.

Now David became
   commander
Of all Saul's men of war. He
Vanquished many Philistines,
And came back for more.

The women from the towns,
When he returned their way,
Danced and sang in pleasure,
And this is what they'd say.

Saul is a mighty king with
Thousands of enemies slain.

David is mightier in battle;
Tens of thousands, his game.

To say the King was unhappy
Would be a grave mistake.
Saul feared for his kingdom
And planned for David's wake.

Soon thereafter came the day
When by spirit distraught,
Unsoothed by David's harp,
Death he would have wrought.

Threw a Javelin at the boy
To pin him to the wall.
But David dodged the thrust
And avoided death's grim call.

Another time he tried,
And once again he failed. So
He hated David more each day
As to himself he railed.

Saul feared David very much,
For he was Jehovah's man.
Saul had lost much status;
It really crimped his plans.

So Saul demoted David to
Captain of a thousand men.
But David still was loved
By folks where ere he went.

Saul promised his daughter
Would soon be David's prize.
All he'd have to do was cut
Philistines down to size.

But before David's wedding
Saul gave her to another.
Yet David still continued
A favorite of her brother.

Saul had a younger daughter
With love for David strong.

So he promised him Michal
But hoped to do him wrong.

He asked a hundred Enemies
By David be put to death
Hoping his youngest daughter
Would be soon bereft.

But David took his men and
Two hundred enemies killed.
Then Saul worried even more,
His hatred never stilled.

He gave Michal his daughter,
Who now became David's wife.
Still Saul went on planning
And plotting on David's life.

David performed with honor;
His fame greatly increased.
People all loved him more,
Saul's hatred never ceased.

CHAPTER 19

So Saul spoke to Jonathan
And all his servants too,
On ways to murder David
And thus prevent a coup.

For he was sure that David
Would end up on the throne.
He was saving the kingdom
To be his family's own.

Jonathan, being David's friend,
Warned him of the danger.
He would have had him run
From Saul's deadly anger.

Saying, "I'll talk with dad
And try to calm him down."
So Jonathan talked to Saul,
And he actually came around.

Now things were good again,
Just as it had been before.

It lasted quite some time,
Then David went back to war.

Again the victory was his;
He put the enemy to flight.
Then he enjoyed his home
Everything seemed right.

As he played the harp one day,
And Saul was listening there;
The evil spirit struck again
And left Saul's nerve ends bare.

Then he flung his spear
Which was ready to his hand.
But David dodged so it missed,
And he left there then and ran.

Now to his home he crept
And explained all to his wife,
Who said that he must leave, or
She feared he'd lose his life.

So through a window he
  crawled,
And then dropped to the
  ground.
Now she put a dummy in his
  bed,
For when soldiers came around.

Now when the soldiers came
She said he was abed and sick.
Saul had bid them, "Bring the
Bed, he cannot make it stick."

When they found an idol there
Saul was angry with Michal.
So she claimed fear of David,
While he went to visit Samuel.

Now Samuel heard his story
Of persecution and of threat.
So he invited David to stay,
As Saul plotted his death.

Many soldiers followed him
To fall under Jehovah's spell.
Then Saul arrived in person,
And he prophesied as well.

Now this was quite unusual
For a man like Saul to do.
Men again in amazement asked,
"Is Saul a prophet too?"

CHAPTER 20

David fled from Nioth, for
Saul and soldiers were there.
So he returned to Ramah and
Fears with Jonathan shared.

But Jonathan couldn't believe
His father denied his word.
So he offered help to David
As soon as proof he heard.

Then once again they vowed
Their friendship not to cease.
And nothing could ever change
Or make their love decrease.

They thought of a method for
Jonathan to warn his friend,
If he learned his father's
Plans included David's end.

So by the stone of Ezel he
Awaited Jonathan's bid. So
Jonathan shot an arrow
Beyond where David hid.

Saul missed him at dinner,
So son Jonathan he quizzed.
Angered at the answer
Saul's javelin whizzed.

So Jonathan knew his
Dad was determined to kill.
Thus he was committed, his
Friendship pact to fulfill.

As a lad gathered arrows,
He shouted, "Farther away.
And hurry to fetch it now,
There's no time for delay."

The warning was for David,
And he knew he must flee.
So, soon as the lad left,
He fell upon his knees.

It was a sudden goodbye.
Jonathan returned to the city.
The time had come to separate,
And David could only flee.

CHAPTER 21

Now David soon learned
That to be on the lam was
Not the least bit of fun.
And that any man

Must live by his wits
And often denigrate himself,
To be always on the move
While trying to stay well.

He went to priest Ahimelech
Who lived in the city of Nob.
He lied about his purpose for
His presence would raise hob.

For a man as famous as he
To be traveling all alone
Was almost beyond belief;
He'd be expected nearer home.

Now David was very hungry,
And probably tired too. Plus
Trying to keep his profile
Low while passing through.

He asked a priest for food;
That worthy could only say,
"We do have some Holy bread,
It was replaced today.

If your men are clean and
Undefiled of late, take these
Loaves of Shew bread
For it's now out of date."

Still David needed a weapon;
He mentioned it to the priest,
Who brought Goliath's sword
Which made David very
    pleased.

It must have revived thoughts
And memories of better days,
When he was growing up and
In history found his place.

He'd gone down the mountain
So early in the morn, and
Then he'd climbed another be-
ond the valley floor.

A giant's voice had thundered
But his God was on his side.
And when his sling he used
How the Philistine had died.

That had been the beginning
Of a time of pomp and fame.
But now he'd been reduced, so
He feared to give his name.

He noticed a young man here,
Chief herdsman for King Saul.
So it seemed almost certain
That he hadn't better stall.

He hurriedly pressed on,
There was need to get away
To King Achish of Gath for
He needed a place to stay.

The soldiers of this king
Knew something of his past.
So it became clear this
Sanctuary couldn't last.

So he pretended to be mad
To expedite an early escape.
The king then threw him out,
And he left before too late.

CHAPTER 22

Then to the cave of Adulam
He made good his escape.
Soon family and relatives
To his hideaway traipsed.

Many of those in trouble
Or preferred him over Saul,
Followed him into hiding,
Four hundred strong in all.

Then they journeyed to Moab
Where he dealt with the king,
For his mom and dad to stay
Till he got a grip on things.

"Get up and go to Judah,"
The prophet Gad did say;
They got up and went
To a forested place.

Saul still waited in Gibe-ah
Sitting under a tree, and
There was always a weapon
In his hand to see.

He felt servants disloyal
And might take David's side.
But then Doeg, the herdsman
Told Saul how he had spied.

David had gone to Ahimelech
To acquire a weapon and food.
Saul then sent for Ahimelech
And Nobs other priests too.

Ahimelech said he'd helped
But reminded Saul that day,
His son-in-law was honorable
And had always been that way.

But Saul, in arrogant anger,
Ordered the death of this man.
No man lifted a weapon or
Wanted a priests blood on his
    hands.

But Doeg stood waiting to act
When Saul gave the word, by
Murdering all those priests,
Eighty-five men of the Lord.

Now to the city of priests he
Went and his army laid it low.
So Nob was all a shambles
When Saul dealt his next blow.

No person or animal escaped
But Abiathar, son of a priest.
He hurried to David's hideout,
To relate Saul's horrible deed.

David then answered in sorrow;
He'd feared about Doeg before,
But now he really felt guilty
For all the casualties of war.

To Abiathar he offered
Shelter or food if in need.
Saul wanted them both, and
They were fugitives indeed.

CHAPTER 23

David heard Philistines were
At Keila stealing grain.
He asked God if he should go
And rescue Israel again.

His answer was affirmative,
The Lord said he should go.
But his men were afraid
And resoundingly said, "No."

David asked the Lord again,
And his answer was the same.
So they wiped the enemy out
And honored Jehovah's name.

For Abiathar went along
With David, to intercede.
Thus God could always help
David do great deeds.

Saul heard where David was,
He wanted to go for the kill.
David called on God again,
And He was with him still.

David left with six hundred
Around the country to roam.
Saul then heard he had left
And decided to stay at home.

Then one day at Horesh in
Caves among the hills, he
Heard Saul was hunting him
And moving in for the kill.

The Lord was with our hero
And kept him safe and sound.
Saul marched high and low
Searching the country `round.

Then Jonathan, his old friend,
Came on a peaceful mission.
He encouraged him to trust in
God; he had true religion.

Men of Ziph were treacherous
And betrayed him to the king.
David fled to the wilderness
Making search another thing.

But no matter where they ran
It was to small avail. For
Every place that David went,
The king closed on his trail.

It seemed David was caught,
But Saul got a sudden call.
Philistines had attacked;
The people had need of Saul.

So the pressure was off;
Again our hero was saved.

Thankfully he named this
Place "The Rock of Escape."

Then he went to live
In the Caves at Engedi. But
All the time he had to be
Alert and ever ready.

CHAPTER 24

But Saul returned again once
The Philistines he'd chased,
To continue to hunt for David
In that rocky, barren place.

With three thousand men, he
Looked among rocks and goats.
He entered a cave in passing
And then turned to go.

On his way he was followed,
And David showed himself.
When Saul was in the cave
David had been there as well.

Now David held a cloth from
The skirt of the King's robe.
Saying, "This I took, when
Your life I could have smote.

God gave you into my hand;
But you're his anointed king.
I will not cause you harm
Or trouble to you bring."

Saul was badly shaken, as
I'd certainly think he'd be.
If things had been reversed
'Twould've ended differently.

Now he called David, "Son,"
And asked that he swear to
Keep the faith in future;
Then he left from there.

So David and his men went
Back to the caves of Engedi.

It had been a wonderful day;
I'd bet he felt quite heady.

CHAPTER 25

Samuel was old and tired,
For he was up in years.
So when he died at Ramah
All Israel came in tears.

They buried him at Ramah in
The family plot owned there.
He went to rest in God with
Whom his life he'd shared.

David went to the wilderness
To a place they called Paran.
He knew of a rancher there
Who was a wealthy man. He

Owned three thousand sheep,
And a full thousand goats.
He was a churlish type who
Was known to brag and gloat.

David sent some men to him
To ask for a small donation.
He treated them quite badly;
No way he'd share rations.

When David heard his answer
He was quite antagonized.
Nabal was a real jerk who'd
Get whittled down to size.

For while they'd been around,
They'd been guards for him,
Had never asked a favor,
Nor ever against him sinned.

His flocks and herds grazed
Peacefully on the land. The
Way he'd treated David's men
Stamped doom upon this man.

David strapped on weapons;
His men all did the same.

All were bent on vengeance
And Nabal was fair game.

But Nabal had a wife who
Was beautiful to behold. She
Also had good sense, and
This story has been told.

One of her husband's herdsmen
Said, "Please hear what I
Say; David asked a donation,
But Nabal sent him away.

Now David was our friend,
He's been often in Carmel;
And whenever he's around we
Can count on him for help.

They've been a protection
Behind which we were safe.
But your husband insulted
Him, he'll be in a rage."

So Abigail did journey to
Head off David on the trail.
Taking supplies and gifts,
A mission she dare not fail.

When they met upon the trail,
She bowed low, and said, "I
Heard of all that's happened,
And you surely must see red.

I know that Nabal is a nerd,
And as stupid as they come.
Please, my lord, have mercy;
For he is just plain dumb.

Now you have done much
  good;
The Lord is at your side. So
Please don't be a murderer
Because of your hurt pride.

May all your enemies be
Cursed just as Nabal is.

And God always protect you,
For you are obviously His.

So please belay your hand;
Do not a murderer be. When
God does great things for
You, please remember me."

David answered, "Thank God
For you, you've saved much
Sorrow. If I'd had my way,
They'd be dead tomorrow."

So Abigail returned
Back home to bunk. That's
Where she found her husband,
And he was roaring drunk.

She didn't tell the news
Till after morning's light.
And it was such a shock;
He passed out from fright.

About ten days he lay there
Thus and then suddenly died.
David heard it happened, and
In thankfulness he cried.

"God saved me from myself,
Serving Nabal for his sins."
Now David sent for Abigail,
And bade her come to him.

She came in haste
And then became his bride.
His other wife was Ahino-am,
So the two were at his side.

Michal was his first wife;
He'd left her behind to
Avoid King Saul's anger when
He ran to save his life.

Saul gave her away it seems,
To Palti, son of Laish.

He took her away to Gallim
Regardless of her wish.

Of wives, he now had two
'Though promised four.
Often one's a great plenty!
So why should he want more?

CHAPTER 26

Now again the Ziphites had
Told Saul where David hid.
He took three thousand men
To search the hills of Ziph.

He pitched camp on Hachilah,
A hillside where he'd rest;
Davids spies were watching,
Yet Saul they'd not molest.

He knew they were there, and
He knew why they had come.
Now he devised a way to
Make them all look dumb.

Abner was Saul's general
And a mighty man was he
In the center of camp where
David wasn't expected to be.

In the darkness of night,
David and Abishai crept in,
Stole Sauls spear and water
Jug and got away with them.

Abishai wanted to kill Saul,
But David spared his life.
Saying, "Let God handle him,
He'll always do what's right."

Then they stood upon a hill
At a distance safe to be
From which to be heard
And also quickly flee.

Then taunted General Abner,
Saying he was fit to die.

For he'd been sound asleep
As they'd stood by his side.

And they could send a man
For the water jug and spear.
But David and Abishai
Would be no longer here.

Then Saul recognized his
Voice, and instantly repent-
ed; he apologized to David
Who knew he was demented.

Saul wanted to make amends
For he'd had quite a fright.
In any case he went home;
He'd lost his yen to fight.

CHAPTER 27

Now David was very weary
Of running from King Saul.
So he devised a strategy
Which should change it all.

Saul would surely get him
If he stuck around. His
Faith in God never lapsed,
And his plan was sound.

They all moved to Philistia
Favored by the King of Gath.
So with six hundred men he
Escaped King Saul's wrath.

He got permission to move far
Beyond the ruling city and
Attacked Philistine towns
To which he showed no pity.

He let King Achish think it
Was Israel whom he fought.
He killed every inhabitant
And so their silence bought.

He still fought Philistines
In an area so remote,

King Achish never guessed
'Twas his people David smote.

Saul heard David left the
Country so abandoned chase.
Then David was left in
Peace to set his own pace.

Achish believed the stories,
And he was prone to think;
David served him always and
Accepted him as king.

Sixteen months it lasted;
He lived in enemy land. But
If King Achish had known,
He would have been banned.

CHAPTER 28

Philistines lusted for blood
Against all Israel's people.
Saul, when he heard the news,
Felt awfully weak and feeble.

Now he asked the Lord
What method he should use.
But Jehovah never answered,
So Saul was in a stew.

Saul who'd killed mediums,
And familiar spirits too,
Asked advice of servants;
What else could he do?

There was a woman at Endor
Who'd spoken to the dead.
Saul then searched her out,
And this is what she said.

"The King kills my kind,
It's death for me to speak.
This may be a trap for me
If I do what you seek."

By Saul she was reassured
Such was not the case.

He'd cause her no trouble,
If this job she'd take.

She accepted the challenge,
For what it was worth. Now
Then, she conjured Samuel,
Who rose up from the earth.

She realized who Saul was;
Her voice raised in fright.
He soothed her fears again
Telling her all was right.

He talked with Samuel,
But what he learned there,
Meant his and his sons'
Deaths, a terrible scare.

He fell down on the ground
For strength he had none.
He'd no food a day and night,
And many miles had come.

His hostess offered food,
Which he tried to refuse.
She talked him into eating;
Nourishment he could use.

So she killed a fatted calf
And kneaded unleavened
  bread.
After they had eaten, into
The night Saul's party fled.

CHAPTER 29

The Philistines all gathered
For battle with Israelites.
It seemed David and company
Might get into the fight.

King Achish invited them;
He knew they were good men.
His leaders had other plans
And were not changing them.

They felt that in battle
These men might fight them
All and do great harm just
To get in good with Saul.

They'd heard songs of David,
And he was a warrior of note.
Not sure of his allegiance,
None wanted to be smote.

They left at dawn unhappy;
In Philistia David stayed.
The Philistines marched and
This was Saul's last day.

CHAPTER 30

Three days of traveling
It took to go home.
With hopes of resting
Before they would roam.

It wasn't to be, to their
Sorrow they learned. Famil-
ies and herds were stolen
And homes had been burned.

His men were grieving and
Threatened David with ston-
es. They needed a scapegoat
For the loss of their homes.

So David called on Abiathar,
Who was the son of a priest.
He asked God for advice
As well as for relief.

The answer was, "Go to war,
For you've nothing to lose.
You will save your families
And the rest of the loot."

So they left there quickly;
All six hundred men he took.
They raced after the enemy
And came to Besor Brook.

A third of the company was
Faint and weary of the trail.
So he left them at the brook
Rather than have them fail.

So with four hundred left,
He hit the trail again.
And then out in the field,
They found an Egyptian man.

He was a slave of the enemy,
Who had been left behind, so
David fed and nourished him
With treatment fair and kind.

And that young man in turn
Showed them where to march.
So found the enemy quickly,
To attack him just at dark.

Twenty-four hours of battle,
Caught the enemy in disarray.
They wiped them out except
Four hundred who got away.

They recovered all the stuff
The Amalekites had taken, and
All the enemy owned, which
In death he had forsaken.

Now they retraced their steps
And headed back to Ziklag.
The two hundred at the brook
Still where they'd sagged.

Some would return their fami-
lies and send them all away.
But David said, "It won't do,
They'll get all their pay."

It was that way in Israel,
And I'd say David was right.
Those who guard supplies get
Paid like those who fight.

All the spoils they'd won
Were given to David by his

Men. It seems appropriate,
The thing that he did then.

He divided all the spoils,
And sent them down the trail
To serve as welcome gifts
For many towns in Israel.

To some they were welcomed
But not in other places. In
Many towns in Israel, they
Feared to show their faces.

CHAPTER 31

Meantime back in Israel, the
Enemy pushed the battle.
They overwhelmed Saul's army
And got his warriors rattled.

The battle became a route;
Israeli's died like flies.
No escape from Philistines
No matter how they tried.

Then the archers attacked;
They zeroed in on Saul.
He was mortally wounded
And his armor bearer called.

He preferred to die
Rather than a prisoner be.
He could expect torture
And could no longer flee.

He told his man to kill him
And remove him from the war.
But that worthy refused,
So he fell upon his sword.

On the battle field he lay
Next morning cold and dead.
The enemy took his armor,
And then cut off his head.

In the temple of Ashteroth
His armor they placed. And

With his body, the wall
Of Beth-shan defaced.

When Jabesh-gileads people
Heard of the enemies deeds,
All believed that of action
They were in dire need.

So their valiant warriors did
A midnight requisition, and
Stole Saul and his sons from
Such infamous positions.

They cremated the bodies and
Buried the bones under a tree.
Then seven days they mourned
But from Saul all were free.

**THE END
OF FIRST SAMUEL**

SECOND SAMUEL

CHAPTER 1

Only three days ago David
Smote the Amalekites. But
Now he was resting and
Relaxing from the fight.

A messenger came with torn
Clothing and dirt upon his
Head, a sign of mourning
And respect for the dead.

He told a wild story of an
Army in headlong flight. How
Saul and Jonathan had died
In that deadly fight.

When asked how he knew that
The king was really dead,
He certainly caused surprise
When this is what he said.

"I climbed up Mount Gilbor
And stood there in fear.
For there was King Saul
A leaning on his spear."

Come over here" he cried,
"And end all my pain.
I shall soon die anyway,
And I've no more to gain."

"So I did as he asked and
Took his bracelet and crown.
I give both to you, my lord,
The most deserving one
    Around."

He hadn't heard the saying
Kill the bearer of bad news.
But David gave the order,
And he got his just dues.

He claimed to have killed
The anointed of the Lord,
So it was too late
If he ever got the word.

Then David and his men rent
Their clothes and cried. For
It was a matter of sorrow
That their King had died.

Long they did lament over
Jonathan and his father Saul.

Israel's King was slain;
They'd seen the mighty fall.

Keep it quiet in Ashkelon,
Nor let it be told in Gath.
Do not tell the Philistines;
For they would only laugh.

Keep dry upon the mountain;
Let no dew fall on the field.
For Saul the anointed King
Fell dead upon his shield.

The mighty bow of Jonathan,
The sword of Israel they used.
They both died as a team;
Lives in death both fused.

Swifter than the eagle;
Strong as the lion were they.
Daughters of Israel, lament,
For they have gone away.

The mighty fell in battle,
"Jonathan I miss thee most.
We were like brothers,"
Cried David, "we were very
    Close."

CHAPTER 2

Then David prayed to God,
As to what he should do.
Word was, "Go to Hebron,"
So that was his next move.

All his wives and families
And warriors he took along.
The house of Judah gathered
To anoint him by the throng.

He heard Saul and Jonathan
By Jabeth's men were buried.
So he showed them kindness;
Lasting friendship curried.

Abner was the son of Ner, and
Saul's commander-in chief. He
Appointed Saul's son as king,
And this caused much grief.

The eleventh tribe he ruled;
He came to battle David's men.
Now a civil war erupted, when
Peace there could have been.

So the two armies fought each
Other until the end of day.
Now Abner lost the battle
And tried to run away.

Asahel was fleet of foot,
And doggedly he trailed.
Abner tried to dissuade him;
In this he utterly failed.

Abner stopped to kill him
With the handle of a spear.
That young man, so fast of
Foot, too bad he had no fear.

David's men had won this bout
For only twenty they'd lost.
Three hundred sixty of Benj-
amin had paid a final cost.

Abner, chased up a mountain,
Called down for a truce.
So Joab and Abishai stopped;
They thought it was no use.

Their brother's body by his
Father's was interned. Abner
Travelled all night long,
And to Hebron he returned.

CHAPTER 3

Thus started a civil war
That seemed to have no end.
Israeli against Israeli, for
They were no longer friends.

Now David had several sons;
His power as king did grow.
Abner went into politics,
And his fame grew also.

As David's strength increased,
Saul's house began to fade.
Now Abner changed allegiance
And offered David a trade.

So David accepted his offer
But demanded a favor first.
He wanted Michal returned;
For her he still had thirst.

Now Abner became friendly
With one of Saul's concubines.
And, although it was taboo,
With her he spent much time.

King Ish-bosheth had noticed,
And to Abner made complaint.
When Abner turned on him,
The king became quite faint.

Thus Abner was still angry;
His Allegiance he would sell.
He wished to be commander-in-
Chief of all tribes of Israel.

So Ish-bosheth brought Michal,
As her husband wept in trail.
But no matter how he cried,
He was doomed to fail.

Abner sent him packing,
That was the way it must be.
For any whim of the king
Became an instant decree.

Now Abner came to David and
Explained the progress made;
In turning the nation over,
He'd continue to persuade.

But soon after Abner left
General Joab returned. Now
He was Asahel's brother
And revenge still burned.

Sending men to call him back,
He took him quietly aside.
He stabbed him with a dagger,
And that's how Abner died.

Joab avenged Asahel's death.
Was it from sorrow and grief?
Or did he want to make sure
He'd be Commander-in-Chief?

David heard and sadly cried
He wanted the nation to know;
He hadn't planned the murder
And would not have had it so.

They agreed with his actions;
Whatever he did, they agreed.
For he was God's chosen,
And no fault could they see.

CHAPTER 4

Ish-bosheth was Saul's son,
When Abner died, he cringed.
For his future with David,
On Abner's style had hinged.

Baanah and Rechab were cap-
tains of Israeli bands,
And they put much effort
Into an infamous plan.

In the heat of day, into Ish-
bosheth's house they came.
Then killed him and ran
All night across the plain.

Bringing Ish-bosheth's head,
David's blessing to gain.
Their scheme, ill advised,
Won death instead of fame.

David thought them murderers,
And he sentenced them to die.
For he had honored the king,
And his reaction was to cry.

CHAPTER 5

All the tribes of Israel,
To David at Hebron came.
Saying, "Saul was our king,
But you were a man of fame.

We'd make a deal with you,
And have you be our king.
We know God is with you;
He has you under his wing."

Over Judah for seven years,
He had been the ruling head.
And now the rest of Israel
Would by him be led.

The Jebusites in Jerusalem
Had insulted him no end.
They said he couldn't win
Against lame, blinded men.

Through the water tunnel
Went his warriors bold,
Surprised the enemy, made
The city his stronghold.

So Jerusalem became well-
Known as David's city.
For those who denied him
Entry, he had shown no pity.

Then King Hiram of Tyre
Sent cedar wood and men
To build a new palace.
He lived much better then.

With wives and concubines,
With many sons was blessed,
But Solomon was the one
Whom we'll remember best.

For a third of a century
David ruled the nation, a
Total of forty years and
Improved internal relations.

The enemy heard he was king
And decided to go after him.
They soon in force arrived
At the valley of Rephaim.

Then David asked Jehovah
If he should do them battle.
With God's "Okay," he killed
Philistines like cattle.

They fled the battle field
But soon came back for more.
David asked the Lord again
And differently waged a war.

Wind in the tops of balsams
Sounded like marching feet,
He attacked from behind and
Wiped them out with ease.

CHAPTER 6

Thirty thousand David took
To fetch the ark, from near
The home of Abinadab, with
Oxen and a brand new cart.

From the house of Abinadab,
His sons the ark escorted,
And the oxen shook the load;
They feared it had aborted.

So Uzzah put out his hand to
Steady the precious prize.
He fell upon the ground
And beside the ark he died.

They played music and danced
Rejoicing before the Lord.
But when Uzzah suddenly died,
It hit them like a sword.

David felt that God was angry,
And they all felt great fear.
So at the house of Obed-Edom,
They left the Ark right here.

For three months they left it,
And its host was blessed.
David brought it to Jerusalem
Where it was now his guest.

As they brought it home, they
Danced and shouted with glee.
Now Michal was watching,
So thus she happened to see,

David was nearly naked, and
She felt, acted like a fool.
So she gave him much advice,
But then he treated her cool.

So her days were lonely; she
Must have known much grief.
Apparently David ignored her
For she never did conceive.

CHAPTER 7

The time of war was over;
The land in peace did rest.
Then David said to Nathan,
"Israel is truly blessed.

I dwell in a house of Cedar,
While God's Ark is in a tent.
It's time to show our thanks
And to work for God we went."

Nathan encouraged him
In what he wanted to do.
But God said "No," to Nathan,
"To tell him is up to you.

All the years the children
Wandered wilds and plains, I
Lived in a tent and led them;
I heard the cries and claims.

I thwarted your enemies kept
You in health or war. I'll
Always favor your kingdom; it
Is what I'm planning for.

I'll not banish my children;
Saul will have been the last.
Earth will know your history;
You'll be heroes of the past.

Your family will rule Israel,
David will be famous of men.
From him will issue a son, who
Will make israel great again."

Now David went in to worship;
To God this is what he said.
"You've done wonderful things,
Through the years you've led.

And now you promise much
    more,
Although I am only a man, for
I am the means you'll use
To carry out this great plan.

You are the God of my nation,
And we can count on you.
So bless my people forever;
We know your word is true."

CHAPTER 8

David's armies ranged the land,
And he conquered all around.
He subjugated the Philistines
Brought Moab to the ground.

The army of Hadadezer lost in
His attempt to regain power.
It seemed David couldn't lose,
His dynasty in full flower.

Seventeen hundred cavalry
Were captured by his men and

116

Twenty thousand infantry.
Some battle it had been!

A hundred chariot horses he
Kept, laming all other teams.
Nightmares the enemy must've
Had instead of normal dreams.

Twenty-two thousand Syrians
Died in this battle too, who
Came to help King Hadadezer
But fell before Davids troops.

In Damascus he put garrisons;
The Syrians, tribute paid.
The Lord gave him victories
Wherever he went on raid.

Hadadezer's gold was brought;
It came from enemy shields.
They also got much bronze;
All won on the battle fields.

Now when King Toi heard how
Ignominiously Hadadezer fell,
He sent brass and silver gifts
And gold by his son, as well.

Then after his return, he
Fought in the valley of salt.
Killing eighteen thousand Ed-
omites brought raids to halt.

On everything that David did
God's smile blessed his work.
A rule of love and justice,
A history of kindly words.

His old friends were trusted
Generals, ministers and such,
Guards, and secretaries, with
Good jobs for all his sons.

CHAPTER 9

Now David remembered
  Jonathan,
How like brothers they'd been.

Then he located Mephibosheth,
A lame son of his late friend.

So now he bid him, "Come,"
  and
Mephibosheth came in fear.
But the king comforted him
Making plans to keep him near.

Saul's property he returned, so
Mephibosheth was a wealthy
  man
Who moved to the City of
  David
According to royal plan.

He moved into David's palace
And lived like royalty.
For he was like a son
Who owed the king his loyalty.

He had his own servants,
And things went much his way.
It was now a pleasant life
That brightened up his stay.

CHAPTER 10

Now the King of Ammon died,
And his son Hanun reigned.
David tried to comfort him;
Hanuns advisers were pained.

They told him David's men
Were spies to set him up. So
They took David's messengers,
And gave them a roughing up

Shaving half their beards,
Cutting short their clothes.
David heard of their plight
And understood their woes.

So he said, "Stay at Jericho
Till your beards have grown.
Then you'll feel much better,
And you can come back home."

Now the Ammonites could see
That they had made an error.
So they enlisted help to
Stave off future terror.

They hired mercenaries from
Other countries 'round about.
Hoping to put the Israeli's
To an ignominious rout.

Joab, captain of Davids host,
Set forces for best effect.
They marched, enemies fled,
Their morale badly wrecked.

Joab took his men back home;
Syrians regrouped the force,
And Hadadezer faced David
Who also had marched forth.

In the war that followed
Israel's enemies were beat.
The Syrians failed in battle
To their total defeat.

All of Syria's allies
Became Israel's friends.
So the children of Ammon
Were in trouble no end.

CHAPTER 11

In spring when wars begin,
David sent armies to fight.
He must have been uneasy;
He couldn't sleep one night.

Joab and his men went to
Rabbah to lay siege. Back
In Jerusalem David waited
And gave up trying to sleep.

So for a walk he went,
Upon the palace roof.
And there he saw a sight
That made him stop and look.

For that at which he gazed,
A woman of striking beauty
Bathed; his eyes now glazed,
He forgot his kingly duty.

He must have surely heard
That she was Uriah's wife.
But kings got their wishes;
Who thought of other lives?

So he told her, "Come over."
She did, for he was King.
Maybe it was love right now
Or just the call of spring.

Then one day she sent a note,
Saying, "I'm in a family way."
He thought and was distraught
And wondered what to say.

Finally he called his friend,
Said, "Joab, send Uriah here."
Her husband came home but to
Her he never came near.

Now this put David in a bind,
So he used his wits and wile.
He tried to get Uriah drunk,
But he was free of guile.

He slept on the palace steps,
For his friends had to fight.
To sleep at home at ease
Did not to him seem right.

So the king, frustrated, sent
Uriah to the front of battle.
He made sure his problem he'd
Cure; Uriah's life was chattle.

Uriah's wife did mourn
For memory of dreams gone by.
But quickly she recovered
And became King David's wife.

David solved that problem
As only a king could do.
But God was not too happy,
And he let him know it too.

CHAPTER 12

Nathan came to King David
And this story told, with
David becoming very angry,
As he heard the plot unfold.

A poor man had a little lamb,
The only one he owned.
It was a family pet and
Considered part of home.

His neighbor was a rich man
With flocks of notable size.
When a guest stopped to visit,
They ate the poor man's prize.

David decreed that he should
Pay the poor man four for one.
Then Nathan said, "In essence,
That's just what you have done.

You murdered your man Uriah
Because you wanted his wife.
In future your family will
Rebel; you'll know strife."

Now David knew he had
   sinned,
By his own words should die.
But God would let him live
By his enemies despised.

Bath-sheba's baby was sickly,
He lived only seven days.
David lay upon the ground
And fasted long and prayed.

The baby died anyway,
So David gave up the fight.

As he said when asked, "It's
Too late; my child has died."

Bath-sheba had a second son
And Solomon was his name.
He would be a man of wisdom,
A king of lasting fame.

God smiled upon this child,
"Jedidaiah" David named him.
Jehovah loved this child, it
Was as it should have been.

Murder was a constant threat
With his family in shadow.
David's wives were in danger,
His future now was shallow.

For Jehovah was displeased
That David had fallen short.
This had shaped his future
Causing happiness to abort.

Meanwhile back at the battle,
Joab was winning a war. So he
Sent for David to take credit,
As that's what kings are for.

So David led the conquerors
On the final pillaging sweep.
Now all of Rabbah's jewels
And crown were his to keep.

Then he returned in honor
With many slaves and loot.
Ammonites now were subjects
And bearing tribute to boot.

CHAPTER 13

Prince Amnon, David's son,
Fell desperately in love.
He played a dirty trick on
Her that he was not above.

Told his father he was ill,
Asked Tamar serve his food,

When she brought the meal
He was in a sexy mood.

He raped her then pushed
Her from his room. She tore
Her blouse and wailed; now
She faced a life of gloom.

She was half sister to Amnon;
Absalom was her full brother.
She was now contaminated
   and
Considered unfit for others.

Now David was very angry
   when
The story he finally heard.
But Absalom hated silently
And never said a word.

Two years later in Ephraim,
Absalom's sheep were sheared.
He threw a big party
Making sure Amnon appeared.

At his signal they moved,
And his men did Amnon in.
So Amnon paid a big price
For such a foolhardy sin.

The story got back to David
All of his sons had died.
He was prostrate with grief
Rent his clothing and cried.

It soon was obvious to see,
All sons returned but two.
Absalom fled to King Talmai,
Until David shed the blues.

Three years Absalom hid till
David got over the death.
But he yearned for Absalom;
It got worse at every breath.

CHAPTER 14

To unite the king and Absalom
Was the object of his friend.
Joab bargained with a woman
For this estrangement to end.

She told of her two sons of
How they fought and one died.
Her family wanted to execute
The one who was still alive.

But if this should happen,
She'd have no sons at all.
David listened with pity;
Said he'd carry the ball.

For he'd make sure they'd
Never harm her other son.
He agreed whole heartedly
She was entitled to one.

Now she let the king know
That it would be real nice;
If he'd call Absalom home,
It would break the ice.

Then he suspected Joab,
And she admitted it was so.
So he called Joab in
And told him he could go

Tell Absalom to come home
But stay out of his sight.
Two more years it stretched
To Absalom it wasn't right.

He kept asking Joab to come
And intercede with the king.
But Joab continued to stall;
He didn't gain a thing.

Absalom burned Joab's grain,
And that got his attention.
So he came by asking why,
And Absalom made mention,

Saying, "Why call me back if
I can't see my father's face?
Five years I've not seen him,
I should've stayed in place."

Then David relented at last
And asked Absalom to return.
For he was a loving father
Who for his family yearned.

CHAPTER 15

Absalom came up with a plan
To usurp his father's throne.
He stole people's allegiance,
And claimed it for his own.

He bought beautiful horses,
A magnificent chariot too.
He sympathized with everyone
And made a great to do.

He sent spies over the land
To incite rebellion there; so
Many friends deserted, for
What looked like better fare.

David got the message, his
Kingdom claimed by his son.
So with his kin and army
He left there on the run.

Now Ittai, the Gittite, came,
He commanded six hundred
   too.
David bid him stay in safety,
But he just plain refused.

Ittai promised allegiance
And swore that he'd stand by.
Whatever fate's decision he'd
Stick by his friend or die.

The city was sad as they left
And fled from their homes.

They faced a future of fear;
Who knew where they must
   roam?

Over Kidron brook and then
Into the country they went.
The Ark they took along, till
Part of the journey was spent.

They set the Ark by the road
Until everyone had walked by.
The king bid Zadok return it,
And then he told him why.

"If the Lord sees fit, I'll
Be back to see it again; but
If he has forsaken me,
I'll just do the best I can."

Back again Zadok and Abiathar
Went the Ark they took along;
David and his people all were
Weeping for much was wrong.

When someone brought word
His advisor had deserted too,
David prayed to God, saying
"Lord, I need help from you."

The king arranged with Zadok,
Ahima-az and Jonathan to ret-
urn for the spark of liberty
Within him still burned.

They'd return to the city to
Sample the mood of the land.
So they'd know about Absalom
No matter where they ran.

Toward the mount of olives
Trudged David and his group.
Hushai the Archite waited
And was ready to follow too.

David sent him back, saying,
"Give Absalom bad advice,

I have others planted there,
To keep me well apprised."

CHAPTER 16

Jonathan's son, David
Treated like a prince, and
Ziba, his loving servant,
Guarded his going out or in.

Now Mephibosheth held back;
He thought he might be king.
Ziba brought David supplies
And many other things.

Then David gave Ziba all he
Had to Mephibosheth before.
It was the king's prerogative,
And they were facing a war.

Now as they passed Bahurim,
A small town along the way,
A man now cursed them and
Had unpleasant things to say.

He called David a murderer,
Who'd killed Saul's family.
Abishai offered to kill him,
David said, "No let him be."

David thought God planned
To give him a bad time.
He'd take his medicine, God
Just might excuse his crime.

A wild eyed man named Shimei
Threw stones, calling names.
But they trudged wearily on
Refusing to play his games.

Absalom came to Jerusalem,
And Hushai the Archite, who
Once had been dad's friend
Seemed just a little cool.

But he convinced Absalom
He had now switched sides,

And Absalom never guessed
He'd been taken for a ride.

Ahithophel, David's advisor,
To Absalom's camp deserted.
Absalom hung on every word
No matter what he asserted.

Now he asked Ahithophel's
Advice on what to do. The
Word of his advisor was
Just what he would choose.

He lay with David's wives,
In the open for all to see.
Word should reach his dad,
For the break to be clean.

The people would choose;
He hoped they'd follow him.
The way things looked now
His dad's chances were slim.

CHAPTER 17

"Twelve thousand men," said,
Ahithophel "to take David to-
Night; he'll be very weary
And unable to fight."

They agreed but asked if
Hushai had a better thought.
He said, "David's a mighty
Warrior who won't be easily
   Caught.

He'll be holed up, hard to
Find, ugly as a mother bear.
You'll need your whole army,
Personally lead them there."

So the army was mobilized
From both far and near. And
Ahithophel sent David word
To get his flight in gear.

Zadok and Jonathan, priests,
Then went to carry warning,
Get David to the wilderness,
And do not wait till morning.

At En-rogel those two stayed,
So movements caused no alarm.
Their reason for being there
Was to keep David from harm.

But as they left the city
A boy there saw them go,
Who then went to Absalom
And of course told him so.

But when soldiers arrived
Friends hid them in a well.
They covered it with grain
So that none could tell.

The messengers got through
And carried word to the king.
Saying, "Go right now and
Put flight over every thing."

They crossed the Jordan fad-
ing into wilderness at dawn.
Ahithophel hanged himself;
He'd been publicly wrong.

David came to Mahanaim and
Welcome by his good friends,
Who brought food and comfort,
With time hope would mend.

Absalom led his army in a
Feverish search of the land.
He appointed Amasa as general
Of this mighty warrior band.

CHAPTER 18

Now David divided his troops
To three different commands.
Planning to lead himself but
Gave in to popular demand.

His friends didn't want him
In the thick of the fight.
And convinced him that to
Chance it wouldn't be right.

So at the city gates
The kingly warrior stood.
He watched them all pass by
Like a human river in flood.

And as his troops passed he
Gave his commanders a charge,
Saying, "Deal gently,
Don't cause Absalom harm."

In the forests of Ephraim,
The battles raged that day.
Twenty thousand lost, the
Slaughter there was great.

For every one who died,
Many others ran away. Not
All of those were heroes
In the battle that day.

David's men were warriors,
Fighters of known fame.
They beat their pursuers,
Winners in a grisly game.

Absalom happened on them,
While in headlong flight.
So turned and fled, try-
ing to escape the fight.

He rode beneath a mighty
Oak, his hair in branches
Tangled. His mule kept on
Running; in air he dangled.

That beautiful hair, in
Which he took such pride,
Held him high and dry, no
Chance to save his hide.

Soon one of Joab's men
Saw him hanging there.

He hurried to the general,
This great news to share.

"Why didn't you kill him?"
His commander inquired;
He'd heard David's charge
And was not so inspired.

"Not for a million dollars,"
That young man said, "you'd
Be the first to accuse me;
I'd surely lose my head."

So then Joab did the deed
His man had just refused.
He dispatched young Absalom,
Who finally paid his dues.

And then Joab's men returned
As he sounded a trumpet call.
Now the battle was over
With peace the hope for all.

Then into a deep pit,
Absalom's corpse they threw.
They covered it with rocks,
And started lives anew.

To their homes they fled,
Absalom's army totally beat.
Their only worry, reprisals,
Which usually follow defeat.

Absalom had built a monumen
In a place called Kings Dale.
And yet his life and death
Were just another sad tale.

When David heard the news, he
Asked for word of his son.
Learning of Absalom's death
Nearly struck him dumb.

"Oh Absalom," he cried,
"Oh Absalom, my son,
I'd rather I had died;
Oh where did I go wrong?"

CHAPTER 19

Now the king was so sad
And his sorrow so deep,
That he cried and moaned
And continued to weep.

His sorrow, so encompassing,
Soon got every one down.
Even the soldiers who'd won
Slipped sadly back to town.

Then Joab went to the king
And thus vented his anger.
"Your friends and soldiers
Placed themselves in danger.

Many of us risked our lives
To keep you healthy and well.
If you appreciate our efforts,
It's certainly hard to tell.

You should go out there and
Appreciate their love. They
Feel you've forgotten them,
Handle them with kid gloves.

Do something now, or in the
Morning they'll be gone. Your
Troubles will begin; for they
Feel you've done them wrong."

Out to the city gates he went
To make the people pleased.
The sacrifices they'd made all
Worth it at times like these.

Now there was much
   discussion
Going on across the nation.
People wanted David back; it
Seemed their only salvation.

From our enemies he saved us;
We made Absalom king
   instead.

He drove David from Israel,
But now Absalom is dead.

Let's call him to lead us,
We want David to rule again.
He is our rightful king
According to God's plan.

Zadok and Abiathar, priests,
He sent to Judah, saying,
"Everyone else welcomed
Me; why are you delaying?"

Amasa convinced the leaders
Who answered as one man.
"Please, come back to us,
We want you as king again."

So David returned in honor
To be their king once more.
Then he forgave his enemies
Welcomed them as before.

His old friend Barzillai,
Who'd fed them when hiding,
Came to him across the river,
Their friendship was abiding.

David invited him to come
To stay the rest of his life.
Barzillai said, "No thanks,
I'd only cause you strife."

Old tribal jealousies caused
Common sense to wear thin.
Israel versus Benjamin and
Judah in arguments no one
Could win.

CHAPTER 20

Sheba was a hot head
And also a Benjamite. He
Deserted the camp of David
Followed by all ten tribes.

Those of Benjamin and Judah
Were to David true.
Men of Judah followed David
So ended in Jerusalem too.

Those ten wives he'd left,
By Absalom had been spoiled.
He bannished them to widow-
hood to him now soiled.

"Go and mobilize the army,"
The king to Amassa did say,
"Bring all our warriors here;
You have three whole days."

And so Amassa went; he sear-
ched throughout the land. To
Mobilize the army, he called
On every fighting man.

They were widely scattered,
And took much time to find.
Those three days passed,
So his schedule was behind.

David called Abishai, saying,
"Stop Sheba at any cost. He
Is more trouble than Absalom.
If he gets away we're lost."

With David's own bodyguard,
Joab and Abishai made chase.
At the Stone in Gibeon met
Amassa face to face.

Joab, dressed in uniform
With a dagger at his belt,
Now drew Amassa aside;
A deadly thrust he dealt.

That would-be General fell
In the road and died. Joab,
With a young officer's help,
Was again the army's pride.

They moved Amassa's remains
Out of the soldiers sight.

With little encouragement,
They followed Joab to fight.

Sheba had traversed Israel
Trying to avoid pursuit.
He'd run back to his clan
To hide under their roof.

Joab surrounded the city
Before Sheba could organize,
Was battering down walls;
His army of mammoth size.

There was a woman within
Wise beyond her years. She
Knew that for her city, a
Siege would end in tears.

So now she called to Joab
To approach the city walls.
For she had things to say,
And he must hear it all.

"They say," she said, "In
Abel, we gave good advice.
This is a God-loving town;
Before wrecking it, think
    twice."

"Give me the man I'm after
And peace is yours," said
He. "Sheba defied the king,
And we cannot let this be."

Then quickly she replied,
"Call off your men of war,
We'll throw his head over
A wall; can we do more?"

David appointed friends
With wisdom and expertise.
Joab, his true friend was
Again commander-in chief.

CHAPTER 21

Three years of famine was
Upon the land. So David
Spent much time in prayer
Learned the fault was man's.

God was punishing a nation
For stupid sins of Saul's.
He'd killed Gibeonites
Nationalistic to a fault.

David went to Gibeon to
Ask what he could do to
Remove the curse on Israel
And once again have food.

Money was not the answer;
Human lives they'd accept.
Seven of Saul's sons, only
Those lives for the debt.

Impaled on the mountain to
Pay for Saul's evil ways,
All seven died together
At the first harvest days.

Two were Saul's grandsons;
Step sons were others. Five
Adopted sons of Michal's,
She'd raised like a mother.

Rizpah, the mother of two
Stood guard upon the mount,
Keeping birds at bay
For too many days to count.

David learned of her vigil
So had the bodies gathered,
Buried with Saul and sons,
For protection from weather.

God answered their prayers;
The land produced once more.
With the Philistine enemy
They were still at war.

Now on the field of battle
David slipped and faltered.
A giant Philistine charged;
The outcome nearly altered.

He faced David with a spear;
It weighed a dozen pounds.
But Abishai attacked him,
And he won that round.

David's men were worried
For he was a beloved king.
To keep him from a battle
Was no little thing.

Three more giants fell to
Israel in battles fought.
And Israel won those wars
With many miracles wrought.

CHAPTER 22

The Lord had rescued David
So many times in life; he
Knew his God was there in
All his trials and strife.

So he composed a song to
Prove his love and trust.
How he knew God's presence
Was definitely a must.

"He's my fortress and my
Savior, Jehovah is my rock.
He is my place of refuge,
And I will hide in God.

Thank you, oh my Savior,
My shield and salvation
Saved me from my enemies
Scattered all the nations.

I'll call upon the Lord
He is worthy to be praised.
If evil days come on me,
It will be me he'll save.

Floods of evil trapped me,
Bound by hell and death.
But I called upon Jehovah;
He answered in my distress.

He heard from his temple;
My cry reached his ears.
Earth shook and trembled;
The heavens quaked in fear.

Smoke came from his nose;
Fire leaped from his mouth.
All burned before him, and
Earth knew great drought.

He walked on dark clouds,
Rode on wings of wind.
The fog was thick about;
Darkness surrounded him.

His love lighted the world;
From heaven he looked down.
From arrows of lightning
He gave a mighty shout.

He routed all his enemies;
His breath split the sea.
He drew me from the waters;
From above, he rescued me.

He saved me from enemies
Who were for me too strong.
In the days of my calamity,
He did not do me wrong.

The Lord is my salvation,
He rescued and set me free.
I was his delight, and for
My goodness he rewarded me.

To those who are blameless,
Lord, and those who are pure,
You are all perfection, and
Your help to them is sure.

The haughty you bring down
And evil you'll destroy.

You watch their every move,
And see their every ploy.

Your power crushes armies,
Your strength leaps walls.
For you alone are God,
I hear no other calls.

He shields those who abide
In Him, and our Lord is God.
He has kept me safely
Wherever I have trod.

In war he was there gave
Me muscle to bend the bow.
Gently He gave me strength
Eased my steps where I'd go.

Helped me crush my enemies,
He put them under my feet.
From rebels he preserved me;
They were dust on the street.

He's the rock of salvation,
I will praise his name. He
Shows mercy to his anointed
Helps make life a game."

CHAPTER 23

Here are some words that
David, son of Jesse, spoke.
A man of great success, to
Whom God gave such hope.

I was anointed by the Lord,
A sweet Psalmist, I was he.
His word was on my tongue,
Israel's Rock said to me:

"One will come who is just,
To rule with love of God. He
Will be as the morning light;
His life will mean a lot.

When tender grass comes up,
A cloudless sunrise will be.

My family he has chosen
In dynasty to follow me.

A lasting covenant made,
Eternal, final, sealed. He
Will be with me forever to
Be my life and shield.

The Godless are as thorns;
They tear all they touch
To be cut and thrown away,
Just too un-godly much."

David seems to have mused,
As old men are known to do,
Of many days gone by and
Experiences gone through.

Of thirty great men he told
And great deeds they'd done.
Many of those he told as
He named them, one by one.

There were seven others
Greater than the rest.
Three of those stand tall
The finest of the best.

CHAPTER 24

The king in all his glory
Was moved to add one more.
He ordered taking a census,
And Joab's advice ignored.

Across the Jordan they went,
And counted on that side.
Nearly ten months it took
For a king's ego and pride.

Both sides of Jordan, the
Coverage of Israel replete,
Thirteen thousand warriors
Ready to bow at his feet.

Bothered by consience, he
Knew that he'd done wrong.

He asked for forgiveness
Because he was headstrong.

David was given a choice,
Three things hard to take.
Seven years of famine
Or three days of plague.

For three months he'd flee,
As enemies hunted him down.
But he was getting old and
Feared he'd run aground.

So David chose the plague;
He'd rather take a chance
On God's tender mercies
Than on the whims of man.

And now the plague came on,
As Israel took its thrust;

Seventy thousand succumbed,
And they returned to dust.

God stopped at Jerusalem by
David on a threshing floor.
David begged him earnestly,
"Why must they suffer more?

I'm the one who sinned and
Should be the one who pays."
God showed mercy to David
And brought him better days.

Now David offered sacrifice;
It must have gone to heaven.
God's blessings he had lost
Back to him were given.

END OF SECOND SAMUEL

FIRST KINGS

CHAPTER 1

The king was getting old,
And spent his days in bed.
He felt always cold under
All those covers spread.

His aids were convinced
They must keep him alive.
For if he were there, all
Fortunes would thrive.

So painted a pretty picture
Of a young, innocent girl.
She'd be nurse and playmate;
To warm his bed she'd curl.

So all Israel they searched
Until a beauty they found.

But it was to no avail for
He'd lost too much ground.

Meanwhile in the kingdom, it
Must have seemed the time,
For Adonijah, David's son,
To royalty wished to climb.

Hired chariots and drivers,
Men to run ahead and claim,
That he would soon be king;
At least that was his aim.

Of those who took his side,
Blood-letting General Joab,
And Abiathar, David's ex-
Priest, both waiting to
Make a grab.

Zadok, Beniah, the prophet
Nathan and other army chiefs

Were loyal to the king and
Wouldn't follow these.

Adonijah went to En-rogel,
Sacrificed at the Serpents'
Stone, called his brothers
And officials from home.

He didn't ask brother Sol-
omon or any true to the king.
Nathan called on Bath-sheba
With current news of things.

So they laid their strategy,
To make sure everything went,
According to David's plan
Instead of twisted and bent.

So David appointed Solomon
To be next king of the land.
Then took him to Gihon, an-
nointing him as per plan.

It was necessary to move
With speed and much finesse.
For if Adonijah became king,
It would be an awful mess.

Solomon and his followers
Would most surely be killed.
And nothing would have gone
As the king had willed.

Adonijah had thrown a party
To celebrate his power grab.
Jonathan, son of the priest,
Brought news to stop that.

Of how Solomon had ridden
To power on David's own
   mule
With a bodyguard's protection
And a nation under his rule.

Adonijah and friends now
Fled in confusion and haste.

After committing a crime,
They preferred another place.

Adonijah hid 'neath an altar
At a church where he'd fled.
He knew it'd be a miracle
If he didn't end up dead.

Solomon ordered him brought
From hiding where he was. He
Thought his chances gone, so
His heart within him paused.

But to his relief Solomon
Said, "Go home and stay." For
He hadn't really expected
To see another day.

CHAPTER 2

As David's time approached
He gave Solomon this charge,
Nothing harmful would he do,
No job of faith too large.

For his covenant with God
Must be carried on. The
Commandments to be
   followed
And the dynasty to be won.

After forty years of rule,
King David went to rest.
Then Solomon was truly king;
His rule was greatly blessed.

Adonijah never gave up
Just planned and schemed.
To become the king was a
Goal of which he dreamed.

He approached Bath-sheba,
Solomon's doting mother,
Asked her a favor desi-
gned to replace a brother.

She was to ask Solomon,
Give him Abishag to wife.
Solomon soon recognized a
Plot against his life.

He'd forgiven him once;
This was just too much;
Again he'd gone too far,
And got himself in dutch.

Now he sent Benaiah, who
Was a messenger of death.
He killed Adonijah, so
There was one enemy less.

Abiathar who left David,
To the wily priest, he
Said, "Go home now and
Stay, or you're dead."

I'd kill you now, but you
Travelled years with dad.
You bore the Ark on trail,
At your death I'd be sad.

For safety at the altar,
Joab, who'd murdered men,
Fled there for refuge,
To live, he had a yen.

Benaiah went to find him;
He refused to face fate,
So was executed there; he
Changed his way too late.

Benaiah he made captain;
Zadok became his priest.
Shimei, who insulted David,
From death was released.

With orders however, never
To leave the place. Shimei
Understood the sentence
Accepted with good grace.

Three years later it seems
Two of his servants fled.

Shimei saddled a donkey
And after them he sped.

Now word came to Solomon
About Shimei's travels.
If he had future plans
They soon unravelled,

Because Benaiah was sent
To lower the boom. For
Shimei in this kingdom,
There was no longer room.

So this left Solomon with
No enemies of the crown.
He could build a dynasty
To one of great renown.

CHAPTER 3

Now to Egypt's Pharaoh, he,
Went on a trip for peace,
Made a pact of friendship,
From war to be released.

Now Pharaoh's daughter he
Married to seal the pact.
He brought her to Jerusalem
With great wisdom and tact.

Their altar of worship had
Always been in the hills. So
He worshipped there until
One in Jerusalem was built.

He loved God as David had
And many offerings he made.
He often went to Gibeon
To sacrifice and pray.

One night he had a dream
And Jehovah God was there.
He said, "What can I do for
You, how can I be fair?"

Power Solomon didn't seek;
For riches he never asked,
Or the death of enemies, or
Much glory in which to bask.

For he felt inadequate
To rule this mighty throng.
So he asked for much wisdom
To keep from going wrong.

So God smiled and said,
"Great wisdom you asked;
You'll have your wish
And shall rule with tact.

Since you chose so wisely
Nor asked for other things,
You shall receive them all
And be greatest of kings."

He awoke and 'twas a dream,
But knew he'd spoken to God.
So he returned to Jerusalem
And ruled with wisdom's rod.

Two women came to him with
A problem to be solved.
They could not agree, so
The king must be involved.

Both were young mothers,
One's baby had just died.
Each claimed the live one,
So their cause they cried.

Solomon called a swordsman
Saying, "Divide this child
In two. Each can have half
When you are through."

The one claiming unjustly
In selfishness agreed, but
The other gave in, saying,
"Don't, there is no need."

He knew how love reacts,
Said, "Give the child to her.

She's the rightful mother
And justice will be served."

He gained fame far and wide
His wisdom became well-
    known.
He was respected by friend or
Foe, especially by his own.

CHAPTER 4

Now King Solomon's cabinet
Members, too many to count,
Came from famous families
Were men of great renown.

From all tribes they came,
Each month of the year. With
Food and taxes for a palace
And without fail appeared.

Everyone gave to government,
A king they loved to please.
For he ruled wise and justly,
So they knew peace and ease.

It was almost unbelievable,
The daily food consumed;
But no one ever complained
For they were not abused.

He was fair and just with
Knowledge beyond his years.
It's a record of proportion
No other ruler came near.

Three thousand proverbs are
His; over a thousand songs
He wrote, a lover of nature
And all things that grow.

He helped those in need;
To kings, he gave advice.
He ruled in total wisdom
Was always just plain nice.

CHAPTER 5

King David was well-known
And by all men admired. One
Of those who looked to him
Was good Hiram, King of Tyre.

To them he sent ambassadors
To welcome a neighbor king.
And for the late King David,
He let his praises ring.

Solomon took advantage of
Friendship with other lands.
The building of God's temple
Was foremost of his plans.

King Hiram agreed to help
Sending cedar and fir trees,
Too. If Solomon needed labor,
He'd send skilled men to do.

Cut trees on the mountains,
Float them along the shore,
Around the Mediterranean
And up to Solomon's door.

Wheat and olive oil in trade
For the lumber Hiram brought.
Every month they changed;
Ten thousand workers
  wrought.

For a month each one labored
Then for two he'd rest,
While other groups took over;
This way it worked out best.

Many thousand workers toiled
And artful skills employed,
From men who cut the stones
To those who laid the joists.

One rock upon another, as
All great works are done.

And on those walls of stone
Went the logs of Lebanon.

CHAPTER 6

Four hundred eighty years
Ago, from Egypt they'd fled.
A Rag-tag band of emigrants
Who suffered, died and bled.

A promised land was found
After forty years enroute.
And to trust their Lord,
That is what it was about.

Solomon started to build a
Great temple for the Lord.
They had grown in strength;
Beauty they could afford.

Four years he'd been king,
When he started this job.
He was anxious to build,
For he truly loved his God.

Ninety feet in length, he
Built, about half as high.
Of logs on rocks it stood
And about thirty feet wide.

A porch along the front
Was thirty feet in length,
Was built on solid stone,
So had great strength.

Many rooms were added
And annexed to each side.
They fastened to the walls,
Were three stories high.

Stones were cut and finished,
At the quarry or the mines.
Timbers were all pre-cut
Done at an earlier time.

So as it was being erected,
No hammer or saw was heard.

It makes me wonder if talk
Was in muted words.

Panel walls, winding stairs
Served for all three floors.
Posts of solid olive wood
Supported olive-wood doors.

Figures of angels, palm trees
And flowers carved on walls
With main rooms of the Temple
Overlaid, pure gold on it all.

He built the inner court with
Three layers of hewn stone.
With a row of cedar beams,
The walls came into their own.

Seven long years they labored;
It seems a long time at task.
But built to God's glory
And certainly built to last.

CHAPTER 7

Then thirteen years it took
Building a palace for himself.
Of course we do not know, but
Perhaps with much less help.

This was a fabulous palace
Surpassing any of its day.
Read the seventh chapter of
Kings, here we lack the space.

Back to the building of the
Temple our story stresses,
With the beauty and grandeur
The Old Testament expresses.

Utensils, lamps, snuffers or
Cups were of finest gold.
And what David dedicated to
That day'd been kept on hold.

CHAPTER 8

Now all of Israel's leaders
Were called to convocation.
The Ark of the Tabernacle in
Zion was to change location.

Under the Temple Angel
In the Holy Place it went
With all holy vessels that
Were once within the tent.

The king and the multitude
Came and assembled there.
Sheep and oxen sacrificed,
For of God they were aware.

The Ark seemed to be empty,
Save the two slabs of stone
Moses brought down the
  mount
When he came back alone.

Priests had placed the Ark,
And they turned to go out;
The Holy Place of God filled
With a beautiful white cloud.

So the glory of the Lord
Filled the Temple with light,
And every one who saw was
Witness to God's might.

Solomon spoke to his people;
The Lord God, he blessed.
He felt a sense of triumph,
For he had passed the test.

His father David had wanted
To build the Lord a house.
But he fought so many times
That he had to do without.

The Lord had promised David
The time would surely come;

His house would be built by
The ruler who'd be his son.

Solomon faced the Temple
Up to heaven held his hands.
Then he made this prayer
To improve the lot of man.

"Oh Lord, you promised,
When my father was the king,
Through our future history;
To let words of wisdom ring.

We know you need not live
In a house we built for you.
For you abide in heaven,
Or wherever you may choose.

But now we face the Temple,
And in sincerity we pray,
For you to grant our needs
Whether it be night or day.

And if we follow faithfully
Those precepts set by you,
May David's house always by
Justice and wisdom rule."

Two weeks they celebrated
And sacrificed much indeed.
From all Israel they came,
"Oh what a sight to see!"

CHAPTER 9

Everything was done,
Solomon finished the task.
God appeared again, said,
"I heard what you asked.

I'll love this Temple always
In my innermost thoughts.
So follow my commandments
Do as you know you ought.

If you walk before me
As your father David did,

Only good will befall you
And you'll need only bid.

But if your people forget,
And turn away from me, I'll
Drive them from the Temple
With no place to flee."

Twenty years of building,
By King Hiram he was aided;
He traded twenty cities,
For which he was upbraided.

Those cities he gave Hiram
Were run-down at the heel.
He must have made amends,
For they made other deals.

Then Solomon levied taxes,
To make the cities better,
Conscripted a labor force,
Became a real go-getter.

Now many cities he built to
Support his growing nation
And he cast slavery's yoke
On enemies of lower station.

No Israelites were conscripts
But placed in posts of trust.
There were many labor forces
With supervision a must.

Three times a year he put
His sacrifices on the altar.
He also offered incense for
His faith never faltered.

In Ezion-geber,
Near Eloth on the red sea,
He built many ships;
In fact, he built a fleet.

King Hiram brought sailors
To teach Israel to navigate

Sailed to Ophir and back
With gold their main trade.

Hiram must have gained
By this exchange of aid;
Solomon, who was wealthy,
Was even richer made.

CHAPTER 10

Solomon's fame had spread
Considered rich and wise.
Sheba's Queen heard stories
And in due time arrived.

She asked many questions
To test knowledge and skill.
He answered with wisdom and
Showed the palace built.

She realized he was greater
Than all the stories she'd
Heard. And so she let him
Know in just so many words.

She'd brought many camels,
And he gave all she asked.
Their hearts were lifted as
In friendship they basked.

Three million five hundred
Thousand in gold she gave.
No such gift had any known;
It exceeded the wildest rave.

She gathered her people about
And returned to her own land.
With pleasure she'd remember
This wonderful man.

His ships brought much gold;
He lived a life of splendor,
Ruled by wisdom and justice,
Was always gentle and tender.

The kings of earth bowed to
Wisdom surpassing their own.

Brought gifts of many riches
Paid tribute to his throne.

Many chariots he owned with
Cavalry and horses too. He
Bought and sold at a profit
A typical business-man Jew.

CHAPTER 11

God had always warned them
Marry no foreign wives. Now
Solomon married many,
But of course he was wise.

Seven hundred wives and prin-
cesses, three hundred conc-
ubines, they naturally got
Attention. Was he so wise?

Many were from those nations
Who worshipped pagan gods.
  So
Solomon fell to their snares,
And in their paths he trod.

Some gods he worshipped -
To others built a high place.
As from Jehovah he retreated,
He naturally fell from grace.

So in anger the Lord decreed
His dynasty would fade away.
Israel to be divided again,
She'd come on evil days.

Twice God had appeared and
Warned of this very thing.
But he loved strange women!
Even if sorrow they'd bring.

When David conquered Edom,
He killed all men at hand.
But Hadad, who was a boy,
And servants did scram.

Through Midian and Paran fled
Until in Egypt they paused.
Israel was his mortal enemy,
The result of misery caused.

Now Hadad got news of Joab's
Death, and David was gone;
He headed back toward Israel,
Planning to avenge a wrong.

Back in Hadadezer's days Is-
rael had spoiled their land.
Eliadah had deserted a post
Escaped with a small band.

To Damascus they ran, and
In time his son Rezon took
Command, gained much power
In Syria but chafed at the
Loss of their land.

Jeroboam was a servant's son,
A man of valor and industry.
Solomon put him in charge of
Joseph's descendants families.

Now Ahijah, the priest who
Served in Israel those days,
Was wearing a brand new robe
As they met along the way.

Then he ripped that robe
Into a dozen strips.
And with this message he
Then came to grips.

"Each represents," he said,
"A tribe of Israel, you see.
So take ten for yourself,
For thus it was told to me,

Solomon failed the faith
As his father never did.
And if he loves the Lord
He keeps it well hid.

For he follows other gods,
And fails Jehovah's law. So
I'll take all tribes but one;
He's not done as he ought.

But as long as he's alive
I will let him reign supreme.
For sake of my servant David
Who was faithful to me.

But from his son who'll reign
I'll give ten tribes to you.
You will be on Israel's
Throne if to me you're true."

Benjamin and Judah, two tribes,
Were generally counted as one.
So thus we have twelve total,
If the tally is correctly run.

God will punish David's
Descendents for a limited
time.
For they'll not suffer forever
Because of Solomon's crime.

For forty years Solomon ruled
And then went to his rest.
Then Rehoboam, his son,
As king would face the test.

CHAPTER 12

At Shechem was the
   coronation,
And all Israel did attend.
Jereboam was urged to come at
The wish of all his friends.

A hard master was your father;
He urged the people to cry.
So for more humane treatment,
It is now your chance to try.

We don't want you for our king
Unless you show more care.

We are tired of being beaten,
And you should be aware.

Rehoboam called councelors,
Old men who were wise.
They all thought the king
Should heed the people's cries.

He refused old men's councel,
Asked advice of men his age.
They told him to get tougher,
That caused his subjects' rage.

Let Rehoboam rule a tribe;
We'll go our way instead.
We won't have him as king;
This, in essence, they said.

The tribe of Judah stayed;
The Lord had said it would,
The only tribe, who for
The house of David stood.

Rehoboam sent Adoram for
Men, as kings so often do.
To conscript from tribes,
Of course from Judah too.

Adoram they stoned to death;
The king's chariot was fleet.
He made tracks to Jerusalem
And stayed in near defeat.

He called up his army, one
Hundred eighty thousand
Strong. God sent word to
Fight Israelis was wrong.

Don't fight your brothers,
Shemaiah the prophet, said.
For this was God's will,
And He wants no blood shed.

In the hills of Ephraim
Jeroboam built his throne.

And Shechem, he built too;
He made this his home.

He did not want his people
To visit other tribes. So
Councelors offered a plan
To con people with bribes.

Two golden calves he made,
Said, "You can worship right
Here, not journey to Jerusa-
lem, and no reason to fear."

He thought he'd lose control
If they visited other tribes.
He wanted to keep them home
So they'd only hear his side.

And so he led his people,
Not to God, but far astray.
For he worshipped idols, too,
And from Jehovah fell away.

He even ordered a feast and
Devised a time of his own.
For God's help and kindness,
His chances now had flown.

CHAPTER 13

Now he approached the Altar
Where incense he would burn.
A man of God came close
And tried his ways to turn.

The prophet shouted loudly
So King Jeroboam could hear.
"Oh Altar, now split open,
And ashes here appear.

A child will be born into
David's family line. He'll
Sacrifice on you, priests
Of un-godly shrines."

The king quickly angered
And shook his fist at him.

His arm suddenly paralyzed,
It wouldn't draw back again.

That same moment a crack
Split the Altar open wide.
Ashes poured on the ground,
And a king in terror cried.

He begged the man of God
To make it well once more.
Then even as he prayed,
His arm was again restored.

Now the king was gracious;
With reward he tried. But
The man of God refused.
In answer, this he cried.

The Lord was definite, for
He did order me, that I
Should not eat or drink,
Nor tarry here with thee.

So he took another road
And went his way, was ac-
costed by another prophet,
Who led him far astray.

He offered food and rest
Claimed to be God-sent.
So he foolishly accepted,
And the rules he bent.

Suddenly while at table
The prophet loudly shouted.
You won't see your fathers;
God's orders you've flouted.

You ate and drank and
Did those things taboo.
Honor of burial with your
Fathers is not for you.

He sent the man away, who
Journeyed along, and was

Killed by a lion. I would
Say, "His day went wrong."

Now some who saw the sight,
Told the story in Beth-el.
The old prophet living
There heard it all as well.

So he traveled out
Upon that road to see
The lion and the donkey
On the scene of tragedy.

They both stood by as if
To guard the remains. So
He took the man's body
And brought it home again.

In his grave he buried it
And asked that if he died,
His sons would bury him
So they'd be side by side.

"The prophecy," he said,
"Surely will come true."
With the prophet's warning,
Jeroboam played the fool.

God's word he flouted and
Wouldn't do things right.
His kingdom soon would end,
None can face God's might.

CHAPTER 14

Jeroboam had a beloved son;
The boy was very ill. He
Sent the queen to Ahijah
Who was a prophet still.

This old man was blind,
And he was up in years.
The Lord had let him know
Jereboam's wife was here.

This was still the prophet
Who'd helped make him king.

What he told the woman must
Have made her ears ring.

He prophesied the child
Would die when she arrived.
And of all Jeroboam coveted,
He would soon be deprived.

He'd received his blessing;
All had started well. But
He had slipped rapidly,
And then he really fell.

He had built high places
And altars to other gods.
But causing Israel to sin
Had really botched the job.

Now when his wife returned
His son Abijah died.
And all Israel mourned,
For his son they cried.

Twenty-two years he reigned
And with his fathers slept.
Nadab his son became king,
So he ruled Israel instead.

Solomon's son Rehoboam rul-
ed In Jerusalem those days.
He did evil in God's sight,
And in the same old ways.

They worshipped pagan gods
And became as depraved as
Any nation around them or
The ones they had displaced.

By Egypt they were attacked;
The city of Jerusalem fell.
They plundered the Holy Tem-
ple stole it's gold as well.

Rehoboam substituted bronze
In place of golden shields.

War was quite commonplace
Upon those rolling fields.

When he'd run his course,
Now his son Abijam reigned.
And it would seem that he
Might end a country's pain.

CHAPTER 15

But Abijam was no better
Than his wicked father was.
He spent his time in sin
Rather than brotherly love.

He was constantly at war
With Jeroboam all his life.
In fact his ruling days
Were a time of strife.

God still honored the pact
He made when David was king.
So Asa, son of Abijam ruled,
He did honor to them bring.

He destroyed pagan statues,
Ran sodomites off the land.
Even toward his mother
He took an unusual stand.

Because she made an idol
And placed it in a grove,
He made her queen no more,
And the idol he broke.

He ruled with zealous
Justice, and her idol burned.
Many things he dedicated
And to the Temple returned.

Into the house of the Lord
He brought silver and vessels
Of gold, and some glory too,
More like the days of old.

Jeroboam had been replaced;
His son Baasha ruled instead.

He was at war with Asa; they
Wished each other dead.

Baasha built a fortress city
In Ramah to eliminate trade.
For his people to go to Judah
Was one thing he forbade.

So Asa depleted the treasury
Took from the Temple things
That had taken years to ass-
emble to bribe another king.

So Ben-hadad of Syria agreed
To break a pact with Israel.
He also sent armies to fight,
So King Baasha hit the trail.

King Asa called his people to
Tear the city in Ramah down,
To use it to build up Mizpah,
So now it became their town.

Even though he was king,
Asa finally did expire;
For kings cannot change
This order to retire.

His son ascended to rule;
Jehoshephat was his name.
Meantime in Israel, a son
Of Jeroboam did the same.

Nadab wasn't much account;
He led Israel to more sin.
He only lasted two years,
And then Baasha did him in.

This was in King Asa's day
During his third year. All
Jeroboam's kin he killed;
So royalty held no fear.

Baasha, as bad as Nadab,
He too led Israel astray.

Twenty-four years of rule
He angered God each day.

CHAPTER 16

Jehu was a prophet, and
Now this he had to say.
"The Lord knows Baasha
Has led his people away.

God lifted you from dust
And helped make you great.
But you have been sinful;
Your future is at stake.

You lived like Jeroboam,
And you'll die the same.
Your family will follow,
Not honoring your name."

Elah, Baasha's son, ruled
In his place. But he was
Sinful too showing no
Love or grace.

There was General Zimri
Of Royal Chariot troops.
He coveted Ela's crown
And to murder stooped.

Killed Elah's relatives
Just as the prophet said.
So all of Baasha's kin
Paid the price in death.

Two years Elah reigned
And by Zimri was blasted.
Seven short days as ruler
Was what Zimri lasted.

Philistines they fought as
They heard of Zimri's coup.
Army voted General Omri as
King, so one thing to do.

Besiege the capital city,
So Tirzah was bottled up.

Zimri knew warfare and
Now held the poisoned cup.

He burned down the palace
And died in the flames.
For he'd been sinful too,
Had been a king of shame.

And now those ten tribes
Were split by war again;
Half of Israel followed
Tibni in a time of pain.

Thirty-eight years in Judah,
Asah was the reigning king.
Then twelve and a half more,
King Omri was another thing.

He was worse than the others
So led Israel farther astray.
Then Ahab his son took over,
Driving them even more away.

He was more wicked still,
In fact their sins he paled.
He married infamous Jezebel
And began worshipping Baal.

At this time Jericho was built
By Heil, a man from Bethel.
As he laid foundations his
Eldest son sickened and fell.

As he finished the town, he
Celebrated by setting gates;
His youngest son died too,
It seemed he'd tempted fate.

Remember in Joshua's day, as
The walls came tumbling down,
The Lord put a curse on any
Who ever rebuilt this town.

CHAPTER 17

Now Elijah came from Tishbe,
From Gilead he was sprung.

He tried to tell King Ahab
Change his ways or be done.

He made prophecy of drought;
Such he said would surely be,
In which not even dew
Would fall among the trees.

He said for three years
That they'd see no rain. So
The message should be clear,
A future of trial and pain.

Then God directed him, so an
Easterly direction he took.
He went toward the Jordan
And hid by Cherith brook.

For the bearer of bad news
Was anathema to the king.
What Elijah had forecast,
Certain death could bring.

From the brook he got water;
The ravens brought him meat.
One day the brook ran dry;
The land was parched by heat.

Arise and go to Zarephath;
Then to him came word. For
There's a woman there who
Heard the will of the Lord.

There he found a widow
 woman
Where the Lord said she'd be.
He asked her for some water
And just a little to eat.

"My son and I are starving,"
She said, "with a little meal,
And with very little oil
It looks like our last deal."

"Just bake a small cake for
Me and don't fear," he said.

"There will be enough left
To make us all more bread."

The Lord has said today a
Cruse of oil will not waste;
Grain on hand will replenish
To surely please your taste.

And so the Lord provided to
Take them through drouth,
With food or drink as needed,
Many days within her house.

Then one day that lady's son
Fell sick and actually died.
"Why must I suffer so, and
Why must he die?" she cried.

Then Elijah took the child;
Up to the loft he climbed.
He prayed fervently to God
And leaned upon him thrice.

Then the spirit returned
Into his body that day. He
Was united with his mother
And also to his play.

So she knew without a doubt
This stranger who had stayed,
Was surely a prophet of God
Who answered when he
    prayed.

CHAPTER 18

Elijah did return after
The passage of many days.
And he met Obediah as he
Travelled along the way.

Obediah loved his God and
Strove to serve him well.
He once saved many priests
From the clutch of Jezebel.

He was searching for water
To save their dying herds.
Elijah said, "Tell the King,"
(They were shocking words)

"I've returned from hiding
And with him I would speak."
Now Obadiah shook with fear;
His knees were suddenly weak.

"You know," he said, "that it
Would be a serious thing for
Me, if I tell him you're here
And then you up and flee.

For three years you've eluded
All those who searched. So
If you disappear again, you
Will leave me in the lurch."

"Before my God I swear, you
Can tell the King I'm here.
I'll not cause you trouble,
You haven't a thing to fear!"

King Ahab came to meet him;
With angry words he greeted.
But Elijah told him quickly,
"Twas you whom you
    defeated.

For if you followed Jehovah
Instead of those other gods,
Your problems would be minor,
But your sins play hob.

Call the people to Carmel
And all of the prophets, too,
Who are supported by Jezebel,
And those who belong to you."

Elijah asked of them, "How
Long will you procrastinate?
Will you follow God or Baal?
Best decide before too late.

Now I'm a prophet of God,
The only one who's left. Let
Us find out which God lives,
The one who's most adept.

So bring two bullocks forth
To the Altar of sacrifice.
Let your priests prepare one,
And I'll do so with mine.

I will pray to Jehovah,
And they can pray to Baal.
We'll both ask for fire
And see which one prevails."

Jezebel had four hundred who
Were her paid priests. Ahab
Owned four hundred fifty, and
Baal they tried to please.

So they prepared their altar,
With the sacrifice in place,
And feverishly prayed to Baal
In effort to save face.

All day long they prayed and
Danced and begged and cried.
No fire warmed the offering
However hard they tried.

This was a test of their God,
If he could produce a flame.
At noon Elijah started taunt-
ing, "Perhaps Baal doesn't
Like your game."

Though they danced and raved
And cut themselves and cried,
No one answered. It was time
For the evening sacrifice.

Now Elijah took twelve stones,
One each for Israel's tribes.
And he built an altar there
With a ditch around all sides.

He piled wood upon the altar,
Then a bullock he prepared.
Next he summoned help to
Bring barrels of water there.

Poured water on the bullock,
On the altar and the wood.
They poured so much water
That the ditch did flood.

Elijah called upon Jehovah,
"You've always been our Lord!
So bring fire to our offering,
And prove your powerful
    word."

Then fire flashed from heaven,
As a bolt that split the air.
It consumed wood and bullock,
The stones and water there.

Now there was no altar left!
The people were amazed. But
They knew that God does live
And pledged a change of ways.

Then he ordered the people,
All false prophets to detain.
They took them to the brook,
Where he ended all their pain.

Then Elijah said to Ahab,
"You can eat and drink again.
Because from all the signs,
There'll soon be ample rain."

He climbed Mt. Carmel and
For rain his servant looked.
Seven times he said, "Try,"
And that was what it took.

Elijah told Ahab, "Speed the
Chariot down the mountain,
Because the rain that comes
Will be no minor fountain."

So the King sped homeward,
And Elijah ran on ahead.
The Lord gave him strength,
As before the horses he sped.

CHAPTER 19

When Ahab told Jezebel how
Elijah killed her priests,
She promptly sent a message,
In which she promised grief.

He fled to Beer-sheba and
Left his servant there. Then
Traveled alone all day, be-
cause he'd had quite a scare.

Now he became very downcast
And prayed to God for death.
For he was terribly weary,
And then he finally slept.

As he slept beneath a bush,
An angel came to him.
He bid Elijah, "Rise and eat."
And then he slept again.

Again the angel awoke him,
And then to him he said,
"Arise and eat some more;
It's a long trail ahead."

He rose to eat and drink
Readying for a trip to come.
He traveled forty days and
Nights, for he was on the run.

To the mountain of God he
Ran and hid within a cave.
For he was only human
With his own life to save.

The voice of God came to him
Asking, "Why tarry here?" He

Answered, "My enemies, and
Of you they have no fear."

Thus Elijah excused himself
For hiding in a cave. But
Standing upon the mountain,
Jehovah before him came.

Wind blew a terrible blast;
An earthquake shook the land.
"Why are you still here?"
The question came again.

"All your prophets are dead!"
He said, "I'm in danger too."
God said "Return to Damascus,
Where you've a job to do."

By the desert road he went,
To Anoint Hazael as Syria's
King. Jehu he anointed, who
New rule to Israel'd bring.

Then Elijah found Elisha,
Where in a field he plowed.
He threw his coat upon him
Who accepted priestly vows.

Elisha sacrificed some oxen
And bade his parents good bye.
Then arose to follow Elijah,
And never did ask why.

CHAPTER 20

Ben-hadad was a mighty king
Who commanded Syrian hosts,
Thirty two kings for allies,
Chariots and horses to boast.

This multitude surrounded
Samaria with much ado. He
Said, "Silver and gold are
Mine; wives and children too."

Ahab, king of Israel, answered.
"My lord and king, I am thine.
I am subservient unto you,
So you own all that's mine."

Ben-hadad sent him word
    again,
"What I claimed is not enough.
My servants will return and
Take their pick of stuff."

"Now listen to this guy,"
Ahab, to his advisers cried,
"The way he's carrying on
He'll soon ruin our pride."

Then his people said to him,
"What he asks is a crime. So
Tell him where to go; the
Option is entirely thine."

"You're counting chickens
Early," Ahab now retorted.
"You're getting greedy; our
Friendship you've thwarted."

Ben-hadad had his legions
Besiege Samaria in battle
Array. God sent word to Ahab,
Which would his enemy stay.

Two hundred thirty-two princ-
es of Israel went that day,
And each man slew an enemy
Before the Syrians got away.

Then the army followed after,
And Ben-hadad barely escaped.
I'll bet he often wondered
How he got in such a scrape!

A prophet came to Ahab, and
Said, "Train your army well,
For Ben-hadad will try again,
With men too many to tell."

Syrians wishfully thought of
Israel's God as of the hills.
Surely down in the valleys
They'd be easily killed.

The army marched the valleys;
They numbered like the sands.
Israel's army was puny,
But God was in command.

A man of God came to Ahab,
Saying, "Look at the enemy
Force! God will give them to
You today; they have run the
Course.

The Syrians believe Jehovah
Is only strong in the hills.
So God will bowl them over,
And you'll cause their spill.

He knows your chance for
Victory seems very slim. But
You must believe in Him,
And He will help you win."

Seven days they were arrayed;
Armies facing the other side.
Then the day they fought, a
Hundred thousand Syrians
    died.

In panic the rest all ran; to
The city of Aphek they fled.
A wall crashed down leaving
Twenty-seven thousand dead.

Ben-hadad fled into the city,
Hid in inner chambers there,
Then planned strategy,
Hoping their lives to spare.

So with sackcloth they gird-
ed and ropes on their heads,

Begged King Ahab for mercy,
Better be slaves than dead.

Ahab called him, "brother,"
Inviting him aboard. Into
His chariot climbed the ene-
my he'd been told to kill
By the Lord.

A prophet met him on a road
With wounds and ashes on his
Face. He said, "My Lord I
Lost a prisoner whom I was
Bound to keep in place.

For he was in my charge,
And with my head I'd pay, if
I failed to do my duty and
Allowed him to get away.

I was busy at other things,
And he escaped." "It's your
Fault," the king replied,
"With your life you'll pay."

The prophet revealed himself,
And said, "So unto you it
Shall be. You had a mission,
But you gave in to an enemy.

In his place you'll die, and
Your people will perish inst-
ead." So Ahab went in sorrow
Facing tomorrow in dread.

CHAPTER 21

Close to the palace of Ahab,
Naboth owned a vineyard in
Jezreel; Ahab wanted the land,
So he offered Naboth a deal.

To Naboth the land had desc-
ended; his father owned it
Before. Ahab went into a sulk
For he was unhappy once more.

Jezebel, his wife, asked him
Why he should fast and be sad;
He told her his unhappy story.
She said, "It can be had."

So she cooked up a scheme
Loaded with intrigue and lies.
Naboth was taken to the city
Gates and stoned, so he died.

Ahab went to claim the vine-
Yard! He let them kill a man
And was ready and willing to
Step in and take his land.

God sent Elijah to Samaria
To upbraid Ahab there. Saying,
"For what you did to Naboth,
His final acts you'll share.

The dogs will lick your blood
Right there where Naboth died.
You have done much evil; life
You've spent at Satan's side.

Jezebel will lose her life;
The dogs will tear her apart.
You have followed her lead
With a crooked, lying heart."

Now when Ahab got the word,
In sack cloth he then dressed.
He went about very softly
In great sorrow and distress.

Then Elijah heard God's word,
"See how much Ahab's
   improved!
So, evil to his sons instead.
This much I'm telling you."

CHAPTER 22

The next three years were
Peaceful for Syria and Israel;

To Ahab it must have seemed
The end of a long dry spell.

So he called his prophets,
All four hundred strong,
And from what they told him,
He just could not go wrong.

Now King Jehoshaphat visited
From Judah where he ruled,
And he thought those prophets
Had King Ahab fooled.

"Where are God's prophets?" he
Asked, "Micaiah is the only
One," Ahab said, "I hate him,
He makes me often see red.

He's very pessimistic, often
Says I'm wrong." But called
A messenger anyway, and
Micaiah came along.

The king asked Micaiah, if
Against Syria he should go to
War. Micaiah said, "Why yes,
You should go for sure."

Ahab was doubtful now and
Asked, "Is this God's Actual
Word?" Micaiah said, "Yes Of
Course, you're under a sword.

He wants you to go to battle
Where fate decrees your fall.
That's why your prophets lied;
The Lord controls them all.

He wants you in the battle;
There you'll meet your end.
When you should do His will,
You refuse to bend."

"Guards take him," cried Ahab,
"For he always treats me so.

Now haul him off to prison,
While away to war I'll go.

Feed him bread and water
Until I come back in peace.
But until that day arrives,
He's not to be released."

"Return in peace," Micaiah
Said, "prove for sure I lied.
But all you people take note
Of what I've prophesied."

And so those kings led off
Headed for the enemy lines.
Jehoshaphat wore royal robes,
But Ahab left his behind.

The Syrian king had
     commanded,
"Kill Ahab, but not the rest."
Ahab, disguised as a soldier,
Was soon put to the test.

Then an arrow shot at random
Struck where armor was not.
He retired from the battle;
The fight was getting too hot.

Now as the day wore on the
Battle grew steadily worse.
Ahab's chariot rejoined the
Fray, soon carried a corpse.

And then the cry rang out,
"To your homes you may
     return,
For the wicked king is dead,
And peace again we've
     earned."

In Samaria they buried him
And washed his chariot clean,
While the dogs lapped up his
Blood as had been foreseen.

All the things Ahab did are
Enrolled in the book of kings.
His son Ahaziah reigned then;
He was sinful in everything.

Jehoshaphat walked straight,
And all his life did good.

Removed sodomites from them,
For justice and honesty stood.

END OF FIRST KINGS

SECOND KINGS

CHAPTER 1

Moab rebelled against Israel
Wouldn't pay tribute anymore.
The King fell from a balcony
Was broken, injured and sore.

A captain and fifty soldiers
Went to Ekron to ask his fate.
God sent Elijah the prophet
To check his religious state.

Meeting those messengers, he
Asked, "Is there no God in
Israel; is that why you ask a
Statue will a king get well?

His faith is thus displayed,
So God has made it plain;
Your king will die where he
Lies, upon his bed of pain."

Now the messengers returned
Unto their king in haste.
For quite near death he lay,
They wished to win this race.

He was surprised by an early
Return and asked how this
Could be, so when told about
The prophet, said, bring him
Here to me.

They went to fetch him from
Where he sat atop a rise.
To the captain and fifty
He answered in this wise.

"You say I'm a man of God
Whom you would take by force.
If it's true, I ask heaven
To send its fire forth."

Even as he asked it should
Came a bolt from the blue.
That captain and his forty
Men were instantly consumed.

Then the king, in anger, sent
A second company of men. And
When they met the prophet,
This also happened to them.

A third time the order came
They begged Elijah, "Hold;"
For after what had happened,
No one felt that bold.

He returned to the king with
Them; his prophecy was true.
The king died upon his bed.
Ahaziah had paid his dues.

Now Elijah's time had come;
His work was done on earth.

Elisha stayed by his side,
A companion of great worth.

CHAPTER 2

"Please stay at Jericho,"
Elijah said "Over Jordan I
Must go." The second time
Elisha begged, "I will miss
you so."

At the river they arrived
Watched by students from afar.
Elijah struck the river with
His cloak; waters moved apart.

So they crossed on dry land
And traveled on their way.
"What can I leave?" Elijah
Asked, "Please have your say."

Elisha said, "This I'd ask
That you would leave to me
A double portion of Spirit,
Which always goes with thee."

Elijah said, "It is a tough
Thing that you ask. But if
You see the way I go, you'll
Have your way at that."

As they walked and talked,
A miracle happened there.
It separated them instantly;
Elishah could only stare.

There appeared from heaven
Horses and a chariot of fire.
They whisked Elijah away, as
Elisha watched them go higher,

He cried, "My father!" As they
Disappeared from view. They'd
Been very close but today
Would start life anew.

He picked up Elijah's cloak;
His friend had left it below.
Smote the waters of Jordan
And made a place to go.

Once again the mighty river
Cleared a place to walk.
So on dry land he crossed
And would cause some talk.

The young men who watched
Had witnessed all this, too.
They knew he had the spirit
Which would see him through.

Now they sent fifty athletes
To search for Elijah about.
For three days they looked,
But they had to do without.

The city fathers of Jericho
Came to Elisha in distress.
Their city had a problem,
And they were under duress.

The water supply was bad;
Their women miscarried, too.
They needed a cure quickly
Hoping he'd have a clue.

So he threw a bowl of salt
Into that poisoned water.
And then prayed a few words
To his heavenly father.

As to Beth-el he walked,
A young gang called names.
They called him baldy, for
This perhaps he was famed.

At last in God's name, he, his
Hecklers damned. Two bears
Left the wild; forty-two kids
Wouldn't heckle again.

On to Mt. Carmel he went,
Finally to Samaria he came.
After the miracles performed,
He may have been quite famed.

CHAPTER 3

Jehoram, who was Ahab's son,
Ruled Israel a dozen years.
He was evil like his father,
So he had cause to fear.

Mesha, King of Moab, paid tri-
bute ever since Ahab's time.
But now he decided to rebel;
This Jehoram thought a crime.

For seven days they marched,
Three Israeli kings and hordes.
The wilderness was dry,
This they could not afford.

"Why has God brought us
  here?"
Jehoram in panic cried.
"Will he defeat us at Moab's
Hands? What can we decide?"

But Jehoshaphat then asked,
"Is there a prophet here of
God?" So they went to ask El-
isha who was on the prod.

"Why not ask pagan prophets,
Whose praises your family
Sings?" "We're victims of the
Enemy," answered the Kings.

"I couldn't care less," said
Elisha, "If it were only you
Two, but about Jehoshaphat,
I know he's honest and true.

Dig ditches in this valley."
He said, "Tomorrow you drink.

And this is only a beginning;
You'll beat a Moabite King."

So they ditched the valley;
Next day the waters came, and
The Moabites started a battle,
But they soon lost the game.

The King even offered a son
As burnt offering on the wall.
But he couldn't win the fight
And suffered a serious fall.

Then the kings of Israel
Went home to their own lands.
Leaving Mesha, King of Moab,
A broken and bitter man.

CHAPTER 4

A seminar student's widow
Came to Elisha and cried,
"I have only a pot of oil,
And my husband recently died,

While he lived and worked, he
Left some debt I cannot pay.
My creditor wants to collect
By taking my sons away.

I don't want to see them go,
For virtual slaves they'll be.
So if you can only help,
It will mean so much to me."

"Borrow from your neighbors,"
He said, "collect pots and
Pans. Fill them from what you
Have 'till you no longer can."

So they did as told
Pouring olive oil with zest.
Until they had enough on hand
To sell and pay their debts.

One day he went to Shunem;
A lady invited him to eat.

Then it became a habit
To stop for bread and meat.

So they built a shelter for
Him, this woman and her man;
Now he had a place to rest
All according to their plan.

Now when Elisha offered
Payment for all she'd done,
She'd never accept a thing,
From his thanks she'd run.

Now Gehazi his servant, said,
In answer to his quest,
"She's never had a son;"
Now you can guess the rest.

Elisha made a promise; she
Had the son he'd prophesied.
But one day as he grew
Older he took sick and died.

She laid him on Elisha's
Bed the couple maintained,
And rode in reckless haste
So Elisha's audience gained.

He followed her back home,
And her son did live again.
Now she could watch him grow
Until he'd become a man.

There was a case of poison
When many suffered ptomaine;
He added flour to the stew
And thus relieved the pain.

As you may have guessed,
A famine was upon the land.
And with all the shortages,
Food came slow to hand.

From Baal-shalishah, a man
Brought some grain, saying,

"Give it to these people,
So they may eat again."

It seemed a weakly morsel
To the man about to serve.
He said, "To feed a hundred
Men takes a lot of nerve."

Elisha said, "Serve what is
There; it's what God said to
Do." After eating some was
Left and they were through.

CHAPTER 5

Naaman, a captain in Syria,
Was a favorite of the king;
For he'd saved the country
From a war and ravaging.

When they'd been at war he
Led a raid on Israeli land.
They'd had occasional war
Almost since time began.

One of his spoils of war,
When he had battled there,
Was a young Israeli girl
Extremely bright and fair.

She served Naaman's wife
As a servant and friend.
Noting Naaman had leprosy,
Said, "He can make it end.

If he'd go to a prophet
In Samaria that I know, God
Would heal him completely,
And he'd never again be so."

So the King of Syria sent a
Letter to the King of Israel
Asking for a favor but
Sending many gifts as well.

The King of Israel cried,
"Is Syria causing a storm?

They're asking a miracle,
And I surely can't perform."

But Elisha sent him word,
Saying, "Send the man to me;
God's blessing of Israel is
Something he should see."

Elisha said to go wash
In Jordan when he got home.
Naaman felt slighted and
Away in anger strode.

But some friends prevailed,
Saying, "It does sound weak;
But perhaps you should try
To find the cure you seek."

So at the Jordan river
Seven times he washed. Then
His leprosy disappeared as
From the river he walked.

Back to Elisha he trekked,
With apologies profound,
Admitting that God is great,
The only living one around.

Gifts he offered Elisha
Were all firmly refused.
His ability came from God
And was not to be abused.

His servant Gehazi thought,
"This guy is going free,
So I'll take care of that;
It certainly shouldn't be."

So he followed Naaman and
Committed unpardonable sin.
Naaman gave cloth and cash,
Which would all go to him.

On the way back he hid them,
For Elisha would reprove.

To stay out of trouble now,
Evidence must be removed.

When he returned, Elisha,
Who knew of his plot, said,
"You sinned and stole; now
Leprosy will be your lot."

Gehazi left the house. As
He turned to go, it was
Obvious to everyone there,
His skin was white as snow.

CHAPTER 6

Sons of prophets grew, and
As time went past, they
Needed a larger seminary
So went to Elisha to ask.

They cut trees by the river
To erect a building ashore.
But an axe head fell in
And could be seen no more.

It was borrowed, he panicked,
Until Elisha made it swim,
The worker reached for it;
It was thus returned to him.

The King of Syria plotted
To take Israel by surprise.
But when he would attack,
Elisha put Israel wise.

This happened several times
Till Ben-hadad finally cried,
"Whatever is going on here?
Who's helping the other side?"

One of his servants told him,
"The Prophet tells the king
Even what you say in bed,
For he knows of every thing."

So Ben-hadad ordered his men
To go spy Elisha out.

One day they found him and
Encompassed the city about.

Elisha's servant asked in
Fear, "How will we survive?"
Elisha caused his eyes to
Open; it was a big surprise.

Around Elisha's people were
Soldiers, horses, chariots of
Fire. So he now felt safe;
Jehovah's army never tires.

Elisha prayed to God, when
The invaders surrounded him,
To cast a spell on the enemy
And make his sight grow dim.

The enemies were afflicted
With blindness to every man.
And then Elisha told them
He'd lead them by the hand.

This city is not the one;
Neither is this the trail.
But I will lead you there;
In this I will not fail.

So to Samaria he led them
To the capital of the land
In the midst of Israeli's,
Who could decimate the band.

The King of Israel asked,
"What shall I do with these?"
For Elisha had prayed again,
And now the enemy could see.

"They're prisoners of war," he
Said, "and must be treated so.
Food and drink provide them
And then let them go."

For a time Israel had peace
Because Syria left them alone.

But then Ben-hadad returned
And surrounded their homes.

Soon all supplies exhausted;
Prices zoomed to the sky.
Food was impossible to find;
A woman was heard to cry,

"My neighbor and I made a pact,
Our son's will boil for broth.
But after mine we had eaten,
She gave me the double cross.

She hid him away from me,
And I don't think it's fair.
She ate of mine then
But now refuses to share."

The king rent his clothing,
Desperately then, he cried,
"It must be Elisha's doing;
I swear he's going to die."

He knew the king sought him
And was planning his death.
Divining the king's actions
Faced trouble like an adept.

CHAPTER 7

So Elisha told the king,
"Tomorrow the siege will end.
Prices will again be normal,
On this you can depend."

The king's man doubted, said,
"I reject what you say, if
God made windows in heaven,
Your words I'd still weigh."

Then Elisha replied, "It
Will be, but when the time
Arrives, you'll be there
But unable to pay the price."

Now at the city gates there
Were four men with leprosy.

They said, "Why wait we
Here, let us go and see.

If we're killed by Syrians,
We would have died anyway.
But if they feed and keep
Us, we'll have won the day."

The Syrian camp they spied
And this is what they found.
The ground was littered
With castoff's all around.

Night had closed upon them
To sound of chariots and
Armor clash; Syrian fears
Led to a desperate dash.

God had played on fear, un-
til their spirits failed.
In haste to get away, those
Goods were left on the trail.

So those four men went back,
And broke the welcome news
Of the abandoned supplies
For all to pick and choose.

The gatekeeper, he who'd
Denied Elisha's prophecy,
Tried to control their race
For the available property.

As he stood in the gateway
To calm the people's urge,
He was trampled to death in
Their uncontrollable surge.

Elisha had prophesied truly
Yesterday, when he'd said,
You will see it happen; but
Then you'll soon be dead.

CHAPTER 8

Elisha spoke to the woman,
Who's son he'd given life,

Advising she move elsewhere;
This land was due for strife.

Seven years of famine to
Soon be Israel's portion.
So she moved to Philistine
Land for a better fortune.

Seven years later, as Gehazi
Talked to the king, he spoke
Of her again and of other
Remarkable things.

Now the woman returned, and
Just arrived at the scene.
The king helped her fortunes
As Elisha must've foreseen.

Elisha went to Damascus for
Ben-hadad, sick with disease,
Had sent Hazael to meet him
With many gifts to please.

Before Elisha Hazael stood,
Presenting Ben-hadad's plea,
Asking, "Will the King reco-
ver, or die of his disease?"

"His condition's not fatal,"
Said Elisha, "But he'll
Surely die." Then, looking
At Hazael, he began to cry.

"You'll be King of Syria,"
Said he, "to rule with iron
Hand, laying Israel waste,
Being a scourge to the land."

Hazael returned to his king
Telling him he would recover.
But while visiting him, the
King he brutally smothered.

King Ben-hadad died, and
Hazael reigned instead.

But not by accession, he
Murdered the king in bed.

Jehoram, Jehoshaphat's son,
In Jerusalem then reigned.
He was also a wicked king
Who caused Jehovah pain.

He married Ahab's daughter
Who was a wicked lass. But
God had been David's friend,
So he let the matter pass.

During his time of rule,
Edom rose in angry revolt.
Jehoram would crush them
But was left out in the cold.

Surrounded by Edomites, he
Would have lost the fight
But broke through ranks
And escaped into the night.

His army now deserted him,
And he was left alone.
So Edom went its way,
And he went on back home.

Then Jehoram died, and
Ahazia reigned instead.
He and Joram fought Syria;
A year later he was dead.

He came over from Judah
To help Joram fight, but
This did not mitigate
The sadness of his plight.

King Joram was wounded,
Quit the battle to heal.
Ahazia came to visit, and
Troubles then were real.

CHAPTER 9

Elisha called on Jehu
To be king of all Israel,

To smite Ahab's house
And also that of Jezebel.

The army accepted him
As king of all the land.
He enforced God's wishes
With an iron hand.

In his chariot he rode to
Joram's camp in Jezreel,
For the king was waiting
For his wounds to heal.

Joram saw them coming
And sent couriers to
Find out what this visit
Was all about.

But Jehu hid each one
Behind him as they came.
Joram and Ahazi met him
To figure out his game.

With Jehu it was war
Instead of peace. As
Joram got the message,
He turned about to flee.

Then Jehu drew his bow,
And let the arrow fly. It
Pierced Joram's heart;
That was how he died.

So they followed Ahazi;
He also died that day.
Next, Queen Jezebel,
For an evil life she paid.

So it came to pass, as
God had said it would,
The wicked people paid
Who did so little good.

CHAPTER 10

Then Jehu sought out
All of Joram's kin,

And Joram's relatives
Fell victim to him.

Jehonadab he spared
Made watch the sight,
Tricked Baal's people,
Tried to do it right.

He called to assembly
All who followed Baal.
How he wiped them out
Is really quite a tale.

"Give special vest-
ments," he told Baal's
Priest. He'd save God's
People but kill these.

He faked sacrifice to
Baal who was their god.
But sent in soldiers
Told to do their job.

They broke many idols,
Tore down Baal's house.
Baal and his followers
Were about cleaned out.

So the Lord's commands
Jehu did complete;
From idol worship and
Sin, he made them retreat.

Twenty-eight years Jehu
Ruled and went his way.
Now Jehoahaz his son
Took over in his place.

CHAPTER 11

When Athaliah learned
Of son Ahazia's death,
She rose in power and
Struck competitors dead.

So all of Ahazia's sons
Died at that time, but

Joash, who was saved
From her ugly crimes.

Aunt Jehosheba took him
Ere he was put to death.
She hid him in God's
House six years instead.

Six years Athalia ruled,
Ploying immoral gains.
Only a matter of time
Till another must reign.

Jehoiada the priest
Called in fighting men.
Then he gave this order
Unto all of them.

"With weapons in hand
Form three rings for
Protection at all times
Around and about the king.

If any man shall fail
By letting an enemy past,
He'll not live to regret;
Retribution will be fast."

Each commanding officer
And those in his command,
Be at temple this Sabbath,
As per Jehoahaz's plan."

The Priest brought forth
The prince who'd been hid.
Declared him King of Judah,
Thus they made their bid.

Now Athaliah heard a noise
And came to check it out.
She wised up to the facts,
"Treason," was her shout.

Then the priest commanded
The captains of the host,

"Stop this woman quickly,
In your duty be not loath."

She ran into the stable,
And she breathed her last.
With her execution, her
Usurpers role was past.

Jehoiada made a covenant
With people of the Lord.
They'd follow Jehovah
To thus become his wards.

The people went on rampage
And on Baal declared war.
Killed Mattan, his priest,
His altars ripped and tore.

That little boy of seven
They placed on the throne.
By their changed behavior,
The past they would atone.

CHAPTER 12

For forty years he reigned
As priests instructed him.
Following Jehovah's command
As he kept free of sin.

Some high places remained,
Sacrifices often burned.
But some people's priests,
Priestly duties spurned.

God's house was now old,
And in places needed work.
So Joash asked the priests
Why the jobs they shirked.

They agreed to take no pay
But still not do repair.
Jehoiada made effort then
To pay the builders fare.

Twenty-three years it took
To repair the house of God.
After that was done, they'd
Still not finished the job.

No vessels of silver or gold,
Snuffers, basins or such,
Nor any new trumpets, for
It still was lacking much.

Then the King of Syria
Declared war on the land;
Joash paid him tribute so
He would stay his hand.

The gold and silver his
Forbears dedicated before
Were taken from the Lord's
House to head off the war.

Now trusted servants com-
mitted murder on the king.
Of course others before
Did this sort of thing.

Once a boy king, in his
Forty seventh year was
Dead. So his son Amaziah
Now reigned in his stead.

CHAPTER 13

Israel had many kings
As Judah also did; they
All sinned and failed;
They were on the skids.

Jehoahaz ruled Israel as
King Joash of Judah died.
He was wicked, too, but he
Changed or really tried.

For a time he prayed and
He did seek the Lord. So
Their problems were less
Because of his accord.

People didn't change,
But continued as before.
Sinful, repenting not,
And painful to the Lord.

Jehoahaz died in Samaria,
And his son Joash ruled.
A Joash also ruled Judah;
By these names I'm fooled.

So Elisha died and was
Buried in an open tomb. A
Strange thing happened; it
Should dispell any gloom.

They were burying a man
Who dropped on Elisha's
Bones. They saw Moabites
Much too close to home.

What a surprise! When the
Corpse rose to his feet,
They'd seen a miracle not
Likely on a street.

They didn't seem shaken
Still sinful as before.
Hazael died in Syria after
Years of intermittent war.

CHAPTER 14

While Joash ruled Israel,
Amazia in Judah reigned.
For nine and twenty years
The same old story again.

For sacrifice and incense
In high places burned.
When time to worship God,
He had to wait his turn.

Yet the kings did much
As kings were wont to do.
Doing well occasionally,
But that was all too few.

He executed those servants
Who had murdered his father;
But their sons and daughters
He did not bother.

For 'tis written no father
For children's sins shall die;
Or children for father's pay,
For his sin he'll be tried.

In a Valley of Salt he slew
Ten thousand Edomites in war.
And in the flush of victory
Decided to battle some more.

He sent messengers to Israel,
They tried to calm him down.
Amazia ignored all reason
Like the bully of the town.

Israel and Judah went to war
At Beth-shemesh faced off.
Amazia should have listened
For this battle Judah lost.

The king was taken prisoner;
The capital of Judah fell,
Jerusalem's walls breached,
With other problems as well.

From the temple went gold
Cups and silver and gold.
Ahazia also gained hostages;
He had stopped Amazia cold.

Joash died in time and son
Jeroboam reigned instead.
Amazia lived on for fifteen
Years after Joash was dead.

They worked against Amazia,
And to Lachish he ran,
But lost his life in the race,
His son became ruling man.

Jeroboam reigned in Israel,
In battle he did fine. Re-
covered Damascus and Hamath,
God was shorted on his time.

At sixteen they crowned him,
So in Judah Azariah ruled.
He built Elath and saved it;
His time as king was cool.

Israel was safe from enem-
ies through Jeroboam's hand.
He sinned against Jehovah,
But was good for the land.

CHAPTER 15

For fifty-two years of rule
Judah's Azaria was good.
He didn't stop the heathen,
Although it seems he could.

And then the king fell ill
As leprosy decided his fate.
So lived in another house,
As his son ran his estate.

Jotham ruled for his father
Until the old man died.
Meanwhile back in Jerusalem,
Jeroboam's son tried.

Only half a year he lasted;
Shallum killed him publicly.
A month he reigned and then
Fell victim of his policy.

Menahem was from Tirzah
And to Samaria came. It
Was Shallum's turn to die
Like a never ending game.

Ten years he did evil; he
Followed Jereboam's way.
Did things he should not,
While he held kingly sway.

Then Pul, King of Assyria,
Set his army on the land.
Menahem paid him duty he
Collected from every man.

The Assyrians turned back,
They had no need to fight.
He won the battle without,
With only a show of might.

In time his turn came too;
With his fathers he slept.
Pekahia, his son, reigned
In Israel in his stead.

Pekahiah ruled two years,
Then got his just dues.
He sinned as Jeroboam had,
To Jehovah was not true.

Pekah headed a conspiracy,
Pekahia's life they took.
The story of his reign
Is written in the book.

Twenty years Pekah ruled
With no change in story.
For he too ruled in sin
Falling short of glory.

Assyria sent armies to
Take Israel's people away.
Cities and treasures lost,
Jotham over Judah reigned.

Hoshea, son of Elah slew
Pekah, took his throne.
Hosheas' story in the
Kings' chronicles is shown.

Jotham, much like David,
But people still did burn
Incense and sacrifice in
Groves, all slow to learn.

Pekah fought against Judah,
King Rezin of Syria too.
Jotham flunked the race,
So son Ahaz then ruled.

CHAPTER 16

Now Ahaz at twenty years
Became king. For sixteen
Years he ruled and did
Little good at anything.

He copied heathen ways
With neighbors he did war.
Did most everything wrong,
As so many had before.

Syria and Judah fought
Battering at his gates.
Again God's treasure was
Used to stave off fate.

At the Temple they got a
Store of silver and gold.
They sent it to Assyria
To get them out of a hole.

Ahaz died and was buried
In Jerusalem with the kings.
Again an Israeli Monarch no
Lasting peace could bring.

CHAPTER 17

Many long years since David,
Few good kings there'd been.
All lustful and irreverent,
Followed not God, but men,

In spite of God's prophets
Whom He had sent their way,
Stiff necked, intolerant,
Not listening to His say,

Going the ways of heathen,
Burning children to their

Gods. Finally in anger He
Turned; many would die on
Foreign sod.

Their enemies conquered and
Carried them to far lands.
They'd lost contact with God
By placing all trust in man.

For centuries they'd slipped;
So righteousness was a joke.
No wonder God scattered them
Till they wore an alien yoke.

CHAPTER 18

At twenty-five was Hezekiah
As in Judah he began to rule.
Twenty-nine years he reigned,
And surely was no fool.

He broke images and idols,
And cut down the groves
Where people had sacrificed
With the heathen in droves.

He broke the brazen serpent
Moses had made back when.
He led people to follow God
Rather than whims of men.

He trusted the Lord, whom
He knew to be true and just,
So ruled with righteousness
Rather than sin and lust.

Again Syria invaded Israel;
People were carried away.
They ignored Jehovah's will
And listened not to His say.

Sennacherub of Syria took
Judah's walled-in cities,
Then tried to scare them so
They'd be objects of pity.

He threatened and blowed.
Many fearful things he told
Within the people's hearing,
After taking all their gold.

On the wall they could hear,
Every word of what was said.
But the king had warned to
Stay calm, keep their heads.

Some messengers returned and
Gave the king the word. With
Clothing torn and fearful,
They told what they'd heard.

CHAPTER 19

His clothing Hezekaiah tore,
To the Temple went to pray,
While sending men to Isaiah,
To hear what God would say.

Soon his answer came down,
"Ignore this General today.
He'll return to die at home,
And not come back this way."

But when the General went,
He left behind a note: Of
How invincible Syria was,
That God was only a boast.

Hezekaiah took the letter
Into God's Temple there; he
Unburdened a troubled soul
In deep and solemn prayer.

"Lord, up above the angels
Please give us aid today.
This man boasts and claims
He'd take our heritage away.

Hear him threat and boast
How he'd jerk you around.
Assyria's a powerful nation,
Don't let him put you down.

They've ravaged our country
Till few are left to strive.
So we need your help today
To prove that you're alive."

Isaiah got word to Hezekaiah,
"To Sennacherub now reply,
Why think you're so great,
Or God won't take our side?"

"You've conquered mountains,
Ridden rough upon the land.
You've ridiculed the Lord
And will go the way of man.

Sennacherib is no problem,
You'll soon have good yields.
For our God is here to help,
And your wounds he'll heal."

That very night the enemy
Was devastated by the Lord.
Sennacherib went to Nineveh
And was slain by the sword.

CHAPTER 20

Then King Hezekiah fell ill
Was told that he would die.
But he cried aloud for mercy,
As for more time he cried.

As the prophet left, after
Saying to set things right,
God spoke to Isaiah again
But now in a different light.

Isaiah returned to the king
To impart the latest story.
For fifteen years he'd live,
So God would reap the glory.

They made a paste of figs
And placed it upon his boil.
Three days later he was well
And returned to his toil.

But the fifteen years added
Seemed too good to be true;
So he asked a sign be given
To serve as a positive clue.

For a miracle Isaiah asked
Earnestly praying to God. So
The sun moved west to east,
Which you'll think is odd.

Ten degrees the sun returned,
Proof is in science found.
Then again from east to west,
The normal way around.

From far Babylon messengers
Came to wish him good health.
So Hezekiah became expansive,
Showed them all his wealth.

Isaiah asked what he'd shown,
He said, "They've seen all."
Isaiah in consternation said,
"One day the kingdom'll fall."

"But later," thought Hezekiah,
"Peace will be in my time.
If I live in thankfulness,
That will be no crime."

History records many deeds
And of how he went his way.
His son Mannasseh followed
And brought on evil days.

CHAPTER 21

Twelve year old Manasseh,
In Jerusalem began to reign.
He was Hezekiah's son and
Hephzibah, his mother's
name.

All the acts of wickedness
Were those things he did.
If he did anything good,

From history it was hid.

He built up groves and
Places of evil sacrifice
And spilled human blood;
He just wasn't very nice.

God named him a renegade
Apt to wipe a nation out.
Yet ruled half a century
While swinging evil clout.

Then one day he died, and
His wicked son carried on.
For two years he ruled,
This son he'd named Amon.

All the things he did, he
Followed his dad's lead.
All that history records
Is a series of evil deeds.

His servants conspired to
Kill him in his house. So
The people all converged
To wipe the servants out.

Now his little son Josiah
Was crowned king instead.
He did a better job and
Turned not right or left.

CHAPTER 22

They came to the Temple
To count the money there,
For materials and workers
To get the place repaired.

He got the job well done,
It should've been before.
A book of law was found
Within the Temple stored.

Shaphan, the scribe, read
The book of David's time.
The king suddenly realized

There had been much crime.

Law of knowledge is sin,
Else it might be excused.
But now he knew the facts
And felt like one accused.

To Huldah the prophetess,
He sent to ask advice. For
She would know God's plan
And tell him what was right.

She told him God was angry
At sins of all those kings.
But the young King of Judah
Would never feel the sting.

Josiah would spend his days
And get his reward in peace.
For he was upright and just,
So God would grant relief.

CHAPTER 23

All the people of Jerusalem,
Prophets, priests, and more,
Assembled at God's Temple,
For a reading of His word.

Beside a Temple pillar the
Young king reverently stood.
He swore to do the things
As written in the book.

So he commanded the priests,
And those who kept the door,
That heathen vessels in the
Temple be brought forth.

Those things of corruption
The kings had earlier built,
He tore down and destroyed
Trying to reduce the guilt.

With all the things he did
God still was full of wrath,

He said, "This land is poll-
uted, by fire needs a bath."

Assyria and Egypt warred,
So Josiah joined the fray.
Proving his undoing, for
He died in battle one day.

So after thirty one years
Son Jehoahaz ruled Israel.
Pharoh of Egypt appeared
To lock him away in jail.

Now Pharoh made
Eliakim, his brother, rule.
Israel payed tax to Egypt
To keep peace and stay cool.

Like many kings before him,
He did much that was wrong.
We know the Lord had reason,
For his disgust so strong.

CHAPTER 24

Jehoiakim ruled Judah when
The king of Babylon came.
He invaded, for Judah's
Subjection was his aim.

Chaldeans attacked Judah,
Moabites and Syrians too.
They all joined in battle
Against Judah's few.

The Lord helped them not,
For Manassa, it was said,
Made the land run bloody
With innocents he bled.

The King of Judah now died,
Son Joachin ruled instead.
Scuttled Israel's treasure,
He tried to save his head.

Stripped God's Temple and
The king's palace too. He

Must have really panicked
As to what to do.

Babylonians took it all
And much more, by the way,
For all people of quality
Were taken to be slaves.

The helpless and the old,
All the sick and weak,
Were left by the way,
Their survival to seek.

Through anger of God in
Jerusalem, it came to pass
That out of His presence
They were actually cast.

Nebuchadnezzar of Babylon
Made Mattaniah king. And
Now named him Zedekiah,
So had a different ring.

CHAPTER 25

Two years Babylon laid siege
And then Jerusalem fell. For
They were out of food, and
Things had not gone well.

Now the king and all his men
By way of the garden escaped.
Across the plains of Jericho,
In great haste they traipsed.

But his army scattered
And prisoners they were taken.
Then his problems multiplied,
By fortune he was forsaken.

His sons were slain before
His eyes; then they blinded

Him. Carried away to Babylon
To reward his life of sin.

All the treasures of Judah
Were taken from the land.
All homes in the city were
Razed by the hand of man.

Many were taken to Babylon
Where execution they faced.
Only the poor and the weak
Were left home in place.

Babylon left a ruler to
Take care of what was left.
Gedaliah, governor of Pale-
stine, in death now slept.

He said, "Serve the enemy,"
To sons of the royal seed,
Who'd come for advice of
Which they were in need.

They were obviously unhappy
With the advice he gave,
For seven months later they
Came back his life to take.

After thirty seven years
In Babylon it came to pass,
That the King of Judah had
Been in prison cast--

Was finally released and
Better times he faced. He
Was given a regular income
For the rest of his days.

END OF SECOND KINGS

FIRST CHRONICLES

CHAPTER 1

From Adam's line to Noah's
And sons of Ham and Shem.
From his line to Abraham,
To Ishmael's sons and then,

We meet the sons of Keturah
And of her generations. She
Was a concubine to Abraham
While building up a nation.

Also of Abraham and Isaac,
And the sons of Esau too.
The early kings of Edom,
Here first we read of dukes.

CHAPTER 2

Sons of Jacob, known as Is-
rael, of Judah and of Jesse
Caleb, Jerahmeel of Shesban
With no sons for posterity.

He gave his servant a daugh-
ter, so his line might go on.
Another Caleb, son of Hur,
Also had many sons.

CHAPTER 3

Six sons had David, while he
In Hebron reigned, and
Several more in Jerusalem,
As size his family gained.

Then his son Solomon, his
Sons, and their son's sons,
All the way to Zedekiah,
And on and on and on.

CHAPTER 4

With so many successors to
Jeconiah, Solathiel, and

More, Shemaiah, and Beriah,
So many you lose score.

Judah descended from Caleb,
Was known as the son of Hur.
Now as we remember the list
Many names become a blur.

There was Ashur of Hezron,
And Jabez who made a prayer.
That's all it says he did
And God was always there.

All were potters or herders,
Wood workers and such, some
Dwelt among the plants, as
Close to a king they stuck.

Living in cities and towns
As many had done before.
They moved to other places
Though this might mean war.

CHAPTER 5

Then Reuben, the eldest, he
Lay with his father's wife.
Tribal punishment
Was loss of his birthright.

Joel was his descendant,
A cattleman of known fame.
Who near the edge of Judah
Staked out a place of claim.

For he and his descendants,
All warriors fierce and bold,
Took over enemy territory
They meant to have and hold.

The half tribe of Manasseh
Had many descendants too,

Spread throughout the land,
At whatever they wanted to do.

They scattered far and wide,
For they honored not the Lord.
Much as we of today, yet
His wrath cannot afford.

CHAPTER 6

We remember the sons of Levi,
Priests they would be, the
Families of Gershom and
Kohath, and also of Merari.

'Twas also the duty of Aaron,
And all of his kin as well.
There were so many involved
It's a long story to tell.

There were cities of refuge,
Where a fugitive could go,
Cities of priests and Levites,
And the cities of the coasts.

CHAPTER 7

The sons of Issachar were
Rulers and mighty men. Also
Those of Benjamin, Naphtali,
Manassah and Ephraim.

All those sons of Asher, by
The thousands they numbered.
During times of war, what
A way to be encumbered!

CHAPTER 8

Fine warriors were Benjamin's
Seed, Saul and Jonathan were
Of this line. Expert bowmen
With many of their kind.

CHAPTER 9

In the annals of the kings
Every family was recorded.

So according to their works
Many were rewarded.

Judah worshipped idols
Much against Jehovah's will,
So were slaves in Babylon
To savor the bitter pill.

Then they straggled back,
Or some descendants did. A
Homing instinct was strong
To finally make their bid.

Some were chiefs and sub-
Chiefs, priests and warriors
Too, Gate keepers and more,
With special jobs to do.

Descendants of Asher were
Thirty-six thousand men of
War. That was of one family
Imagine how many more.

CHAPTER 10

Saul had failed Jehovah, so
Went his sinful way. His
Errant will caught up with
Him upon that fateful day.

For those were days of war
When he was sorely pressed.
Philistines were charging;
The Israelis needed rest.

Saul's three sons and he
All died upon that day. It
Wiped out his whole family,
So the scriptures say.

The Philistines came back,
After the Israeli army fled.
When finding Saul's body
There they cut off his head,

Put his body and his sons
Before a Temple of heathen

Gods. Some Israeli warriors
Brought them to Israel's sod.

CHAPTER 11

Israel's leaders gathered
And to David made petition
That he become their king
To help a nation's condition.

But the Jebusites refused
To let him enter their town.
For a Jebusite executioner,
David now looked around.

So Joab made his move, and
The Jebusites rued the day.
Joab became commander-in-
Chief after his power play.

David became rich and famous
As along life's path he trod.
And fortune smiled upon him,
For he was a friend of God.

Three of David's warriors
Were greater than the rest.
They all won great honors,
When put to test.

Jashobeam was greatest,
A man who knew no fear, he
Killed three hundred enemies,
With nothing but his spear.

Then Eleazar was next, a
Great warrior was he. Before
The Philistines Israel ran,
But he wasn't one to flee.

In a barley field he stood
And fought them man to man.
He gave his army courage;
The victory there was grand.

Abishai was Joab's brother,
He killed three hundred too.

Chief of thirty warriors
And a spear he also used.

Those three came to David
Where he hid within a cave.
The deeds they did that day
Proved that they were brave.

They fought through enemy
Lines, got water from a well,
Which they brought to David;
It's a story I love to tell.

Beniah was another hero, two
Giants from Moab he slew.
In a pit he killed a lion
With slippery snow there too.

There was an Egyptian giant
Seven and a half feet tall.
He faced Beniah with a spear,
But Beniah caused his fall.

Now there were many others,
Thirty brave men all told.
Captains of his legions,
Wonderful warriors of old.

CHAPTER 12

Many warriors came to
David where he hid. They
Came to fight his battles,
And do as he would bid.

Expert with the sling and
Bow and arrow as well,
Fought with either hand
And with either could excel.

All Benjamin's tribe, which
Was also the tribe of Saul,
Wanted David for king,
So worked at Saul's downfall.

Swift as deer of the field,
Ready for battle to a man.

They'd take David's orders,
And fit well into his plan.

All this time he'd hidden
In the Philistine realm,
Raiding the distant borders,
He was at the bandits' helm.

On his way to war with the
Philistines against King Saul,
The generals became wary
And didn't trust him at all.

So they sent him back
Because they had this fear,
He might desert to Saul, and
That could cost them dear.

Some brave and able warriors
At Hebron joined him there.
They'd fought the Amalekites
And always did their share.

From the tribe of Benjamin,
Three thousand were a few.
They also came from others;
Many Levites too.

From north, south, east and
West, mountain and vale they
Came, equipped and ready to
Fight, dreaming of war games.

From each corner of the land
In great numbers and supply,
Israel was ready for change
And this was the time to try.

They'd found a champion who
Had answered God's call.
Joy was rioting in the land;
They'd soon be rid of Saul.

CHAPTER 13

Then David asked his people,
"Why not invite others now?"

And we'll bring back the Ark;
It waits at Abinadab's house.

In a new cart they hauled it
By Uzza and Ahio driven.
Now an ox stumbled, and by
Uzza sudden help was given.

God had warned them before.
The Ark must not be touched.
When Uzza instantly died,
David felt it was too much.

In anger at Jehòvah then,
For Uzza he named the place.
The title has always stuck,
Is known by that name today.

Now David was afraid of God,
Asking, how to get it home?
They left it with Obed edom,
And David his fate bemoaned.

Now God smiled on Obed
  edom
Three months it was there.
Obed's blessings multiplied
Daily his fortune flared.

CHAPTER 14

Remember King Hiram of tyre?
Cedars, masons and help he
Sent to build a palace for
David, much skill and
Material was spent.

God smiled on this Kingdom
With David obviously pleased.
The family of Israel improved;
No signs better than these!

Philistines attacked, so David
Asked for God's advice. Then
Jehovah helped him repel them;
Soon he'd repulsed them twice.

With God's help David won all
Seemed equal to any situation.
His fame spread over the land;
He was feared by every nation.

CHAPTER 15

Many priests David sent with
Cymbals, psalteries and harps.
They danced with joy that day,
As they returned the Ark.

Michal, his first great love,
Saw David dancing before the
Ark. Watching him in public,
She despised him in her heart.

CHAPTER 16

Now David had pitched a tent
In the middle the Ark was set.
All were given meat and drink
And to each, a loaf of bread.

Offerings, sacrifices made,
Celebrating joyfully that day.
He even called a choir, where
Many instruments were played.

David made a prayer of thanks
For on this day to be living,
For those years of protection
Sang a song of thanksgiving.

Ministers, porters and prie-
sts he caused to tend the Ark.
Musicians to make glad noise
As with God's joy they'd hark.

CHAPTER 17

David had a dream; he wanted
To build Jehovah a house. But
The Lord spoke through
  Nathan
Saying He would do without.

Like the children of Israel,
Many years he dwelt in a tent.
From their midst he'd led his
People everywhere they went.

But in time, He said that
From David's line He'd bring
A famous ruler forth,
Who'd be forever a King.

David thanked God again for
Wonderful things He'd done.
For the miracles performed
And for battles they'd won.

For he recognized Jehovah
As God of all the universe.
He thanked the Lord for every-
Thing, for what he was worth.

CHAPTER 18

David built up his Kingdom;
The Philistines he subdued.
As many other nations fell,
He became a famous Jew.

Very much wealth he gained,
Horses, chariots, silver and
Gold. From all the lands of
Enmity, came riches untold.

He reigned over Israel with
Honest justice supreme.
A fantastic reversal from a
Young shepherd boy's dream.

Those kingdoms of enemies,
He'd fought only yesterday,
Now gave of their wealth
As much tribute they paid.

Past enemies were servants,
His friends in high places.
His people all adored him;
He enjoyed the good graces.

CHAPTER 19

Ammon's king died one day,
Uncertain life even then.
David sent his sincere good
Will to a son of a friend.

Hanun's advisers thought
That this was a sham, and
These were all spies come
To scout out the land.

So cut short their garments
And shaved their heads
 smooth.
Then sent them back to Israel
In the sorriest of moods.

But David heard of the deed,
For bad news travels fast. He
Told them to slow the return
Till their shame was past.

Now the children of Ammon
And their not so smart king,
Realized they had goofed and
Had done a bad thing.

So a thousand talents of
Silver King Hanun sent forth.
He paid three other countries
To help fight his war.

But David and Joab
And their legions of men,
Went to battle once more
And won once again.

CHAPTER 20

War clouds covered Ammon,
As Joab and men raided there.
Riches and people despoiled,
No inhabitant was spared.

David arrived upon the scene,
And Milcom's crown tried on.

Seventy-five pounds of gold
And precious stones he'd won.

The people he put to work
With saws, harrows, and axes,
Now for many years to come,
They'd pay him their taxes.

They fought Philistines
It was that time of year.
Did battle with giants,
Whom they greatly feared.

The giants fell to them,
And Israel was now freed.
It must now be peaceful;
Of war there was no need.

CHAPTER 21

David wanted a census
To see how many he ruled.
Joab argued the point, but
His argument soon cooled.

For David was determined
They should do this thing.
And he soon won his point;
After all he was the king.

So Joab counted people,
Judah and Benjamin lacked.
He knew God would be ang-
ered by this stubborn act.

God's man came to David,
Said for this he'd pay;
Three years of famine
Or three days of plague,

Three months of disaster,
From enemies of the land.
"Now give God an answer,
Which will you withstand?"

None of these did he like;
We know that for sure.

But he decided to chance
The mercies of the Lord.

God sent pestilence on
Israel that day. Seventy
Thousand died, the result
Of a terrible plague.

David cried desperately
For the carnage to cease.
Saying, "Lord, save your
People, the sinner is me!

Please do with me and my
Family as you will, but
Too many of your people
Already've been killed."

He saw the Lord's angel
With sword fully drawn.
He better get this right;
Israel would be the pawn.

So he built an Altar on
Ornan's threshing floor,
To make burnt offerings
And plead with his Lord.

On Mount Gibeon was a
Tabernacle Moses built;
David didn't go there be-
cause of fear and guilt.

CHAPTER 22

On this spot he'd have
Solomon make God's House.
He collected materials to
Give his plan more clout.

He'd won wars and brought
The land great peace, so
Solomon must set a Temple
And do so with more ease.

He gave them skilled workers,
Gold, silver, and wood. To

Son Solomon, he declared,
"I've done all I could."

CHAPTER 23

"So do the job up right
And do it in lively fashion.
For the honor of our God, of
His love and his compassion."

So David stepped down, as
He made Solomon the new
  King.
Each one had a job, whether
To work, pray, or sing.

Now David took a census
Of all those who would work.
The numbers were impressive;
At jobs they'd never shirk.

The priests, descendants of
Aaron, were in great demand.
Charged with the building
And spirituality of the land.

CHAPTER 24

By coin toss they chose them,
For the jobs they would do.
The chief men of the tribes
And of the Levites too.

CHAPTER 25

With zithers, harps, or cymb-
als some were called to play.
Others made prophecy, as
In thankfulness they prayed.

Many were trained families
In music and singing praise.
Two dozen dozen in number,
Ignoring reputation or age.

CHAPTER 26

Guards around the Temple
Were captains of the clans.

They were able bodied men
And dependable to a man.

Many men were appointed to
Guard the different gates.
They were rotated regularly
To fill in every date.

Every chosen man was famous,
Appointed to rule the clan,
Guide religious ceremonies,
Or steer the destiny of man.

CHAPTER 27

Twelve regiments had Israel,
One each month of the year.
Twenty-four thousand men,
Whose captains knew no fear.

Politicians there were too,
From every tribe and group.
Tax bureaus were entrenched;
Some made wine from fruit.

Others cared for vineyards,
Herdsmen, shepherds as well.
Wise men, teachers, scribes,
Others too numerous to tell.

CHAPTER 28

David called them together,
Those valiant men of old,
The men of war and others
Who'd always done as told.

"My people and my brothers,"
He said, ``God smiles on us;
We survived and prospered
In spite of all the fuss.

I have been His favorite,
And He has made me king. My
Son Solomon will follow me;
We're blessed in everything."

Then to Solomon, he said,
"My son, God has chosen you
To build His Holy Temple,
So do well in all you do.

God is just and generous
So long as you do his will.
His loving care of you will
Keep your life fulfilled.

I give you all the plans
To build the Temple with,
As well as gold and silver
With which to furnish it.

Let this task not cause you
Fear; He'll be at your side
To help you finish the job
If with Him you'll abide.

You have men with skills
For every possible job. And
They're all at your command
To do this work for God."

CHAPTER 29

Then to the assembly
The king turned, and said,
"My son is still very young
And there's much work ahead.

I've gathered all my riches;
They are at God's command.
And because of my devotion,
I place them in His hand.

Now who will do as I? Who'll
Give of his wealth?" Then
Many gave of their worth, and
Others gave of themselves.

All the people were happy,
And many helped the king.
They were thoroughly sold on
The rightness of this thing.

David praised the Lord; with
Food and drink they feasted.
The people of Israel pledged
Solomon their allegiance.

At a ripe old age he died,
David, King of the clans;

Then Solomon took his place
To carry on God's plan.

END OF FIRST
CHRONICLES

SECOND CHRONICLES

CHAPTER 1

He was king all powerful of
The richest nation on earth.
Horses, chariots, soldiers,
Gold and silver of worth.

A thousand burnt offerings
He sacrificed upon the hill
At the Tabernacle of Moses,
For it stood there still.

Then God appeared, one night
And asked, "What can I do?
For anything you wish, I'll
Certainly give to you."

Solomon did not look about,
For he had nearly everything.
He said, "I'll sure need wis-
dom to be your favorite king."

God promised this request
And so much more than that.
He'd be wisest king on earth;
His fortunes would grow fat.

Silver and gold in Jerusalem
Was as plentiful as could be.
He dealt in lumber, horses,
And shipping on the seas.

CHAPTER 2

King Solomon finished plans
For the Temple of the Lord;
'Twould be a thing of beauty
Which he could well afford.

He felt quite unworthy per-
forming his work of love. For
He felt God rated better
Than even heaven above.

To his friend, King Hiram,
He made his request. Saying
He could pay very well, and
Would Hiram be his guest?

Hiram answered quickly, "We
Will do as you require. We
Have wood and clever
    workmen
Whom you can certainly hire."

CHAPTER 3

In the city of Jerusalem, on
Mount Moriah's crest, here
He built the Temple, where
Jehova's house would rest.

For God had visited David on
Ornan's threshing floor, so

Jehova's Temple site would
Be here evermore.

The roof was twice as high
As the building was long.
With so much inlaid gold,
It had to be quite strong.

Beautiful jewels inlaid in
Gold with which 'twas plated,
Even golden nails were used;
The wonders never abated.

Within the innermost room,
The Holy of Holies was there;
Much gold and finest linens
Two sculptured angels shared.

At the front of the Temple
Mighty pillars he built too.
Named them Jachin and Boaz,
As he was pleased to do.

CHAPTER 4

An altar also he built,
Thirty feet across each way.
And a huge round brass tank
Wherein priests would bathe.

Twelve metal oxen held it,
Facing all four directions,
Ten vats to wash offerings,
According to instructions.

These things and much more,
He built as he was told. Out
Side the Temple was brass;
Nearly all within was Gold.

CHAPTER 5

As the Temple was finished,
Gifts were brought forth,
Put in the Temple treasury,
And people praised the Lord.

The Covenent Ark was placed
In the Holy of Holies that day,
And all the people rejoiced
Who thought it here to stay.

Priests and Levites there,
Singers and trumpeteers too,
Each joined in the chorus
To give Jehovah his due.

"God is good," was the theme,
"May kindness forever last."
Glory filled the Temple and
Quite overcame the cast.

CHAPTER 6

He stood before the people,
This was Solomon's prayer.
To renew his people to God,
He had called them there.

"Lord, you never asked for a
House so big and grand. But
You've granted me the honor
To build upon this land.

My father David would have,
But you bid him wait for me.
And now our faces are turned
Toward heaven and to thee.

You are the one, almighty,
Whose laws we would obey.
Please think upon our needs,
And help us when we pray.

We will face this place
To ask forgiveness for sin.
If what we do is pleasing,
Please be sure to listen in.

Now if your people backslide,
And who has not done so?
Please give them another try
Before you let them go.

So Lord this Temple is yours,
The Ark of your power's here.
Please give us all salvation;
May the kingdom be ever
  near."

CHAPTER 7

As Solomon finished praying
Fire from heaven flashed
Consuming all the sacrifices
And worshippers fell flat.

"He is good," they exclaimed,
"So loving and kind;"
They praised and sacrificed
During this exciting time.

Seven days they celebrated,
Coming from over the land.
Solomon finished the Temple
Just as he had planned.

Now the Lord appeared to him
As he lay asleep one night,
Saying, "I heard your prayer;
I will treat my people right.

Make your Temple sacrifices,
Remember in times of drought,
If people have forgotten me
That is what it's all about.

If locusts eat your crops,
Or epidemics should befall,
Then humble yourselves and
Pray; I will hear your call.

This Temple I have chosen,
Here my heart will ever be.
Your fortunes will prosper,
If you always follow me.

If you fail to heed my words
And listen not to me,

Catastrophe will befall you
For all the world to see."

CHAPTER 8

Now for twenty years as king
He built to his content. Sol-
omon improved and fortified
Making friends where he went.

He built cities in the desert;
Here chariot horses were kept.
Getting labor from erstwhile
Enemies he proved adept.

His people were his officers,
Cavalry men and charioteers.
Two hundred fifty others
Administered Israel's affairs.

He built a fancy palace for
Pharoh's daughter whom he
Married. And now to her
New home she was carried.

She'd not be on sacred ground
With honored customs bent.
She was of another religion,
And not of Jewish descent.

Instructions Moses had given
Solomon executed with finesse.
He sacrificed and prayed to
God and never went to excess.

He launched a fleet at sea,
And with King Hiram's help,
Traded in goods and gold
And ended with great wealth.

CHAPTER 9

Now the queen of Sheba heard
Of this great and unusual man;
So she set out to visit him;
'Twas her most important plan.

She asked him many questions,
As some women seem to do. And
He answered every one, his
Wisdom showing through.

She brought jewels and riches,
So much t'was hard to believe.
And he gave her gift for gift
For all that he received.

She complimented him lavishly
For all that he had done,
She was very impressed;
Her heart he'd obviously won.

He drew a billion each year
In gold and precious stones,
Temple steps of sandalwood
And a beautiful ivory throne.

All countries paid tribute
Till he was richest of all.
For Solomon heard God's word,
And he answered to the call.

For forty years he reigned,
And died a popular man. Then
His son became their king,
And Israel's troubles began.

CHAPTER 10

Now all Israel came, to
Attend a king's coronation.
They asked better treatment
As standard for the nation.

But he took bad advice from
Peers with whom he'd grown.
Threatened harsher methods
Than any they had known.

All but the tribe of Judah
Deserted the king in anger.

So he sent his man Hadoram,
But he sent him into danger.

He was after forced labor;
It would increase his might.
Hadoram was stoned to death,
And Rehoboam left in fright.

CHAPTER 11

Now he mobilized his armies,
A hundred eighty thousand
Strong. Not a popular king,
He knew this might go wrong.

He wanted to force Israel
To live within his rule.
But God sent word, "Desist,"
And not to play the fool.

He beefed up many cities,
Armed them with shields and
Spears. Still a despot king
Who lived in constant fear.

Of many sons and concubines,
One son he'd groom to rule.
So spread the rest over the
Land to let jealousies cool.

CHAPTER 12

For five years he was popular,
And Rehoboam his power
built.
But he had abandoned the Lord
And would pay for his guilt.

Attacked by king Shishak, the
Egyptians engulfed the nation.
Then Rehoboam met a prophet,
To assess the situation.

Shemaiah told the leaders,
"You have failed your Lord.
You must change your ways;
His wrath you can ill afford."

They admitted their sins and
Cried, "We're a bunch of rats.
God has a right to abandon us,
And that is where we're at."

God regretted His anger, and
Relaxed in spite of their sin.
So they plea bargained and
Took advantage of him.

So, though Shishak conquered
Them, he took mostly treasure.
For God in his great mercy
Reduced the punitive measures.

The kingdom still was strong
In spite of a recent defeat.
For seventeen years he ruled,
From God did a steady retreat.

He was an evil king who
Never really honored his job,
Worshipped idols and things,
And denigrated the living God.

In Jerusalem he was buried
When he'd finally done his
Thing. So then his son Abijah
Became the reigning king.

CHAPTER 13

Now the new King of Judah
  was
Quite strong upon the throne.
And he found a way to make
His enemies feel alone.

When Israel's King attacked,
He hurled insults and taunts;
Until for nerve and valor
Jeroboam was in want.

So of Israel's mighty legions,
Many fell in battle that day.

For the rest of Jeroboam's
Life, he never got his way.

Young King Abijah, of Judah,
Waxed stronger throughout his
Life. He sired many sons and
Daughters by his many wives.

CHAPTER 14

Ten years Judah was peaceful
As King Asa called the shots.
For he was Abijah's son, who
Followed his father's plot.

He wrecked the heathen idols
And the altars upon the hills.
Peace of God was upon Judah,
So made it practical to build.

He walled the cities of Judah
With towers and guarded gates.
With the energy of peacetime,
Advanced at a successful rate.

Now General Zerah of Ethiopia
Charged with a million men.
King Asa cried for God's help,
For he really needed it then.

The Lord defeated the enemy
And the Ethiopian army fled.
Decimated to the last man
By the army Asa led.

Judah collected much plunder
And attacked the cities about.
All the natives were fearful
Resulting in a total route.

CHAPTER 15

Asa returned from battle and
Asariah the spirit possessed.
He hurried to meet the king
To advise him of the best.

Saying, "God has been here;
He has treated us all well.
In whatever we have done
He has always been our help.

When in distress you searched,
It was He who came to you.
And if you stay with Him, He
Will always see you through.

Israel doesn't follow God,
As Judah and Benjamin have.
They've had no peace while
Worshipping golden calves.

No one can fight our Lord,
Neither nation or man, for
Problems will grow every-
Where and on every hand.

For if you honor God, use
Good will and courage; He
Will carry the burden, and
You'll not be discouraged."

Asa rose to the challenge,
Destroyed ungodly things.
People celebrated joyfully,
Worshipped God and King.

Thirty-five years of peace,
Asa led Judah and Benjamin
Clans. Brought much to the
Temple, lived well for God
And man.

CHAPTER 16

But next year he slipped
Baasha of Israel attacked.
He asked Syria for help;
Faith he suddenly lacked.

"Why not ask God for help?"
Hanani a prophet asked,

Put man ahead of Him, and
By Him now you'll be last.

So Asa was angry and had
Hanani thrown in jail. The
Remainder of Asa's reign
Is truly a sorry tale.

At forty one years he died
By disease and things galore.
The Annals of Benjamin and
Judah tell a whole lot more.

CHAPTER 17

Now Asa's son Jehoshaphat
Was pious and sincere. In
His father's footsteps he
Walked and devoutly feared.

His people paid their taxes;
His wealth began to build,
Knocked down heathen altars
That were in the hills.

He educated his people with
The help of many priests;
Using the law of the Lord,
They went about to teach.

Former enemies feared him
And had no thought to fight.
They paid annual tribute,
So really treated him right.

CHAPTER 18

Jehoshaphat's son now married
Ahab's daughter in Israel.
Marriage between these two
Should seal the borders well.

So in time he visited there
And King Ahab threw a party.
Asked he be an ally in war,
He accepted hale and hearty.

"I'd say yes," he said,
"If it's what God's wish is."
Ahab called his priests;
Jehoshaphat doubted this,

They said war would be won
With no dissenting priest.
He wanted to hear a man of
God, not so sure of these.

So Ahab admitted now, there
Was one he didn't like; he
Often prophesied against,
As if Ahab's plans to spike.

Finally he called Micaiah,
Who was God's chosen man.
Word he gave was negative
So Ahab was angry again.

He ordered Micaiah jailed;
The priest was hauled away.
His prediction, sure death,
If Ahab fought that day.

So those kings went to war;
Ahab died in the fight. So
Once again the word of
The Lord was proven right.

CHAPTER 19

Jehoshaphat came, from Israel
To a new prophets greetings.
Jehu chastened him severely
For his Israeli meeting.

So Jehoshaphat stayed home
And looked after his land.
He did his very best, for
He was a God-fearing man.

He went among his people
As a teacher of God's way,
Appointed judges as leaders,
Would allow no foul play.

"You're appointed by God,"
He said, "So keep your head
Up high. Avoid partiality or
Dishonesty, take no bribes.

Defend all innocent people,
Do God's work on earth. Of
Injustice, crime and misery,
There is never a dearth."

CHAPTER 20

As time went on it happened
All his enemies converged.
When impending attack was
Sure, total fear emerged.

With legions of warriors
Charging at them that day.
Jehoshaphat called on God,
With all sincerity prayed.

He asked, "Lord of heaven,
Help, we face problems
Sore. We're looking to you
And asking aid once more.

You gave this land to us,
Will it be taken away? You
Are our great help in need,
Please hear us we pray."

From all across the nation
People were gathered there.
I doubt if any other time
Were so many in prayer.

Jahaziel, a Levite, im-
bued by the Spirit of God, said,
"Be calm, have faith,
For you've no need to sob.

This battle God will wage,
Trust Him and be sincere.
He will decimate the enemy;
You've not a thing to fear.

Armies of Amon and Moab,
And those of Mt Seir, set-
tled old scores out of
Distrust and fear.

So God won Judah's battle;
It was a great slaughter. He
Hadn't needed any help
As they fought each other.

Judah had only to plunder;
By God they'd been blessed.
He was obviously with them;
They'd survived the stress.

He'd loved the Lord always,
But very late in life, he
Allied with sinners, and
His projects met strife.

With Israel's King Ahaziah,
For Tarshish his ships set
Sail. God smiled not, then,
And the venture failed.

CHAPTER 21

Before Jehoshaphat died,
He made son Jehoram king.
But Jehoram was evil; he
Thought of only one thing.

For great power he lusted
And no consience he had.
He killed all his brothers
And did every thing bad.

Most of their rulers died
As his brothers had done.
Thus he wrested power from
Practically every one.

In the hills he built idols,
His people, forced to bow.
If not for David's covenant,
God would destroy them now.

Then Edom revolted,
And Libnah joined in.
He almost subdued them but
They're still free of him.

Then Elijah the prophet
Was shocked at his ways,
Said to clean up his act
For he'd numbered his days.

"Your nation and people
To you will be lost with
Your children and wives
All at very high cost.

The Philistines and Arabs,
Who lived next to Ethiopia,
Struck across the borders
And cured his myopia.

They stole his treasures
And carried families away.
Only Jehoahaz his youngest
Son got away that day.

Then as Elijah had warned
He was struck by disease.
He died in great pain, for
The Lord he'd displeased.

So at forty years of age
He died totally unmourned.
For in the side of God he
Had been a prickly thorn.

CHAPTER 22

Ahazia, the new king, was
Evil and vile like his dad.
With advice from Ahab's fam-
ily, he could only be bad.

He allied with King Jehoram
Who over Israel then ruled.
And if he sought fame, he
Most certainly was fooled.

Jehu, son of Nimshi, whom
By the Lord had been led,
Found him hiding in Samar-
ia, and soon he was dead.

For Jehu had been given the
Job, to clean up the place,
And as for serving God,
Ahazia had been a disgrace.

Burial was with pomp, for
Jehoshaphat had been
King. Joash, Ahaziah's son,
Survived and followed him.

Rescued by Jehoshabeath, an
Aunt, and wife of a priest
From Athalia his grandmother
Who was greedy as a beast.

Six years Joash was hidden
In the Temple, out of sight,
By his nurse, aunt and uncle
Who were trying to do right.

CHAPTER 23

For seven years of tyranny
Queen Athalia reigned, she
Who by murder and treachery
Controling power had gained.

Then Jehoiada, the priest,
Got his act together.
He knew if he didn't
It wouldn't get any better.

Secretly he called Levites
And leaders of the land.
They circulated to organize
Then carried out their plan.

Some priests and Levites,
Coming off shifts that day,
Instead of going home, at
The lower gate now stayed.

So three groups of leaders
On that Sabbath to arrive,
With officers, spears and
Shields formed on all sides.

Now brought the little pri-
nce, a crown upon his head.
And all the people cheered,
Declared him king instead

Of Athaliah the queen, who
Was suddenly alarmed, for
She was being replaced by
The small boy she'd harmed.

She was forcibly removed
And sentenced to death.
In spite of her status
You can guess at the rest.

Then Jehoiada made a pact
They all meant to keep;
They'd all be the Lord's,
His blessings to reap.

They wrecked baal's temple,
And killed his high priest,
Gloried in their fortune,
From greatest to the least.

They took the Boy King and
Placed him on the throne.
Rejoiced in a quiet city,
For it was all their own.

CHAPTER 24

At seven years of age
Young Joash became King.
So he tried to please God
In work and everything.

Jehoiada chose his wife so
He had daughters and sons.
He also ruled Benjamin and
Judah as it should be run.

He'd build on the Temple
And he would not relax.
He called on the leaders
And then levied a tax.

The people came from near,
And they came from far,
At rebuilding the Temple,
Jehoiada was the star.

He coaxed and goaded
Made sure it got done.
One of the finest men
Living under the sun.

He lived a long life,
Righteous and fine, One
Hundred thirty years;
That's a long time.

After Jehoiada's death,
King Joash did slip. He
Listened to his leaders
And became a real drip.

He failed to worship
The God of his fathers;
Went chasing after idols
And listened to others.

God sent his prophets to
Bring them to the fold.
But they wouldn't listen
To what they were told.

Zechariah then said,
"God you've forsaken.
He's tired of your sin
You had better awaken.

So the leaders plotted
For Zechariah's death,
But the order came
From the king instead.

So this was the way
Jehoiada was paid back.
For his son was executed
By this dastardly act.

Then Syria attacked,
And Judah was over run.
The leaders were killed
As the country succumbed.

The king badly wounded,
Lay sick on his bed, and
Some of his officials
Made sure he was dead.

Joash was gone, and his
Son Amaziah became king.
Now the rule over Judah
Would have a new ring.

CHAPTER 25

Twenty-nine years in Jer-
usalem Amaziah reigned,
And to do what was right
Was his major aim.

Did in his dad's killers,
Let their families live,
For Moses' law requires
Each to pay for his sin.

He organized his army,
Hired Israeli mercenaries,
But God sent his prophet;
This message he carried.

"Israel is on my list, so
They must not fight for
You. They'll lose the
Battles; you will too."

So he sent them home,
Unhappy at rejection, but
Led his army out against
The Lord's objections.

To Salt Valley they went,
Slew twenty thousand of Seir.
The Israelites, still angry,
On rampage to Judah steered.

Three thousand they killed,
And much booty they grabbed.
Amaziah angered God by wor-
shipping idols brought back.

God's prophet warned him of
This dangerous road. But Ama-
ziah was angry; this only
Served as a goad.

He declared war on Israel,
King Joash tried to reason,
Amaziah would self-destruct,
Good sense was out of season.

So his army was defeated,
And prisoner he was taken.
His luck all ran out, when
By the Lord he was forsaken.

They breached Israel's walls
And much booty Joash took.
There is more about Amaziah,
It's all written in the book.

In the Annals of the Kings,
It tells of his turning away,
How he fled from his people,
Of how by them he was slain.

To Lachish they followed,
And killed him there. Burial
In the Royal cemetery was
The only honor they spared.

CHAPTER 26

His son Uzziah was sixteen;
Fifty-two years he reigned.
As long as he followed God,
In fame and power he gained.

He fortified Jerusalem's gates,
And parts of the city walls.
He gloried in his wealth
And took credit for it all.

He fought the Philistines
And captured the city of Gath.
Was often blessed by the Lord,
And also earned His wrath.

Entered the Lord's sanctuary,
Refused to leave when told,
Suddenly infected by Leprosy
He no longer felt so bold.

He was banished by his people,
Lived in isolation. Though
Son Jotham became Vice
   Regent,
It must be small consolation.

At death was buried Royally,
And Jotham became the King,
As must have happened often
And was a common thing.

CHAPTER 27

Jotham reigned sixteen years,
In most things he did well.
He managed God's
   requirements,
But his people's morality fell.

His people became corrupt,
He built cities in the hills.
Built fortresses and towers
And strove to do God's will.

He was successful in his wars;
Three years the Amonites paid
Tribute of silver, wheat and
Barley, his armies to allay.

Now in the Annals of Kings of
Israel and Judah we're told,

Of Jotham and other kings
In those golden days of old.

CHAPTER 28

He was twenty years of age,
When he began to reign. Six-
teen years he ruled, and his
Son Ahaz, a new king became.

He left a legacy of evil
And worshipped the idol Baal.
He sacrificed his children,
As the job of king he failed.

He lost the war to Syria; his
Warriors fell like flies. His
Son and some close officers
At Israel's hand also died.

Women and children were capt-
ured; but finally returned.
The enemy feared God's wrath;
He knew they might get
    burned.

The King of Assyria arrived;
He'd come to Judah's aid. But
Judah became a liability,
From mistakes King Ahaz
    made.

If things weren't already bad
He nailed up the Temple doors.
Forced on all heathen Gods,
And again insulted the Lord.

In Jerusalem he was buried
When he finally died. Then it
Was his son Hezekiah's chance
To make an honest try.

CHAPTER 29

Hezekiah was a good king, who
Started the job out right. He

Restored the Temple and furn-
ishings--rose in God's sight.

Organized priests and Levites,
Returned Judah to the Lord,
They sang and sacrificed, re-
newing love of God's word.

People came from far and near;
Across the land they trekked.
Renewed the old religion the
Wicked kings tried to wreck.

CHAPTER 30

The passover celebration had
Been a thing of the past. But
Hezekiah was determined to
Bring those good days back.

Across the land he sent them
As they passed the word along.
The news was widely acclaimed
With pleasure and with song.

Seven days more they noted
This grandest of occasions,
The finest thing to happen
Since Solomon ran the nation.

They confessed and sacrificed,
Sent prayers toward heaven,
So God would hear their pleas
And sins would be forgiven.

CHAPTER 31

In the days to come they tore
Down all obelisks and idols,
Shame images and worship
    centers,
Things of heathen title.

Hezekiah the King organized
The Levites and priests.

So now each one had his job,
To the very last of these.

Now all would tithe and
Burnt offerings would make;
Of all increase offer of new
Wine, and grain and grapes.

They gave so willingly; there
Was extra of everything. For
They were much happier than
They'd been under many kings.

Great surpluses were divided
Among young and old alike.
There was plenty for everyone
Including priests and Levites.

So the rewards of labor
Were divided fairly to all.
For Hezekiah was a noble King
Who heeded Jehovah's call.

CHAPTER 32

From Assyria came Senacherub
Who boasted battles and wars,
Would put Judah to tribute,
And probably even take more.

Hezekiah did not cringe; he
Beefed up and built double
Walls. Sennacherub boasted
Loudly to scare them all.

He tried to scare the army
On the plains before the city.
He made threats and did his
Best to sound wise and witty.

The King and Isaiah a prophet,
Unto God, for help then cried.
God leaned hard on the enemy,
So many men and officers died.

King Hezekiah prospered
In every thing he did.
He was greatly honored
Until his ego made its bid.

God turned against him but
He humbled himself in time.
So the Lord did not bear down
Or cause him any strife.

For he'd been seriously ill,
And God had heard his prayer.
But when he was well again,
He gave little credit there.

From Babylon came emissaries
To hear of his miracle cure.
So the Lord let him explain;
Of his answer I'm not sure.

Most stories of Hezekiah,
Of wealth and praises sing.
When he was buried with
   honor
His son Manasseh became king.

CHAPTER 33

Fifty-five years he ruled,
From when he was twelve.
He un-did his father's work
And cast an evil spell.

He erected heathen idols
And made obeisance to Baal.
Much of what his father did
Became of no avail.

On and on it went, as
He sinned more and more. The
Lord's warnings didn't reach
Him or were just ignored.

So God sent the Assyrian army,
And by chains he was bound.

They carried him to Babylon
Where he finally ran aground.

At last common sense emerged,
And he knew the Lord was
  God.
He meekly asked forgiveness,
Repented, cried, and sobbed.

The Lord listened to him
And finally sent him home.
We know not how long it took
To penetrate his dome.

But he changed his ways for
He rebuilt all he'd destroyed.
And Judah's future glowed;
Now it's hopes were buoyed.

When Manasseh died, he was
Buried 'neath a palace floor;
His son Amon became king,
But the job he did was poor.

For two years he lasted, but
His sins increased each day,
Till his officers rebelled,
And with his life he paid.

Some citizens eliminated them
Because of this awful thing,
Then made Josiah, his son,
Their next and honored king.

CHAPTER 34

Things looked up in Judah as
Eight year old Josiah reined.
At twenty he cleaned house,
Eliminating erstwhile shame.

The obelisks he chopped down,
The heathen altars destroyed.
Across Israel they marched,
As troops of change deployed.

He built up the Temple, as
People brought in their gifts.
He undid the damage of those
Other kings who'd slipped.

Hilkiah the high priest, as
He accounted for the tithes,
Found a book God had given
Moses, and he was most wise,

For he sent it to the king.
It was read to Josiah there,
Who, hearing what it said,
Tore his clothes in despair.

God promised destruction
If Israel deserted his way.
Josiah knew they'd slipped;
The situation was grave.

He ordered them to pray
God to forgive their sins,
Called Hulda, the prophe-
tess, so she said to him,

"Israel's past is spotted,
Before the Lord, we've run.
He'll destroy this nation
But He's not yet begun.

If you do your very best
And follow His every law,
Until after your death,
His anger He will thaw."

The rest of Josiah's life
He now heeded God's will,
Led the people of Judah,
The law he did fulfill.

CHAPTER 35

With greater zest now
Josiah assigned the tasks,
To Levites and priests,
And no one ever asked--

"Why must we try so hard
To do this thing just so?"
For everyone was willing,
All minds and hearts aglow.

A passover feast in April,
As in days of yore, was
All completed in a day, as
When Moses called score.

For seven days thereafter,
Unleavened bread they ate.
This was the finest program
They'd ever had to date.

Now Neco, King of Egypt,
With Assyria went to war.
Josiah joined the battle,
King Neco asked, "What for?

God is with me," he said,
"Your help I do not need."
Josiah was strongheaded,
Good advice he'd not heed.

By archers he was wounded,
And death rang its knell.
He'd have lived longer
If he had listened well.

Many a heart did sorrow; as
A great king they mourned,
His good deeds were legend;
Many friends he'd formed.

CHAPTER 36

So Josiah's son Jehoahaz
Became ruler of Judah next.
For three months he lasted,
By Egypt's King was hexed.

Carried away a prisoner, a
Quarter million demanded,
Brother Jehoiachim, now
King, was heavyhanded.

For eleven years he ruled,
It was an evil reign. His
Brother was taken to Baby-
lon, to prison in chains.

Golden bowls and many things
Were from the Temple taken.
In general the Jewish people
By Jehovah were forsaken.

Jehoiakin, son of Jehoiakim,
Became the king of might.
And he did very little that
Was good in Jehovah's sight.

So he was summoned to
   Babylon,
As per Nebuchadnezzar's will.
Jehoiakin was deposed, his
Brother called, a job to fill.

Now the people of Judah, inc-
luding many high priests, had
Forsaken their father's God
And no longer kept his feasts.

He sent prophets among them,
To make them change some
   ways.
But the King of Babylon intr-
uded making sorrowful days.

The Temple was demolished; it
Became a pile of junk. What
Was left was burned, and
God's hopes for Judah sunk.

Seventy years Judah slipped;
People were evil inclined.
But then King Syrus of Persia
Put them back on line.

For he had conquered Babylon,
And the earth was his to rule.

He wished to set things right
Let the nations' tempers cool.

So all who followed God, he
Set free and homeward bound
To go rebuild the Temple, in
Their beloved Jerusalem town.

The prediction of Jeremiah,
That prophet of olden days,
Had truly shown the people
That God would have his way.

END OF SECOND CHRONICALS

EZRA

CHAPTER 1

Now all the Jews in Persia
Heard a welcome declaration.
King Syrus gave them leave
To go rebuild their nation.

Seventy years it was, since
The land had been laid waste,
And many had never expected
To actually see this day.

But the king gave many gifts,
Required the same of Jews,
Who wished to remain behind
And this way pay their dues.

Those who craved their land
Could take the gifts and go
Rebuild Jerusalem's Temple,
For God had willed it so.

CHAPTER 2

From all the Persian cities
And all across the land
Came many Jewish people
From all the different clans.

Now it had been so long ago
Some genealogies were lost.

To claim priestly status now
Could be at very high cost.

For they were not allowed
The rations given to these,
Until proving their estate,
Or if God closed the breach.

Over forty-five hundred Jews
Returned to ancestral homes,
A half million dollar value,
Animals, gifts and robes.

To Jerusalem many returned
And other cities of the land.
This would always be home
And a future they could plan.

CHAPTER 3

They returned to Jerusalem
In September that year; they
Sacrificed burnt offerings
For attack could be near.

Some priests rebuilt altars
In place as they were before.
They celebrated and feasted,
And worshipped the Lord.

Rebuilding started; masons
And carpenters were hired.
Then cedar logs and lumber
Came from Sidon and Tyre.

Food, wine or olive oil was
Paid for supplies; Their
Own priests and Levites
Were those who supervised.

The building progressed
Amid singing and shouts.
Many celebrated joyfully;
Much noise was all about.

CHAPTER 4

Foreigners had settled their
Land while they were away.
So they were now the enemy,
Who had much to say.

They sent letters to Syrus,
Or some who sat the throne,
To cause trouble for those
Who'd come back home.

King Ar-ta-xerxes, who
Over Persia then ruled,
Got a convincing letter
And he became their tool.

So Temple work stopped,
And that was how it stayed.
Until Darius ruled Persia
The second year he reigned.

CHAPTER 5

Those prophets of Jehovah
Encouraged them to build.
Men of God were anxious
That they fulfill His will.

In spite of meddlers, the
Work progressed. They met

Hecklers now with authority;
The work of God was blessed.

They asked a record search
To see if there'd ever been
A decree by King Syrus to
Let the people build again.

CHAPTER 6

King Darius issued orders
To check the record books.
Sure enough they found it;
A search was all it took.

King Darius answered them,
"Don't interfere with those
Jews; they're doing the job
That they were told to do.

You will pay the bills for
The Temple building there.
Pay it out of taxes that are
Normally my share.

Give them bulls and rams
And everything they need,
So they can do the work with
Greater skill and speed.

This order you'll follow so
For my sons and me they'll
Pray. This is an order, so
See that it's obeyed.

Give them trouble, and I'll
Tear your houses down. With
The lumber I'll build a gal-
lows and hang you clowns.

So those characters complied
And heeded the king's
  command.
The Temple was later finished
As joy washed over the land.

Once again the passover feast
Was in the spring of the year,
A week of unleavened bread,
In a spirit of joy and cheer.

The King of Assyria helped
In the building those days.
For God in heaven interceded,
So that he changed his ways.

CHAPTER 7

If Ezra's ancestry is traced
It is quite easy to see;
His genealogy went back all
The way to Aaron, the priest.

He knew the law of the Lord,
Was a man all could trust. So
As he'd asked about returning
To King Cyrus, it seemed just.

For Ezra was a priest and
A student of God's command.
He was prime material to lead
His people back to their land.

CHAPTER 8

As they assembled to travel,
No Levite showed his face. So
Ezra sent for their leaders
Before he'd leave the place.

They found not only Levites
But Temple assistants as well;
And then they started back
All the way to Israel.

He never asked for soldiers;
God would keep them safe.
And now to show timidity
He surely would lose face.

Now as Ezra had forecast,
God travelled in their midst.

Though carrying much wealth,
They never lost a bit.

No attack or theft occurred,
And now when they returned,
In joy they'd rebuild the Te-
mple for which they yearned.

CHAPTER 9

This was the cry of Ezra, as
Before the Temple he prayed.
He sought the help of God
That a nation might be saved.

"Some of our men have married
Into the nations of long ago
The very thing you warned,
Would bring our nation low.

The heathen ways are winning
As pollution affects the race.
And I am greatly embarrassed
Your awful wrath to face.

Oh Lord, how can we face you
After doing such things? You
Showed us loving kindness,
Friendship of Assyrian Kings.

Our history is full of sin;
We've even flaunted your laws.
If you meted out Justice
None would favor our cause."

CHAPTER 10

Then as he wept and prayed,
Many people joined him there.
A man called Shecaniah spoke,
Those sinners really cared.

He'd give up foreign wives,
Send them and children away.
For they agreed to do what-
ever the leaders should say.

So Ezra went into the Temple
After Shecaniah made it clear;
They all would meet the need
To eliminate problems here.

December the fifth they came,
Trembling with fear and pain.
Not only afraid of punishment,
They stood in cold wet rain.

They agreed to follow rules.
Many a man that day must've
Suffered like the damned to
Send wives and babies away.

END OF EZRA

NEHEMIAH

CHAPTER 1

This is the autobiography of
Jehovah's servant Nehemiah,
Another Jew in Persia
And the son of Hecaliah.

As cupbearer to Ar-ta-xerxes,
One of Persia's great kings.
I asked about my country men.
The answer, an ominous ring.

Jerusalem's walls are down,
The gates there were burned.
Then my heart was heavy
   laden;
My thoughts within me
   churned.

So I prayed to Great Jehovah
To hear the prayers of we few
Who attended unto God
And in our hearts were true.

CHAPTER 2

Now four months later, as
I served the King his wine,
He noticed I was silent
And soberly inclined.

He asked me what was wrong,
Why I was so sad of face.
Now in my heart I trembled
As I answered to his grace.

"In the country of my people,
In Jerusalem, that city fair,
Everything is a shambles,
And I wish that I were there.

I would rebuild the city,
Lead my countrymen to God.
The condition of my home
Land makes me want to sob."

In amazement did I hear,
As the King answered me,
"So will you be long?" As
He sat beside his queen.

Letters of authority he
Gave me; I was on my way;
So in a time of trouble,
David's city I'd save.

And in time I did arrive
But found some there who
Would block my progress,
So to me would be a snare.

First I checked in secret,
But then I told them all
I had heard God's wish; I
Came to rebuild the wall.

They all got excited and
Were anxious to commence.
Enemies were against me,
But God was my defense.

CHAPTER 3

High priests and others
Started the work along,
Aided by groups of fami-
lies, a veritable throng.

Gate to gate they built,
Corner to tower, and on.
Priests, mayors, workers,
Others led the throngs.

CHAPTER 4

Sanballot was very angry
We were rebuilding the wall.
He and his army officers,
We, by names were called.

They'd like to fall on us,
To wipe us from the earth,
Our work, we felt import-
ant and was of great worth.

I asked God, "Repay our enem-
ies as they richly deserve."
For half our men stood guard
As others worked and served.

By each man stood weapons;
Everyone was ready to fight.
Each family was prepared for
War morning, noon or night.

From the rising of the sun
To the end of light of day,

Every man with weapons near
Worked and guarded time
   away.

Dressed and ready for battle,
We slept all clothed in bed.
To fail in preparedness we
Might suddenly end up dead.

CHAPTER 5

Some of our Jews were rich
Wishing to be richer still.
So loaned money to the poor
And urged they pay the bill.

Soon they mortgaged homes;
Children into slavery sold.
But creditors hounded them,
So they felt tired and old.

"We're not foreigners; our
Children are like theirs."
Cried the poor in distress,
"We're about to despair."

Now I was very angry when I
Heard these plaintive cries.
I called them all together
And took them down to size.

"Why charge a brother?" I
Asked, "and call it a help-
ing hand? You are really
Robbing your fellow man."

So they agreed to help the
Poor, return usurous gains.
Make loans with no interest,
And drop all usury claims.

Now I called on the priests
To make them keep their word.
I added a curse for failure;
They'd get it from the Lord.

Twelve years I was governor
With no salary from people.
Government self supporting,
But costs were unbelievable.

Many ate at my table plus
Visitors from far away. I
Never levied a special tax,
But to my God did pray.

"Oh Lord, I've done my best
To treat your people right.
Please keep me in your heart
And spare me, in your might."

CHAPTER 6

Now when our enemies
   realized
That our wall was nearly done,
They used all their power
To make me cut and run.

Vainly they wrote letters
To call me out upon the plain.
I knew within myself 'twas
My death they hoped to gain.

With threats and lies galore
They gave me such a time;
Dirty tricks they engineered
Were nothing short of crime.

Four times they sent notes,
And each time I made reply.
I knew within their clutches
That I would surely die.

Now to God I prayed, they
Would get their just reward.
For I was in His service;
I was working for the Lord.

They tried to run me into the
Temple, but there, I'd not

Flee. I knew the law of Judah,
And I was not a priest.

In fifty-two days we finished,
The work was then all done.
With all the lies and threats,
It had been a trying run.

CHAPTER 7

After the wall was finished,
We hung doors in the gates,
Named gatekeepers, Levites,
Singers, all were in place.

I gave Jerusalem's rule over
To Hanani my brother to do.
He commanded the fortress
Was also of the same school.

I instructed them with care,
Also the guards at the gates,
Lock up early in evening,
Keep them next day till late.

Each must guard his section
And would care for his share.
To do the job with precision,
A time for each to be there.

These are some people who
Came with us from Babylon;
Clans, sub-clans, individuals.
The list goes on and on:

Some descendants of Solomon,
Officers and officials too.
Over fifty thousand in all
And to their homeland true.

Horses, camels, mules, donk-
eys, all were brought along.
They gave gifts and wealth
With hearts full of song.

Now the people went back to
Towns from which they'd come.

But in fall they returned
During the passover month.

CHAPTER 8

In mid September we rallied,
God's law Ezra read, from
Scrolls Jehovah gave Moses,
And explained what it said.

People all began sobbing as
They understood the law. We
Encouraged them to happiness;
It was a good time for all.

So in joyful celebration,
They ate the festival meal.
Ezra and the Levites studied
The scrolls in great detail.

Of olive and myrtle branches,
Of fig and palm trees too,
We built huts where possible
To live that week through.

Ezra finished reading as
We feasted there,
Quietly closed the ceremony,
Just as Moses had declared.

CHAPTER 9

During the month of October
Once again we held a meet.
And to Israeli people, the
Laws of God did read.

For hours we confessed our
Sins, worshipping with song.
For he is our Lord forever,
We've known it all along.

He is greater by far
Than we can think or say.
So love the Lord our God,
Stand up, give Him praise.

Then Ezra prayed. "Oh God,
Maker of heaven and earth.
Of deserts and seas, with-
Out you, we have no worth.

Forever you have been God;
We'll always belong to you.
You've kept your promises;
Your word has been true.

Father Abraham you chose,
To give all this land. You
Led our people over a sea,
When only a fleeing band.

You came down the mountain
And gave them your command.
Led them to this country
Helped them make a stand.

Food you sent from heaven,
They drank out of the rock.
Yet when they rebelled,
Your love never stopped.

Forty years you led them
Through wilderness there.
Their feet did never swell;
Their clothes did not wear.

Often they've complained
And went their stupid way.
You always took them back,
To learn another day.

Now again we are in trouble,
And in prayer we come to you.
For we reap the wages of sin,
And there is much to do.

We are slaves in Caanan,
That land you've let us share.
We pay tribute to other kings,
But your punishment is fair.

So now we sign this covenant;
We promise to serve you again.

We princes, priests, and
Levites, and I too say, "Amen."

CHAPTER 10

So then I signed the document,
And many another signed too.
We signed for our nation;
Our covenant was thus
    renewed.

We'd follow His
    commandments!
In marriage, foreigners not
Take, heeding His law to the
Letter to avoid any mistakes.

We'd not deal on Holy days
Or do work in a seventh year,
Forgiving all Jewish debts,
And pay Temple tax with cheer.

The Temple we would
    maintain,
The bread of the presence too.
The atonement of Israel was
Our most important work to do.

We tossed a coin to determine
A time of year 'twas right, to
Supply wood for the altar
By every grown-up Israelite.

The first of each increase
Was the Temples, whatever it
Be, of herds or crops or such,
Or from our olive trees.

Every eldest son was given
To serve the Lord for life.
In sacred containers they
Gave the best of crop or wine.

We all maintained the Temple
Just as the Lord decreed. And

Everyone shared the burden
The way we'd all agreed.

CHAPTER 11

All the officials of Israel
Lived in Jerusalem those days.
One of ten living elsewhere
Were to come there to stay.

Some were chosen by lot, and
Others were volunteers, but
Solomon's servants' people,
Lived as they had for years.

Many leaders and priests,
Levites, gate keepers and
Such, moved to Jerusalem, so
They'd be readily in touch.

Some Levites living in Judah
To the tribe of Benjamin went.
This may have been permanent,
Perhaps they were only lent.

CHAPTER 12

Priests aided Zerubabble.
Many a Levite went to help
With leaders of many clans,
Clansmen of theirs as well.

A family record was made, as
King Darin of Persia reigned.
In Chronicles many are shown,
And in other books again.

Priests and others were act-
ive; Ezra taught in the place,
When I governed in Jerusalem
By His willingness and grace.

While dedicating a new wall
Leaders came from far and
Near. We paraded upon it and
Sang, wonderful sound to hear.

The people and events we
Organized as told in Moses'
Law. And celebrated with
  many
Happy songs, as fine a thanks-
giving as one ever saw.

CHAPTER 13

In the midst of celebration,
Moses we read, Amonites and
Moabites were forbidden to
Worship, so did as it said.

Always at odds with Israel,
They cursed us as well.
So when the reading was done,
'Twas decreed all foreigners
Be expelled.

Another threat to the Temple,
Caused by Eliashib, a priest.
Changed use of a store room
Without a lawful release.

I had been in Babylon, but
On my return cleaned house.
Levites portions were shorted;
They'd been almost pushed out.

I changed the status at once
Got things as they should be.

"God remember I was
  righteous,
Please send blessings on me."

They'd desecrated the Sabbath,
Those who peddled their wares.
I closed the gates on Friday
So they quit coming there.

I closed them Friday eve;
A guard was put on each one.
"Oh God please remember the
Good things I have done."

Some Jews married foreigners,
Children in Jewish couldn't
Speak. I argued, and cajoled
And threatened bones to break.

King Solomon's downfall was
By women of other lands. They
Will steadily contaminate
And cause the collapse of man.

I purged all our foreigners,
Again did things as should be,
"Remember, Lord, I'm your
  man;
In your kindness, remember
  me."

END OF NEHEMIAH

ESTHER

CHAPTER 1

Three years Ahaseurus reigned;
His kingdom was vast indeed,
A hundred twenty seven prov-
inces of Persians and Medes.

Six months he celebrated,
To show his glory and wealth,
And an orgy for his servants,
I'd also bet for himself.

On the last day of the party
He wished to parade his queen.
He ordered her to appear; she
Must have felt demeaned.

She didn't answer his summons,
A great shock to his pride!
He called advisers and aids,
To quickly come to his side.

What penalty did law allow,
For queens who failed to obey?
Should he ignore her rebuff
And let her have her own way?

"Ignore impunity," they said,
"And set a precedent for all.
No wife will honor a husband;
None will listen to our call.

You should issue an edict of
Law; Queen Vashti shall be
Banished from your highness;
Choose a more worthy queen."

Each province got a letter
Giving home rule to men,
To stop the foolishness, they
Wished this woman's lib to end.

You and I know the difference,
For they will never say die.
One day women will rule earth
As some men wonder why.

CHAPTER 2

After the king's anger cooled
He'd never see Vashti again.
His pride had caused problems;
The edict caused him pain.

His aids thought of a scheme;
Replace Vashti with a beauty
Who would succeed the Queen
And never fail in her duty.

Over the land they challenged
A beauty contest of all time.
So Esther, who was a Jewess,
As a beauty socially climbed.

Now Esther was a young
  orphan,
Whose parents were both dead.

She ended up in the palace,
A short hop to the king's bed.

He was thrilled with Esther,
Who was by beauty endowed.
Her wisdom a thing of great
Pleasure, carriage most proud.

Now Mordecai was her cousin,
Who had raised her as his own.
And she had done his bidding
As in the years she had grown.

He tutored her like a father,
Took pride in her rapid climb.
Nor mentioned being a Jewess
During this exciting time.

Hegai the eunuch, King Ahase-
urus' harem controlled. He
Was quite taken by Esther,
Beauty and talents extolled.

Seven ladies in attendance he
Assigned, and all the finest
Clothes. He gave her lovely
Jewelry from head to toes.

When she was thus presented,
The king stared with delight.
He was happy in her presence,
To him a beautiful sight.

Another big party he threw,
Gifts to every one he gave.
He was the target of murder,
By Esther and cousin saved.

CHAPTER 3

Haman was made prime
  minister,
Now second most powerful
  man,
Authoritative and arrogant,
Next to the king in the land.

Mordecai bowed not in his
Presence as required to do.
So Haman, in a fit of anger
Vowed to eliminate all Jews.

So by a roll of the dice, a
Date for slaughter was chosen.
And Haman talked to the king,
But the word Jew was
  unspoken.

A date was set for slaughter,
To rulers all over the land.
Haman sent official orders
To carry out his deadly plan.

They would wipe out the Jews,
Every man, woman and child.
In Sushan it became known,
Every Jew in town was riled.

CHAPTER 4

Mordecai learned of the plot;
Ashes and sackcloth he wore.
With sorrow other Jews joined,
Their kind would be no more.

Esther heard of his sorrow,
And by servants the cause.
So fully aware of the problem,
She had reason for pause.

Haman was a deadly enemy,
  who
Twenty million offered to pay,
To finance killing the Jews,
If he had his wicked way.

Forced presence on the king
Could cause untimely death.
Mordecai insisted she risk it,
In consideration for the rest.

CHAPTER 5

So Esther took the chance,
Entered the king's inner court.
He held out his scepter in
Welcome as she came forth.

He asked about her problem;
She stalled and led him on.
Inviting him and Haman to a
Banquet, their best to don.

So they hurried to Esther's
As wine was being poured;
The king again inquired
What they were gathered for.

Again she pledged her love
Asked them back next day.
She'd make her wishes known;
Wisely she'd planned her way.

A happy man was Haman! As
  he
Bragged and stalked about.
Invitation by the queen was
Very important without doubt.

Mordecai still failed to bow
As he passed him at the gate.
Again Haman's temper flaired;
In his heart was deadly hate.

But he controlled his temper
And went home to blow.
For he was very important
And wanted every one to know.

Yet told them of his anger
When Mordecai failed to heel.
His wife said, "Build a gall-
ows so your wrath he'll feel."

Haman was pleased with this
Because he foresaw the day,

When Mordecai would hang,
And he'd have had his way.

CHAPTER 6

The king slept fitfully; he
Tossed and turned all night,
So read historical records,
Found things not just right.

Mordecai had saved his life
By disclosing a murder plot.
He had never been rewarded
Or even improved his lot.

Haman wished Mordecai
     hanged
And was on his way coming
Through the outer court
To get the king's okay.

The king asked his opinion
On what he should do for
A man who'd served him well
Had been honest and true.

Haman thought, "Of course,
It is I of whom he speaks.
I'll suggest the very best,
For he'll surely honor me."

He said, "Bring royal robes
The king himself has worn.
Seat him on a royal charger,
As if he to rule was born.

Let a most noble prince go
Before him on the way, say-
ing we remember our heroes
And homage to him pay."

The king was mighty pleased
With Haman's brilliant plan.
Said, "You may do the honors;
Mordecai the Jew is the man."

Haman took the royal robes,
And placed them on that Jew.
Mounted him on the charger,
To parade the city through.

To all along the way he
Shouted out the speech as
He'd told the king, but had
Himself thought to receive.

Then back home he went with
His spirits mighty low. For
After what had happened, he
Had little of which to blow.

Alarmed, his wife received
Word. The plot would fail
She knew. It could be fatal
If Mordecai was a Jew.

Now even as they talked the
King's messengers arrived
To take him to the banquet
Queen Esther had contrived.

CHAPTER 7

Again they were guests of a
Wise and beautiful queen.
Haman would be elsewhere
If he had his future seen.

Again the king asked, "What
Can I possibly do? For you
Have only to ask, a half my
Kingdom I'll give to you."

"If I'm in your favor," she
Said "there is a thing I'd
Like, you to save my people
And also my own life."

"What are you saying?"
The king wanted to know.
"Who would ever harm you
Or treat your people so?"

Esther pointed to Haman,
Pale and sick with fright.
Saying, "He's my peoples
Enemy and not doing right.

If it were only slavery, I
Might not have said a word.
But that would do you harm,
My King, my love, my Lord.

He sentenced us to death;
To slaughter we're to go.
Because he hates one Jew
We'll all be treated so."

Haman pleaded with Esther;
He was terrified of death.
Sickened by the sight,
The king got up and left.

Then as the king returned
In total shock he stared.
Haman was on the couch with
Esther; he had fallen there.

In shock and pain Ahaseurus
Looked, now in anger cried,
"Will he even rape my queen
Right before my eyes?"

A veil was placed upon his
Face, at the gallows built
For Mordecai, so roped and
Tied, right there he died.

CHAPTER 8

King Ahazuerus did that day,
Summon Mordecai to court. He
Gave Esther Haman's estate,
And then got a full report.

Learned of their relationship,
Mordecai, prime minister made.
Esther put Mordecai in charge
Of Haman's erstwhile estate.

Once again Queen Esther came
And knelt before the king.
She'd stopped a plot to end
A most terrible thing.

Again the king did listen
For her argument was strong.
Haman's decree of death to
Jews was definitely wrong.

So Mordecai and Esther sent
Word to all the Jews. It was
Legal now to fight for life,
And this was welcome news.

Through each province of the
Land, word was coursing forth,
From Ethiopia, west and south,
To India far east and north.

So the word did spread, their
Enemies they now could fight.
Many claimed to be Jews, for
They were wracked with fright.

CHAPTER 9

The day when Haman's decree
Would have wiped out all Jews,
They were told to fight back,
So to them this was good news.

Now all rulers of the land
Had to help the Jewish side.
For they really had no choice
But help, or run and hide.

Mordecai was very powerful;
He gained more power still.
So on the day of reckoning
Many of the enemy were killed.

In the city of Shushan, five
Hundred of the enemy fell.
All ten sons of Haman were
Hanged on the gallows as well.

Now at all the Jews had done,
The king was quite surprised,
So asked Queen Esther, "Now
What bargain will you drive?"

So she asked for one more day
The Jews might do their thing,
So the freedom of her people
Might even stronger ring.

Three hundred enemies died as
The balance of power changed,
Seventy-five thousand more,
As fortunes were rearranged.

Now to this very day they
Celebrate that time, when

What might have happened
Could have really been a crime.

CHAPTER 10

Mordecai, leader of the Jews
Was considered of high degree.
King Ahasueras took tribute
From mainlands and the seas.

And so those two did rule
With honor in every way. And
The stories of their doings
Brought glory to that day.

END OF ESTHER

JOB

CHAPTER 1

In the land of Uz lived a man;
He did as God wanted him to.
He owned camels, donkeys,
Sheep, oxen
and servants too.

Each year he gave a party for
Each of seven sons he had. He
Sanctified his children just
On the chance they'd been bad.

He offered up burnt offerings
And blessed them every one.
For he was a family man who
Loved his daughters and sons.

One day the angels came
And appeared before the Lord.
Satan came along with them
To pass his wicked word.

"Where were you?" The Master
Asked. "Patrolling the earth"
He replied. God knew the ans-
wer, and He probably sighed.

Satan never did a thing if to
Others it meant no trouble,
And if they hadn't enough,
He'd surely cause them double.

"Have you seen my servant Job?
He will no evil think or do.
In every thing he does, he is
Loyal through and through."

"I know him well and that he
Is," Satan then replied. "But
I'm sure the only reason is
Because you have him bribed.

Look how you've protected
  him.
You gave him all he owns.

Take away his riches, he'll
Curse you and your throne."

So then the Lord replied, "Do
As you wish with his wealth
But do not take his life or
Seriously impair his health."

So Satan went away, and Job's
Problems then began. A farm
Hand soon reported that he
Was the only remaining man.

For the Sabeans had raided
And driven his cattle away.
They'd killed the farmhands
Out in the fields that day.

Another messenger arrived.
The first one still stood by,
Saying, "Fire swept your pas-
ture; sheep and herdsmen
    died."

"It never rains, but it pours,"
Must have been Job's thought.
Another messenger rushed up,
Saying, he only wasn't caught.

Bands of Chaldeans attacked,
Camels ran off, servants kil-
led. Next word to come most
Men's faith would chill.

"Your children were feasting,"
He said, "at the eldest son's
Home, a mighty desert wind
Swept in, it left me alone.

The roof fell in, and they
All died and I alone am left."
Job arose and tore his robe
As in grief he was bereft.

Upon the ground he knelt, and
This is what he said. "Naked,

Into this world I came. And
With nothing I'll be dead.

The Lord gave it to me,
And he can take it away.
So blessed be the Lord, for
He owns the night and day."

To revile the Lord or sin
Was a thing he wouldn't do.
But Satan couldn't be happy,
So he'd mix another stew.

CHAPTER 2

Once again Satan came, and
God spoke, as before he had.
"Have you noticed my man
    Job?
He still has not gone bad."

Satan said, "Oh sure I have,
But he still has his health.
Touch his body with sickness,
And he'll be first to yelp."

"Do with him as you please,"
God replied, "only spare his
Life." Satan left again to
Brew another batch of strife.

Now Job was suddenly stricken
With boils from head to toe.
But he did what he could
And never cried out in woe.

His wife asked, "Why be so
Good, why not curse God and
Die?" But he'd not give up
As long as he could try.

For he would never expect all
Good and nothing to go wrong.
He trusted God in everything;
That's what kept him strong.

Job had three good friends,
All trusted men and true.
They came to visit him now
To see what they could do.

He was in such a sorry strait,
With pain and boils so bad,
They hardly recognized him;
The meeting was very sad.

Tearing their clothes they
Cried, threw dust on them-
selves, sat beside him all
Week. Sympathy should help.

For seven days and seven
Nights, not a word was said.
Maybe sharing the thought,
'Twere better to be dead.

CHAPTER 3

At last silence was broken,
As Job said what he thought.
The day of birth he cursed,
As for sanity he fought.

"Oh I should have died the
Day I was born. My days
Are full of pain; my nights
Are so forlorn.

In death I'd be at ease,
My pain would be no more.
Death would make us equal,
The sick, the rich or poor.

Why must man be born
If he must suffer so? I
Cannot eat in my misery,
Like water pours my groans.

I most feared what happened,
But I never lay around.
I work from morn to night,
Yet trouble struck me down."

CHAPTER 4

Now Eliphaz, the Temanite,
To Job made reply. "You've
Encouraged others, why
Should you give up and cry?

Others with great trouble
You told to hold fast.
To those who love the Lord,
His mercy will always last.

This truth was given me, as
Though whispered in my ears.
A voice came to me at night
As I shook with fear.

For men, it said, are weak,
And not long for this earth.
This applies to everyone
No matter what his worth.

He goes forth in morning
Strong, and brave and well.
But he may not last the day;
It's a thing none can tell."

CHAPTER 5

"He cries for help in vain,
For no man seems to hear.
If a man turns from God,
He will in time know fear.

He may seem successful;
Things to him come faster.
But it never really pays,
In time he'll see disaster.

To you my friend I recommend,
That you confess your sins.
For God will do great things
If you'll only go to him.

He will save the penitent
From any form of trouble.

And if you'll ask forgiveness,
He'll help you on the double.

So listen to my counsel, for
I've found that it is true.
God will come to your aid but
Will wait to hear from you."

CHAPTER 6

Job's Answer

"You can't weigh my problems;
My troubles are very great.
God's terrors are aimed at
Me; deep sorrow is my fate.

I'd prefer to die right now
Than live this constant pain;
To be free of its horrible
Grip would surely be a gain.

Why does my strength sustain
Me? Can I be patient till I
Die? I am utterly helpless
As unto God I cry!

If friends are all like you,
My enemies need never show.
You've prejudged me already;
How can you treat me so?

I've always been a righteous
Man in all I say or do!
So why should I be judged
Even by a friend like you?"

CHAPTER 7

"A man's life is a struggle;
His trials last days on end.
Time seems to drag slowly
When it takes so long to mend.

My nights are long and weary,
And my days go hopelessly by.

I'm only allotted frustration,
I'm sure I shall soon die.

Oh God am I a monster,
Why must you burden me? For
To dust I'll soon return, and
Then anonymous I shall be."

CHAPTER 8

Bildad Replies

"Job, why do you blow? For
You know that God is just.
If you've read the chronicles,
Then you really have a crust.

Those who are truly good, the
Lord will handsomely reward.
But if you've hidden sin
You cannot expect accord.

Man's days on earth are short;
Those who forget God will die,
Awaking strong in the morning
But at evening can only sigh.

A good man He'll remember
Will not cast him away, Will
Fill your life with laughter,
Your enemies put to shame."

CHAPTER 9

Job Answers

"All you say is true,
I will not argue that.
For God is wise and mighty,
And I know not where I'm at.

A thousand questions He could
Ask, the answers to which I'd
Fail. For He made all that
Is, but I am weak and frail.

His miracles are unbelievable,
He holds earth in his hands,

Can move mountains and seas,
Or change the shape of land.

The great destroyer who can
Multiply wounds without
   cause,
He alone is strong and just,
And this will give me pause.

For I am only a man
With no future on this earth.
And if I complain to God,
It would be of little worth.

If He'd stop testing me,
In terror I'd no longer be.
I could speak without fear,
That's what I really need.

Boldly I would tell him,
I'm His innocent servant,
The only defense I have at
Which I'm really fervent."

CHAPTER 10

"I'm so weary of living in
Pain, in bitter sorrow I'd
Cry, and unto God I'd ask,
Please Lord, tell me why!

Are you as bad as men;
Is life so short and mean?
Life is not worthwhile,
If on you I cannot lean!

Did you make me for sport,
To wreck what you created?
My cries seem weak to me,
My suffering underrated.

It seems every time I gain,
You knock me down again.
But You are God almighty
And I am just mere man.

Oh! let me have a moment
That I may rest with ease,
Before death befalls me,
So sickly life will cease."

CHAPTER 11

Zothar Replies to Job

"If talk were only purity
You'd be as white as snow.
But I will not sit quietly
And listen to you blow.

If God would talk to you
And make you see your self!
For He sees all your sins
And knows you need His help.

You've probably been so bad
He should punish you more.
Why should He reward you?
You don't know the score!

If you'd get right with God
And approach without fear.
It'd be like morning, and
You'd always feel Him near.

Hope and courage you'd have,
Time to catch your breath.
The wicked shall not escape,
Their only hope is death."

CHAPTER 12

Job's Reply

"Yes, I'm very sure there's
Nothing you don't know!
And on the day you die
All wisdom will surely go.

There's a possible chance
That there's a thing or two
Of which I am aware
And should explain to you!

You are no better than I,
No matter what you say.
Yes, I asked for His help,
And he gave it every day.

But now I'm just a joke, my
Neighbors laugh at me.
Many scoff at righteousness,
Yet they go scot free.

I know His ways are strange,
And all men are His slaves.
When He closes in on a man,
Then no one can escape.

Now men my age are wise;
Many things we understand.
But God has greater wisdom
Than any living man.

Wise men are as fools
Wherever he is concerned.
He overthrows the mighty if
His anger they have earned.

He will raise up a nation
And of good men rulers make.
Then reduce them to nothing
If selves they overrate."

CHAPTER 13

"To show greatest wisdom,
Silent you should be. But
I'm not totally stupid, so
Please now listen to me.

I would speak with God; you
Put words in his mouth. If
You think you can fool Him,
You are being stupid now.

Only two things I would ask
When I speak to Him.
I'd be terrified by either,
If He'd point out my sin.

Oh Lord, do not abandon me,
Or too close to me approach,
As by your awesome presence
You become my coach.

I am helpless and adrift
Like a leaf upon the wind.
I clutch at useless straws
And am terrorized within."

CHAPTER 14

"How frail is man, oh Lord,
And how few his days! He's
Often stalked by trouble
In so many ways.

He blossoms like the flower,
Then withers and he dies.
Like the shadow of a cloud
His presence swiftly flies.

Age tires and wrinkles him,
In misery he passes in vain.
Sons as men he may not see,
Thought of which is pain.

His life is so brief a span,
There's not much he can do.
Please withhold your anger
Until I'm called by you.

I would hide among the dead,
Until your anger fades. And
Then arise to answer, Lord,
Upon the judgment day.

For when I die, I'll live
Again, it's my dearest hope.
But now my life is so beset,
In faith I only grope."

CHAPTER 15

Eliphaz's Answer

"You talk like a foolish man
Who all the answers knows.

You have no fear of God!
Why should you treat Him so?

Why should any man, such
Total righteousness claim?
Eyes flashing and bitter
Words, at God you take aim.

He can't even trust angels,
So why should He trust you?
A wicked man is in trouble;
It follows his life through.

His life is one of fear;
In worry he spends his days.
He fights against the Lord
In all conceivable ways.

His gains all ill-gotten,
What, he has won't last. For
Gods anger will destroy
All that he holds fast.

Let him not trust in riches
And not deceive himself. For
The godless are often barren;
They'll not get his help."

CHAPTER 16

Job's Reply

"If you're a friend, I can't
Tell, the words go on and on.
I'd like to think you'd help
But believe you've over done.

If our roles were changed
Then I might do as you. But
I think I'd try to cheer
And be a friend more true.

My comforters are all busy
Tearing my life apart.
Even God is on my back,
Won't someone have a heart?

Here I sit in sackcloth,
My eyes red with weeping. I
Am innocent, my prayer pure;
To God I give my Keeping."

CHAPTER 17

"Unto death I draw near, I
See my mockers everywhere.
None confirm my innocence,
How can this load I bear?

But pure hearts shall win
And stronger they shall be.
But you my fickle friends,
Remove yourselves from me.

For my hope within me dies,
You've made my day more sad.
The night seems pitch dark,
My future sure looks bad."

CHAPTER 18

Bildad Again

"Now Job you make no sense,
Who are you trying to fool?
If you were all that good
You'd be playing it cool.

When calamity falls, it's
Because one sinned so much.
If you were really perfect,
You'd have better luck.

The sinner will always lose,
For things just go that way.
His enemies are on his trail
And will hound him every day.

His relatives will die, and
He shall do so too. No one
Will remember him, in death
His trials are all through."

CHAPTER 19

Job Says

"If I'm guilty as you claim,
Why don't you prove it now!
You say that I'm a sinner,
But I just don't see how.

My situation is desperate;
I cry for help in vain. Even
God has abandoned me
In this world of pain.

Friends look at me in horror;
My best friends put me down.
I'm an object of ridicule,
The sorriest man around.

But if I had an iron pen,
Upon a rock I'd write,
That I'm eternally certain
My God is by my side.

In spite of the persecution
Toward me you eagerly give,
I know that I am God's,
And my redeemer lives.

But you insist I am guilty
No matter what I say.
I warn you of your danger,
If you continue this way."

CHAPTER 20

Zophar's Speech

"I hasten to answer you,
For I am the one who knows!
The godless shall not win
As in wickedness he grows.

What he gets is often ill-
gotten; all he does is vain.
His sons will pay his debts
And he'll lose all he gains.

For a time he flourishes,
Eats and drinks to excess.
Suddenly it turns upon him,
To cause his early death.

Then he'll soon realize that
He has no power. The world
Will turn against him,
Nor will God be his tower."

CHAPTER 21

Job's reply

"Go ahead and mock me, for
I know that you're all wrong.
God never seems to limit the
Ways of the rich and strong.

They grind poor folk under
Foot and have it their way.
They laugh and libel God
In much of what they say.

And while I'm discussing man,
It's God to whom I complain.
Everything the wicked touch,
It seems becomes their gain.

You say their children will
Pay, but I'd not have it so.
Let the guilty suffer, I say,
That's the way I'd see it go.

You can show me one or two
Who has paid for stolen gain.
But God gives rich or poor,
What he sees fit in pain."

CHAPTER 22

Eliphaz Again

"Is man of any value? What
Is his worth to God? It's
Got to be your wickedness,
Perhaps the poor you rob.

You may have refused to help
Friends who were in need.
You must have been a terror
In your un-godly greed.

You think God sits in heaven,
By thick clouds is screened.
But every dastardly act you
Do, by Him is easily seen.

You seem to forget, sinners
By Him are fated to fail.
The righteous will be there
To hear the despairing wail.

Do not quarrel with God but
Admit that you were wrong.
Give up your lust for riches;
Your thoughts will be a song.

He will hear your prayer,
If promises to Him you keep.
What you wish will happen;
A light will guide your feet.

You'll be a help to sinners
And you'll have pure hands.
God will be your champion,
And you'll be a better man."

CHAPTER 23

The Reply of Job

"Today I still complain,
For my punishment is unjust.
If I could talk to God, I'd
Be willing to let Him judge.

But He's nowhere to be found,
I search for Him in vain. But
I'm sure He knows my
   problems,
Yet still leaves me in pain.

There is no changing God,
What's on His mind He'll do.

No wonder terror grips me;
Darkness surrounds me too."

CHAPTER 24

"Oh, for my day in court,
When God will judge my fate.
For crime is running rampant,
And it seems a hopeless case.

The rich debase the poor,
And the godly wait in vain.
The poor have no shelter
To ease the cold and pain.

They eke out a frugal living
As the rich waste much food.
The wicked cause much sorrow,
For murder is their mood.

In secret they commit sins,
On their faces wear a mask,
As they prey upon brothers,
But are seldom taken to task.

How quickly they disappear,
Like heat consumes the snow.
All they own is cursed when
It comes their time to go.

At death they're broken, as
They treated the poor. From
The earth they'll disappear,
To be remembered no more.

Yet God smiles upon them,
Or leastwise so it seems.
Now can you prove me wrong
Or tell me it's a dream?"

CHAPTER 25

Bildad Says

"Can you count the angels?
He's light in darkest space!

Can a man stand before Him
Or see His glorious face?

No man is perfect,
How can you hope to be?
Do you think you're better?
I think you're kidding me!"

CHAPTER 26

Job's Eighth Answer

"Wonderful friends you are!
Stupid you must think I am.
How are you so brilliant? The
Dead naked, before Him stand.

He made heaven in empty
   space,
On nothing He hangs the earth.
His throne he hides in cloud,
And to the rain gives birth.

By power He calms the ocean
Is skilled at crushing pride.
He directs the fate of man;
No one can change its tide."

CHAPTER 27

"I vow by the Living God, who
Has taken away my rights,
My lips shall speak no evil,
My tongue shall speak no lies.

Though my soul is bitter, my
Conscience is certainly clear.
For I am not a sinner,
And I'll repeat it here.

What hope has the godless,
When God takes away his life?
But why should God listen
When he cries out in fright?

For our God he had no use,
Except when under duress. So

His fate is naturally bleak;
He can't expect much less.

Like dust he gathers riches
With closets full of clothes.
He goes to bed a rich man,
To find his wealth has flown.

Terror overwhelms him as
In death he is blown away.
The righteous boo him into
Eternity; he has had his day."

CHAPTER 28

"Men have much knowledge
For things they wish to do,
Like making light in darkness,
Or cutting a mountain through.

They can mine the earth in
Search of precious stones. Or
Dam up streams of water,
To hunt for gold are prone.

But for wisdom or understand-
ing, men know not where to go.
They cannot trade in riches,
So search both high and low.

Death and destruction are
Clues, and God shows up there.
For he causes storms upon the
Oceans or makes weather fair.

He steers the paths of rivers
And guides the lightening bolt.
He knows where wisdom is
And declares it to us dolts.

He speaks to mankind thus
But he is not demanding. To
Fear the Lord is wisdom, for-
saking evil is understanding."

CHAPTER 29

"Oh, for the days gone by
When God took care of me.
He lighted the path before,
And I walked safe and free.

Those were the golden days,
When an honored spot was
  mine.
I was judge against all evil
And kept justice on the line.

By the elders I was honored,
From the young I had respect.
For I was an honest judge,
Who could hold his head erect.

All waited upon my council,
From the day they were born.
My smile caused rejoicing,
Even by those who mourned,"

CHAPTER 30

"Younger men are strong,
But in dismay, we find,
Although strong of back,
They're so weak of mind.

There are many outcasts,
Also social dregs. To
Eat at civilized tables,
They would have to beg.

Their children behave
Like Satan's tools.
They lack common sense,
And act like total fools.

Now I am the subject of
Their taunts and ribald
Songs. And everything I
Do seems to go so wrong.

In jeopardy my life
By God has been placed.

He offers me no help
As the heathen I face.

In terror I live, and my
Property is all gone. My
Weary heart is broken,
As so much goes wrong.

All night I'm in pain,
As I toss and turn.
Then, Oh my God, I cry,
Tell me why I'm spurned.,

I am in a whirlwind,
In a storm to dissolve.
I reach out hoping my
Troubles You will solve.

I grieved for the needy
And wept for the poor. I
Looked forward to light,
But He closed the door.

My heart is troubled, and
Affliction is my estate.
I cry out for help, but
Nothing is my fate."

CHAPTER 31

"If I'd left His pathway,
Looked at a woman in lust,
But He knows I'm innocent
Or I'd deserve to go bust.

If I've harmed the poor
Or caused widows to weep,
Saw anyone cold and
Left him to freeze,

Then all of these evils
I deserve and much more.
So God's great punishment
Would surely be in store.

If I've trusted in money
Or if I live for wealth,

Or worship moon or stars,
I deserve poor health.

I've never cursed anyone
Or laid wait for revenge.
I never denied my sins,
Or ever showed contempt.

Can you prove I'm wrong
Or committed these deeds?
That I am guilty of envy,
Of murder or of greed?

I'll stand before a Judge
And my case I'll plead. Or
Let the thistles grow to
Choke my land with weeds."

CHAPTER 32

The friends had failed to
Prove that Job was wrong.
They thought him guilty,
But his mind was strong.

Elihu, son of Barachel of
The Clan of Ram, was angry
With them all but he
Was a younger man.

So he held his peace till
Others spoke their minds.
It was plain to him, they
Were baffled and blind.

"It seems," he said, "wis-
dom's not just to the old.
God gives intelligence,
If I may be so bold.

I've heard your arguments
Which on Job make no dent.
My pressure's up like a
Wine cask with no vent."

CHAPTER 33

Elihu Continues

"Please listen Job, and
Think of what I say. For
I am a kindred spirit
And am also made of clay.

You've said it often and
Repeated it oft' again.
You have done no wrong
And are a righteous man.

You say God is trying to
Find some sin you've done.
Thereby to find a reason
To put you on the run.

You ask a middle man to
Stand between you and Him,
So you can query God
About your alleged sin.

God is greater than man,
Why should He account, for
A wrong you have fancied
As your misery mounts.

God often speaks to men
In visions and in dreams.
Often gives them answers,
Or shows them other means.

He opens minds to visions
Or saves them from a trap.
Keeps them oft' from sin,
And teaches men to adapt.

Sometimes sends sickness,
Often accompanied by pain.
He splits the heavens
With lightning and rain.

If a messenger in Heaven
Intercedes for a friend,

God pities him and says,
Now let his misery end.

His body will be healthy
As any child's again. In a
Realm of light he'll live
And will be a better man.

If the man has sinned he
Will soon admit it all.
And when he prays to God
He will hear his call.

Mark well my words Job,
And listen carefully, for
These are words of wisdom
You shall hear from me.

If you wish to speak, now
Say what's on your mind.
For I am on your side;
Justification I'd find."

CHAPTER 34

"Oh listen to me men,
I will tell you true. You
Listen to certain sounds;
Special foods you choose.

So choose what is right,
But let it be understood.
We must first define and
Choose only what is good.

God said, 'You are guilty.'
Job said, 'That's not true.
I'm being greatly punished
For what, I have no clue.'

Now who else is as arrogant
As Job has proven to be? He
Says, 'God is so difficult;
He is too hard to please."

Now as His people know,
Our God is truly just.
He can raise a mere man
Or leave him in the dust.

He makes kings or beggars,
So try to understand,
That if He hated justice
He could not govern man.

If He withdrew His Spirit,
Life would turn to dust.
There's no truer statement,
God's not wicked or unjust.

Why should He form justice
Just to fit man's whim? For
Man in his arrogance won't
Come repent to Him!

Job, you're speaking like
A fool, a half-wit will ag-
ree. The way you talk you
Deserve a maximum penalty.

You add rebellion and igno-
rance with blasphemy to
Your other sins. You better
Change; it's time to begin."

CHAPTER 35

"You say, I don't sin, but
No matter if I had, for
God treats me like dirt,
I'm in trouble just as bad!"

Just look up at the sky,
Can a sin shake His throne?
Or if you should sin again
Would it make Him moan?

Sin may oppress a man,
Good deeds give him ease.
Do you think He doesn't
Hear, or if He's pleased?

Do you think He's happy?
Does He always keep cool?
Must He quickly respond?
Job don't act the fool."

CHAPTER 36

Elihu Continues

"Now, if you will listen
I will tell you true. For
I'm a man of knowledge
Which I'll impart to you.

God is always just will
Do what's right for man,
Has many ways to lead him
According to His plan.

If man heeds His word in
Victory his life will end.
If he ignores his maker,
Before life he will bend.

Do not try to shame God
By complaining about fate.
He sent you this suffering
To make you walk straight.

He's after your attention,
Often teaches by distress.
So glorify Him in earnest;
His method is the best.

Our God is wonderful, He
Makes vapor into rain. He
Spreads it on the earth
And calls it back again.

Blessing us through nature,
In His hands are lightning
Bolts. So do not be wicked
Or act like stupid dolts."

CHAPTER 37

"Listen to His thunder as
He shouts across the land.

We cannot comprehend the
Awesome power of His hand.

For He directs the storm,
Snow and showers to fall.
The wonder of His power
Should be obvious to us all.

If you, oh Job, are wise,
Tell us how it's so.
For God is not impressed
With how much you know.

We tremble if His voice,
In heaven as thunder rolls.
From south He sends rain,
From north He sends cold.

Can you tell the secret of
How God controls the storm,
Or clears skies of clouds?
For Him it is the norm."

CHAPTER 38

From a wind God answered,
"In your ignorance Job, my
Providence you denied. Now
I'll demand some answers,
To these you must reply.

Where were you when water
Filled seas to great depth?
They were allowed to come
So far, not another step.

Have you commanded a silent
Dawn to appear? Putting a
Stop to the night with its
Darkness and fear?

Have you measured earth,
Can you tell me its size?
Can you define darkness,
Or how the sun does rise?

Who dug the valleys for
The torrents of rain?
Whatever causes water to
Ice make its change?

Why does rain on a desert
Make grass to spring forth?
Now stop Orion or Pleades;
Move the star of the north!

Can you guide the planets
Or decide the seasons? Name
The laws of the universe,
And recite their reasons?

Can you stalk prey, like a
Lioness for those younger?
Who feeds the young ravens
When they cry in hunger?"

CHAPTER 39

The Lord Continues

"Do you happen to know how
A mountain goat gives birth?
Why is a wild donkey wild
In her place upon the earth?

Will a wild ox be a servant;
Can you trust him on the job?
The Ostrich has no wisdom;
She was made that way by God.

What about the horse of war;
Did you decree he leap ahead?
For he glories in the battle
And has no fear of death.

What makes a hawk to soar,
Or an eagle to ride the wind
Where she lives in mountain
Majesty, and feeds her young
Through thick and thin?"

CHAPTER 40

"Do you still want to argue,
Or do you concede?" Now with
His hand upon his mouth,
Job then had to plead.

"I am nothing at all the
Answer I'd never find."
For he recognized his better
And knew he was in a bind.

Then from out the whirlwind
God spoke to Job again.
"Stand up and brace yourself
For battle like a man.

Now you would condemn me
To make yourself seem wise?
Will you discredit justice
So to take me down to size?

Are you as strong as God;
Can you shout loud as He?
So put on your royal robes
And have a go at me!

Give vent to anger; let it
Flow against the proud.
Humiliate the haughty;
Step on the wicked crowd.

Knock them into the dust
Stone faced in death.
If you can do all that,
I'll believe the rest.

How about the behemoth;
Him, I also made. He
Rests down by the rivers,
Sleeps there in the shade.

He is high and mighty,
Nigh impossible to kill.
Your sword need be sharp,
More than normal skill.

He won't fret the torrents,
When floods sweep hard.
No one will ring his nose,
For he always is on guard."

CHAPTER 41

"Can you catch a leviathon
By using hook and line?
Tie him with a noose
Or imprison him for life?

He cannot be netted, a head
Too hard to harpoon. And if
You try to catch Him, you'll
Not forget it soon.

His jaws are terrible, his
Scales nothing can penet-
rate. To stand against him,
One would seal his fate.

He's king of all he rules;
He blows fire on his breath.
He is totally fearless and
Strikes with sudden death.

I owe nothing to anyone,
All under heaven is mine.
If you have aught to say
Now let me hear your line."

CHAPTER 42

Job Replies to God

"I've heard of you before
And now I hear your voice.
But when I made complaint,
That was a reckless choice.

You are God most powerful
And much too great for me.
In sack cloth I repent and
For mercy call on thee."

After speaking to Job, God
Was angry at those friends.
If Job had not prayed, it
Could have been their end.

God told them to sacrifice,
And Job would pray for them.
For they had spoken meanly
To Job their good friend.

Now his relatives visited
And brought him many gifts.
Since he prayed for friends,
God made his fortunes shift.

God smiled on later life
And blessings freely flowed,
With daughters, sons, and
Riches for good old Job.

END of JOB

PSALMS

CHAPTER I

Joy to those who avoid the
Paths of evil men. They
Meditate all their lives
On His great work to them.

Like trees along the river,
Bearing fruit in season,
They believe in justice
And need no other reason.

Their lives will not wither;
Their deeds will never die.
How different from sinners,
For they don't need to cry.

PSALMS 2

What fools the nations are
Who rage against the Lord.
Any plots against Him
They can ill afford.

For God will put His Son
Upon Jerusalem's throne. So
Rule them with an iron hand,
Break their sinful bones.

Oh rulers of this earth,
Listen while there's time.
Fall down before His Son
And kiss His feet sublime.

For if you rouse His anger
His wrath will soon begin.
But Oh, the joys of those
Who put their trust in Him.

PSALMS 3

As David fled from Absalom,
His faith was tried. His
Life in deadly danger by
A son who'd been his pride.

He cried out to God in
Loneliness and shame. "You
Are my strength and shield;
You'll always be the same.

And if ten thousand enemies
Surround me on every side,
You'll always be my savior
And my strength and pride."

PSALMS 4

"Lord, you always helped
Me when I was in distress.
Now please listen again,
As my troubles I confess.

The Lord asks sons of man,
Will you always turn away?
Why do you worship idols?
God rules night and day."

The Lord has set apart
Those whom he's redeemed.
And I am His forever, so
I know He listens to me.

Stand before God in awe,
In silence before Him wait.
Sacrifice and pray, and
He will keep you safe.

PSALMS 5

"At dawn I look to heaven
And earnestly send my plea.
Lord lead me as promised,
Ere my enemies capture me.

You enjoy no wickedness;
Any sin you cannot stand.
Bear down on sinners, Lord,
Protect the righteous man."

PSALMS 6

"Lord, I'm growing tired,
As my enemies multiply. In
Your loving kindness save
Me as on my pillow I cry.

Lord, in your kindness
Please take away my pain.
For if I'm alive and well,
I will praise you again.

Leave me now, men of evil,
To God I've made my plea.
He will trap you in sin
While he's protecting me."

PSALMS 7

Don't pounce on me, Lord,
As a lion would surely do.
For I'm not hurting others,
But to you I'm true.

Arise, oh Lord, against the
Evil my enemies aim at me.
And in truth and honor
Only justify me publicly.

Evil, sinful man conceives,
And labors toward its end.
Let him fall into his trap
Unless his ways he mends.

How thankful I am, Lord,
Because you are so fine.
So I will offer praises,
For I know you are mine.

PSALMS 8

The majesty of your name,
Oh God, the heavens show.
May it silence our enemies
Wherever mankind goes.

Oh Lord, when I look up,
Heaven's glory I see. Why
Do you ever bother with
Mere mortals such as me?

Only a little lower than
Angels you made man. And
Over all the lower animals,
You let him rule the land.

Your glory fills heaven; it
Is in mountains and trees.

It flows o'er the earth
And washes in the seas.

PSALMS 9

In my heart I praise you,
For wondrous things you do.
I am filled with joy, oh
Lord, just because of you.

Enemies shall not conquer;
God will destroy them all.
My Lord lives forever; the
Meek will hear His call.

Sing out God's praises, who
In the Holy City dwells. He
Is a refuge in all trouble,
To give you peace as well.

Now Oh Lord, have pity
And send my enemies away.
Protect the needy forever;
Please hear me as I pray.

Lord mete out your justice;
Let the wicked gasp in awe.
Let wayward nations see
They are weak and flawed.

PSALMS 10

Lord of all the worlds,
Why stay so far away, as
Wicked men of the earth
Lie stealthily in wait?

Pour upon them, the evil
For others they've planned;
For they think God is dead,
So are safe from His hand.

They mouth curses; murder
And robbery is their game.
The truth they do not know,
And they profane your name.

Lord, help of the helpless,
Who is trusted by the poor,
Make retaliation swiftly,
Justice quick and sure.

PSALMS 11

Why do they tell me flee
To mountains to be safe,
The wicked lie in ambush;
My enemies lie in wait.

But God is in His heaven;
I depend on Him for help.
He hates all violence
And He will keep me well.

PSALMS 12

Good men are disappearing;
There's no sincerity left.
Oh Lord, be quick and sure
To defend the oppressed.

Wicked men have strung their
Bows aiming arrows at me.
But you speak no idle word,
In ruling the land or sea.

PSALMS 13

Why do you forget me Lord,
How long look the other way?
I'm hiding in great anguish
While my enemies hold sway.

They'd like to know I'm down;
Don't let them know I'm low,
And I will sing your praises,
Lord, for I trust you so.

PSALMS 14

A man is a fool who says,
There's no God or He's dead.
He is stupid and evil and
Heaps trouble on his head.

But all have fallen short;
They don't know how to pray.
God has come from Zion,
His people for to save.

PSALMS 15

Who can share your refuge,
Lord upon your holy hill?
Any one with blameless life,
A man who does your will,

Never harms his neighbor
And speaks against all sin.
Who always keeps a promise
Even if it ruins him.

PSALMS 16

Save me now, oh God, as to
You for refuge I come.
You are my only savior,
When all is said and done.

Pleasant brooks I'm given,
Green meadows as my share.
He calms me in the night
Councils me while there.

He will never leave me, the
Needs of life He'll give.
The joys of life eternal
Will be mine to live.

PSALMS 17

I follow in your pathway;
Please listen as I pray.
Show me your eternal love
As I follow in your way.

PSALMS 18

My enemies surrounded me,
And I cried in my distress.
I was trapped and helpless;
I stared at certain death.

The day when I was weakest,
You came, Savior, to my aid.
And only because of you,
Did I ever make the grade.

You prepared me for battle,
Helped me draw an iron bow.
So if I am great, oh Lord,
It's you who've made me so.

My enemies quail before me,
Fall defeated at my feet.
You make them turn and run
Destroying him who hated me.

You rescued me from enemies,
Kept me safely out of reach.
I praise you to the nations;
Your love I'll preach.

PSALMS 19

His craftsmanship is there;
The heavens tell the story.
Without word, silent skies
Teach His wondrous glory.

Cleanse my heart Oh Lord,
Keep me from doing wrong.
I shall sing your praises;
Redemption will be my song.

PSALMS 20

In your day of trouble,
May God be on your side,
To answer all your prayers
And with you always abide.

So give victory to our king,
Lord, listen to our prayer.
We know you hear in heaven,
And we would meet you there.

PSALMS 21

The king's glory is strength;
You welcomed him to success,
Set a crown of gold on him;
You've granted his requests.

In majesty you clothed Him
And you'll be at his side.
His enemies will suffer,
But in grace he'll abide.

Accept our praise, Lord,
For your glorious power.
We'll sing songs for ble-
ssings you have showered.

PSALMS 22

My enemies mock and jest
And laugh at my belief.
I am worn and scorned,
And I sadly need relief.

They're like raging bulls,
Or even a lion fierce. Like
A pack of dogs they circle,
To rip, tear and pierce.

Save me from them, Lord,
And also from their horns.
I have always trusted you,
From the day I was born.

Let all men praise you, for
Great things you've done.
The poor love and trust you
So be joyful, everyone.

PSALMS 23

Because He is my shepherd,
I have all I need. He lets
Me rest in meadow grass; He
Leads me by a quiet stream.

I shall want for nothing,
For I know He is there.
He will restore my soul,
And His glory I will share.

The valley of the shadow
Holds no fear for me.
He prepares my table in
The presence of my enemies.

He fills my cup with calm;
His mercy fills my life.
I'll dwell in Him forever,
And have no inner strife.

PSALMS 24

On a flood He established
Earth built upon the seas,
It all belongs to God, to
To do with as He please.

Who climbs His Holy Hill,
Or stands in a Holy Place?
Only those generations,
Who seek His loving face.

Lift your heads, oh gates,
Lift your everlasting doors,
For he is our eternal King
Who rules forever more.

PSALMS 25

You are my salvation, Lord,
So show me how to know,
The pathway that is right,
With me, Lord, please go.

Look at me with kindly eyes
And forgive my stupid ways.
Teach me what is right, Oh
Lord, don't let me go astray.

My problems go from bad to
Worse, save me from them all.
See my pain, feel my sorrow,
Oh please Lord hear my call!

PSALMS 26

Dismiss charges against me,
Lord, I try to keep your law.

Test my life and motives,
My hands from sin I wash.

I trust truth and kindness;
They've been my goal in life.
I sing in great thankfulness;
You've led me out of strife.

PSALMS 27

He'll hide me in His Temple,
In His presence every day.
I want this most of all,
If I could have my way.

From tormentors He will hide
Me and send help I need.
I expect He will save me,
And for that I plead.

PSALMS 28

I lift my hands to heaven,
Lord please hear my cry.
Don't punish me as wicked;
My trust you'd then belie.

Blessed be my Lord,
You have heard my voice. You
Are my strength and shield;
My heart will ever rejoice.

PSALMS 29

Give the glory unto Him,
For he deserves the best.
Worship Him in beauty
And in His mighty holiness.

God's voice is wonderful
Full of power and majesty.
It shakes up the mountains
And rips up the cedar trees.

PSALMS 30

Lord, I'll sing your praise;
You've saved me from the foe.

I'm back among the living,
And I want all men to know.

I thought it was forever
When I was riding high.
That you would always favor
Me, for I was so alive.

But my courage suddenly left,
As you turned your face away.
Then I knew abject terror
Through dark and dreary days.

Then I cried to you, oh Lord,
Oh how I begged and pled,
How can I ever praise you,
If I am cold and dead?

Joy replaced my sorrow,
As you smiled on me again.
Now I'll sing His praises
Of loving kindness to men.

PSALMS 31

Into thy hand I give myself,
For I need to be redeemed.
I trust I will be rescued
From all of my enemies.

Slander of many I've heard;
I knew fear on every side.
As my downfall was plotted
I nearly lost my pride.

Blessed be the Lord, He's
Marvelous, kind and strong.
In haste I felt abandoned,
But He proved me wrong.

PSALMS 32

Blessed was the day when
My sins were all forgiven.
Dishonesty was keeping me
From any hope of Heaven.

He's promised to teach us;
We're surrounded by song.
Oh rejoice in His love
And nothing will go wrong.

PSALMS 33

By His word it happened:
He spoke, and earth began.
Yes, in all its splendor,
It appeared at His command.

Blessed is the nation,
Whose God is the Holy One,
Whose people He has chosen
As His daughters and sons.

From heaven He gazes down
And He watches all they do.
He keeps them safe from evil,
Even as He will for you.

PSALMS 34

Bless the Lord and praise
Him from morning to night.
I will praise His name and
Teach that which is right.

From fear He delivered me;
His angels encamped nearby.
They heard and saved him, as
For help the poor man cried.

The Lord is close to those,
Of a broken heart. Many
Righteous are afflicted, but
God will take their part.

PSALMS 35

Draw thy spear, oh Lord, and
Stand between my enemy and
Me. Let them be confounded,
For 'tis my soul they seek.

They told lies against me,
Like friends I treated them.
Now I need your help, Lord,
To stand in my defense.

PSALMS 36

Now to the chief musician,
A fitting psalm was made.
About the wicked man, who
Scorns God's wondrous aid.

For he flatters himself,
As he builds up his ego.
Then becomes overbearing,
As self esteem grows.

Like a mighty mountain,
Righteousness is strong.
Thy faithfulness Oh Lord,
Gives hope to the throng.

With thee is the fountain,
And life is its stream.
The light of your love
Will keep us in its beam.

PSALMS 37

Never envy the wicked,
Like grass he disappears.
Trust the Lord instead;
With Him there is no fear.

In the light of justice
He'll show you free of sin.
Don't be envious of evil,
For that doesn't always win.

PSALMS 38

Lord, rebuke not or anger,
For that I cannot stand.
It would surely haunt me;
It is too much for man.

PSALMS 39

I pledge to hold my tongue,
To bridle my angry retort.
My heart is hot within me,
But cool is my report.

Lord, help me in my future,
I'm so weak and frail. My
Time is only a hand-breadth,
And my vanity to no avail.

Man accumulates his riches,
That he may not get to spend.
He may walk life in vain
And quickly come to the end.

So hear my prayer, oh Lord,
And give ear unto my cry.
Oh give me understanding
Before my time to die.

PSALMS 40

Patiently, Lord, I waited,
And then you heard my cry.
You lifted me from the pits,
And then set me high.

I'll praise you to all men
With a new song in my heart.
With pleasure and with joy
I'll always take your part.

Wonderful, thy works, Lord,
A multitude are thy ways. Do
Not spare thy mercies, Lord,
I will not spare my praise.

PSALMS 41

My enemies wish me evil;
They wait for me to die,
As all of them against
Me, my injury do devise.

He who was my friend,
Whom I trusted and I fed;
Now raises up against me
And wishes I were dead.

But please be merciful
Lord, raise me up again,
So I can live to forgive
Such a fickle man.

PSALMS 42

Lord, please soon come,
For you my heart yearns.
Day and night I cry, as
My soul within me burns.

I went to thy house,
And I kept thy Holy day.
I raised my voice in joy,
As I sang thy praise.

PSALMS 43

Oh send out your truth,
And send out your light.
Oh lead me my Lord,
In your pathways bright.

I shall go to your alter
In love, and in hope.
I'll praise you, Oh Lord,
No longer will I grope.

PSALMS 44

We heard glorious stories
Of winning Caanan, of old.
How those battles were won
With your help, we're told.

Please stand at our side
And help us to win again.
I trust not in my weapons;
Without you we're only men.

Lord, sincerely we follow,
In all things worship you.
Yet our name is an epithet;
Our enemies hate us Jews.

PSALMS 45

My heart overflows with
Poetry for my Lord and King.
So I'll tell my story which
With true blessings rings.

Of all, He is the fairest;
His words are full of grace.
God blesses you forever,
All that's wrong He hates.

Arm yourselves mighty ones,
Go forward to great deeds.
Defend truth, humility and
Justice, win with all speed.

Swiftly draw your bow, Lord,
Your arrows sharp and true.
Justice is a royal scepter;
Enemies will fall to you.

With myrrh, aloes, and cassia,
Your robes are well perfumed.
In your ivory palaces, music
Is made with beautiful tunes.

I advise you now, Oh daughter
From your home land far away,
Don't fret your parents, your
King delights in you today.

Your bride awaits, Oh king;
She is lovely and well clad;
What a beautiful procession,
It is joyful and so glad.

Your sons will all be kings,
God, around earth to reign.
Nations of earth will honor;
Forever you'll be praised.

PSALMS 46

Let oceans roar and foam,
Mountains fall into the sea.
God is refuge in trouble; He
Gives strength to you and me.

In His city a river flows
With love from shore to shore.
It's where He lives eternally,
With peace forever more.

In anger the nations battle;
Their young to war they send.
But with only a gesture, He
Could cause the world to end.

He commands heaven's armies,
The God of Jacob at our side.
Stand silent knowing He is
God; Forever with Him abide.

PSALM 47

Come rejoicing, everyone,
For the Lord of Gods is nigh.
He is King of all the earth,
Subdues nations with might.

He blesses all His people,
The best to those He loves.
He ascends with mighty shout;
Sing praises to God above.

He rules the world with love
Sitting on His holy throne.
Gentile nations adopted Him
And praise Him for their own.

His trophies, battle shields
Of armies from all the world.
He is honored everywhere,
Where ere His flag unfurls.

PSALM 48

How glorious mount Zion, how
Glorious God's name, on the
Mountain north of Jerusalem
High above the plain.

A great defender of the city,
That earthly kings must see.
The marvels they saw there
Caused them to turn and flee.

They were filled with panic,
Like a woman in travail. For
He can cause mighty warships
To founder and to fail.

We have heard of the cities,
Built, Lord, by your love. For
Your name is praised forever,
In earth and heaven above.

So, our children, go and look
At castles and towers tall.
Go and see these marvels
And walk upon their walls.

Remember a great God is ours,
He'll protect us from on high.
He will be our Lord forever,
Long beyond the day we die.

PSALMS 49

All people of earth take heed,
You high, low, rich or poor.
Listen carefully, everyone,
To the wisdom in these words.

Yield not in time of trouble;
The Lord will see you through.
Love and trust Him always;
Then He'll be true to you.

Riches are no answer; money
Can never save a soul.
Rich and poor alike will go,
When our Lord calls the roll.

A soul is far too precious
To be ransomed by mere
   wealth.
You must love and cherish God,
The way to spiritual health.

If a man be rich and famous
And rides roughly over all,
Then be thou not dismayed,
That he's riding for a fall.

PSALMS 50

In Zion's glorious temple,
God in glory shines forth.
He brings noise of thunder
Amid a terrible fire storm.

He comes to judge a people.
To us on earth He shouts,
"Gather together my people,
Gather ye, all about!

I have come to judge you,
In all fairness I declare.
For sacrifice or offerings,
I really do not care.

Cattle on a thousand hills
Have always belonged to me.
In fact I own the world; I
Want only trust, you see.

A word to evil men is this:
Recite my laws no more;
You commune with evil, as
You curse, lie, and whore.

You refuse my discipline
And you go your wicked way.
When I list my charges,
The fiddler you shall pay.

Praise is the honor due me,
Those tried and true will

Receive salvation from God;
They've paid their dues."

PSALMS 51

"Don't sentence me to death
Or take the Holy spirit away.
Do not toss me aside forever;
Let my heart not go astray."

This was King David's plea as
He looked back upon his sin.
For adultery with Bath-sheba,
Belated repentance set in.

"Cleanse me from all guilt,
Make me pure as driven snow.
I am guilty as can be,
Thus in life I cannot go."

PSALMS 52

Now his enemy Doeg,
   murdered
Eighty-five priests and fam-
ilies. David was in sorrow,
But it sounded like a plea.

"Why do you boast of evil,
Why do you follow this rut?
You're riding high today;
You'll soon be out of luck.

The truth you seem to hate
And wickedness you love, but
God will strike you down, Oh
Man with the lying tongue.

As for me, I praise the Lord,
For His punishment is just.
I will wait upon His mercies
And in His love I'll trust."

PSALMS 53

Only a fool would say to him-
Self, "I think God is dead."

Now his life is full of sin
Or sickness in his head.

It must be hard for God
To find a man who's true.
None of us is good; we're
Corrupt through and through.

Oh if God would save us now
And take us to Zion with him!
For we will never be happy
Until we're free of sin.

PSALMS 54

Men of Ziph betrayed me,
Told my hiding place to Saul,
Oh save me with your might;
Oh Lord, please hear my call.

Wicked men out there, Lord,
Seek a quick end to me.
They are ruthless men
Who have no love for thee.

PSALMS 55

Listen to my prayer, Lord,
Don't hide if I call to you.
I groan beneath my burden;
It seems more than I can do.

My enemies shout against me;
They threaten me with death.
Hateful fury engulfs me; in
Terror I fail for breath.

Oh, for wings to fly away
To a quiet resting place,
Where once again, oh Lord,
You'd smile upon my face.

Had my enemy reproached me,
Then the burden I could bear.
But it was my trusted friend,
Whose confidence I'd shared.

As for me, I'll call on the
Lord, I know He will save.
All day and night I'll cry;
He'll hear me when I pray.

For my God has been forever,
Has been since olden days.
He will condemn them, for
He knows their sinful ways.

PSALMS 56

To me Oh God, be merciful
Ere my enemies swallow me.
There are many who jest;
I'll put my trust in thee.

Unto thee I send my praises;
Thy vows I know you'll keep.
You saved my soul from death,
And you will guide my feet.

PSALMS 57

I hide beneath your wings
In the shadow of your love.
Until the storm is past,
I will pray to God above.

PSALMS 58

They've no sense of fairness
But live out lives of crime.
Make them disappear, oh Lord,
Into the mists of time.

PSALMS 59

Around the home of David,
King Saul had set his men,
To capture and to kill him,
So this psalm David penned.

Hide me from enemies, Lord,
Who would shorten my life.
Don't spare these murderers
For they cause much strife.

Put them in jeopardy, Lord,
Let them slink home at night.
As for me, I know Your mercy,
And you'll set things right.

PSALMS 60

Oh God, you've corrected us;
Our ego's suffered a blow.
You caused us to re-assess.
You've really laid us low.

But you've given us a banner,
For all who love the truth.
And we'll depend on help
We expect to get from you.

Help us to do mighty things
And keep us on our toes.
With your wonderous help,
We'll trample on some foes.

PSALMS 61

Listen to my prayer, Lord,
No matter where I may be.
For when in need I cry
And I know you'll rescue me.

I shall live forever, Lord,
In the shadow of your wings.
And for your loving kindness,
My heart your praises sings.

PSALMS 62

Why do I stand silently and
Wait for Him to rescue me?
And why, when trouble comes,
Do I grow tense, and flee?

My kingdom is tottering, and
They force me from my throne;
He is my refuge and my rock,
And I'll trust in Him alone.

The greatest and the lowest,
Are alike in His sight.
So, my people, make your plea,
He will treat you all alike.

PSALMS 63

Lord, how I search for you
In this thirsty, weary land.
How I long for sanctuary
And need your protective hand.

How I lay awake at night,
How oft' I've thought of you.
So often you have helped me,
You're a friend so true.

PSALMS 64

Lord, hear my complaint,
In secret they make plans,
To ambush the innocent and
Plot evil to the godly man.

But You will put them down
To show sin does not pay.
Your people will rejoice
And to you give the praise.

PSALMS 65

Oh Lord, we wait upon you
In love fulfilling our vows.
Because you answer prayer,
All mankind before you bows.

Though we are often sinful,
You will forgive them all.
Oh what joy we'll know and
Those who hear your call.

PSALMS 66

With power He rules earth
And watches over the land.
Everyone sing His praises;
Our lives are in His hands.

He purifies us with fire,
Like silver in a mold. We go
Through flood and mire, but
He saves us from the cold.

PSALMS 67

Now look down on us, Lord
And smile upon our work.
Send us around the earth,
So we can spread the word.

With all His saving power
And His eternal plan, earth
Has yielded abundantly
With blessings made for man.

So, ye people, all give thanks
For blessings from God above.
Even those from other lands,
Be ye thankful for His love.

PSALMS 68

Let the godly man exult;
May he rejoice and be merry.
Sing praises to the Lord
For as far as voices carry.

Oh yes, He led our people
In a wilderness forty years,
Safely past the enemy, and
Calmed their greatest fears.

The enemy failed to stop us;
Their jewelry our women wear.
And he lives upon Mt. Zion,
Close to His people there.

"Oh Lord, bring all nations
With tribute in their hand,
Singing praises to the Lord,
All kingdoms of the land.

He rides the ancient heavens;
His voice comes from the sky.
He gives power to His people,
And He answers to their cry.

PSALMS 69

Leader of heaven's armies,
You know how stupid I am.
You also know I love you;
My religion is not a sham.

I keep on praying, Lord,
I know my day will come.
They cannot overwhelm me,
Although I'm on the run.

They even gave me poison
And vinegar for my thirst.
This hatred bows my spirit;
My heart within me hurts.

But rescue me oh Lord,
From poverty and pain. For
All who seek God will
Know gladness once again.

PSALMS 70

Rescue me oh Lord,
Hurry to my aid,
For only you can help me;
Oh please do not delay.

PSALMS 71

You were my trust and
Hope since I was a boy.
I know that I am yours;
That is my secret joy.

My lips sing your praise,
Though I was close to death;
You helped me once again,
Raised me from the depths.

PSALMS 72

Psalms For Solomon

Give the king wisdom, God,
Righteousness to his son.

With wisdom he'll rule,
Poor, wealthy, everyone.

Yea He shall have dominion
From sea to shining sea.
And He shall always deliver
Righteous ones in need.

Kings of earth will aid him;
All will bring their gifts.
He will rule in peace and
Wisely heal all rifts.

For helpers he will care,
The poor and weak defend;
He will rescue the needy
And call God his friend.

May the king be blessed in
The cities across the land.
Honor his name forever
As a wise and gentle man.

PSALMS 73

How good God is to Israel,
To those with pure hearts.
But I nearly slipped and
Cast my soul afar.

I envied the wicked. All
Seems to go their way.
They grow fat in sin, and
They never seem to pay.

They seldom have problems;
Their road seems smooth.
They boast against heaven
Cheating lifetimes through.

Godly people are confused,
"Why even try," they sigh.
"The wicked have it easy,
And their riches multiply."

When I stopped and thought
I knew this was not true.
One day God will tell them
Their debts have come due.

So all those days of power
Will be like a dream. For
They will suddenly realize
They've lost their steam.

How could I be so stupid
As to wish them wrong? My
God does surely love me
Keeps me well and strong.

He will guide my life
With wisdom and with love.
My feet will be directed
By a heavenly father above.

PSALMS 74

Jerusalem is your home;
Lord walk the ruin through.
Why be so angry against us?
How can we placate you?

An enemy gave a battle cry
Tore your sanctuary down.
It's an awful shambles now;
He burned it to the ground.

The prophets are gone;
Enemies dishonor your name.
How can you let it continue,
Why not put them to shame?

Oh God, you are our King;
You guided us in ages past.
To the Red Sea you led us,
Through it you made a path.

The land is dark, Lord, your
People are trodden down.
Arise, Oh God, and state your
Case, enemies curse aloud.

PSALMS 75

Oh Lord, we do thank you,
We know you really care.
"Oh yes," the Lord replies,
"You can bet I'll be there.

I know the earth trembles
And people live in terror,
Firmly I set its pillars.
It was not built in error.

I warn proud and stubborn
To lower an insolent gaze,
Power comes only from God;
There are no other ways."

PSALMS 76

No wonder He is feared, who
Can stand before His rage?
All men tremble before Him
As He appears on stage.

He cuts down princes and
Does awesome things to kings.
So revere Him in fear, He
Does justice in everything.

PSALMS 77

All night long I pray, with
My hands both lifted high.
There can be no joy for me
Until He heeds my cry.

I recall the good old days;
They ended so long ago. My
Nights were filled with song;
My heart is filled with woe.

Oh God, your ways are holy;
Your great power is complete.
No one else can ere compare,
No one can compete.

PSALMS 78

Listen to my teaching, as I
Reveal truths to you. For
Generations to come, please
Teach them to your youth.

So they need not be rebels,
As their fathers were. Make
Them see His glory; in their
Memories make it burn.

From Egypt He led them with
Great miracles wrought. Yet
So often they rebelled and
Did not as they ought.

He refused Ephraim's tribe,
Who were Joseph's descendents.
And chose His servant, David,
Whom to sheep was attendant.

David had a heart of gold,
Hands strong and skillful.
It was his greatest wish
To do Jehovah's will.

PSALMS 79

Your temple is in ruins,
The enemy is razing the land.
He is butchering your people;
When will you take a stand?

Like water blood is flowing;
Few are left to bury the dead.
All nations around us scoff,
Heap contempt upon our
  heads.

Save us, Lord, pardon our sins,
Oh please Lord, hear our cry.
They've taken many prisoners,
And many are condemned to
  die.

Take vengeance on the enemy,
Save your people from despair.
Then we'll sing your praises;
We'll know you really care.

PSALMS 80

God of Israel, lead us,
God enthroned, bend your ear.
Show your power and glory;
Rescue us from hurt and fear.

Turn us back to you, oh God,
Look on us with joy and love.
Only then shall we be saved,
Oh Lord in heaven above.

A tender vine you planted; we
Took root and filled the land.
You're treating us like weeds,
Because we failed your plan.

Come back, we beg, Oh God,
Protect the things you made;
Guard the sons you love, for
Only then shall we be saved.

PSALMS 81

How strong He has made us;
Sing praises to Jehovah's name.
Sound the trumpet in joy
And for all the days of fame.

For I heard a voice that said,
"I'll lighten the heavy tasks.
I saved you from trouble;
I gave you all you asked.

From Mt. Sinai I answered you,
Where rumbling thunder hides,
Tested your faith at Meribah;
Where does your faith abide?

Oh my people watch and listen,
Worship no God but me, no

Idol in your home and my
Beloved children you shall be.

But my people will not listen;
They seem not to want me near.
So I'll let them go their way
To live with all their fears.

But if they'd only follow
Me and walk within my paths,
Quickly I'd subdue their foes,
So they'd have peace at last."

PSALMS 82

He is judge of heaven's court;
God judges all judges there.
Why do people fail to listen,
Why don't they judge fair?

Why not rescue poor and needy
From the traps of evil men?
When destitute men need help,
Where, oh where, are you then?

I've called you sons of God,
Of Him who is most high. But
In death you are merely men,
And even a prince must die.

Stand, oh God, and judge the
Earth, for it belongs to you.
All nations are in your hand
To judge as you must do.

PSALMS 83

Enemies degrade our nation;
Against Israel they're allied,
Assyria, Ammon, Amalek,
  Gebal,
Tyre, and more on their side.

Now they all work together,
Lot's descendants there too.
They not only want us, Lord,
They're also out to get You.

They must learn you are God
In charge of all the earth.
In all that mankind does
Your Holy name comes first.

PSALMS 84

Lovely is your temple, Lord,
With hints of heaven above.
I would enter your courtyard
Back to your eternal love.

A day in your temple beats
A thousand anywhere else.
I'd gladly be your doorman,
For I'd be near your help.

PSALMS 85

Amazing blessings, oh Lord,
You've poured upon the land.
Restoring Israel's fortune
And forgiving sins of man.

Pour out your kindness God;
Grant us your salvation. We
Will listen carefully Lord;
Bring peace to this nation.

Truth and mercy have joined;
Justice and peace have met.
They go before the Lord to
Make a pathway for His steps.

PSALMS 86

Be merciful to me, oh God,
As near your throne I grope.
For I worship only you, my
Lord; you are my only hope.

Listen carefully, oh Lord,
Oh hear my urgent cry.
For I will call on you
Whenever trouble strikes.

Send me a sign of favor, Lord,
So those who hate me can see
That you are on my side,
And will help and comfort me.

PSALMS 87

High upon His holy mountain
The city of Jerusalem stands.
Oh wondrous City of God,
What tales are told by man.

My friends all boast of birth,
Of many places they've been,
Egypt, Babylonia, Phylistia,
Tyre, Or Ethiopia, so myster-
ious to men.

But I know the day will come,
When highest honor obtains,
To be born in Jerusalem with
A special mark by the name.

For God will personally bless
The city of ancient kings. So
My heart remains in Jerusalem,
And the wonders they'll sing.

PSALMS 88

Jehovah, God of my salvation,
I cry before you day or night.
My life is full of trouble
And death is drawing nigh.

For my life I plead, oh Lord,
And I'll do so day by day.
Without you I'm helpless,
Oh why turn your face away?

PSALMS 89

Honesty is your character;
Lord, you rule land and sea.
Oceans cease their fearful
Storms when you merely speak.

You promised me an heir,
Who'd always fill the throne.
So why do you cast me off
And leave me so alone?

You promised a kingdom Lord,
Like no other under the sun.
"He will be my son," you said;
"Yes, he will be the one".

"No matter what the future
Holds," a remnant cried again,
"We'll praise and bless the
Lord, Amen, Oh Lord, Amen".

PSALMS 90

A Prayer of Moses

Oh Lord of the generations,
You have been our home.
As long as we have been,
Wherever we have roamed.

You've been God forever,
Before you formed the earth.
We know you will never die
With no record of your birth.

Like green grass in morning
That grows fresh and tall,
We're mowed down at mid-day,
To wither ere evening falls.

Seventy years you gave us;
A few get even more. Some of
Those are quite painful with
Sorrow and regrets galore.

Oh, Jehovah God, do bless us
And teach us how to pray.
Please turn away your anger
And be with us every day.

PSALMS 91

Within a sheltering shadow
Of our Lord's mighty wing
Is a place of refuge, where
I hear the words of my King.

He rescues me from trouble
And protects me from plague.
I'll not fear the darkness,
Nor have any dread of day.

His angels He has ordered
To protect us where we go.
They will hold us steady,
So we don't stub our toes.

PSALMS 92

I sing of your miracles for
My cup you keep so full.
You give me your blessings;
I'm strong as a wild bull.

The wicked seem to flourish;
They grow much like weeds;
Eternal destruction awaits;
They'll pay for evil deeds.

PSALMS 93

Our King's robe is strength;
The world is His throne;
From the everlasting past,
Eternal future is His home.

He's mightier than breakers
On all shores of the world.
Nothing will ever change
His holy flag unfurled.

PSALMS 94

When doubts assail me, and
With the world I can't cope,

Let me listen and be still,
And He will give me hope.

The Lord God is my fortress,
The rock where I hide.
He'll destroy the enemy,
For sin He'll not abide.

PSALMS 95

He is shepherd of our lives;
Please listen to His call.
Ignoring Him as Israel did
Will precipitate your fall.

For they doubted Him while
Practicing greed and lust.
Yet forty years He led them
In sorrow and disgust.

In anger He swore they'd
Not enter the promised land.
So forty years they wandered
To miss all they'd planned.

PSALM 96

Sing to all men His praises,
Oh bless His holy name. Tell
All about His miracles,
Each day tell how He saves.

He'll judge all men fairly
When He judges the earth.
All who heed His word will
Rejoice in their rebirth.

PSALMS 97

His fire goes before Him;
His lightning cuts the sky.
Let His people rejoice for-
ever; they shall never die.

Let honor of useless gods,
And of idols be disgraced.

Every god most bow to Him,
And they will be displaced.

PSALMS 98

Sing a song of victory won,
By His power and holiness.
For Israel is His own, whom
He promised He would bless.

Let the sea in all power
Roar with wildest glee.
God is coming to judge, to
Return the world to peace.

PSALMS 99

May all the nations tremble,
Mountains and valleys shake,
In majesty He sits in Zion,
And evil men will quake.

A great king brings justice;
It's in everything He does,
Across the blazing desert,
Through the raging flood.

PSALMS 100

All men enter his gates,
Singing praises to His name,
Shout with joy to the Lord;
Faithfulness is His game.

PSALMS 101

Sing of loving kindness, of
His power and holiness. Help
Me control my vulgar self;
May I show no selfishness.

Do not approve the slanderer,
Save me from deceit or pride.
Godly heroes of the land,
To my home I will invite.

Good shall serve me well,
Tricky liars I can't abide.
It will be my daily task to
Rid God's city of crime.

Those Psalms when made
Were promises to His savior,
As he fought lifes battles
And sought Jehovah's favor.

PSALMS 102

When I'm in serious trouble
Lord please hear my plea.
Bend your ear to my distress,
Don't turn away from me.

Enemies taunt me day by day;
I eat ashes instead of bread.
My tears fall into my drink
And I'm as good as dead.

We know, Lord, we are passing;
Soon we'll hear your call.
So love us Lord and be near,
As evening shadows fall.

You are true and famous, Lord,
Your name goes on forever.
So please bless Jerusalem
And help from us don't sever.

People love her every rock,
Each grain of sand and dust.
Nations tremble before you
As Israel proves its trust.

PSALMS 103

With kindness He surrounds
Me, with hope fills my days.
His mercy to those who love
Him, indeed is very great.

He is like unto a father; He
Is tender and He's strong.

He knows we are only dust,
Our days on earth not long.

PSALMS 104

Mountains rise and valleys
Sink, to levels you decree.
You also set the boundaries
For all the lakes and seas.

PSALMS 105

A thousand generations He
Kept His covenant of old;
He upheld a treaty made,
Just as Abraham was told.

Abe was only a visitor, to
A fair and bountiful land,
And when trouble followed,
God gave a helping hand.

To Jordan now came famine,
But Joseph, God had sent
Ahead. His family followed,
Here was meat and bread.

In time they multiplied,
The people filled the land.
Now a multitude from that
Small and weakly band.

Their landlords feared
The people they'd saved,
So Egypt in its fear now
Converted them to slaves.

God had Moses free them
And miracles brought about,
Sent trials and pestilence,
Till Egypt let them out.

He spread a cloud above
To shade them from the sun.
By a pillar of flame at night,
He guided them on their run.

When they asked for meat,
He gave them manna and quail.
No matter what they asked,
He helped them without fail.

When they thirsted for water,
Brought it gushing out a rock.
Then He led them into Caanan,
A land of bountiful crops.

PSALMS 106

How good you are, oh Lord,
Your love will never die for
Those who are fair and just,
And we know have really tried.

We've been such sinful people,
Almost from the day of birth.
We often wonder why He
  thinks
We could be of any worth.

Our fathers did rebel, yet
He led them with loving care.
God had every right on earth
To have just left them there.

On gaining the promised land,
They still did not do as told.
Rather than kill an enemy, he
Was accepted into the fold.

So they learned heathen ways,
And to idols they sacrificed.
On the altars of heathen gods
Children lost their lives.

Thus they added murder
To a multitude of evil deeds.
But in time God softened up,
And listened to them plead.

PSALMS 107

From afar He brought them
This wandering exile nation.

Thank God for all He's done;
It's time to offer oblation.

They fell, none could help,
Panicking, cried their need.
And He saved their lives
In pity for urgent pleas.

Many sailors on the oceans,
Tossed by wind and gale, cry
For help from God with pit-
teous cries and visage pale.

Safely home He brings them,
As He calms the mighty seas.
They soon forget those times
Again to do as they please.

He has power to enrich, or
Make slave of prince or king.
Will mankind heed his ways
Or thank Him for such things?

PSALMS 108

Above earth your glory is,
From mountains to the seas.
Hear my cry, I'm your child;
You promised to champion me.

PSALMS 109

It is hard to love a man
Who curses you as you pray.
This could make me doubt
He'll ever change his ways.

Show him it's no fun to be
The butt of vicious lies.
Evil he returns for good,
And justice he decries.

PSALMS 110

Unto my Lord, said the Lord,
"At my right, you shall be.

In the midst of enemies
You shall represent me.

In the day of thy power, in
The holiness of thy might,
You'll be as morning dew
After resting all the night.

Forever to be a priest,
Much like Melchizedek.
Your God will be with you,
To love and to protect."

PSALMS 111

The power of His works to
His people He has shown.
His deeds are just and fair
To those who are His own.

Men can be thankful
With reverence to Him.
Only in love of our Lord,
Can wisdom begin.

PSALMS 112

Happy is the man who finds
Delight in God's command.
His tomorrows will be bright;
Misfortune he'll understand.

He knows that what happens
Is always for the best.
And that all pain and sorrow
Is part of God's great test.

When darkness over takes him,
He knows light will show thr-
ough. He knows God is near
Will help him bear bad news.

PSALMS 113

Oh you saints of Jehovah,
Arise and praise His name.

His loving self of yesterday
Will forever be the same.

He stoops to lift the poor;
The hungry ones He feeds. He
Answers the childless mother
In her bitter time of need.

Hallelujah to the Lord, for
He's the only God there is.
And we are very happy,
Because we know we're His.

PSALMS 114

Once upon a time, when these
Chronicles were young, when
Israel escaped from Egypt,
That land of foreign tongue--

The Red Sea saw them coming
And its waters did divide.
So they crossed over safely
And gained the other side.

The Jordan River opened
A way for them to pass, and
Over the plains and mountains,
They crossed the land at last.

Oh tremble mighty earth, at
The presence of our God. For
He brought forth gushing
     water,
When Moses struck the rock.

PSALMS 115

Oh glorify the name of God,
For we know that He's not
     dead.
He has given the earth to man,
But of heaven, He's the head.

Oh Israel trust Him well; He
Is your helper and your shield.

And all you priests of Aaron
To our God your praises yield.

PSALMS 116

Death, I surely looked upon;
It stared me in the face.
He brought me back from fear,
And I'll give Him the praise.

I love my Lord, because He
    Hears my Prayers and
    answers them.
So as long as I can breathe,
I'll sing His praise, Amen.

PSALMS 117

Praise The Lord all nations,
All you people of the earth,
For He loves us very dearly,
Our King of royal birth.

PSALMS 118

His kindness is forever, so
How can I be afraid? He
Answered and rescued me,
When in distress I prayed.

Beneath His royal banner
I'll battle for my friend.
It's better to trust God,
Than put confidence in men.

A stone refused by builders
Is the basis for His church.
He'll be with us always,
Never leave us in the lurch.

The Lord has made this day;
Let us rejoice therein. For
With Jehovah on our side,
We know we'll surely win.

PSALMS 119

Happy are all those who've
Always done His will. They
Live as we should live,
And His wishes they fulfill.

So oh blessed Lord of all,
Please lead me by your rule.
For I would live by wisdom;
Let others play the fool.

Help me Lord to overcome
The scorn that I receive,
For loving your holy word
By those who don't believe.

Make me want your word, Lord,
As I struggle on life's way.
Help me to show my love
In all I do and say.

So when I am discouraged,
Revive me by your word. Let
The world know you spoke,
And I was there, and heard.

Never forget your promises
Lord, they are my only hope.
As unbelievers torment me,
Then I'll be able to cope.

I know every law of God
Is just and it is fair.
It has a logical purpose,
Or it would not be there.

PSALMS 120

In troubled times I called,
And He listened to my plea.
The wicked counciled war;
But I who cried for peace.

PSALMS 121

Shall I seek aid from gods
Who, on a mountain were set?

No, not from them, for I'm
Sure that none I'd get.

I will call upon Jehovah;
By Him mountains were made.
Over me He watches, and He
Will always give me aid.

PSALMS 122

Thankfully we are standing
In the Temple of the Lord.
We're in crowded Jerusalem
With judges holding court.

These are Jehovah's people
Worshipping as law requires,
To praise and thank God;
Let us hope they never tire.

PSALMS 123

Oh, Lord, who art in heaven,
We lift eyes on high. We'll
Look to you for kindness,
Hope we never need to sigh.

PSALMS 124

The Lord was on our side;
Israel should be aware, or
We'd fall to the enemy, if
His violent anger flared.

Oh blessed be Jehovah
Who helped us to escape.
Oh blessed be our God
Who decided heaven's shape.

PSALMS 125

Let goodness rule the godly,
Be we steady as a mountain.
Lord protect our people;
Lead us to life's fountain.

PSALMS 126

We were once all exiles
In Egypt so far away.
But then the Lord rescued
Us; Oh what a happy day!

Many other nations looked
And were all amazed.
Our Lord had done so much;
It left them in a daze.

PSALMS 127

If the Lord is not with you
Your labor's all in vain.
If you work only for riches,
Your future is a pain.

Children, a gift of God,
Sharp as arrows will defend.
If you've had a quiver full.
Will protect you to the end.

PSALMS 128

Blessings to you my friends,
Who trust in God today.
Your lives can be contented,
If you love Him and obey.

Home will be a happy one,
So follow our blessed Lord.
A healthy, vigorous family
Will be your just reward.

PSALMS 129

The whip has cut repeatedly;
It has not kept Israel down.
God has broken the chains
That kept men bound.

PSALMS 130

If you keep in mind our sins,
For what can we ever hope?

But in your loving kindness
Lord, we can always cope.

PSALMS 131

I am not proud or haughty,
Great knowledge don't claim.
I will be calm and quiet;
To trust you is my aim.

PSALMS 132

Once my heart was troubled,
And my mind would not sleep.
I would build a Tabernacle,
A home on earth for thee.

The Ark was in Ephratah,
And then the country of Jaar.
But next in the holy temple,
For we have brought it far.

It's a symbol of your power;
We'll dress priests in white.
Don't fail your son David;
You vowed to treat him right.

Lord, you have promised that
His son would follow him. So
If we obey your will, his
Dynasty will never dim.

You shall live in Jerusalem;
Praises, priests will sing.
David's power will grow,
So he'll be a mighty king.

PSALMS 133

Pleasant and joyful a life,
If in harmony brothers dwell.
It's like anointing oil,
Or fresh water from a well.

PSALMS 134

Every night the watchmen who
As Temple guardsmen serve,

Bless the Lord of heaven,
The one who made the earth.

PSALMS 135

He brought His people out of
Egypt and into the promised
Land, by way of many miracles
That they might understand--

That idol worship of heathen
Gods, who cannot see or hear
Is a hopeless substitute for
Knowing Jehovah God is near.

PSALMS 136

Now to the Lord give thanks
For all the good He's done,
Who made the heavenly lights,
Earth that's warmed by sun.

Praise Him who won over
  Egypt,
Led His people through a sea,
Saving them from mighty kings;
Yes, their Savior, it was he.

PSALMS 137

Beside the River Babylon, we
Dreamed of Israel far away.
In sadness we were slaves,
In war they carried the day.

PSALMS 138

The Kings of earth, oh Lord,
Shall tell a wonderful story
Of Jehovah and His love,
Of Jehovah and his glory.

PSALMS 139

Oh Lord, you've examined me;
You know my every thought.
  So

Place your hand on me and
Make me do as I ought.

If I go up to heaven, or
If I stay here below,
You always will be there,
No matter where I go.

If I could saddle the wind
And to far oceans ride,
Or even into the darkness,
All those places you abide.

Search me out, oh God, test
My thoughts and my heart.
Always be beside me, for I
Would be where thou art.

PSALMS 140

Don't let the wicked prosper
Anywhere within our land.
But please help the godly;
Hold out your helping hand.

PSALMS 141

Answer my prayers to help
As I pray for sinners' lives.
Help me escape their traps;
Lord, for my soul I strive.

PSALMS 142

Hear my lonely cry; for ref-
uge you are my only place.
Save me from persecutors;
Only you can keep me safe.

PSALMS 143

I run to you for help, Lord,
Please listen to my plea.
My enemies have followed
And they want to capture me.

PSALMS 144

God is the blessed rock,
In battle He gives us skill.
In kind and loving ways,
He binds us to His will.

Oh Lord, why do you bother
With frail and feeble man?
He bends before the breeze;
He is hardly worth a glance.

I find myself a dreaming of
The wonderous land you rule.
There's no room for evil,
And no man plays the fool.

Daughters graced with beauty
Like pillars of palace walls.
Sons healthy and vigorous,
Who heed their parents' call.

Our barns are full of crops,
Thousands of sheep afield,
Great oxen loads of produce,
That glorious land will yield.

Where no enemy dares to tread,
There's peace upon the street.
For happy are the ones who'll
Be there for God to greet.

PSALMS 145

His awe inspiring deeds will
Be told by every tongue.
His strength sustains the old,
Gives dreams to the young.

He will judge the wicked
And heed His people's cries.
I'll praise His name forever,
From the valleys to the skies.

PSALMS 146

Unto Him I'll sing praises
Until my dying breath. For

With him lies eternal life,
And there's no fear of death.

He keeps every promise; He
Opens the eyes of the blind.
He gives hope to the hopeless
And food for every mind.

PSALMS 147

Hallelujah, bless the Lord,
Oh let His praises ring.
He heals the broken hearted,
And mends the broken wing.

His power is absolute; His
Understanding is too. He
Covers heaven with clouds
And sends the evening dew.

Praise Him Oh Jerusalem,
Be sure to praise His name.
He protects the City walls
And fills barns with grain.

PSALMS 148

Praise Him to the heavens
And to the sea below. His
Miracles are in the fire
And also in the snow.

PSALMS 149

Jerusalem, rejoice in God,
Praise Him in all you do.
Do His will in the nation,
For He takes pride in you.

PSALMS 150

Hallelujah, praise our
Lord with music and song.
Give praises, all living
Men, He's good, and strong.

END of PSALMS

PROVERBS

CHAPTER 1

He wrote to teach a people,
An effort to make them wise,
To give them understanding,
And not be taken by lies.

"Honor father and mother,"
He said, "hear what they say.
They've travelled the road
And can smooth the way.

Only fools will not listen;
Wisdom is for the taking. If

You think you're brilliant,
It's time for your awaking.

Do not do a dishonest thing,
Though so-called friends may
Lead down paths of crime
Though easy seems the deed.

Now wisdom often calls to
Keep you from distress. And
If you listen not, your
Lives will be a mess.

If you turned the other way
When wisdom beckoned, "Come!"

You found a life of crime,
And now you're on the run."

This, and more did Solomon
Write, to make a people wise.
To keep them well and happy
With no discouraged sighs.

CHAPTER 2

"To all people I say listen,
Good sense will be given you.
It's like hidden treasure, if
Reverence for God is true.

His word, a book of knowledge,
Good judgment He will reveal.
Wisdom and truth will follow;
Heaven's blessings will peal.

They'll keep you from evil,
And on the pathway of love.
Let stupid thieves stoop low;
You take the high road above.

Follow the steps of the godly;
Stay on a path that is right.
In evil we'll lose what we had
And succumb to the fight."

CHAPTER 3

"Never forget this my friend,
If happy and long you'd live.
Always be truthful and kind
And never fail to forgive.

Never trust only your wisdom;
It is just your best guess.
Seek first the will of God
Crown effort with success.

We're not wise enough to live
Conceited by what we know.
Follow God, refuse to do evil,
Success will be down the road.

Help the poor and helpless;
Honor the Lord with tithes;
With good health and success,
You'll drink the best wines.

If ever you are chastened
Accept it as proof He cares.
As a father He is teaching,
So you'll be alive and aware.

Wisdom is better than riches;
It gives a life of good cheer.
Pleasure in honor and peace,
Of quality better than years.

Wisdom established the earth,
In knowledge weather is made.
So rightly use common sense,
Don't let them slip away.

If you practice them well
You'll be safe on the trail.
Trouble won't hound you;
He will protect without fail.

Withhold no payment of bills,
Or offer to pay another time!
Or harm friend or neighbor,
That would surely be a crime.

Do not envy men of violence,
Nor get in needless fights.
Such things are abominable
To good men or in His sight.

The curse of God is on evil;
His blessing is on the good.
A wise man is given to honor,
A foolish is misunderstood.

CHAPTER 4

Young men, listen to me, as I
Once heard my father's voice.
He often talked with me
In the days when I was a boy.

For I was once a son, loved
Like an only child. And he
Told me many things of which
A good life is compiled.

"To be wise," he said, "good
Sense and judgment attain.
Love and cling to wisdom, she
Will help you time and again.

Be sure to learn this lesson;
Good living is best of all.
Be honest, wise and forgiving,
Or you may stumble and fall.

Avoid all evil men; they can
Not abide goodness as such,
But grope and stumble in sin
And blame it all on bad luck.

Walk the straight and narrow,
A kiss of prostitutes reject.
Stick to your path to be safe,
And God will guide every step."

CHAPTER 5

Run from the wayward woman;
Her charms are double edged
Swords. Smooth flattery her
Weapon, to make you get care-
less with words.

Betraying friends and home
Land are part of her trade.
Strangers she'll lead to your
Wealth; you may become anoth-
er's slave.

Later in shame you may reflect,
As you nurse a bad case of V.D.
Why didn't I take good advice,
For now disgrace is upon me.

Honor your father and mother;
Be considerate in all you do.

Their love, as a beam of light,
Is showing the pathway to you.

Lust not for beauty of women;
Don't let coyness seduce. They
Can bring a man to poverty;
His pride and honesty reduce.

CHAPTER 6

We might excuse a thief if
He stole for his family to
Eat. But a man is sure a fool,
If a wife or a man he'd cheat.

CHAPTER 7

Love wisdom like a sweetheart,
Walk with her the narrow path.
Let not a wayward woman
    spoil
The hard earned honor you
    have.

She'll be ready to seduce you,
And it soon will be too late.
You best resist her flattery,
Or you will be tempting fate.

CHAPTER 8

Now have an ear for wisdom;
She stands patiently in wait,
At every corner along the
Road and at the city gates.

To everyone she offers the
Knowledge of good and true,
Of the use of common sense
In everything you do.

Her words, clear and simple,
Carry the formula for life.
Greater than precious jewels,
Keep your heart from strife.

Wisdom and good judgment
   are
Partners in everything. Give
Knowledge and understanding
With power to godly kings.

She hates evil and deception
And every kind of vice, arr-
ogance and corruption; she
Helps you do what's right.

In ages past, wisdom was,
It is a universal thing. In
The starry light of heaven,
As soft as an angel's wing.

So listen to her counsel,
A wee small voice within.
Let her light your pathway
Away from the road to sin.

CHAPTER 9

Revere and fear our God;
This is basic wisdom for all.
Now if you listen carefully,
You will hear her gentle call.

CHAPTER 10

These are Solomon's sayings;
He warned of ill gotten gains.
Lazy men will soon grow poor
And often know great pain.

Happy are the parents
Of level-headed sons.
Sad, the mother of the rebel,
As from the law he runs.

When the sun is shining,
The wise man makes the hay.
But he'll miss opportunity
If he sleeps away the day.

A wise man you can teach,
For he makes his own luck.
With a fool you can try, but
You can't teach him much.

Only sorrow can result
If you wink at sin.
But if you boldly reprove,
You will know peace within.

A good man speaks with truth
For that is what he loves.
Curses come from evil men,
   who
Wear them much like gloves.

A wise man holds his tongue
And trouble often avoids.
A fool blurts his ignorance
And pleasure is destroyed.

One who can stand correcting
Is walking the path to life.
But he who refuses council,
Is on his way to strife.

To hate is to be a liar, to
Slander, a blithering fool. So
Keep your feet out of your
   mouth
And always keep your cool.

CHAPTER 11

For cheating and dishonesty,
God will let the wicked fall.
To honesty and righteousness,
The good man hears his call.

The whole city will celebrate
A goodly man's success.
And it will do the same when
A bad one's in distress.

A ruler who uses wisdom is
A good thing for his land,

For safety is in good council
By the quiet, thoughtful man.

Never vouch for credit
For a man you do not know.
That can cause you trouble
No matter where you go.

In giving you'll get richer,
In pleasure you'll be first.
But if you are miserly, no
One can quench your thirst.

Holding crops for profit,
If leaving others in need,
Is classed as a wicked act,
For such an evil deed.

If you search for good,
The Lord will smile on you.
But if you search for evil,
Then trouble will accrue.

If money is all you trust
You are riding for a fall.
But if you trust in God,
Then hear the Savior's call.

He who angers his family,
If he drinks and misbehaves,
Will lose all he loves,
And become another slave.

Men of godly wisdom plant
Trees that grow good fruit.
And winning men to God is
A target at which to shoot.

CHAPTER 12

Good men love animals and
Give them tender care. An
Evil man is mean to them
Even if trying to be fair.

A wise man hides wisdom,
As calm and quiet he goes.
A fool shows stupidity, as
Brilliance he would show.

Good men heed advice, and
Work for the good of all.
But the lazy man, or evil,
Plunges ahead and falls.

The good man keeps busy
Upon the road of life.
So what is there to fear?
He'll be free of strife.

CHAPTER 13

If you're in control, you
Also control your tongue.
This is true for you or
Me, or the old or young.

A good man hates all lies,
And all lies are the same.
They bring the liar down,
Cause the innocent pain.

Some who have great riches
Are poor in other things.
Poor men fear no ransom or
The problems riches bring.

Gamblers' riches don't last;
Wealth earned will grow. So
Forget hopeless dreaming
And earn wealth as you go.

We like plans to succeed,
'Tis a very pleasant dream.
Criticism is hard to take;
It tends to make us steam.

To accept it as we should,
It can mean lasting fame.
Only a fool refuses help if
He thinks he lost the game.

If you love your children,
Use authority as you should;
Discipline they need, so's
To know wrong from good.

CHAPTER 14

With kind mercy all day,
A wise woman makes a home.
Lacking love or calmness,
A dumb one wrecks her own.

Our blessed God we honor,
When we do what's right.
But to sin is to show,
That His laws we despise.

A rebel's foolish prattle
Can ruin his stupid pride.
But a wise man's speech
Is respected on all sides.

Men of wisdom and truth
Will not tell a lie. A
False one tells no truth,
Nor does he even try.

Take a wise man's advice,
Who always considers his
Acts. Stay away from the
Fool, who ignores facts.

The main bond of rebels is
Their guilty feeling. The
Common bond of people
Is good will in dealing.

Wicked works will perish
Though they seem to grow.
Down the wide and easy
Path none should ever go.

The backslider slides
And gets bored at himself.
To live well is exciting
And improves his health.

To scorn poor neighbors
Is a sin without end.
But blessed are those
Who show pity for them.

Those who brew trouble
Shall wander and stray.
Those who do good will
Find a pleasanter way.

Work is profitable, and
Doers are easily pleased.
Talk only is useless; it
Will not a debtor release.

A wise man has wisdom; a
Fool's folly is despised.
Honest witness can save;
False witness can demise.

CHAPTER 15

Both heaven and hell
Are to God an open book.
So are men's minds
Wherever He looks.

Cheerful is the man who
Meets life with a smile.
A sad look on a face
Invites unhappy miles.

A wise man looks forward
To the truths of the day.
A sinner lives on trash
To which he's a slave.

I'd rather be poor in the
House of the Lord, than
Have riches by the ship
Load with trouble aboard.

With humility and reverence,
Wise and honored you'll be.
And this will help you face
Most problems you meet.

CHAPTER 16

Everything is per His plan,
All things fulfill His need.
Honor God in all you do,
And you surely will succeed.

Wisdom is a fountain that
Waters the flowers of joy.
But a fool's burden is folly,
Life and love it destroys.

Without the pangs of hunger
And no incentive to labor,
Many idle hands and tongues
Would be in Satan's favor.

Evil begets much strife;
Gossip separates friends.
Wickedness seeks company
Brings pleasantness to end.

Better to control yourself
Than an army to command. We
Can toss a coin or hope;
God holds the winning hand.

CHAPTER 17

Better eat a crust in peace,
For it is a better break,
Than with dispute or strife
To every day eat steak.

A wise slave will control
His master's errant sons.
And one day he will share
In the estate they've won.

Silver and gold are pure
From the smelter's fires.
God will clear men's minds,
Of that He never tires.

Do not mock the poor for
The Lord made them too, or

Ignore their misfortunes;
They may turn back on you.

If a man rebels too much,
He may just seal his fate.
Many will rise against him;
He may get wise too late.

Better to meet a she-bear,
Whose cubs were just taken,
Than to confront a fool
Whom wisdom has forsaken.

To hide behind wickedness,
Or condone one who does, we
Are anathema to God
And will end up in the dust.

It's hopeless to teach one
With no use for truth. A
Brother helps when needed;
Friends are loyal too.

If you often co-sign for
Someone you don't know,
You may soon own his debt;
Your progress may be slow.

Sinful men love to fight;
Trouble follows a boast.
Evil men suspect everyone,
And they row a leaky boat.

To be a rebel's father
Is to be in constant pain.
No matter what one does
He sees no positive gain.

Like a dose of medicine, a
Cheerful face brings smiles.
But a sad one is heavy
And drags along for miles.

A man who takes a bribe
To pervert a law's intent

Is wicked in his heart,
And justice he has bent.

CHAPTER 18

A selfish person quarrels;
They always want their way.
Facts never please rebels;
They love a dreary day.

A fool is contentious;
Sudden revenge he proposes.
His mouth is his problem
More than he supposes.

He who bears a tale that
Would better be untold, may
Find his friends are not
And have left him cold.

No matter how broken a body,
As long as courage holds,
But once that courage fails,
The will to continue folds.

One side of any story is
That man's version only.
If the other side is told,
It may sound truly phony.

To flip a coin can save an
Argument between friends.
Let not a petty speech
An honored brother offend.

If a man is truly blessed
With a wife God did give,
He finds she's a helper
Who makes it good to live.

CHAPTER 19

Better be a poor man with
The problems that entails
Than to be a rich one
Upon a godless trail.

A man without knowledge is
Often a blithering fool. He
Rushes in where angels fear,
And cannot keep his cool.

There are many who entreat
The man who has much more.
He's everyone's "friend,"
Who's begging at his door.

When a man is down and out,
And brothers pass him by,
You can be pretty sure his
Friends won't hear his cry.

Wisdom is a bank account;
Good interest it will earn.
Liars will be caught; false
Witness should be spurned.

It seems quite strange
That a fool should succeed;
And for a fool to rule,
It seems strange indeed.

A wise man holds his anger,
He overlooks small wrongs,
He sits above mere malice,
Peaceful minded and strong.

A son who's prone to rebel
Is a pain in every sense.
A wife that always nags
Keeps a man tired and tense.

A lazy man sleeps soundly
With stomach lean and gaunt.
If he's too lazy to work,
He deserves to be in want.

Keep God's commandments
They give life and breath.
Despising and ignoring them
Can culminate in death.

Remember to help the poor;
His God is your God too.
The more you give to him,
The more He'll give to you.

While your son is young,
Discipline him as he needs,
Or maybe ruin his life, so
He'll commit unworthy deeds.

It's hard to try to help a
Man who is anger prone. He
Will face himself one day,
So leave him on his own.

Learn all you can in youth,
And all your life be wise.
Listen not to rebels,
Don't be taken in by lies.

Man proposes many things,
But only God can make it so.
Kindness is as kindness does;
Honesty makes beauty grow.

To love our God is life
In all its golden beauty.
It guides our every effort
Making safe our daily duty.

When a scorner is smitten,
Then the stupid understand.
But reprove a wise one,
And he'll be a better man.

When a father and a mother
Are mistreated by a child,
'Tis a blighted community
With all against him riled.

A witness who will lie will
Never change his ways. With
Mockers and with rebels,
He should be chased away.

CHAPTER 20

Wine holds false courage;
Hard liquor leads to fights.
It often masters drinkers;
Only foolish men imbibe.

If you are too lazy to
Plow in the planting season,
You'll have less at harvest,
For very obvious reasons.

Many things are wonderful,
When at your beck and call.
But having an honest father
Is probably best of all.

Every kind of cheating
Is to God a sinful fact.
Even a child's character is
Revealed by daily acts.

If you have good hearing,
Eyesight clear and strong,
Be sure to thank your God
In serious prayer and song.

No matter what it is, the
Buyer calls it junk or old.
But once it is his to sell,
It's like pure gold.

CHAPTER 21

The ways of man are right
As far as he's concerned.
But in the eyes of God
Was his pleasure earned?

He smiles down upon us,
When we are just and fair.
In His sight that is better
Than all the gifts we bear.

If lust and pride govern,
If evil is your way, if you

Often harm your neighbor,
Far from God you'll stray.

Meanness to his neighbors
Comes easy to a wicked man.
It seems to be his pleasure
Like part of a daily plan.

Proud and haughty, a mocker,
As his arrogant way he wends.
The evil man is stubborn;
But the godly man will bend.

Many things a lazy man covets,
But for work, he has no time.
The godly man gives to others,
For he knows it is no crime.

God hates the hint of bribery,
Even packaged as a gift.
A liar should be punished, if
False witness passes his lips.

No man can stand against him,
No matter how well prepared.
So you can plan for victory;
Only God can take you there.

CHAPTER 22

If I were to make the choice,
Then a good name I would
  hold.
For it is a better thing
Than diamonds, silver or gold.

In the eyes of God we're one,
Rich, poor, old or young.
The prudent man plans life,
But the fool will go unsung.

Raise your gaze to God, then
Riches or honor will be yours.
If you walk a rebellious path,
It will be a rocky course.

Much rather than a borrower,
Would I a lender be. For
When I borrow from another,
I'm subject to his greed.

He who plants but trouble
Shall harvest there in vain.
He who helps the poor shall
Know blessings for his pain.

Knowledge is the magic word;
It keeps men alive and well.
To resist the Lord's will,
Can make your life a hell.

I cannot go to work today;
The lazy man will cry.
For I might meet a lion,
And I'm not ready to die.

Painted women are traps,
Who'd set your lust athirst.
If you are that gullible,
Your life will be a curse.

He who bribes with earnings
Stolen from the poor will
Certainly be impoverished
Before his days are o'er.

Listen to good advice; all
Things to God entrust. Do
Not hide your faith, for He
Is righteous, and He's just.

Defend the poor and sickly,
And He'll be on your side.
Kick no man when he's down
Or God will have your hide.

CHAPTER 23

When dining with a ruler,
Do not a glutton be. Be
Aware that his delectable
Food may be stolen meat.

Why hurry to get rich, why
Should you your prime waste?
You may put riches first,
Just to have them fly away.

When you know a man is evil,
Then hold yourself aloof.
The food and favors offered
Cause upright men to stoop.

Discipline your child; do
Not from perseverence fly.
So by wisdom he shall live;
His soul shall never die.

He will speak with learning;
The world will smile on him.
So love the Lord completely;
Don't envy those who sin.

Be wise, my child, and keep
Away from drink or gluttony;
This is a form of laziness,
The surest way to poverty.

CHAPTER 24

Godless men are plotters,
Don't envy them their ways.
At cheating and in violence
They spend endless days.

A man of wisdom is mightier
Than the biggest one around.
Rebels known as wise men
Just do not abound.

Always rescue mankind;
Don't ever let him die.
And do not shirk your duty;
Do not ignore his cry.

God knows man's thoughts; you
Can bet He's aware of yours.
So do your job with wisdom;
It is your best course.

Many times he'll fall, but
Each time he'll return. For
The help of his God, the
Good man's work has earned.

If your enemy is down, don't
Rejoice at his defeat. The
Lord may turn on you, if
With your acts displeased.

So watch your step, my son,
Walk the straightest path.
Be friends to honest people
And avoid societies wrath.

When righteous are accused,
Help them stand their ground.
When man's sins are ignored,
Let them know you're around.

All good men are angered,
When money can buy a judge.
Blessed is the honest man,
Who in fairness won't budge.

Probity is honor's mark
A frank reply that's true.
Don't lie about a neighbor,
Even if he lied about you.

I spied a field one day where
Weeds grew above the grain.
Walls were crumbled down;
The sight gave me a pain.

As I looked, I knew the man
Who owned the field would be
A dozing and a resting,
Beneath yon shady tree.

A little time for slumber,
A few more minutes of rest,
Now poverty is upon him,
For he has failed the test.

CHAPTER 25

In the days of Solomon,
When Hezekiah was a priest,
Scrolls found in the Temple
Were copied and released.

These are some wisdoms app-
ropriate to that day. And
In these present times they
Still guide us on our way.

God, in all His glory, has
Secrets no one knows. It's
An honor worthy of kings,
To discover as you go.

When silver is refined, the
Sterling is ready to work.
Take cheats from government,
To help clean up the earth.

Keep problems with a friend
Just between you two. Being
Hot-heads and going public,
Is a bad thing to do.

Words of wisdom used with
Care, are like apples of gold.
He who listens with care
Reaps pearls of truth untold.

Those willing to earn a wage
Are like a breath of fresh air.
If they do not keep a promise,
Real truth may not appear.

Don't visit a neighbor's home
Till your welcome wears thin.
Nor tell a lie about another;
It will wound and trouble him.

Confidence if misplaced,
Is like a broken tooth. And
He with a heavy heart may
Resent the mirth of youth.

If your enemy is thirsty,
Make sure he gets his fill.
By practicing human kindness,
His hatred you can kill.

Always control your spirit
No matter where you go.
For unbecoming behavior
Will surely bring you low.

CHAPTER 26

Snow is strange in summer,
Or heat stroke if it's cool,
As is rain at harvest time
Or wisdom from a fool.

Why enter another's argument,
If you've problems of your
Own? It's like kicking a dog
Who is chewing on a bone.

Lying to a neighbor is
A sure way to start a fight.
And gossiping to others
Will never set it right.

Words can hide a wicked heart,
Just as paint will cover rust.
But like rust under the paint,
All too soon it will show up.

Beware the trap you set for
Others, you may be a victim.
Flattery to cover hatred
Is a certain contradiction.

CHAPTER 27

Don't brag about tomorrow,
Or of what you plan to do.
You never know for sure what
Tomorrow will bring to you.

To your father's neighbor and
Yours, stick with him to the

End. He'll be like a brother,
When you need a friend.

Always look ahead, my son,
And make your father proud.
Do not a simpleton be, who
Goes along with the crowd.

Pleasant visiting a friend
Is like sparks from flint.
It's a satisfying fellowship,
Which warms the heart within.

The beauty of a face does
Not a perfect person make.
Friends you choose can prove,
You have made a bad mistake.

A man who works for another
Must a living wage be paid.
Honor speaks for itself,
In a fair and even trade.

Diligent man is honor bound,
To work for reasonable gain.
To insure a families welfare,
So his work is not in vain.

CHAPTER 28

The wicked man is fearful
Watching the trail behind.
The honest man goes forward
Without a fear in mind.

With a dishonest government,
A country can easily fall.
But with honest leadership,
The land is good to all.

Oppression by the rich,
A poor man might expect. But
If exploited by the poor, his
Hopes will all be wrecked.

Complaint about a good law
Only helps an evil man.

To support a righteous rule
Is to fight all evil plans.

To the criminal element,
Justice is only a word.
But to the man of God
No better word is heard.

Better to be a poor man
With honor a known fact,
Than to be a rich one
With honesty only an act.

Young man, obey the law,
And make your father proud.
Those who exploit the poor
Are just an evil crowd.

Can those who flout the law,
Expect God to hear prayer?
Or if leading others astray,
Should their lives he spare?

Conceited rich are known, by
The poverty of their souls.
Their arrogance in success
Leaves the poor man cold.

When the wicked grow strong,
The poor and good must hide.
But when the wicked perish,
Goodly men must rise.

CHAPTER 29

Those who do what's right
No matter how much the cost,
Have met God's requirements;
Their names are not lost.

A ruler with good judgment,
Upright, just and fair, will
Have his people's blessings,
God's good will he'll share.

CHAPTER 30

Agur, son of Jakeh wrote,
These things did he write;
I am weary, and I'm tired,
In fact, I'm ready to die.

I feel I'm a stupid man,
In humanity out of place.
I know God is mystery who
Understands the human race?

God is one who can travel
From here to heaven and back.
Who else could the world of
Wind and water keep track.

His word is life itself,
And all he says is true. To
What he said in days of old,
We can add nothing new.

Two things I ask, oh Lord,
Grant my wish before I die.
Give me only enough to eat,
And don't let me tell a lie.

Don't ever feed me Lord, so
Well I forget thy name. Do
Not make me so poor I steal,
Or take thy name in vain.

Four things never satisfied,
The grave, flames of fire,
The desert sands for water,
And a barren womb's desire.

Many things I do not know;
Others I wish to understand.

How eagles glide across the
Sky, or serpents slide over
The land.

The ways of man and maid, the
Ship that navigates the sea,
And the adulterous woman
   who
Says, "There's no wrong in me."

CHAPTER 31

Kill not the days with women,
Nor things that destroy kings.
But for the poor and needy,
Let words of justice ring.

Find a virtuous woman, one
With love and honor to give.
Trust honor and truthfulness,
As long as both shall live.

She'll aid you with problems,
Help the poor and needy too;
She'll always do what's best,
All the while protecting you.

She'll have strength and love
And wisdom on her tongue.
   She
Will rear children in honor
And in your sight, stay young.

Let her know she is loved;
No other could take her place.
That her love and patience
Are stamped upon her face.

END OF PROVERBS

ECCLESIASTES

CHAPTER 1

King Solomon was wise; a
Very honest man was he. He
Was also King David's son;
How could one much wiser be?

He spent much time in thought,
Always returned to this theme.
To live this life without God,
A hopeless event would be.

Nothing is done these days
That hasn't been done before.
No matter how rich one gets,
He keeps wishing for more.

In spite of power and wisdom
The king so often displayed,
Evil and trouble abounded;
Suffering left him dismayed.

CHAPTER 2

So to himself, he said, "Now
A life of mirth I will find,
A time of peace and happiness,
But 'tis a figment of my mind.

Great riches I accrued with
Wealth more than any before.
I took all I desired, yet
My heart still vexed me sore.

I dreaded to think wisdom
Will no more than folly last.
And when they both shall die,
Memory is a thing that's past.

Things I'd labored for,
At my demise would be, by
Another with no effort,
All inherited from me.

I wondered what he'd do
With the loot he'd gained?
That thought bedeviled me;
It caused too much pain.

Now God's word came clear;
Man must work for wealth,
With wisdom and honesty,
To rest and good health.

CHAPTER 3

Everything has a time,
A time that's truly best,
A time to do great works,
Or to stop and rest.

To plant and to harvest,
To destroy and rebuild,
To laugh and to cry,
To heal or to kill,

To grieve or to dance,
To hug or to hate,
And for learning to love
It is never too late.

To scatter or gather,
Or to tear or repair,
A time to speak out,
Or be silent and share,

To find or to lose,
To keep or throw away,
For peace or for war,
To charge or to pay.

Then I asked of myself,
What is the object of work?
Would I be as well off,
If all duty I'd shirk?

Then the answer I found
As I thought on this theme,

If all men were lazy
This earth would be mean.

For the reward of a man
Is the work he has done.
Of the food and the drink,
And the pleasure he's won.

It seems often that justice
Gives way to the bad.
And that many good men
Have really been had.

So eat, be happy, enjoy
The fruits of your labor;
Earn good things of this
Life; enjoy a sweet savor.

CHAPTER 4

I observed the sad plight
Of the oppressed with many
Against them but none to
Fight at their behest.

The thought then came to me,
How much better to be unborn.
So you'd never see misery
Or have reason to mourn.

Envy and jealousy seem to
Be the driving force. So the
Fool refuses to work, for it
Seems a hopeless course.

The man with no kith or kin
Who works hard to get wealthy,
Where will it go when he dies?
The very thought is unhealthy.

Two can work so well, why
Should any alone grow old?
For often two can snuggle
And easily ward off cold.

If a man is young and willing,
And if he's able, and wise,

He can even become a ruler
And cut the world down to
  size.

Or if he's old and foolish,
And already is a king still
Both get old and perish;
It seems a hopeless thing.

CHAPTER 5

When to the house of God you
Go, take care in what you say.
Worship him sincerely but
Don't promise your life away.

If you give your word, but
Make promises you can't keep,
You'll lose face with God
And make your word seem
  cheap.

Better to make no promise
Than make a vow that's broken,
For to God and man, your word
Should not be just a token.

Be not at oppression dismayed,
But to government be alerted.
Bureaucrats run the system
Which is thoroughly perverted.

Each answers to a higher up;
No two see things the same.
The law applied to a poor man
Is usually a different game.

A spendthrift is never happy
No matter how much he earns.
He spends as much as he
  makes
And never seems to learn.

The man who labors diligently
Seldom misses a night's sleep.

But the rich man worries much
Protecting riches he'd keep.

Naked to this life he came
And without riches he will go.
So what do riches accomplish,
Except to cause him woe?

Eat and drink, be thankful
To God for all he gives.
For this is your portion,
So be thankful that you live.

CHAPTER 6

Some who are very rich don't
Live to spend their gain. And
Some who live for many years
May die in poverty and pain.

For into vanity man is born,
And the same he oft' departs.
So just what has he gained
If not peace in his heart?

CHAPTER 7

A reputation for being good,
Is a worthwhile goal to seek.
More valuable than riches, it
Makes stronger one who's
   weak.

It is better to be serious
Than be merry like a fool.
Why mourn the "Good old
   days",
They weren't all that cool.

To finish is much better,
Than still having to start.
Do not be quick tempered,
It tears a man apart.

Wisdom is better than wealth,
But so little money can't buy.

He can get more than riches,
Who is ambitious and wise.

You may suffer a sad fate if
You're too certain of yourself.
So take things as they come
And be thankful for Gods help.

A man of wisdom is stronger by
Far than most any group of men.
And not any man is sinless,
Not even one in ten.

I have searched all the people
And found wise men very few.
Although God made men
   upright,
We all are prone to stoop.

CHAPTER 8

He who thinks of judgment
And considers things sublime
Is indeed a man of wisdom,
Who will keep away from
   crime.

Judgment of an evil act
Does not often instantly come.
So that sinful acts are
Easily forgotten by some.

Judgment is often meted to
Those who much better
   deserve.
Doing good is superior to bad,
So at least most observe.

No matter how I search, I
Find that this is always so;
Rich or poor, fool, or wise,
Our futures only God can know.

CHAPTER 9

A man may be powerful, even
The strongest in the land.

Yet when called by death, he
Is helpless as any other man.

None can stop that call
No matter how they try.
For to each and every man
There comes a time to die.

So often we tend to believe
God rewards us here on earth.
And so the mighty battle
To increase our worldly worth.

I saw too, upon this earth,
Speed doesn't win all races.
And prizes don't always go
To those with handsome faces.

One can be most wise
And do great things for man,
But if not already famous,
Recognition may be banned.

All men should have wisdom,
The greatest of nature's tools.
In silence it speaks louder
Than a shouting king of fools.

CHAPTER 10

In ignorance a fool may dwell,
For he really doesn't know,
That although he feels wise,
His lack of wisdom shows.

These are the kind of men,
Who often rule the land.
So thus there is a problem,
Till wisdom takes a stand.

Never curse a man for things
Wherein you think he's failed.
For he is sure to hear, and
You'll wish you hadn't railed.

CHAPTER 11

Of your wealth be not greedy,
But help those in dire need.
The day may soon come, when
You gain from this good deed.

If we hide behind excuses,
The job will never get done.
So keep on doing good;
It will surely help someone.

It is wonderful to be young
And of fun to get your fill.
But keep in mind that God
Expects you to pay your bills.

CHAPTER 12

Remember the days of youth;
Prepare for the onset of age.
As Life's desires are failing
You're nearing a final stage.

Let wise words be heeded, and
May they your consience goad.
For all your acts he'll judge
At the end of your road.

END OF ECCLESIASTES

THE SONG OF SOLOMON

CHAPTER 1

Girl: "Kiss me again my king;
Your love is better than wine.
You brought me to your palace,
And your presence is devine!

I'm tanned by the summer suns,
For I'm a keeper of the sheep.
But my king thinks I am
Beautiful, even in my sleep.'

Oh tell me my love, where
Lead your flock today?
For I am prone to join you,
Wherever you lead the way."

So the king would make
    answer,
"Oh, beautiful woman, to me,
Bring your flock and follow;
I will care for your needs.

For thou, my love art fair,
Thy beauty a thing to behold.
I'd drape thy neck and arms
With chains of pure gold."

"Oh yes, my king," says she,
"When at your table we meet,
Your presence is an aroma of
Balsam and myrrh so sweet.

For behold, fairest of all,
Fresh and green is our bed,
As through the pleasant night,
You lie betwixt my breasts."

CHAPTER 2

She's the lily of the valley,
And of Sharon, she's the rose.
He's the apple of her eye,
As in splendor there he goes.

He leaps over the mountain,
Comes bounding over the hills.
He says, "Arise my love, come,
Spring is here, winter stilled.

So come to me, my love, let
Me hear your lovely voice. For
You're the fairest of them all;
You're my darling of choice."

CHAPTER 3

"Once I awoke in fear, for I
Found my love not there. But
With diligent love I searched,
And found him ere despair.

I took him to my mother's bed,
And I left him in deep sleep.
Girls of Jerusalem, let him
Rest as long as he please.

He made himself a chariot
Adorned with silver and gold.
With three score warriors to
Guard and his safety enfold.

Oh, daughters of Zion, behold
His glorious crown enthroned.
'Twas his mothers wedding gift
On the most glorious day he's
    known."

CHAPTER 4

"How fair you are, my dear,
Eyes as soft as turtle doves.
Your lips full and ruby red,
Your speech of unending love.

So come with me, my darling,
To the garden of our delight.
Amid frankincense and myrrh,
And glory that is bright."

CHAPTER 5

Solomon calls from his garden,
A place most fair to the eye.
She now had a dream, and of
This dream she cries.

"I heard my love at the door,
And he asked me to let him in.
But I fumbled as I did
And thus committed sin.

For before I opened up,
He had long been gone.
I had tarried in my welcome;
I had taken much too long.

Then I searched the city over,
I searched in fear and pain.
I asked the help of others,
But my plea was in vain.

I asked Jerusalem's daughters
To send him to me. Now
They asked me why my love
Could ever, so special be.

I told them all the things
That set him above others.
What made him surpass
  friends,
Champions, or brothers."

CHAPTER 6

"Whither is thy beloved gone?"
The girls I asked would know.
"We will help you find him,
Since you love him so!"

"Among lilies he pastures his
Flock; that is where he'll be.
For I am his, and he is mine;
He is all good things to me."

"Oh beautiful shulamite girl,"
He cries, "I'm in love with

You; you're fairer than the
Lily and fresher than dew.

Three score queens are mine
And eighty concubines, you
Are fairer than all virgins;
You, my love, are truly mine."

CHAPTER 7

"Your eyes are deep as pools;
Your lips sweeter than wine.
Thy form is stately and royal;
Your love, my dear, is mine."

"Oh come my love," she cries,
"I'd truly please thy desire.
So let us go to the vineyards
And to our love aspire."

CHAPTER 8

"If you had been my brother,
In public we could kiss.
For in the house of my mother
They'd have expected this."

At Baal-hamon, his vineyard
Earns a thousand silver pieces.
"Let me be a vineyard for my
Darling to do with as he
Pleases."

"Thou beautiful, lovely woman,
Who under an apple tree I
Loved; set my seal upon thy
Heart, for thou art fair as
That above.

Of thee, I am jealous, which
Is as cruel as the grave,
It is a thing that does not
Help, nor does it ever save."

END OF THE SONG OF SOLOMON

ISAIAH

CHAPTER 1

In those days of long ago,
From God people fell away.
Those of Jerusalem and Judah
Scoffed and did not obey.

Uzziah, Jotham, Hezekiah, and
Ahaz, were kings those days,
And Isaiah was a prophet who
Tried to change their ways.

He had a very real vision
In which God spoke to him
Of the nation's waywardness
And of people's outright sin.

Your land is in ruins;
Your cities are in flames.
Why won't you confess
And admit to your blame?

Why waste your time
With sacrifices and gifts,
For unless you do repent,
God has no use for this.

Your gifts are a mockery;
Sacrifices are in vain. You
Have blood on your hands;
You've caused much pain.

I will redeem you, my people,
And your judges I'll return.
But the sinners, the scoffers,
And rebels I will spurn.

CHAPTER 2

It shall come to pass,
In the days of tomorrow,
There'll be no widows of war,
None will know such sorrow.

For beaten into plowshares
Will be the engines of war.
Armies and their battles
Will be seen here no more.

Then Zion will be known
As the seat of God's rule.
And when that time comes
'Twill be a rebuke to fools.

For those who've forsaken
The Lord God of their fathers
Will be in great trouble and
By His word will be bothered.

The lofty shall be humbled,
And the haughty will bow low.
Into clefts of rocks and
High mountains they will go.

CHAPTER 3

I will take away the water;
No longer will food be there.
Commoners and kings will die
Fighting for an equal share.

All the land of Judah
Will be ruled by fools.
Every man of wisdom
Will have lost his cool.

Thy women who were
  haughty
Shall come to a sorry end.
Their ways were abominable,
Which they refused to mend.

By the sword your men shall
Fall, all mighty men of war.
You will have more trouble
Than you ever had before.

CHAPTER 4

When days of trial are past
And time of judgment over,
With seven women to each
  man,
The land will be in clover.

God will clean Jerusalem
By taking all her sins away.
With a halo of fire at night
And a cover of smoke by day,

They'll be shaded from sun,
Sheltered from storm or rain.
'Twill be the city of love
With God's protection again.

CHAPTER 5

If my love owned a vineyard
And grapes in it were sour,
It would be a sad experience,
An exceedingly bitter hour.

He might rip out the fences
And tread on all the vines.
For they'd be of little use
In the making of sweet wine.

"This is Judah and Jerusalem,"
Says God in great distress.
"Why should I ever help them
Or their efforts bless?

They dance and drink all night
And don't try to do my will.
Like a harvest of sour grapes
They do not fill the bill.

They have spurned the help
I've given all these years. So
I'll withdraw from them and
Let them drown in their tears.

The enemy shall come from far
And captives will be taken.

To common sense and
  godliness,
Their minds would not
  awaken."

CHAPTER 6

The year King Uzziah died, I
Saw the Lord upon His throne.
The Temple filled with glory
And also filled with smoke.

"Oh woe is me,"
I cried in fear,
"Unclean am I,
What am I doing here?"

A seraphim flew to me with a
Live coal in hand. Touched
My lips with fire, and said,
"Your sins are purged, oh man."

Then I heard the Lord of glory,
I clearly heard him ask,
"Whoever can I send
Who is equal to this task?"

"Here I am, send me," said I;
"On this job I'll go." "With
Much to tell," He said, "they
Will never believe it's so."

"How long do I tell them,
How long this sorry state?"
"Until the cities empty," He
Said, "and the land desolate.

Just one in ten shall live;
Only the holy shall return.
Even though you prophesy,
Only a very few will learn."

CHAPTER 7

When Ahaz of Judah ruled,
Israel and Syria attacked.

And Ahaz was badly worried
By their warring acts.

Then Isaiah was sent so the
King might fear no loss. For
Those fighting against him
Must never be his boss.

By Isaiah came the word that
Ahaz would win the war, but
Ahaz wouldn't bend and show
Thankfulness to the Lord.

Then Isaiah spoke to them in
Some exasperation. "Why do
You provoke your God? You
Are a very trying nation.

Now listen to this prophecy,
A child, a virgin will bear.
Long before He's born, your
Enemies will not be there.

She'll call His name Emanuel,
Which means that God is near.
Because these words I preach,
You refuse to really hear.

In time your luck will fail;
Your land will be over thrown.
With only a few people left
To herd and till their own.

The conqueror will come; he
Will rip your land to and fro.
Back to brush and thorns
In time it will all grow."

CHAPTER 8

I made a sign as commanded
That I'd soon father a boy.
His name would mean, "Your
enemies will be destroyed."

And soon as time went on,
My good wife conceived.

And I named him as directed,
For my Lord I truly believed.

Then again His voice I heard,
Decrying their lack of faith.
Some were joining the enemy.
A war they could not face.

They doubted all His promises
Of no deaths or wounds. So He
Would overflow the Euphrates
And they'd all perish soon.

Syria and Israel ready for war,
Their efforts are for naught.
Let no one surrender in Judah;
This war need not be fought.

I know that I am safe; the
Meaning of "Isaiah," my name,
Is a symbol from God saying
"Jehovah's will be saved."

Why ask mediums or witches!
Why not listen and learn?
The very name, "Shear Jashub,"
Means "A remnant will
    return."

But people will not listen.
When weary, hungry, and cold,
Shaking fists at the king, at
God they mutter and scold.

CHAPTER 9

People who walk in shadow,
Shall not forever thus go.
The light of God will shine,
So Israel's people will glow.

For in the days to come,
When a child to us is born,
Twill be a day of peace with
No reason for any to mourn.

From David's line to descend,
In justice and peace to reign.
For now God chastises from
Philistia and Syria with pain.

In spite of all their trials
Israel will refuse to repent.
The Lord will quickly purify;
He will not soon relent.

But his hand is reaching out
Hoping they'll see the light.
For God is ready to forgive
If they'll do what's right.

CHAPTER 10

Woe to a crooked ruling class
Who lie in wait to steal from
Widows, orphans and the poor;
Their fate they'll surely seal.

Where will they find haven if
War comes from distant lands?
Yet God's help is waiting, if
With Him they'll take a stand.

Syria's King thinks himself
The greatest king around.
But even while he's bragging,
The Lord will bring him down.

The enemy will advance in
Strength and powerful array.
But God will pass judgment,
And plague will put them away.

CHAPTER 11

From the Royal line of David
(It was cut off like a shoot,)
A new branch will sprout; it
Will grow up from that root.

A tremendous spirit of wisdom,
Good counsel with God's
  might,

Clothed in truth and fairness;
Duty to God is His delight.

There'll be peace on earth
Such as man cannot recall.
No creatures shall be enemies;
A child shall lead them all.

Cows will graze with bears;
Calves and cubs will play.
Babes will handle adders and
Play with poisonous snakes.

From the lands of the earth
God will bring people home.
They will then believe Him
And soon come to their own.

CHAPTER 12

On that day you will say,
I know that God loves me.
He was angry with me once,
But now His love I see.

I'll trust and never fear;
He is my strength and song,
So with my Lord to lead me
I just cannot go wrong.

So I thank the Lord and
Praise His name.
I will tell of His love
And shout His fame.

CHAPTER 13

See Babylon lose to an
Enemy straight and tall.
The Gentile sinners
Will suffer, faint and fall.

Heaven is dark above them;
No light from stars or moon.
Fighting men will stumble,
Their time is here too soon.

A city where sin was master,
To rise and shine no more,
It will suffer the ravages
Of a thoroughly angry Lord.

CHAPTER 14

He'll have mercy on people,
For they are still His own.
He'll bring them back again
To occupy the ancient home.

As for that evil King, you
Know he played the fool. So
God has crushed his power
And broken his evil rule.

At last the earth is quiet;
Nations with you've joined.
Lucifer, you have fallen
From power you purloined.

For you said you'd ascend
To be mightier than our God.
But now you are buried with
No rights, a hopeless clod.

Word came through Isaiah,
When King Ahaz died. "The
King you smote is dead, but
By his son you'll be tried."

So Israel's trial will end,
And a new era will begin
Behind Jerusalem's walls;
All will be safe within.

CHAPTER 15

This was the message to Moab:
Cities and people will die.
The bravest of your warriors
In utter terror will cry.

Your people will be scattered;
Rivers will be red with blood.

Some to be food for lions;
Disaster has come in a flood.

CHAPTER 16

To Judah send gifts to sooth
And beg for asylum there. Ask
Protection in their shadow,
Sanctuary they may share.

Moab was so proud, its
Arrogant insolence all gone.
Enemy warlords have struck;
It's singing a different song.

They pray anguished, to idols.
For Moab I'll weep in sorrow;
Their days of glory are gone;
All is bleak for tomorrow.

So oft' your people were told
About courting total demise.
In three years your glory will
End with few if any alive.

CHAPTER 17

Now this message to Damascus,
To Syria's capital city,
Once proud and so arrogant
But now an object of pity.

Like Israel you will fade;
Your glory a thing long past.
Even your largest cities
Will be emptied out at last.

Your idols will have failed,
Things your hands have made!
So now you'll turn to God,
For only He can save.

CHAPTER 18

You people of the Nile may
Assemble your armies and go

268

Attack Israel's ruined lands
And hope to find them so.

As you plan your wicked coup
God will intercede. You'll
Be casualties upon the field
Where you planned your deed.

Then in time to come, from
Lands far and near, to the
Holy God of Israel men will
Bring much hope and cheer.

CHAPTER 19

On a cloud He swiftly rides,
The avenging God of Israel.
Egypt fights each other,
Which in time will tell.

Five cities accede; even the
Hebrew language they adopt.
Jehovah will hear their plea,
And He will be their God.

From Egypt to Assyria, there
Will be a common path. Three
Nations He'll accept, who'll
No longer feel His wrath.

CHAPTER 20

The King of Assyria captured
Ackdad of Philistine land.
God told Isaiah to disrobe,
And go about a naked man.

He said, "My servant, Isaiah,
Who's gone naked three years,
Is a symbol of trying times,
Ethiopia and Egypt in tears.

As prisoners of Assyria, un-
covered and naked in shame.
Philistines will be dismayed
Due to their earlier fame.

If this can happen to them,
What chance have we to stand?
We counted on their help in
Order to hold our land."

CHAPTER 21

In an awesome vision I saw
Babylon's time would come,
Its mighty army vanquished,
The survivors on the run.

A watchman on the wall, at a
Banquet we prepared to eat,
Called, "They come to attack,"
So we scrambled to our feet.

He cried, "Babylon is fallen!
Idols broken on the ground.
Oh come rescue its fugitives
From being hunted down.

Yet a year the war will wage,
And Kedar's power will fade.
Few mighty archers will live;
This word the Lord has made."

CHAPTER 22

Now this message to Jerusalem,
"Why are your people amazed?
Bodies all over the street,
Your city is being razed!

Tell Shebna the ruler that
He is building in vain. For
God is removing His blessing!
His future is exile and pain.

I'll replace you with Eliakim.
Your uniformed title he'll get.
He will be a good leader,
Better than you, you can bet."

CHAPTER 23

"Before Israel's rescue, men
Of Tyre you should know, you

Will find utter destruction
When back to your home you
   go.

You've had a glorious history,
A great seaport of the world;
Babylon will defeat you as
His conquering anger unfurls.

Babylon was God's tool to
Defeat you, oh wicked Tyre,
So flee to Tarshish, but
You'll not avoid His ire.

He commands Heaven's legions
To get His Royal way. All
The final word is His, and
He will surely make our day.

Seventy years you'll drift,
And awake to another king.
The Lord will see the day
When His praise people sing."

CHAPTER 24

The city will be in chaos;
Homes will be locked tight.
Over all the land it's thus,
All men frozen with fright.

When only a remnant is left,
Shouts of joy they'll raise.
From east to west will come
Giving tongue to praise.

From His throne in Zion He
Will govern earth in glory.
Justice and beauty will rule
His people of ancient story.

CHAPTER 25

Mighty cities are in ruins;
Strong forts are torn down.
Ruthless nations fear your
Name for many miles around.

All mankind will proclaim,
You are God in whom we trust.
You will crush all evil works,
And grind the enemy to dust.

CHAPTER 26

We wandered from your love;
To other gods we paid respect.
We missed a loving presence;
Our lives we nearly wrecked.

Yet we have assurance that
This life is temporary pain.
For those who live for God
Will surely live again.

CHAPTER 27

That day the Lord will take
His swift and powerful sword.
In the day of our freedom
Let this then be His word.

"Israel is my vineyard, the
Lord will tend their vines.
I have lost my anger toward
Them; they are truly mine."

CHAPTER 28

You drunkards of Samaria, in
The valley of delight, your
Priests and prophets stagger,
No sober leaders in sight.

Often you made mistakes,
Just as drunkards always do.
You don't listen to the Lord;
He tries to plead with you.

How long can a farmer plow
Without planting the field?
How long before you realize
You must eventually yield?

CHAPTER 29

Jerusalem, your future is woe!
For year by year you claim
To pay service to God, but
Your deeds are only in name.

Your God will be your enemy
With legions camped about.
And suddenly with no warning,
He will put your foes to rout.

Your future will be veiled,
Like walkers in your sleep;
Not knowing what is coming,
For knowledge is too deep.

CHAPTER 30

Write this down for proof,
This message you received.
Your road is rough and rocky
Because you won't believe.

But your Lord is waiting
For you to see the light.
For this is His main hope, to
Help you set things right.

CHAPTER 31

Friends and enemies alike,
The Lord's sword will smite.
All the people of Israel
Will know that He is right.

CHAPTER 32

A righteous king is coming
With honest sons to reign.
A mighty rock in the desert,
To shield His own from pain.

Erring tongues will steady;
By man's behavior he's known.
Shiftless and lazy women
Will reap as they have sown.

CHAPTER 33

Now to the Assyrian hoards,
Whom God used to His ends,
You gloried in your strength
And in pity would not bend.

Strength will turn against
You; you'll no more prevail;
And wherever you put your
Hand, you will surely fail.

He will to His people be, a
Fortress upon the mount, for
They'll have food and water,
Blessings they can't count.

God is a swift river our en-
emies cannot cross. He'll
Forgive our every error;
We shall not suffer loss.

CHAPTER 34

Isaiah tried to warn them
Of Armageddon days to come.
Many nations waging battle
Before the Lord would run.

The dead would be unburied;
Blood would flow in streams.
Weak and strong would fall,
As in a horrible dream.

For many generations desol-
ation shall rule the land.
Tested and found wanting,
This is the fate of man.

CHAPTER 35

Yet Zion's hills and vales
Will bloom and rejoice. The
News will cheer His people,
For the blessings employed.

He will bid them all come,
The weak, deaf, and blind.
No evil men will go there,
Only the good and kind.

CHAPTER 36

To Judah in wars of victory
Sennacherib's armies came.
The Assyrians camped at the
Gates in Hezekiah's reign.

To a team of truce they met,
The leader bragged and blew,
That the alliance with Egypt
"Will be no help to you.

Don't expect help from God
Who with idols was replaced.
The nations who've resisted
Have fallen in disgrace.

Your army's badly beaten;
Winners you just won't be.
It'll be a total disaster,
If your city we besiege."

Israel didn't want people
In great fear, so they
Said, "Speak Aramaic for
Our walls all have ears."

Now Sennacherib's speaker,
With voice loud and harsh,
Spoke in Hebrew to plant
Panic in their hearts.

He shouted to the walls,
"Just what can you do?
Our armies are stronger
Than what is left of you.

Come out to us now, and
We will treat you well.
But if you resist, we will
Make your lives a hell."

Now many people listened;
They answered not a word,
And Hezekiah's committee
Were very much disturbed.

CHAPTER 37

The king sent servants to
Isaiah and anguished said,
"Sennacherib threatens and
Heaps abuse on God's head.

So please pray to God, so
His people he will save.
Our demise seems very near;
These truly are bad days."

Isaiah answered, saying,
"Your king need not worry;
The enemy will get a call
And leave here in a hurry."

A crown prince of Ethiopia
Was leading an army his way.
King Sennacherib prepared
For the coming of that fray.

To Libna, Sennacherib and
The besiegers returned. But
They left a message with
Jerusalem, who they spurned.

"We've left you for now,
But you should be warned
That we shall return, and
Your walls will be stormed.

You know we've won against
Those we've fought before.
Gods and idols didn't stop
Us, neither can your Lord."

The answer went back to
Their challenger so rude,
Saying, "Boasting is empty;
Your thinking is crude.

Why do you think it was
So easy to win,
If you didn't have help
On the job from within?

You scoffed at our Lord
Who helped in your coups;
You can bet your life
He'll take care of you."

That night the Lord's angel
Came and visited his camp.
He left Sennacherib's spirit
Chagrined and damp.

A hundred eighty-five thous-
and next morning were dead.
It must have been a warning
And a sign of things ahead.

Then to Nineveh he returned
And to a pagan god prayed.
Two of his sons killed him
And made good their escape.

So the prophecy came true
In which Isaiah had said,
"He will never return
For soon he'll be dead."

CHAPTER 38

Now quite some time before,
The king was sick and frail.
Isaiah now spoke to him
Causing his heart to quail.

"Set your affairs in order;
Your time has come to die."
Now Ahaz faced the wall and
He sure prayed and cried.

"Lord, I'm only started on
Things I want to do. I'm
Just not ready to go, and I
Am most faithful to you."

The Lord sent a messenger,
And this in essence said.
"God has heard you, you'll
Do more alive than dead.

I give you fifteen more years,
And I'll come to your defense.
You're safe from Syria's King,
And this will prove my intent.

Ten degrees I'll move the Sun,
It will go from west to east.
So you'll know without doubt,
From death you're released."

Then Hezekiah was so happy
That in thankfulness he wrote;
"I felt, in the prime of life,
I most surely would be smote.

Then I cried, I wailed and
Lay awake all night, saying,
Oh Lord your plans are good,
But I need a longer life.

Then He answered my prayers,
So all my life I'll sing.
For He surely is my God, and
In Jerusalem I'm still king.

For the boils that I had
He made an ointment to heal,
And the sign I had asked
Was part of the deal."

CHAPTER 39

Babylon's King congratulated
Him, for He was now well. So
The king showed his treasure;
He'd fallen under their spell.

Now Isaiah in dread told him,
"Those spies came to observe.
They'll loot your kingdom and
As eunuchs your sons will
Serve."

"Oh well," said Hezekiah,
"The harm's already been done.
But I'll not face the music,
We'll leave that to my sons."

At least that was the gist
Of what Hezekiah said. For
He knew when it happened
He'd be already dead.

CHAPTER 40

"Speak softly to Jerusalem,"
The word came to Isaiah then.
"Her sins will be pardoned,
And her punishment will end."

I heard a voice of shouting,
"Make a road in wilderness.
Fill hollows, level the bumps,
Remove all of travel's stress.

Make a highway for the Lord,"
I heard a voice call, "Shout."
Then the thing I asked was,
"What shall I shout about?"

"Shout of man, who like grass,
Dies and his image fades. Who,
Compared to the beauty of God
Is of dust, a mere charade.

He strengthens the tired
And encourages the weak.
They who wait upon the Lord
Will always hear Him speak."

CHAPTER 41

Oh listen to me now
You islands of the sea, let
The people draw on strength;
Have them come close to me.

Who raised this conqueror who
Drives kings before His sword?

Who said from the beginning,
You must know, "I am the
  Lord."

They said to one another,
"Cyrus is God's and so are we.
Perhaps he'll give us quarter,
Or so at least it would seem."

So they helped each other,
As new idols they did make;
For before the warrior Cyrus,
All the land did quake.

But you Israel are my servant,
The seed of Abraham, my
  friend.
And I'll be with you always
Even to the end.

But Israel will thrive to
Witness for the world to see.
The Lord will show His hand;
The world will know t'was He.

Now what of all those idols,
Did they prophesy anything?
Was there any warning or
Help that they could bring?

Not one could give answer;
They had no knowledge within.
Just witless, foolish things
And as empty as the wind.

CHAPTER 42

See my servant, my chosen one,
In whom I much delight.
I've put my spirit upon him;
He will make the nation right.

He will not shout or yell or
Rouse rabble in the streets,
Will not damp a gentle heart,
And only truth he'll mete.

He'll bring a blinded people
By a path hitherto unknown.
He will smooth and straighten
The road and protect His own.

But those people He had hoped
Would bring glory to His name
Are prisoners in their land,
Trapped and for all fair game.

They refused to listen and
Went on their erring ways. So
That is why He punished them,
He made difficult their days.

In ignorance they pushed on
In spite of the hints He sent.
It seemed they'd never guess;
He wanted them to repent.

CHAPTER 43

So my people do not fear, for
I'll be with you all the way.
I'll bring you all together
For that future glorious day.

When I call the nations of
The world I'll say, "Come.
Can idols tell your future?
I am God and the only one!

Around the earth I'll make a
Road to bring you back home.
You've been a sinful people
Where on earth you roamed.

You've caused your problems,
Not seriously taken my name.
So then I destroyed Israel;
I let her struggle in shame."

CHAPTER 44

Oh pay attention, Israel,
Be sure you return to me.

For I have paid your price,
It is I who'll set you free.

CHAPTER 45

Now this message to Cyrus
Who is God's anointed man,
With power at his disposal
To conquer many lands.

He shall go before you, but
God shall open up the gates.
He will smash the iron bars
Of Babylon the great.

There are hidden treasures;
Secret riches will be yours.
He'll call you by your name,
As He guides your course.

He made the darkness and
Caused the light. He will
Guard your step by day and
Remove your fear at night.

Who makes up idols? Who
Are those fools who say
They hope to get results
As to idol gods they pray?

All the world shall know
Of Jehovah's great name.
All who were angry at Him
Will come to Him in shame.

Every man shall know Him
And every knee shall bow,
As everyone on earth
Will total allegiance vow.

Israel shall be justified,
In triumph they shall see,
Of all the gods of name,
None are as great as He.

CHAPTER 46

Babylon, Bel and Nebo are
Taking the idols away.
When they fall down, that
Is where they'll stay.

I'm the one who made you;
I'll carry you all the way.
From your time of birth
Until your dying day.

If you trust in idols, can
They tell what to expect?
Remember, I'll protect and
Save you who are my elect.

CHAPTER 47

Your judgment day, Babylon,
Is a thing you must face.
For your days of honor and
Glory will be taken away.

You punished my people
Which they richly deserved.
But you went too far to
The point of being absurd.

You ground their faces in
Sand; they had no recourse.
Now they show repentance,
But you show no remorse.

So, oh wicked kingdom, call
Your demon hordes whom
You worship all the time
In preference to the Lord.

Star gazers and astrologers
Tell you all is well. But
Beware of what they say for
They can't save themselves.

CHAPTER 48

Hear me, oh my people: you
Claim allegiance to me, but

Brag of living in Jerusalem;
Your convictions are weak.

I've told you often certain
Things would come to pass,
But you are deaf with iron
Necks and heads of brass.

CHAPTER 49

Then Isaiah told of Jesus,
The Holy One God would send.
He would be all powerful
Yet meek and kind with men.

He'd restore Israel to God
And bring the Gentiles home.
He'd bring God to every man,
So none need stand alone.

He'd smooth mountain trails,
Cross deserts without thirst.
But they'd still complain,
Yet God would put them first.

In time of feast or plenty,
They'd see signs on the wall,
That God the mighty redeemer
Is the Savior of us all.

CHAPTER 50

If God spoke to you today,
These questions He might ask,
"Did I cause your problems,
Or with misery fit your task?

Was I too weak to save you;
Are your needs too great for
Me? You know that is not so,
For I can calm the sea."

If man only trusts himself,
And doubts God's tomorrow,
He is being deluded and will
Surely know much sorrow."

CHAPTER 51

Listen! Israel, don't fret
That your numbers are small.
Now your God is with you,
And you will hear His call.

Remember Abraham and Sarah;
That is whence you came.
They sired a mighty nation,
And you will do the same.

He'll rule nations after
Cleansing earth with fire.
Your land will be an Eden
In pure salvation attired.

CHAPTER 52

Beautiful on the mountain
Is the bearer of good news.
The God of Israel reigns;
He has redeemed the Jews.

Shed your bonds of slavery
And leave Babylon behind.
You are redeemed of God;
He has cleansed your mind.

Though my servant be beaten,
He'll stand bloodied alone;
He will cleanse the nations,
And they shall all atone.

CHAPTER 53

Oh how few believed it, for
He is rejected and despised.
He was not attractive
To our jaundiced eyes.

In His Father's sight He
Was like a tender shoot in
A dry and sterile desert
Sprouting from a root.

Oppressed and afflicted,
Yet not once complained, He
Died for our afflictions; and
Bore our shame and pain,

Following God's great plan
As they led Him to His death.
Even when He prayed for us,
For we sinful ones He pled.

CHAPTER 54

The mountains may fade away,
And the hills may disappear,
His promise of peace is good,
So you never shall know fear.

You'll live in houses with
Precious jewelled walls.
You shall know no terror
With God on instant call.

CHAPTER 55

If you'd eat at a full table
Or drink from a flowing well,
Then come to me and listen;
I've great things to tell.

The Lord will accept you no
Matter how dark your past.
And only things He promises
Can you be sure will last.

For as He was to David,
A friend in times of need,
You can depend on Him
To rescue you in deed.

Let all men turn to Him,
For he is standing by. He
Will guide your lives and
Set your thoughts on high.

Seek Him while you can for
You know that He is there.

If you wait too long there
May be no time to spare.

To those who heed His call
Good things come to pass.
For only by His word
Will any good thing last.

For those who love the Lord
There's beauty on all hands.
His name will be famous, as
It sweeps across the land.

CHAPTER 56

If you keep His sabbaths and
Attend His house of prayer,
He will bring us together;
There'll be no hatred there.

The leaders of the people
Who would lead men astray,
Who lie abed in morning,
And at night want to play,

Blind to every danger,
They're as greedy as can be.
Themselves an only interest,
And they covet all they see.

CHAPTER 57

If a godly man dies young, he
Shall certainly rest in peace.
But ungodly ones who scoff
Will never know release.

You give no thought to God;
You steep yourselves in sin.
Even all your gold and idols
Cannot give you peace within.

But he who trusts in me shall
Walk the highway I will build.
He of humble heart will know
Hopes and dreams fulfilled.

Those who stir up trouble,
Who are restless like the sea,
Will never know my comfort;
They never will know peace.

CHAPTER 58

All you who worship loudly,
Who make a show of
  godliness
Yet cheat and lie in daily life
Do not God's way profess.

For He would have you help a
Poor brother along the way.
To feed the one who's hungry,
And help improve his day.

Honor those you work with; do
Not the sabbath profane; you
Will get your blessings,
And God will honor your
  name.

CHAPTER 59

The problem is your sin,
From God it has cut you off,
For you're often party to
Murder and at Him you scoff.

No one cares about fair play;
There's no justice in courts;
And you think dirty dealing
Is akin to national sports.

You look for God to help you,
But He has turned away.
So if you want His blessing,
Then it is time you pray.

Now God knows what is
  wrong;
No one else is stepping in.
So He wears righteousness as
Honor and will battle sin.

CHAPTER 60

Let your light shine, and
My glory you will radiate.
As a shadow covers the earth,
All nations watch your state.

Look across the land and see
Your children return to you.
They'll come from many lands
And bring much treasure too.

God will be your glory;
Your land will know peace.
Your sun will never set,
And wars will cease to be.

CHAPTER 61

The spirit of God is upon me,
As to sad people I speak. To
Cheer the brokenhearted and
Tell good tidings to the meek,

So He might teach them honor,
Like great oaks among trees,
To cry liberty to captives
And set prisoners free.

Foreigners will help rebuild
The ruins or feed flocks.
You shall be called priests
And ministers of God.

The Lord God hates injustice;
He loathes the doing of wrong.
So He will bless His people
And make their lives a song.

CHAPTER 62

Nations call you righteous
As you shine forth in glory.
For God will uphold you,
And this will be your story.

No more will foreigners rule
Or take away your grain.
He has spoken with integrity;
It shall not happen again.

To every land He has said,
"I bring my people gifts, as I
Bring them back to Jerusalem
And heal up erstwhile rifts."

CHAPTER 63

God, who marches like a king,
In crimson robes and strength,
Is He who crushes His enemies,
Keeps evil nations at length.

Alone He avenged His people,
Caused wicked nations to fall.
Israel will rejoice in good,
And they will answer His call.

So many years He carried them,
And thus made famous His
    name.
They rebelled and grieved Him,
So He gave them years of pain.

Oh Lord, look down on us from
Heaven, see that we have need.
If Abraham and Jacob disown
Us, you are our God indeed.

Why would you disown us?
    Why
Let us fall from grace? You
Treat us like heathen nations
When we would seek your face.

CHAPTER 64

There is no greater God
Ever since the world began.
Therefore your wrath is heavy
When you turn away from man.

We know that we are sinful;
Please help us when we pray.
For Lord you are the potter,
And we are only clay.

CHAPTER 65

Now the Lord sadly answers,
"Look who's calling me now.
Many who never looked before
Are suddenly learning how.

Though my chosen people are
The ones I've tried to reach,
They're rebels, arrogant
And very difficult to teach.

Yet I'll not destroy them all,
For as in a clump of grapes,
There's an occasional bad one;
You don't throw them all away.

The wicked ones are destined
To the avenging sword to fall.

But those who are deserving
Will be to glory called."

CHAPTER 66

"The earth is my footstool,
And Heaven is my home.
Those men who are contrite
I consider as my own.

In flaming fire I'll try them,
All those people of my own,
Those who pass the test will
To far-off lands have flown.

They'll have seen the light,
And my glory will declare.
They will collect my people
To bring them back from there."

END OF ISAIAH

JEREMIAH

CHAPTER 1

Jeremiah was still a boy,
Whom God chose to lead, a
Battle against the world
With all its evil deeds.

He said, "You will not fail;
I'll put words on your lips.
Be not afraid of the enemy
Or allow your faith to slip.

Warn kings and nations I'll
Punish for their wrongs.
The good ones I will bless,
And help them to be strong.

Like boiling water on Judah
From out the north I'll
Bring enemies down on them,
Their gates they will storm.

This is fitting punishment
For when they deserted me.
So tell them without fear,
There is no danger to thee.

For I have made you strong,
And no man can do you harm.
I will back you every day
With my strong right arm.

All the Kings of Judah, the
Priests and men will fail.

Fear not, I'll be with you;
They will not prevail."

CHAPTER 2

"So give this message now; let
Your voice sound in the street.
Ask why they failed Jehovah,
Why they've been so indiscreet.

I led them through the desert,
In wilderness gave protection.
What did I do so wrong that
I should merit your rejection?

The rulers turned against me;
Their prophets worship Baal.
Yet I'll not give up on them;
I don't want to see them fail.

Why is Israel a slave to evil;
Why does she her God forsake?
No other nation changes gods.
Why does Israel make
    mistakes?

Servants you made yourselves
To idol gods you've chosen.
All those promises you made
And every one you've broken.

Yet for all your perfidy when
In danger you call on me. But
To win approval of wicked men
You plot and plan and scheme.

You flit here and there and
Bargain for another alliance;
You'll end up in despair for
Soon you'll meet defiance."

CHAPTER 3

Like an unfaithful woman
You've left me once again.
You always give your love
To that other man.

Like a harlot beside a road,
You sit and wait alone.
But when loneliness affects
You, you come back and moan.

Saying, "Father we sinned,
But have we done so wrong?"
And yet you continue to sin
And go thoughtlessly along.

When King Josiah reigned,
God's word came once more.
"Look at sinful Israel, she
Is acting like the whore.

She seeks her pleasure daily
And sins beneath every tree.
Giving herself to idol gods
And every day offends me.

I hoped that she'd return,
But she never did come back.
Judah turned faithless, too,
And followed Israel's act.

Now Judah is most guilty, so
Israel gets another chance.
Please come back to me my
Children, obey my word again.

I'll bless your people and
Will hear them cry to me,
"Father we have sinned, but
We'll come back to thee."

CHAPTER 4

Israel you must return
And live an honest life.
For your alternative is
Untold misery and strife.

So change your ways or you
Will be destroyed. You'll
Know much terror because
With God you toyed.

I could see their failure;
They'd no talent for good.
So valleys became deserts;
Mountains heaved and shook.

Cities they fled in terror
As enemy armies drew near.
People gasped for breath
And were weak with fear.

CHAPTER 5

"Run through the streets,
Search for an honest man,
I'll not destroy the city"
I heard, "if you only can."

But I could not find a one
Who was willing to change.
But those were ignorant
People within my range.

So I went to the leaders
And gave the word to them.
But they were all the same,
Refusing the ways to mend.

Prophets were a joke to them;
Calamities they couldn't see.
"Oh foolish senseless people,
Why do they turn from me?

I, who formed the oceans and
Made the mountains appear.
You should be smart enough
To know I'm one to fear.

So I'll let the enemy attack,
Who'll do vengeance for me.
Disaster should be a lesson,
Perhaps a truth they'll see."

CHAPTER 6

"Run you people of Benjamin,
Flee Jerusalem while you can.

Evil shepherds surround you;
The enemy around you camps.

You are really helpless; by
Their swords you'll fall.
They'll use trees for rams
To batter down your walls.

This warning is your last,
And then I'll empty the land.
I'll destroy all evil doing;
I've found no deserving man."

It seems the more I tried to
Bring reason to their minds,
The more they were determined
To be wicked and so blind.

Yet frustrated but patient,
I'd give them another chance.
But with all the lying evil,
They won't give me a glance.

Let the cost of evil sift
Through the greed for gold.
I see no chance of rescue;
They've been so often told.

They are insolent and hard,
Their ways refuse to mend,
Try my patience to the
Hilt and deserve the end.

CHAPTER 7

God told Jeremiah to stand
Before the Temple again and
Say, "I gave you one more
Chance to change your ways."

They think they are safe be-
cause my Temple I will save.
Don't expect them to listen;
They all behave like knaves.

Stop robbing the poor, let
Them on the land remain. Do

Not abuse my house for it is
Called by my Holy Name.

It's become a family rite, as
To idol gods they bake cakes.
It is not me they harm; they
Must pay for their mistakes.

But they ignore your efforts,
Will go their unholy ways,
They forfeit their children,
And to idol gods they pray.

In the valley of Ben Hinnom
They sacrifice their little
Ones. Bones there pile deep
With bodies by the tons.

In Jerusalem they won't sing,
No, or laugh in celebration.
Wreckage will be complete,
With the land in desolation.

CHAPTER 8

Their teachers are at fault,
And more dearly they will pay.
For they're only after profit,
As they lead my people astray.

And while God in sorrow waits
For them to see the light,
His people deplore their fate
And fail to admit He's right.

CHAPTER 9

Tears like fountains flow. I
Weep for people day and night.
Adulterous and treacherous,
They don't try to do right.

Each an enemy to his neighbor,
But he claims peaceful intent.
So I'll test them in the fire,
Hope toward good they're bent.

Nothing seems to change, so
I'll scatter them over earth.
The wise perish in wisdom;
The rich, counting his worth.

People, like heathen nations,
Give me lip service but no
More. I will punish them and
Life will be a burden sore.

CHAPTER 10

Fear not those predictions
By people who worship stars,
Nor those idols of wood who
Can do no good or harm.

From wood they make idols,
On them royal colors drape.
But they can't move or speak
Or man's destiny shape.

But you, Lord, oh mighty God,
Can do things no other can.
You shaped mountain and sea
And made earth fit for man.

CHAPTER 11

God always kept His word to
The Children of Israel,
Who showed no inclination
To do their share as well.

They even plotted my murder;
God showed me their plan.
And while they plotted, I'd
Been trusting as a lamb.

I thanked my Savior, saying,
"Lord, reward their wicked
Ways." "I will," He said,
"Whole families will pay,"

CHAPTER 12

"Oh Lord," I cried, "why do
Wicked men succeed? In any

Business they thrive
Much aided by their greed.

Why not cause them despair,
Expel them from this place?
Birds and animals have left,
Yet they think they're safe."

"If the men of Anathoth,"
God to me replied, "can get
Your goat and make you wroth,
Why should I take your side.?

You've greater trouble ahead,
Your family's tossing you out.
Your brothers plot your death,
So listen to them with doubt.

They turned my beautiful vine-
Yard into a barren wilderness.
The land is really desolate;
They've made it a total mess.

So they will be overrun, and
Their enemy who does the job,
May even stay upon this
Land if he accepts me as God."

CHAPTER 13

Then Jeremiah got the word to
Get a loincloth for himself.
Not place it near the water
But to wear it like a belt.

Then take it to the river
And in rocks hide it there.
So by the River Euphrates he
Hid it from curious stares.

Then after time had passed,
He was told to bring it back.
But it was moldy and weak
And any strength it lacked.

The Lord explained, "This
Is happening to Judah's pride.

Destruction to the nation
Will all good override.

They will not honor God, for
Like the leopard is spotted,
Their lives are not in tune;
Their integrity has rotted."

CHAPTER 14

The people cry for rain,
All the land is tinder dry.
But they've ignored the Lord,
And he will only sigh.

Now they make good promises
And ask Him for quick relief.
But only if they're hurting
Do they really claim belief.

CHAPTER 15

God told Jeremiah that even
Moses and Samuel couldn't do
Things those sinful people
Were trying to get Him to.

Hezekiah had done so much
That was wicked and wrong,
God knew very well that as
Rebels only were they strong.

CHAPTER 16

He warned Jeremiah, "You
  must
Not marry such as these. For
Children born here will be
Prone to sickness or disease.

There will come a time when
Worldly nations will say,
Why did we ever build those
Idols of wood and clay?

Man's creations cannot think
Or move, or answer prayer.

When they come to that deci-
sion I will meet them there."

CHAPTER 17

My people sin so easily,
Their children do so too.
Others inherit your wealth
For it's too good for you.

Cursed is the man who from
God has turned away. His
Life will be a problem as
If living on barren plains.

One who trusts the Lord will
Live in confidence and hope,
Like a tree on a river bank
With drought need not cope.

CHAPTER 18

He said, "Even as a potter,
I'd like to change your ways.
And if you would only change
I'd gladly extend your days."

So He sent Jeremiah again
To bend His people's ears.
But they cried, "Go your way,
To us you hold no fears."

They set a trap for Jeremiah;
His preaching raised their ire.
He asked the Lord to stop them
Before their plans transpired.

CHAPTER 19

Yet he told them of the future,
How the population would die.
For they'd sinned and angered
God who'd not heed their cry.

These people would see the day,
When more evil they'd turn.

They had greatly sinned when
Sons in sacrifice they burned.

Ben Hinnom, would "Valley of
Slaughter," be named. It would
Be a "Place of Death." That
Would be its only fame.

And then as he'd been told, he
Smashed an earthen pot, saying,
"As you see this vessel broken,
That will be your lot."

CHAPTER 20

Now before the Temple, as he
Made his claim, Jeremiah was
Arrested, whipped, in stocks
And Pashur villified his name.

The next day he was released
And was finally free to go.
But then turning to his
Tormenter addressed him so,

"Pashur, I have word for you;
God has changed your name.
You will live in terror, and
Your friends will do the same."

"So I turned back to Jehovah,"
Jeremiah then proclaimed, for
He felt that he'd been had,
And by people could be
  maimed.

But when I refused to preach,
I felt driven by fire within.
And I had to do the job that
God had caused me to begin.

I knew that He'd be close in
Spite of threats and fear. He
Would guide and protect me
And from danger keep me clear.

Yet inwardly I cursed that
Day that I'd been born be-
Cause of people's treatment
I was sad and felt forlorn.

CHAPTER 21

Pashur and Zephaniah, a priest,
Went to Jeremiah for the king.
To ask God's protecting hand
In this new and fearful thing.

For the mighty
   Nebuchadnezzar,
Who ruled Ethiopias land was
Threatening Jerusalem's walls,
At her gates had made a stand.

They hoped for a miracle such
As others He'd done before.
That God would stop the
   enemy,
So they'd avoid a fearful war.

"Tell the king," Jeremiah
Said, "this, God does say,
I'll be on the enemy's side
Unless you change your way.

If you stay within the city
From plague you'll soon die,
Surrender to Nebuchadnezzar
And be prisoners for life.

He'll reduce it to ashes;
You'll be killed or starve.
Quickly change your ways
Or come to greater harm."

CHAPTER 22

Again word came to Jeremiah
"Go face the king, tell him
To be fair in his mind and
Change about everything.

If he'll stop cheating and
Enslaving those he rules, I
Will save his nation from
War, he'll be no one's fool.

Now if you do these things
And honestly rule the land,
You will get His blessings
And riches at your command.

But ignore my word again
And fall upon your face.
Feet first to be carried
Out through the city gates.

Woe to you King Jehoiachim
Who wished riches to build.
Those objecting to slavery
Were taken out and killed.

You are selfish and ruthless
And making a big mistake. A
Beautiful palace or riches,
Doesn't a worthy kingdom
   make.

Your father Josiah was good,
And he ruled just and fair,
But while you are alive your
Subjects will know despair.

Like an animal you'll die and
Be thrown on the dump beyond
The gate. None will mourn you;
It will improve their fate.

And, Coniah, you are useless;
Your life has been in vain.
Your children shall not live,
For you've caused only pain."

CHAPTER 23

On the leaders of my people,
I'll put my biggest curse. For

They lead a nation to slavery;
There's not much that's worse.

They're prophets I'd not send
Who tell people all is well.
But this, the Lord has spoken,
"They lead people toward hell."

Yet in time, in days to come,
He'll save them from the mess,
And this will be His name,
"Lord of our righteousness."

God says to His people, "The
Prophets are not from me;
They tell you, you are safe,
Yet in sin you cannot be."

CHAPTER 24

I stood before the Temple;
God sent this vision to me.
I saw two baskets of figs,
And it was easy to see,

One was delicious and ripe,
The other moldy and spoiled.
Like people who do right,
Or those wicked and soiled.

Thus the Lord compared them
To Jeremiah that day. "Good
Ones I sent to Babylon but
Will bring back this way.

For their good I sent them,
And some day they'll return.
Common sense may set in, so
My will they'll not spurn.

Figs, inedible and spoiled
Like Zedekiah and friends,
I'll banish over the earth;
In misery they will end."

CHAPTER 25

Twenty-three years elapsed,
Since Jeremiah began to warn,
People were displeasing God
In word, manner and form.

Oh turn from evil to good,
Help the poor, sick and old.
Abandon idols, follow God,
You, His arms will enfold.

You're too willful to listen;
Seventy years will go your way.
If you must dance to idols,
There will be the devil to pay.

This beautiful land of Caanan
Will be desolate, arid and dry.
Conquerors will be conquered;
In turn they will also cry.

Atrocities done on my people,
On the masters too will return.
For no one can play with fire
Without in time getting burned.

At cries of leaders and people
All the earth will know fear.
There will be no place to hide,
No Savior who listens or hears.

Now you are safe in your
  homes,
But soon in the midst of a war,
Everything will be wasted
Because you angered the Lord.

CHAPTER 26

Again word came to Jeremiah
  to
Return to the Temple to speak.
As before he'd call the nation
To their Lord and reason seek.

As told, he laid it on them,
Every humbling word from
    God.
In a serious last ditch effort,
So Jehovah could spare the
    rod.

Those false prophets, priests
And people became an angry
    mob.
Shouting, "Kill this crazy Man,"
And they wanted to do the job.

Officials of Judah heard
And came rushing there.
Now they could hold court,
And publicity share.

The priests and prophets
In turn made the claim.
Jeremiah, the traitor, at
Their city had taken aim.

Now in his defense he was
Allowed to take the stand.
So in detail he told them
Things God had planned.

How he was sent to speak
To Temple and city too.
They should follow God
For all had much to lose.

"As for me, I am yours to
Do with however you plan.
But God has truly sent me;
You'd kill an honest man."

Now his accusers conferred
And doubted he should die.
Wise old men in the crowd
Declared the decision wise.

Remembering long ago, when
Micah, God's man, held forth,

Much the same had happened,
And many favored the Lord.

"If we kill Jeremiah, and
He is a man of the Lord,
Who knows what God will do;
His anger we can't afford."

Now Uriah, son of Shemiah,
Gave that message to all.
He, too, was God's man
Who heard the master's call.

Jehoiachim and his officers
Sentenced him to death;
Uriah heard of their plans,
And away to Egypt fled.

Jehoiakim sent men to bri-
ng him home. There he fell
To the king's sword, who'd
Have better left him alone.

The king's secretary then
Argued with the court, so
They let Jeremiah live in-
stead of cutting life short.

CHAPTER 27

Now when Jehoiakim, son of
Josiah, began to reign,
Jeremiah heard from God;
To him this message came.

"Put a yoke on your back,
Like an ox about to plow.
Send a message to the king,
Which I will tell you now.

To Edom, Moab, and Ammon,
To Tyre, and Sidon too:
God, who owns all things,
Will do as He wishes to.

Bow to Nebuchadnezzar, give
Allegiance to him, or he

Will destroy you so do not
Argue, for you cannot win.

All nations shall serve him,
His son and grandson too.
Don't believe false prophets,
For they are lying to you.

Submit to this Babylon King,
And you'll be let alone.
Don't fight as they advise,
For at lying they are prone.

If they are God's prophets,
As they so like to claim;
Let them pray to God that
Some treasures will remain.

Bronze pillars at the Temple,
Great basin before the court,
Will all go to Babylon's King,
With all people of import.

There all these will stay un-
til God sends for them. For
The time will one day come,
He'll bring them back again.

CHAPTER 28

Now Azzur, a prophet false,
And his son Hananiah, too,
Denied Jeremiah's claims,
As his kind were wont to do.

He broke the wooden yoke,
From Jeremiah's back and
Tried to steer the people
Upon a different track.

Saying, "God will rescue us,
The people and our goods.
Within two years He told me,
We'd be out of the woods."

So Jeremiah said to him, "I
Sincerely hope this is so.

If you are His messenger,
Then we'll all soon know."

Then God spoke to Jeremiah,
Who went to Hananiah in turn.
Saying, "You lied to people,
God's word you've spurned.

You have chosen your fate,
God won't stand for lies.
As a result of your perfidy,
Within the year you'll die."

As Jeremiah had prophesied,
In two months Hananiah died.
It happened that same year,
'Twas the year he'd lied.

CHAPTER 29

Many people were banished,
King, family and friends.
Even prophets and slaves
Were taken in the end.

Zedekiah sent ambassadors
To the conqueror. To Jewish
Slaves Jeremiah wrote and
Told the reason therefore.

"Do seventy years as slaves,
And God will bring you back.
Listen to word I send, and
Be sure to clean up your act.

Pray now for Babylon and
Work hard for her peace. For
If all is well with her, it
Will also be good for thee.

Give and take in marriage,
Increase our numbers there.
Ignore all false prophets;
At lying they have a flair.

You'll find God if you seek
Him; He promised to be found.

He does have plans for you,
If you'll only stick around."

Those who weren't captured
Will find life a curse.
Sinful and adulterers, but
Shemiah, a prophet, is worse.

For he sent letters back
To Jerusalem's priests, say-
ing, "Jeremiah lied to us,"
This was the story released.

"He says that we'll be here
For many long years to come.
So put him in the stocks,
In short, imprison the bum."

Zephaniah took the letter
And gave Jeremiah the word.
He delivered the message
As it was given by the Lord.

"Shemaiah is a dreamer who
Prophesies things untrue.
He shall not see the good
Or future planned for you."

CHAPTER 30

Then again a message came,
As the Lord of Israel spoke.
Saying write this down, "In
Time I'll bring people home.

One of your own will rule;
He'll be a priest for me.
My dedicated people and my
Friends you will surely be.

But now my wrath will rule,
Destruction is the norm.
Later you'll understand why
You must weather the storm."

CHAPTER 31

"When the time comes your
Families shall know, that
Through those ages past,
I have loved them so.

Upon the hills of Samaria,
Watchmen will call to say,
'Let us all go up to Zion,
And praise the Lord today.'

No longer will children pay
Debts their fathers caused.
I'll lead them by the hand,
Love them without pause.

In each heart my law will
Be, I'll forgive all sins.
Their cities will be safe,
Where none shall break in."

CHAPTER 32

For eighteen years now
Nebuchadnezzar had reigned.
And King Zedekiah of Judah,
Was just a royal pain,

He put Jeremiah in a dung-
eon under the palace of the
King, because his prophecies
Had an ominous ring.

He'd predicted to the public,
That the future was in doubt,
If their king wouldn't give
In and submit to the rout.

In prison he was visited by
Landowner cousin, Hanameel,
Whose field was for sale,
And he offered a good deal.

The land became Jeremiah's
By legal deed. To prove to a

Stubborn king that again
There'd be a need,

In time to come they would
Buy and trade and sell. And
If they'd listen to God,
They'd get along quite well.

CHAPTER 33

Men asked why He'd chosen
Them once but now denied
Them. But he'd not broken a
Covenant; He would take them
Back again.

In peace and plenty they'll
Be tending flocks and fields.
Grapes will make good wine,
Labor, much good will yield.

CHAPTER 34

Then even as the battle raged
By Nebuchadnezzar the great;
Only three cities undefeated,
Chaldeans camped at the gates,

God said, "Tell the king, he
Will be in the enemies hands;
As captive of the Chaldeans
They'll devastate his lands.

He won't die in the carnage;
In peace, later that will be.
His death will bring sorrow;
His people will truly grieve."

Many a Jew held others slave,
And did as the king demanded.
Freeing brothers and sisters,
As God by Jeremiah
    commanded.

But their freedom was short,
For to slavery they returned;

The Lord rescinded his mercy
For the bridges they'd burned.

"Bodies will feed vultures,
No one will bury your bones."
Said God in indignation,
"Cities a rubble of stones."

CHAPTER 35

Came a message to the prophet
Who did as he had been told.
The Rechabites were brought
Who were abstainers of old.

Saying, "We drink no wine,
Our lives in tents we spend.
We have done as God asked,
Will keep faith to the end."

"So why won't Israel do," He
Asked, "as these have done?
Instead of upright and good,
To great evil she has run.

So thus I'm determined to do
All the things I have warned.
And only after it's too late,
Will she look back and mourn.

Because of Rechabite faith
In doing as they were told,
They'll always worship God
And remain within my fold."

CHAPTER 36

Now Baruch, who was a scribe,
Responded to Jeremiah's call.
For they were very worried
That all Israel would fall.

The Lord had bid him to note
Terrible deeds they'd done.
To try to show this people
The fearsome risk they'd run.

God had said to show them
The errors of their way,
In hopes they would change,
So a hand of fate He'd stay.

Fasting day at the Temple,
Many people were around.
Baruch read God's warnings
To change or be shot down.

He read the same account
To the officers and scribes.
When he'd finished reading,
All were shaken with fright.

They bid Baruch and Jeremiah,
To hide and not be found, for
The king would hear of this,
And they must not be around.

So the king soon sent for
The warning they had written.
He burned it as he read; by
No conscience was he smitten.

Scribes who had penned it
Were marked for quick arrest.
But with God's help they hid
To live for another test.

Now to Jeremiah came word,
"Make up a scroll again, and
Tell that wicked king he's
Bought himself much pain."

So again they did write, all
They'd written before. Now
They told the king he'd die
And a good deal more.

CHAPTER 37

Coniah didn't follow as the
King upon the throne, for
Nebuchadnezzar chose
    Zedekiah,
For God, Jeremiah stood alone.

Zedekiah sent to Jeremiah,
Saying, "For us please pray."
But of course no change,
No one heard what he'd say.

Jeremiah went out the gate
To see that land he'd bought.
By the guard was stopped, who
Claimed a traitor he'd caught.

It did no good to argue, and
Into a dungeon he was cast.
He was there for days, but by
The king was called at last.

He asked if God would help
Keep an enemy from the gates.
But Jeremiah told him, "No,"
Total failure lay in wait.

For Pharaoh's army would flee,
No stopping the enemy now.
Jeremiah pled for freedom,
From the dungeon to stay out.

But they sent him back with
A crust of bread each day.
Enough to keep him alive
And also out of their way.

CHAPTER 38

Several of the princes knew
About Jeremiah's claims. They
Thought him against the cause,
And to ignore it was a shame.

They begged the king to give
Him into their tender care.
They found a slimy cistern,
And he was lowered there.

But an Ethiopian friend and a
Palace official of standing,
Pled his case to the king;
His reasoning was
    commanding.

He was given thirty men to
Save Jeremiah ere he died.
'Twas God's will to save him;
The Ethiopian gent complied.

To the palace prison he was
Sent and there he did remain.
Until one day when the king
Requested his presence again.

"I want to ask something,"
The king then said to him,
But Jeremiah was skeptical,
Before he would begin.

So the king made a promise;
He'd not lower the boom,
Even if Jeremiah's answer
Added to his gloom.

Jeremiah said surrender, so
His family and he could live.
But the king feared the Jews;
His faith was like a sieve.

How Jeremiah tried, in vain
To save the king that day.
But the king was filled with
Fear and sadly sent him away.

"If the princes come, don't
Tell what you said. Say you
Begged off from the dungeon,
It would cause your death."

Just as the king had feared,
The princes' came and quizzed.
But Jeremiah's story held, so
The princes' plotting fizzed.

CHAPTER 39

Two years the battle raged,
Before David's City fell.
With God on the enemys' side
She didn't do so well.

They sat in victory staring,
Conquerors at a middle gate.
The other side of town, king
And princes tried to escape.

But the enemy trailed, they
Were quickly brought to bay
And forced to watch murders
Of all his children that day.

Then his eyes were blinded
And to Babylon he was sent.
There in slavery he'd live,
And all his life repent.

Meantime the beautiful city
Fell in wreckage all around,
Walls and gates a shambles,
All the homes burned down.

Those who surrendered were
Shipped to Babylon as slaves.
Only the sick or very poor
Were allowed to live or stay.

Given fields and vineyards,
They were the luckier of all.
Nebuchadnezzar wanted safety
For Jeremiah, so made a call.

The Captain of the guard
Was told to bring him out.
He was left on his land
To live in his own house.

CHAPTER 40

Jeremiah was taken to Ramah
When captured with the rest.
But was given the choice of
Doing what he thought best.

He returned to live in Judah
Where Gedaliah was in charge.
Those who'd been dispersed
Came in from near and far.

Guerrilla bands and others
Came in to tend crops, All
With Gedaliah's blessing
Before the visiting stopped.

Some guerrilla leaders came
To warn of Ammon's king. But
Gedaliah couldn't believe
Ishmael would do such thing.

One named Johanan asked,
 "Why
Don't I go and kill him first?
For he is seeking murder,
And for your life he thirsts."

But Gedaliah refused the
Plan of rubbing Ishmael out.
He thought it was a subject
They were all wrong about.

CHAPTER 41

Ishmael, of royalty, came
To Mizpah with a ten man crew.
Gedaliah asked them to dinner,
The polite thing to do.

As they dined and visited,
Those eleven suddenly arose,
Surprising trusting Gedaliah,
Brought his life to a close.

They slaughtered all Jews
And Babylonians in town. Next
Day they killed seventy more,
Ere the awful news got around.

Now ten of eighty who came,
Bartered their goods away,
To stay alive to another time
And to worship another day.

The bodies of those murdered
In a large cistern were thrown.

It was built by King Asa to
Hide from enemies long ago.

Ishmael and his men took the
King's daughters and others too,
Then headed out toward
 Ammon,
And boy, how they did scoot!

Johanan and guerrilla leaders
Heard and took up the chase.
At Gibeons pool they caught
 up
And should have ended the
 case.

Ishmael and eight men escaped,
And for safety quickly hiked.
They got away from Johanan
To the land of the Ammonites.

To Chimham Johanan then
 went
With the people he had saved.
They left to go to Egypt
Because they were afraid.

CHAPTER 42

Johanan and his captains,
And people they had saved,
Came looking for Jeremiah,
For his intercession craved.

"Oh what to do?" they cried,
"Please ask God what is best;
Just tell him of our problem,
And we will do the rest.

For whatever he should say,
We will consider it a must.
Be sure to tell the truth.
For He is harsh but just."

Ten days later he heard,
So they all gathered round.

You asked me to check with
God; this he did propound.

He's sorry that He treated
You so bad in days gone by,
But He'll save you in the
Future if you will only try.

Babylon's King won't harm you
If you stay to work the land.
But if you cut and run,
You will be sorry, every man.

If you flee to Egypt, your
Troubles are sure to follow.
All hope of a better life
Will prove very hollow.

"Never forget this warning,"
The prophet Jeremiah pled.
"If you insist on going,
You'll soon all be dead."

CHAPTER 43

They all raised a clamor,
Claiming Jeremiah had lied.
He was leading them astray
With a story cut and dried.

He'd plotted with Baruch
To get them all enslaved.
He must be so treacherous,
His speech with lies paved.

So word of help he'd given
Fell upon deaf ears. For
The thought of Babylonians
Made them wild with fear.

They gathered the people,
Those rescued from Ishmael,
And those who had returned
To that part of Israel.

They hit the road to Egypt,
Even Jeremiah and Baruch,

With those other people,
Were forced to travel too.

They arrived in Egypt, and
Jeremiah called them round.
He buried rocks amid stones
On Egypt's palace grounds.

"This spot the Lord vows
Nebuchadnezzar will be; he
Is God's loyal servant who
Will do as the master seeks.

Some will die of wounds,
Others from the plague.
Captured will be many, and
There'll be no help or aid.

He'll plunder Egypt, its
People carry away, temples
And obelisks destroy,
Gods of Egypt he'll break."

So said Jeremiah to those
Who'd made him come along.
Words fell on deaf ears;
They thought he was wrong.

CHAPTER 44

All Jews in Egypt got this
Word through Jeremiah. "Why
Insist on being wicked? To
God you'll become pariahs.

Years you've worshipped
Idols and 'Heavens Queen.'
You think God don't know?
Your sins he hasn't seen?

He's sent so many prophets
To save the day. But you
Are all determined that
You will have your way.

That is why He wiped out
Jerusalem and Judah too.

He will do that in Egypt,
And all because of you."

Then to Jeremiah came the
People's reply. "We do
Not believe your story; we
Don't believe we'll die.

Yes we worshipped idols and
Burned incense to 'Heaven's
Queen,' grapes made good
Wine; gardens were green.

Since we failed to do so,
By bad luck we're overtaken.
We'll go on doing our thing,
Your God we have forsaken."

Jeremiah warned them that
Babylon would strike again
And scorch the earth leav-
ing no woman, child or man.

Though they'd cry for help,
He would turn a deaf ear.
Idols could not help them
In time of death and fear.

CHAPTER 45

When Jehoiachim was king,
And Baruch was feeling low,
Jeremiah told God's word so
All these things he'd know.

"This the Lord has promised,
He will be on your side. So
Don't fret about the future;
Do not overdo your pride."

CHAPTER 46

Jeremiah learned of all
Those nations going to war.
Descriptions of the battles,
What they're fighting for.

Beside the Euphrates River
Egypt and Babylon clashed.
Egypt's Pharaoh Neco turned
And homeward dashed.

The sword of God is sated;
It drips the enemies blood.
Egypt expected victory today,
A swelling militant flood.

In shame they lose a battle,
Against each other they fall.
Your bull god Apis is use-
less he can't hear your call.

CHAPTER 47

Through the City of Gaza a
Flood of terror gushes forth
To desolate the Philistines
It flows from out the north.

Hooves clatter loudly, and
Chariot wheels roar. Fathers
Will flee helpless children,
Before the sword of the Lord.

From Tyre and Bilon, from
Caphtor and Ashkelon too, the
Anger of the Lord will rage,
And it will eliminate you.

CHAPTER 48

Against the land of Moab
And her cities he assailed.
For her people fell short;
In His sight they've failed.

"Flee for the hills," He says,
"While cries of terror spread.
For the cities are a shambles
They speak of war and death.

You boasted mighty men
And smiled at Israel's fate.

Your destiny overtakes you;
You are wising up too late."

CHAPTER 49

I'll destroy the nations
With idol worshipping ways,
And I will cut you short,
Making sorrowful your days.

You thought you were safe
In valleys fertile and fine.
Neighbors will run you out
And own your land in time.

Weep for your cities, but it
Was Israel I gave them to,
And they will get them back.
In time I'll smile on you.

Where are Edom's wise men
Of the days gone by? If any of
Them are left, they should
Be smart enough to fly.

The land of Edom will be
Ruined and stripped bare.
The terror of the land all
Her inhabitants will share.

Here live desert tribes
With flocks and tents. Neb-
uchadnezzar will kill them,
For this purpose he was sent.

They claim self-sufficiency
And need no gates or walls.
So I'll scatter the heathen
In all directions to fall.

CHAPTER 50

Against the Babylonians
And the Chaldeans, too, God
Told Jeremiah to prophesy;
They'd soon reap their dues.

From north destruction comes;
None will survive that day;
Men and animals flee; Judah
And Israel ask the way--

Back to Zion and God's will,
They have fallen from grace.
Are persecuted by the enemy
And vainly seek His face.

They try His love to keep,
His law, to themselves bind,
Never more to stray or seek
Another god of any kind.

Babylon, you conqueror, were
Fattened on other's stores,
To be overrun by enemies
Who come from out the north.

CHAPTER 51

Against the land of Babylon,
God will stir the nations.
Her cry of terror is heard
By all of His creation.

Israel has been forgiven
And can go home at last.
Babylon is being judged by
Heaven for a sinful past.

Year after year you'll hear
Of wars and insurrections.
For sins against you she'll
Die, all at His direction.

Do not stand and watch but
Get yourselves away. Terror
Will walk the land, for it
Is Babylon's judgment day.

Get yourselves to Jerusalem,
Where you can start anew.
For I am still your God,
And I will go with you.

Jeremiah delivered the word
To an officer of Zedekiah's
Troops, and it is written
For a record and a proof.

CHAPTER 52

Zedekiah was a wicked king
And he was only twenty-one.
He went from bad to worse
For anyone so young.

The ninth year of his rule
Nebuchadnezzar hit the city.
Two years later it was capt-
ured and was shown no pity.

He and his children all fled
Across the plains. The Chal-
deans captured them and
Subjected them to much pain.

Before Nebuchadnezzar they
Were all brought and tried.
Death to the princes, and
Zedekiah lost both eyes.

Meantime back at Jerusalem,
It was sacked and burned,
Many people kidnapped, only
The very poor were spurned.

A few were left behind
To till and work the land.
But the best craftsmen were
Taken by the enemy's band.

All officers and councelors
Formerly at Zedekiah's call,
Came before Babylon's king,
There they killed them all.

In prison thirty-seven years
Was Jehoiachim, Judah's ex-
King, then he was released,
A most unusual thing.

The new King of Babylon
Treated him kindly that day.
Gave him food and clothing,
And in the palace let him
Stay.

END OF JEREMIAH

LAMENTATIONS

CHAPTER 1

Jerusalem, City of David,
Often remembers better days.
Into exile she's been led;
All of Judah now are slaves.

Long she lay in splendor,
Immorality and wantonness.
She despised God's name
And failed His every test.

Joyous throngs are no more;
She tries to hide her face.

Enemies she once despised
Dragged her to disgrace.

"My sons and daughters are
Gone." she cries, "When I
Ask for help, only the
Sound of jeers arise.

I know you promised, Lord,
To test my enemies as me.
Look upon their sins, Lord,
And give my heart relief."

CHAPTER 2

The beautiful city is gone;
In dust and ashes it lies.
Its walls crumbled down; in
Other lands her people die.

He has judged a fortress,
Without mercy tore it down.
People long rejected Him,
So now must bear His frown.

Jerusalem's gates are down,
Kings and princes no more.
Children die on the street,
More weeping than before.

Your prophets lied to you;
They said all was well. Now
They say, 'Twas your fault,
They led you into hell.

Now, oh people of Jerusalem,
Weep and pray at the walls.
Plead for starving children;
Pray God to hear your call.

Lord, why must children die?
We bounced them on our knees,
Priests and prophets in the
Temple, youth on the streets?

CHAPTER 3

To black of night I've been
Sent, in dungeons dark. God
Is against me day and night;
I'm His bow and arrows mark.

His hands are heavy upon me;
The cup I drink is strong.
My people laugh and rail me
By way of ribald song.

And yet we have a hope, for
God does have compassion.

We'll accept His discipline
Or feel it in this fashion.

We cower in fear, oh Lord,
Which we thoroughly deserve.
But we ask another chance,
'Tis you we now would serve.

CHAPTER 4

The finest gold is tarnished,
And the city walls are broken.
The best of our youth is gone,
And you can not find a token.

The animals feed their young,
For ours there's nothing left.
Our sins surpass Sodom's
where
All was paid by sudden death.

Our people starve; they are
Nothing but skin and bone.
Normal tender loving mothers
Often cannibalize their own.

We thought kings infallible,
And those allied to us, were
Less help than a shadow and
Of less substance than dust.

CHAPTER 5

Strangers own our homes; our
Sorrow is too much to bear.
Of foreigners we beg to eat,
Who don't ever treat us fair.

Our fathers sinned and died
Before the hand of judgment
Fell. Widows and children are
Slaves, lives a living hell.

Women and children are raped
On city streets. Beneath our
Loads our backs are bent, for
Our sin we bitterly weep.

EZEKIEL

CHAPTER 1

Beside the Chebar Canal
In far off Babylon land,
Ezekiel, a Jewish priest,
Was totally God's man.

This is the story he told
Of a wondrous vision he saw.
"Heaven suddenly opened;
I stood and watched in awe.

Out of the north in glory,
A tremendous whirlwind came,
Accompanied by a great cloud
Of fire and of flame.

Out of the midst thereof
It showed amber bright. And
Four strange creatures of
Which I never saw the like.

Four faces, one on each side
Of their heads did they have,
And hooves of polished brass,
Much like those of calves.

With hands like a man
Just under their wings,
And strangly enough they
Had four of those things.

On one side of their heads
The face of a man did shine.
The right side, a lion's, an
Oxen left, an eagle behind.

With wings on each side
And attached in such a way,
That they never need turn,
But could always go straight.

Their appearance was light
And the likeness of flame,

Which went up and down as
They left and they came.

I looked at them and beheld
Four wheels on the ground,
Like a wheel within a wheel,
Many eyes in the ring around.

They were high and dreadful,
Each creature with his wheel,
Of rainbow colors, as they
Moved loud noises pealed.

There was a voice from the
Heavens high over our heads,
Such colors of bright beauty
That I stared in great dread.

Under the heavens they stood
With wings outspread. And
They moved with great speed
To a voice overhead.

They lowered the wings, then
In heaven a sight to behold,
A throne with a man, a light
Round about like unto gold.

A throne like sapphire, that
Most precious of stones. He
Had the appearance of fire
From His head to His toes.

The likeness of the Lord
Was what it appeared to me.
I fell flat on my face and
Heard a voice to me speak."

CHAPTER 2

"Stand on your feet," The
Spirit said, and gave me
Strength to get off my face
And listen there at length.

"Now Son of man," said He,
"I'm sending you back home
To those rebellious ones
With opinions overblown.

So go tell them what I say;
They may listen not at all.
They'll see you as a prophet
Who's heard Jehovah's call.

Walk boldly among them; do
Not fear what they say.
Among thorns and scorpions
I'll lead and keep you safe.

Nor must you rebel, but do
That for which you're sent.
Teach a stiff-necked people,
Their only hope is to repent.

A hand put forth a scroll of
Lamentations, mourning, and
Woe, written there quite pla-
inly, things I should know."

CHAPTER 3

Then He said to me, "Eat my
Words, oh son of man."
So I took the scroll,
And He bade me eat again.

Now when I took a bite, it
Was like honey to my taste.
And having been told by Him,
I thought it no disgrace.

"I'll send you to your own,"
Were the words He then said,
"They speak your language
But are very hard of head.

If I sent a foreigner, they'd
Listen and try to understand.
It is a known fact, prophets
Lack honor in their own land.

They would not listen to me;
You'll have no better luck.
But you're as tough as they,
So do not come unstuck,

Let my words sink in and
Take them to your heart.
Now go back to your people,
Be sure you play your part."

Then the Spirit lifted me up,
And God's glory moved away to
A sound of great earthquakes,
While I stood there amazed.

Now by the Spirit I was taken
To my people at Tel Abib. But
I was bitter and angry and
Felt not very glib.

Seven days I sat among them
Overwhelmed beyond
   compare.
Now the Lord searched me out
And spoke to me while there.

"Now don't refuse to warn
Them, when I say it's time.
For if you shirk your duty,
It will be a personal crime.

But if they fail when told,
The onus will fall on them.
I'll expect your very best
As this evil you try to stem.

For if a good man slips, and
You don't set him straight,
If he dies because of sin,
You will fall from grace.

But if you warn him in time,
So he could make amends,
You will have saved his life
And God will be your friend."

I was helpless in His hands;
When He beckoned me I came.
He showed me His great glory,
As I fell again upon my face.

And then He said to me,
"Go stay within your home.
Only come forth when I call,
Do not about the colony roam.

I will paralyze your tongue,
So you can't yell at them.
And I'll only let you speak,
When I've a message to send."

CHAPTER 4

"Now on a piece of tile, draw,
Oh son of man take heed, a
Picture of the beautiful city
And show it under siege.

With the enemy encamped
  about,
And siege mounds all in place.
Indicate Jerusalem's capture,
Unless it seeks Jehovah's face.

Each detail is a symbol; it
Has meaning for its time.
It's a warning unto Israel
Of payment due for crimes.

For three hundred ninety days,
Upon your right side now lie.
Each day means a year of
  doom,
As in captivity they will cry.

Now you'll turn to your left;
Forty days, each equals a year,
When Judah will have to pay
With captivity, pain and fear.

Bare your arm to signify her
Enemies' power and will. I'll

Paralyze you in that pose,
Till those days are fulfilled.

While on your right side bake
Your cakes of various grains.
Eat eight ounces each day
And a quart of water plain.

Over a fire bake your cakes
With flames from human dung
To signify unclean food where,
In Gentile lands they've run."

But then I cried, "Oh Lord,
I've never eaten things un-
clean. Your order seems,
That I would be demeaned."

So He let me off the hook.
"All right," He said, "You
May use old dry cow chips
To fuel the fire instead.

Bread, use in portions,
With water in great demand.
Starvation and thirst will
Reign across the land."

CHAPTER 5

Then again He said, "Shave
Your hair and beard all off.
Divide the hair by weight
Even as the watchers scoff.

Divide in three equal parts,
Center one on a map. Spread
Another across your drawing,
And with a knife then slash.

Scatter some upon the wind;
Throw some into the fire.
Tie more into your robe,
To illustrate Jehovah's ire.

These things will happen to
The people who have failed.

They shall be destroyed
The day when God prevails.

A third will die of famine;
Disease will take another.
Enemies will murder the rest;
Fathers, children, mothers.

You will be an example to
All nations great and small.
I'll not be appeased until
I've avenged them all."

CHAPTER 6

"Turn toward the mountains;
Make this prediction known.
Even in the river valleys
Must this prophecy be shown.

Cities will be demolished;
Your idols will be burned,
Idolaters silenced to death,
For God has been spurned."

CHAPTER 7

"Go tell your people their
Last chance they've blown.
And I will not pity them;
The fault is all their own.

The day of judgment comes
Just as surely as the dawn.
The time speeds ever closer;
You'll regret all wrongs.

Rich men gloat and count
All the gold they've saved.
But with idol worship and
Sins, they have paved

A path to death and ruin.
But even if they'd lived,
There'd be no hope left;
God no help would give."

CHAPTER 8

After six years as captives
Some of Judah's elders came
To visit at my home, and it
Seemed I saw a man of flame.

He reached out taking me by
The hair, took me by vision
To Jerusalem, as if He
Whisked me through the air.

At the north gate entrance,
The idol of jealousy stood.
He said, "Oh son of man,
Now will you take a look?

They worship a man made
God and push me from my
place."
Then He said, "Come with me
And see even more disgrace."

He brought me to the gate,
So I dug a hole in the wall.
He ordered me to dig again;
I uncovered a hidden hall.

Seventy ancients of Israel
Honored idols and beasts.
They had all forgotten God
And practised pagan beliefs.

"So you see," He said, "how
Great sins they do?" He sho-
wed me another gate where
Women wept for Tamuz,

A supposed god of fertility
Who was said to be deceased,
So they moaned and wailed
This idol to appease.

He showed me another place,
Some who worshipped the Sun,

Turning away from the Temple,
From their God they'd run.

CHAPTER 9

In a loud voice He thundered,
"Call those men of war, have
Them bring weapons; revenge
Is what I want them for."

Each one carried a sword
And carried a writer's case.
They came into the Temple
Looking ready for the chase.

This one, He gave an order,
To walk out upon the streets,
To mark the forehead of each
Righteous man he'd meet.

Then He told others to fol-
low the first one's path. To
Show all who weren't marked,
The vengeance of God's wrath.

He said, "Fill the Temple
With the bodies of the dead."
And they proceeded then
To do as He had said.

Now they were busy, so I
Fell upon my face and cried,
"Will there be any left?
So many have already died."

"Their sins are great," He
Said, "Murder is the norm.
I won't spare or pity them;
Their futures are forlorn."

The man with the writer's case
Returned with his errand run.
Saying, "I've done as told;
I declare my job is done."

CHAPTER 10

Suddenly above the cherubim
Appeared a beautiful throne.
It was a most marvelous sight
Like unto a sapphire stone.

Then he of the linen clothing
Who carried the writer's case,
Went among the whirling
    wheels
To the live coals at the base.

He took a hand full of them
And over the city he spread.
While I gazed in awe with
A wonderful sense of dread.

Those cherubim were the ones
I'd seen beside the Canal,
Hands beneath their wings,
Faces on all sides as well.

When they rose into the air,
The wheels went right along,
God's glory went with them as
Beautiful as sight and song.

CHAPTER 11

By the Spirit I was lifted,
To the east gate transported.
Twenty-five men were there
Who'd still not been deported.

The Spirit said to me, "The
Leaders are the wicked ones"
They say, "Listen not to God;
Our own business we will run."

They'd rebuild and stay in
This city they have destroyed.
Where they murder and sin and
With the devil have alloyed.

"So prophesy unto them, both
Loud and clear speak the
　word."
Suddenly one dropped dead,
As the fearful truth he heard.

For I told them God knew all
The sinful deeds they'd done.
And the fearful consequences
Which they could not outrun.

Then the glory of the Lord
Over the Holy city rose. The
Cherubim lifted their wings
And with their wheels did go.

The Spirit took me back to
Babylon and the exiles there.
So I told them my experiences,
Visions, prophecy I shared.

CHAPTER 12

Again God's word came down,
While Israel was still free.
"You live among the rebels,
So tell them this for me.

They know that I am calling
But don't really want to hear.
So pack up your belongings
And make it to appear

Like an exile in the night,
You are trying to steal away,
That you fear the sad results,
If you try to stay."

So I did as I was told and
Worked the day well through.
In the wall I dug a hole and
At night went out there too.

Next morning He said to me,
"Now you've got them curious;

Tell them, it's a sign from
Me and I am deadly serious.

They will be driven out, and
Exile will be their lot, even
Their king to be driven away,
His future a hideous blot.

To the land of the Chaldeans
He will go in captivity.
There in exile he will die,
But the land he'll never see.

His people and his servants
Will scatter far and wide.
From God's veangence they
Will find no place to hide.

I'll save a very few, who'll
Believe evidence in time
Of all their wayward ways
And of their many crimes.

Now they are saying, these
Threats are for future days;
Tell them it will happen now,
And with no further delays."

CHAPTER 13

"They give people messages;
Good things press to hear.
The truth they do not tell;
That would cause much fear.

These prophets are false
And are not sent by me. They
Claim that all is well
When it was not meant to be.

They claim to have visions
And the blessings of God, who
Says, 'You lie in all you do,
And I will apply the rod.'

A wall you'd have them build
Is flimsy with no strength.

You whitewash all its flaws,
And lie to all at length.

I'll cause a storm of terror
To destroy the wall and you,
Who said "Peace," and it was
not and the facts you knew.

Against those women prophets,
Who damn young and old
   alike.
You pay for news they sell,
Thus they make their strike.

You pave a way to destruction,
By cheating and your charms.
But you will meet your maker,
For you have done great harm.

I will deliver my people
From your conniving hands.
You will know that I am God;
I'll wipe you from the land."

CHAPTER 14

Some elders of Israel came
By to pick my brain. But I
Knew they would not listen;
What did they have to gain?

"I, the Lord will answer,"
Was the message I received.
"While they worship idols,
There'll be trouble with me.

I'll send great punishments,
Wipe evil from the land. If
Noah, Job, or Daniel lived,
I would save no other man.

Godliness would save each
But would not save another.
For they are so bad that
Other help they'd smother."

CHAPTER 15

Word came again, "Oh son of
Man, they are useless vines.
No matter what we tell them,
They all have evil minds."

CHAPTER 16

Then again He said, "Speak
To Jerusalem of her sins.
Something must be done
For she is rotten within.

Like a lost babe I found her,
Whose mother'd cut and ran, I
Cut the cord and bathed her,
And took her by the hand.

She was bloody and bruised,
And had been left to die.
No one wished her well or
To help her would they try.

So I gave to her the will
To make her way alone.
And when next I passed that
Way she was fully grown.

She'd become a raving beauty;
In marriage I made her mine.
I gave her precious jewels,
Dressed her in fabrics fine.

She ate the richest foods
And wore the finest silk.
She was a beautiful queen
In a land of honey and milk.

Then she trusted her beauty
And others more than me.
She followed all the nations
Like a harlot on a spree.

The very jewels I gave her,
And golden ornaments and
   such,

She used to dress pagan idols,
With behavior just too much.

Beautiful clothes I gave her
She used on idols as drapes.
My oil and incense burned to
Them; she is a total disgrace.

She took my children and she
Sacrificed them too. Is
There no possible end to the
Terrible things she'll do?

She's worse than a harlot;
She pays them to come to her.
I will turn her out in anger,
And their homes I will burn.

She's thankless and arrogant,
Her allies ashamed of her too.
Assyria, Philistia and Egypt,
Will give her, her just dues.

Like mother like daughter,
That is what they'll say.
Despising husband and child-
ren, as you go a sinful way.

You follow Sodom and
   Gomarrah
In all the sins they've done.
But you are much worse,
And a greater risk you run.

In time a day will come
When I'll favor you again.
Then you will live in plenty
And according to God's plan.

That day you'll have charge
Of those you have despised.
The fact that you're forgiven
Will be a great surprise.

You do not deserve my smiles,
With shame will be overcome.

I will be your God again
In spite of all you've done."

CHAPTER 17

"This riddle give to Israel,"
His word then came to me. "A
Mighty eagle snipped a shoot
From the top of a Cedar tree.

He carried it to a busy city,
By a river broad and fair,
Planted it in fertile ground
And awaited growth to flair.

It became a spreading vine,
Grew beautiful to his gaze.
Another great eagle arrived,
Appeared to seek his praise.

So shall I let it grow
Or shall I tear it out?
I will do the latter
For my word it flouts."

Then He said, "Now ask them,
What means this riddle to you?
Now I'll explain the meaning,
And believe you me, it's true.

Into Babylon's beautiful land
You were brought to live. And
King Zedekiah was honored
But allegiance he'd not give.

So he'll be rooted out, and
In a foreign land he'll die.
For he has caused much grief
And the loss of many lives.

I, the Lord, shall punish him,
For he took my name in vain,
When he vowed to obey me
But then rebelled again.

Know that I am God; I strike
The high and exalt the low. I

Can make a green tree wither
And the dead one grow."

CHAPTER 18

Again the message came,
"Why in Israel do they say,
For the fathers' sinfulness,
Children will have to pay?"

"You should know," God says,
"No longer will this be;
Souls of fathers and sons,
They all belong to me.

He who sins and dies in sin,
He shall surely die. But
He who changes all his ways
Shall get another try.

If he is honest, fair and
Just in all he does, then he
Will certainly live no
Matter what his father was.

The secret is you see, not
How pious he acts or tries,
But how he actually lives,
And especially how he dies.

If he was raised honestly,
To live and help in need,
Yet fails in time of stress
And dies doing evil deeds,

He'll pay as charged."
God goes on to say, "His
Soul will face the facts of
How he spent his last days.

So, why do the people cry,
"The Lord is so unfair?"
For they have no reason to
Complain or feel despair.

I would, that everyone
Could live forever blessed.

So all men were guaranteed
A life of peace and rest.

But my people, in effect,
The decision is up to you.
A chance for eternal life,
Is decided by what you do."

CHAPTER 19

The leaders of Israel sing
A lamentation for death.
Princes, like young lions,
Wasted youth and breath.

When Jehoahaz was the king,
He ruled surrounding lands.
They rebelled against him
When tired of his demands.

Jehoiachin ruled next, who
Much like a King of beasts,
Became a killer of men, he
Loved not God, the least.

His enemies surrounded him
And brought him to bay.
In far off Babylon for his
Follies was forced to pay.

Mother Israel was strong,
And comely as a green vine.
She is rooted up and moved;
Now she withers and pines.

CHAPTER 20

Six years after Jeconiah,
Israeli elders felt it wise,
To ask His help by coming
To me for God's advice.

But now God said to me,
"There is no way that I
Will speak to them, or
Offer the time of day.

They burn little children
To worship idol gods, and
Now in all my fury, I am
Going to apply the rod.

Tell them, Son of man, my
Fire will scorch the world;
All the earth shall see
The flag of God unfurled."

"But, oh God," I said,
"They think in ignorance I
Meddle," they say of me,
"He only talks in riddles."

CHAPTER 21

This message then came,
"Toward Jerusalem face;
Make a serious prophecy
Against that wicked place.

From Negebs borders, I'll
Clean up across the land.
Sigh and groan before
Them, I won't spare a man.

Draw a map for them showing
Routes of the enemys thrust.
He'll turn toward Jerusalem
And level it to dust.

Babylon is an ally, so the
Word you speak they'll repel.
But Babylons king remembers
The times when they rebelled.

Ammonites too are targeted;
They laughed at Israel's woe.
I'll pour my fury upon them;
They'll fall before my blow."

CHAPTER 22

This message came decrying
Jerusalem's terrible deeds

Of lust and murder, idol
Worship and fantastic greed.

Every leader in our city is
Bent on murder and on power.
Mothers and fathers defied,
And evil rules every hour.

They deserve all they get;
Full penalty they'll receive.
I'll consume them with wrath;
My people they've deceived.

CHAPTER 23

Now I heard His voice again,
"Son of man, listen well. It
Is of two beautiful sisters,
And I have much to tell.

The elder was Aholah, and
Aholibah was the other. I
Married them both, and of my
Children they were mothers.

Aholah turned to other gods;
Dashing Assyrians pursued,
Captains and commanders,
Most attractive men in blue.

She worshipped their idols
And prostituted herself.
She did the same with Egypt;
She sinned with them as well.

The Assyrians stripped and
Killed her, and her children
Stole. It served her right;
She played the harlot's role.

Aholibah saw what happened,
You'd think she would change.
She went the same old way,
But covered a wider range.

Even fell for pictures of
Chaldean soldiers on a wall.

Her lust became so great
That she sent out a call.

She forgot the Assyrians and
With Babylonians went to bed.
Soon she tired of them all;
Her lust for them went dead.

So she turned to Egypt where
She'd done this thing before
And sinned more than ever;
She was rotten to the core.

Now Aholibah was Jerusalem;
Aholah was Judah, you see.
Both chose their sinful paths
In preference to following me.

And now Jerusalem, Aholibah,
Those very nations you spurn,
Will attack you on all sides,
When in anger they return.

From the land you'll be taken
And cut down in your prime.
They can have my share, for
I'd not give you the time.

I will leave you to your fate,
Which you very richly deserve.
And you will get no help from
Those heathen god's you serve.

You ignore my Sabbaths, and
My Temple you have defiled.
You only came to pray after
Sacrificing your own child.

To distant lands you sent
For priests to take my place.
For lovers you even bathed
Wore jewels and painted face.

My judgment against idolatry
Will be a lesson to see. The

Just will judge them fully,
And justice they will mete."

CHAPTER 24

Nine years of captivity had
Been King Jehoiachin's lot.
God said, "Mark the date;
Jerusalem is getting hot.

Babylon's King at her gates,
And all her plans he'll foil.
Tell them to put on a pot,
Fill it with water to boil.

Fill it with choice meats,
The best of every cut.
Cook it till well done, and
Then I'll tell you what!

Heap fuel on the fire till
Flesh falls off the bones.
See the scum upon the water
Like blood upon the stones!

Dump contents on the rocks,
The scum and rust remains.
If you burn it in the fire,
It'll never get clean again.

Like the sin of Jerusalem,
The pot will not be cleansed.
Nor will I be mollified till
I've dealt with evil men."

Then God took my lovely wife
And told me not to mourn. So
I told them when they asked,
It was a sign from the Lord.

He says "My temple I'll des-
troy, your children claim.
It's no use to grieve; it's
Because of your great shame.

To each other you may sorrow
And be sorry for your sins.

When you realize I am God,
Then true wisdom has set in."

CHAPTER 25

"The people of Ammon scoffed
At my Temple's loss. They'll
Be captives of Bedouin tribes;
They'll know that God is boss.

Moabites hate all my people;
They will breach her borders.
They shall know that I am God
Making changes, giving orders.

Edom I will smash, for they
Sinned against my own. When
Israel carries out my edict,
Edom's doubt will have flown.

Philistines hold grudges and
Avenge long-forgotten feuds.
I'll wreck coastal cities;
With sorrow they'll be imbued.

All these will feel my hand
And bend beneath the rod.
So through the haze of sorrow,
They will know that I am God."

CHAPTER 26

"Now Tyre has rejoiced at
The sound of Jerusalem's fall.
For she controlled the trade,
And now they'll have it all.

But I will stand against her
As nations bring her down.
Her suburbs will fall, then
They'll wipe out the town.

Cities will choke on dust as
Many Horsemen gallop
  through,

Hammers and battering rams,
Chariots and warriors too.

They'll plunder your riches,
Destroy your beautiful homes.
They'll throw your rocks and
Timbers into the ocean's foam.

All the world shall tremble
At attrition visited on you.
None will see you again, for
On this world you're through."

CHAPTER 27

"Now sing this song for Tyre,
Mighty seaport on the coast,
Who of your great beauty
You are prone to boast.

You deal riches of the world
In beautiful ships and style,
Your soldiers from many lands,
Your sailors from far isles.

You are courted by merchants
Of exotic lands o'er the sea.
Bringing commerce and gifts,
Your goodwill to appease.

Your ships of trade with
Others like mighty caravans
Trade throughout the world,
In all that's known to man.

But now your sailors weep at
This world's terrible loss.
Your city is sunk beneath the
Sea at an unbelievable cost.

Beneath the waves you lie,
All your people too. No one
Understands your awful fate;
How could it happen to you?"

CHAPTER 28

Again God told me, "Speak to
The prince of Tyre; tell him
He is only a man although
He claims to be much higher.

In splendor he was born to
Live like that evil one, and
To the very day of his fall,
He was honored like a son.

He used his wisdom for gain
Corrupting his soul thereby.
So from my mountain I'll cast
Him like a common man to die.

I am also Sidon's nemeses; you
Will be struck by enemies and
Disease; you'll know I am God,
To me you'll make your pleas.

All your neighboring nations
Will no more be Israel's foes.
Every one will know I am God
And no longer cause her woes.

I will gather all my own, and
I'll bring them back again.
They'll have prosperous homes
And return from foreign lands."

CHAPTER 29

After Jehoiachin fell, from
God this message I received.
"Now look toward Egypt;
Give her this word for me.

Oh Pharaoh, King of Egypt, you
Bragged to have made the Nile.
Now for your provocation,
You have my temper riled.

I'll take you from the river
To be food for wild beasts.

You failed my people Israel;
They trusted you before me.

I'll bring Babylon's army to
Destroy your lands and homes.
And for forty years to come,
Through Egypt none will roam.

For forty years a waste, her
People exiled to other lands.
But at the end of that time,
They'll be no longer banned.

Yet she'll be a minor kingdom;
Never more with pomp or
    power.
All will remember her failure
In Israel's darkest hour."

CHAPTER 30

"Now prophesy and say to her;
Doom clouds cover your face.
Your dead cover the ground;
Your wealth is taken away.

The land of Cush, Put, Lud
And of Libia and Arabia too,
All those countries shall
Fall who're allied with you.

From Migdol all the way to
Syene they will fail, all
Those desolate nations on
Hearing my name shall quail.

The great King of Babylon
Will destroy them as he goes.
And Ethiopia will see terror
In this time of woe.

There'll be anarchy in Egypt;
No king will live to reign.
Cities of the Nile ruined,
Pelusium and Thebes in pain.

Heliopolis and Bubastis, by
Foreign swords shall die.
The women gone into slavery,
And Tehaphnehes will cry.

Among nations I'll scatter;
Egypt will know I am Lord.
In Nebuchadnezzar's hand I
Place the fury of my sword."

CHAPTER 31

"Tell Pharaoh, King of Egypt,
And all of those he rules,
That even as Assyria did,
They play the part of fools.

As a great cedar of Lebanon,
Standing straight and tall,
Looked down on neighbors
And felt too strong to fall.

Its head is in the clouds;
Egypt is haughty and strong.
But I will bring it down to
Show the world its wrong."

CHAPTER 32

"Mourn for Egypt's King
Strong like a lion he feels.
As a crocodile of the river,
I'll throw him on the field.

Birds and beasts will feast
Upon Egypt's flesh and bones,
Scattered over hill and dale,
Like many weathered stones.

Blood will run like rivers;
Heaven will show no stars.
Lands you never knew will
Feel terror cold and stark.

For all the pride of Egypt
Will fall to Babylon's sword.

When she hits the bottom,
She will know that I am Lord.

To be buried in Sheol by
The side of those of yore.
With allies by your side you
Will know retribution sore.

The princes of Assyria, and
All who rode rough shod, over
Neighboring countries and
Over those who trusted God.

Now they lie undone in hell
In nether parts of earth.
They thought to be almighty
And over valued their worth.

Edom is there with all her
Kings and those others too.
They all worshipped idols;
They'll be company to you."

CHAPTER 33

Now tell my people that if
An attacking army draws nigh,
If a watchman is on the wall,
Then heed his warning cry.

One who hears the warning
And refuses to take care,
Deserves death that waits,
For he didn't do his share.

To me He gave notice that
Like a watchman I would be,
There to warn the people
Of disaster reported to me.

And if I failed my job of
Course they'd die in sin.
But He also warned me; my
Troubles would just begin.

With deaths I'd be charged,
For unprepared, they'd die.

For I was not alert and
Didn't give a warning cry.

"I know my people cry," He
Says, "and pine away in sin.
But I say change your ways,
This is the time to begin.

No matter if you're good,
Sin will erase it all. Even
If a saint should slip,
He is heading for a fall.

But he who is a sinner, who
Repents and changes his ways,
Will see a better tomorrow,
And I will brighten his days.

Tell them I have no pleasure
In unnecessary pain or death.
They determine their own fate,
So why not save their breath?"

Then one who escaped from
Jerusalem came to me, saying
"The beautiful city is fallen,
And now it ceases to be."

For some time I'd been mute,
But then my voice returned.
So I gave forth God's word,
For within my mind it burned.

For they knew how Abraham
Won Caanan with so very few,
And they, who were so many,
Thought they could do it too.

But God said, "Not a chance,
You are murderers and thieves.
You worship heathen
   idols,
My word you won't believe.

So those within the ruins
Shall surely die by the sword.

And disease will be the fate
Of those in caves and forts.

They'll fall to wild animals
Who escape into the fields.
They'll know I am the Lord,
For now they lack my shield."

He said to me, "Your people
Make of you a laughing stock.
They'll know you were my
   man;
They'll feel wrath of God."

CHAPTER 34

He said to prophesy against
The wicked leaders of Israel.
"You get fat at my expense;
In all ways you've failed.

For you feed upon the flocks
And wear the finest clothes,
But you never tend the weak,
Nor mend the broken bones.

You never seek the lost,
Nor feed the starving ones.
With cruel force you rule,
And to your pleasures run.

So I'll hold you accountable
For all my sheep you've lost.
You'll pay for your folly,
And you'll decry the cost.

I will be their shepherd
And show them a better way
Through mountain and valley,
Toward a brighter day.

Then I'll send a shepherd
Who will lead my people well,
A descendant of David
And the ruler of all Israel.

They will know I'm God as I
Lead them by life's stream.
The time of fear and sorrow
Will be a fading dream."

CHAPTER 35

Against people of Mt. Seir,
He said I should prophesy:
"I will smash you utterly;
The world will hear you cry.

I'll demolish your cities
And desolate the land. My
People took a bad beating
At your bloody evil hands.

In mountains and valleys,
You'll get your just dues.
Death will take your people;
There'll be no out for you."

CHAPTER 36

"To thy mountains, Israel,
God would have you know the
Enemy claimed your heights
And called them all his own.

Now to Edom who mocked
   you,
And took you away as slaves,
At every turn they murdered
You, till my anger is ablaze.

So speak to Israel, tell on
Mountains, hills, and dales,
I am angry at your enemies,
With me they made no sales.

But people will increase and
Flocks and crops will grow.
No longer will nations laugh,
For I will bring them low."

CHAPTER 37

The hand of God was upon me,
And this vision I was shown.
I was down in a valley full
Of bleached and aged bones.

They were withered and dry,
But He said, "Oh man, this
Is my question, can these
Old bones live again?"

"Only you oh God, can know,"
I said, and He replied to
Me, "Tell them to live
Again, and it shall be."

So I did as told, and those
Old bones drew together and
Grew flesh and skin though
Bleached by years of weather.

Then He bid me call the wind
To bring the breath of life.
So they became a living army,
Men who once died in strife.

Now He explained the vision.
"Israel is like those bones,
Separated from each other,
They're scattered and alone.

But tell them I will gather
Them unto me again, and
They will rise and prosper
And not be scorned by man.

Carve upon a stick to show
Judah and her tribes. And
Then upon another stick,
This I shall describe.

This stick will represent
All other Israeli folk. And
Like these sticks in hand,
They'll all be in one boat.

God will gather His people
From nations of the world.
Under one king they'll live
With His holy flag unfurled.

The world will surely know;
Who my people will be.
For I have set them apart,
They're all special to me."

CHAPTER 38

"Face north, speak against
Meshech and Tubal's King Gog.
He'll lead the final battle
To try to overthrow your God.

After many years of peace,
Down on Israel he'll descend.
Many nations will join him
In battle toward the end.

There are those who will ask
Merchants, princes, friends,
Why would any rob or seize,
To make them poor in the end?

In future years of history
Gog will do his wicked worst
To wipe Israel and godly men
From the face of the earth.

Gog will be my tool to
Right my score with man. But
I will be against him when
He tries to take their land."

CHAPTER 39

"Now, Son of man, prophesy
Against this evil Gog the
King. Tell him I am angry
Because of this evil thing.

On fields and seacoasts
He has been safe before.

I'll rain fire from heaven,
So he'll know I'm the Lord.

Israelis of the cities will
Gather supplies and spears.
They'll need no other fuel
For a period of seven years.

In the valley of travelers,
Just east of the dead sea,
I'll make a graveyard there,
Where Gog's armies will be.

Every Israeli will turn to,
To bury the warriors of Gog.
This is their great victory;
They'll know that I am God.

Seven months they'll labor
To clear their land of dead.
And send more to make sure
All's been done as said.

A feast of birds and beasts
Will be a sacrifice to me.
Call the animals and fowl;
Invite them to the feast.

All nations will know that
For Israel's sins she paid.
There'll be an end to debt,
Her future boldly assayed.

Earth's nations will know
God takes away and gives,
Israel will be certain proof,
Jehovah is God and lives."

CHAPTER 40

Eleven years of exile, then
The city of Jerusalem fell.
Fourteen more had passed
Before this vision I tell.

Back to Israel I was taken
And set on a mountain high.

A city appeared beside me,
A bronze hued man nearby.

A Temple of beauty, and
This man stood by the gate.
He held a measuring stick
And also a measuring tape.

"Son of man, stand by and
watch," He said to me, "for
You must go to your people;
Tell them all you've seen."

He measured the outer walls
At ten and a half feet high.
And by measure once again,
They were equally as wide.

Walking through the passage,
Was impressive and fine.
Nearly a hundred feet long
And just about half as wide.

Guard rooms along the walls,
Outer gates, there were three,
A large court, other walls,
And a Temple for priests.

A place to kill sacrifices
And to wash and prepare, a
Beautiful inner court and
A glorious Temple there.

CHAPTER 41

Into the nave he took me
And went on measuring there.
The room that he measured
Was thirty-five feet square.

"This," he said," is Holy."
As he taped the Temple wall.
The rooms were set in tiers
And were three stories tall.

The columns at the entrance
Were very well built.

Three tiers of rooms here
With no lean, sag, or tilt.

Each wider than the lower
None attached to the wall.
With a series of girders,
And they supported it all.

A stairway at the side led
Up from floor to floor. On
Each side in there were
Other rooms in the court.

Two doors led to a terrace;
Both were of imposing size,
One toward the south, an-
other on the opposite side.

On the west another building,
It faced the Temple yard.
The inner walls were paneled;
Upon those walls were carved

Cherubim and palm trees all
About the inner Temple walls
With an altar made of wood
Five and a half feet tall.

"This is Jehovah's table." he
Said, as we crossed the floor.
The nave and Holy of Holies
Both had double doors.

Those doors were decorated
Just as were the inner walls.
There was a wooden canopy
Which covered the entry hall.

CHAPTER 42

The next building he measured
Was back in the inner court.
It was much like those others
You've read in this report.

Again, three tiers they were
But reversed in size, with

The smaller at the ground,
The larger toward the skies.

"Now," he said, "those tiers
Of rooms facing north and
South are really very holy,
For when the priests go out,

They must leave all clothes,
For their robes are holy too,
So others they must don be-
for mingling with other Jews."

He measured the other wall,
A square of imposing size,
Eight hundred seventy-five
Feet long and equally wide.

CHAPTER 43

Later we returned through
The doorway facing east. The
Sound of the Lord approached,
And His glory could be seen.

Much as it was at Chebar, and
The other times before, with
Sight and sound of Jerusalem
Was the presence of the Lord.

Then into the Temple came
The glory and the light.
And I fell upon my face in
Great awe if not in fright.

Then the spirit lifted me up,
Taking me to the inner court,
Now from within the Temple I
Heard the voice of the Lord.

He who did the measuring
Still stood by my side, and
The Lord said, "Son of dust
In this Temple I will abide.

My people and the kings will
No more defile my name. Once

They made idols and totems,
Their conduct was a shame.

Tell them of this Temple,
See if they note their sins.
If they prove deserving,
Describe this place within.

Write the laws to follow
If I shall be their king.
This hilltop is most holy
So let the praises ring."

He showed altar measurements
And steps that led thereto.
I was told of Zadoc's family,
What the Levites should do.

CHAPTER 44

To the eastern passageway,
The Lord now brought me back.
Saying, "This door must not
Open, not even a tiny crack.

The prince may gain entrance
Only on his feasting day. Be-
cause the Lord God of Israel
Entered through this way."

By the north passage we came
To the front of the temple
There. Of His glory filling
The Temple I was well aware.

Again, I fell upon my face,
And He said to me, "Now use
Your head and listen, and
Remember all you see.

Remind people they've sinned,
By accepting heathens ways.
It is the way of strangers,
Who do not give God praise.

No one may enter my Temple
Unless he accept what's right.

He must be circumcised, and
Love God with all his might.

The priests of Levi's tribe,
Who worship idols or abandon
Me, will sure be humiliated
For everyone to see.

They kill animals for offer-
ings and guard Temple gates.
They may do menial work but
Never gain an exalted state.

But the sons of Zadoc, who
Too from Levites descended,
Shall serve me and my table,
For by them I was befriended.

They'll wear special clothing
As in my presence they stand.
And then wear other garments
To mingle with normal man,

Wearing their hair modestly,
Drinking no wine before.
Present themselves to me
Within this inner court.

Marrying only a Jewish maid-
en, or the widow of a priest.
And what is right from wrong,
To my people they will teach.

As judges of my people, they
Will arbitrate all claims.
To do according to my word
Shall be their only aim.

In everything they do,
They shall all obey my ways
In all the sacred festivals
And keep the Sabbath day.

Property they shall not own,
For I am all they need. On

Sacrifices by my people
They shall in plenty feed.

Animals dead of natural cause
Are a food to priests, taboo.
But they may eat of offerings,
Of harvest grains and fruit."

CHAPTER 45

"First of this holy portion,
This land you must provide,
Eight and a third miles long,
Six and two-thirds miles wide.

Then measure an area eight
Hundred seventy-five feet
Square, a strip a tenth as
Wide around the Temple there.

This equals half the area or
Three and a third miles wide.
The Levites will live on the
Equal half of the other side.

Next to this Holy Land, but
One and two-thirds miles wide,
Will be for a city of Israel,
Where anyone can abide.

Then on each side of these, a
Strip my prince will possess,
Who shall not rob my people
Or cheat or otherwise oppress.

You must use honest scales, a
Homer the unit of measure to
Be. All measures, wet or dry,
To derive from that, you see.

An ephah for dry equals a
Homer; a tenth homer, a bath;
For liquid measure, a shekel
Is not an ounce but a half.

A shekel is always a shekel;
No matter how many there are.

Twenty gerahs equal a shekel;
Fifty shekels a maneh is par.

Give a tax to your prince for
You cannot expect him to toil.
A bushel per sixty of grain,
One percent of your olive oil.

Give a sheep of each two hun-
dred. If all people comply,
Plus offerings for atonement,
The needs will never run shy.

You'll make up for your sins,
Reconcile Israelites to me.
Do this religious feast, for
Other occasions it shall be

A bullock offer at New Year's,
To purify the Temple, you know.
A priest offers for sin some
Blood on the door posts.

The fourteenth of this month
There'll be a seven-day feast.
With beef, mutton, and goat,
It'll be bread without yeast.

As an offering for sin the
Prince will also supply, a
Bullock for the passover, for
Himself and the tribe.

Each day of that week they
Will offer a bullock and ram,
Also a goat for sin, that
Well-known frailty of man.

A prince will give fourteen
Bushels of grain for a meal,
Twenty-one gallons of olive
Oil, this is also the deal.

Early October each year the
Prince will make a feast, of

Burnt offering of meal and
Oil for sins great or least."

CHAPTER 46

During the week, inner gates
Of east walls will be closed,
But be open for celebrations,
Or other events then posed.

Only the prince shall go or
Return by the way he went.
These rules go on and on
With no quick or simple end.

Each day required offering
And a sacrifice from all.
Even as it is today
When we hear the call.

The prince could give land
To any one of his sons.
But it must be from his own
And not just from any one.

He could own it forever;
'Twas His in special trust.
But if given to a servant,
Then in time he surely must

Return it on that day when
Seven years was complete.
For then he'd be free to
Relinquish and retreat.

The prince shall not take
Land or property of another.
It must be of his own and not
Impoverish an Israeli brother.

Then he showed me other
    rooms,
Saying, "Here they boil meat."
And he showed me boiling vats
With ovens underneath.

"They make sacrifices here,"
Was what he told me then.
"The Levites offer to God
To atone for the sins of men."

CHAPTER 47

Back to the Temple door, a
Stream flowed under it there.
Passing south of the altar,
Eastward it flowed most fair.

Onward it flowed its course,
Becoming wide, full and deep.
And back toward the Temple it
Was a beautiful wooded sweep.

"The river flows in Jordan
And desert to the Dead Sea.
It will heal where it flows,"
Was the thing he told me.

The sea will abound with fish;
Drying nets adorn its shores.
But the marshes and swamps
Will always be salty and poor.

Along the banks of this river
All kinds of fruit will avail.
With a new crop every month,
Always plenty without fail.

For food, fruit will be used
And medicine made from
   leaves.
The water from this river
Will benefit all who believe.

"Now these," he said to me,
"Are instructions you'll use,
To divide the land of Israel,
None to be shorted or abused.

Each tribe will own a share
Divided and chosen by lot. He

Proceeded to order boundaries;
Each tribe must own its plot.

Those from other lands whose
Children born in our midst
Were counted good Israelis
The land's length and width."

CHAPTER 48

Then he listed all the land
That the tribes would get.
With Dan on the north, to
The south they would stretch.

Ashur was next, with Naphtali,
Manasseh, Ephraim, Reuben in
Line, Judah next to the south,
The Holy Land, one of a kind.

It is the land of the temple
And with the Temple therein
With thousands of acres, for
Those sons who fought sin.

They're the sons of Zadoc,
Who stood straight and tall.
Each entitled to much land
Outside the Temple walls.

And there's the land
Where Levites will live.
Sized as above, which none
Can sell, trade or give.

Holy is that land where
God's priests will abide.
It lies to the south with
Its borders on each side.

To the south is the land
All Israelis may use free.
For pasture use or garden,
Or for parks and trees.

In the center is a city
Where anyone may live.

For all are Israelis
Who have talent to give.

Then the land of Benjamin
From east to west border,
South of this are Simeon's
Boundaries on this order.

Next, Issachar and Zebulon
And Gad is farthest south;
Egypt's brook is a boundary,
With other markers about.

On each side of the city,
Will be three city gates.
Each one named for a tribe,
In honor of each estate.

The length of city walls
Will be six miles around,
Called "The City of God,"
"What a beautiful sound!"

END OF EZEKIEL

DANIEL

CHAPTER 1

Three years into sinful reign,
King Jehoiakim lost a battle.
Nebuchadnezzar of Babylon
Captured Jerusalem's chattel.

From God's Temple he took
Back to his homeland afar,
Of the Temples sacred cups,
Away to the land of Shinar.

To his palace chief, he gave
Orders to recruit, some young
Israelis of noble mien, bearing
And wisdom to suit.

Strong and healthy they'd be,
Handsome and willing to learn.
In the palace to live and
Study, not to be spurned.

Daniel was named Belteshazzar
Hananiah now was Shadrack.
Abednego, known as Azariah,
Mishael now became Meshack.

So they'd live with royalty
And eat the very best foods.

With many wonderful things
Their king, allegiance wooed.

Daniel, a vegetarian at heart,
Begged off all the rich fare.
He told the king's steward,
Who was worried and scared.

The king ordered the best
For the young men he'd adopt,
And for his angry attention,
No one was willing to opt.

"You'll become thin and wan;
Others will put you to shame.
So eat the best on the table;
Don't fail to be in the game."

Thus admonished the steward,
Who'd protect his position.
But a vegetarian diet easily
Won Daniel the decision.

For the four did succeed in
Growth, health and learning.
Their minds clear and alert,
Effort superior to yearning.

After the king communed with
These boys of high pedigree,

Astonished by wisdom and wit,
Intellect was easy to see.

Three years of study under
Tutors the king did provide.
Appointment to his advisory
Staff was now easy to decide.

About seventy years Daniel
Served all Babylon's Kings.
Until in Syrus's Reign, his
Opinion counted on things.

CHAPTER 2

Nebuchadnezzar had dreams in
The second year of his reign.
Causing him much puzzlement
And considerable pain.

He called the magicians, his
Soothsayers, Chaldeans and
Such, and said, "Interpret my
Dream or run out of luck."

They answered, "Oh king what
You ask is grossly unfair.
Without knowing your dream,
We just don't have a prayer."

"The dream I've forgotten,
But you claim to know all.
So Tell me its meaning, or
Prepare for a serious fall.

For if you cannot produce
An answer I can believe, you
Will be torn limb from limb
For your attempt to deceive."

But they only repeated,
"There's no man that's alive,
Who can give you an answer
To that for which you strive."

So the angry king ordered a
Mass execution to take place.

So as a matter of course,
Fate met Daniel face to face.

To the executioner, he asked,
"Why is the king angry, pray
Tell." Then Arioch told him,
And he understood well.

"Let me talk to the king,"
Was the next thing he asked,
And they granted his wish,
Which might well be his last.

"Give me some time," he said
"And I'll tell you your dream,
While I'm about it, oh king,
I'll explain what it means."

So then he went home, and to
His friends he explained. So
They all prayed to God, so
Their lives they'd retain.

Then Daniel told Arioch,
"Spare the lives of these
Men, for I have the answers,
If the king's ear I can bend."

Then Daniel explained to the
King how it was. How no man
Could know unless revealed
By his God from above.

"You saw a huge statue of
A man shining brightly. He
Was made of silver and gold,
And of iron, very slightly.

His feet were of iron
But were partly of clay.
And then what you saw nearly
Turned your hair gray.

For a rock from the mountain
By unnatural means was cut.

It rolled toward the statue
As though following a rut.

Then it crashed into those
Feet of iron and clay.
So it was ground into dust,
And the wind blew it away.

Then as you watched in awe,
That rock grew large, until
It became a great mountain,
Covering earth near and far.

Now that head of pure gold
Is the empire you now rule,
Even the birds and beasts,
The wise men and fools.

Your empire is very great;
You rule lands far and near.
And God is your friend,
So you have none to fear.

But there will come a time
When your empire will end.
And to another great power,
All the world will bend.

Then the third great power
Will rise to rule all. Indicated
By the bronze belly,
Which in time too will fall."

The king fell to the ground,
And worshipped there in awe.
He called his people to witness
That God rules it all.

Daniel became Babylon's ruler
And chief magistrate became.
He remembered his friends,
Who all became men of fame.

CHAPTER 3

As he grew more powerful the
King began feeling his oats.

Made a ninety foot like-
ness as his ego suffered bloat.

It was a golden statue, and
It was nine feet wide. He
Forgot about the living God;
His ego swelled with pride.

He sent word to officials,
The rulers of his realm, to
Come worship his likeness,
They'd sure be overwhelmed.

When the band struck up, and
Everyone else bowed down,
Shadrach, Meshach and
Abednego weren't on the
    ground.

Of course some one tattled;
The King in anger declared,
Jews too would pay homage;
Not a soul would be spared.

A chance he would give them,
Or in the furnace they'd be
Thrown. They had no fear,
And they let it be known.

"No way we'll worship idols,
Definitely not one of you."
Then the king grew violent;
The air must have been blue.

He threw them in the furnace
It was hot with raging fire,
It devoured their tormentors
Before they could retire.

The king couldn't believe it,
As he watched them amazed.
Not even a hair was singed,
As they walked in the blaze.

With these three was another,
Obviously the angel of care.

Nebuchadnezzar shouted to
"Hurry, come out of there."

He claimed future allegiance
To God the father of all men.
Shadrach, Meshech and
Abednego prospered even
    more then.

CHAPTER 4

"Unto all people of earth,
Countries, lands and nations,
God has shown me wonders."
The King made proclamation.

"His signs are most wonderful,
Truly great are His deeds.
His kingdom is everlasting
And He has proven it to me.

As I lay on my bed taking my
Time with great ease, a
Dream came to me that com-
pletely shattered my peace.

So I called all my magicians,
Soothsayers, astrologers and
Such. When told of my dream,
They just couldn't tell much.

But Belteshazzar, the master
Magician, I told of my dream.
And I asked him to interpret
Just what it could mean.

Now this was my dream;
It was like a vision to me.
A tree grew to be mighty
With fruit and foliage green.

High it grew, tall and great,
'Till all the world could see --
It served animals and people
With good fruit and leaves.

Then from heaven, there came
An angel of God with a shout.
Cut the tree, trim branches,
Get birds and animals out.

But bind its stump tightly,
With bands of iron and brass,
With roots in the ground
Beneath tender green grass.

Let heaven's dews drench him,
With cattle may he eat grass.
Seven years with an animal's
Mind," said God, "let it pass.

This will prove to the world,
As the holy ones all know,
God dominates world
    kingdoms,
Calls score for man's show.

Now that was my dream, oh
Belteshazzar, magician, true,
The wisest man here failed;
The explanation's up to you."

Then Daniel was stunned,
And he sat staring aghast.
The meaning of this dream
He'd tell the king at last.

"If the meaning of the dream
Could on your enemies fall!
For the tree that you saw
Growing fruitful and tall

Your majesty, your fate is
Indicated by this tree.
What will happen to you
Was decided by holy decree.

From your kingdom you'll be
Taken to pasture like a cow.
You'll think like an animal
And be parched by drought.

But the stump and the roots
Were left in the ground. So
You'll get the kingdom back
And again will be around.

You must change your ways;
Stop sinning and do right.
Be merciful to the poor
And honest in God's sight.

A year later, as the
Palace roof I strolled,
A voice came from heaven,
And this I was told.

This message is for you;
You are no longer the king.
You will live in a pasture,
Seven years of this thing.

And then behold, it was so,
For seven years it was thus,
Then my wits were restored
And in God I now trust.

Now toward heaven I gaze
To worship the father above,
Forever he and his kingdom
Stands, a monument to love.

Officers and others returned;
My kingdom was restored to me.
Forever I'll honor and praise
My God who gave me reprieve."

CHAPTER 5

Now Belshazzar the king, one
Of Nebuchadnezzar's offspring,
Offered feast for a thousand
With much food and drink.

He sent for the cups, those
Cups of silver and gold,
Taken from Jerusalem's Temple
In those far off days of old.

They drank from silver and
Of iron, wood, gold and stone.
Then a strange thing happened,
The king felt fear and alone.

For a hand suddenly appeared,
And wrote words upon the wall.
His heart knew such terror
That he feared he might fall.

Then he sent for his wise men
To tell him what it meant.
But they knew not the answer;
It was wasted time they spent.

The queen mother then heard,
And she rushed into the hall
Saying, "You've a man who's
Able and available on call."

So Daniel was brought in to
Explain the sign they'd seen.
He was promised great riches
Such as often come in dreams.

But he answered, "Keep your
Gifts, or give them to another;
A great king was your ancestor,
Whom this occasion ushered.

High God gave him great glory,
Nations held him in fear.
And so he took the high road
For many glorious years.

Then his heart was hardened;
He took credit for success.
God took him from his throne,
He suddenly counted for less.

Though you knew this my king,
With stolen cups you imbibed,
You ignored the God most high,
And to man-made gods
   ascribed.

So he sent writing on a wall,
And this it means. God has
Weighed and found you
    wanting;
Now to exit life's main stream.

Daniel was made third ruler;
On his neck a golden chain.
He was robed in royal purple;
This had been his day of gain.

As all of his prophecies were,
He'd told the king quite true.
Darius, the Mede, became ruler
At the age of sixty-two.

That very night the king, obv-
iously in an enemy coup, was
Murdered and lost his kingdom,
So that part also came true.

CHAPTER 6

Darius split the kingdom,
A hundred twenty ways. Each
Ruled by a governor to keep
His treasure safe.

He placed three presidents
Who'd rule over all those.
With Daniel to be first,
Was the way the king chose.

For he was very capable, and
Very few mistakes he'd make.
Yet the king did foul up,
Perhaps not fully awake.

For all of those others were
Jealous and full of deceit.
They were out to get Daniel
And cause his defeat.

Now they conjured a law and
Got the king there to sign.

So it really did look like
They had Dan in a bind.

For the king signed a law
Making it illegal to pray
To any other but the king
For the next thirty days.

But Daniel, though he knew
The king signed the decree,
Faced toward Jerusalem and
Prayed to God on his knees.

So they all gathered round
And caught him in the act.
Then they lost no time tell-
ing the king of the fact.

They reminded him he had
Signed a decree into law.
He could see for a fact he
Had drawn the short straw.

So the king gave the order
To put Daniel under arrest.
He was thrown to the lions,
Though Darius did his best.

Though Daniel was a friend,
And he hated this thing,
He had to uphold the laws
As the duty of a king.

"May God whom you worship
Be with you to night." Was
The best he could offer
In his turmoil and fright.

No entertainment that eve
Could the king now enjoy.
As he seethed in knowledge
Of their guilt or the ploy.

So early next morning at
The den Darius arrived.

He'd never dared hope his
Friend Daniel had survived.

So when he called out
And was answered in kind,
The Joy that he felt was
Enough to blow his mind.

For God had sent an angel
To keep the lions at bay.
So the king ordered Daniel
Released and whisked away.

He ordered the presidents,
Governors, and families too,
To be thrown to the lions,
So they met their just dues.

He issued a decree, which
Through his kingdom did ring,
Daniel's God was almighty,
From whom good things spring.

So Daniel prospered greatly
While Darius held reign, and
While Cyrus, a Persian ruled,
His life was quite the same.

CHAPTER 7

Daniel lived in Babylon the
First year of Belshazzar's
Reign. A dream he put to pen
Caused him concern and pain.

This is what he wrote,
The way he dreamed it there,
But he told no one then, for
It gave him quite a scare.

"Upon a mighty ocean, I
Observed a powerful storm.
Winds blew in all directions,
Causing waves in many forms.

Then four mighty beasts
From out of the ocean came,

Every one was different,
No two at all the same.

The first was like a lion,
And it had an eagle's wings,
But they soon pulled off
And made it a lesser thing.

It could no longer fly, so on
Two feet like a man it stood.
The mind of a man was given it,
I know not if for bad, or good.

The next appeared like a bear
With its paw about to strike.
Its teeth held three ribs,
And its voice sounded like--

"Get up, and people devour,"
Which seemed strange to me.
Perhaps it had dreamed of
Meat between its teeth.

The third was like a leopard,
On its back it had four wings.
It also had four heads, and
Great power was in this thing.

Then as I watched in terror, a
Vicious thing from the deep
Arose. Vastly strong, tearing
Or crushing as it chose.

Ten horns grew from its head,
And it was more vicious by far.
If meanness could win a prize;
This one would surely star.

Then as I stood agape another
Small horn started to grow.
Three others were ripped out
To make room for that to go.

The little horn had a bragging
Mouth, eyes of a man to boot.

Wherever on earth it went, it
Eagerly gathered loot.

Thrones were put in place.
Great God, Ancient of days,
Sat down to judge the people
By the book's open page.

Upon a fiery throne He sat,
Came forth on wheels of flame
With hair like whitest wool,
Into this world He came.

He rode a river of fire, in
Clothes white as driven snow.
With millions of ministering
Angels wherever He would go.

That fourth brutal animal
Was killed and burned. It
Had challenged Almighty God,
Its evil fate had earned.

The other three animals had
Their kingdoms taken away.
In time they were let live,
For a short unhappy day.

Next I saw a man arrive,
Or so it seemed to me. He
Approached the Ancient One,
This ruling Prince to be.

His power will never end,
His government never fall.
Nations of earth will obey;
People will heed His call.

I was so confused that I
Approached one standing near.
I asked him what it meant,
And then he made it clear.

"The four animals are kings
Who will rule earth. One day

God's people will reign
Through their rebirth.

The fourth animal," he said,
"Will rule for a time and
Destroy all within it's path
And leave a legacy of crime.

Ten more kings will rise
From the empire he spawned.
One will rise more vicious
Than any since times dawn.

He'll counter the will of God
And change many ways on
  earth.
Then God will levy justice,
And this king won't be first.

Then God's people will rule,
And those who rule will serve.
Justice will be the byword
In heaven and the earth."

Then I awoke disturbed, I was
Pale and sick with fright.
I told no one what I'd seen,
For who would think me right?

CHAPTER 8

Three years into Belshazzar's
Reign and a similar dream
Again. At the capitol, Suza,
In the province of Elam.

Beside the Ulai river I stood;
A ram with two horns was near.
As I watched, one grew longer,
And nothing did he fear.

As I stood there watching,
One horn began to grow. He
Butted all within his path
And quickly laid it low.

It did exactly as it pleased,
Became very powerful indeed.
From the west a goat appeared
And came with blinding speed.

Only one horn, this goat had,
But it was of mammoth size.
He rushed upon the ram
And in battle won the prize.

The victor was very powerful
And had all things his way;
At the height of his glory,
His horn broke off one day.

In its place grew four more;
Four directions they pointed.
One grew large and battled
Others, also God's anointed.

Against God's people he
fought,
And some of them he defeated.
He defiled the Temple of God
And blasphemies repeated.

He challenged heaven's army,
But they fought not to win.
Truth perished from earth;
The world succumbed to sin.

Now two angels I heard speak,
"Why wait so long? Daily
Sacrifice must be restored,
For this all seems so wrong."

The other one replied, "Six
Point three years must go by."
A superior type stood near,
Over the river, another cried.

"Gabriel, speak now to Daniel,
You must explain his dream."
But I had fallen upon my face,
Too scared to speak or scream.

"Son of man," he said, "this
Vision please understand,
Not 'till near the end of time
Such things'll sweep the land.

Those two horns of the ram
Are Median and Persian kings.
The shaggy goat is Greece;
They will do mighty things.

The horn that broke off,
Four smaller ones grew there,
Small kings will follow
But not with so much flair.

Now as kingdoms grow and
Become rotten to the core,
Another king shall ascend;
He'll amass a terrible score.

He'll conquer all opposition
With no regard for strength,
Will devastate God's people,
Go to unbelievable lengths.

He'll cry 'Peace,' as he does
Murder, all across the land,
Battle the Prince of Princes
And think he's more than man.

But in doing this latter
He will seal his fate.
For against the will of God,
He will not be so great.

The twenty-three hundred days
That you in your vision heard,
Will be near the end of time,
But that number is God's word.

It will be a very long time
Before this comes to pass.
So keep it to yourself; it
Shouldn't be a great task.

I was sick for several days
Thinking about these things,
Before I could do my duties
To be of service to my king.

CHAPTER 9

Darius was son of Ahazuerus.
Darius, a Mede, became king.
His first year in Chaldea
I learned an exciting thing.

I read in Jeremiah's records,
How for seventy years of time,
Jerusalem would in ruin lie,
In payment for its crimes.

And so I pleaded our case
For our people to be returned.
We'd go back to our homeland,
For which all Jews yearned.

So I prayed and fasted in
Sack cloth covered with ash,
Asked forgiveness for Israel
For all mean, despicable acts.

"Oh Lord of love and mercy,
Of great and awesome deeds,
We've rebelled against you
Disregarding our real needs.

For years you've warned us,
Nobles, and the common man,
We drifted from your grace,
Refused to honor your plan.

So your curse has followed,
Moses' warnings came true.
You led Israel from Egypt,
Please lead us back to you.

We deserve no nod or smile,
But save your interest there.
Oh send us back to Jerusalem,
To rebuild your city so fair."

Gabriel, from my other vision,
Flew to me as I prayed. Said
"God loves you very much, but
It will not happen that way.

Four hundred ninety years,
The people will know no rest.
At last they'll be cleansed,
As by sin they're put to test.

In time a prince will come,
An age of decency begin. Jer-
usalem's walls to be rebuilt,
As well as streets within.

The Prince will die as savior,
A king, his army will deploy
And break a seven year treaty,
The Jews' fond hopes destroy.

For he will break his pledge
And harass the Jews again. So
God's judgement will descend
And pour upon this evil man."

CHAPTER 10

After three weeks of mourning
Three years into Cyrus' reign,
With fasting and much prayer,
Daniel had a vision again.

"Beside the Tigris River," he
Wrote, "I looked up and saw
A person standing there who
Put me in fear and awe.

In linen he was robed with a
Golden belt around his waist.
His skin glowing and lustrous,
Blinding flashes from his face.

His eyes like pools of fire,
Arms and feet of polished brass.
Voice like roaring multitudes,
And I was alone on the grass.

For my friends were fearful,
And ran away to hide, when we
Saw this fearful vision, I
Was weak and pale with fright.

And when he spoke to me
I fell face down, in a deep
Unknowing faint,
Oblivious to all around.

He touched and lifted me
Trembling to hands and knees.
Then I heard him say, "With
You, oh Daniel, God is pleased.

Now do not be afraid," but I
Stood trembling with fear.
"Listen carefully," he said,
"For God has sent me here.

In heaven you were heard
The day you began your fast.
I've come to help you under-
Stand, and I am here at last.

For evil blocked my way,
It rules that Persian land.
The Jews' guardian angel came,
And Michael gave me a hand.

So I'll tell you of the fate
Of the Jews of future years."
I still stared at the ground,
For I was weak with fear.

Then someone touched my lips;
He appeared like a man to me;
And though I had been mute,
I now could finally speak.

"I'm scared," I said, "I find
No strength to speak." He who
Seemed a man, touched me, and
I no longer felt so weak.

"God loves you very much," he
Said, "So do not be afraid."
And I felt much stronger
Since he came to my aid.

"I'll tell you of the future,"
He said, "for it is written
That Persia and Greece
Are lands by Satan smitten."

CHAPTER 11

"I was sent to help Darius
The year he first was king.
But I'm here now to show you
Some things the future brings.

Three kings will rule Persia,
But a fourth one will succeed,
Much richer than the others
And foment war against Greece.

A mighty king will rise, but
At the crest of power fail,
His empire divided among
    many,
A king of Egypt will prevail.

Yet his own people will rebel;
They'll take his kingdom away.
They'll make it more powerful,
And hold much greater sway.

Then Syria and Egypt will
Allies be in time, through
The marriage of a daughter
But hopes will be a blight.

Her brother will seek revenge,
March against Syria's king.
He will bring back Syria's
Idols and many other things.

Syria's king will tackle Egypt,
But his time will be short.

His sons will march again
And take an Egyptian fort.

Egypt then in anger will
Rally and conquer them. He'll
Kill thousands of the enemy;
Success will soon be stemmed.

In time yet to come, Syria
And allies will return. Some
Jewish insurgents will help,
And Egypt will fall in turn.

Onward the Syrians will march,
Pillaging Israel's land. To
Egypt's King, give a daughter,
Another failed political plan.

Coastal cities he'll conquer,
As he seeks the road to fame,
Only to meet a general from
Whom he'll retreat in shame.

Homeward he will turn, but
With trouble where he steers.
And somewhere along the way
He will totally disappear.

No better his successor, he'll
Send a tax collector to Israel.
His reign is brief; life is
Short; everywhere he'll fail.

An evil man is next to power,
But not of the line of kings.
With intrigue and flattery,
He'll get control of things.

With promises, deceit, a few
Followers, he'll be strong.
Rob rich, bribe the poor,
And in many ways go wrong.

He'll capture feudal lords,
And against Egypt will march.

Egypt prepares against him;
He'll stop before he starts.

His staff plots to stop him;
The army deserts, many die.
Two kings are skilled at
Deception, and they'll try.

But neither will succeed till
The Lord's appointed time. So
He'll turn his armies south,
While he's still in his prime.

Roman warships will threaten,
And he'll withdraw in fear.
Jerusalem will be pillaged,
As Syria's angry king appears.

He'll stop daily sacrifice
And pollute Jerusalem's law.
Leaving godless Jews in power,
Who righteousness never saw.

Some who actually understand
Will teach the ways of God.
Many will be robbed or killed
For doing a righteous job.

In time it will improve, when
For help they're due. But the
Helpers will take advantage
Of poor and persecuted Jews.

Some good ones will stumble,
Till trials make them strong.
So that when it comes their
Turn, they will do no wrong.

The arrogant king will boast
He's even greater than God.
Claiming with the fortress
God, he can do a better job.

The southern king'll return
And attack this king again.

But his enemy will come back
To fight this and other lands.

Ethiopia and Libia servants
Will be. With danger north
And east, he'll stay between
Jerusalem and the sea.

Here a royal camp he'll pitch,
Until his time runs out, he
Will be a great pretender but
Will lose his powerful clout."

CHAPTER 12

"Michael, the mighty prince in
Heaven, will plead your cause.
For he is the Jews' champion,
A guardian without pause.

Jews will suffer greatly, yet
Those with names up there,
Will endure to battle on, for
In heaven they own a share.

Those righteous who have died,
Will rise up and shine again.
Others will rise to contempt,
For they are the shame of men.

Those people who are wise,
Who've shown others His love,
Will shine like stars forever
In God's holy firmament above.

But do not tell this prophecy,
Oh Daniel, you have seen, keep
It secret to the end, till
More learning you've gleaned.

Then I saw two men, standing
Upon each river shore. And
Standing now above the river,
In linen, there was one more.

The one on shore asked him,
"How long will this terror be?"
He said, with hands toward
Heaven as if help to seek,

"Three and a half years, after
God's people are crushed," But
I understood it not, for
Truth, it seemed was hushed.

I asked, "What does it mean?"
He said, "Don't try to under-
stand. Till the end of time,
It will not be known by man.

Wickedness will continue, and
The persecuted be cleansed,
Only be wiser than others are
Until the very end.

When they ban daily sacrifice
And pagan worship proclaim,
There'll be a period of time,
Of twelve hundred ninety days.

They'll be blessed who await
The thirteen hundred thirty-
Fifth. Live your days out now,
So future life will be a gift."

END OF DANIEL

HOSEA

CHAPTER 1

Four kings reigned in Judah
During Hosea's time on earth.
God bade him marry a prostitute
To have stepchildren by birth.

To show a parallel to Israeli
Worship of idols of stone. For
To slip in allegiance to God
They had proven quite prone.

Jezreel, he named the first
To punish Israel's king. In
The valley thus named, Jehu's
Defeat God would bring.

Then Gomer had a daughter
And Lo-ruhamah she was
  named.
God said, "I'll show no mercy;
I'll not forgive Israel again.

I'll help the tribe of Judah;
They won't need a war machine.
For when they face enemies, I
Will always stand between."

Then Gomer had a son,
  "Lo-ammi,"
God decreed his name. For He
Said, " Israel is not mine;
She's caused me too much pain.

And yet she will see the time
She'll be great and strong
Like sand along the sea, when
She's overcome her wrongs.

Judah and Israel will unite
Under rule of a single king.
From exile they'll march, as
New-found freedom rings."

CHAPTER 2

"Change your name, Jezreel"
God says, "in time to be mine.
But plead now with your
  mother,
For she's no longer my wife.

Beg her to give up harlotry
Before I cause her to pay.
I'll not favor her or her
Children; this is not her day.

For she has lived in shame by
Chasing heathen gods and men.
I'll refuse her peace or plenty
'Till she returns again.

Confused, she'll run in circles
Searching for what she seeks.
And I'll expose her nakedness
For all her lovers to see.

In time to come I'll court her,
And I'll bring her back to me.
As in days of long ago, when
From Egypt I made her free."

CHAPTER 3

"Now go get your wife again,"
The Lord then said to me
"And love her once more,
Though she prefers adultery."

For a price, I got her back,
Bade her spend time at home.
Israel will have no prince
Or a king upon the throne.

But in time they will submit
And return unto their Lord.

In the end being willing
To listen to His word."

CHAPTER 4

"Hear these words, oh Israel,
You lie, steal, and kill. The
Land is filled with sorrow,
You list' not to God's will.

All living things will die,
And you can not blame another.
Priests have led you astray
Ruining Israel, your mother.

Daughters are prostitutes,
Sons and fathers, no better.
Oh Judah keep your distance
And avoid this fate forever."

CHAPTER 5

"Listen, priests and elders,
You've led Israel far astray.
In sin and idol worship, you
Have turned their minds away.

I've seen your godless deeds;
Your sins go deep within. You
Better change your ways, for
My patience is wearing thin.

Hear a warning cry, Israel!
For destruction you are bound.
It will be wherever you go;
You'll find no help around.

When you've lost the race
And winning cards are gone,
Then you'll come back to God
And sad will be your song."

CHAPTER 6

"Let's return to God, for
He has given us these wounds.

He'll be glad to heal us,
And He will do it very soon.

Sacrifice I'll shun," He
Says "I only want your love.
You're just a gang of robbers
Who've left a trail of blood."

CHAPTER 7

"Only outlaws live in Samaria,
In thievery, lies, and lust.
Their deeds of evil cover the
Land; it's like a coat of dust.

Kings are foolish drunkards;
The princes practice intrigue.
My people mingle with heathen;
They are a sorry mess indeed.

Idol worship weakened them,
Ephraim's hair's turning gray,
Like a dove flutters about
Who has truly lost her way."

CHAPTER 8

"Enemies are coming, Israel,
The worst you've ever seen.
I'll punish you with them
For you are small and mean.

I reject your golden calf
You made with human hands.
You will find my requests
Have now become demands.

Grain stands wan and weak.
Even if it richly yields;
Strangers will be reaping
Food within your fields.

You'll be of the nations
Much like a discarded pot.
To buy your only friends
Will be your sorry lot.

The wind you have sown,
A whirlwind you will reap.
I'll send you off to exile
So you'll be clear of me.

Israel built great palaces,
Judah, her great defense
But ignored their maker
And are facing recompense."

CHAPTER 9

"Rejoice no more, Israel,
For God you've left behind.
You pray to other gods
At every excuse you find.

You resorted to wickedness
As you did in Gilgal long ago.
I'll drive you from my land
For I cannot stand you so."

CHAPTER 10

"The more I give Israel, the
More idols and statues she
Makes. She must be punished;
Heathen altars I shall break.

When their king is taken,
They'll claim not to care. As
Slaves they'll go to Assyria
And drag their idols there.

They will know great shame;
Their trust is all misplaced.
Samaria's King will disappear
Like a chip on an ocean wave."

CHAPTER 11

"As a son I raised them, and
When I called they rebelled.
I held them in my arms, and
When sick, I made them well.

But in spite of all my effort
They will not return to me.
So as slaves in far off Egypt
And Assyria they will be.

My heart cries for Ephraim,
But I'll punish him as I must.
He ignored that I healed him;
My words were less than dust."

CHAPTER 12

"Come back to me my people,
So love and justice can be.
But you're like crafty men
Who'd rather lie and cheat.

Many heathen altars stand
Like furrows in a field;
Gilead is full of fools
Who to idol worship yield."

CHAPTER 13

"Once when Israel spoke
Nations shook with fear.
They worshipped idol gods
And the power disappeared.

For idols they melt silver;
Golden calves are built;
Ignoring the word of God
Is their greatest skill.

Like morning dew drying
Or mist that's blown away,
They'll soon grow weak and
Rue the shortness of the day.

Into Caanan I brought them,
A land of easy leisure. So
Now they've forgotten me
To only seek more pleasure.

I gave them kings in anger;
I took them back in wrath.

Sin has paved their way,
They'll walk a rocky path.

Ephraim showed promise
But resists like the rest,
Will wither in desert wind,
Instead of being blessed.

Samaria is no better; she
Rebelled against my will.
An invading army will come;
Her people they will kill."

CHAPTER 14

"Oh Israel, return to God,
Come to Him now and say,
Our sins have done us in,
We need your help today.

Our allies cannot help us;
Our Idols are useless too.

We'll only know your mercy,
If we sincerely follow you.

I will cure your doubts,
So relax in my love, being
Fruitful as the harvest,
When you turn to God above.

But stay away from idols,
For I, your God, lives. The
Wonderful fruits of mercy
Are only mine to give.

If you're wise, you'll be-
lieve and listen well.
The paths of God are true,
The only way for Israel."

END OF HOSEA

JOEL

CHAPTER 1

"Listen, you men of Israel,
In all life you've not heard,"
Says Joel the son of Pethuel,
"Listen to his prophetic word.

Tell all your children this,
Your children's children too.
For in the days to come this
Word surely will come true.

Awake, playboys and drunks,
And everyone else as well.
For locusts invade the land
In numbers too great to tell.

They'll strip the grain and
Debark the trees. All life on
Earth will suffer; nothing
Of worth will they leave.

Ministers of God will hunger,
Farmers stricken and shocked.
With nothing but sadness left,
The land'll be bare of crops.

A land once known for plenty
To soon be scorched and dry.
Animals will have no pasture;
All will wither and die."

CHAPTER 2

"Sound the warning trumpet
Upon God's holy mount, his
Judgment now approaches in
More ways than one can count.

Invaders number like locusts;
Their kind never seen before,
Sweeping the land like fire;
Great changes are in store.

'Twas like Eden before them,
Like a battle raged behind.
Like horses racing overland,
Destruction on their minds.

Terror is on the people as
God's army strikes them down.
They swarm upon the city, the
Most fearful enemy around.

This is the day of judgment,
An awesome thing to face. Oh
Come to the Lord today, and
Be a winner through His grace.

Bring the people and children;
Bring priests, ministers, too.
The Lord may still show mercy
And save this land and you.

He will turn this army back,
Restore the crops and lands.
Again he'll send the sunshine;
Rain will cleanse what stands.

Rejoice, people of Jerusalem,
Be happy in God's will. He'll
Send crops, grain and wine,
A cup of blessings He'll fill.

His spirit He'll pour on you,
On master and slave alike.
For all who'll call upon Him,
He has chosen to keep alive."

CHAPTER 3

"All of Israel will prosper,
When in judgment I stand."
He says, "I'll judge earth's
Rulers, my people and land.

They traded good for evil as
They pulled my people apart.
But I'll bring them back,
So all Israel can take heart.

They will regret treachery,
And be slaves in their time.
Take them to judgment valley,
Where they'll pay for crimes.

Harvest is due and waiting;
Their wickedness overflows.
The day of the Lord is near
And time of judgement close.

I am The Lord of Zion, and
The enemy must pass me first.
The land is of milk and honey,
Fresh water to slake thirst.

Edom and Egypt will fall, for
Innocent people they killed.
I will avenge my own; the
Enemy's voice is stilled."

END OF JOEL

AMOS

CHAPTER 1

Near Tekoa village, a shepard
Who was watching his flock,
In a vision saw the future,
A true revelation from God.

Two years before an earthquake;
Pastures withered and dried.
Shepherds mourned and wailed;
The Lord, like a lion cried.

"Again those people of Damas-
cus are making my people poor.
They've treated Israel like
Grain on a threshing floor.

I'll burn Hazael's palace,
Kill aggressors where they be.
Syrians return to slavery;
I have spoken; listen to me!

They put my people to slavery;
The walls of Gaza I'll burn.
I'll kill those of Ashdad, for
Israel's treaty they spurned.

Philistia and Tyre have sinned;
Walls and palaces I'll destroy,
Set fire to Teman and Bozrah,
There'll be little to enjoy.

Ammon has tried me again as
Borders she tried to enlarge.
The walls of Rabbah I'll fire,
And a great battle will start."

CHAPTER 2

"I'll not forget Moab's sins,
She wiped Edom under foot.
So I'll destroy her leaders
And rip her up by the roots.

Or do I forget Judah's evil,
And Israel also has erred.
Though I did much for them
The sins were not deterred.

You locked my prophets up,
This, Israel cannot deny.
Your warriors will stumble;
Strong men in weakness cry."

CHAPTER 3

"Hear! oh Israel and Judah,
You are the children I love.
But listen now and fear, for
I'm removing the kid gloves.

For a partnership to work,
Each must do his job. But
You have shirked your duty
And angered the living God.

People have in their homes
Loot of bandits and thieves,
They'll lose all they own
They've sinfully received.

When I punish Israel, idol
Altars of Bethel go too,
With homes of the wealthy
For the wickedness they do."

CHAPTER 4

"You aggressive women who
Make husbands rob or steal,
Crushing those with too lit-
tle who can't count on meals,

I sent blight and insects to
Decimate your olive trees. I
Took sons in plague or battle;
Yet you'll not listen to me."

CHAPTER 5

"Though men she sends to war,
Israel the beautiful will die.
A very few will live, ninety
Percent will not survive.

Bethel, Gilgal and Beer-sheba,
Your people will know grief.
Seek the Lord and live, or
You, with fire He'll sweep.

To you who mete not justice
And honesty is only a word,
Seek Him who made the stars,
For he is truly the Lord."

CHAPTER 6

"Woe to Jerusalem and Samaria
In luxury and idleness live.
You eat well and know comfort,
But the poor no help you give.

Behavior decrees your fate;
'Twill befall great and small.
To be surprised on every side,
There'll be no escape at all."

CHAPTER 7

Now the Lord showed Amos in
A vision as big as life, how
He'd send a plague of locusts
To add to Israel's strife.

Amos pled with God, saying,
"Please, don't treat them so,
They're such a little nation,
And they will have no hope."

So then God changed His mind,
Saying, locusts He'd withhold.
But with a terrible fire
Their land He would enfold.

But Amos begged again, saying,
"Lord, they are so weak;
Your forgiveness for them
All, I most sincerely seek."

The Lord stood beside a wall,
And in His hand held a line.
Now he said He'd punish them
With problems of another kind.

Prepare, oh Israel, for worse;
You think life is only a game.
But God made the earth, and
Jehovah is His name."

"Amos is a traitor," cried
Amaziah, a priest of Bethel.
"A rebel who plots for the
The king's death as well."

Then he sent word to Amos
To flee the land at once.
But it was quickly obvious
That Amos was no dunce.

He'd been called a prophet,
Amos said 'Twas just a name,
For he was only a herdsman,
He could not claim such fame.

He'd been sent by the Lord,
Israel's fate to tell,
And his duty to his God
Was to speak to Israel.

CHAPTER 8

"God showed me fruit," Says
Amos, "a full basket heaped,
Which represents Israel
And is ready to be reaped.

They're ripe for punishment
With dead bodies everywhere.
They trample on the needy;
The poor they do not spare.

They will tremble, awaiting
Doom, everyone will mourn.
It will get dark at noon,
And all will be forlorn.

People wander o'er the land
Thirsting for the Holy word.
Idol worshippers will fall
And never again be heard."

CHAPTER 9

He stood beside the altar,
Said, "Shake the Temple down,
They run, still to be killed,
For the Lord has frowned.

They cannot dig so deep
That they can get away,
Nor ever hide from me
Where I do not hold sway.

I can touch the land so
It melts and people burn.

Or flood the Nile River,
Until they drown in turn.

God is at home in heaven,
Earth, His basement floor.
He pulls vapor from the
Ocean, on earth as rain
It pours.

Israel, I loved as others,
I've helped Ethiopia too.
Also Philistia and Caphtor,
But I've got my eyes on you.

Your sins are mounting up,
Judgment day will arrive.
If in sin, you feel safe,
By the sword you'll die.

I plan to bring you back,
The City of David rebuild.
I'll smile upon their crops,
The granaries I will fill."

END OF AMOS

OBADIAH

CHAPTER 1

Now Obadiah had a vision,
And this report he gave.
It concerns Edom's condition,
Its future looks grave.

This is word from God to
The countries round about.
Cut Edom down to size, for
She's too arrogant and proud.

"So you live on high cliffs
And feel safe in this place;
Though you soar with eagles,
You can fall on your face.

If a thief had robbed you, at
Least a little would be left.
If he stripped your vineyards,
You'd not be totally bereft.

But everything you own, Edom,
Will be searched and taken.
Allies will turn against you;
By friends you'll be forsaken.

There'll be no wise men left
For which you were known.
Stupidity rules your lives;
Your mighty warriors flown.

You can't stop the slaughter,
You helped in Israel's demise.

You helped brother invaders
And thought you were wise!

When he was forced to slavery,
You helped divide the spoils
Killed, maimed and plundered,
And added misery to his toils.

On the Gentile nations God's
Vengeance will surely fall.

Like a cup you gave others:
Yours is filled with gall.

All the nations of Israel
Will return to do their thing.
Edom to be ruled by Jerusalem,
And God shall be the king."

END OF OBADIAH

JONAH

CHAPTER 1

Jonah, the son of Amittai,
Heard God's urgent call. "Get
On over to Ninevah, prophesy
Within their walls."

Jonah had fear of preaching
To the gentile hoard. So he
Boarded ship in an effort
To escape the Lord.

As the ship did sail along,
Great wind came upon the sea.
All the sailers panicked,
Jonah was in the hold asleep.

So the captain woke him up,
For sailor's gods had failed
To calm the tossing ocean;
The ship was loud with wails.

Then they all drew straws
To see who caused the storm;
Jonah drew the short one; to
Him this seemed the norm.

Then they wanted to know
Who he was and where from.
So he admitted being a Jew,
Who from God was on the run.

This really shook them up,
The storm was getting worse.
He said, "Throw me overboard,
I'm the one who's cursed."

They tried to row the boat
Were losing against the sea.
He said, "Throw me overboard;
No need to die because of me."

They prayed for forgiveness
And threw Jonah over the side.
Waters suddenly calmed, as if
This had saved their lives.

They stood in sudden awe of
This God who had such power,
Sacrificed and praised his
Action in this troubled hour.

God had sent a monster fish,
Which gobbled Jonah down.
And I'll bet his earnest wish
Was to be in Nineveh town.

CHAPTER 2

As he sank beneath the waves
His prayer went up to God,
For he knew why he was here,
As the Lord applied the rod.

He knew he'd never worship
Anyone other than the Lord.
For when he'd lost all hope,
He thought of God once more.

God ordered the great fish
To spit Jonah upon the beach.
And that was how it happened
That Jonah lived to preach.

CHAPTER 3

Jonah heard the voice again,
"Go, warn Nineveh of doom."
So went to preach the word
But with a heart of gloom.

It was a mighty city, but
He no sooner began to talk,
When people listened avidly
From lives of various walks.

His message fell on willing
Ears, "Forty days you've
Got to change your ways,
Or destruction is your lot."

Even the king sat grieving,
Ashes and sackcloth wore,
And ordered his people to
Fast and pray to the Lord.

God noted the change; they
Were now honest and true,
So gave up on destruction
And didn't carry through.

CHAPTER 4

But Jonah complained, for
Now he felt like a fool.

Sulked under shade trees,
Here 'twas shaded and cool.

God asked, "Why be angry?"
Jonah bitterly complained,
"You got softhearted, and
Didn't do as I'd claimed."

Those leaves withered, died
And afforded no more shade.
But he was protected again by
A broad leafed plant God made.

And now there came a worm,
It chewed that plant in two.
The sun beat upon his head
Until weak and faint he grew.

"Why make me suffer so?" Were
The words to God he cried.
"Death is better than this,
Why don't you let me die?"

Then God asked, "Why is
It that you feel so burned?"
Jonah said, "it's because
My anger has been earned."

God said, "It is obvious
You act like a little boy,
Because the sun's hot, and
Your shelter was destroyed.

Why shouldn't I be sorry
For Nineveh and its folks,
When they were in darkness
And didn't know the ropes?"

END OF JONAH

MICAH

CHAPTER 1

Under three kings Micah prop-
hesied. It came in the form
Of visions, as to tell the
Truth he always tried.

Jotham, Ahaz, and Hezekiah
Were kings of Judah then. But
To Samaria too he pled, to
Change ways and be cleansed.

The Lord stalks in vengeance
For Judah and Israel's sins.
He'll tear down forts and
Walls because of sin within.

Because of people's efforts,
Which will be to no avail,
Lament in desperate sorrow
As for the cities they wail.

Flee the towns and cities
With no hope of saving them.
Weep for those in slavery
Whom you'll never see again.

CHAPTER 2

To you who lie awake at night,
To plot with the wiles of man,
To assume a certain house, or
By fraud that piece of land.

By threat and violence you
Steal what belongs to others.
God meant for you to treat
All men as brothers.

You'll find no sympathy, as
You wail a dirge of despair.
Your weak hope will disappear
As God brings anger to bear.

You do not want to listen,
It's easier to ignore facts.
But this you can be sure of,
You'll all pay for your acts.

And yet the day will come,
My people will see the light.
The Master will lead you back
To paths of peace and right.

CHAPTER 3

"Attention! Leaders of Israel,
All of you know what's right.
But the way you treat my
People certainly is a fright.

You cheat, lie and filet them
Like meat for the cooking pot.
Then you pray to God for help
When trouble is your lot.

Do you think He'll listen
When for His help you pray,
When all of your prophesy's
Will lead my people astray?

You who claim peace, when
You'll not preach till paid,
Have to admit you were wrong
When you can't make the grade.

This message is for you
And from God above.
I prophesy of the Lord
And the power of His love."

CHAPTER 4

That mountain known as Zion
Will be famous the world o'er,
Praised by all the nations,
Visited by rich and poor.

Come visit God's Temple, for
He'll tell us what is right.
From Jerusalem He'll rule the
World in holy, powerful might.

He'll judge among the nations
Convince those far away to
Beat armor into plowshares;
We'll know peace that way.

In his home each will live
With peace at last a verity.
And as a result of no wars,
We will know prosperity.

Forever we will follow Him,
In a day when all's right. He
Will save the lame and poor,
Protect them by His might.

Though nations 'round about
Still worship idols and sin,
God's people see no sorrow,
Because of peace within.

But now you live in terror,
A king is dead, wise men too.
Nations are at your throats,
Not knowing His plan for you.

One day God will gather your
Enemies like sheaves of grain.
With horns of iron, hooves of
Brass, He'll inflict the pain.

CHAPTER 5

Rise, mobilize your forces,
For the enemy is at hand.
And he'll strike with vigor
As he moves across the land.

Bethlehem is small, yet to
Be the birthplace of a king,
Who comes from ages past,
His voice with freedom rings.

God will abandon His people
For a time 'till they reform.
But one day He'll return,
And peace will be the norm.

Then He will feed His flock,
And we'll know lasting peace.
If the enemy invades our land
God will lead us to release.

He'll appoint seven shepherds
To watch over us that day.
He'll give us eight princes
To lead us all the way.

With the strength of a lion,
Israel will suppress her foes,
A gentle rain of freshness
Where in the world she goes.

"Weapons I'll destroy," says
God, "defenses I'll tear down.
Put an end to fortune telling;
There'll be no witches around.

You'll worship no more idols;
Shrines must also go. I will
Pour vengeance like fire
On those nations who do so."

CHAPTER 6

Listen, my people, let your
Complaints cover the land!
God is also grieved by your
Thieving, arrogant stand.

Oh Israel, what have I done
To make you turn away?
For I cut your bond to Egypt
And rescued you as slaves.

I sent Moses to lead you to
A land of plenty, most fair.
With Miriam and Aaron to help
Forty years of journey there.

Remember Gilgal and Acacia,
All the blessings I bestowed?
Now you ask, "What can we do
To pay back what we owe?"

But God says, "No to you, I
Don't want sacrifice or pain.
Just be merciful and humble
To walk with your God again."

God could say, "I'll overlook
It; go ahead, lie and cheat.
But that would never do, it'd
Only add to people's deceit."

So He says, "I'll wound you;
You will eat but hungry be.
All you earn will be useless;
From want, you'll not be free.

You follow commands of Omri
And Ahab who are your Gods.
So you're the world's laughing
Stock as I apply the rod.

CHAPTER 7

Men will cry in woe, "Where
Have all the good men gone?
Those left are murderers
Who do nothing but wrong."

The rich and those who rule
Make misery for the poor.
Men of honesty and honor
Just plainly are no more.

Friends cannot be trusted,
Your brother, or your wife.
With enemies in your house,
You're in danger for life.

The only choice I have is
Look to God for help. Wait
Patiently as He punishes me,
For I am a sinner as well.

Then my enemies will surely
See that God is on my side.
I'll see them in confusion
While in safety I'll abide.

I'll hear the Lord remark,
"Good times for you I caused.
As when I led you from Egypt,
The world will stand in awe."

He'll bless, as he promised
Our father Jacob, long ago.
He also promised Abraham
He will keep us in the fold.

END OF MICAH

NAHUM

CHAPTER 1

Nahum preached this message;
He prophesied Nineveh's doom.
To those at whom he aimed,
It must have forecast gloom.

God is slow to anger, and
Doesn't easily forgive.
Taking vengeance if earned,
You'll wish you'd never lived.

His power is in the cyclone,
In billowing clouds of storm.
Rivers dry at will, earth-
quakes rumble, silence born.

Before His mighty anger, no
Man of the world can stand.
He is the author of beauty
But can decimate the land.

How can mortal man stand be-
fore His might? Nineveh, he
Can strike you dead, when He
Has barely begun to fight.

Though your armies are great,
You'll vanish before Him in
Flame. When punished enough
He'll just break your chains.

Assyria's King will perish,
And his dynasty will fall.
You will be forever free if
You'll listen to His call.

CHAPTER 2

You lost the battle, Nineveh;
The enemy breached your walls.

In panic your warriors run;
They have ignored your call.

Your queen naked is led away,
The king's guard is too late.
Like a leaking water tank,
The soldiers try to escape.

Oh Ninevah, great city, you
Who were the lion of them all,
You once collected booty from
Others, it's your turn to fall.

Your finest youth defeated,
Your treasures are taken away.
Never will you rule again, for
Nineveh, you've had your day.

CHAPTER 3

There's blood on your streets,
As chariots rumble and roll.
The dead are there in heaps,
As total carnage unfolds.

You were a beautiful city,
A mistress selling her charms,
Who sold out to God's enemies
To do His people harm.

You taught them to worship
False Gods along the way.
Now he stands against you;
Your actions earned your shame.

END OF NAHUM

HABAKKUK

CHAPTER I

Little is known of Habakkuk
That prophet of long ago.
Concern with Israel's holin-
ess it seems was his alone.

He cried out in bewilderment,
"Oh God, please listen to me?
All is bribery and oppression,
Injustice, the worst of these.

Why is a cry of the helpless
Hopelessly lost to your ears?
Why are you silent, as murder,
Plunder and idolatry appear?"

Then as in a vision, a reply.
"I have an answer for you;
You'll really be surprised
At what I'm going to do.

The Chaldeans, so violent and
Cruel, will sweep on the prey.
The power of Kings or princes
Will simply melt away.

They claim power of idol gods,
So they'll raid and disappear.
Cities and kingdoms will fall,
Warriors paralized with fear."

"Oh my Lord and savior,"
Habakkuk then implored,
"How can you let them destroy
    Us?
For you are a merciful Lord.

If you are against us Lord,
Then who will our champion be?
For they'll praise many gods,
As we in terror, mercy seek."

CHAPTER 2

"I'll climb up high, oh Lord,
To await your decision there."
Then the word quickly came.
"Write my answer, very clear.

Then men will read and tell
The thing that they have seen.
For it will surely happen
Without much time to dream.

A time will soon arrive when
Your enemy will pay his bill.
With his arrogance and greed,
His appetite is unfulfilled.

Though he works night and day,
His servants in time will cry,
'You've plundered many nations,
And now you deserve to die.'

For God has so decreed
That those shall work in vain,
Who rob and murder for profit,
And cause their neighbor pain.

Now you have made your idols
Of wood and speechless stone.
When you await their answer,
You'll find you're all alone.

But the Lord is in His Temple;
Let the earth in silence tell
That man who lives with God
Knows at heart all is well."

CHAPTER 3

In triumph, Habbakuk sang,
"Oh Lord, the God of all,
In time of terrible need,
You have heard our call.

In your mercy Lord,
And in your power to save,
Your glory reaches to heaven;
The earth sings your praise.

Your power is glorious;
Your word shakes the earth.
My strength and redeemer,
Your love brings rebirth.

Guide me on my journey
Over mountain and vale.
Beside your living glory
All other gods are pale."

END OF HABAKKUK

ZEPHANIAH

CHAPTER 1

A Jew was Zephaniah, and
His father was Jewish too.
He'd seen a vision from God,
So this job he had to do.

And so this prophet warned
Of Gods impending wrath
To befall this wicked nation
Here in Nebuchadnezzar's path.

You've had plenty of time
To abandon your wicked ways.
But if you insist on folly,
It will imperil future days.

God says, "I will crush Judah
For wicked things she does,
Fish, fowl, animals, worship-
pers of sun and moon above.

You claim to follow God, but
You worship idols too. Stand
In silence in His presence,
`Twas all brought on by you.

Judah's judgment day has come,
He'll punish all who kill and
Rob; so think not to escape,
For no one trifles with God.

Gold and silver is useless;
This land will perish by fire.
He will punish His people,
Who've richly earned His ire."

CHAPTER 2

Gather yourselves together
And pray as never before.
Ere His terrible wrath begins,
Let us beg mercy of the Lord.

Walk humbly every day and do
Only what is right. It is
Possible He'll protect you,
If you trust His holy might.

You Philistines in the cities,
And who live beside the sea,
Your land will be desolate, He
Says, "You will answer to me.

My tribe of Judah will live
In the homes you left behind.
Moab and Ammon will also fall;
My people, safety will find.

Ethiopia and Syria stumble,
The arrogant people be slain.
Nineveh, the capitol of Syria,
Will become a crumbling plain.

A city of security and wonder
That lived a law unto itself
Will be mocked by passersby,
Can look for no one's help."

CHAPTER 3

Jerusalem, a beautiful city,
Is full of violence and crime.
She is drifting far from God
And is running out of time.

Her prophets lie and cheat;
Her priests, a Temple defile.
Your Lord is a living witness;
He sees their sinful style.

All day they see my judgment
Heedless, they show no shame.
All the time their borders
Are losing the survival game.

These evil nations will fall,
Soon all the earth shall see.
Says this waiting, angry God,
"They'll pay the price to me.

I'll pour out my fierce anger;
The earth shall know my ire.
I'll not need to strike again;
If I consume them with fire.

I'll change their language,
One tongue will tender praise.
They'll be from all the earth
And no longer feel ashamed.

In peace and quiet lie down
And not one will be afraid.
When God brings them back,
You'll all know better days.

Then He will live among you,
And the victory will be yours.
Enemies will be vanquished
For making rough the course.

He'll gather you together,
Will bring you home again.
He'll restore your fortune;
You'll be a wonder of man."

END OF ZEPHANIAH

HAGGAI

CHAPTER 1

The Lord sent word by Haggai,
In days of Darius, the King,
To rebuild Jerusalem's Temple,
A timely and important thing.

He says "You live in houses
That are luxurious and fine.
You plant enough for an army,
But for good harvest you pine.

You cultivate and reap but
Have little left of your own.
As slaves you work for wages
But cannot maintain your home.

The Temple lies in ruins, but
You just don't seem to care.
I'll send drought to the land,
And we'll see how you fare."

Finally they got the message,
Started changing their ways,
Began rebuilding the temple
Darius's second year of reign.

CHAPTER 2

Haggai asked this question,
As the Lord told him do.
"Is it really as fine as it
Was; does it seem so to you?"

The governor and High Priest,
And all those others there,
After careful thought agreed
It once was much more fair.

So now you can take courage
And work with God's goodwill.
For He's been with you always
And will help you still.

The temple in the future will
Be greater than it was before.
For God has gold and silver,
He'll give peace forever more.

Your lives once were selfish
And were dominated by greed.

So everything you did
Was a contaminated deed.

But now that you are working
The temple is being redone;
He will give you better crops
With greater blessings won.

"Now tell Governor Zerubbabel,"
God says, "He will surely be,
As a signet ring on my finger,
For he's found favor with me."

END OF HAGGAI

ZECHARIAH

CHAPTER 1

Zechariah was a prophet in
The days of Darius's reign.
The job that God assigned him
Had been tried before in vain.

For none had really listened
As prophets suggested cures.
Those were now long dead, but
They'd known His word
    endures.

They realized they'd gotten
Just what they deserved. And
When the Lord had punished
Them, justice had been served.

Then Zechariah saw, in a
Vision in the night,
A beautiful red horse
And a man who sat astride.

Then behind him other horses
And men upon their backs. "An

Angel stood beside me," he
Said, and it was him I asked,

"What do these riders mean?"
The red horse rider replied,
"They were sent to patrol the
Earth, and this they spied."

Now all those riders reported,
As God's angel listened there.
The world seemed at peace, and
His angel made this prayer.

"Lord God of hosts, seventy
Years you've punished Israel;
How long must she endure,
When will you wish her well?"

Words of comfort came from
The Lord to the angels there.
He said, "Shout this message
Abroad, for God really cares.

With your nation I was angry,
And the heathen enforced my

Decree but went far beyond
What was planned by me.

So now I have returned
With mercy for my own, and
Israel will see prosperity
Such as it has never known."

Then I saw four horns of an
Animal as I gazed at them;
Representing nations that
Crushed Judah and Jerusalem.

Then I saw four blacksmiths
And once again I asked,
"Who are these people,
And what then is their task?"

Then again the angel replied,
"They came to wreck the horns,
Representing the power who'll
Wish they'd never been born."

CHAPTER 2

Then I looked around again,
And I saw a man with a
Measuring stick which
He carried in his hand.

And then I asked of him,
"Oh whither are you bound?"
He said, "I will take Jerus-
alems measure all around.

One day it will be filled
And spilling over its walls.
There'll be so many people,
It will not hold them all.

The Lord will be here then;
He promised to reward us well.
He will he a shining light
To Guard all Israel.

Hasten from your slavery and
Toward Jerusalem hurry forth.

Abandon the land where you
   are,
If east, west, south or north.

And any who give you trouble
Will have me on their case.
Israel is the apple of my eye;
Her enemies, I'll give chase.

Then many nations will join;
By our Lord they will be led.
And from His Holy Habitation,
By His word they will be fed."

CHAPTER 3

In my vision I could see old
Satan and Joshua were there.
Satan was accusing Joshua
Of things and deeds unfair.

Then the Lord rebuked Satan,
Saying, "You Listen now to me,
I reject your accusations, for
Mercy to Israel I've decreed."

Joshua's clothing was unclean,
As before God's angel he stood.
The angels changed his attire,
I said "A turban will be good."

So they did that too, and to
Joshua one did say, "If you
And other priests follow God,
You will learn a better way.

Joshua represents a servant;
That one He'll surely send.
To be a Temple cornerstone,
So of peace will be no end."

CHAPTER 4

Then it seems I'd been asleep,
And the angel had awakened me.

So he addressed me again, and
Said, "Tell me what you see."

"Seven lamps on a lampstand,
With a reservoir above. And
Seven tubes to feed the lamps
Like the fingers on a glove.

And I see two olive trees
Carved upon each side, and
Whatever that does mean, for
I know not what it implies."

So then he explained to me,
It was a message and it meant,
Only through God's spirit
Can successful word be sent.

And before Zerubbabel not
Even a mountain could stand.
He will finish the Temple
With God's grace on the land.

Then the Lord spoke, saying,
"Zerubbabel started this job.
He'll finish it; you'll know
This message came from God.

Small steps accomplish much.
These seven lamps, like eyes,
For the Lord around the
World many deeds can spy."

"How about those olive trees
Carved on the lamp," I asked.
"What do they represent,
And what then is their task?"

"They are like anointed ones
Who help the Lord of earth."
I understood without a doubt
That they were of great worth.

CHAPTER 5

I looked up and saw a scroll;
It was flying through the air.

"What do you see?" He asked,
Said I, "A scroll flies there."

Thirty feet long it appeared
And about a half as wide.
"It's like a scroll of God,"
He Said, "that item you spied.

It says, that all who lie or
Steal are now wasting breath.
The homes that harbor such
Are courting certain death.

Look up again, there's some-
Thing flying through the air."
When I asked, He answered, "a
Basket of sin is everywhere."

The basket lid was lifted;
I saw a woman seated within.
"An act of evil" He said,
And pushed her back again.

Now two women came flying,
Each upon a stork's wings.
They took the basket and
Flew away with the thing.

"Where are they taking her?"
The next thing I asked Him,
"Off to the land of Babylon,"
He said, "It's a home of sin."

CHAPTER 6

The next time I looked, four
Chariots were coming near
From between two brass-like
Mountains that had appeared.

A team pulling one was red,
One of blacks next that way.
The third team was white and
The last were dappled greys.

Again I asked the meaning
Of this, and he explained.

"They patrol the earth,
Over land and sea or plain.

The black ones will go north;
The whites will follow there.
Those dappled ones go south;
The reds both do their share.

These four heavenly spirits
All do our father's work;
When the Lord bids them go,
They're not going to shirk."

Then I got word from God
That those heading north,
Had calmed the Lord's anger
By their going forth.

Then again His message came,
"Three soon will come. Heldai,
Tobijah and Jedaiah to bring
Gold and silver from our sons.

From Babylon to bring gifts,
Do a crown of silver and gold,
Put it on Joshua's head, and
God's word he'll be told.

In lieu of the man to come,
His name will be "The Branch,"
Oh Joshua, you'll be crowned,
And you'll represent that man.

For He shall rise to glory;
The Temple of God He'll raise.
Then crowns will they deserve,
Whom gold and silver gave.

They'll come from far or near
To help at building there.
You'll know I came from God
And diligently do your share."

CHAPTER 7

Jews from Bethel came with
Priests and prophets to ask

About the custom of mourning,
Considered by them, a task.

The Lord's word to Zechariah,
Similar to this plan, "Tell
Them God was never in their
Hearts, as much as the
Pleasure of man.

You think much of fun; mour-
ning and fasting is a sham.
You cheat strangers, widows,
Orphans, counter to His plan.

Although you've been told by
The prophets down the years,
You refuse to stop and listen,
Thus you had lives of tears."

CHAPTER 8

"Oh yes, I'm really angry,"
Again God's message came,
What Israel's enemies did
Is really a dirty shame.

I'll return to Jerusalem, and
I'll dwell within her walls.
"Holy Mountain, Faithful City,"
Are names it will be called.

A city of peace it will be
Until the young grow old.
Children play in the streets;
Pleasant adventures unfold.

Don't worry or be discouraged,
Or fear I'll change my mind.
But build up the temple and
To your neighbors be kind.

There'll be joyful festivals
If you cherish a fellowman.
Then men from over the world
Will visit from other lands.

You'll receive His blessings;
All men will be your friends.
They'll know God is with you
And will be until the end."

CHAPTER 9

Lands of Judah and Jerusalem
Are doomed to feel the sword.
Those left will worship God
And listen to His word.

Temple guards protect them;
No evil will tread the land,
God's Prince upon a donkey,
Our savior in form of man.

He will rule the earth from
Sea to shining sea. Judah and
Ephraim (His bow, and arrow),
And sword you will also be.

The Lord will lead His own;
They'll know no defeat. Yes
God will save His people as
A shepherd protects his sheep.

Wine will be abundant from
A wonderful harvest of grapes.
All peace and happiness for
God their part will take.

CHAPTER 10

It is stupid to ask idols
For such a thing as rain. And
Fortune tellers' predictions
Are nothing but a pain.

He'll make his people strong;
From them will come the hope
That holds the world together
And helps all men to cope.

Pastmasters have no power;
My people I'll give strength.

Wherever they go I'll be, the
Width or breadth or length.

CHAPTER 11

Oh Lebanon listen now, your
Judgment rages like fire.
Cry in fear, wicked leaders,
For you have raised God's ire.

Then I received more orders,
To go take a shepherd's job--
Of a flock being fatted,
And this word came from God.

It'd show the way his people
Are bought, sold and slain.
"Thank God," they say, "I'm
Rich," (leaders causing pain.)

He'll not help them either,
Land will again be wilderness.
Now God bade me help again
With this terrible mess.

So two shepherd staves I took,
Named them Union and Beauty.
And then I fed that flock,
Which was of course my duty.

I got rid of evil shepherds,
Grew impatient with them all.
I'd not be their conscience,
Saying, "Ok, take your fall."

I broke the staff called
Beauty, for my job was done.
We had no use for each other,
And I could cut and run.

So they settled up with only
Thirty pieces of silver paid.
As the Lord advised, I put it
In the Temple treasury plate.

I broke the staff named Union.
This was a token that the

Bond between Juda and Israel
Had definitely been broken.

Then my orders came to play
The shepherd's part once more,
A useless, lying, conniving
One, undoing work of the Lord.

"This will show them," said He,
"They'll get no help from me.
Pity leaders who fail flocks!
A sad thing for all to see."

CHAPTER 12

Says He who made heaven and
Put man on earth, "I'll make
Judah and Jerusalem poison
To enemies, a prize of no
worth.

They'll send armies to subdue,
And though nations all unite,
I'll bewilder their warriors;
They will be unable to fight.

Victory first goes to Judah
To curb Jerusalem's pride. I'll
Destroy the attacking nations;
I will be on Jerusalem's side.

More power to Jerusalem! they
Will sorrow for one spurned.
Those lonely ones will grieve
In sorrow they richly earned."

CHAPTER 13

There'll be more cleanliness
Available to Judah and Israel.
I'll destroy all idol worship;
Idol names will go as well.

None will claim to be prophets;
False claims none will try.
He who claims to be a prophet,

It's written, will surely die.

Two thirds of Israel will
Fail and fall by the way.
Others will live through fire
And call their God by name.

CHAPTER 14

The day is soon to come
When Jerusalem will be taken.
Homes looted, spoils divided,
Women raped by evil awakened.

Half the cities populace will
Be carried away as slaves.
The rest will be left in Jer-
usalem where they'll remain.

The Mount of Olives will be
Where He will stand and fight.
It'll split from east to west,
And they'll take flight.

It will be an avenue through
Which His people shall escape.
It will form a great valley
Reaching to the city gate.

The sun, moon, and stars
Will no longer shine.
But it will be like day
Throughout evening time.

And from the Holy City
The waters of life will flow.
Half to the Mediterranean,
Half to the dead sea will go.

Over all earth He'll reign,
My Lord, the King of all.
Those who fought Jerusalem,
By terrible plague will fall.

To fight against each other,
And lose everything there.
Those who survive the war
Will come each year for song,
And prayer.

All nations will honor Him,
And homage they will pay.

All things are His property
When comes that Holy day.

No more grasping trades
Will be in the marketplace.
All services will be free;
We'll gaze upon His face.

END OF ZECHARIAH

MALACHI

CHAPTER I

After seventy years of
Captivity, Malachi made this
Claim, saying, "The honor you
Owe God is high over your aim.

Your sacrifices are imperfect;
Your service is only by lip.
A thing your human governor
Would surely never forgive.

Look around the world, and
You'll be forced to believe
That God is much greater
Than you are willing to see.

A father and a master,
Are both honored names.
(And He is both to you)
So why do you play games?

His name will find much honor
Throughout the Gentile world.
You ask mercy and blessing
With lips in derision curled.

All sacrifices sick or stolen,
His needs will not slake.
Cursed is any man
Who continues that mistake."

CHAPTER 2

"Priests had better listen,
This warning is meant for you.
If you don't change your ways,
Then misery will be your due.

He'd like to bless you now,
But curses are all you'll get.
You do not take Him seriously;
With God you're out of step.

He'll rebuke your children
And rub your noses in dirt.
You ignore the law of your
Fathers to your eternal hurt.

We're the children of Abraham,
And by God were created equal.
Yet you violate His covenant,
And treat our brothers evil.

You defile God's Holy Temple;
With heathen women you wed,
Divorcing wives of your youth,
Who more than shared your bed.

Our God loves good men,
Not those prone to divorce.
Rear godly children who'll
Cherish Him for the course.

Do not weary Him with talk
That makes evil seem good.
The straight and narrow path
Is travel where you should.

CHAPTER 3

God will send before Him a
Messenger to prepare the way.
And He will suddenly appear
Bringing great joy that day.

Who'll stand before Him as he
Washes ministers and Levites
Clean? For He'll refine the
Pure and isolate the mean.

Though you scorned Him often,
He'll be Lord when you return.
God is loving and unchanging,
Or in your sins you'd burn.

You say you gave to God; your
Tithes and offerings are shy.
Bring all gifts to the temple;
Great blessings He'll supply.

It seems that evil prospers
Over those who would be fair.
But God has a book of record,
All good names are there.

CHAPTER 4

The day of judgement comes
As heat from a furnace fire.
All those who are wicked will
Be ashes of His ire.

But you who fear God's wrath
In freedom will leap with joy.
You'll tread ashes under foot,
Songs of thanksgiving employ.

Remember Moses on Mt. Horeb?
Commandments given him
  there?
God will send one like Elijah,
Who'll be honest and fair.

He'll unite fathers and sons,
They'll work for all men. But
He will destroy what's dear,
If they don't soon repent.

END OF MALACHI

AND OLD TESTAMENT.

MATTHEW

CHAPTER 1

Forty two generations ago
God promised Abe, His friend,
His family would prosper and
Grow like stars by the end.

Joseph and Mary were engaged
And happily planning to marry.
But news that she was pregnant
Had him sleepless and harried.

Into the night he fretted, as
Restless, he rolled and turned.
He must have felt like a lover
Who has suddenly been
    spurned.

According to Hebrew custom
In practice in those days, he
Could denounce her publicly
And then send her away.

But finally he fell into
A Troubled and fitful sleep.
And an angel stood beside him,
An important mission to keep.

"Joseph, David's son," he said,
"Waver not, take Mary as wife.
Her child is from God, so
Take your place with pride.

`Jesus,' you shall name him,
It means `Savior of mankind.'
And as forecast through the
Prophets, will change things
For all time."

CHAPTER 2

Jesus was born in Bethlehem
During King Herod's reign.

Seeing His star in the east,
Three wise men now came.

"We seek a King of the Jews!"
They said, "We saw His star,
In the east two years ago,
And we have come afar."

The king was troubled for he
Feared a threat to his crown.
"Where can I go to worship
Him? Where is He now?"

The Jewish leaders told him
That Bethlehem was the place.
Here the baby would be born,
A king of the Jewish race.

Then the wise men left there,
And a star went on ahead. And
The little town of Bethlehem
Was the place to which it led.

There they found the child,
Worshipped with loving pride.
For He'd be the Mighty King
The men of old had prophesied.

They returned back home again
But by another path. For
They hadn't reported to Herod,
Because they feared his wrath.

He'd tried to trick them, to
Tell him where the babe would
Be. Joseph listened to angels
And that same night did flee.

He took the mother and child
And into the night they fled.
Herod had many babies killed
Because he wanted Jesus dead.

In Egypt they lived for years.
The prophets had proclaimed,
"I'll call my son from Egypt
That great and glorious day."

Herod's brutal action now
Proved what Jeremiah'd said.
Rachel weeps for her children!
Uncomforted, for they're dead.

Then one day King Herod died,
So the angel called them back.
Now Joseph brought His family
And trod the homeward track.

But hearing that Herod's son
Had ascended to the throne,
They diverted into Galilee
Rather than go directly home.

And so they lived in Nazareth,
Lending meaning to the theme
Which said "The Great Messiah"
Would be a Nazarene.

CHAPTER 3

Through the Judean wilderness,
One, "John the Baptist," came.
He preached repentance in
The Kingdom of Heaven's name.

"Prepare the way of the Lord;
Make His pathway straight.
The Kingdom of Heaven is near,
And the time is getting late."

Centuries before, Isaiah
Had said John would come.
And now those seeking baptism
Had developed into a run.

But Sadducees and Pharisees
He very strongly denounced.
Called them, "Sons of vipers,"
And practically ran them out.

"You can't escape His wrath,"
He said, "because you're Jews.
If you would do a worthy deed
That would be better news.

With water I baptize the rep-
entant but one much greater
Follows me. With Holy Spirit
And fire, He will purify thee.

He will burn away the chaff,
But the grain retain." Now
From Galilee to the Jordan
River, for baptism Jesus came.

Now John the Baptist said to
Him, "You should baptize me.
For you are greater than I,
So how can this ever be?"

Then Jesus answering, said,
"It was so decided long ago.
And we must fulfill the word,
In righteousness it is so."

Now when rising from baptism,
All the heavens opened to Him;
God's Spirit descended, and
A voice from heaven broke in.

"This is my beloved Son,
In whom I'm truly pleased."
There is no written record
Of a grander press release."

CHAPTER 4

Then out into the wilderness
By the Spirit Jesus was led,
Hungry, was tempted by Satan
To, "Change rocks to bread.

It will prove you are God's
Son." By Satan He was told.
"No, God's words," He said,
"Are what feed men's souls."

So to the City of Jerusalem,
To the Temple spire there.
Now Satan told him, "Jump,
For the scriptures declare,

His angels will protect you
From dying on rocks below."
Jesus looked Satan in the
Eye saying, "Absolutely no.

It also warns every man not
To put God to foolish tests.
So I'll consider your tempt-
ation as just another jest."

Then atop a mighty mountain
Satan ushered Him again. The
Earth lay spread in beauty
Before the eyes of man.

"I'll give it to you!" he
Said, "just to worship me."
Jesus said, "Get behind me
Satan; such will never be!

The scriptures are specific,
And they quite clearly say,
Worship the Lord God only
And only Him, obey."

So finally Satan left Him,
And the angels then arrived.
Buoyed Him up and fed Him
And kept Him very much alive.

Soon He heard that John had
Been arrested and put away.
From Judea to Nazareth, He
Now moved near Galilee lake.

So Isaiah's prophecy was true,
Saying, "Zebulon and Naphtali,
By the lake and land beyond
Where He often spake--

This land of sin and sorrow
Might now be set aright. So
Those people in darkness,
Soon would see the light."

As He walked upon the beach,
Two brothers fished there.
He called to go fish for men
And was followed by the pair.

So Simon, known as Peter, and
His brother Andrew too, would
Be joined by James and John,
For there was much to do.

They traveled in Galilee,
Sickness, disease, He healed;
Crowds followed everywhere,
His doctrine truly appealed.

CHAPTER 5

He preached a famous sermon
One day upon the mount. Now
Many people listened, and
This, it was about.

"Blessed are the humble, for
Heaven will surely be theirs.
Also they who mourn, for
Comfort will be their share.

Blessed are the righteous;
Goodness shall come to them.
And those merciful to others,
Will see mercy return again.

All those shall see the Lord
Who are pure in their heart.
Peacemakers are His children,
For they are doing their part.

The Kingdom of Heaven awaits
Any persecuted for good deeds.
You will be double blessed if
Cursed or reviled for me.

So rejoice and be most happy,
For great will be your reward.
For so were treated prophets
Who walked this path before.

You are the salt of the earth,
So keep your flavor high.
You'll be trodden under foot,
If you don't sincerely try.

You're the light of the world
Like a city built upon a hill.
Don't hide it from men's sight;
Let it shine God's goodwill.

I came not to destroy law,
Or the prophet's word to kill.
As long as the earth exists,
The word shall be fulfilled.

So the commandments do not
Break or teach others to.
But live and teach them well,
And heaven will smile on you.

You must improve on scribes
And on pharisees too. Or you
Will not see Heaven's kingdom,
No matter what else you do.

You know you shall not kill,
I say now to you, neither
Shall you say, "You fool,"
Or woe will be your due.

Gifts to God are worthless
Given when angry at another.
So be at peace with God by
Getting right with brothers.

Never insist you were right;
Better to forgive and forget.
You may skip judge or prison,
If you don't fume or fret.

You know adultery is wrong,
Something men should not do.
I say, if your eye wanders,
Heaven will not forgive you.

If your eye causes you sin,
Pluck it and cast it away.
If your right hand causes
Trouble, cut it off today.

Better one member to perish,
Than a whole body go to hell.
If one continually sins, on
Others it casts evil spells.

A man can divorce his wife;
This is the law of the land.
Only as a result of adultery
Can it be right for man.

Break not your vows to God,
So the law of Moses goes. Do
Not swear by heaven or God,
Say a simple "Yes," or "No,"

Those words will do the job,
You need not make it strong.
And if you swear a vow, it
Shows that something's wrong.

An eye for an eye was law,
A tooth for a tooth was too.
With forgiveness violence
Meet, more good it will do.

If a man wants your shirt,
Let him also have your coat.
There is always room enough
For another in your boat.

If one needs to be carried a
Mile, then carry him for two.
Let those who need to borrow,
Feel free to come to you.

Love friends, enemies hate,
Thus the saying goes. But
If others cause you trouble,
Be sure to pray for those.

Be the heavenly father's son;
He puts down evil or good. Be
Friends, to friends or enemies;
This is the way you should.

CHAPTER 6

Don't brag about your deeds
Even when they seem good.
For you're only doing those
Things you normally should.

So do not be a hypocrite,
Thus demanding attention.
Nor cause a lot of trouble
And so promote dissension.

Secretly do your kindnesses
For God who sees it all.
He'll rally to your cause
When otherwise you'd fall.

If you pray aloud in public
To impress on all your piety,
You'll get no help from God,
For you are lying to society.

When you pray to God, don't
Repeat it o'er and o'er,
For those things you need,
He knew about before.

Pray within a closet; pull
The door behind you closed.
He'll reward you in public
For needs you shyly posed.

In this manner pray: "Our
Heavenly father we honor you,
May your will, as in heaven,
Also be on earth the rule.

Feed us again today, oh Lord,
And keep us from sin as well.
Help us forgive detractors,
As you save us from ourselves.

Allow for our shortcomings.
As we are tempted and when,
Our earthly days bring sorrow,
Give us greater faith, Amen."

Now if you wish forgiveness,
Then grant the same to others.
You will get from God the
Love you show your brothers.

If you seek public attention
With face so wan and drawn,
It's like declaring piety
With a bugle and song.

Expect no reward in heaven
You've had it here on earth.
But if you fast in secret,
It will be of greater worth.

Wealth you gain while here
May rust or corrode away.
But the credit you store up
There, will never fade.

If in your heart is darkness,
Then evil rules your life. But
With sunshine in your heart,
You can overcome all strife.

None can serve two masters.
You'll fail one in the end.
So don't fret food or money;
All important needs He sends.

God knows all our problems,
And He will see us through.
So do not live in fear,
For He'll take care of you.

CHAPTER 7

If you wish good treatment
Then treat others well.
If you criticize a brother,
He'll be the first to tell,

If you saw a spot in his eye
And told the whole world.
You were surely blinded by
The charge you hurled.

Gifts you give to wastrels,
They waste and ask for more.
You may even be attacked if
They don't know the score.

Whatever it is you need,
Do not fear to ask. Your
Needs will be fulfilled,
If you'll accept your task.

We give well to our children
Many gifts of lovely things.
How much joy we'll know for
Our father's gift of kings.

We know the road is narrow
To our father's home above.
Sin's way is wide and smooth
But therein lies no love.

Many will claim Him leader,
But when the great day comes,
Only those of integrity will
The winning race have won.

Amazement gripped the crowds
At the things Jesus had said.
For authority and wisdom
Were words He deftly spread.

CHAPTER 8

Down the hillside Jesus came
With large crowds in His wake.

A leper now approached,
And thus to Jesus spake.

"Sir, I know you can heal
Me, if only you should wish."
Then Jesus gently touched him,
And he was healed that quick.

"Now immediately," Jesus said,
"The priest must examine you.
And as per the law of Moses,
Your public testimony is due."

Now an army officer asked His
Help, as to Capernum He came.
His servant boy was paralysed
And in terrible pain.

So Jesus said, "I'll come,"
But then the officer replied,
"I know you can heal him from
Here, if you should so decide."

"I haven't seen such faith as
This," Jesus said, amazed.
"If all Israel had your faith,
A whole nation could be saved.

It seems that many Gentiles
Believe like this one has,
So for whom the kingdom is
Into darkness may be cast."

He sent the man home, saying,
"Your son has been healed."
And Jesus continued His work
In this His appointed field.

He arrived at Peter's house,
Whose mother-in-law's fever
He Healed. She arose from bed,
And prepared for them a meal.

Several people were brought
Who were demon possessed.

Then he spoke a single word,
And all those demons fled.

So the sick He healed and
Fulfilled Isaiah's prophecy.
"He healed our sick, and He
Took away our disease."

Then a Jewish teacher said to
Him, "I'll go where you go."
He said, "Birds and animals
Have homes; for me, not so."

Another said, "I'll come Lord,
But after my father's wake."
"Let the dead of spirit carry
On," He Said, "My father's
Work is at stake."

The crowd got large, and our
Lord soon needed rest, so
They set off across the lake
In a boat at His behest.

The wind got much stronger;
Waves rolled high and wide.
Like a babe, Jesus slept, but
His disciples in terror cried.

"Oh Lord and master, save us
Ere we founder in the deep."
Jesus said, "I often wonder
What little faith have these."

He stood and calmed the wind,
And the ocean became serene.
And they in amazement gaped
At all they'd seen.

"What sort of man is this? He
Calms winds or rising seas?
Takes time for common folk,
Least of all for such as we!"

They sailed across the lake
And gained the other side;

Then they went ashore where
The Gadarenes abide.

Travelling past a cemetery,
Two men were demon
   possessed,
Whose natures were so violent,
None dared that area tread.

Those two came dashing out,
"Son of man," they screamed,
"Why must you torment us, who
Even suffer in our dreams?"

The demons begged of Jesus,
"Please, if you cast us out,
Let us enter a herd of swine
Which is feeding here about."

So Jesus bade them "Go", and
Those pigs in panic fled,
They rushed over a precipice
And died a watery death.

"Only the sick," said Jesus,
"Really need a doctor's call.
While those who are healthy
Don't need him there at all.

So go and learn the meaning
Of what the scriptures say.
It's time to be merciful; it
Is time to change your ways.

I've come to urge sinners,
Not righteous to the fold.
Self-righteousness is its
Reward, and it will be told."

John's disciples came to ask
Him one day, why His follow-
ers never fasted as was of
Course the normal way.

"Because I, their servant, am
Still with them," Jesus ex-

plained. For John had been
Murdered which caused pain.

"In time," He said, "I will
Walk that path, and when that
Day arrives, then my discip-
les too will fast."

This parable He told them.
"Who would patch old cloth
With new? Who uses old
Containers to hold fresh brew?

The patch will wear away
From where it was sewed in.
The wine would be spilled
Because of ruined skins."

Herdsmen rushed to the city
And told their story there.
So the populace barred Jesus'
Entry, for they were scared.

CHAPTER 9

So back across the lake to
Capurnaum on the other side,
They brought Him a young man
With palsy and paralyzed.

"Cheer up" to the lad he said,
"Your sins I have forgiven."
But some religeous leaders
Thought, "Blasphemy to
   Heaven."

Jesus knew their thoughts, so
Said, "Have you such evil mi-
nds? I can forgive their sins
And know no bind."

Then turning to the boy, with
Words akin to these, He said,
"You're cured, arise and walk;
Be sure to take your bed."

So the lad picked up His bed,
And into his house he went.
The multitude all marvelled;
Such power God gave men.

Now Matthew, the tax collector,
Was sitting at his booth,
And he got up and came along,
When Jesus invited him too.

They ate at Mathew's home and
Pharisees grumbled that night
About sinners there, they
Thought that was not right.

A rabbi came for help whose
Small daughter had just died,
And he knew that she'd live,
If Jesus should so decide.

But as they were on their way,
A sick woman came from
   behind,
Just to touch Jesus' robe was
Foremost in her mind.

Twelve years of hemorrhage,
Always looking for a cure,
Now Jesus was her only hope;
Of this she was very sure.

He felt her touch and turned,
And told her she was healed.
The beauty of her faith, to
His sense of right appealed.

To the rabbi's house they came
Where all the mourners wailed.
When he said she only slept,
Scoffing sneers prevailed.

When He led her forth alive,
The news then swept the
Land. As they left for home,
Another adventure began.

Two blind men had followed,
Both begging for a cure.
He asked if they believed
And were they really sure?

"Oh yes Lord," they said, "of
Course we do." "Your faith
(Now touching their eyes,)
Will make it happen to you."

Suddenly they could see and
Real joy they knew. So despite
His plea for silence, they
Promptly spread the news.

Then Jesus cast out a demon
From a man who could not walk.
The crowds greatly marveled
And the Pharisees did balk.

"He posses demons," they said
"From Satan comes His power."
But Jesus just ignored them,
He knew they'd had their hour.

Then He travelled extensively
Through cities and the land.
Teaching and preaching good
News of the Kingdom at hand.

Many sicknesses He healed;
How He pitied those that came,
For their problems were great.
They were sick, halt and lame.

"There's so much to do," said
He, "And so few to do the job.
For help upon the harvest
Field, let us pray to God."

CHAPTER 10

Jesus called his disciples,
An even dozen if you please,
To cast out evil spirits
And heal all kinds of disease.

Simon, known as Peter, Andrew
His little brother, too, and
James, the brother of John,
And Philip and Bartholomew.

Thomas and Mathew the tax
Collector, called the
"Publican," then Thadeus and
James who was Alphaeus's son.

Simon the Zealot who'd be
Called "Subversive," today.
And Judas Iscariot, who for
Thirty pieces of silver
Jesus, would betray.

With these words He sent them,
"Avoid Samaritan and Gentile.
Preach only to Israel's people,
Others are not worthwhile.

Announce Heaven's Kingdom;
Heal the sick, raise the dead.
Give freely to all in need;
Do it only for daily bread.

Do not worry about wages
Or take extra food. For
Those you are there to help
Should take care of you.

When in town or village
Find one who believes in God.
Then live in with his family
Until you've finished the job.

Be friendly if they let you;
Give blessings where you will.
Shake the dust off your feet,
If bad treatment is your bill.

Cities of Sodom and Gomorrah
Will fare better judgment day,
If they don't give you shelter
And send you safely on the way.

Like sheep, go among them, be
Wary, but as gentle as doves.
Expect arrest or whipping; in
Synagogs, you'll see no love.

Governors, kings will try you,
Don't fret about what to say.
The Spirit will direct, His
Wisdom will show the way.

Families will betray members,
Deaths be caused by their own.
They'll harass because of me,
A result of love you've shown.

Stick it out; endure it all,
Stand straight, do not bend.
For you will surely be saved,
If you'll hold out to the end.

Spread the news city to city
As you flee hither and yon.
I'll return before you finish
The cities you're working on.

No servant's more than master;
Neither is master of his fate.
They both are tied together
And share the same estate.

Since they called me Satan,
How much will they do to you?
But the time will surely come,
When all will know the truth.

What I tell you now in secret,
Shout from the roof above.
Fear not the pangs of death;
He'll keep your souls in love.

If a sparrow's feather falls
God knows it right away.
Your very hairs are numbered;
He'll help you win life's race.

To my father I'll present
All who to men presented me,
But not recognize in heaven,
Any who seek me not in peace.

I came to offer better times,
But conflict rather prevails.
Families will turn upon them-
selves; family ties may fail.

He who loves earthly things
More than he loves me,
Cannot expect in heaven,
My great friend to be.

You must not love your family
More than you love me.
You'll not make it to heaven,
If you let them come between.

If you protect your life
And limb at any cost, rather
Than my righteous name, then
Eternal life you've lost.

Whom you welcome in my
   name
Is done so in my father's too.
And a welcome you've thus
Given will be returned to you.

If you give a little child
A drink of water in my name,
You'll be rewarded in heaven
And be ahead of the game."

CHAPTER 11

Now in time the job was done;
His disciples he had trained.
So he left the dozen behind
And went out to teach again.

When John was still in prison
He heard of Jesus' fame. So

He sent two of his disciples
To check out certain claims.

Asking, "Are you that Messiah?
Or do we still look and wait?"
Jesus answered the questions,
"Go tell it to him straight.

The blind are given sight;
The lame are made to walk.
The dead are brought to life;
The deaf now hear and talk.

The poor now hear the gospel,
So do not be offended in me."
Then to the multitude He said,
"Tell me what in John you see?

For he is not a reed to
Be shaken in the wind. He's
Not clothed in soft apparel,
Nor one who's steeped in sin.

He's not only a prophet,
But a man of love and grace.
For of him it's been written,
God sends him before thy face,

He'll prepare thee to announce
The kingdom is at hand. And
He may not be great in heaven
But is more than mortal man.

You are like children, who
Are unhappy with their games.
John fasts; he drinks no wine,
You say, `His brain is lame.'

I, the Messiah, eat and drink;
You object to company I keep.
You don't like the way I live
Whether I'm awake or asleep.

You do not see the miracles
Taking place in your sight.

It matters not whatere I do,
You say it is not right.

Woe to you, wicked cities, for
Miracles you wouldn't accept.
Had it been in Tyre or Sidon,
They would be marveling yet."

Then this prayer He offered,
"Oh Father, Lord of earth and
Heaven, you know me, I know
You, so my life is leavened.

For those who suffer burdens,
Come, I will make them light.
For my load is easily carried
If you will do things right."

CHAPTER 12

About that time He walked
In fields of grain one day.
Pharisees saw His disciples
Picking and eating grain.

So they said to Jesus, "Your
Disciples break the law." So
He explained to them it
Was in the way they thought.

"Recall what King David said?
Into the Temple he went, and
He and friends, because of
Hunger, ate the Holy bread.

It was the Sabbath day; that
Is what they complained about.
Pharisees tout the law, which
Gives them political clout."

He reminded now of Moses'
    law;
The Sabbath was for no work.
"One here is greater than the
Temple, you misunderstand
Scripture verse.

God prefers you'd show mercy,
Than give offerings and such.
He is master of the Sabbath;
You judge innocents too much."

Over to the Synagogue he went,
To a man with withered hand.
Pharisees still plotted ruin
And carefully laid plans.

"Is it legal to heal on the
Sabbath?" He was now asked.
Quick and honest He answered,
And thus took them to task.

"If you lost a lamb in a well
And it was on the Sabbath day,
Would you pull it out now,
Or let it drown where it lay?

A human is more valuable than
The price of a sheep. It is
Doing good on the Sabbath."
This pulled the fangs of
The Pharisees.

He bid the man stretch forth
The hand so withered and bent.
It was now well and healthy,
So Pharisee plans were spent.

So then they called a meeting
To plot His arrest and death.
Fearing his purity and power
With all the energy left.

He healed sick and ailing,
Asking his secret to keep.
Fulfilling Isaiah's prophecy
Of shepherd of all the sheep.

"This is my beloved servant,
In Him my soul takes delight.
He Judges nations in justice;
All conflicts without fights.

In Him I'll put my spirit; in
Gentlest of voices He speaks.
His name is joy to the world;
He gives hope to the weak."

One was possessed of a demon,
Blind, and unable to talk.
Jesus healed and cured him.
People in amazement gawked.

"Perhaps a Messiah," was said,
This angrily, Pharisees den-
ied. "He's Satan, King of
Demons, that's why He's so
Successful," they cried.

He read the thoughts and said,
"A house divided cannot stand.
If Satan threw out evil,
It would destroy his own plan.

If I expel demons through
Satan, how do your priests
Cast them out? But if I do so
Through God, His Kingdom has
Arrived without doubt.

You must be for or against me,
Your backbiting won't help.
Sin can be forgiven, but aga-
inst God, disaster it spells.

You dress in clothes of men
But display a viper's heart.
For you feign deep religion
Tearing God's kingdom apart.

By action, a thing is obvious;
A tree by its fruit is known.
Mans feet always follow the
Path his speech has shown.

Consider every word you use;
Your future is what you say.
Words can point toward heaven
Or divert you the other way."

One day some Jewish leaders
And pharisees came to ask if
Jesus would show a miracle,
But He took them to task.

"Only a faithless nation
Would need convincing more.
Jonah spent three days in a
Whale, yet proof you implore.

For three days I'll be deep
Within earth's environs. And
Long ago they believed Jonah,
But you'd put me in irons.

Who listens and believes
Will condemn you in the end.
You fail to trust one greater;
Your stiff necks won't bend.

You're like a man who slipped
And is by a demon possessed.
It leaves his heart and body
In a hopeless pursuit of rest.

But in time the demon returns
And finds a vacancy there.
So he calls in seven friends
To the man's greater despair."

Now someone brought Him
  word
As Jesus spoke to the crowd,
That His mother and brothers
Were awaiting him without.

"My disciples," He said, "are
Like mother and brother to me.
Obey my Father in heaven, and
I will be greatly pleased."

CHAPTER 13

From a house He went one day
To sit by the sea in peace.

But a multitude gathered, so
He boarded a ship for relief.

He preached now from the deck,
Talked in parables like these.
"Behold, a farmer did plant
And sowed a great many seeds.

Some scattered as he planted,
And the fowl feasted that day.
Some fell where soil was thin,
Sprouted, then wasted away.

Some fell in weeds and thorns;
They choked and died. Others
Took root in good earth, grew
Strongly and quickly like rye.

If you've ears and hear, then
Listen to my words with care."
Disciples asked, "Why speak in
Parables, is it really fair?"

"Mysteries of heaven's
  Kingdom,"
He said, "are given to you to
Know. They'll listen and hear,
But knowledge will not grow.

You're fortunate indeed, for
Heaven's mysteries are yours.
Those without knowledge won't
Learn. Wisdom will get more.

This was Isaiah's Prophecy;
They hear but don't understand.
They are lazy of learning and
Asleep where they stand.

Many a good man of learning
Has longed to know what to do.
I will explain these parables;
They'll be no mystery to you.

This is of the seeds that fell
On the path that's packed hard.

They're like preaching to a
Man who is hard of heart.

He understands not God's word
For Satan snatches it away.
The shallow, rocky soil will
Root and grow plants in days.

The word is rooted shallowly,
And though received with joy
When the road gets rough and
Rocky, is rejected like a toy.

Ground covered with
Thistles in his grain, it
Made no sense to pull; he'd
Lose more than he'd gain.

They grew together; he burned
Thistles at harvest time."
They asked him to explain;
His answer followed this line.

"There are people much like
Thistles, like the devil's own.
The good folks of the world
Are a crop that God has sown.

Harvest is worlds end when
Good and bad will be divided.
So if you have ears, please
Listen well," He chided.

"Those evil will be thrown
Into the pit of fire. They've
Always caused trouble and
Have raised the Father's ire.

Angels will be God's reapers
When the glorious day appears.
When they separate the tares,
There'll be sorrow and tears.

Heaven is like a treasure a
Man discovered in a field. He

Coveted that property and
Sold assets to swing the deal.

It's also like a fine pearl
A merchant considered best.
To buy it he sold his all
When finally put to the test.

Again it's like the fisherman
Who sorts the fish within his
Net. He casts away the bad
And only keeps the best.

In like manner angels will
Come and sort good and bad.
There'll be much weeping and
Sorrow on that day most sad.

Do you understand?" He
  asked,
As he taught that little band.
Bravely, each answered "Yes,"
As only men of sincerity can.

"Some of you," He said, "know
Jewish law and scripture, too,
You'll have treasures from
The Old Testament and New."

Back to Galilee he journeyed,
In Nazareth's synagog taught;
He astonished everyone there
By wisdom and miracles
  wrought.

"How can this be?" they asked,
"We knew him since a child."
As they watched and envied
Him, jealousy was soon riled.

He did few miracles there, as
He sojourned with His band. A
Prophet has honor everywhere,
Of course, except in his land.

CHAPTER 14

When King Herod heard of
Jesus he confided to his men.
"It must be John the Baptist
Come back to life again.

How else can he do miracles,
Lest he's back from the dead?"
John had known Herod's wrath;
That was how he lost his head.

Jesus heard of John's murder
And went by boat to be alone.
His grief some what lessened;
He returned toward His home.

Many people waited for him
Needing His healing powers.
He pitied and healed the sick;
He labored many hours.

That evening disciples came.
"It's past eating time," they
Said, "we've two fishes and
Five small loaves of bread."

He seated them on the grass,
Prayed over bread and fishes.
He told the heavenly Father
About their needs and wishes.

About five thousand men and
Women and the children ate.
About a dozen basketfuls
Were gathered from that place.

He told His trusty disciples
To row off across the lake.
He'd stay to dismiss people,
For the time was getting late.

Into the hills He trekked; it
Was a place to relax and pray.
Out upon the water night fell,
And wind whipped up the
 waves.

In wee hours of the morning,
Jesus, upon the waters walked.
Disciples in terror screamed,
Fearing a ghost there stalked.

But Jesus told them, "Have no
Fear, for what you see is I."
So Peter said, "If it really
Is, bid me come to your side."

So Jesus said, "Do come." And
Upon the water Peter walked.
But at angry water he looked
And by disaster was stalked.

Looking away from Jesus, he
Was by faith now unsupported,
Sinking beneath the waves, in
Terror his aplomb aborted.

Jesus reached and saved him,
As for anyone he'll do. And
As they climbed into the boat
The sea calmed; no wind blew.

Jesus said to Peter, "You
Are a man of little faith."
The knowledge, "This is God's
Son," left them all agape.

At Gennesaret they landed,
The news spread of His fame.
They brought the sick, and
He healed halt and lame.

CHAPTER 15

From Jerusalem many Jewish
Leaders and Pharisees came.
"Your people ignore tradition,
So tell us what's your game?

They do not wash their hands,
When food they partake." He
Said, "Some of God's direct
Commands you people violate.

You tell children, give the
Church money parents need.
God says, Honor father and
Mother. You teach evil deeds.

It is not what you eat, it's
What you say that matters."
Those questioners went away,
But they were mad as hatters.

"Let them go," He said, "the
Blind lead the blind. They'll
Fall in the ditch, for they
Have closing of the minds."

"Kosher food," He said, "can
Not make you good or bad.
It is useless bitter speech
That makes it all so sad."

Fifty miles or so they walked
To cities of Tyre and Sidon.
A woman from Caanan called to
Him, but He continued on.

He paid no attention, but she
Followed to implore. His Dis-
ciples said, "Send her away
For she's becoming a bore."

"I only help Jews," He said,
"Not Gentiles such as you.
You don't qualify for help;
It's a thing I shouldn't do."

"Dogs beneath the table," she
Said, "get crumbs that drop."
"Your faith is strong," said
He and took the time to stop.

"Your request is granted, the
Demon departs your child now."
Thankfully she returned to
Her daughter and her house.

He went back to the sea, and
Sat by Galilee's shore.
Many people gathered around,
Trailed by many more,

Bringing sickly relatives,
The blind, diseased and lame.
He healed them all, plus
The halt, crushed and maimed.

For three days they came, and
For three days He healed.
They were tired and hungry
After so much time afield.

Again He performed a miracle
From seven loaves and a few
Fish, fed four thousand folks,
And they ate all they wished.

He sent them back home, went
To the Magadan coast by ship.
If a place ever needed His
Presence, this was surely it.

CHAPTER 16

Saducees and Pharisees came,
Asked Him to show them a sign.
"You tell tomorrow's weather
By sky color at evening time.

But with man's problems," He
Said, "You can't read signs
Of a wicked, adulterous world,
Or that you have little time.

A wicked nation seeks a sign,
But none will be shown to you.
You had one by the prophet
Jonah; it will have to do."

Jesus was concerned His dis-
ciples get good instruction.
He spoke of man's traditions
As per Pharisee introduction.

In Caesarea Philippi He said,
"Whom do men say I am?"
They answered, "John the Bap-
tist, Elijah, or another son of
  man."

"Who do you say?" He asked,
As he did quest and prod. And
Peter answered promptly, "You
Are the son of the living God."

"Simon Peter, son of Jonah,
My Holy father smiled on thee.
Human flesh has not revealed
Those facts you know about me.

And you, oh Peter,
Are like a rock of faith.
And upon this rock I'll build
My church in future days.

The keys I'll give to you
Of earth and heaven above.
And what you lock on earth
Will never know heaven's love.

What you free down here will
Be free up there. Now tell no
Man I am the Messiah, for I'm
Forced to travel with care."

Thence forth He often spoke
Of the things that were to be.
Of fate awaiting in Jerusalem,
A trial He would not flee.

Peter could not believe his
Lord would have to suffer so.
And did his very best
To soften up the blow.

"Get thee behind me Satan,"
Were words that Jesus used.
For He must follow destiny;
He couldn't pick and choose.

To His disciples, He said,
"If any would be my friend,
He must carry a cross and fol-
low me to the final end.

One who lives only for himself
Will lose the best in life.
But he who gives all he has
Will be saved from strife.

What profit to gain the world,
If eternal life you lose?
And aside from life eternal
What more can one choose?

For I shall come in glory
And judge men by their past.
And some of you standing here
May see this come at last."

CHAPTER 17

Now nearly a week had elapsed;
Much had obviously gone on,
When Jesus climbed atop a hill
Taking Peter, James and John.

His face glowed like the sun;
His raiment white as snow, as
Moses and Elias talked to Him,
Imagine what a sight to behold.

Peter wished to build shelter;
Bright cloud came overhead.
"Meet my son in whom I'm
pleased." God from heaven said.

Think of their consternation,
The disciples prostrate fell.
Jesus touched and soothed,
And assured them all was well.

Alone again with Jesus, as
Down the mountain they went,
He pledged them all to secrecy
About the strange event.

But they wondered why
The Jewish leaders claimed
That Elias must first return
Before the Messiah came.

"True," He said, "it is writ-
ten, Elias must set things
Right. In fact He was here,
But he suffered many slights.

And I, the Messiah," He said,
"Shall suffer at their hands."
Now they realized that John
The Baptist was the other man.

At the foot of the mountain a
Demon heard Jesus call and
Let a boy who'd been hopeless
Now stand straight and tall.

The disciples had failed
This sad young man to heal.
And Jesus in some distress
Put forth this appeal.

"How long must I endure your
Doubt and lack of faith? By
It you can move a mountain,
By just telling it to go away.

But any particular demon can
Pose a hopeless task, unless
You spend much time in prayer
And in all seriousness fast."

Then while still in Galilee,
He told of things to come.
He'd be killed to live again,
But never did He mention run.

Now they were distressed at
This awful thought. So when
A tax collector accosted them,
It seemed they were caught.

Jesus said, "Go down to the
Lake and throw in your line.
In the first fish caught will
Be pay for your tax and mine."

CHAPTER 18

The Apostles argued who'd be
Greater when to heaven they
Got. Jesus drew attention to
An innocent little tot.

Saying, "Lest you become as
Children, with loving innoc-
ence too, you'll find Heaven
Is very far from you.

The world is full of evil,
And if you go along, no
Matter what is your excuse,
You'll know it is all wrong.

So deny those things of evil,
Pull them out, cast 'em away.
Better go to heaven without,
Than burn in hell each day.

Despise not little children
Whose angels are heaven's
choice; treat them right, or
Have no reason to rejoice.

The son of man came to save
A soul which before was lost.
A shepherd will leave ninety
Nine to find one at any cost.

If perchance he finds it,
Joyfully he'll carry it home.
It gets more love than the
Rest, so it no more will roam.

If a brother offends you, go
Talk it over to his face,
And if you win him over
It will be no disgrace.

But if he listens not, take
Others and try again. If
In the church he refuses,
He may then be banned.

Whatever you ban on earth
Will also be banned up there.
If two or more pray, and
If sincere in their prayers--

Then I'll be in their midst.
If they truly belong to me,
Whatever it is they pray for,
My father will cause to be."

Peter asked Him "How often
Forgive my brother's crimes?
For he has sinned against me
A minimum of seven times."

Jesus said, "Not just seven
Times, seventy times seven.
Thus you treat your brother,
If you hope to reach heaven.

Heaven's Kingdom compares to
A kings debtor unable to pay.
The king demanded payment in
Full or he'd be put away.

He fell down and begged and
Promised fully to reimburse.
He went to his debtor and
Threatened and cursed.

He demanded full payment now
And would accept no excuse.
The man was unable to pay;
Time he asked was refused.

To prison he was sent, now
Friends informed the king.
They thought this behavior
Was an unforgivable thing.

So that king in great anger
Requested his debtor to show.
This man he'd forgiven, and
Now his chance he'd blown.

The king sent him to jail
Until his debts were paid.
Always forgive your debtors;
You may be treated that way."

CHAPTER 19

After He said these things
To Judea's coast He came.
Healing many who followed;
Many knew of His fame.

Pharisees heckled, saying,
"Is it legal to divorce?"
He said, "You know how it
Was before of course.

Husband and wife were one
As they were meant to be.
Moses allowed divorcement,
For men are small and mean.

This can only be for cause,
Such as adultery or deceit.
Anything less, with the
Frowns of heaven will meet."

Disciples thought to marry
Was a poor thing to do. He
said, "Not for everyone, of
Course, everyone isn't you."

He blessed little children
His disciples would send away.
He said, "Of such is heaven's
Glory; they brighten my day."

Now a young ruler came to ask
The way to heaven's fair land.
And Jesus answered him gently,
"Be true to all God commands."

"I have since a child," he
Said, "what must I do more?"
"Give your riches to the poor,"
The answer vexed him sore.

He was rich in many things
And could not abide the loss.
His authority was very great,
And he enjoyed being the boss.

"It's as hard for a camel to
Pass through a needle's eye,"
Jesus said, "as for the rich
To deny their wealth and get
To heaven instead."

"So who can be saved?" the
Disciples asked in distress.
Jesus answered, "With God's
Help, more than you'd guess."

Peter said, "We followed you,
Our very lives we have given.
So just what will we be
When we get to Heaven?"

Jesus answered, "When I, the
Messiah shall sit my throne,
You shall all be beside me
Where none is ever alone.

Each to be a judge of Israel,
For you gave lives and homes.
Many rewards and eternal life
Will be yours on the thrones.

Many who are leaders now,
Will be the least up there.
Those who listen to me here,
Will there as leaders fare."

CHAPTER 20

Now an owner hired some men
Very early in the day,

To work on his vineyard,
To tend his grapes.

Then he hired others, and
Still others later yet. For
The job must be done quickly;
He had little time to fret.

Then when the day was over
And work for now was done,
He paid each man his wages,
The same amount to everyone.

They who worked and sweated
Through the heat of day
Complained about long hours
For the same short pay.

The landlord said, "Be happy,
I did as agreed to do. You
Bargained for those wages in
Advance; it's no wrong to you."

Thus in Heaven's Kingdom those
Who would be first are last.
And they'll find the time to
Change was a time gone past.

Then on the way to Jerusalem
He took the twelve aside.
And He told them once again
Of what would soon betide.

He told of coming betrayal,
Of condemnation to die.
Of the coming crucifixion, of
How in three days He'd rise.

Now the mother of James and
John, came to Jesus' side. To
Seat her sons on right and
Left; this she had in mind.

"You don't know what you ask,"
He said, "it's not mine to

Give. They'll share my burdens,
And for others we must live."

The others were indignant,
Thought those two had a nerve.
Jesus said, "We're all equal;
To be great we must serve.

For I came not to rule men
But to be a servant to all.
And if you would follow me
You'll heed humanity's call."

When they departed Jericho, a
Multitude followed along. Two
Blind men calling for help
Were ridiculed by the throng.

They begged for their sight.
Again He touched and healed.
Because they now could see
Followed Jesus far afield.

CHAPTER 21

Now as they neared Jerusalem,
He sent two disciples ahead.
As they'd been told before,
This they did and said.

Found a donkey's colt tied
And loosed him to lead away.
Answered when asked, "The
Master has need of him today."

"This is done," He said, "to
Fulfill prophecy of long ago,"
Saying, "Jerusalem, meet your
King riding a donkey's colt."

They put their robes upon the
Colt and set Jesus on it too.
With branches of palm, the
Way to Jerusalem was strewed.

People lined the way shouting,
 "Hosannah to Davids Son.

He's the prophet of Nazareth,
And in God's name He comes."

To the Temple Jesus went and
Made the money changers leave.
Saying, "Father's house is for
Prayer, not a den of thieves."

In the temple he healed them,
The halt, the sick and lame.
For many sought His services;
From all directions they came.

Now this caused annoyance to
The chief priests and scribes.
They asked pointed questions
And heckled Him with jibes.

He calmly quoted scripture
And rebuked their guile. Say-
ing, "Don't you know? Praise
Is perfected through a child."

He spent the night in Bethany.
He walked back to Jerusalem
Next day, and spied a fig
Tree growing along the way.

Now He was very hungry so
Walked over to the tree but
Found no figs to eat, for
It grew naught but leaves.

"You'll not grow fruit again!"
In exasperation He cried. And
The tree promptly withered;
While they watched, it died.

The apostles, awed, now asked,
"Why did it die so soon away?"
"You can move a mountain," He
Said, "If you've enough faith.

With faith and prayer, if
You'll truly believe,

Anything can be yours, if
You'll thankfully receive."

While teaching in the Temple,
Priests and leaders asked, by
What authority he taught, as
A way to take Him to task.

"I'll tell you if you answer
Me," He said, "Was John sent
By God or man?" They dare not
Answer either way, so they
Could not His actions ban.

"If we say from God,"
They said, He'll ask, "Why
Not believe in me? And if
We say from man, the mob will
Have us treed."

For they think Him a prophet
Ordained from long ago. So
They were forced to answer,
"We just don't really know."

"So I won't answer," He said,
What think you of these two?
A father sent two sons to work,
Where they had much to do.

One said "I won't go!" but did,
One said "I will!" but failed.
"Which one obeyed his father,
Which one the right assailed?"

"The first obeyed," said they,
Jesus said, "You failed the
Test. Others will see heaven;
You're no better than the rest.

You doubted John the Baptist
And even as you saw the signs,
You refused to repent and
So lived on in common crime.

A planter owned a vineyard,
He rented it and moved away.
When harvest arrived, he sent
Servants to collect his pay.

But the renters beat his men
And killed some others he sent.
Then finally killed his son
Who for his father went.

Now when that owner returns,
What do you think he'll do?"
The Jewish leaders replied,
"Tear those renters in two."

"Do you read scripture?" Jesus
Asked, "The stone the builders
Rejected was a corner stone
When the building was erected.

It was the will of God; what
A marvelous thing to see. It
Means heaven is not for un-
Believers, only those who be.

Who falls on this stone shall
Be bruised and broken. But
Whom it falls on will fail,"
They knew to them He'd spoken.

In anger and indignation
They'd have liked to take Him
Away. But feared the crowd too
Much; He was popular that day.

CHAPTER 22

He described heaven's Kingdom
By a story of a wedding feast.
The king sent invitations, as
The good news was released.

Many guests were invited,
But not a one of them showed.
So he sent more invitations
As for a gala event he strove.

Many laughed and ignored him
As they went their way.
Some beat and killed messen-
gers, totally ruined his day.

Angry, he destroyed the city,
Hanged those murderers high.
They deserved no invitation,
But once again he'd try.

Again he sent his servants
To invite whoever they would.
But one invited guest didn't
Dress the way he should.

This one wore no wedding robe,
And when the king asked why,
(It was furnished by the host,)
So of course he made no reply.

"Bind, and throw him out,"
Cried the king, "where there
Is weeping and pain. Many are
Called, few chosen, with no
Chance to try again."

Pharisees and Herodians met,
Agreed to set a trap,
And asked, "Is it really legal
To pay the government a tax?"

"Show a coin," He said, "and
Tell whose likeness is there"
He knew they tried to trick
Him and wouldn't play fair.

A coin they had was inscribed
With Caesar's image on the face.
"So give to Caesar what is His
And give God His with grace."

Baffled and beat by His answer,
They soon went on their way.
The Sadducees would question
Him later on that day.

One said, "Moses said a man,
Should marry his dead brothers
Wife and raise heirs to that
Brother during his own life.

Now we knew of seven brothers;
Each followed through but died.
Not one fathered a child, yet
Each took the girl to bride.

So the question we ask you now,
Whose wife is she in heaven?
For while here on earth, she
Was married to all seven."

His answer fitted the people
Who doubted the resurrection.
"You're ignorant of scripture
And overdue for correction.

At resurrection, as in heaven
There's no marriage or divorce.
Not believing in resurrection,
You don't know that of course."

God said, "I'm the God of Abr-
aham, of Isaac and Jacob too.
You don't seem to realize; He
Was speaking directly to you.

For He is God of the living,
He is not God of the dead.
This word I speak is true,
For that is what He said."

The multitude who listened
To his doctrine were amazed.
But pharisees still heckled;
This question they now raised.

"Which is the greatest comm-
andment?" a lawyer inquired.
"Love God with all your being,
The greatest, most inspired.

The second is nearly as great,
Love your neighbor as yourself.
Keep those two to perfection,
You've kept the others as well."

"Who's son is the Messiah," He
Asked pharisees gathered there,
"He's only the son of David,"
They were quick to declare.

"David called Messiah, `Lord,'
When under the spirit's spell.
Saying, God said to my Lord,
Sit, while your enemies I quell.

Since David called Him `Lord,'
How can He be only David's
    son?"
They dared not question more,
And so they held their tongues.

CHAPTER 23

To disciples and crowds He
Said, "Pharisees and Jews,
Make many rules and laws,
Which are only made for you.

In public they sit, where they
Smile and fawn and preen. They
Make many laws to keep; their
Main ambition is to be seen.

They love fancy titles, would
Be called `Master,' and `Rabbi,'
Too. Keep no rules they make
But expect so much from you.

Only God call "Rabbi," you
Are all brothers here on earth.
Only the "Messiah" is master;
This warning is of great worth.

Call no man "Father," except
God, who is the Father of all.

He who would be great will
Be humbled but wiser, fall.

To be great in heaven, on
Earth you must a servant be.
Woe to hypocritic leaders with
Long prayers on the streets.

Blind guides swearing by gold,
But not by the Temple itself.
Those followers you convert
Become twice the sons of hell.

You carefully do your tithing,
But you miss things that count.
Polished and pious outwardly,
But dirt on the inside mounts."

You say, "Fathers killed proph-
ets, thus accuse yourselves.
You'll kill those I send among
You but not escape the judg-
ment of hell.

Jerusalem, You wicked city,
How to protect you, I've tried.
You stoned and killed prophets,
As justice or truth they cried.

Now your house will be empty
And a home land you will yearn.
And you'll not see me anymore
Until you welcome my return."

CHAPTER 24

Leaving the temple grounds, a
Few disciples wished to stay
Behind. The buildings were so
Beautiful, as to capture minds.

Jesus said, "Why stay? This
Beauty will not long endure.
Twill be strewn among rocks,
Of this you can be sure."

They asked Him if the end of
The world was near. "Don't let
Anyone fool you," He said,
"False prophets will appear.

They'll perform miracles and
Will cause many to go astray.
But no matter what they claim,
Don't listen to what they say.

For there will be wars and
Rumors of many more, earth-
Quakes, famines and trouble
Like you've never seen before.

This is only the beginning,
For if you'd follow me,
Those who live in Judea, to
The hills must quickly flee.

Ignore secondhand reports
That the Messiah is here or
There. "When I come in glory,
It will be for all to share.

Angels will go forward with
Trumpet blast; tell the wond-
rous story and gather in my
People to join me in glory.

In spring you always know
Summer is around the bend.
And always keep in mind that
This could forecast the end.

Heaven and earth will fade,
Only my words will remain.
None knows when it will be;
Only our God can say.

As in Noah's time, people
Will play, party and booze,
As if time would never end
So they had nothing to lose.

Two men will work together,
One will stand, another fall.
Two women working at homely
Tasks, one will get the call.

So always be prepared,
For you will never know
When that time will come,
And you will suddenly go.

So be my faithful servant;
Feed my children day by day.
If you are lazy and evil
You will surely pay."

CHAPTER 25

To reach the Kingdom can be
Likened to these. Ten brides-
Maids awaited the bridegroom,
Whom all wished to please-

But five not prepared, took
No oil for their lamps. So
When they heard him coming
Found their style cramped.

The wise ones were ready;
The others must go for oil.
So some went to the party;
Others' plans were foiled.

Late to attend the party,
Now the doors were locked.
Readiness not their virtue,
They had no trade in stock.

So watch, always be ready,
You know not at what time
Your number may be called;
There'll be no warning signs.

`Tis also like a man who
Travelled far and wide. He
Sent for his three servants
And called them to his side.

He divided up his goods;
To one, ten units he gave.
To another he entrusted two,
Only one to another slave.

Now after he had left the
First two doubled the stake.
The third one buried his,
And that was his mistake.

When the master returned,
Two had made his money work.
The other had been timid;
His duty he had shirked.

Two who'd shown profit were
Invited to the master's home.
The one who'd hidden his
Was left to grieve alone.

The unit that he had hidden
Was taken from him forthwith.
Now the lesson most obvious
Here is stated like this.

Take those talents you were
Given; make the most of them.
For if you fail to use them,
They may be taken back again.

When the son of man comes
With angels and great glory,
He will separate the nations,
And this will be the story.

He'll separate us right and
Left like goats and sheep.
And to those on the right
He will make this speech.

"I was hungry and thirsty
You gave food and water too.
You visited me in prison;
God's blessings rest on you."

The righteous ones shall say,
"When did we do such things?"
He'll say, "You did them when
You took the needy under wing."

He'll tell those others, "You
Were not your brother's keeper,
When brother's needed help,
You were heavy sleepers."

They will be cast aside to
Eternal punishment. But the
Righteous will be given
Into heaven's firmament.

CHAPTER 26

The high priests of Jerusalem
Met in secret that day, even
As Jesus took three disciples
And climbed the mount to pray.

Two days away was passover
When they planned His death.
Judas arranged to betray Him,
His trickery swift and deft.

For thirty pieces of silver,
Judas traded his soul. He'd
Soon realize his treachery,
Regret would take its toll.

There was Mary of Bethany,
As they were visiting there
She poured oil on Jesus' head;
Very expensive oil she shared.

The apostles felt it should
Be sold to feed the poor! But
Jesus rebuked them, saying,
"They'll be here forever more.

But I'll not be here long, so
What she did is quite apropos.
For she is anointing my body
Because she knows I must go.

So history will treat her well
Wherever this story is told.
For she prepared my body for
Death with heart of gold."

Into Jerusalem they went and
Spent a day of passover there.
A gentleman of that city, his
Home was willing to share.

As they ate the evening meal
Jesus gave them great concern.
Saying one would betray Him
And thus damnation earn.

Each one asked, "Is it I who
Would do this terrible deed?"
He said, when asked by Judas,
"Yes my friend, it is indeed."

He took of bread and wine,
Invented communion of today.
`Twas on the night of passover,
This custom that came to stay.

"This," He said, "is my body,
To be broken for sins of man.
And this wine is for my blood;
It will wash him clean again.

This is my last meal with you;
I'll be in God's kingdom soon."
Now they sang a song and left
Under a pall of gloom.

For He warned them they would
Weaken and soon flee in fear.
"The shepherd will be smitten,
And the flock will disappear.

For thus the word is written,
But you will again see me;
For after I have risen, I'll
Go ahead of you to Galilee."

Of course they assured Him
That none of them would flee.
"No matter what should
    happen,"
Peter said, "Depend on me."

"I know you mean well," said
Jesus, "and it would be nice,
But ere the rooster crows in
Morning you'll deny me thrice."

Then those faithful disciples
Gave assurance He did not seek.
But they'd soon learn of
Strong intent, flesh too weak.

In Gethsemane He left Peter
And the sons of Zebedee.
"I must go and pray, please
Guard this path for me."

Then He left them there and
Knelt and prayed, "Heavenly
Father, if it is your will,
Please take this trial away."

Three times He returned; each
Time they were asleep. He
Knew intentions were good, but
Their bodies were too weak.

The mobs sent by the priests
Suddenly burst upon the scene.
And we can only ask ourselves,
"What makes people so mean?"

Judas came directly to Jesus,
Greeted Him as an old friend.
The Messiah said, "Do as you
Must." He knew it was the end.

They grabbed Jesus roughly, a
Prisoner of bias and fear.
Then one who'd protect Him,
Drew a sword, cut off an ear.

But Jesus told him to desist;
To live by a sword is to die.
This was all prophesied to be;
It's not ours to ask why.

If He'd ask God in heaven, He
Would send angels to protect,
But it was in scripture to be
And was not for Him to object.

His disciples so true soon
Wavered and failed the course.
Scattering, they ran in fear,
When facing a superior force.

Peter, perhaps more loyal and
True, followed the crowd. He
Made himself small and incon-
spicuous, as the time allowed.

The high priests of the Jews,
Supreme judges were there,
To testify against Jesus, of
Whom they were scared.

Answering sneering questions,
"Yes, I am the Messiah," Said
He, "and upon clouds of glory
Returning to earth I'll be."

"Blasphemy," cried the priest,
"Hear Him, I let my case rest.
What about His sentence?" The
Answer in unison, "Death!"

As a common prisoner, He was
Treated, struck and spat in
The face. To hide their guilt
They showed him as disgraced.

Peter trailed, heart quaking,
The picture of timid fear. A
Girl indicated to soldiers,
"This is another here."

In terror he denied his Lord,
As if he doubted what she said.
Again later out by the gate,
His innocence once more pled.

Later when others accused him,
He cursed, swore and denied.
When a rooster crowed that
Morning, bitterly he cried.

CHAPTER 27

When the morning dawned
again, Priests and leaders met
To Convince the Roman
   government
To sentence Jesus to death.

So in chains they sent Him to
Face great Pilate's stare. For
They wanted the Roman
   governor
Their guilty deed to share.

Now Judas who'd betrayed Him
Knew he'd cost Jesus His life,
And that what he had done
Was anything but right.

So he tried to return money
He had gained through perfidy.
But the priest laughed and
Said, "Let the onus be on thee."

Then on the temple floor
He threw the money down. And
He went out and hanged him-
Self, a deed of sad renown.

Then those cheats and liars,
Gathered up the silver pieces.
But suddenly became concerned
With law the scripture teaches.

They must not use money that
Had paid for death of another.

It was a Jewish religious law
That politics could not cover.

So they bought a field of clay
From which pottery was made.
They made it into a cemetery,
In which foreigners were laid.

Potter's field, field of blood,
Is the name it carries today.
Fulfilling words of prophecy
That prompted Jeremiah to say,

They valued Him in silver,
Thirty pieces worth, used
To buy the potter's field,
As prompted by the Lord.

Now before the Roman
   governor,
Our Lord stood uncowed. When
Asked if He was the Messiah
Answered "Yes," firm and loud.

But when others accused Him,
He stood silent and strong.
As Pilate queried and listened,
The less He thought Him wrong.

In vain He tried to save Him,
Pilate's wife would too, but
He was a victim of politics
With nothing they could do.

Each year at passover, by
Custom a prisoner was released.
So Pilate asked them, "Jesus,
Or Barabbas, which will it be?"

The Jewish rulers and priests
Had done their insidious worst,
Stacked the cards against him
And did great harm to our Lord.

So the crowd cried, "Barabbas,
And Jesus you must crucify."

Pilate said, "I give Him to you,
For I think it's wrong He die."

He was whipped and given to
The soldiers to crucify. In a
Robe of scarlet and a crown
Of thorns, He suffered and died.

Insults and epithets flew
As Jesus in patience forbore.
I'm glad I didn't see the
Tortured death of my Lord.

A Cyrenian they forced to car-
ry His heavy cross up the hill.
There they crucified my Master;
Jesus said it was God's will.

Over His head this sign hung,
"Jesus, King of the Jews." A
Mob has no rhyme or reason; it
Is governed by perverted views.

Upon the "Hill of the Skull,"
Was where the Lord was killed.
So that in every way that day,
The scriptures were fulfilled.

Many watched Him suffer,
Cast lots for his clothes.
He was offered drugs, but
Answered a positive "No"

Two robbers were crucified,
One upon either side.
One joined the cursing mob,
A part of the angry cries.

Darkness covered earth from
Noon till three o'clock.
As if the light of the sun
Had mysteriously stopped.

Jesus cried out in agony;
The world got light again.

The Temple curtain split a-
part, putting fear in men.

Earth shook and rumbled;
Great rocks split apart.
Many men trembled who
Were famous "lionhearts."

Jesus dismissed His life,
As these things came about.
Many graves opened up, and
Saints came walking out.

Soldiers standing by were
Terrorized by those events.
They decided Jesus really
Was "The Son God had sent."

There were women who gazed
In horror from far away.
They were greatly saddened
By the infamy of that day.

Joseph of Arimathea, a rich
Man, got Jesus's body released,
Wrapped and placed it in his
Own tomb, in spite of these.

Mary Magdalene and the other
One sat by the Sepulchre
Wall and watched from afar,
So they had seen it all.

The chief priests and leaders
Managed a guard upon the tomb.
They meant to give no quarter
During these hours of gloom.

Charged disciples with tricks
To fake that Christ had risen.
They sealed a rock-bound door;
By suspicion they were driven.

CHAPTER 28

The Marys visited the tomb
Early that Sunday morning. To

Be shaken by an earthquake
As if in holy warning.

For an angel came from heaven,
He rolled the great rock away.
Those guards promptly fainted
In the sudden light of day.

The angel told those women,
Do not fear, all is well. For
Your Savior has arisen, go
Find the disciples and tell.

In fright but with great joy,
They ran to tell their own.
Jesus appeared before them;
They no longer were alone.

They worshipped at His feet.
He said "My dear ones do not
Fear, go tell my brothers
In Galilee to meet me there."

Temple police returned and
Told bosses of this affair.
It had made a big impression;
They still were badly scared.

So all the Jewish leaders met,
Decided to bribe the guards.
It threatened their positions,
From which they feared to part.

So claimed the disciples came,
Stole Christ's body as they
Slept, this story is widely
Believed in Jewry yet.

All eleven disciples left and
Met upon the mount in Galilee.
Yet some were not quite sure
That this was really He.

"I've been given all power," He
Said, "in heaven and on earth.

So go and teach all nations,
Of Jehovah Father's worth.

Baptize all men in the name
Of Father, Son and Holy Ghost.
Teach them to observe all
Things, no matter where you go.

For what I've commanded you;
I'll be with you all the way.
Even unto the world's end
And to a brighter day, Amen."

END OF MATTHEW

MARK

CHAPTER 1

According to Isaiah, God
Would send His son to earth.
The son of Joseph and Mary,
The result of virgin birth.

According to the same Isaiah,
A messenger would announce,
Each should prepare his life,
So Jesus' work would count.

He'd be a man of action; he'd
Eat locusts and wild honey.
With clothes of camel's hair
And little use for money.

He baptized many with water
In Jordan's cleansing flow.
He said another was coming
Whom he was grateful to know.

He said, "I baptize with water,
But one who follows me will
Baptize with the Holy Spirit;
Free from sin you'll be."

Then in the days to come He
Baptized many in the land.
Came the one called Jesus, the
Son of God and Son of man.

From the town of Nazareth in
The land of Galilee. In the

Moment when He was baptized,
Heaven opened for Him to see-

The Holy Spirit in the
Form of a beautiful dove,
Alighted on His person and
A voice from heaven above-

Said, "This is my beloved son
In whom I am greatly pleased."
Then He went into the desert
And Satan tempted and teased.

Forty days and nights, listened
to Satan's tempting whims.
Wild things and desert were
Company; angels cared for Him.

Now John was put in prison
For things that he had done.
Preaching God's word had
Never been all games and fun.

Jesus retreated to Galilee
To Preach good news to men.
Here He saw Simon and
   Andrew
And promptly called to them.

"Forget your fishing, leave
Your friends and follow me."
Then likewise He called James
And John, the sons of Zebedee.

To Capernaum they followed,
In the Synagogue He taught,
As no scribe but with author-
ity, all listeners were awed.

An unclean spirit possessed
A man in their midst, and
He cried out to Jesus, for
He feared that this was it.

"Oh Lord let us alone,
We beg of thee, we know
You're the Holy One of God,
So please let us be."

Jesus rebuked him, saying,
"Hold the peace, come hence."
With a loud voice he came
As he tore and wrenched.

Then everyone was amazed,
Asked, "Who is this man?
Even the evil spirits flee
At His spoken command."

His fame spread abroad as
Word went from city to sea.
He became quite famous
Throughout all Galilee.

Now Simon's wife's mother
Took very sick with a fever.
Jesus took her by the hand
And immediately healed her.

By evening people came from
All over the land. For word
Was rapidly spreading about
This very remarkable man.

He cured many diseases, and
Numerous evils exorcised.
Asking them to keep silent,
For they knew He was Christ.

Rising up in the morning
Before the dawn of day, He
Found a place of solitude
Where He knelt to pray.

His followers told Him,
"Many await your return."
The mission of His life
In His breast still burned.

In Synagogues He preached
Throughout all of Galilee.
Casting out many devils
And healing much disease.

Then he healed a leper who
Beseeched Him while there.
He pledged him to silence
About the whole affair.

But when the man left all
Clean and no doubt proud,
He told all who'd listen
In voice clear and loud.

It made Jesus so famous, He
Was forced to avoid cities.
But they followed into the
Desert for help and pity.

CHAPTER 2

To Capernaum he journeyed;
People near beat Him there.
They pressed so close about;
There was no room to spare.

Four men with a palsied one
Couldn't get in the house.
So tore a hole in the roof
And thereby let him down.

When Jesus saw the faith of
The intrepid ones, He said,
"Go, thy faith has healed
Thee, go in peace my son."

To others it was blasphemy.
He knew their thoughts, so
Asked, "What if I forgive
Sins or say, get up and walk?

The Son of God has power
To heal or sins forgive."
They marveled to themselves,
"We never thought like this."

He met a tax collector, Levi,
As he traveled by the sea.
He said, "Come leave your
Job and go along with me."

The pharisees and scribes
Followed this unusual man.
For they'd been looking for
Trouble once His fame began.

So when He sat to eat, in
Company of Publicans and
Sinners, they played trouble-
Shooters, natural winners.

Sure, He sensed the rumors,
Said, "No doctor is needed
For the well, the sick and
Sinful I came here to help."

Now part of Jewish religion
Said one should often fast.
People came to Jesus and
About this practice asked.

"John's disciples fast,
Not those who follow you.
Yours don't do so; why
Aren't they fasting too?"

"Friends of the bridegroom
Fast when he is gone. One day
I'll be taken," He said, "and
Then my disciples will mourn.

That old custom is ancient as
Patching new cloth with old.
It won't last much longer, so
Will still be prone to holes."

Walking one day in the grain
His helpers shelled to eat.
Some leaders objected to the
Sabbath day harvest of wheat.

Jesus mentioned King David,
How Temple shew bread he ate.
That was illegal too but was
Forgiven in the hungry state.

"The Sabbath is to benefit
Man, not the other way round.
I have authority to decide,"
He said, "to use or put down."

CHAPTER 3

While in Capernaum He went
Back to the Synagogue again;
He noticed a gentleman there
With a badly deformed hand.

He knew His enemies watched
In hopes He could be accused.
And if they could trip Him up,
He'd be badly abused.

His ready accusers, He asked,
"Is the Sabbath for good or
Bad?" They would not answer,
For by answer they'd be had.

"Hold out your hand," He said,
The sufferer put it forth.
With that much faith in Jesus,
Results were certain of course.

The hand was instantly well.
Now Jesus was beloved by all,
Turning none in trouble away,
Always tuned to their call.

His enemies quickly regrouped,
To plot and plan His death.
His fame spread like fire;
Enemies had little time left.

Later He climbed the hills,
Took others too by invitation.
He chose twelve for disciples,
Who'd be as dear as relation.

Peter was he who'd been Simon,
James and John, sons of Zebed-
ee, known as "Sons of Thunder,"
A compliment, I believe.

Another James, son of Alpheus,
Andrew, Philip and
   Batholomew.
Thomas, Thaddeus, Simon and
Judas and one called Matthew.

Simon was of the resistance,
He advocated the Roman
   demise.
Judas was the one who betrayed
Jesus, then took his own life.

Returning to where He stayed
Great crowds gathered again.
There wasn't room to sit or
Eat, most unpleasant to man.

Friends wanted to rescue Him;
Enemies saw it another way.
"He's owned by Satan," They
Said, "so the demons obey."

"Can Satan defeat Satan?" He
Asked, "A house divided can't
Stand. Satan must be bound,
Before I can hope to save man.

I allow blasphemy against me;
Against the Spirit you will
Cower. None is forgiven who
Doubt the Holy Spirit's power."

His mother and brothers came
Asking that he come and talk.
What He told the messenger
Might seem that He balked.

"Keep my Father's command,"
He said, "do His will; forget
All others. These are father,
Mother and also my brothers."

CHAPTER 4

Again the crowd gathered upon
The shore of the sea. Until
He fled to the deck of a boat
And proceeded to preach.

In parables He taught them,
Though slow to understand.
In the evenings He explained
Hidden meanings to man.

"A man planted grain in paths
Of birds eating that day.
Some fell on sand and rocks;
The sun soon wilted it away.

He also planted among thorns
Where they smothered to death.
Some he planted in good soil
Which grew to be the best."

Disciples that evening asked
The meaning of these stories.
"The Kingdom of God," He said,
"Is explained in its glory,

You are able to learn things
Of heaven that others miss.
How can you fathom the future,
If you cannot see this?

The man in my story is one,
Who gives the word to all men.
It often falls on deaf ears,
And these people won't bend.

The story of rocky soil is
Of those with characters weak.
Joyous, they hear the message,
Only to forget what they seek.

The one of weeds and thistles?
People who listen in delight!
Daily problems crowd them out;
Good intentions take flight.

Seed falling in good soil is
Like people steady and true.
They accept the word in glory
Spreading it to everyone anew.

It makes a plentiful harvest,
Often sixty or a hundred fold.
The good news multiplies, as
By good people it's retold.

A lamp hidden from man, can
Never light up his way. A
Good light will be seen, and
What is in darkness betrays.

Listen carefully and do all
Good things that you hear. So
Practice sincerely and often
And understanding will appear.

To him who has understanding,
Good things shall be given.
Of such is the pathway upward,
A key to the gates of heaven.

He who is happy in ignorance,
What he has may be taken away.
He lacks wisdom to hold it,
Will lose what he has one day.

The Kingdom is like a farmer;
He sowed crops and left there.
In summer they grew mature;
He returned to harvest fair.

Heaven's Kingdom," He said,
"Is like mustard seed, small.
Yet it grows very large,
Beautiful, bushy and tall."

Then as the day was waning,
As evening shadows closed;
They started across the lake,
And a terrible storm arose.

Over the transom water came,
Surging up from the deep.
Wildly they called to Jesus,
For He was peacefully asleep.

He rose and with equanimity
Told the wind to be still.
The tempest quickly calmed;
The wind quieted to His will.

Then He chided them gently
For Lack of faith this day.
They in awe asked each other,
"Who is He, even wind obeys?"

CHAPTER 5

They arrived on shore, and a
Wild man came from the tombs,
Crying, "Help," suffering from
Self-destruction and gloom.

Muscular, stronger than most,
None could keep him in chains.
He ran through the country
Hurting and crying in pain.

Far off he saw Jesus coming,
Running toward him, fell down.
Jesus's power over demons in
That whole area was renown.

So Jesus spoke to the demon,
"Come out, leave this man be."
Screaming in fear it cried,
"Son of God help me,"

"What Is your name?" Jesus
Asked. It replied, "Legion
We are, let us stay near,
For we wish not to go far.

There's a herd of swine near
By; let us enter into them."
Jesus granted their wish, and
In that herd caused mayhem.

In confusion they bolted,
Fell into a lake and drowned.
Is it any wonder that Jesus
Wherever he went was
   renowned?

Now the news quickly spread;
Folks came from far and near.
Seeing the ex-lunatic sitting
There sane caused them fear.

They begged Him to leave, but
The new man asked to go too.
Jesus advised he tell people
Of the wonders God can do.

Ten nearby towns he covered,
Doing as Jesus had insisted;
The people were truly amazed
At all the things he listed.

They arrived on the far shore;
A crowd formed on the beach.
A Synagogue leader implored,
"Come before you preach."

His child was sick and dying;
He asked Jesus come and heal.
He knew of Jesus' power and
To Him tearfully appealed.

So Jesus went with Jairus, as
They pushed through a throng,
A woman of years of sickness,
Her faith was unduly strong-

Grabbed His robe then moved
On, knowing she'd be healed,
Heard the Master say, "Who
Touched me?" For He'd felt
The power slip away.

Some wondered at His words,
How, in this pressing throng,
Could He ever notice just one
And think anything was wrong?

Fearfully she drew near and
Admitted what she had done.
He said, "Go your way; your
Belief for you has won."

Then a messenger drew near,
Saying the girl had expired.
Jesus said, "Have faith,
Sir! Your daughter's tired."

They arrived at Jairus' home,
Found all in utter confusion.
For parents and disciples,
He changed their conclusion.

Jeering met His statement,
She was only asleep. He took
Her hand, said, "Arise little
Girl, join friends who weep."

Imagine the shock of parents;
How happy they must have
   been,
When she arose to their joy
To continue life with them.

CHAPTER 6

To His home he returned, but
Friends and neighbors compla-
ined, Envious of His powers,
So he made but little gains.

Lack of belief robbed them of
Many miracles, caused grief.

A prophet with honor at home
Is just too much to believe.

He sent His disciples out;
Two by two they went. Healing
The sick, casting out demons,
No money or extras were sent.

"In villages" He said, "with
Only one family eat and sleep;
If not accepted in that town
Shake its dust off your feet.

This signifies abandonment
To its well-earned fate.
And on the day of judgment,
It will be in terrible shape."

Thus they went about, healing
And teaching across the land
Anointing many with oil and
Spreading good news to man.

Herod took a brother's wife,
John the Baptist lectured him.
This, he said was not right;
It was surely a matter of sin.

So Herodius waited her chance,
On Herod's birthday struck.
He admired her daughter's da-
nce, must have drunk too much,

For he offered a fine gift of
Whatever she might ask. Then
Her mother advised her ill;
John lost his head to the ax.

Herod was sad but beaten, for
He'd known John was right.
But He kept his word to his
Stepdaughter, the word he
Could not slight.

John's disciples heard of his
Fate, took the body in their

Gloom, wrapped and prepared
It, and laid it in a tomb.

When Herod heard of miracles
Jesus and disciples performed,
He thought John had returned,
Was taking the world by storm.

Some claimed it was Elias,
Others a prophet, believed.
Perhaps Herod quaked in his
Boots, felt he was deceived!

Jesus' disciples returned
Telling of what they had done.
He suggested a vacation, obv-
iousy, a rest they had won.

They headed up-shore by boat,
The crowd onshore was large.
Many had recognized Jesus;
Ahead on foot they charged.

All those people were waiting,
As they anchored near shore.
Jesus took pity, taught them,
They all thirsted for more.

Disciples suggested dismissal;
Day was advancing toward eve;
They had no groceries at hand,
Inadequate food for the needs.

Jesus said, "We must feed
Them." They said, "A hopeless
Wish, with all these people
Are five loaves and two fish."

To heaven He was thankful,
And blessed what was there.
Passed it around and each
Was filled with his share.

They gathered the scraps, and
Twelve baskets were left. So

Five thousand ate that day
By a miracle timely and deft.

Jesus sent His disciples over
The lake to Bethsaida by boat.
But He stayed behind to send
Those people back home.

Then into the hills He went,
Where He spent time in prayer.
That night it became windy;
His disciples were scared.

Across the lake He walked,
Undaunted by wind and waves.
They saw him moving out there,
Heedless of storm or spray.

In the wee hours they saw Him,
And in terror they screamed,
Thinking they'd seen a ghost,
Or perhaps it was a bad dream.

To calm their fears He came,
Saying, "Be cheerful, not af-
raid."While boarding He
Calmed the wind and waves.

Some did not recognize Jesus
Or remember a miracle ashore.
He fed five thousand people
And could have fed many more.

They landed at Gennesaret;
People in multitudes came,
Begging to touch His garment,
For they'd heard of His fame.

CHAPTER 7

The Jews sent out parties
To investigate Jesus again,
His disciples ate some bread
Without washing their hands.

Jews questioned this practice
For the custom was well known.

They washed pots and pans
And many things in the homes.

But Jesus informed them, "what
Goes into the mouth isn't bad,
But what comes from the heart
Is often wicked and sad.

The law of Moses also says,
Honor mother and father, sick
Or well. Give of your wages
To keep them in good health.

You say, give to the church,
And let parents grow old. For
It's not that important if
They're hungry or cold."

His disciples were confused
And asked Him to explain.
So patiently He took time
To make it more plain.

"What you eat isn't so bad, as
What you think and say. Lust,
Murder, envy, gossip, pride
And folly, lead you astray.

What you eat, washed or not,
Cannot hurt your soul.
But a tongue that is loose
Can take a vicious toll."

They neared Tyre and Sidon
From His home in Galilee,
Many were assembled waiting
For Him to heal and preach.

A woman cried for help; her
Daughter was demon possessed.
She was a Gentile whom
The Jews normally detest.

Now Jesus was there to teach
Only those of His own kind.

This woman had great faith,
Very obvious to His mind.

"For even puppies," she said,
"Are given crumbs at a table.
Please Master, heal her,
For I know you are able."

"So go in peace," He said.
"For your daughter is healed.
Such faith you have
To my heart appeals."

He met a man near the sea, as
He journeyed back to Galilee,
Who had an impediment
Of speach and also was deaf.

They brought the man forth
And to Jesus appealed.
If He'd lay on His hands,
They knew he'd be healed.

Then again he did the thing,
For which He was so famed.
Though He begged for silence,
Those wonders they proclaimed.

In amazement they noted
All those things they saw;
They could only marvel, so
The news spread fast abroad.

CHAPTER 8

Three days many had attended
Wonderful things He taught,
Without food in the desert,
Where nothing could be bought.

To disciples he said, He just
Couldn't send them away. But
They scoffed in irritation,
"What, food in a desert today?"

He said, "Gather from among
The people what you can find."

Seven loaves and a few fishes,
Given by some who were kind.

Jesus blessed what they had
Asked His disciples to serve.
Four thousand ate their fill,
Found seven baskets, reserve.

They sailed to Delmanutha.
And Jews met Him ashore. They
Came to argue religion and
To heckle him some more.

"Do us a miracle," they said,
"We'll believe by your deeds."
"Most certainly not," said He,
"How many do you need?"

Into the boat they climbed,
Back across the lake to go.
Disciples brought no food,
They had only one loaf.

He warned of Philistine yeast;
They thought he meant food.
They missed His meaning, He
Asked, "Why are you so obtuse?

Why don't you listen or hear?
Heed the five thousand I fed,
Or those four thousand later,
Why would I worry about
    bread?"

They arrived in Bethsaida and
People met Him with a man. He
Was blind wanted a miracle
To heal by touch of a hand.

Leaving the town, He healed
And made him whole again.
Bade him go home to his
    family,
Not tell his story to man.

Jesus asked His disciples,
"Whom do others think I am?"
They said, "John the Baptist,
Elijah, a prophet back again."

"What do you think?" He asked,
"The Messiah," Peter claimed,
Jesus warned, "Keep the word
Low, or I could be detained."

For He'd soon be rejected by
The Jewish leaders and prie-
sts. He would be put to death
By such people as these.

In three days He would rise,
And they'd see Him again. But
Peter couldn't believe Jesus
Was in for so much pain.

He took Jesus aside saying to
Him that it couldn't be true.
Jesus said, "Get behind me Sa-
tan; I've no time for you.

This is only your wish with
Out a thought for God's will,"
For Peter found it hard to
Believe Jesus would be killed.

Jesus called His disciples
And the crowd to come too.
Saying, "If you'd follow me,
This you must first do.

Put aside your treasures
And shoulder your cross.
Remember, all you have
Can very quickly be lost.

If you give of your life to
Promote the good news.
There is much more to gain
Than it's possible to lose.

How much good can you win
If you should lose your soul?
Much better to lose your life
With your name on the roll.

Anyone who is ashamed or
Afraid of my message or me,
When I come in my glory,
Ashamed of him I shall be."

CHAPTER 9

"Some of you may be living
When His kingdom comes in
power. So be sure you are ready
And prepared for that hour."

Six days later Jesus led them
Up a mountain nearby. There
Were Peter, John and James,
Jesus' face began to shine.

His clothing, dazzling white,
More glorious they'd not seen.
Elijah and Moses appeared,
Spoke with Jesus as a team.

Peter babbled like a child;
He was flustered and shook.
But the next thing that hap-
pened was one for the book.

A cloud covered the mountain;
The sun was blocked from view.
Then came a voice from heaven
Saying, "Attention; all of you.

This is my beloved Son, in
Him I am well pleased." Then
Moses and Elijah were gone,
As if they'd left on a breeze.

Jesus said, "Don't tell until I
have risen from the dead."
All the way down the mountain
Marveled at what He'd said.

They'd heard from the Jews,
Elias, Messiah would precede.
And Jesus said, "That is true
And more, so listen to me.

Elias has already been here,
Subject to malice and death.
Predicted of long ago, they
Would hound my every breath."

At the foot of the mountain,
The people waited in suspense.
Disciples had failed to heal
And were agitated and tense.

One in the crowd had a son
Who was by a devil possessed.
But when the disciples tried,
Their efforts were unblessed.

Jesus rebuked them, saying,
"Your faith is small and weak.
So where now is the child?
Please bring him here to me."

Following an order from Jesus,
The demon left, and fled
After he'd convulsed him, and
Everyone thought he was dead.

Jesus raised him by the hand;
His disciples could but stare,
Asked, "Why couldn't we do it?"
Said He, "This takes prayer."

They traveled through Galilee's
Land, secretly as they might.
He wished to teach well in
All things that were right.

He said, "Soon I must die,
In three days I'll live again."
Not sure of His message, they
Didn't dare ask what He meant.

On the way to Capernaum they
Argued who would count most;
When the journey was finished,
Folly'd trailed like a ghost.

For when arrived in Capernaum
Safely where they'd stay,
Jesus asked about the argument,
They were too abashed to say.

He called them to listen, saying,
"A man unwilling to serve,
Can never be great in heaven;
It takes dedication not nerve."

He took a child in his arms,
Said, "Welcome these in my
Name. Thus you are welcoming
Me pleasing God the same."

A disciple said, "We saw a
Man casting out demons today.
He was using your name, so
We told him his hand to stay."

"Forbid him not," said Jesus,
"For if he works on our side,
He cannot be against us, a
Thing we can easily abide.

But if one little child were
Made to lose faith, that man
Had better be dead at birth,
Than face heaven's rage.

If your hand or foot or eye
Will keep you from God's will.
Destroy them, get on with the
Job, or your chance for heaven
is killed.

Better to arrive maimed or
Blind than be cast into fire.
Be at peace with neighbors;
Do not try to raise one's ire.

Think of value of salt; keep
Flavor of its goodness high,
As you conduct your person.
Actions you'll be judged by."

CHAPTER 10

Now southward they journeyed
As they left Capernaum behind.
Jesus was true to His nature,
Always gentle and kind.

They crossed Judah's border
East of the River Jordan. The
Crowds still did follow, and
As usual He still taught them.

The Pharisees came to heckle,
Asked questions about divorce.
Jesus said, "Yes, Moses gave
Them a writ, but there's more.

Hearts are cold and hard, but
God never meant it that way.
For man and wife should be
One; thus they should stay.

They may abandon a family if
Necessary and their friends.
A couple should be together
And stick it out to the end."

Later He told the disciples,
To divorce and marry again,
Is to commit adultery,
For either woman or man.

Mothers brought the children
While crowds gathered one day.
His disciples, very indignant,
Started shooing them away.

But Jesus said, "Oh no, do
Not deny any child; heaven
Is made up of such, treat
Them gentle and mild.

Any man who denies a child a
Right to heaven and to love
Will not make it himself
To that glorious home above."

He took them in His arms and
Placed hands on their heads,
He blessed them with love
To enforce what He'd said.

When ready to journey again,
A man fell to his knees, say-
ing, "Good Teacher, how can I
Enter heaven; tell me please."

"Only God is good," He said,
"First, God's bidding obey,"
And he answered,
"I've done so, every day."

Then the Savior looked down
On the young man of no guile,
And with love in His heart
He gave him a smile.

Said, "Sell all that you own
And give to the poor. Come
Follow me and help carry my
Cross to live ever more."

But sadly the man turned
And walked slowly away.
For the price was much more
Than he was willing to pay.

To his disciples, Jesus ob-
served it was a sad situation.
Too few rich men trade wealth
For the promise of salvation.

"Tis easier for a camel thr-
ough the eye of a needle to
pass." They asked, amazed,
"Then who has a chance?"

"Without God it's impossible,
For rich, poor or anyone, but
With Him in your life," said
Jesus, "all things can be done."

Then Peter reminded Him they
Had given all they held dear.
"Give your all; you'll gain
Much more." It was very clear.

"And in the world to come
After this world of strife,
You can be sure of a place
Of eternal life.

Famous people on earth may be
Of small consequence up there.
He who is a servant down here
Is homing in to heaven fair."

As they neared Jerusalem, the
Disciples were quite scared.
For the word of coming trials
Jesus had recently shared.

Sons of Zebedee requested,
In heaven to sit by His
Side. He asked, "Can you al-
so suffer as I am tried?"

"Yes," said the dreamers,
"We'd be true and unafraid."
"You may follow," He said,
"But the person's been named."

Ten who were left
Were now aware, brothers
James and John had tried
For the lion's share.

Jesus called them together
And said, "As you know, the
Arrogant of earth rule men
But to serve them are slow.

Among you it is not thus.
For if anyone will command,
He must start at the bottom
And be a servant to man.

Even I, the Messiah, am not
Here to be served but to
Help those in sin and
Give my life for the word."

Now later that day, when
Leaving the town of Jericho,
Bartimaeus, a blind man,
Was sitting by the road.

Hearing it was Jesus who
With a crowd was coming by,
Raised voice strong and
Loud, to Jesus he cried:

People called for silence,
But he called all the more.
Jesus said, "Send him here."
Asked, "What cry you for?"

"Oh teacher," he said, "I
Do so wish to see." Now
Jesus said, "You're healed,
You've great faith, indeed,"

Bartimaeus was overjoyed,
His sight was bestowed. He
Immediately followed Jesus
As He went down the road.

CHAPTER 11

At the Mount of Olives He
Sent disciples into town,
For a colt that was tied,
Said, "Bring him on down."

"What is this?" They were
Asked as they got the steed,
And answered as told, "Our
Master sent us; He has need."

They brought the colt to
Jesus, "A Royal charger," I
Might say, He rode down the
Street on that unusual day.

"Hail to The King,"
The multitude cried,
"He is kin of King David
And our national pride."

Thus He entered Jerusalem,
And to the Temple He went.
Then returned to Bethany
For the day was nigh spent.

Next day they returned for
There was much to do. Jesus
Was hungry on the way and
Checked a fig tree for fruit.

The tree was barren with
Not even a fig on a branch.
He said to that tree, "You
Will not bear fruit again."

Again to the temple, where
He ran money changers out,
Saying, "This is for prayer,
But thieves fill the house."

Then the priests and Jewish
Leaders decreed he must die.
But feared public opinion if
Not careful how they tried.

Next morn they were bound
For Jerusalem once more. As
They passed the fig tree,
A surprise was in store.

For it stood withered and
Dead, never again to bear.
Brought to His attention,
This wisdom he shared.

"If you have faith enough,
Tell this mountain to move
Away, if you truly believe,
Your command will be obeyed.

Anything you pray for will
Surely come to pass, if you
Forgive as you should and
Believe in what you ask."

When they entered the Temple,
The leaders came again, asked
Why He'd thrown the merchants
Out and a business stemmed.

Jesus answered, "Tell me this,
Was John the Baptist from God
Or man?" They couldn't answer,
For here the problem began.

People thought John a prophet
Who had been sent from God.
And with any other decision,
They'd raise pure hob.

If they sided with the people
Jesus would ask, "Why did you
Not believe him then?" With
Explanation a difficult task.

So they were stuck without
An answer at all. And Jesus
Didn't answer them, for they
Were effectively stalled.

CHAPTER 12

Now Jesus told a story of an
Entrepreneur of vision. He
Bought a vineyard to rent out
With servants in supervision.

When the harvest time arrived,
He sent others to collect.
But they ran into opposition
And barely saved their necks.

So he sent still others yet,
Hoping for a change of heart.
But those in possession
Were off to an evil start.

So he tried again, but they
Killed those he sent next.
So then he sent his son, sure
They'd show more respect.

But they planned to keep this
Business so illegally gained.
So they killed his only son,
To his great grief and pain.

You know what the owner will
Do! He'll not treat them well,
He will kill them one by one,
Rent the farm to someone else.

Jesus asked, "Do you remember
The stone builders rejected?
It became an important part
Of the building they erected.

This is the way of God, a
Fine thing to see." Then the
Jewish leaders who listened
Were very much displeased.

They recognized characters
In the stories that He told
And being cast as heavies
They felt was too bold.

They dare not move upon Him,
The people favored Him strong.
So got more spies and heck-
lers to show Him in the wrong.

"Is it right," they asked,
"For a man to pay a tax?"
Jesus, wise to the trickery,
Beat them at their own act.

Of the likeness on a coin,
He said "Engraved there is
Caesar, to him give his own,
It is his and only fair."

The Sadducees tried next
With a statement Moses made.
A widow should have children
With her brother-in-law's aid.

"Seven brothers took a wife,
Yet none produced an heir. If
She died too, which brother
Will be her husband up there?"

"You don't know scriptures,"
He said, "In resurrection,
(which you deny,) There is
No husband and wife.

You doubt the resurrection,
So about the burning bush
Moses saw, God claimed Ab-
raham, Isaac and Jacob, so
Give that some thought.

Though long go they died, `I
Am their God!' He said. That
Makes Him God of the living
And not a God of the dead."

A scholar who stood nearby
Approved of Jesus's retort. So
He asked Jesus, "Which law is
Of the greatest import?"

He said, "Love God with all
Your heart and soul Israel;
And the next is very like it,
Love all others as yourself."

The scholar smiled and said,
"I'm sure you've spoken true,
For there is only one God
And we owe Him our dues.

I know our allegiance to Him
Is more than sacrifices or
Temple Rites." Now Jesus said,
"You're worthy in His sight."

Those who'd been detractors
Started to keep profiles low.
Beside His wit and language,
They felt ignorant and slow.

"Your religious leaders say,
Messiah is of David's descent?
And if that is so," He added,
"Then what did David intend-

Through the Holy Spirit, He
Said, `God said to my Lord,
Sit here, I'll quell enemies,
And you'll have none to fear.'

Now if he said, 'My Lord,'
How could it possibly be,
That He be David's son or
Spring from his family tree?

Beware of scribes, pharisees,
Who devour widow's
    inheritance.
Who love to sit in full dress,
Make long prayers of pretense."

They watched the treasury;
Lavishly some people gave.
A poor widow gave a farthing,
All she'd been able to save.

Jesus said, "Note, she gave
The very last of her wealth.
Others gave of surplus, but
She gave all she was dealt."

CHAPTER 13

As they left the Temple one
Said, "Master please observe

All the beautiful buildings,
The craftsmanship superb."

"Yes," He said, "that's true.
But it will all collapse." "What
Will be a sign of this; how can
We know?" They asked.

"Many shall be the signs," He
Answered, "many be misled.
Many will claim God-hood
But belong to Satan, instead.

There'll be wars, rumors of
Wars, yet it shall not be
With famines and suffering
Across the land, over seas.

You'll be called into courts,
Urged to deny my name. Fami-
lies will spy on each other
In times of infamy and shame.

It will be an opportunity to
Show them when they're wrong.
But no time for weakness,
Trials will face the strong.

You'll be hated by all men,
And all for my name's sake.
But He who triumphs to the
End surely will be saved.

This will be that desolation of
Which the prophet Daniel told.
It has been long predicted
Since those days of old.

So when you see it coming
Quickly run for the hills.
Just thinking of those trials
Will give strong men chills.

Never has there been
Greater infamy in the world.

Nor will there ever be
In time to come unfurled.

Many times they'll tell you,
Here is Christ or there. To
Believe all signs and wonders
Means capture in their snares.

Take heed of all I say, for
They'll try to trip the elect.
But you've been pre-warned
Of what you can expect.

Now after the tribulation, the
Earth and heavens will change.
The moon will disappear, and
The sun will become orange.

Heavens shall be convulsed
And the stars appear to fall.
Then I will come in glory,
A living proof to all.

Then I will send angels over
The lands and farthest seas.
They'll find my people
And bring them all to me.

Remember now the fig tree.
It grows buds and leaves in
Season. When signs are
Right you'll have reason-

To know I have come. Heaven
And earth will disappear;
My word will stand forever,
And you'll know I am near.

But no one knows just when,
So watch for my return
And always be prepared by
Having salvation earned."

CHAPTER 14

Two days away was the feast
Of unleavened bread. Chief

Priests were planning, how
They'd put Christ to death.

They knew better than do it
During the time of feast, for
Then the people would cause
Trouble to say the least.

Mary of Bethany came to Simon;
At his house they stayed, he
Who'd been a leper before
Jesus improved his fate.

She put expensive perfume
In reverence on Jesus' head.
Then some disciples grumbled,
Not really under their breath.

They'd have her sell it and
Give the money to the poor.
Jesus said, "She did well;
The poor are here ever more.

My fate is already written,
She readies me for the grave.
It is a thing most fitting;
To this purpose it was saved."

Judas offered his services
To give Jesus to the priests.
They offered him a reward to
Carry out this infamous deed.

On the first day of passover,
Jesus sent disciples to town
To arrange for the meal on
This Jewish day of renown.

They found all as He'd said,
Down to the last detail. But
It always worked that way,
His words true without fail.

That evening as they ate,
He passed the startling word.

For one of them eating there
Would betray the Lord.

They were all concerned, and
Each pledged undying fealty.
In fact they went so far as
To stretch a fact of reality.

"Prophets forecast long ago,
He said, "I must die, of cou-
rse, he who will betray me
Will be sorry he was born."

He broke a crust of bread
And gave to each a piece. He
Asked blessing on it, saying
"This is my body, take, eat."

He passed the wine around,
Saying, "This is my blood,"
And told them all to drink
Of this cleansing flood.

"For this is shed for many
That they may live in love.
I'll not drink again 'til I'm
With my father above."

After a song they retired
A way up the mountain side;
He said, "The time is near,
So I'll be caught and tried.

You'll be scattered after
They've finished with me.
I'll go on ahead," He said,
"And meet you in Galilee."

Peter informed Him he'd be
Only true. Said Jesus, "Be-
fore the cock crows thrice,
I'll be denied by you."

Peter said vehemently, "No
Lord, I will die instead."
The others felt brave too,
At least so they all said.

At the garden of Gethsemane,
With Peter, John and James,
He went a little farther,
Left them while He prayed.

His spirit was sagging, for
He knew danger was near.
After an hour of praying,
To the three he reappeared.

They were sound asleep, and
They'd been left to guard.
"I left a chore to you,"He
Said, "and it was too hard."

Twice more He went to pray,
To go a different course.
"My will doesn't count," He
Prayed, "I bow to yours."

Each time He returned and
Found His disciples asleep.
Intentions were good, but
The flesh was totally weak.

He'd have said, "Sleep on,"
But it was time to rise, for
Camp was already breached
By that one who spied.

The soldiers came with all
Those priests and knaves.
Judas' kiss betrayed him to
Those with swords and staves.

As a criminal they took Him,
That prophecy be complete.
His disciples ran in terror
And in ignominious retreat.

But Peter stood his ground
And cut off a servant's ear.
Then mingled with the crowd
As he too succumbed to fear.

Yet he followed well behind,
To the palace of the priest.
Who was asking for a witness
To perjure himself at least.

Many bore false witness, and
Their claims did not agree.
Then two they found who'd try,
But still were not home free.

Then the high priest asked
Jesus, "Why not answer these
Claims?" But He answered not
And blunted the dirty games.

Then he asked Jesus, "Are you
The son of the blessed one?"
He said, "I'll be in clouds
Of glory when I come."

The priest rent his clothes,
Said, "Hear ye, what He said?
Blasphemy," they cried, and
Called out for His death."

Then He suffered their abuse;
They struck and spat on Him.
Thus they treated our Lord
Who was guilty of no sin.

Three times that night Peter
Was accused as Jesus' friend.
Twice he denied the claims,
And a third time once again.

The rooster heralded the morn;
Peter who had thrice denied,
Recalling Jesus' words, bowed
His head in shame and cried.

CHAPTER 15

Early next morning they met,
Elders and priests in debate,
A kangaroo court to assure,
Jesus' death to be His fate.

They sent Him to Pilot, who
Would have taken his side,
But they twisted the facts,
So by custom He was tried.

He was delivered under guard
And whipped and belittled.
They berated Him with curses,
The object of their spittle.

But He refused to recant for
Those things He had done.
And He truly did behave
Like the Great Father's Son.

Pilot tried to give them
Barabbas, the thief instead.
But the high priests were
Anxious to have Jesus dead.

So the mob was incited to
Demand Jesus' life. And
When Pilot asked why, they
Yelled "Crucify. Crucify."

To the cross He was nailed,
Amid remarks that were lewd,
Over his head hung a sign
Saying, "KING OF THE JEWS".

Two robbers were crucified,
With one on each side. Thus
He was counted as evil
On the day he died.

Darkness now fell at a time
Of normal light. From nine
In the morning until mid
After noon, like night.

He cried with a loud voice;
His spirit he dismissed. And
Now the veil of the temple
Was full length of it split.

A Roman officer on guard
Was impressed and surprised.
He said, "This man truly was
God's son the Christ."

Some women who'd followed
And administered other days,
Now watched in fear
But stayed well away.

But Joseph of Arimathea be-
longed to the court of the
Land, appeared now to Pilot
With a gentle demand.

And Pilot obliged by giving
Jesus' body to him. With
Fine linen and great care
He wrapped the body within.

To his own tomb, hewn from
A stone and one of the best,
He took Jesus tenderly
And laid Him to rest.

CHAPTER 16

After the Sabbath was over
The two Marys brought spice,
And they embalmed the body
Of their Savior the Christ.

As the sun rose next morn
They hurried to the tomb; it
Was full of horrors past,
Minds fogged by gloom.

They worried how they'd move
A great stone before the door.
But upon their early arrival,
Angels had been there before.

The rock was rolled aside, a
Young man sat there in white.
He said, Jesus had arisen,
Thus assuaged their fright.

Saying, "Go pass the word;
He lives and is in Galilee,
Send His disciples there;
It's where they will meet."

They were bewildered and
Too frightened to speak. I'm
Sure such an experience, and
My knees would grow weak.

Mary Magdalene saw Him first,
Hurried to spread word about.
Disciples were normal people
With minds still in doubt.

Later two disciples walked
And met Him on the road. But
Recognized Him not, though
Quite pointedly He spoke.

Then at the evening meal as
They were eating, appeared
He among them and rebuked
Their unbelieving.

He sent them into the world,
To give good news to men.
"Baptism and belief will
Save you, not condemn.

They'll have my authority,
Who believe and go my way.
Face danger, cast out demons,
Preach the word every day."

When He'd finished talking,
Up toward heaven did arise.
To sit at God's right hand
On a throne up in the skies.

Disciples roamed the land,
Taught and healed every
Where. Miracles performed,
Proves that He was there.

END OF MARK

LUKE

CHAPTER 1

Luke, the beloved physician
Tried to search out the truth.
In Revelations he wrote of
Jesus and John, in childhood,
And youth.

Zacharias was a Temple priest,
His wife of Aaron's descent.
Both of the priesthood but
Lives barren and far spent.

It was Zacharias' turn, the
Service of the Temple to per-
form. But an angel beside the
Altar was not the norm.

"Fear not," he told Zacharias,
"God has smiled on you today,
And He's sending the son, for
Whom you've so often prayed.

He will bring you joy you've
Missed but must be raised as
You're told. A child of wild-
erness like Elijah of old.

He'll be great in God's sight,
No drinking or gambling sin.
Many children of Israel will
Return to God because of him."

Zacharias doubted, said, "Can
You prove this to me?" "I am
Gabriel, whom God has sent,"
He said, "This way it will be.

You've doubted God's word!
`Till that day you'll be dumb."
As Gabriel'd said, Zacharias
Lost the use of his tongue.

With Temple services over, he
Returned again to his wife.
She knew in time she was
Giving the world new life.

"How wonderful," she said, "I
Appeared destined in life, to
Be incomplete and childless,
Failing my mission as a wife."

Now Gabriel was dispatched to
Galilee where a young lady
Lived. He told Mary, a virgin,
The best news He could give.

Soon she'd bear a child, such
As never known before. His
Fame would cover the world.
Loved by man in peace or war.

He shall be King of Israel,
Son of God, and son of man. A
Lineage of King David, prom-
ised of God ere Israel began.

He told her also of Elizabeth
Who'd bear one named John.
Mary visited, "Aunt Elizabeth,"
Who with pleasure did respond.

Three months she visited and
Then returned to her home.
She'd have God's Son, whose
Destiny was the royal throne.

Elizabeth's time was up, and
Her son was born one day. So
On the day of circumcision,
He was expected to be named.

She chose the name John, to
All the neighbors surprise.
And to the baby's father,
The name seemed right.

Wonder of wonders, he spoke,
His tongue in control again.
Everyone thought and remarked,
Sensing the Lord's hand.

Zacharias prophesied and pra-
ised the Lord for this deed.
"My son," he said, "will help
Guide mankind toward peace."

As Gabriel had said, John was
Rugged and strong. And as he
Grew up, his wilderness vis-
its were often and long.

CHAPTER 2

Caesar Augustus, the Emperor,
Decided he'd been too lax.
And to live the way he'd like,
He'd levy another tax.

So everyone must return to
His ancestral home. A long
And tedious journey for those
Who far afield had roamed.

Joseph, being of David's line,
Returned home to Nazareth.
Mary bore that precious babe
By whom all men are blessed.

There was no room in the inn,
So lodged in a stable nearby.
Cattle are said to have lowed
Answering the infants cry.

Shepherds on the hills were
Guarding their sheep at night.
When an angel appeared near-
by and calmed their fright.

"Do not be afraid," he said,
"I bring the most joyful news.
The Messiah is born tonight,
Who'll be King of the Jews.

You'll find Him in a manger,
In the town of Bethlehem."
Suddenly the hosts of heaven
Sang of good tidings to men.

The shepherds hurried to town,
To view this Holy Child. They
Told of heaven's choristers
And gazed with loving smiles.

Mary listened carefully to
The things she loved to hear.
Great things were ahead for
This child she loved so dear.

Upon the day of christening,
The name "Jesus" He received.
That was the angel's message
Even before He was conceived.

There were Simeon and Anna,
Who at the Temple spoke. They
Prophesied wonderful things
This child of God would show.

They fulfilled the law and
Returned to Galilee. There
Jesus grew strong and tall,
And the truth did early seek.

When He was twelve years old,
To Jerusalem they had been.
On the way home they realized
Jesus wasn't with them.

Three days they searched, and
In the temple He was found,
Amazing those learned men
By the knowledge He'd
  expound.

And so He returned with them,
Obedient to their every wish,
Gaining favor with God and
Man, Mary cherished all this.

CHAPTER 3

Tiberius Caesar reigned when
Pontius Pilot ruled in Judea.
Herod was Tetrarch of Galilee,
Phillip, a brother of Iturea.

John, known as the Baptist,
Preached the baptism of man.
Isaiah prophesied long ago,
This was part of God's plan.

"Make way through wilderness
The pathway of our Lord.
Repent all you vipers of sin,"
Was the message of his word.

"Change all of your ways
And look up to the heights;
Prove to our God before man
That you seek what is right.

Abraham is your father but
Cannot save you, you know,
And the ax of God's wrath
Can still lay you low."

People then asked, saying,
"What can we do?" John said,
"You can give of yourselves,
Give your coat and shoes."

The Publicans came also, say-
ing, "Now show us the way."
He replied, "Take only your
Due and adhere to fair play."

Even the soldiers did ask,
"How do we do what is right?"
He said, "Do violence to
None or worsen his plight."

All of them wondered, "Is it
The Christ who is sent?" As
They followed and listened
Wherever he went.

"I baptize with water," he
Said, one comes who's higher.
He'll bring the Holy Ghost
With the Spirit and fire.

His fan in His hand, He'll
Purge wheat from the chaff.
Salvation is His work,
And justice is His staff."

As time did unfold, Jesus
Came to Jordan's fair stream.
His baptism by John must
Have been like a dream.

As He prayed unto heaven
God opened the windows wide,
Saying, "This is my beloved
Son, in whom I take pride."

Jesus was of age about
Thirty years old, a direct
Descendant of God, as in
Scripture it's told.

Now John had made an enemy
Of Herodius, Phillip's wife,
Who'd married Herod, but
Now she sought John's life.

He was thrown into prison
Because of Herodius's urging.
When John said her behavior
Was in need of purging.

CHAPTER 4

When Jesus left the river,
The Holy Spirit urged Him
Go into the waste lands of
Judah; Satan got Him in tow.

For forty days of temptation;
Old Satan offered it all.
Jesus need only before the
Devil in worship fall.

Jesus knew of those wiles
And put Satan in his place.
"All riches belong to God,"
Told the devil to his face.

Finally, His temptations all
Over, back to Galilee came,
Preached in the Synagogue,
Enjoying near instant fame.

In Nazareth His early home,
Where He'd become a man, He
Got no credit as a prophet,
And here the trouble began.

He reminded them a prophet
Is not honored in his home.
They drove Him from the city;
Toward Capurnaum He roamed.

He taught with authority; and
Exorcised a demon one day.
People asked in awe, "What
Kind of man do devils obey?"

Stories spread like wildfire
Of one who healed at a word;
After a day at the synagogue,
There were others who heard.

Simon's mother-in-law, who
With high fever was in bed,
To health was restored when
He spoke and it fled.

They asked Him to stay, for
They'd like to have Him near.
But He said He must go, for
Reasons He made clear.

God's word he must spread;
Throughout Judea He must go.
In the synagogues and by-
ways He often taught it so.

CHAPTER 5

On shore of Lake Gennesaret
The multitude got so large,
He used Simon Peter's boat;
Here He made His charge.

When He'd finished speaking,
Told Peter, "Fish farther out."
Peter'd fished for nothing
All morning, tried in doubt.

So he moved the ship and
Cast the nets again. They
Caught so many fish as had
Scarce been seen by men.

It took two crews and boats
To hold the fish that day.
Peter suggested to Jesus
That He should go away.

"I'm such a sinner," said he,
"You'd best steer clear of me."
"You can be fishers of men,"
Said Jesus, "only follow me."

So now upon the shore, on
This auspicious day, Simon
Peter and Zebedee's sons
All adopted Jesus' way.

One day within a village He
Healed a palsied man. Many
The crowds that followed
As He taught across the land.

Often He retired into
The wilderness and prayed.
He needed to talk with God
To keep his strength all day.

Wherever he went, Jewish lea-
ders and teachers dropped in.
They tried hard to catch Him
In what they considered sin.

There was a sick man, whose
Friends lowered him through
A roof. As a fact of faith,
This should have been proof.

Jesus forgave his sins and
Immediately caused a rift,
Teachers and leaders cried
"Blasphemy; only God forgives."

"You should know," said Jesus,
"I can forgive men's sins. So
I'll say that he is healed
To show fallacy in your whims."

Now the man who'd been
  healed
Took his bed and walked away.
The people all marveled at
What they'd witnessed today.

Jesus met a tax collector, a
Man called Levi by name;
He invited him to follow,
And with alacrity Levi came.

Tax collectors were notorious
In those times as today.
Now Jesus and His disciples
Were invited to Levi's place.

The leaders and others cried,
"He eats with sinners." Jesus
Said, "I'm here to help these
Who are not social winners."

Next they complained His
Disciples did not fast, while
Others did so quite often,
So they took Him to task.

"The day will come," He said,
"My disciples will fast too.
As long as a I am here, it's
A thing they don't need to do.

One day I will die, and then
They'll want no food." Now
He quoted these parables
In an apparent change of mood.

"You'd not patch old garments
With cloth that is new;
It would tear too easily,
And little good would do.

Nor would you put new wine
In a wine skin that's too old.
The old skin would easily
Tear, little wine would hold.

So keep the old with the old
And the new with the new.
They will both keep better,
And taste better too."

CHAPTER 6

One Sabbath as they walked
In a field of ripened grain,
His disciples picked and ate
To assuage the hunger pains.

The Pharisees were watching,
As it seems they always were,
And quickly remarked, "Your
Disciples are illegal, sir!

Jewish law is explicit, says
Do not work the Sabbath Day,
But you people thresh and eat
The ripened kernels of grain."

"If You read the scriptures,
You would surely know, that
David's men ate shew bread
Said He, "Many years ago,"

"That was illegal too. But
For man was made the Sabbath
Day. I'm Lord of the Sabbath
And not the other way."

Again they questioned as He
Healed a man's withered hand.
Then He asked them a question,
Left no point to stand.

"Which is right, to heal or
Harm on the Sabbath day?" He
Asked. They could only grind
Their teeth and walk away.

Up the mountain he climbed,
Where He went to pray, and
After He returned, He chose
Twelve disciples that day.

Returning down the mountain,
A multitude gathered there.
Many wished to be healed;
His reputation had flared.

They vied with one another
To touch Him if they could.
For thus they were healed,
His mere presence was good.

To His disciples He said,
"Be not sad you're poor,
For the Kingdom of Heaven
Will one day be yours.

For you who weep there'll
Be happiness ahead. And if
Now you are hungry, your
Future promises bread.

If you lack friends on earth,
Are reviled because of me,
Count your blessings because
You're in good company.

Remember the early prophets;
They were treated thus too.
They will be waiting up in
Heaven to welcome you.

But pity the rich man here,
For he has all he could ask.
He sees no one in need; if
He did he'd leave real fast.

Consider the false prophet,
Whom the crowds praise. He
Will know sorrow in future;
It has always been that way.

Pray for God's blessings
On he who causes you pain.
If he hits you on the cheek,
Turn the other side again.

If he demands your coat,
Give your shirt as well.
If you love your enemies
Your godliness will tell.

Give gladly what you have,
By giving you'll get more.
Treating others as you'd be
Is always a pleasant chore.

If you only give to those
Whom you think will give to
You, there's no reward in
That, for so the sinners do.

Remember when you give, if
You measure, count and sift,
Your reward may be the same,
For it really wasn't a gift."

Jesus used illustrations,
"Can the blind lead the blind?
A student who is smarter than
His teacher will be in a bind.

How can you remove a speck
That blinds anothers eye,
If you can't see the log that
Is blocking your own sight?

A good tree produces fruit,
Is a joy to the taste, but
Brambles and thickets
Are nothing but a waste.

Good deeds from good hearts
Are most certain to flow.
A wicked man's skulduggery
Just naturally will show.

Why call me Lord, if you
Listen not to what I say? But
You build a strong foundation
As you listen and obey."

CHAPTER 7

So He preached to the people,
While back to Capernaum
  bound.
Then was met by Jewish elders
From that ancient town.

This centurion had a servant
Who was sick and near death.
And Jesus had become
The only hope he had left.

The pleas were urgent, for
He loved the Jewish nation.
He'd built them a synagogue,
Was a man of worthy station.

Just before Jesus arrived,
The man's friends came forth,
Saying that he felt unworthy
To impose upon the Lord.

He said, "Just say the word,
He'll be healed." Jesus mar-
veled then. "Such faith, is
Quite unusual among men."

So Jesus sent them home, and
This the scripture tells,

When next they saw that
Servant, he was hale and well.

The next day in His travels,
He went to a city called Nain.
They carried out a dead boy
As He came before the gates.

It was a sad procession, for
He was his mother's only son.
Jesus felt compassion, and
Said, "Back to life now come."

Of course, the boy revived,
Returned to a mother's love.
Then everyone did marvel
And feared great God above.

Jesus became famous as
He went about His mission;
John sent two disciples
To make a final decision.

"Are you the true Messiah?
Or look we for another?"
"Tell him what you've seen;
We see all men as brothers.

The lame are cured,
The sick are healed," said
Jesus, "and to the poor
The gospel is pealed.

The deaf are made to hear;
The dead, from death are
Raised. Blessed are they
Whom the Lord does praise."

When John's messenger left,
Jesus praised him to one and
All. "He is a true prophet,
Greater than duties call.

Yet the least in heaven
Is still greater than he."

And many there He baptized
Because they all agreed.

Pharisees, and teachers
Now did not follow Him.
"What can I say?" He said,
"They follow their whims.

John fasts and hungers,
And I eat whenever I can.
They claim John is crazy,
And I am a gluttonous man.

But one can always justify
His own inconsistencies."
He accepted a Pharisee's in-
vitation to his home to eat.

A woman of the street came
With some expensive perfume.
She poured it upon His feet
While there within the room.

She rubbed it on His feet
And tears she mingled there.
Simon, the Pharisee was
Amazed; he could only stare.

Then Jesus told a story of
Two men who floated a loan,
Borrowed from the same man,
The money was all his own.

One got five hundred, the
Other ten times as much.
When it came time to pay,
They both were out of luck.

A forgiving man, the Ben-
efactor forgave them both.
The question I ask now,
"Which will love him most?"

Simon answered, "One who
Owed most." "Ah yes, true,"

Jesus said, "it's the diff-
erence between her and you.

You feel no burden of sin,
Showed no courtesy at all.
She, appalled by sinfulness,
At my feet thus falls.

Her sins, which are many,
Are forgiven her today."
The Pharisees at the table,
Angry, had nothing to say.

CHAPTER 8

Then He began to tour the
Cities and towns of Galilee.
Along with disciples, some
Women and Mary Magdalene.

While a crowd gathered He
Told this story one day. "A
Farmer went out to sow,
The story is of that grain.

Some fell on a beaten path;
Birds ate it right away;
Some fell on thin soil, so
Flourished a few days.

Some landed in weeds, grew
But choked to death. Some,
In rich fertile soil and
Grew many times the rest.

Listen carefully," He said.
To His disciples explained,
Prophets predicted men will
Hear, no knowledge gained.

"I'll explain to you; few
Others will understand. So
Gather around, listen, to
Improve your knowledge span.

A hard path is like hearts
Of men. Satan steals words

Away. Rocky ground is any
Who believe but do not stay.

Thorny ground, weeds galore
Is like life's days of care.
Folks hear the words, believe,
Don't have strength to share.

Good soil belongs to honest
Folk, who listen and applaud.
With gladness they receive
And spread the word abroad.

Who would light a lamp and
Hide its light from us?
We know that lamps are
Meant to show light in dusk.

As men get more knowledge,
Light will brighten the day.
To he who has will be given;
From He who lacks shall be
Taken away."

His family visited one day
Couldn't get past the crowd.
When told of the situation,
Said, "It's what it's about.

Anyone who loves good, com-
mits his life to me, is my
Father, mother, sister and
Brothers, is truly family."

In the course of time, once
Again they crossed the lake.
Jesus curled up in the boat,
A much needed nap to take.

Wind and waves arose; the
Ship tossed to and fro. But
He slept on in peace, while
Fear did mount and grow.

"Master, we're sinking," they
Cried, waking Him from sleep.

He calmly addressed the storm,
And quickly calmed the deep.

He asked, "Where's your faith?"
But they were so amazed, they
Could only ask, "What kind of
Man does wind and sea obey?"

In the Gadarenes land one
Came. Homeless, spirit poss-
essed, who knew a world of
Pain and hopelessness.

In chains they'd bound him,
From fetters he broke free.
He fell to the ground before
Jesus, for relief did plead.

"What is your name?" Jesus
Asked, and he said, "My body
Is home to so many devils,
Legion should be my name."

The demons recognized Jesus,
Begged not to be cast in the
Pit. A herd of swine fed near-
by, so they asked to enter it.

Jesus granted their wish, and
Into the swine they did go.
The swine ran over a cliff
And perished in a lake below.

The herders ran to the city
And told the story in fear.
People were terrified and
Asked Jesus, to "Leave here."

The cured man wished to go,
But Jesus sent him on his way
To tell his story to people,
How God healed him that day.

Back over the lake Jesus went;
Many were awaiting Him there,

Those He'd helped in the past,
And more who were despaired.

Jairus, ruler of a Synagogue,
Whose daughter was near death,
Knelt before Jesus, begging
She might longer draw breath.

As they crowded around Him, a
Lady quietly touched His robe.
For years she'd been sickly,
And Jesus was her only hope.

"Who touched me?" He asked,
He'd felt healing powers flow.
Peter said, "In this crowd,
How could you possibly know?"

She who suddenly was healed,
Bowed, and admitted her act.
He said, "Daughter, faith has
Cured you; health is a fact."

Word came from the Synagogue,
Jairus' daughter had expired.
Jesus said, "Be of good faith
And see what transpires."

He went in with her parents,
And Peter, James and John,
Went to the bed of the maiden
Ignoring the wailing going on.

He said, "She lives," But
They knew she had died. So He
Took her hand and said, "Lit-
tle maiden, it's time to arise."

All were amazed as she arose;
She lived and was hungry again.
He told them,"Keep it secret;"
They should not tell any man.

CHAPTER 9

Soon He called His disciples
And gave them power to heal.

Authority to cast out demons
To help those who'd appeal.

"Take no cane," He said, "No
Food, money, or extra clothes.
And stay with only one family
In whatever town you go.

If they harass when you enter,
Shake their dust off your feet."
Thus they began their circuit
Of towns where they'd preach.

Stories of their miracles were
Common, as Jesus' fame spread.
Herod heard `twas John Baptist
Or prophet back from the dead.

The governor was disturbed, for
John he'd had killed. So the
Rumors running rampant
Must have given Herod chills.

Jesus' apostles all returned
And reported what they'd done.
Then slipped away to Bethsaida
As people followed on the run.

Once again He taught them of
A kingdom within their reach,
And always with compassion
Did He heal, and teach.

One evening the disciples
Worried; people had naught to
Eat. Five fishes, two loaves
Was it, and no other meat.

They were duly appalled, when
Jesus said, "Feed this crowd."
Jesus blessed what they had
And did themselves up proud.

Seating them upon the ground,
Five thousand plus ate that day.

Each ate his fill; they carried
Five baskets of scrap away.

One day Jesus asked, "Who do
They think I am?" "Elijah or
John Baptist or a prophet
Risen, says the average man."

"Who do you say," He asked,
Attention on Peter locked,
He answered, "You are Messiah,
The Christ of our God."

"Now then keep it a secret,
Tell no man," He said, "For
My enemies will afflict me
And shall preside at my death.

They'll capture and try me
With trickery and lies.
They also will kill me, but
In three days I shall rise.

If any will follow me,
Let Him forsake all he has.
For only what you give up
Will be yours and will last.

If your life is so precious
That you protect it at all
Costs, what good will it be
If your soul is lost?

One day I'll come in glory of
My Father, angels, and mine,
Too. I'll deny all doubters,
Will embrace those of truth.

Some who stand here now may
Live to see the day,
When the Kingdom of our God
Will brighten up his way.

Now He took Peter, James and
John up the mountain side to

Pray. Was transformed there,
Pure white of dress and face.

He spoke to Moses and Elijah
Of His impending death. Those
Three disciples were asleep
And awoke with baited breath.

Peter cried out in confusion;
He knew not really what, and
A bright cloud covered them;
Terror gripped like a knot.

A voice from the cloud said,
"This is my beloved son,
And if you'd listen to any,
He should be the one."

A long time those disciples
Waited and never told a soul.
Who would ever believe their
Story, if they were told?

Next day, once descended, a
Man came from the crowd, said,
"My son has a demon, your
Disciples couldn't cast out."

In exasperation Jesus said,
"Oh followers of little faith.
How long do I hold your hand
Through every step you take?"

So Jesus called the demon out,
Delivered the son He'd healed.
The people were all amazed;
God's power to all appealed.

He warned of His coming death;
His apostles spoke of heaven.
So He set a child among them,
Proceeded with their lesson.

"If you care for this child,
You have also cared for me.

The more you care for others,
Greater in heaven you'll be."

John told Jesus "We saw a man
Doing miracles in your name.
We forbade him doing this; he
Is encroaching on your game."

Jesus said, "Forbid him not;
He's obviously on our side.
And if he's not against us,
His help with us abides."

These days He traveled toward
Jerusalem and His fate. Some
Towns who knew His destinat-
ion turned Him away.

James and John were irked
And wanted to call down fire.
But Jesus gently rebuked them,
Insisting they hold their ire.

Someone offered to follow Him
No matter where He'd go.
"Animals have dens, birds have
Nests," He said, "But I've
No place called home."

Others would follow but had
Many things to do first. But
Jesus said, "My work must be
Done, for it only, thirst."

CHAPTER 10

The Lord chose seventy more,
As disciples to send ahead
To visit all those towns
Where He soon planned to bed.

Again He gave instructions to
Apostles He'd chosen anew.
Saying, "Pray for more help,
For there's so much to do.

As lambs among wolves I send
You, carry no cash or clothes.
Bless every home you enter,
Don't move from home to home.

If they're worthy of blessing,
It will surely stand.
But if it doesn't take,
Then go elsewhere so it can.

Eat or drink what they offer;
A worker is worth his wage.
Heal the sick and tell them
God's Kingdom is in place.

If a town rejects you, shake
Its dust off your feet. "Say,
"You were very close to God,
As we walked your streets.

Even wicked Sodom will fare
Better, facing Judgment Day.
Chorazin and Bethsaida owe,
And they will surely pay.

If Tyre or Sidon had seen my
Miracles, they'd have repented
Long ago. Even Capernaum's
People shall be brought low."

He said to His disciples,
"Accepting you, they welcome
Me. And if they do that, they
Are accepting God, you see."

Those returning disciples
Reported great success for
The seventy returning, had
Cast out devils with the rest.

"To walk safely with an enemy,
I gave you what you need," He
Said, "if your names are written
In heaven, it's a greater deed."

He said, "I thank you Father,
For all things you've shown
To these with a child's faith,
And to famous men, unknown.

I am my father's messenger,
Whom I know, and He knows
  me.
And no one else can know Him
Unless by me revealed."

Then to the twelve, He said,
"Prophets of days gone by, for
The experience you have had
Would have given a mighty cry."

There was a man of education,
Who this question asked, "If a
Man would live forever, what
Is his most important task?"

Jesus asked, "What do the laws
Of Moses say?" "Love God with
All your heart, mind and
Soul," he said, "always."

"Love a neighbor, as yourself,
But who will that be?"
"There was once a Jew, who
Was mugged by thieves.

He lay beside the road brui-
sed, crippled and bleeding,
A Jewish priest and Levi pas-
sed, didn't heed his pleading.

Then a Samaritan came along,
Who rescued and nursed him
Well. Who then was a
  neighbor?"
"The Samaritan," he answered,
"It was easy to tell."

"That is true," said Jesus,
"And compassion is our game.

So now as you go on your way,
Be sure you do the same."

There were two sisters at
Whose home they stopped.
One listened to Jesus, the
Other did household jobs.

To Martha this was unfair.
Jesus said, "Don't fret,
Come listen to me! Mary is
OK, it's a good way to be."

CHAPTER 11

A disciple asked, "Master,
Please teach us to pray!"
He answered, "When you do,
It should be this way:

Holy Father in heaven, we
Do honor to your name. May
Your Kingdom come soon;
Grant us food every day.

Forgive our sins, as we
Forgive others. Don't let
Us be tempted, and may we
Treat everyone as brothers."

He taught the importance
Of continuing on in prayer.
If you keep on praying,
Your answer will be there.

If you continue to ask,
In time He will respond.
He'll give you the help
If you'll only keep on.

Even sinners who love kids,
Are sure to give in;
Much more, our Father will
Teach you how to live.

Just ask, He will grant the
Holy spirit to those in need.

But you must ask and believe,
To accomplish this good deed."

They said He worked for Satan,
Because of demons exorcised.
He said "No kingdom can stand,
If it's divided into sides.

If I draw strength from Satan,
How do your priests get power?
For they cast out demons too,
Is Satan the man of the hour?

One must be greater than he,
If you would drive him hence.
To be against or for me is
The thing that makes sense.

If a demon leaves a man and
Wanders thirsty with no rest.
And returns to where he was,
Finds it neat and well kept,

So calls seven of his friends
To live where he was before.
The man whose body they enter
Is at least seven times worse."

"Blessed is she who bore you,"
A lady in the crowd cried.
"So are those who listen."
He replied.

"You ask proof I'm the messiah,
But I remind you of Jonah, in-
stead. He proved to Nineveh
God sent him," Jesus said.

"The things you have seen
Should be ample to prove
That I have been sent here
To serve as a prophet to you.

At Judgment, the Queen of
Sheba, who went to Solomon's

Land, will judge you for not
Heeding one greater than man.

Nineveh listened to Jonah;
One greater than man is here.
But you just will not listen;
You've no sense, or fear.

A lamp is made to show light,
Not to let darkness prevail.
If your eyes see Gods wonders,
Your life will love detail."

He was invited by a Pharisee
To eat a home cooked meal.
Jesus did not wash His hands;
His host, surprised, appealed.

It was a Jewish ceremony and
A custom of their land. Jesus
Said, "You can wash the skin,
But still be a dirty old man.

Now God made the inside as
Well as the outer skin. Puri-
ty is demonstrated best by
Generosity of the man within.

You tithe slightest earnings,
Forget about justice or love.
You sit in choice seats and
Leave what is good undone."

A religious law expert said,
"You've insulted my work too."
"Yes," said Jesus, "you make
Impossible rules; Pharisees
Are no worse than you.

You are like your ancestors
Who killed prophets long ago.
You'd have done so yourselves
And are destined for woe."

Of course they were furious
With this man they detested.

They plied Him with questions,
Hoping He'd slip, be arrested.

CHAPTER 12

The crowds grew in size; He
Turned to His disciples, said,
"Beware of pretentious men
Nor let claims turn your head.

Hypocrisy can't be hidden;
The facts will emerge in time.
Don't fear those who'd murder,
For that is their crime.

Fear God, who can kill and
Can cast your soul into hell.
Knows the value of a sparrow,
Hairs on your head as well.

You're greater than sparrows,
Before heaven I'll declare,
You were friends upon earth,
You befriended me there.

I'll deny before the angels,
Any who deny me before men.
But to deny the Holy Spirit
It can well mean the end.

If Jewish rules cause trials,
Don't worry about what to say.
The Holy Spirit gives words
And will show you the way."

Someone called from the crowd,
"Make my brother share with
  me."
"You worry too much," said He,
"Over things such as these.

Never covet what's another's or
Worry about how to get wealth.
Life is uncertain at best; how
Can you count on good health?

A rich man owned a farm, and
Harvest was good one year. He
Tore down the barns and built
Larger to house riches dear.

That night he died; no good
From his wealth would he see.
Earth's riches are fleeting;
God will care for your needs.

Don't fret for what you lack,
For God's plans are for you.
Make His Kingdom your
  concern;
Your life will be happier too.

Heaven is a haven of safety,
Thieves or rust don't abide.
Be ready for the Holy Fathers
Return; enjoy life at His side.

You know not the time of His
Coming; it will be like a joy
In the morning. So be ready
And waiting, don't worry, for
You'll get a warning."

"Lord, to whom do you speak?"
Asked Peter. Jesus said, "To
Everyone dependable and
honest, there's a place in the sun.

He who is drunken and cruel,
The master may give no
  warning.
For him will the party be over,
To face a future of mourning.

One doing wrong unknowingly
May hope for punishment light.
He of knowledge and ability,
Decisions had better be right.

I've come to bring change, and
I wish my job were complete.

My trial ahead is most awesome,
I'm tense, till fate I meet.

Much division will follow me;
Families will split in beliefs.
Some will swear by the law,
But others will follow me.

South wind warms the weather,
Cloud build up precedes rain.
But you notice few warnings
That can cause you great pain.

Meet an accuser half way; try
To settle claims that prevail.
Better to settle out of court
Than chance going to jail."

CHAPTER 13

Some Jews of Galilee died, as
They sacrificed in the Temple.
"Were they great sinners?" He
Asked, "Were they murdered
As Examples?

Recall the eighteen men who
Died when Siloam's tower fell?
Were they terrible sinners?
But you're too wicked to tell!

Change your ways at once,
Look to heaven's fair land.
Else you will surely perish
Like any other sinful man.

Yet, God is like the gardener
Whose master condemned a tree.
For it had borne no fruit for
Years, at least two or three."

"Cut it down and burn it,"
Was what the owner said.
"It has never produced a fig,
So it might as well be dead."

His gardener begged him to
Wait, saying, "I'll weed and
Fertilize. And if it produces,
I hope you agree it was wise."

One Sabbath He preached, as
To the Synagogue a lady came.
Jesus healed her as He had
So many other sick and lame.

The keeper of the Synagogue
Gave an angry shout. "Do your
Healing during the week. Rest
Is what the Sabbath is about."

"Don't be a hypocrite," said
Jesus, "You work on the Sabb-
ath day, you give your cattle
Water and also feed them hay.

So why is it so bad to Reli-
eve this lady's pain? For
Eighteen years Satan had her,
But now she's healthy again."

His enemies were shamed, and
The people impressed by His
Deeds. He told them a parable
About the tiny mustard seed.

"Heaven's Kingdom," He said, "is
Like mustard seed in ground.
It grows like a tree until it
Shelters birds that abound.

It's like yeast that is set
And is kneaded like dough. It
Silently works to do the job
For which it is known."

On, ever onward He travelled;
Steadily toward Jerusalem He
Went, teaching the glory of
Heaven, the job for which He'd
Been sent.

Someone once asked Him,
"How many will be saved?"
He answered, "Many try, but
For many 'twill be too late.

Very hard you must work,
If you would enter there, for
Once the door has been closed,
Very poorly you will fare.

From the darkness you will
Cry to be let in."
He'll say, "I know you not,
So go back to your sin."

You'll say, "Lord, remember,
You taught on our street." But
You'll be stuck where there's
Weeping and gnashing of teeth.

You will see in the Kingdom,
All those prophets of old.
But you may find yourself
Left out in the cold.

But many will make it, whom
You never would have believed.
And others you thought saints
Will be left out to grieve.

Then some Pharisees said,
"Herod is looking for you.
You'd best make yourself sca-
rce, or he'll do you in too."

Jesus said, "Tell that old fox
I'll keep on with my endeavors.
Today and tomorrow with deeds
Of healing as busy as ever.

One day I'll enter the city
That murders God's prophets.
For I've a destiny I'll meet,
And no one will stop it.

Oh Jerusalem, I'd gather you
As a hen protects her brood.
But you will be desolate, be-
cause you're never in the mood.

Never again will you see me
Until that time when you say,
Welcome, to He who comes in
The Lord's name, on judgment
    day."

CHAPTER 14

In the house of a Pharisee
Where Jesus went to dine,
They watched Him like a hawk
To accuse Him of crime.

A man with dropsy was there,
Whom Jesus would likely heal.
So to their querulous natures,
He addressed this appeal.

"Is it lawful to heal, to do
Good on the Sabbath day?"
They all refused to answer,
Not a word would they say.

Soon the deed was done; the
Man was healed and went way.
Then Jesus faced His silent
Accusers and had this to say.

"If you owned an animal, and
On Sunday it fell into a pit,
Must you wait till the day was
Over before you rescued it?"

Again they had no answer to
A man who read their thoughts.
But He was always watched;
His life with danger, fraught.

Now He'd noted how the guests
Had vied for favorite rooms.

He said, "If invited to a wedding and wish the respect of the groom-

Don't choose the best position
Lest your host put you down.
Just keep your profile low;
Your reward may be profound.

For he who would be great,
May find himself brought low,
But he who is humble and just,
Everyone will want to know.

When you would have a feast,
Invite the poor, the halt, or
Lame." To his host He said
"To them it really is no game.

Rich friends and relations
Can return the favor to you.
But help those in need; and
Get their blessings too."

"Blessed is He who will enter
God's Kingdom," one called,
For one there understood,
Within that Pharisee's walls.

Now Jesus told this story of
A man hosting a great feast.
All of those invited guests
Made excuses to be released.

So the master sent a servant
Out into the city streets.
"Bring anyone you find, all
Those you chance to meet."

The servant reported, "It is
Done, with room to spare."
He said, "Search thoroughly,
Bring all you find out there.

So there will be no room
For those I invited first.

And those who honor my offer
Won't know hunger or thirst."

Multitudes followed the Lord;
He turned to them and taught,
Explaining Heaven's Kingdom,
Showing it cannot be bought.

Saying, "To go with me, man
Must leave all else behind.
He'll bear his cross and
Follow, if he would be mine.

So do not make great plans,
Unless you count the cost. If
You start but cannot finish,
All your effort is lost.

What king would rush to war
Without first taking account,
And has men and equipment,
A winning battle to mount?

So if you can't do the job,
Don't try bluffing it through.
Forsaking all you have, is
The thing that you must do.

Salt is good for flavoring.
If it lost its taste, what
Then? It is no longer fit for
Food, nor is it good for men.

Now if you've ears to hear
Be sure you listen well.
For there is much to learn,
More than voice can tell."

CHAPTER 15

Sinners and outlaws came!
Jesus didn't discriminate.
Jewish leaders complained,
Calling it a terrible state.

He told them these parables:
"A man lost one of a hundred

Sheep. He looked for the one,
Went without food and sleep.

When he found it, he carried
It home with great pleasure.
Overjoyed by his success,
As though it were treasure.

To save the one that's lost,
Brings us joy that's untold.
When we know the ninety nine,
Others are safe in the fold.

Another He told of a woman,
Of ten valuable coins she had.
One got lost, she searched
And swept and was very sad.

Diligently she looked,
And when it was found she
Rejoiced and called all
Her friends to come round.

Such is the joy in heaven
When one sinner comes home.
For those others are safe
Who hadn't the urge to roam.

And there was the story
Of the prodigal son. He
Wanted his inheritance now!
Then took off on the run.

To a far country he went, and
His substance he squandered.
Now famine covered the land
To which he had wandered.

Finally he found a job as
The caretaker of swine. But
His mind wandered homeward
In just a matter of time.

What he fed to the pigs
Was appetizing these days.

Soon the good old times at
Home seemed very far away.

So he returned to his father,
Who saw him coming with joy.
He killed the fatted calf,
To honor his returning boy.

His brother who'd been home
Was unhappy to say the least.
He'd worked for his father
Without party or feast.

The father said, "Dear son:
All that I have belongs to
You. So please don't let
Yourself get into a stew.

For your brother was lost,
And we thought he had died.
But now he is back,
And we know he's alive."

CHAPTER 16

Again, He said, "This rich
Man a steward employed. But
While keeping the records
With the figures he toyed.

Word got to the boss, that
Man was on the shady side.
The servant was called in
And questions were plied.

"Get your business in order
And plan to hit the road,"
Said his master, unhappy
Because he'd been snowed.

This steward, being crafty,
Went to those owing the boss.
Reducing their debts to him,
Employed the old double-cross.

Now his master admired this
Mans making of friends,

But didn't appreciate having
To pay in the end.

"So do not buy friends
Through cheating," He said,
"For honesty in all things
Is the best way to get ahead.

If dishonest in small things,
Who'll trust you in more? If
My money's not safe with you,
I can't trust you for sure!

You cannot serve two masters.
You will love one, the other
Despise. Or enter His Kingdom,
If money is all you prize."

Pharisees loved money, and
They laughed Him to scorn.
Pious, noble in public, but
Not willing to be warned.

People saw them as heroes;
God saw their pretense. Be-
fore John the Baptist, laws
Of Moses made sense.

John introduced good news,
God's Kingdom to come soon.
Great multitudes came to
Learn of this great boon.

The law is in full force;
The same has always been,
Solid as heaven or earth,
A certain guide for men.

A divorce without cause
To marry another is wrong.
To marry an adulteress
Is to join a sinful throng.

A rich man lived in the
Lap of luxury, so to speak.
A beggar named Lazarus sick
With sores on the street,

Lay by the rich man's gate,
In hunger did call. The
Rich man lived in splendor,
Paid him no heed at all.

In time they both died,
Each went to his reward.
The rich man went to Hades;
Lazarus went to his Lord.

Now the rich man looked up
From torment he endured, to
See Lazarus in Paradise,
Well and happy, all cured.

He asked Lazarus be sent
To give relief from pain.
Just a drop of water on his
Tongue would be a gain.

"In life," said Abraham, "You
Were rich, things were fine.
Lazarus needed your help, but
You gave no money or time.

And now there is a gulf
Between us and you. So we
Cannot visit each other,
Even if we wanted to."

The rich man begged Abraham,
"Send him back where we lived.
Help to father and brothers,
I would hope he could give."

But then he was told, "The
Scriptures told them before.
It won't do any good
To warn them any more."

CHAPTER 17

"Temptation is present," said
Jesus, "but woe the cause. He
Might better drown in the sea;
That would be a minor loss.

For harming a child, there is
Great punition in store. If a
Brother sins against you,
Always forgive him once more."

Someone asked, "Lord, add to
Our faith!" "With faith as a
Mustard seed," He said, "by
Command alone, you can uproot
A mulberry tree.

Do you thank a servant to do
The job that he ought? As
When you obey me, it is the
Duty which you were taught."

Traveling toward Jerusalem
He met ten lepers one day,
And after healing every one,
He sent them on their way.

They reported to the priests
And realized they were clean.
Then one ran back to Jesus
To thank Him once again.

Jesus noted this paradox,
Only one returned of ten.
This is so true of people,
They behave much like men.

The Pharisees wanted to know,
"When will the Kingdom
  appear?"
He said, "It is something you
Can't see, but it may be near."

None can say, "It's here or
There or now or when. For
The Kingdom of God, you see,
Is within the hearts of men."

To disciples He said, "Soon
You'll look in vain for me.
Hearing I'm here or there,
Those things do not believe.

Like lightning in the sky, my
Coming will be known to all.
I must suffer terrible things,
Ere to my home I'm called.

This nation will reject me,
And people as in Noah's day,
Will eat, drink and be merry,
Expect tomorrow, the same.

As in Lot's day everyone went
About his own fickle life.
Fire and brimstone destroyed
Them, and what about his wife?

Who clings to his life will
Lose it, who gives it shall
Gain. Two may be together and
One shall be taken away."

"Where taken to?" a disciple
Asked, and this He answered,
"Wherever the body, it is
There the vultures gather."

CHAPTER 18

"There was a judge," He said,
"Who feared not God nor man.
He listened to a widow's plea
For vengeance time and again.

At first he did not heed her,
But she pleaded all the more.
Then he finally did give in,
Because it became a bore.

So you see if an evil judge
Can give in, how much more
Your heavenly Father, who
Listens and knows no sin!

God will give justice surely
If you plead day and night.
The question, when I return,
How many will see the light?

There was once a Pharisee
Who felt holier than other
Folks. When He prayed aloud,
Ridicule at others he poked.

But the man he picked on
Beat His chest and cried for
God to forgive his sinful ways
With no arrogance or pride.

This sinner, not the Pharisee,
Returned home forgiven. For
The proud shall not be honored,
But the humble, justice given."

Mothers brought their children
For Jesus to touch and bless.
Disciples ordered them away;
No doubt to save him stress.

Then Jesus called them over,
Saying, "Let children come to
Me. The Kingdom is peopled
By hearts as trusting as these."

A rich young ruler once asked,
"Good master, what should I do?
For I would enter the Kingdom
And be much more like you."

"Only God is good," said Jesus,
"You know what the command-
ments say." "Yes," he answered,
"I've Honored them from early
     days."

"Go sell your wealth," Jesus
Said, "give the money to the
Poor." The man sadly left, for
Just the thought hit him sore.

Jesus sighed, "It's easier for
A camel to traverse a needles
Eye, than for a rich man to
Enter heaven and abide."

"Just who can be saved?"
Someone then asked. He
Answered, "God can do what
To men is a hopeless task."

Peter reminded Him, "We've
Left homes to follow you."
Jesus replied, "You'll be
Rewarded for what you do."

Jesus tried to tell them
Of His fate in days ahead.
They had no understanding
Of all the things He said.

Along the road to Jericho a
Blind beggar sat by the way.
As they were passing by, he
Was heard to loudly say-

"Oh Jesus, Son of David,
Please have mercy on me.
I am blind and wretched,
And you can make me see."

Jesus pausing, said, "Be
Healed. Faith has made you
Free." Instantly he healed
And like others could see.

He followed them praising
God, as all others there.
They had seen a miracle,
And his joy they shared.

CHAPTER 19

Zacchaeus was a rich man,
And a tax collector too.
So he was in ill repute
With most all other Jews.

He wanted to see Jesus so
Climbed into a tree. For he
Was short of stature; it was
The only way he could see.

As they passed by, Jesus cal-
led, "Zacchaeus, come down,
For I would spend some time,
As a guest in your house."

The crowds were displeased
At a sinners home He'd stay,
But Zacchaeus was so happy
He had this to say.

"Lord, I'll henceforth give a
Half of my wealth to the poor.
If I've cheated any a dollar,
I'll surely refund them four."

"A son of Abraham," said He,
"Who's been lost on the way,
I've come to search for such
As he, who's gone astray."

He didn't want the people to
Think the kingdom would now
Appear, so He told them this
Story as Jerusalem drew near.

Now a nobleman was called
To be king of the land. Ten
Assistants he called, and
Gave money to each man.

Someone rebelled, sent word
To him they'd never submit.
When he returned, he called
In the keepers of his mint.

One had multiplied by ten,
Funds entrusted to his care.
Another increased his by five,
But another one was scared.

The king commended the first,
Said, "Ten cities you shall
Govern." Then he listened to
Reports of all those others.

He who multiplied by five
Was given five cities to rule.
He who'd hidden his in fear,
The king considered a fool.

This one had hidden the money
Rather than give usury. The
King said, "You thought I was
Hard; you're right about me.

Take what this one had, give
It to the one with ten." "He
Doesn't need it," they said,
"He's richer than most men."

The King agreed with them,
Saying, "Yes, it's very true.
To he with much will be given
He without may lose that too.

Now go get those other rebels
Who refused to follow me.
Bring them into my presence,
And their execution I'll see."

Travelling toward Jerusalem,
He sent two disciples ahead,
Where they'd find a donkey's
Colt; it was as He'd said.

They found it tied and were
Asked why take it away? they
Answered, "We take it to our
Master," as He'd said to say.

And so they brought the colt,
For Jesus to ride into town.
Upon the road ahead of Him,
People laid clothing down.

Down the Mount of Olives they
Came, a company of disciples
In voice, cried "Glory to God,
For His mighty works rejoice."

Pharisees bade Him quiet them,
He said, "No, let them alone.
Quiet them now, and there'd
Be cheers from these stones."

As they came to Jerusalem, He
Began to bitterly weep, said,
"You rejected my work, lost
The chance for eternal peace."

At the Temple, He made bus-
iness men leave. "This place
Is for prayer," He said, "you
Make it a den of thieves."

In the Temple He taught each
Day, as His enemies contrived;
But they feared the people,
For their hero had arrived.

CHAPTER 20

Teaching there one day was
Challenged by priests. Driving
Merchants from the Temple
Could help people like these.

"Where is your authority,"
They asked, "to throw people
Out? We think you were wrong,
You don't have so much clout."

He said, "I'll show my author-
ity but first answer me this.
Was John the baptist from God,
Or were his reasons only his?"

Now however they answered,
Trouble would be their lot.
If from God, why not believe?
But if not, they feared a mob.

John was considered a prophet.
So answered, "We don't know."
He said, "Nor do I tell you."
So again He stole the show.

He turned to the people again,
This story he revealed. "A man
Planted a vineyard, and left,
After he rented out his fields.

At harvest he sent a servant
To collect a share of increase.
They beat and mauled his man,
Didn't live up to the lease.

And then he sent another, but
The same thing happened again.
And when he sent a third, he
Too returned, a beaten man.

So he finally sent his son,
Of whom he was very proud.
His son was thus exposed
To this deadly crowd.

When they saw him coming,
They plotted his early demise.
Like all other criminals, they
Thought themselves quite wise."

"Let's kill him," they said,
"Then it will all be ours."
"What will the master do, on
Hearing of this wicked hour?"

"God forbid," they exclaimed,
"No man should kill another!
He'll kill them all and rent
That vineyard to others."

"What does the scripture mean,
When it speaks of the corner
Stone, rejected by builders,
But now came into its own?

If any fall upon the stone,
He shall be broken. Whom it
Falls upon will be pulverized,
Leaving not a token."

Those priests and scribes,
Wished Him in their clutch.
They knew He'd ridiculed them
But feared people too much.

They observed His every move,
So to prove Him a wicked man.
They'd give Him to the author-
ities or governor of the land.

One question they asked was,
"Is it lawful to pay taxes or
No?" knowing their game, He
Asked, "Why tempt me so?"

He said, "Show me a coin,"
Caesar's likeness was there.
"Give Caesar what is Caesar's,"
He said, "give God His share."

Again they were foiled and
Beaten at their own game. So
Marveled and kept the peace,
And you'd think were ashamed.

They rejected resurrection so
Asked about the woman who
Married brothers. As Moses's law
Required. Each one died, and
She married another.

Each one died without heirs,
To all as required, she was
Wife. Who would she belong to
In heaven when she died?

"Marriage is common here. In
Life after this one, not so.
But equal then to angels," He
Said. "Back to death can't go.

Dead now live, Moses showed,
At the burning bush. He spoke
To Abraham, Isaac and Jacob's
God, and He made no joke.

He is God of the living," to
The Sadducees Jesus then said.
"His people all live forever;
He is not the God of the dead.

Why call Christ David's son?
For in Psalms David said, the
Lord said unto my Lord, sit
At my right hand, while on
Your enemies I let you tread."

Often He silenced enemies
Much as He did this one. "If
David called Him Lord then
How can He be David's son?"

He said to His disciples,
"They love Synagogue seats;
Beware of pious experts who
Act holy but often cheat.

They devour poor and widows,
Pray loudly on the street.
They'll receive damnation
As God to His face they meet."

CHAPTER 21

A collection box was located
Quite near the Temple doors.
The rich gave of abundance;
There were gifts by the poor.

A poor widow dropped in hers,
Apparently all she owned.
"Her heart is bigger than the
Others," He said, "she's shown."

His disciples admired stone
Work and beauty on the walls.
"It'll all be rubble," Jesus
Said, "it'll crumble and fall."

"When?" they asked, "And how
Can we know the time?" "Don't

Let any deceive you," he said,
"By claims and false signs.

There'll be wars and rumors,
Earthquakes, famines and such.
There will be floods and tyr-
anny not to enjoy very much.

You'll be hunted and harried
Because you trust in my name.
So The Messiah will be known
And also gaining fame.

Fret not what to say when
Before court you are called.
I'll give you words; you'll
Never for wisdom be stalled.

Even brothers will witness;
Your families will persecute.
Because of my name, but
Your soul will live through.

Stand firm, do not waver, as
Toward eternity you wend.
You who follow only me, your
Spirit will win in the end.

When Jerusalem is blocked,
Armies of destruction arrive,
Oh Judah, flee to the hills,
Hurry, escape and survive.

God's judgment day has come,
Prophecies will be fulfilled.
Mothers and families must
Into exile go or be killed.

Gentiles will try Jerusalem
To end in God's own time.
With evil omens and portents,
Raging seas, monsterous tides.

The sun and moon will change;
Earth in turmoil will be. The

Heavens a fearful sight, and
People of earth will see me.

In a cloud of glory I'll come,
Stand straight, do not fear.
This is a sign you can trust;
You'll know salvation is near.

When the fig tree blossoms
You know the season is near.
When you see what I describe,
God's Kingdom is almost here.

Heaven and earth shall pass;
My word will ever be true. So
Watch and pray to be ready
On the day I'll come for you."

Each day at the Temple, He
Taught to great crowds. Each
Evening He was at the place
Of olives called "The Mount."

CHAPTER 22

Now passover time approached,
A big celebration by the Jews.
Leaders wanted to kill Jesus,
But a riot would be bad news.

Then Judas Iscariot weakened
And fell to temptation's spell;
Approached the chief priests
With information to sell.

Of course they were excited
And offered him a reward. So
He went ahead with trickery
That he could ill afford.

Jesus sent James and John,
When the passover day arrived,
To find a room for the feast,
And this He prophesied.

"In Jerusalem, you'll see a
Man carrying water down the

Street. Follow to his master,
And that is where we'll eat."

Sure enough, it was so! And
With a room ready upstairs.
So they prepared the meal for
When all the rest got there.

While at table He said, "Long
I looked forward to this meal,
I'll not eat or drink again,
Until Gods Kingdom is real."

He broke the bread and said,
"Eat, in remembrance of me.
The Wine you drink is a token
Of blood and pardon for thee.

One of you will betray me,
At this table as a friend.
It is God's plan I must die,
I weep for this man's end."

The disciples wondered aloud,
Who this could possibly be,
Each one must have thought,
"It couldn't possibly be me."

But the discussion shifted to,
Who in heaven would be first.
Typical men they were, who
For authority thirst.

"In this world," Jesus said,
"Kings and great men order
Slaves to do as told, no
Matter if freedom they crave.

Among us, in these times, he
Who serves will be great. You
Who've stood by me these days,
In my Kingdom will rate.

You will sit at my table and
Can be there with just pride.

You'll sit on thrones to
Judge Israel's ten tribes."

"Peter, " He said, "Satan has
Asked to make you fail. But
I've prayed you'd have faith
And not follow his trail."

Peter answered, "Lord, I will
Drink of the cup as you do.
I'll follow to jail or death,
I will be there with you."

But sadly Jesus informed him,
"Ere a rooster crows tomorrow,
You will deny me three times
Very much to your sorrow.

When I sent you to preach."
He asked, "with no money, or
Duffel or clothes, did you
Lack anything for your task?"

"Never a problem," they in
Unison declared. "The people
Took us in, and whatever was
Needed they gladly shared."

"Now the time of prophecy,"
Said Jesus, "has come due.
I'll be judged a criminal
And be betrayed to the Jews.

So sell what you have and
Buy a weapon for protection.
Your lives are in jeopardy,
And you'll suffer rejection."

They left the room and went
To the mountain for prayer.
He said, "Pray for faith and
Strength while there."

He left His disciples and
Walked about a stones throw

Away. In sorrow and agitat-
ion, He knelt down to pray.

"Father, if it's your will,
Remove this trial from me.
But if it must be done,
Then let it surely be."

As He prayed in agony, an
Angel from heaven came down
To cheer Him as great drops
Of blood fell to the ground.

He returned to His disciples,
Found them fast asleep. He
Said, "Awake, pray sincerely,
That this vigil you may keep."

Then Judas, leading the mob,
Came, kissed Him on the cheek.
For he had sold his soul
And had a bargain to keep.

Jesus chided him gently for
The awful thing he had done.
The others, reading signs,
Would fight for God's son.

One slashed with a sword,
Cut off a servant's right ear.
Then Jesus bid them be calm
And not shed any blood here.

He touched the wounded man;
The ear was restored. "Am I
A robber?" He asked them,
"Must you have clubs or swords?

Each day I was at the
Temple, you made no arrest!
Today Satan reigns supreme;
You are slaves at his behest."

So they seized and led Him,
To the home of a high priest.

Then Peter following the mob
Came and joined with these.

The soldiers had built a fire;
Peter was miserable and cold.
A servant girl recognized him;
Of course it was she who told.

Peter denied fearfully, say-
ing, "I know not this man."
Later on too he was accused,
And he denied it hotly again.

Another hour of time elapsed;
He was placed as from Galilee.
Peter answered,"Surely not,
You are mistaken about me."

Then the rooster cut loose,
He crowed lusty and long.
Peter saw Jesus look at him
And wept for he'd done wrong.

The guards struck Him and
Treated Him rough. Stoically
He held to His silence, gave
Nothing to these toughs.

At daybreak the Sanhedrin
Met, (authorities of the land).
Jesus was brought out, asked,
"Are you Messiah or man?"

"You won't believe," He said,
"Soon I'll be enthroned by my
Lord." "Aha!" they cried, "Con-
demned by His own word."

CHAPTER 23

Then the council members took
Him to Pilot for interview.
Claimed He led people to ruin
By not paying taxes when due.

"He claims to be our Messiah,
Which is a ridiculous thing."

Pilot asked Him point blank,
"Are you the Messiah, or king?"

"Yes." He said. Said Pilot,
"There's no crime I can see."
They cried, "He has caused
Trouble from here to Galilee."

"Take Him to Galilee," said
Pilot, "Herod's there at this
Time." Herod interrogated Him,
He too saw no sign of crime.

They mocked and derided Him,
Clothed Him in royal dress.
Then returned to Pilot,
Who was somewhat distressed.

Then Pilot and King Herod,
Who'd been enemies to that
Day, put enmities aside,
And let friendship hold sway.

Now Pilot called together
Jesus' accusers and the rest.
Declared Jesus' innocence,
But it was a hopeless protest.

Three times they roared
That His life not be allowed.
Then Pilot finally wavered
And gave in to the crowd.

There was Barabbus, jailed
For murder and insurrection,
Whom the mob wanted set free;
They accepted no objection.

For this was the order and
The custom of the day,
To free another prisoner
And let him go his way.

Pilot freed Barabbus, gave up
Jesus, (doing all he could).

Then sentenced Him to death
To do with as they would.

Now they forced a Cyrenian,
One called Simon by name,
To carry Jesus' cross up the
Hill to where they came.

Crowds trailed behind, and
Many women stricken by grief.
Jesus turned to them, said,
"Ladies, please don't weep;

The days that are coming are
Much worse than this. When
If mountains fell on mankind,
It would seem like pure bliss.

For if they do this today,
To me, the living tree,
Whatever can you hope
That your fate will be?"

Three crosses they prepared,
To carry out the grizzly task.
"Father forgive what they do."
Was all that Jesus asked.

In center, they crucified Him,
A criminal on either side.
The soldiers gambled for His
Clothing by throwing dice.

The Jewish leaders scoffed,
"If you are the chosen one,
Then come down, save yourself,
If you truly are God's son."

Even soldiers mocked Him by
Offering sour wine to drink.
Saying, "Save yourself, if
You truly are Messiah, King."

One hanging beside Him said,
"Save yourself and us too,

Because if you're the Messiah,
It will be simple for you."

The other protested, "Don't
You fear God at your death?
We deserve to die, but this
Man drew no evil breath."

"Jesus, remember me in your
Kingdom," he said, and Jesus
Replied, "Today, you'll be
With me in paradise."

Now when it came noon, dark-
ness took the place of day.
And until three o'clock
It continued that way.

With a loud voice Jesus cried,
"Father, I commit my spirit
To you." the veil in the
Temple then rent in two.

The Centurion watching said
"Surely, this was a righteous
Man." And all the people who
Watched went sadly home again.

His followers and the women
Were watching what transpired.
They must have felt very sad,
And I'd say weary and tired.

Joseph of Arimathea laid
Jesus' body in a sepulchre of
Stone. Women got spices for
Burial after returning home.

CHAPTER 24

Sunday morning they returned,
To find the stone rolled away.
Christ's body was not there,
To their complete dismay.

Now two men stood before
   them,

Clothed in shining dress.
Those women were terrified
And in deep distress.

"Why look in the tomb?" they
Were asked, "for He's alive!
Just as He said He would,
Jesus came back to life."

They were reminded then of
All he'd preached and said
He'd be killed by evil men,
Arise again from the dead.

They hurried to tell the
Others there was no need to
Grieve. It seemed fantastic,
One could scarcely believe.

Peter even checked the tomb;
In confusion he went home.
Two disciples were walking
When joined by a man alone.

They didn't recognize Jesus
As He walked along beside.
They were greatly disturbed
By sorrow they couldn't hide.

He said "You seem serious,
What can your problem be?"
They said, "Have you heard
What happened last week?

It's about a Holy teacher of
God, He did mighty things.
We thought He was Messiah
And our future Jewish King.

Our priests and leaders
Arrested, caused His death.
The soldiers crucified Him;
In confusion we are left.

His body is missing from the
Tomb where it was interred.

Some of our women saw angels,
And He lives, they inferred."

Jesus said, "Why do you doubt
What prophets wrote long ago?
If you'd read the scriptures,
You'd know it must be so."

Many passages He quoted,
Genesis right on through,
Explaining what they meant,
How they affected Him too.

As they neared Emmaus, they
Asked Him to stay the night.
He broke bread at the table;
They suddenly saw the light.

Once they really recognized
Him, He faded out of view.
Telling others in Jerusalem,
Heard, "Peter saw Him too."

The two from Emmaus told of
Meeting Jesus on the road.
Suddenly He was among them;
They thought He was a ghost.

"Why be afraid," He asked,
"Do ghosts have a body like

Me? Look, and touch the nail
Marks in my hands and feet."

In indecision they stood,
Filled with joy and doubt;
He asked to eat some fish,
Gladly they brought it out.

He proclaimed the scriptures,
Saying, "Prophets long ago,
Predicted it would happen to
Me; they affirmed it so.

There is forgiveness of sins
For all who turn to me. The
Prophecies have come true
As you have lived to see.

I'll send the Holy Spirit;
My Father has promised too.
Tell no one yet, wait here
Until He comes to you."

He raised His hands aloft,
Blessed those informed men.
As they worshipped, up to
Heaven saw Him ascend.

END OF LUKE

JOHN

CHAPTER 1

Before anything else was,
There was our Lord.
And God is also known
As the living word.

All that is, He made;
Eternal life is His to give.
His light makes day of night
And life worthwhile to live.

John the Baptist, God sent,
To witness that He was true.
John was not the light, but
Jesus' light shines through.

Later, Jesus came to earth,
To shine His light on life.
But though he made the earth,
It caused sorrow and strife.

For it refused to recognize
That our God He is. His own

People missed the point, that
He has eternal life to give.

Yes, to all those who welcome
Him, He will give eternal life.
Not the result of passion or
Plan, but above human strife.

He became a living person
And visited earth down here.
He showed us how to live
Beyond the reach of fear.

John showed Him to people,
Saying, "He's greater than I".
Jewish leaders and priests
Quickly passed Him by.

Many blessings He brought.
Moses gave rigid law, demand-
ing merciless justice, which
Jesus's love tends to thaw.

Jewish priests and leaders
Wanted to know who John was.
He said, "A voice
Introducing God's love."

"If you aren't the Messiah,
Elijah, or a prophet," they
Cried, "then tell us by what
Authority you baptize."

"I baptize with water," John
Said, "One greater than me,
I'll introduce to Israel as
The Spirit of Peace I see."

As Jesus appeared, John said,
"He is the one of whom I told.
His slave I am not fit to be,
He was, before times of old.

I was a watch for the spirit,
It landed on Him like a dove.
It was He for whom I looked,
The peak of peace and love."

He pointed out Jesus next day,
Saying, "God's lamb is He"
Two of John's disciples foll-
owed Jesus, and Jesus asked,
"What do you seek?"

They asked, "Where do you
Live?" He said "Come." It was
Andrew, Simon Peter's brother,
To him the call was not dumb.

Jesus called Peter "Cephas."
In their tongue means "stone."
And from that day forward,
Peter would never be alone.

Then Jesus found Philip
The very next day,
And by personal invitation
He too followed in the way.

Nathaniel was shown by Philip,
As the scripture explains. "Can
Good come from Nazareth?"
Nathaniel now exclaimed.

See for yourself, Philip said,
Jesus greeted him as an honest
Man. "Do you know about me?"
Was his surprised demand.

Jesus told him he had heard,
What to Philip he'd exclaimed.
Now he called Jesus, Messiah,
And the Son of God, the same.

"If you believe," Jesus said,
"I saw you under a fig tree,
Then you'll see the angels of
Heaven ministering unto me."

CHAPTER 2

At a wedding in Galilee His
Mother noted the wine was low.

441

So she asked Jesus to help,
Surprisingly, He said "No."

For the time was not right,
His miracles to be shown, she
Told the servants, "Obey Him."
Her son, she must have known.

He had them fill several con-
tainers with water to the brim.
To the master of ceremonies,
Said, "Taste some," to him.

"Wow!" said that servant,
When he had tasted the stuff,
"It's the best wine around
And one cup is not enough."

He praised the bridegroom
On the quality of his wine.
It was late to celebrate,
But he thought it was fine.

His disciples were amazed at
The success of this miraculous
Feat. He was the Messiah,
They fully did believe.

The Jews held the passover
At this time of year, Jesus
Entered the Temple as the
Celebration drew near.

He found money changers there;
They sold cattle and sheep. In
General He felt the Temple
Was made tawdry and cheap.

With a whip made of cords,
He belabored them all.
Thus He cleaned out the
Temple from wall to wall.

He scattered coin changers,
Money all over the floor.

He turned over their tables
And chased them out doors.

To sellers of doves, He said,
"Get these out right away.
This house was for prayer
And will be again today."

The disciples remembered,
Written in scripture long ago,
"My concern for God's house
Will in time lay me low."

"Where is your authority for
This?" Jewish leaders cried.
For the error of their ways,
They steadfastly denied.

"If you've authority from God,
Show us a miracle as proof."
He said, "All right I'll show
A miracle especially for you.

Destroy this Temple, (His
Body He meant), in three days
I'll raise it again." "Never,"
They cried, "It was forty-
Three years abuilding by man."

Little they knew of the Temple
He spoke, His disciples rem-
embered when from death He
Arose. He spoke of His body;
They held His memory close.

He convinced many by miracles
On that passover day, that
Jesus was the Messiah, but He
Knew people have strange ways.

CHAPTER 3

Nicodemus came to see Jesus
In the darkness of the night.
Could he be hiding this visit
From the harsh truth of light?

He said, "We know you are a
Teacher, and He sent you here.
The miracles are proof enough,
And your message is clear."

"To enter The Kingdom," said
Jesus, "You must be born
Again. A feat possible with
God, but impossible with man."

"Can a man be reborn from the
Womb, and thus be born anew?"
"Baptism of water and Spirit"
Said Jesus, "is the way to do.

Man can reproduce humans, the
Holy Spirit gets you to para-
dise. The Spirit, like wind
Goes where it will, gives life.

You're educated and respected,"
Said Jesus, "but Still do not
Understand, and you won't
Believe what I tell man.

For I, the Messiah, have come,
Will return to heaven again.
God so loved the world, that
He gave His son to save man.

Those who won't believe do
Their deeds in the dark. And
When the truth is presented
Are too busy to hark.

Those who are doing His will,
Happily work in the light.
Willing to be seen, for they
Know they are doing right."

John, before being imprisoned,
Baptized at Aenon, near Salim.
His disciples were harassed,
Spoke with misgivings to him.

"The man you called Messiah,
Gets more converts than we."
"Don't worry," he told them,
"He is more important than me.

I'm certainly not the Messiah.
Remember, I've said it before.
I will become less important;
He has big things in store.

From heaven He was sent, but
My knowledge is only of earth.
He tells of what He has seen,
But few ever see its worth.

All those who will trust Him,
Will see glory eternal. But
Those who scoff never will,
His wrath will be infernal."

CHAPTER 4

When word came to Jesus, they
Had more converts than John,
Though His disciples did the
Baptizing, He moved on.

He passed through Samaria,
And rested at Jacob's well.
That He was tired and weary,
Must have been easy to tell.

A Samaritan woman drew
    water,
Jesus thirsted in a dry land.
Surprised that he'd ask, for
She recognized a Jewish man.

The Samaritans were despised,
Considered a half breed race.
Most Jews looked down on them,
Seldom spoke to their face.

He told the woman at the well,
Of the water of eternal life.

She'd been with several men,
But had never been a wife.

"You are a prophet," she said,
"Please tell me why this is,
Jews all worship in Jerusalem,
Samaritans, at Mt. Jerazim."

"It isn't important where,"
Said He, "But it must be real.
Without God's help to worship,
There is no Spirit that heals."

"I know the Messiah will come,
And He'll explain all to me."
Said Jesus, "You are correct,
And I am He of whom you
   speak."

Back to the village she went
And told them all the news.
How she'd met the Messiah
They called King of the Jews.

His disciples returned and
Offered Him something to eat.
But He said the food He had
Was pretty hard to beat.

Doing his father's will was
The way he gathered strength.
There are many souls to save
And all must work at length.

Now many who heard her story
Went hurrying out to the well
To see and hear firsthand,
Things they'd heard her tell.

Two days He stayed there,
Before they went away. Then
He returned to Galilee,
In spite of what they say-

Within His own country, a
Prophet gets no honor at all.

But I suppose like many of us,
His homeland always called.

In that land He loved, they
Followed Him on the run. For
Many at the passover had
Witnessed miracles He'd done.

At the town of Cana, where He
Had turned water into wine,
Miracles He performed there
Had not dimmed with time.

An official of Capernaum came
And begged Jesus to come. For
Death was at his door, he
Wished Jesus to heal his son.

Jesus said, "Why must I do
Miracles before you believe?
But go on home, "He said," your
Son is granted reprieve."

As he traveled homeward, He
Was met with reports of joy.
For his son was well again,
Jesus had healed his boy.

So He made another believer,
It only took a miracle to do!
"Am I that slow to convince,
Or is it only folks like you?"

CHAPTER 5

Now He returned to Jerusalem.
Inside one of the city gates,
Beside the Bethsaida pool,
Where many sick folks wait,

It's said an angel often
Came to make the waters heal.
The first one in thereafter
Got the best of the deal.

Jesus saw one there who'd
Been sick nearly four decades.

"Would you like to get well?"
Jesus asked. He answered,
"I cannot move or get away.

When it's time at the pool,
I have no help to move,
So before I can get there,
To someone else I lose."

Jesus said, "Take your bed and
Walk." So he did that Sabbath
Day. He knew not who healed
Him, for Jesus faded away.

Later in the temple, Jesus
Gave him good advice. Saying,
"Lest a worse thing happen,
Live a faultless life."

When the Jews learned, Jesus
Told this man to take his bed,
They started to persecute Him
And covertly plan His death.

For Moses' law declared that
To work on Sunday was taboo.
Even to carry ones bed was
Work according to the Jews.

Jesus said, "My Father works
Good, His will, I follow too."
Placing Himself equal to God,
And their animosity renewed.

"But I can do nothing," He
Told them, "by myself alone.
Only with my Father's help,
Can I bring health to homes.

You will see other miracles,
So much greater than these.
For I can bring the dead to
Life, as well as heal disease.

If you fail to honor the Son,
You've failed the Father too.

If you believe my message,
Eternal life has come to you.

You'll see the day when the
Dead hear my voice and rise.
The sinful ones to judgment,
The good to eternal life.

I pass judgment as He wills;
I judge only as I'm told.
For God it is who sent me;
His justice as good as gold.

What I say about myself,
John told you too. God has
Told you over the years, but
The truth escaped from you.

When John preached here you
Rejoiced and benefited for a
Time. But I have a greater
Witness, miracles assigned.

You read the scriptures and
They all point to me. You'd
Listen to strangers before
Opening your eyes to see.

Yet I'll not be the judge of
You who live by Moses' law.
For you'll be judged by him,
When death's straw you draw.

Moses wrote about me, but you
Wouldn't believe his word.
So He will be your judge to
Apply the law of the Lord."

CHAPTER 6

Crossing the Sea of Galilee,
Many followed where He went.
It was probably plain to all;
They were tired and spent.

Climbing up a mountain, He
Could see a large crowd.

And it would be my guess,
The clamor was quite loud.

Turning to Philip, He asked,
"What do we feed them with?"
He answered "It would cost a
Lot, for a crowd like this."

Now Andrew said, "There's a
Boy with two fish and five
Barley loaves." Jesus said,
"Sit upon the grassy slopes."

Now Jesus took what they had,
Gave thanks for it there.
They fed over five thousand
And had some to spare.

They recognized this miracle
Would put Him on a throne.
But Jesus climbed up on the
Mountain to be alone.

At evening His disciples took
Ship over the Sea of Galilee.
But the water that had been
Benign became a raging melee.

They saw their Savior walk-
ing on the watery waves. And
They cried out with fear, as
Their panicky lives He saved.

He'd just entered the boat,
And they made the other shore.
His coming and His company
Had made a long journey short.

Next morning people sought
But found Him nowhere. So
Decided He'd crossed the sea
And in boats followed there.

Asked how He'd crossed. Said
He, "That's not the point you

See; you followed for the
Food not to hear me.

Do not worry what to eat,
Or to drink or wear. Just
Learn about eternal life,
Which God sent me to share."

Said they, "What can we do,
To understand God's will?"
"Believe the word I preach,
And His will you'll fulfill."

"We need another miracle,"
They said. "Like manna in the
Wilderness. If you can feed
Us every day, we'll know by
God you're blessed."

"I am the manna He said, and
You can forever feed on me.
The trouble is you've seen
And still you won't believe.

Everyone who my Father wills,
Will come and follow me. I
Will not forsake them; from
Fear or hate they'll be free.

This is my Father's will, He
Sent me from heaven to earth,
Any one who believes His son
Has eternal life and worth.

When we reach the judgment
Day, I'll raise him again."
He said He came from heaven
And Jews began to complain.

"We know He is Joseph's son
How can He put on airs?" for
He'd in essence said with
Him there was no despair.

Even His disciples grumbled
This was hard to understand.

446

"What will you say," He asked,
"When I'm in heaven again?

Physical birth is not enough
To make a man follow me. The
Heavenly Father must show him
The righteous path to see."

Many of His disciples left
Jesus and went their way.
He turned to the dozen left,
"Will you go too, or stay?"

Simon Peter answered, "Master,
To whom shall we go? The
True words of eternal life
Are uttered by you alone.

We know you're the one of God;
You're the light and the way."
Jesus said, "I chose you all,
But by one I'll be betrayed."

CHAPTER 7

Now Jesus' own brothers
Still did not believe.
So they urged Him to go
And Galilee to leave.

"You'll draw attention where
People congregate," said they.
"Go ahead," said Jesus, "for
It is only me they hate.

They don't like truth, but it
Is what they hear from me."
So they went on ahead, and
He stayed a while in Galilee.

But soon He followed them,
While keeping His profile low.
His name was on many tongues,
They thought "great," or "no."

Whether He was good or bad,
Few of them really knew.

But none dare speak openly
For they feared the Jews.

Midway through the program
He entered the tabernacle to
Teach. Jews all marveled at
A knowledge beyond reach.

He said, "I only state God's
Will, not ideas of my own. If
I were seeking my own glory
You'd certainly have known.

None of you keep the law that
Moses handed down. But when
I heal a man on Sunday, you
Would like to run me aground."

"You are crazy," they cried,
"To think we'd take your life.
We are kind and good, your
Thoughts are running rife."

He said, "Moses gave you cir-
cumcision, for it was the way.
A thing you often practice
Upon the Sabbath days.

When I heal a man's infirmity,
You treat it as a major sin.
Why not judge fairly, rather
Than according to your whims?"

Someone from Jerusalem said,
"Is it this man they'd kill?
He teaches and preaches bol-
dly and goes about at will.

Are our leaders aware He is
The Messiah who must appear?
But we know who he is, and
He really comes from here."

Jesus cried, "You all know me,
But not God from whom I came.

You do not know the truth,
That He is one and the same."

Jews would have arrested Him,
Only God would pick the time.
Common people of Jerusalem
Felt He'd committed no crime.

He had done only what they'd
Expect Messiah to do. So the
Priests sent officers to take
Him with people in this mood.

But Jesus said, "Not yet, for
The time being I must remain.
And then to the one who sent
Me, I will return again.

You will search but not find
Me, nor can you follow where
I am." They pondered where He
Was going and what His plan.

On the last of the Holidays
He shouted to one and all.
"Come drink my living water,
Believe my word, and call."

Of course this Living water
Was the Holy Spirit to come,
After He'd return to heaven
As God's own Holy Son.

Now many in the crowd quite
Obviously believed. Others
Said, "As per the scriptures,
He cannot come from Galilee."

Even palace police stalled,
Returned with empty hands.
"He says wonderful things."
They said to angry demands.

"We rulers know He's guilty,"
The Pharisees then said. "The

Crowds are just plain stupid
And they have been misled."

Nicodemus tried reason, but
Their hearts were as stone.
So the meeting broke up
And they all went home.

CHAPTER 8

Early in the morning, to the
Temple Jesus came. Pharisees
Brought a woman who'd been
Found adulterous to her shame.

"What do you say?" they asked,
"Moses's law says she must die."
Jesus stooped and wrote in
The dust while they stood by.

Then He answered, " Stone her,
You who've never sinned."
His tempters silently slipped
Away. I'd bet Jesus grinned.

"Where are your accusers?"
She answered, "They are gone."
He said, "Neither do I accuse
You, go your way, do no wrong.

I am the light of the world,
And I will flood your path,
Follow me!" "You are boasting
Now," said the Pharisees.

"Your laws say, if two witness-
es agree, their testimony is true.
My Father witnessed of me
But is a stranger to you."

"Who is your Father?" they
Asked. "If you knew me, you'd
Know Him. Change your ways
And no longer live in sin.

You are from a place below,
And I Come from above.

You are of this world, but
I've come from God's love.

I am the one whom I've
Always claimed to be. I could
Condemn you for much and a
Great deal I could teach.

I only bring the message of
Him from whom I'm sent." But
They still didn't understand
That God was whom He meant.

He said, "After you kill the
Messiah, you'll know that I
Am He. I bring this message,
The words He taught to me."

Many Jewish leaders who
Heard Him did believe. And
Jesus said, "Now listen to me,
The truth will set you free."

"We're Abraham's descendants,"
They said, so what do you
Mean by free?" They thought
Themselves already to be.

"You're slaves of sin," said
He, "and are stifled by its
Bands. You don't heed Moses'
Laws but fickle rules of man.

As slaves you have no rights,
But the Son of man surely
Does. And He can set you free
To reap God's Holy love.

Yes, you are Abraham's desc-
endants, yet we often find
That you are hard of heart
And oh, so narrow of mind.

I tell you of things I saw
When I was with my Father

God. Satan was your father,
After whom you've trod.

Abraham would not kill me,
As some of you have set out
To. And it is all because I
Told the truth to you.

Satan is the father of liars;
You are following his path.
That's why the truth I tell
Meets only with your wrath.

God's children would listen
To word that comes from Him.
Because you don't listen is
Proof you're children of sin."

"Samaritan, foreigner, devil,"
They cried, "You are truly
Demon possessed." He said,
"Only God's will do I profess."

He said, "I have no demon,
And you'll find no sin in me.
I'm here to honor my father,
Not for myself to greater be.

But this, I will tell you,
And I speak with honesty.
You can have an abundant life
Forever, if you'll follow me.

Abraham looked forward and
Rejoiced to see my day." They
Said, "You're not old enough
To make these fancy claims."

He stood steady, facing them,
Gave no ground. "In truth,"
He said, "I was with my God
Before Abraham came around."

Now the Jewish leaders were
Really fit to be tied. They

Were ready to stone Him, but
He escaped their sight.

CHAPTER 9

They came upon a blind man
Who'd been so all his life.
Jesus' disciples asked, "Was
Sin what caused his strife?"

"No," said Jesus, "for God's
Glory we have much to show.
The story must be told
Or the world will never know."

Then He spat upon the ground,
Made mud into a potion. On
Those blind eyes rubbed it
With a gentle caring motion.

Jesus told him "Go and wash."
The man regained His sight.
Neighbors and friends asked,
"Is this he who was blind?"

To queries he answered, "It
Is, I've been healed today.
Jesus told me wash after He
Anointed my eyes with clay."

"But He works on the Sabbath!"
The Pharisees complained, and
To harass the once blind man,
They went to quite some pains.

They approached his parents
Asking the questions again.
They answered, "Go ask him!
For he's a grown up man."

They returned to him with
Questions to harass him more;
He believed, Jesus Messiah,
And also Son of the Lord.

Still they doubted and
Would have sullied his name.

He questioned them in turn
And thus put them to shame.

Jesus found him on hearing
They'd angrily cast him aside.
Saying, "I came to give sight
To those spiritually blind."

He gave allegiance to Jesus,
As Pharisees feigned offense,
And Jesus said in essence,
"They could show better sense."

CHAPTER 10

"If man enters not by a door,
But by another way." said
Jesus, "he's not the shepherd
Who should be there that day.

To a shepherd, sheep respond
And follow wherever he leads.
A stranger they won't know;
At his presence, will flee.

I am the door of entry, and
Yet they do not understand."
For many Jewish rulers were
Determined He was only a man.

"Any claiming to be me were
Robbers, thieves to the core.
I have come to give life to
Believers, sinners and poor.

Hirelings leave on the run
When first trouble appears.
I'll risk all for my flock,
To spare anguish or tears."

There was wonder and fear in
Jewry. Some said, "He's not
As He claims." Others asked,
"Then how did He heal the
Sick and the lame?"

"Who are you?" They cried, He
Said, "I told you; you won't
Believe. You've seen works I
Do, would rather be deceived.

You are not of my flock, or
You would recognize my voice.
My sheep will follow my call,
But each makes his own choice.

Life eternal I'll give my own;
No man shall draw them away."
Again they picked up stones,
To have killed Him that day.

"My Father is more than men,
He and I are both one. So why
Would you stone me?" He asked,
"After the works I have done?"

"Not for works," they cried,
"But for the blasphemy you do.
You call yourself God. That's
Blasphemy for one like you."

"The law is written," He said,
"That men are God's, scripture
Is true. If I say I'm His Son,
It could also be said of you.

If you believe not me, then
At least believe things I do.
Believe I am in the Father,
And that He is in me too."

Again they'd have taken Him,
Killed Him like any other man.
But he escaped from them,
And avoided their evil hands.

He retired beyond the Jordan
To where John first baptized.
And many people came to Him,
His word and power prized.

"John did no miracles, but
What He said of Jesus is true.
He sure is the Messiah," they
Said, "not just another Jew."

CHAPTER 11

Remember how Mary of
   Bethany,
With perfume bathed His feet?
She and her sister sent a
Message, Jesus' help to seek.

Their beloved brother Lazarus
Lay sick and close to death.
Jesus said, "This is no perm-
anent thing." Two days later
He left.

He said, "This will bring
Glory to my Father and Son."
From the Jewish authorities
He still was on the run.

Disciples worried and fretted
He would meet an untimely end.
He said they'd go in daylight,
For Lazarus was His friend.

"Twelve hours are daylight,"
He said, "during which we'll
Walk." He may have felt dark-
ness was when evil stalked.

First He called it sleep, His
People said, "It's OK to rest."
Then Jesus wised them up,
"Our friend is actually dead.

You're lucky it is so, for
It may strengthen your belief."
When they arrived they found
Their friends in total grief.

Martha hurried to meet Him;
Mary'd stayed behind. Martha

Said, "If you had been here,
My brother'd not have died.

But even now God will give
Whatever thing you ask."
Then Jesus answered, "Your
Brother's death won't last."

"I know," she said, "At the
Judgement He will rise again."
"I am resurrection and life"
Said Jesus, "to believing men.

If any believe in me, though
He dies, yet shall he live.
Martha, do you believe the
Son of man has life to give?"

"Yes, Lord Jesus, I believe."
Trusting Martha cried, "to
Live and believe in you most
Surely means I'll never die."

Then she summoned her sister,
Who came to Jesus post haste.
Jews who'd come to comfort
Them followed in her wake.

Mary said, "Lord, if you'd
Been here he'd not be dead."
Jesus asked, "Where have you
Laid him?" and He also wept.

Some said, "Could this man
Who opened the eyes of the
Blind, could He also have
Kept this man alive?"

They came to the grave, and
He said "Roll the stone away."
Martha said, "Lord, think of
The smell after four days!"

But Jesus only reminded her,
"Martha, I told you before!

If you have faith you'll
See the glory of the Lord."

Jesus raised His eyes toward
Heaven saying, "Lord, I had
To show them, so they will
Believe your revelations."

Now in a loud voice he cried,
"Lazarus, come from the grave."
All were witness that day, to
The fact that Lazarus came.

Now many Jews there were
Convinced and did believe.
Others ran to the Pharisees
And reported this final deed.

Chief priests and Pharisees
Gathered for a council of war.
They feared Jesus' miracles,
Would have too many believing
His word.

Caiaphus, high priest thought,
"Best that we kill this man,
Than lose the power that
We command."

He prophesied also that
Jesus' death would combine
All the children of God, who
Had scattered in those times.

They all met in council to
Plot the murder of this Jew.
So Jesus left that area
To start in Ephraim, anew.

The passover drew near,
And they all wondered aloud,
Whether Jesus would stay
Or mingle with the crowd.

Now word was passed that
Anyone should come forth,

If he knew of Jesus' location,
He should quickly report.

CHAPTER 12

Six days before passover at
A banquet by friends. Mary
Washed Jesus' feet with
Perfume of a special blend.

Jesus and Lazarus at table,
Martha served the food. The
House filled with fragrance
And friendly, cheerful moods.

Judas, who would betray Him,
Would sell the perfume, give
To the poor. Jesus said "we
Will have them evermore.

My time on earth is short,
So let her do her thing."
Now the people of good faith
Thought of Him as king.

So they flocked to see him,
And Lazarus, whom He'd raised.
Chief priests and pharisees
Didn't give much praise.

The raising of Lazarus caused
Many more people to follow
The Lord. Another thing they
Felt they couldn't afford.

Lazarus' name was added to
That one they hated so much.
So those Jews made plans that
Wouldn't leave fate to luck.

Next day he entered Jerusalem;
The passover time was here.
Now by great mobs of people,
He was welcomed and cheered.

Jesus rode along the street
Upon a donkey's colt. Just

As the ancient scriptures
Had centuries ago foretold.

Many were stories that day
Of how Jesus brought Lazarus
Forth. And I'd bet many more
Were in that day's reports.

Not until the fateful day was
Over, did His disciples get
Wise to the many scriptural
Prophecies that came true be-
fore their eyes.

The Pharisees were worried;
Where Jesus was, people went.
If not the main attraction,
Their egos were quickly bent.

Some Greeks came to see Jesus,
He said "My time is nearly
Come. My work upon this
Earth is very close to done.

I must fall and die like
A kernel of grain, if
I would live life anew with
My Heavenly Father again.

A life that is coveted
While here on the earth,
In heaven when it counts
Will not be of much worth.

If you lose it down here
For a cause that is pure,
Eternal life is yours in hea-
ven and a haven that is sure.

If the Greeks would come,
Tell them come and follow me.
For wherever I am, that is
Where my disciples will be.

Now I am deeply troubled,
So what shall I pray?

My Father in heaven, please
Take my problems away?

That is the reason I must
Face terror and shame. To
Save souls of this world,
So Father, help me bring
Honor to your name."

Now from heaven came a voice
Which was speaking to them.
"I've given honor already,
And I will do it again."

Now the people all marveled.
A spell, were they under?
Some thought it was an angel,
Or had they heard thunder?

"The voice was for you" He
Said, "and it wasn't mine.
It's judgement day for earth;
Satan is running out of time.

When on the cross I'm lifted,
I'll draw believers to me."
He said this to show that
He would die on the tree.

"What says He?" cried the
Crowd, We thought He'd never
Die." "I'll soon leave," He
Said, "make use of my light.

Darkness will soon fall, so
Use my light while you can.
Then in time to come, you
Will bear light to man."

This gentle man of miracles
Departed from all to hide.
And still for all the proof,
Men's belief did not abide.

As Elias said so long ago,
"Who's believed our report?

Who has been convinced by
The mighty arm of the Lord?

Eyes are blinded; there's
Hardening of the heart. So
They cannot be converted,
Nor can I take their part."

Many rulers did believe, but
They dared not confess. For
They loved the things of men
And cared for God much less.

Jesus cried, "Who believes me
Trusts Him from whom I came.
I came not to judge the world
But to the world to save.

My word shall be judge; it is
My Father's word heaven sent.
That was why I came here, and
It is how my life was spent."

CHAPTER 13

Jesus knew His time had come
To go back where He came. And
Those He'd loved before,
He still loved them the same.

He girded a towel about Him,
Bathed His disciples' feet.
But Simon Peter wasn't sure
He deserved this treat.

Then Jesus said to him,
"It is necessary that I do.
Because if I don't, I can
Have no more to do with you."

Peter said, "Oh Lord, in that
Case I would much prefer,
You'd wash me so thoroughly
There'd be no sign of dirt."

Jesus said, "You were clean,
Your feet complete the chore.

You don't understand now, but
In time you will much more.

You are clean, but that is
Not true of everyone." For
Judas, would betray Him, whom
He considered the Devil's son.

When He'd washed their feet,
He asked them why, "You call
Me Lord and Master," He said,
"But that is certainly right.

You should wash each other's
Feet. No servant is above his
Master. Nor a messenger over
The one who sent him after.

Any who welcomes my
    messenger,
Also welcomes me, but there
Is one who will betray." For
That reason He was grieved.

Then when questioned by the
Disciple known as John, Jesus
Indicated discreetly that
Judas Iscariot was the one.

Jesus gave Judas a bit to eat,
And said, "Hurry, do it now!"
To the others sitting there,
Those words carried no clout.

Jesus turned to the others,
After Judas hurried out, and
Said, "I'll soon see God's
Glory without a doubt.

Dear ones, brief the moments
Are! I will be gone; where I
Will be none can follow,
You cannot come with me.

I give you a new command, to
Love each other as I have you.

That you are my disciples, to
All the world you'll prove."

When Jesus told them, "Where
I go you cannot follow me."
"Where you go," said Peter,
"That's where I want to be.

Where you go I will go, and
For your safety I will die."
"Ere the cock crows tomorrow,"
Said Jesus, "my name three
Times you will deny."

CHAPTER 14

"Many homes are in my father's
Land; I only say what is true.
I'll go ahead to prepare them,
So they'll be ready for you.

Where I go you will follow,
And there we'll be together.
For now you know the way
To the land of love forever."

Said Thomas, "Lord, how could
We know the way?" "I am the
Way to the Father," said He,
"Your path is by words I say."

"Show us the Father," cried
Philip, "I am in He and He
In me. If you'll believe,
His hand in me you'll see.

If that's not enough, what
About miracles you've seen?
And you shall do much greater
If you'll only believe.

If you truly love, obey. My
Father will send the Holy One.
He will be a comforter, and
If you invite Him will come.

The world cannot receive Him,
For it does not know His name.
Now I will not abandon you,
For I don't play idle games.

From this world I'll soon be
Gone, but I shall live again.
And I'll be with you always,
As before, unknown to man.

When I come back to life,
The proof will all be there.
He who obeys because of love
Will all my glory share.

When the Holy Comforter
  comes,
(The Holy Spirit is also He.)
He will teach you very much
And remind you oft' of me.

And so I give you peace,
More than the world has known.
Don't be troubled or afraid,
For you'll never be alone.

The evil prince approaches,
But over me he holds no sway.
I go willingly to my Father
To show you all the way."

CHAPTER 15

"My Father is the gardener
And I am only the vine. He
Prunes, trims, and shapes,
Develop's fruit that's fine.

He has trimmed and pruned,
And shaped you too;
Through the word I carried,
From Him, to earth, to you.

So let me live in you, and
You shall live in me. For a

Branch can't produce fruit,
When severed from the tree.

Branches that are severed
Soon wither and are burned.
Live in me and I in you, ask
What you will, it's earned.

We live in each other, and
If we love my Father too,
A harvest we'll accomplish
Will be the finest fruit.

Your joy will overflow, if
Life is girded by God above.
Risk your life for another,
There is no greater love.

I've called you my friends,
It is I who've chosen you.
You are no longer servants
Who know not what to do.

If you're hated by others
For doing good things, it's
Because you reprove evil,
And are reborn of kings.

Had I not shown them the
Errors of their ways, they'd
Have no burden of sin with
Which they filled their days.

The work I did among them
Shed light upon their laws.
But just as it was written,
They hated me without cause.

The Holy comforter will come;
I will send Him down to you.
He will come from my Father,
The Holy Spirit of truth.

He will testify of me, and
You shall bear witness too.

He will give you strength,
Bear testimony that is true."

CHAPTER 16

"This I've told you, so it
Won't be such a shock. You'll
Be denied and murdered, by
Those who claim to serve God.

They've never known my father,
Nor have they known me. I
Tell you this now, for I'll
Not much longer with you be.

I return to Him who sent me,
You don't seem to wonder why,
Instead you only feel sorrow,
Because you think I'll die.

It is better that I go, then
I'll send a comforter to you.
When He comes He'll show the
World how to pay its dues.

He will show people how
Great God's love and free.
That it delivers from judge-
ment and how easy it can be.

Man committed sin, when truth
He wouldn't accept. But there
Is righteousness available
And much to understand yet.

The Holy Spirit will guide
You, when I am here no more.
For Satan has been judged,
And he has fallen short.

Soon you'll not see me, but
Later you'll see me again.
I go to the Father," said
He, His disciples did not
Understand.

Jesus knew their questions
And answered in this way. "I
Tell you now you will sorrow,
Others will rejoice that day.

You will weep and lament,
But sorrow will turn to joy,
As a woman forgets her pain
Once she's borne girl or boy.

So now when you see me not,
Sorrow will be your portion.
When you see me again, your
Heart will not be broken.

You'll not ask my help, for
My Father'll meet your needs.
Whatever you ask in my name,
That you shall receive.

For the Father loves you,
Because you first loved me."
His disciples said, "We know
How true you are; we believe."

Jesus said, "The hour will
Come you'll despair. And
Yet, I'll not be alone, for
My Father will be there.

So peace be with you then;
The world will weary you some.
But be of good cheer, for the
Same world I'll overcome."

CHAPTER 17

Jesus looked to heaven and
Said, "Father, time has come
For you to reveal the
Glory you've given your son.

It could be given again as
Total authority on the earth,
Giving life eternal to anyone
That you've seen of worth.

For these have recognized me
As the son you sent below,
To show this sinful world
The things it needs to know.

So Father, reveal my glory
As in your presence I stand.
All the wonders we've shared,
Long before the world began.

I've told these men about you,
Who in the world were given
To me. Now they know for sure,
That all is a gift from thee.

So hover over them, Lord,
And keep them safe and true.
For they are my glory, and
They belong as well to you.

The ancient scriptures read,
While here I kept them well.
They were safe within your
Arms, except the son of hell.

For the world hates them as
It does me. Don't take them
From earth but let them safe
From Satan be.

As you sent me into the world,
I sent them out too. I consec-
rated them to you, which gave
Them growth and truth.

I pray not only for them but
For all those others to come.
For there'll be more beli-
evers before the race is run.

Let us dwell within each other,
Just as we do, you and me.
So the world will understand
Our glorious love is free.

And may our love affair be
So obvious to all men, that
They'll know the glory that
Is available to all of them."

CHAPTER 18

Crossing the Kidron ravine,
He entered a grove of trees.
Judas led the soldiers there;
He knew where Jesus would be.

With weapons drawn, torches
Blazing, they came at night,
Jesus went to meet them, and
They fell back with fright.

Now He asked whom they
   sought,
And then answered them again.
"I've told you," He said,
"That is exactly who I am.

Since I'm the one you want,
Please let my friends go free."
To fulfill a prophecy, "I
Kept safe those given to me."

Peter's sword slashed an ear
Off a priest's servant's head.
Jesus said, "Put your sword
Away, I must drink this cup
Instead."

So Jesus was arrested and
Was taken to face the court.
Peter followed after, while
His nerve did a steady abort.

They took Jesus to Annas and
To Caiaphas, the high priest.
It was he who had prophesied
That Jesus must be deceased.

Peter followed behind as did
One who was acquainted there.

Peter came within the gate, a
Fire with soldiers he shared.

The girl who tended the gate,
Said, "Were you one of them?"
"I certainly am not!" he said,
"That is not who I am."

Peter warmed by the fire the
Soldiers built against cold.
Maybe heat slowed his shaking,
I'd not likely be that bold.

Indoors, inquisition began
About His teaching life. He
Said, "I often teach in the
Temple and never have I lied.

Ask any who have listened,
For many have there been."
He was suddenly struck in
The face by one of their men.

"If I did, prove it," said He,
"Do you hit one who tells the
Truth?" Annas sent Jesus to
Caiaphas, to question Him too.

Peter was asked once more,
"Are you a disciple of His?"
And soon another questioner
Again asked him this.

All three times when asked,
Peter angrily denied that
He had ever known this man
They called the Christ.

And then the rooster crowed,
As the nighttime fled.
And it is written elsewhere
That Peter bitterly wept.

Into the hall of judgment,
From Caiaphas, Jesus was taken.

And though they seem so evil,
Religion wasn't forsaken.

They avoided the judgment
Hall, forced Pilot to come to
Them. To enter was defiling,
As bad as being condemned.

Pilot said to them, "Why acc-
use this man?" They answered
"If He weren't a malefactor,
We'd never take this stand."

Said Pilot, "Take Him and
Judge Him by your laws." They
Said, "It's not lawful for us
To kill a man for any cause."

This indicated crucifixion as
Jesus earlier had prophesied.
Pilot entered the hall again
And again with Jesus he tried.

He went back to the priests,
Saying, "He's an innocent man."
For Jesus admitted He was a
King but not one of the land.

"I came," He said, "to bring
Truth to people of this world."
By his actions Pilot showed
That his mind was in a whirl.

To the people he said, "In
This man I find only good.
So I'll release the prisoner
To you, if you think I should."

But they screamed, "You must
Release Barabbas, the murderer
Instead." It was very obvious
That they wanted Jesus dead.

CHAPTER 19

Pilot had Him scourged, and
With purple robe he was clad.

A crown of thorns impaled Him;
The beating He took was sad.

Pilot brought Him out again;
Again he took Jesus' side. But
Jewish officials and priests
All the more for death cried.

"He ought to die," they said,
"He calls Himself God's son."
"You do the job," said Pilot,
"Of this, I want none."

He took Jesus back and asked,
"From just where do you hail?"
But Jesus did not answer,
So Pilot's questions failed.

Pilot said, "If you'd talk, I
Have power to save your life,
Or if I really wanted to, I
Could have you crucified."

Jesus said, "Power is from
God, or you'd have none at
All. But they are even
More prone to Satan's call."

Pilot wanted to release Him
They'd allow no such thing.
"He is Caesar's enemy,
He claims to be king."

So by hidden threats they
Forced Pilot to their will.
Because he would never dare
Against Caesar rebel.

Pilot said, "You take Him,
Why would you crucify a king?"
They said "Caesar's our ruler,
And this one is no such thing."

They forced Him to bear His
Cross upon Golgotha's hill.

Jewish rulers had won; some-
One else would actually kill.

Pilot posted a sign above Him
Saying "Jesus of Nazareth,
King of the Jews." In Hebrew,
Latin and Greek, the news.

Hebrew priests and rulers
Wanted it to say, "He said."
Pilot said, "Nothing doing,"
And he left it as it read.

When soldiers had finished
Their gory task that day,
They divided His clothes;
Then with dice they played.

This fulfilled the written
Word, it said, "They divided
His clothes, and then they
Cast dice for His robe."

Now near the cross in sorrow,
Jesus' mother stood.
And I, John, was close by, as
Close as I reasonably could.

Then He bid her to accept me
And to consider me as her son.
And as far as I was concerned,
A fine new mother I'd won.

I took her into my home, so
Jesus in peace could go away.
Scriptures would be fulfilled
Before the close of day.

He was given sour wine on a
Sponge on a Hyssop branch.
Then He bowed His head and
Died when thirst was stanched.

Next day was the passover, so
Bodies couldn't be left there.

So Jews arranged with Pilot
To end this grizzly affair.

So they broke the legs of
Those other two on each cross.
Jesus' life had already fled,
So they wrote Him off.

A soldier pierced His side,
Blood and water flowed. This
Disciple was a witness, and
My account is true, I know.

So scriptures were complete,
He'd have no broken bones.
Look on Him they'd pierced,
But life and soul had flown.

Joseph of Arimathea came, a
Secret disciple, in fear. Yet
He asked for Jesus' body, so
In the scriptures it appears.

Nicodemus also came, that one
Who visited Jesus at night.
They embalmed, entombed Him
As part of the burial rite.

CHAPTER 20

Early in the morning on that
Sabbath day, Mary Magdalene
Came to the sepulchre and
Found the stone rolled away.

Then she ran to Simon Peter,
And to me, John by name, she
Said, "Someone took Jesus,
I know not where He's lain."

We both ran to the sepulchre
Saw his bindings on the floor.
We now believed He had risen,
We hadn't understood before.

We went home, but Mary ret-
urned to the tomb in grief.

She saw two angels, and Jesus
Appeared to her great relief.

She thought him a gardener;
He set the record straight.
Called her by name, "Master!"
She most joyfully exclaimed.

"Touch me not," He said, "I've
Not yet been to the Lord;"
She went to the disciples
And gave them the word.

In evening of that Sabbath,
In a place hidden from Jews.
He appeared in their midst
And said "Peace be unto you."

He showed them the nail marks
And spear wound in His side.
His disciples were overjoyed
To see the living Christ.

"My Father sent me," He said.
So I'll send you also. Then
Breathed His breath on them,
Said, "Receive the Holy Ghost.

Now whoever you forgive, in
Heaven will be forgiven too.
But if you forgive him not,
In hell he'll pay his dues."

Thomas was not present when
This grand meeting took place.
He really doubted their story
And he said so to their face.

Then eight days later they
Gathered there again. With
Doors and windows closed,
For Jews were not their fans.

Now Jesus stood among them,
And said, "Peace be to you.

Reach out and feel my wounds,"
To Thomas, the doubting Jew.

"Oh Lord my God!" said
  Thomas,
"I believe what I have seen!"
"Blessed are those," said He,
"Who didn't see but believed,"

Many signs and marvels Jesus
Did in His disciples' presence.
These were written here,
That you might know the
Christian essence.

CHAPTER 21

All night without reward, on
This fishing trip we planned,
Ten of us disciples worked
Just a little way from land.

Ashore in the morning mists,
Stood a man who called to us,
"Cast your net to starboard,
You'll catch fish enough."

So we did as we were told,
The net we could not bear.
For it was so full of fish
We feared it might tear.

"It's Jesus," I cried in joy,
Peter dove and swam ashore.
But we rowed a hundred yards
Before we reached the Lord.

Now He had a fire going, and
Bade us bring some fish. Then
Peter dragged the net ashore
With food for many a dish.

"Come have some breakfast,"
He said, none of us refused.
Being served again by Him
Was just the greatest news.

Three times He'd appeared
Since He'd been crucified. So
We knew beyond a doubt, He
Lived again though He'd died.

After breakfast was eaten, to
Peter three times He spoke,
"Son of Judah, do you love me
More than all other folk?"

And He answered "Yes, Lord,
My love for you'll not end."
The third time Jesus asked,
"Peter, are you my friend?"

And again, "Feed my sheep."
"When you were young, you
Did as you pleased, but
When old, you'll be undone."

This, an indication, of the
Way Peter would die. Again
Said Jesus, "Follow me."
Now it was I, Peter spied.

He said, "Lord, tell me now,
What will this one do?" But
Jesus said, "If I let him
Live forever, "What does it
Matter to you?"

I lived in those days, and
What I've written is true.
If all His experiences were
Recorded and read to you-

There'd be a lack of books,
To write it all down. For
More I'm sure happened to
This man of great renown.

END OF JOHN

ACTS

CHAPTER 1

He instructed His disciples
Of the Holy Spirit then
After being taken to heaven,
He often came back again.

Proved beyond a doubt that
Truly it was He, who told
Them of God's Kingdom, and
How wonderful it must be.

He said, "Don't leave Jerus-
alem till the Holy spirit
Comes to you; it's my Father's
Word, you can count on it too.

John baptized with water, but
The Holy Spirit changes lives.
With great power and effect,
Preach and read the signs."

Once they asked, "Will our
Country be free from Rome?"
"Only my Father knows," He
Said, "but this is your home."

Soon after that He rose into
The clouds and disappeared.
In awe they wondered, at this
God they had been so near.

Two angels appeared, saying,
"Men of Galilee why stare at
The sky? Jesus is in heaven,
But will return by and by."

They returned to Jerusalem
About half a mile away, and
Had a prayer meeting upstairs
In the home where they stayed.

All these attended; Peter,
Simon, James and Andrew,

Thomas, Phillip, John
And also Bartholomew,

Mathew, James, Alphaeus' son.
There was Judas, son of James.
Also the brothers of Jesus,
His mother and others came.

For several days of meetings,
Over 100 people one day,
Peter got up, took the stand,
This kind of speech he made.

"Brothers, scriptures tell us
Judas sent Jesus to the cross.
Judas was one of the apostles,
But his gains soon were lost.

They bought a field for money
He earned for treachery done.
He died most horribly as be-
fore his conscience he'd run."

In Psalms David says, "Let
His home be desolate and ob-
solete. May his work be left
For someone else to complete."

We must find another to take
Judas' place in the group.
One who's been through it all,
With care in whom we choose.

Two men were nominated, and
Now they prayed to heaven.
A straw was drawn to decide,
Mathias joined the eleven.

CHAPTER 2

Since Jesus died and rose,
Seven weeks had gone by.
The believers were together
As Pentecost arrived.

Then like a mighty wind from
Heaven, strange sound spread.
It seemed flames or tongues
Of fire were on their heads.

The Holy Spirit spoke through
Them with joy, in strange lan-
guages which some thought was
Nothing but a ploy.

The speech was understood by
People of other lands. "What
Can this mean," they asked,
"From Galilee, every man."

Then Peter shouted them down,
Said, "Listen to what I say,
These you hear are not drunk;
It is too early in the day.

What you see this morning
Was promised centuries ago."
In the last days said God,
As was told by Joel,

"I'll pour out my spirit
On the race of man. Your sons
And daughters shall prophesy,
And God's glory shall expand.

The sun will turn dark, and
The moon will be as blood.
Strange sights from heaven;
Earth will panic and flood.

Any who call upon the Lord
Will that very day be saved.
The terror of those times
Shall not fill his days."

Our Lord Jesus of Nazareth
Was endorsed by God above.
By Him He's shown miracles,
Assured all men of His love.

Then God, according to plan,
Let Jews, by governed Rome,
Murder this remarkable man,
The best earth has known.

God brought Him back to life;
Jesus, death could not claim.
David quoted Jesus as saying,
(By scripture, He's the same),

"I know my Lord is with me,
Helps me with power. My Ton-
gue shouts praise and love;
He's at my side every hour.

You'll not leave me in hell
Nor let my body decay. You
Will give my life back to me,
We'll both know joyful days."

Think, dear brothers, on this,
Of a King looking far ahead.
He prophesied what happened;
God did not leave Jesus dead!

David knew the Messiah would
Surely be born from his line.
We know Jesus arose. We were
Blessed by Him in our time.

In heaven He sits at the
Right of God on His throne
With ability to send the Holy
Spirit we claim as our own.

"I state clearly," said Peter,
"God sent the Messiah, His son,
Whom you killed as a criminal
After the miracles He'd done."

Deeply moved, those sinners
Asked, "Tell us what to do."
So Peter answered their plea
Saying, "This is for you.

Change your ways for better;
Be baptized in His name today.
You can have His gift of life,
If for it you'll really pray.

For Christ promised everyone,
Who has listened to His call,
Even to you in other lands,
God will not let you fall."

Urgently Peter preached, and
Near three thousand he called.
They joined the believers and
Deep awe was a feeling of all.

Often they shared meetings
Worshipped in temple each day.
Met in homes for communion;
Many from the city were saved.

CHAPTER 3

At three P.M. they met for
Prayer, a custom those days.
A lame man was at the Temple,
Where he begged by the gate,

Peter and John approached,
Was asked by him for alms.
They offered a greater gift,
Not just grease his palms.

Looking at him Peter said,
"Silver and gold we've none.
But what we have to offer
Will let you walk or run."

Peter took his hand saying,
"In Jesus of Nazareths name,
We bid you stand and walk,"
And he was no longer lame.

Still holding the hand, Peter
Pulled him to his feet. Now
Those weak bones and muscles
Mended; he stood and leaped.

Into the Temple he walked,
Leaping and shouting for joy;
People were amazed at him
Who was crippled since a boy.

Peter took advantage of this
Interest the crowd had shown
To preach a powerful sermon,
Before much time had flown.

He addressed them thus, "Men
Of Israel, why be amazed? For
We've no power of ourselves;
Do this work by God's grace.

It was done by the murdered
One, whom God gave the glory.
He was promised by Moses and
Prophets of ancient story.

That servant of our God,
The one whom you rejected,
Came to bring eternal life
Man so callously neglected.

John and I are witnesses,
We saw Him die on the cross.
God brought Him back to life
And made victory out of loss.

We are witnesses before Him;
We saw Him again, alive. His
Name has glory and power by
Which He guides our life.

Jesus' name healed this man,
And you know how lame he
  was.
Faith has caused a miracle,
The faith that God gave us.

I realize, dear ones, you in
Ignorance crucified Christ.
God has fulfilled prophecies
Told from ancient times.

So change your attitudes and
Hearts; turn to Jesus' name.
Our fathers' God can save you
And bring Messiah back again.

He must remain in heaven as
Prophesied in olden times,
Until man changes his ways,
To turn his back on crime.

Moses said, "God will send
A prophet who resembles me.
So listen very carefully and
Consider His words decrees."

Every prophet since that time
Has supported Moses' claims,
That those who do not listen
Are subject to hell's flames.

The prophets were our fathers;
You're entitled to salvation.
He promised world blessings
Through the Jewish nation.

God made His son live again;
He sent Him first to you. Now
In turning your backs on sin,
You'd be blessing all Jews."

CHAPTER 4

Chief priests and Sadducees
Listened to Peter speak. And
They became very disturbed
To hear such things as these.

Peter and John were arrested
And kept in jail over night.
It was obvious some of them
Would not go without a fight.

Five thousand now believed,
Annas and Caiaphas in doubt.
The disciples were arraigned
To weed this movement out.

The council questioned and
Tried to find fault with both.
Peter addressed them boldly
Being led by the Holy Ghost.

"Honorable rulers and elders,
Speaking of the man we healed
In the name of Jesus, to whom
Your mercies didn't appeal,

By His will a man is well,
Jesus, Messiah whom you
Crucified, and God brought
Back to life after He died.

Recall the stone discarded,
Of which the scriptures told,
The strength of foundation
And more valuable than gold.

Messiah was referred to here;
None other can save from sin.
Under the canopy of heaven
No one can help you but Him."

The rulers saw boldness with
Which common men did speak.
The cured man stood there, so
Their argument seemed weak.

Soon they called them back,
Saying not to preach in Jesus'
Name. John and Peter said
They must tell of Jesus' fame.

Once again the council warned
Them, and sent them on. For
This miracle of healing had
Spotlighted Peter and John.

Once they were free they told
The other disciples all. Then
The believers united, and in
Prayer they made this call.

"Lord, God of heaven, maker
Of heaven, earth and the sea,
Long ago your servant David
Spoke of days like these.

Why nations against thee plot
Or heathen against you rage?
That is just what's happening
Here in this city today.

The rulers and many people
United against your son. They
Will stop at nothing in their
Power to see your work undone.

Do miracles by your servants;
May wonders be done each day.
Give us words of love to con-
duct ourselves without shame."

After their prayer was over,
The building there shook. The
Believers were all of a mind;
Only faith and prayer it took.

They sold all their property,
And with others they shared,
Preaching the message boldly,
Spending much time in prayer.

Many a "Barney the Preacher"
Sold their property or land
Gave the money to the needy
Through love of God and man.

CHAPTER 5

There was a man named
   Ananias;
He sold a piece of land, then
Indicated his small donation
Was total cash at his command.

Peter said, "Ananias, you
Help Satan. To the Holy Spirit

You lied. The choice was give
Or not! "Ananias suddenly died.

Every one was terrified, as
They well enough might be.
Ananias' wife came in,
Unaware
Of her husband's death you see.

Peter asked "How could you two
Put Gods Spirit to the test?
The young men just buried your
Husband," so knew of his death.

Imagine her instant fear, and
She too fell down and died.
The men Peter had mentioned
Buried her by Ananias' side.

Now terror was the byword of
All who heard the story. Disc-
iples taught at Solomon's Hall,
Did miracles for God's glory.

Sick were brought on beds or
Mats, to be where Peter's sha-
dow fell. From all around they
Came; all were made well.

Sadducees and priests could
See they were losing ground.
As easily seen, the disciples
Must quickly be brought down.

They were quickly arrested and
Into jail were thrown. But an
Angel came to their rescue,
And by morning they had flown.

Back to the temple as God's
Angel had told them to. They
Preached the Holy word of God
To a congregation of Jews.

The Jewish council convened,

Ordered the apostles to trial.
The palace police returned,
And were noticeably riled.

Guards were there, they said,
Jail house doors were locked.
The prisoners had disappeared,
At temple they preach of God.

Again they were arrested, be-
fore rulers and priests were
Taken. It was obvious how bad
Those rulers were shaken.

"We warned you about this
Preaching Jesus, and how we
Caused His death." "We obey
God, rather than men. From
Him comes life's breath."

Apostles answered, "The God
Of our Fathers gave Him life
After you caused His death
And on the cross He died.

God's mighty power exalted Him
To save Israel from sin. We
Witness of the Spirit, whom
God gives who believe Him."

Furious, the court would kill
But a Pharisee named Gamaliel,
An expert on Jewish law, in-
formed them, it'd not go well.

"Remember Theudas, the
    leader,"
He said, "who was said to be
Great. Had four hundred follow-
ers but was killed, and his
People abandoned by fate.

There was Judas of Galilee,
And many who followed his
    way.
He died, and all of his people

Scattered and strayed.

So leave them alone, I suggest,
If what they preach is their
Own, in time it will happen,
Their words will be overthrown.

If it is really of God, your
Chances of winning are slim.
You won't be able to hold out,
You cannot fight against Him."

They beat the disciples and
Sent them away with a warning,
Who were honored to be thought
Worthy, so taught in the
Temple every morning.

CHAPTER 6

Converts rapidly multiplied
Till they were a large crowd.
And as is usually the case,
Some were vocal and loud.

They said those widows, who
Spoke the language of Greece,
Were discriminated against,
Weren't getting enough to eat.

So the twelve had a meeting,
Chose seven, tried and true,
To arrange food to the needy,
All would share in their due.

The rest were left to their
Duties, more able to teach.
Many Jewish priests believed,
So many more did preach.

Stephen, full of the Spirit,
Did great works and deeds.
But was set upon by others
Because of jealousy and greed.

Some known as the "Freedmen",
A cult of the Jewish faith,
Of Cyrene, Alexandria, in Eg-
ypt, Celisia, Ausia, far away,

Banded together trying to dis-
credit his works, but not one
Could match him in wisdom;
In anger they went berserk.

They brought in some liars to
Perjure, put him on the spot,
Swore he spoke against the
Temple, against Moses and God.

Said, "He claims Jesus will
Wreck the Temple and Moses'
Laws." Stephen's face glowed;
They should have been awed.

CHAPTER 7

The high priest asked Stephen,
"Are these accusations facts?"
Said Stephen, "A Glorious God
Told Abraham, when in Iraq-

Leave your land and family,
And travel wherever I say."
So he left from Chaldea and
In Haran of Syria he stayed.

His father died; God brought
Him back to Isreal again. But
He was given no property here
Or even a small tract of land.

God promised him this country
Would go to descendants he'd
Spawn. They'd also be slaves,
A period four centuries long.

Ex-masters would be punished;
People would again worship
Here. A rite of circumcision
At God's insistence appeared.

Abraham circumcised son Isaac,
When he was eight days old. He
Was the father of Jacob, of
Whom great things were told.

Jacob sired twelve sons,
Patriarchs of the nation, who
Viewed their young brother
Joseph with indignation.

So they sold him into Egypt,
And he became Pharaoh's slave.
Now Joseph was very honest
And also totally brave.

So it's good to learn that
God smiled on him every day.
He followed the straight and
Narrow, as many went astray.

God kept him from affliction,
With favor in Pharaoh's sight.
So he became governor of Egypt,
Only Pharaoh had greater might.

A deep famine gripped the land,
But Egypt had full granaries.
His brothers sought food,
And Joseph heard their pleas.

In time he called his kindred;
They came to live in Egypt too.
Seventy-five there were, but
Their numbers rapidly grew.

Jacob died in Egypt and was
Taken home to rest. As God's
Promise to Abraham neared, the
Jewish population did crest.

Those patriarchs, Jacob's sons
Were taken back when they died
Too. The Egyptians felt they'd
Been joined by too many Jews.

A king came to power in Egypt,
Who'd no respect for Joseph's
Name. He plotted against them,
Brought to them great shame.

Things became intolerable, and
Moses was born about this time.
For a spell his father's house
Sheltered this child sublime.

His parents were forced to
Abandon him, to be found by
Pharaoh's daughter fair. Who
Raised him in the royal palace,
And he was educated there.

He became a mighty Prince
And was wise in many ways.
For he'd been tutored by the
Best Egypt had those days.

He went to visit brethren who
Slaved in the masters' fields.
And he witnessed an Egyptian
Giving a Jew a dirty deal.

He struck to chastise him,
The Egyptian fell and died.
He knew God sent him to help;
But his brothers didn't realize,

When men of Israel fought, he
Tried to stop a brawl. "Will
You kill me like an Egyptian?"
One asked, "who needs your
Help at all?"

Now Moses fled in fear and
Arrived in the land of Midian.
Word of his deed had gone
Farther than he had planned.

Two sons he sired while there
And forty more years expired.
Upon Mount Sinai, God spoke
From a blazing bush of fire.

As he gazed in wonder, heard
A voice of God. It said "Take
The shoes off your feet, for
You stand on sacred sod.

I'm the God of your ancestors;
I have heard my people's cry.
I've come to deliver them,
For I won't stand idly by."

God sent Moses to lead them
From Egypt through the Red Sea.
In wilderness forty years they
Wandered, from slavery free.

Moses told, our fathers God
Would send a prophet much like
Him, to keep them in line,
And out of the ways of sin.

Our ancestors rejected Moses,
Would return to slavery again,
Were prone to worship idols,
Made by the hands of men.

God turned away from them, as
They worshipped sun, moon and
Stars. They made a golden calf;
Allegiance had slipped by far.

In Amos' book of prophecies,
The Lord God says in warning,
"You'd rather worship heaven
Than God who made the
    morning.

You made idols forty years in
Wilderness and in sinful ways
Carried on." He said He would
Send them far beyond Babylon.

Stephen told of the Tabernacle
Ark, how ten commandments
    were there.
`Twas Joshua's weapon

In battle and with God's help,
Well they fared.

God blessed King David; he
Would build a Temple to God.
How Solomon finally did, but
Live in Temples, God does not.

"Heaven's my throne, says God,
Upon earth I'll rest my feet.
Anything that man can build
Cannot my requirements meet.

You've always persecuted the
Prophets as your fathers did.
Those who promised a Messiah,
Even the laws of God you hid.

You murdered God's Messiah,
The one whom you betrayed."
Jewish leaders were angered
Ground their teeth in rage.

But Stephen seemed unaware,
This was his awed story. "Look"
He said, "I see Jesus standing
At the right of God, in Glory!"

They grabbed him in fury and
Dragged him beyond a city wall;
They stoned him to death and
Bowed to one named Paul.

"Lord receive my spirit," he
Cried as stones flew at him,
His last words,"Don't charge
Them with this sin."

CHAPTER 8

Now Paul believed it was right
To treat Christians mean.
Threw men and women into jail
And caused many more to flee.

The apostles stayed on
But the other believers fled,

To Judea and Samaria escaped,
And Jesus' story they spread.

In Samaria Philip traveled
With great sermons, miracles
Galore. People listened here
Who'd never listened before.

Demons came screaming,
  tearing
From victims they'd possessed.
He healed paralyzed and lame
And put old Satan to the test.

A man named Simon, a sorcerer
Had bamboozled the crowds.
Because of his amazing acts
He was influential and proud.

Many a good Samaritan thought
Him the Messiah to come. But
Now Philip told about Jesus;
It was truly amazing to some.

Simon too believed Philip,
Followed wherever he went.
When the apostles heard about
Him, Peter and John were sent.

They arrived and prayed the
Holy Spirit would abide with
New baptized believers who'd
Accepted good news in stride.

Peter and John laid on hands;
The Holy Spirit entered there.
Simon offered money, if their
Secret with him they'd share.

"Your money perish with you,"
Peter cried, "God's gift can
Not be bought. Pray that God
Forgives your evil thoughts."

"Pray for me," cried Simon,
So these awful things won't

Happen to me, I'd be rid of
Sin, this you can easily see."

Peter and John returned to the
City teaching all the way.
Philip saw an angel, this he
Heard the angel say:

"Go to the road to Jerusalem
Through the desert at noon."
So he did as the angel said;
He met a man there soon.

An Ethiopian of authority, a
Purser of Candace the queen,
In charge of her riches, when
By Philip he was seen

Riding in his chariot and
The Spirit bade Philip go near.
Reading the prophet Isaiah,
Philip made the picture clear.

He declared belief in Jesus
And his wish to be free of sin.
Then they came upon a pond,
And Philip baptized him.

When the baptism was over, the
Holy Spirit took Philip away.
The Eunuch never saw him
  again,
Though rejoicing from that day.

Philip ended up at Azotas,
So he preached the good news
There; and in the cities
He preached it everywhere.

CHAPTER 9

Paul was still very busy, and
Christians paid the price. He
Called Jerusalem's high priest
So as to increase his strikes.

Men, women and children were
In chains for belief, his
Persecution of the Christians
Was designed for no relief.

Near Damascus on a mission,
Blinded by a light from above.
Paul, like an avenging eagle,
Now became more like a dove.

"Paul, why persecute me?" the
Voice of Jesus asked. He fell
To his knees in fear, still
Thinking persecution his task.

"Lord who are you?" he asked,
The answer was loud and clear.
"I am Jesus, whom you'd kill,
My followers you cause fear.

Now get up; go into the city;
Await instructions I'll send."
Paul was speechless, perhaps
Too frightened to pretend.

As he got up from the ground.
He realized he was also blind.
He was three days in Damascus,
Nor ate or drank in that time.

There was a believer in that
City, one Ananias by name.
He was told to find Paul,
That man of dubious fame.

In a vision he was told, he
Was chosen to make Paul see.
Jesus said, "I must show him
How he must suffer for me."

So Ananias found him to whom
On the highway Jesus appeared.
He who persecuted Christians,
Whom believers feared.

"Paul," he said, "Jesus sent
Me, so the Holy Spirit may be
Yours. And to bring you sight
That you may see your course."

Then laid his hands upon him,
And Paul's sight returned. Now
He ate and regained strength,
As the news within him burned.

In Damascus for several days,
In Synagogue he told the news.
Christ was truly God's son,
Who was crucified by the Jews.

All people were amazed; they
Thought him Christian's foe.
Now a fervent preacher, the
Leaders dare not let him go.

So they plotted murder, but
He learned about it all. Some
Of his new converts helped
Him escape over the city wall.

Jerusalem disciples feared
And considered him still mean.
Barnabus brought him to them,
Saying, Jesus, Paul had seen.

In time he was accepted, and
He spent much time with them.
There was soon a murder plot;
Friends sent him home again.

Throughout Judah, Galilee and
Samaria, they knew a time of
Peace. Growing in strength
And numbers, a great relief.

Peter roamed those countries
Till Aeneas of paralysis he
Cured. Eight years bedridden,
Many converts for God assured.

Dorcas, a kindly woman to all,
Suddenly took sick and died.
They wrapped her for burial,
Learned that Peter was nearby.

So they begged him to come to
Joppa; this he did post haste.
They took him up the stairs,
To the room where Dorcas lay.

Peter asked her friends to
Leave, he prayed and bade her
Rise. He took her by the hand,
And she opened her eyes.

Then he called in her friends,
Presented her alive. Then
Needless to say his converts
Were immediately on the rise.

Peter stayed in Joppa, living
With Simon, a friendly tanner.
You can bet he often raised
God's name in Christian manner.

CHAPTER 10

In Caesarea lived a man,
A captain of exellent renown.
Of prayer and generosity, by
Vision told, "Call Peter now."

The messenger angel left, he
Called trusted servants near.
Saying, "Find the man Peter,
And bid him please come here."

Peter was on his housetop,
Some were flat like a floor.
There he had a vision which
Caused a change forevermore.

Cornelius' messengers drew
Near; Peter stood all alone.
A multitude of things to eat
The Jews would never condone.

Animals, birds, and snakes,
Jews thought unclean. A voice
Said "Eat as you please." He
Said, "It's bad to eat these."

Thrice it was repeated, so
He sensed a message there.
Peter was very perplexed at
The meaning of this affair.

Then the messengers arrived;
He invited them to come in.
For they had inquired if this
Was where Simon Peter lived.

Peter lodged them overnight,
As told by the Spirit to do.
They told of a Roman officer,
Cornelius, respected by Jews.

Now they went to Cornelius;
He'd worship Peter there.
"No," said Peter, "I'm not
God, to hallow me isn't fair.

God gave me a message, that
Other men are good as Jews.
I can enter your home now,
"Gentile," is not bad news."

"Four days ago I prayed," he
Said, "and an angel of light
Appeared, said, call Peter,
The facts will be cleared.

Friends and I are gathered,
To hear you give the word."
Said Peter, "I'll impart
The best news you've heard.

The Jews have Messiah; now
Gentiles are accepted too.
Jesus died for salvation,
For both Gentiles and Jews.

That Jesus of whom I speak
Was murdered, yet he lives.
Heralded by early prophets,
His name is in Holy writ."

The Spirit came upon them,
Upon Gentiles as on Jews.
It was shown to all there;
This truly was good news.

Peter baptized them in the
Name of Jesus, Messiah and
Lord. Cornelius asked him
To stay on as a friend he
Could afford.

CHAPTER 11

The apostles and brethren
Learned the Gentiles received
The word. Those of Judea
Thought this totally absurd.

They questioned his preaching
The word to the uncircumcised.
He recounted his vision at
Joppa and also his surprise.

He told them of things which
He had thought unfit to eat.
And how the Lord let him know
His thoughts were incomplete.

How Cornelius sent for him,
A result of a vision he'd had.
How Peter went to Caesarea
With success anything but bad.

The Holy Ghost's presence
He taught to Gentile friends.
That they were as good as he,
And they must learn to bend.

On hearing these things, they
Objected to Peter no more.

The Gentiles were privileged
Too, a thing to be happy for.

To Phoenicia, Cyprus and Ant-
ioch, after Stephen's death,
Fearing for their very lives,
Many a believer had fled.

In places they'd preached,
But generally only to Jews.
Some preached to the Greeks;
Many Gentiles got the news.

The church at Jerusalem heard
Of the good work going on. So
They sent Barnabus to help;
He soon arrived at Antioch.

Barnabus did great work; his
Goodness and strength paid.
Many a soul was added, due
To his kindness and faith.

Barnabus journeyed to Tarsus;
And Paul, to Antioch returned.
There for a year of success
The name, "Christian" earned.

Prophets came from Jerusalem;
One named Agabus prophesied
There'd be a famine in Israel;
Crops would wither and die.

So the believers sent help,
Each giving all he could. It
Seems the way a Christian
Can walk tall and should.

CHAPTER 12

About now, Herod the King
Killed John's brother James.
Seeing this pleased the Jews
He thought it sort of a game.

So he had Peter arrested and
Thrown into jail. With

Sixteen soldiers guarding him,
An escape attempt should fail.

He would deliver after Easter
To the grasping hands of Jews.
But deep prayer by believers
Caused a change in the news.

During the night Peter was
Waked by an angel at his side,
He followed from the prison
With a swift and eager stride.

Now the angel left him when
He was safely in the clear.
Then he understood that night,
God had been very near.

Still in surprise and shock,
He knocked at Mary's gate.
Many were within in prayer
Who still pleaded his fate.

A damsel answered his knock,
Slammed the door, surprised.
She said he was there; they
Thought her out of her mind.

Peter kept on knocking until
They realized it was he. He
Told them what had happened,
Said, "To safer turf for me!"

At dawn the jail was turmoil
When Peter couldn't be found.
On the hapless guards, Herod
Took vengeance by the pound.

Herod moved to Caesarea, made
A speech of pomp and splendor,
The people called him a god;
It is something to remember.

God's angel struck him down,
With worms his body crawled.

He'd usurped God's glory,
His folly'd caused his fall.

Good news began to spread
And it moved across the land
As men reached out for God,
He lead them by the hand.

Now Paul and Barnabus visited
Jerusalem, and to Antioch ret-
urned, taking John Mark with
Them so he might also learn.

CHAPTER 13

Prophets and teachers there,
Lucius, Barnabus and a black
Man named Simeon. Paul and
Herod's half brother Manaeon.

The Holy Spirit spoke, His
Voice loud and clear, with
A job for Paul and Barnabus
And John Mark too it appears.

They laid hands on them and
Sent them on their way. They
Preached from town to town,
As they traveled day by day.

They crossed over Cyprus
And in Paphos met a fake. He
Was a Jewish sorcerer who
Much trouble tried to make.

The governor of the island
Sought their presence there.
Knowledge of the Lord was a
Treasure he wished to share.

This man urged the governor
Not to give them heed. For he
Was obviously on Satan's
Side in this jealous deed.

Then Paul, in anger flared,
"Son of Satan, enemy of good,

You've caused pain and misery,
Did all the harm you could.

God's hand is heavy upon you,
You're stuck in your own mess.
Your deeds have come home to
Roost, so grope in darkness.

Instant blindness came on him
And in fear he cried aloud.
He begged someone to lead him,
A revelation to the crowd.

When they left Perga, their
Helper John Mark left them.
It seems he yearned for home,
So he left for Jerusalem.

Antioch again they visited;
In the Synagogue were invited
To speak. Paul stood and said,
"To you who love God, I teach.

Israel's God found in Egypt
Our father's aburdened sore.
He rescued them from slavery
So we'd be His forevermore.

Forty years in the wilderness
He suffered ill manners gross.
Yet undid seven nations of
Enemies to keep Israel afloat.

Four centuries He gave judges,
Till the prophet Samuel came
Along. Then for forty years,
By Saul, a king most strong.

When David, God made king,
He was said to be His friend.
God promised, from his line,
Our Messiah Christ He'd send.

The Jews killed our Christ,
But God made Him live again.

Often he was seen in public,
The breath of life for men.

God kept His word to David,
Through Jesus forgives sin.
A thing Jewish law can't do,
And doesn't believe in whims."

Many people followed as
They left that day. The
Temple overflowed; Jewish
Leaders were enraged.

"God meant you Jews to carry
The news He sent you. Now
Gentiles have salvation for
It was rejected by Jews."

Now Jewish leaders stirred,
Caused a condition of hate.
They were run out of town,
Shook dust off at the gate.

Many were the converts that
This pair left behind. For
Many were lifted up and
Were no longer blind.

CHAPTER 14

They preached at Iconium;
Words found willing ears.
They were both convinced
Of truth they held dear.

Jews and Gentiles believed.
The Jews who spurned the word
Spread doubt among Gentiles
Of things not normally heard.

Long they stayed to preach
And proved their message true.
God was with them there, and
Great miracles helped too.

In time they had to flee for
Vicious lies had spread. So

Preaching good news to men,
To outskirt areas they fled.

Now in Lystra there was a man
With crippled feet from birth.
And he was listening to Paul
For all that he was worth.

This man's faith was great,
And such was plain to see. So
Paul bade him "Stand and walk,"
Which he did in obvious glee.

The crowd was suddenly
   shaken,
By this miracle they had seen.
To proclaim this pair as God's,
The whole multitude was keen.

Paul, who was chief speaker,
As "Mercury" was proclaimed.
"Jupiter" they named Barnabas,
As the two found sudden fame.

High priests brought flowers
To these they'd've glorified.
But Paul ripped his clothes
Alarmed and godhood denied.

"Worship the living God,"
They said. "Forget idols of
Stone. We come to bring news
Of our God on the throne,"

They barely convinced people
That they were merely men.
But a few days later, saw
A complete reverse of trend.

Jews of Antioch and Iconium
Riled up a murderous mob.
Tried to kill Paul, and
They nearly did the job.

As friends stood near, he
Got up, walked back to town.

Left with Barnabas next day,
This was unhealthy ground.

Again in Derbe He preached,
Made many disciples there.
Back to Antioch and Iconium,
Strong in faith and prayer.

Entry into the Kingdom is
Through hard work and trial,
Great love for God and each
Other throughout this while.

Much of the world they saw,
To Antioch again. A major
Operation for God to have
Carried out by man.

Glad Gentiles were inclu-
ded in blessings bestowed.
Stayed at Antioch a time,
Preached the word long ago.

CHAPTER 15

Paul and Barnabas at Antioch,
Heard preachers going through,
Taught about circumcision
As if it were something new.

At length they discussed, but
Reason seemed to no avail. So
They were chosen as delegates
To hit the Jerusalem trail.

Now they stopped a while at
The towns they passed through.
Letting Gentiles hear that
They could live forever too.

In Jerusalem they were met
By the church leaders there.
Paul and Barnabas reported
Their ministry most fair.

Now some erstwhile Pharisees
Took the floor and declared,

Gentiles must be circumcised
If eternal life they'd share.

So the elders and disciples
Set a meeting to decide. For
This issue must be settled
Before peace would abide.

Now the meeting dragged along,
Until Peter stood, and said,
"Brothers let's not look back,
But may we always look ahead.

The Holy Spirit freely gives,
God confirms the Gentiles too.
They can believe and trust
As well as a circumcised Jew.

We nor our fathers could bear
This yoke, so why hang it on
Them? Rather than force the
Issue, let us Jews unbend!"

So ended dissension that day,
And Barnabas took the floor.
Told of visiting the Gentiles
And miracles through the Lord.

James agreed with Peter, that
None be forced to adhere to
Rules foreign to nature but
With a heart honest and fair.

This letter they took to Ant-
ioch, where they went. Many
A life was enriched by the
Message thus sent.

Now Paul and Barnabas decided
To visit Turkey, where they'd
Been before. Barnabas wanted
Mark to go, changed the score.

Paul remembered how Mark had
Abandoned them one other time.

Barnabas apparently thought
It was an insignificant crime.

So they argued hotly over
This critical point. Then
Barnabas took Mark and left,
While with Paul, Silas joined.

With friends' blessings, for
Syria and Cylicia embarked,
Where they'd encourage the
Churches by prior work marked.

CHAPTER 16

To Derbe, Paul and Silas went,
Met another believer strong.
His mother was Christian; his
Greek father did little wrong.

They took Timothy in company;
He was circumcised by Paul.
His father didn't favor it,
But Timothy'd heard the call.

To placate Jewish neighbors,
The operation had taken place.
Then they went a traveling,
To spread the word of grace.

In faith and numbers the
Church now swiftly grew. They
Traveled Phrygia and Galatia,
Through much of Turkey too.

As into Bithynia they would
Go, the Holy Spirit bade them
Stay. To Troas they went ins-
tead, going the Spirit's way.

Then Paul had a vision, and
In his dream as seen, a man
From Macedonia, called
For their help, it seemed.

So aboard a boat we went and
Sailed across to Samothrace.

And on to Macedonia's border,
Here we stayed several days.

Several women were upon the
River bank that day. We taught
Them from the scriptures at
The place they'd come to pray.

Now Lydia was a seller of
Cloth of purple shade. A
Worshipper of our God, who
Believed the points Paul made.

Now she and all her household
Were baptized by us there.
Urged us to stay and visit,
Her home with us she shared.

Once, down beside the river,
We met a girl slave. She told
Fortunes for her master who
Took payment for the same.

She followed close behind us,
And her cry was heard afar.
"These men are here from God;
I'll tell you who they are.

Their mission is to save us
From our sinful wicked ways."
Thus she followed, and called
Out, it seemed for many days.

Soon it got annoying, until
Paul, in anger cried, "Come
Out in Jesus's name, you evil
Spirit, who dwelleth inside."

A spirit came forth that hour,
Her talent was whisked away.
Her master became our
Enemy from that very day.

They captured Paul and Silas,
Who were into prison thrown.

Their feet were put in stocks,
All hope for freedom flown.

But Paul and Silas prayed and
To God sang praise, suddenly
The prison was rent, as
The earth shook from a quake.

All the doors were opened;
Every band was loosed. The
Jailer would have killed him-
Self, as he sweat, and stewed.

Paul bade him stay his hand;
Every prisoner stood by. Then
The keeper knelt before him,
With all his heart he cried-

"Oh please save me sirs just
Tell me how to do." Paul said,
"Believe in Jesus Christ;
Salvation can be yours too."

Then he brought his family,
And all were baptized there.
Now their food with Paul and
Silas was gladly shared.

On the following morning in
Secret, so nobody would know,
Their erstwhile jailers would
Have had them quietly go.

But Paul refused to run, said
"Let them lead us out them-
selves. For as Roman citizens,
We weren't treated well."

They entered Lydia's house and
Calmed all the brethren down.
Then preached another sermon
Before they left the town.

CHAPTER 17

Amphipolis, Appolonia were
Towns they passed through

Going to Thessalonica,
And a Synagogue of Jews.

Three Sabbaths in a row,
Paul preached Christ arose.
Many of those of Greece
Believed it was so.

Some Jews did not believe;
They formed gangs of hoods,
Causing trouble, for friend
Jason it did little good.

Jason and friends sent
Them away at night. In
Berea where they arrived,
Paul did as he felt right.

Now people of Berea were
Nobler than those before.
They took them in, were
Willing to listen more.

The Jews from Thessalonica
Would not let Paul be. So
Again, he went his way,
Only this time by sea.

Brethren now conducted him
To Athens, the city state.
Paul asked the other two
To join within its gates.

Waiting for his friends,
He saw idolatry everywhere.
So preached at the market
To all who'd listen there.

Now some philosophers and
Others argued at length. For
They feared this new religion
Was gaining too much strength.

On Mars Hill he said, "Men
Of Athens, I see you prize

`The unknown God,' we know
As Him we call `The Christ.'

He gave all you have, and He
Dwells within your hearts. He
Made heaven, earth, and men.
He does nothing just in part.

Handiwork does not interest
Him; He needs not idols you
Make. But follow Jesus, whom
He sent for the future's sake.

From death God raised Him,
For assurance to all men.
Many mocked and doubted, so
He departed once again."

Some believed those truths
Which Paul held forth. In
Faith and love they walked
Upon this shining course.

CHAPTER 18

Soon Paul arrived in Corinth,
Here Aquila and Priscilla he
Met. Jews, once of Italy
Who were tentmakers yet.

At Synagogue each Sabbath he
Preached to Jews. But they
Mocked and doubted Jesus, so
He taught Gentiles the news.

"Your blood be upon you," he
Told the Jews, "I preach,
To Titus Justus, a Gentile,
And to many others I teach."

Some time Paul stayed next to
The Synagogue in Crispus'
House. For others in Corinth
Were believers most devout.

In a vision one night, God
Appeared to him, saying "I

Am with you in thick or thin for
Jewish displeasure is a whim.

Many have I here and I'll
Keep you from harm. So for a
Year and a half he stayed,
Knew his life was charmed.

Achaia's new governor refused
All claims, so Sosthenes,
The Synagogue's leader, was
A victim of Jewish frames.

They grabbed him outside the
Courtroom, beat him up there.
Gallio the governor ignored
Them, for He didn't care.

Several more days Paul stayed,
Then to them bid adieu. So
Now he sailed for Syria, and
Priscilla and Aquila went too.

In Ephesus he paused to visit,
And his hair he had shorn,
For a vow he had made, but we
Aren't sure of its form.

He was invited to stay, but
Had a date to keep. So from
Ephesus to Caesarea to Ant-
ioch, he must have lost sleep.

In Galatia, and Phrygia, he
Met Christians there. He met
Apollos a Jew of whom Aquila
And Priscilla were aware.

Apollos preached John's bapt-
ism, spoke convincingly too.
Priscilla and Aquila helped
Him, for there was much to do.

Jews were hard to convince,
Yet he seemed able in a trice

To prove by scriptures that
Jesus was truly the Christ.

CHAPTER 19

On Paul's travels he asked if
The Holy Ghost they had
  known.
Negative, the answers, their
Ignorance they now owned.

They'd been baptized by John
To repentance, Paul said. And
They must believe in Jesus,
And that He wasn't dead.

So now they were all baptized
In Jesus's loving name. Paul
Put His hands upon them and
The Holy Spirit quickly came.

In tongues they then spoke,
And they prophesied as well.
They prophesied in Jesus' name
And numbered about twelve.

In the synagogue Paul spoke
Boldly, disputing some there,
As the Kingdom of God, in
Their minds they compared.

Some spoke against Paul and
Belittled his work, so
He separated from them and
Found another place to report.

Thus for two whole years, he
Taught very well for the Lord.
Both the Greeks and the Jews
All over Ausia got the word.

The Lord was with Paul and
Many miracles he performed.
The sick were quickly healed;
Great things were the norm.

Some conjurors then came,
Jewish brothers of no repute,
Who tried to cast out demons
And were severely rebuked.

They were beaten for their
Trouble, when using Paul's
And Jesus' name, by the same
Devils they tried to tame.

Now many people came and
Gave up the pagan ways. Even
Burning evil charms and books,
Confessing sins most grave.

Greatly grew God's word in
Ausia during Paul's stay.
For to speak diligently and
Boldly seemed to be his way.

The spirit whispered that
New scenery was in order. So
He sent two of his followers
Across the Macedonian border.

Yet for a season he stayed
In Turkey to teach. But his
Preaching caused trouble for
Some men of greed.

Some silversmiths who worked
Making shrines or false Gods,
Lost money to Christianity,
Were fearful for their jobs.

They occupied a theater with
Two hostages, Paul's friends.
And great was the bedlam, as
His mission they'd end.

Now the mayor of the town
Got their full attention,
Said "This illegal meeting
Has no reason worth mention.

So take it to the court, or
You're in danger of the law."
He broke up a near riot and
Their cold anger thawed.

CHAPTER 20

After the uproar had calmed,
Paul called his people near.
He embraced them, every one,
To him they were very dear.

So to Macedonia for the Lord,
Three months later to Greece.
Now hearing Jews lie in wait,
Back to Macedonia to teach.

Now seven of his followers
Had gone on before.
All of them met in Troas
To carry on once more.

Then we sailed once again,
After the passover days.
Five days we sailed and
In Turkey, a week we stayed.

Sunday, Paul was preaching,
His friends gathered around.
One who fell asleep, fell
Three stories to the ground.

Now the fact that he died,
Is testified in the book.
And everyone there except
Paul was badly shook.

Taking Eutychus in his arms
Said "Fear not, he's alive."
In joy we ate the passover;
Another sermon we'd abide.

Tenacious were those people!
How God's word they loved!
After half an hour's sermon,
We think of hats and gloves.

All that night he preached!
A journey ahead next day.
He'd have had little rest,
And much time he prayed.

Though Paul was in a hurry,
At Miletus spoke to friends.
"I've willingly served and
Been faithful to the end."

CHAPTER 21

"I know danger awaits me, but
The Holy spirit beckons so I
Go. You will never see me
Again, this is a fact I know.

And now I leave you all, whom
I've striven to educate, for
I've taught you with dilig-
ence, and it's getting late."

He'd warned of coming trials
And to teach God's own love.
He prayed with them earnestly
For guidance from above.

So we sailed toward Jerusalem,
Past Cos, Rhodes and Patara
Too. On another ship to Syria,
Great places to pass through.

Many believers urged Paul to
End this voyage. For the Holy
Spirit warned them, by the
Jews he might be destroyed.

Paul pushed determinedly on,
And many came to see us sail.
So Tyre was left behind on
Our long and tedious trail.

At Ptolemais we greeted some
But only stayed a day. Then
Stopped at Caesarea, where
For several days we stayed.

Philip, an evangelist, had
Four daughters with the gift,
And a man named Agabus,
Warned Paul much like this.

"If you go to Jerusalem,
In great danger you will be.
The Jews are plotting daily;
Your downfall they would see."

Paul said, "Weep not for me,
For Jesus I'll die or go to
Jail. The Holy Spirit leads;
My mission I shall not fail."

He could not be dissuaded, so
We said, "God's will be done."
Then we packed our things and
Left to face what might come.

Other disciples came with us,
At Mnason's home we stayed.
At the church of Jerusalem
We met the elders and James.

Paul recounted many things
With the Gentiles he had done.
They said, "It is wonderful;
Here is problem number one.

We have many good Jews, who
Of course, are believers too.
They want more Jewish customs
To be followed by you."

So Paul shaved his head, and
For some others he also paid.
Customs of his Jewish friends,
He did not attempt to evade.

His vow almost complete he
Fell afoul of Turkish Jews,
Who grabbed him at the Temple
And spread erroneous news.

They took him from the Temple,
Would have killed him there.
The Roman garrison
   commander,
Paul's life quickly spared.

The soldiers, to protect him,
On shoulders, held him high.
Amid shouting and clamor,
The mob in frustration cried.

"Away with him, away with
   him,
Take this man away!" He said
To the commander, "Please
Sir! Let me have my say."

Now the commander was
   amazed,
Because Paul had spokenGreek.
He wished to talk to the mob;
The soldiers quickly agreed.

CHAPTER 22

In the silence that ensued,
In Hebrew he proclaimed, how
Having been educated a Jew,
All the christians he'd had
Killed or maimed.

He'd hounded and jailed many
For faith which they believed.
And on the road to Damascus,
He was plotting more grief.

The light from heaven blinded
Him, and life greatly changed.
For his deeds in future were
With those martyrs arraigned.

How a Jew named Ananias,
A man both tried and true,
Cured him of his blindness,
And told him what to do.

For Paul had been chosen to
Do God's work on earth. To
Spread to all the world, the
Story of Jesus' royal birth.

"To Jerusalem I returned. At
The Temple, as I prayed, I
Had a Vision, saying now
From Jerusalem go away."

"Lord," I said, "these Jews
Know on their side I fought.
And the fact that I'm a Jew,
Does it all stand for naught?"

"They'll not believe you here,
So I'll send you far and wide.
For if you tarry here, these
Jews will have your hide."

God said, "I'll send you far;
To Gentiles you will preach."
Now when he said this, those
Jews all began to screech.

"Away with him" they shouted,
"The Gentile lover's not fit
To live. Throw him out of the
City; show him short shrift."

Inside the soldiers took him;
The lash was quickly applied.
But Paul asked why a Roman
Citizen was lashed, not tried.

Now afraid, they left him and
Next day he was set free. So
They brought him into session
With council and priests.

CHAPTER 23

Paul began to state his case
But a high priest interfered.
If we'd heard Paul's comment,
We just might have cheered.

Paul was duly corrected, and
His apology seems quite clear.
Yet we know, not always
Are things as they appear.

Accusers were Pharisees and
Sadducees, each about half.
The way he handled hecklers
Makes me want to laugh.

"Men and brothers," he said,
"I was a Pharisee all my life.
I believe in the hereafter, so
I'm being caused this strife."

Sadducees believe not this,
So were split down the center.
Paul was nearly torn apart by
The contest of his tormentors.

The chief captain rescued him;
God appeared to Paul at night.
"You honored me in Jerusalem,"
He said "to Rome take light."

Now certain Jews conspired,
To rid the world of Paul. His
Nephew heard them plotting,
And to Paul he told it all.

Paul called an officer, the
Chief commander listened well.
Then sent the boy away with
A warning not to tell.

Late at night Paul was taken
Away, guarded by the officers
Men. To the governor was del-
ivered, and a note was penned.

"This man, rescued from a mob,
Was I think, unjustly accused.
I'm sending him to you, who
Will good judgment use."

To the Governor they brought
Him, asked from ere he hailed.
"From Silicia," he said, from
Which long ago he'd trailed.

"I'll hear the case," said the
Governor, "when your accusers
Come." He stayed in Judgement
Hall until his trial was done.

CHAPTER 24

Five days came and went, and
Ananias, a chief priest, showed.
Some other Jewish leaders and
Tertullus, their lawyer spoke.

"You have been so good as to
Give much peace to us Jews. We
Do not wish to bore you, but
Please listen to our views.

This man is seditious and
Profaned the Temple, we saw.
We captured, would have judged
Him according to our law.

But this captain came upon us
And violently took him away."
The Governor motioned to Paul,
To rise and have his say.

Paul got up and refuted all
The things they'd claimed. He
Knew that Felix might ignore
All the barbs they'd aimed.

"I followed Jewish tradition,
Have obeyed laws and rites.
Was born a Pharisee," He said,
"And believe in an after life.

Now these men accuse me, but
They cannot prove their claim.
Jews found me in the Temple
And tried to distort my aims."

Felix put them off because
He knew of their perfidy. And
Though keeping Paul a prisoner
Allowed him a lot of liberty.

Felix and Drusilla visited;
Paul taught about temperance.
"Go ahead," said Felix, "but
I'll keep you in remembrance."

Felix visited quite often,
Hoping for a bribe. But that
Was one of those things to
Which Paul did not subscribe.

Two years Felix kept him a
Prisoner with his fate unclear.
Portius Festus became Governor,
And Felix still left him here.

He sought favor with the Jews
Used this means to gain. So
Paul again would face the men
Who'd already caused him pain.

CHAPTER 25

Festus went to Jerusalem; the
Jews again presented a claim.
If he'd bring Paul to waylay
And kill him was their aim.

But Festus said, "You come to
Caesarea, I'll return soon.
You'll get your chance for
Your claims to prove."

Again they hurled charges,
Which Paul, of course denied.
Festus asked, "In Jerusalem
Would you be tried?"

"No, I'll appeal to Caesar,"
Paul said, so Festus agreed.
King Agrippa with Bernice
Came to hear Paul speak.

Festus said "This man, Jews
Would put to death, what do I
Tell the Emperor? For I see
No charge to press.

So please, oh King Agrippa,
Listen to what he has to say.
I know nothing to tell Caesar
When I send Paul his way."

CHAPTER 26

King Agrippa said to Paul,
"Go ahead, speak your piece."
Paul said, "It is good, oh
King, that you listen to me.

For the Jewish laws you know,
Their various customs as well,
So if you'll be patient sir!
I do have much to tell.

You know well and so do they,
As a Pharisee I was raised.
But there is a reason why,
For my death they are crazed.

Because I believe and teach
That Jesus whom they killed
Still lives. Is it strange
That God new life can give?

Once I was on their side and
Delivered Christians to die.
A great light shown upon me;
God spoke to such as I.

God sent me on a mission, to
Tell this glorious truth.
I've been true to the vision
From that day of my youth.

I preached first in Damascus,
Then Jerusalem, and in Judea.
Now these Jews would kill me,
For telling this great idea.

God protected me, as I told
What Moses and the prophets
Said, the beloved Messiah
Would suffer, and in three
Days rise from the dead."

Festus shouted, "You studied
Too hard and lost your mind."
Paul answered, "I'm sane and
Sober; you are very unkind."

Agrippa asked, "Do you expect
To convert me with words like
These?" Paul said, "If you all
Were saved, I'd be pleased."

They agreed they'd not heard a
Thing to warrant Paul's death.
Had he not appealed to Caesar
They'd put his trial to rest.

CHAPTER 27

Now they made arrangements
To take our group to Rome.
So Julius, a Roman officer,
Headed us toward our new
    home.

Aristarchus of Thessalonica,
A Greek, came with us by boat,
Which made a number of stops
Along the Turkish coast.

Julius was very kind to Paul,
Even letting him go ashore.
But due to treacherous winds,
It was hard to keep on course.

Near Cyprus and the mainland,
All along the coast we passed
Provinces of Pamphilia and
Celicia, landing at Myra last.

A ship from Alexandria, bound
For Italy took us on our way.

The sailing was very rough
Due to winds and giant waves.

Now as we neared Cnidus,
The wind became too strong.
So we ran across to Crete
Passing the port of Salmone.

So slowly against the wind,
We gradually made our way. We
Finally landed at Fair Havens,
Near the city of Lasea.

It was dangerous to go far;
The season was too advanced.
Paul told the officers aboard;
It was an unwise chance.

The crew was getting anxious,
Fair Havens was a poor winter
Port. Aiming next for Phoenix,
This harbor they'd abort.

The wind switched to south,
And the trip seemed more safe.
So close along the shore and
Northerly, they made way.

Soon there blew a northeaster,
Which forced them out to sea.
They couldn't buck the wind,
Before it were forced to flee.

Waves grew high and angry,
As the windy tempest roared.
The crew threw into the angry
Sea, all cargo found aboard.

Now two weeks or so, they'd
Gone with very little to eat.
Paul took this opportunity
Once again to speak.

"If you hadn't sailed you'd
Have had no injury or cost.

Last night God spoke to me;
There'll be no human loss.

However we will lose the ship,
And on an island will be cast.
Take heart and believe God's
Word, one thing that lasts."

As darkness turned to dawn,
Paul begged everyone to eat.
"For you haven't eaten much,"
He said, "for nigh two weeks."

He had a piece of hardtack,
Shared with every one aboard.
Two hundred seventy-six, how
Could it feed this hoard?

They felt much better and
Dumped more load into the sea.
And in the growing light they
Noted a bay with sandy beach.

They headed between rocks and
Steered for the calmer bay,
But ran aground on a sand bar;
The ship was wrecked by waves.

Prisoners, some soldiers would
Have killed, but Julius said
"No! Grab whatever floats
And head for shore, let's go!"

We clung to planks or flotsam,
Quite safely escaped to shore.
The ship, demolished by the
Storm, soon was there no more.

CHAPTER 28

It was the Isle of Malta,
By the natives we were told.
They kindly built a bonfire
To protect us from the cold.

As Paul helped gather fuel,
A snake bit him on the hand.

He shook it off into the fire
And continued as he'd planned.

People watched expectantly
For Paul to sicken and die.
But when he showed no signs,
They couldn't quite decide.

They said he's a murderer,
But now they thought, a deity.
And so with food and gifts
They performed a fealty.

The Governor of the island
For three days fed us all.
His father, who was sick,
With prayer was cured by Paul.

So then the sick converged
And came to Paul for cures.

They brought us many gifts
And were our friends for sure.

Three months we tarried there,
Before we again set sail. For
A ship, "Twin Brothers" shelt-
ered out of winter gales.

We visited several other
Places on the Adriatic sea.
But we finally got to Rome,
Where Paul wanted to be.

He could live where he wished
So long as he stayed in Rome.
For though guarded by a
Soldier, this was now his home.

END OF ACTS

ROMANS

CHAPTER 1

Dear friends, this is from
Paul, a ready slave of Christ.
I was chosen as His messenger,
To set a great truth right.

Long ago scriptures promised
A king from David's line. As
A tiny baby he came and grew,
Triumphed over death and time.

So He proved to be God's son
With God's holy nature too.
We've been around the world
To show His love for you.

Wherever I go I hear, what
Wonderful Christians you are;
I thank God for this report;
His love has reached so far.

Day and night I pray for you
And serve the God of light.
Telling others of God's son,
A product of His might.

I pray that I might visit you,
That I may give you strength.
And it also is a truth, that
I need your help at length.

Many times I would have come,
But I've always been detained.
Now I'm ready to come to you,
Of His truth I'm not ashamed.

All you of the Gentile church
Are as deserving as the Jews.
Just believe in Jesus Christ;
You too can share this news.

Scriptures have always said
You trust God through faith.

If you trust in His word,
From ruin you'll be safe.

From early days men have seen
God's wonders on the earth.
Yet Men do work wickedness
With no interest in rebirth.

God shows His anger from
Heaven against all evil men.
For they push away the truth
And sin again and again.

Knowing who He was of course,
They kept driving Him away,
When they should have been
Obeying Him every day.

Their minds they perjured
With confusion of thought.
Turned their efforts to idols
Which men had wrought.

God finally let them go, in
Their violence, sex and sin.
They left the way of natural
Life, for Satan's every whim.

There were Gays and Lesbians,
Even in those far off days.
For every kind of wickedness
Their souls in time would pay.

Greed, hate and envy became
Their normal way of life.
Disobedient to their parents
And too often causing strife.

Aware God's penalty is death
Yet evil through and through.
Forged ahead in wickedness,
They tempted others too.

CHAPTER 2

Well you may be saying, those
People were certainly bad.

But if you think you're so
Perfect, that is also sad.

Punishment for sin is certain,
Whether you're a Gentile or a
Jew. How long do you think
God will be patient with you?

Thus far he has tolerated all
The terrible things you've
Done. Hoping you'd wise up
And back to God you'd come.

For you've done things
You condemned in others.
Remember, in God's sight
Gentiles and Jews are brothers.

God gave us all a conscience,
And it tells us how to behave.
He will punish sin by anyone;
The good ones He will save.

God will judge secret lives;
He knows all thoughts and
Aims. This is part of His
Great plan which I proclaim.

You teach Jewish rules to
Others; you do it very well.
But you break God's laws, so
Why not teach yourselves?

God welcomes those who
Are right in heart and mind.
But those who only pretend,
He will surely leave behind.

CHAPTER 3

Now what are the advantages
For a man to be a Jew? If he
Is true to Jewish laws, in
Fact there are quite a few.

Some of course are unfaithful,
But His word God won't change.

Honesty in everything we do
Is the end for which He aims.

Tongues are prone to lie;
No one has ever been good.
No one has ever really tried,
Although we know we should.

Men are quick to kill and
Hate those who disagree,
Caring nothing for our God,
Nor for what He sees.

The wonderful laws of God
Can lead us to a perfect end.
It's clear, all has failed;
His laws and will we bend.

All we learn from law is
That we're sinners, every one.
But now we can know His grace,
Just by believing in His Son.

Scripture told us many times,
As did the prophets of long
Ago. But God sent us His Mes-
siah to show the way to go.

So we boast of earning the
Salvation for which we strive.
But if we believe in Jesus,
He will change our lives.

For only if we trust in Him,
His laws can we obey.
And then as God has planned
Can we be saved by faith.

CHAPTER 4

God Promised Abraham a son;
Abe was nearly a century old.
Abraham never doubted but
Believed what he'd been told.

And Abraham became the father
Of many nations, as we know.

Abe knew before it happened
For He'd said it would be so.

God accepted Abraham on faith,
On faith will accept us too.
Brought Jesus back from death,
And thus He paid our dues.

CHAPTER 5

Through faith we've gained,
Made better in God's sight.
We have peace with Him,
By the work of Jesus Christ.

Because of our faith He has
Brought our privilege high.
And we look joyfully forward,
To all God has in mind.

Trials should cause rejoicing,
Build patience and strength.
Each time it happens, we grow
To have more faith at length.

We know how God loves us; the
Holy Spirit is our proof.
In the light of all His love,
How can we be aloof?

Adam brought death from sin;
Jesus in mercy brought life.
As Adam brought death to us;
Jesus brought hope and light.

Commandments were given to
Show man how badly he failed.
Much like a mirror they show
How Satan so often prevailed.

Sin once ruled over life, now
God's kindness rules instead,
Giving us hope with Him, and
Of life to which Jesus led.

CHAPTER 6

Now shall we keep on sinning
Because our God forgives? Nay!
The alternative is goodness,
Which guarantees we live.

The power of sin was broken,
As unto Him we were baptized.
Our sinful natures He buried,
As He bore our sins and died.

End your bodies of evil doing
And stand upright every day.
For now you're dead to sin,
So go seek the godly way.

No more need sin be master;
You can choose the way you go.
So choose your Master Christ
And in His goodness grow.

Any master will accept you;
Make sure your choice is wise.
Become slaves of what is good,
Instead of cheap acts or lies.

When you were slaves of evil,
Doing good was not your forte.
But do not shame yourself
Now, by what you do today.

CHAPTER 7

When a person passes on, the
Law no longer applies. As a
Woman is no longer married,
When her husband dies.

The Mosaic law died to you,
When Christ died on the cross.
Since you are dead to sin,
You are also dead to law.

The law is not your worry, so
Serve God with heart and mind.

God's laws are not evil,
They only show sin's bind.

My heart had known no evil,
Nor the sin lurking within.
The fact that law was there
Tended to show my sins.

So I was fooled by sin for
By law, I should have died.
The law, although it's good,
Would have had me tried.

So sin is using God's good
Laws to put us in a bind. Oft'
I fail to do what's good,
For sin that's in my mind.

The love of God compels me
To want to do what's right.
But my old basic sinful self
Controls me like a blight.

So now you see my problem,
Who will save and set me free?
Thank God Jesus has done so
When He died for you and me.

CHAPTER 8

There is no condemnation for
Those who walk in the light.
The spirit, in which I now
Live, has given me new life.

Knowing God's commandments
Cannot save you from sin.
For only through Jesus' power
Can you possibly win.

Only through the grace of God,
Which His Son bought for man,
Can we obey God's laws more
Fully, the only way we can.

If a base nature controls you,
His will you cannot obey. But

When God's Spirit lives within,
It gives peace every day.

All who live by faith in Him,
Will share His glory too.
Release from sin, death and
Illness, will also be our due.

We are patiently waiting, for
That bright and glorious day,
When all evil will disappear,
Thorns, death and decay.

We who are Christians look
Forward with hope and pray,
To be released from suffering
Pain and so rejoice each day.

Now the Holy Spirit knows
What it is for which we yearn.
And He intercedes each day to
Help us God's benefits earn.

How can we think to fail with
Such great promises as these?
From all the pain and toil on
Earth, He promised release.

Scriptures tell us be ready
For Him; be prepared to die.
But He will always be at hand
If we're accused or tried.

None can keep His love from
Us, of this I've seen proof.
For when we cry in times of
Trouble, He never seems aloof.

Tomorrow we need not worry,
Nor today to live in fear.
For when our Lord died for us,
He made the promise clear.

CHAPTER 9

Now my people Israel,
You cause me great distress.

You number in the millions,
But so many have digressed.

Cheerfully I'd be punished,
If you'd accept God's love.
But you spurn His laws and
Offers, refuse to look above.

Our fathers were men of great
Renown, and Christ was one of
You. His promise was made for
You who are also Jews.

Even Abraham's children are
Not all of his mind. When the
Promises were made for Isaac,
All others were left behind.

Isaac's wife was told, "Your
Sons will be twin boys. The
Older will serve the younger,"
She may have known mixed
    joys.

The Bible says quite clearly
That God chooses whom He
    will.
And if you'll only note, whom
He chooses fills the bill.

He even said to Moses, "I'll
Be kind to whom I choose."
So it does seem that some
Are preordained to lose.

Do not question His actions,
For God made us as we are.
To second guess his reasons
Would lead us astray too far.

Even Pharaoh, King of Egypt
Was used to show God's power.
Some He may ignore, others
With fortune shower.

Remember the potter's work,
How he chooses to form clay.
Making one vessel beautiful
And another a different way.

His is the right to exercise
His fury and destruction, or
Show great mercy to us with
Kindness and instruction.

He can call the heathen His
And shower on them His glory.
But His chosen who only kept
The law, may be another story.

Christ became a stumbling
Block for many Jews. But
Those who believe in Jesus
Are recipients of good news.

CHAPTER 10

I would love to see you saved,
Brothers of the Jewish faith,
You show great honor for God
But in a misdirected way.

Christ died to set us right,
A thing you cannot see. You
Think to follow Moses' law
Is the only way it can be.

Moses taught that by the law,
Was salvation's only chance.
But on the cross Jesus died,
By faith, salvation's grant.

No need to search heaven or
From the dead bring Him back.
Salvation is in trusting Him,
In hearts and minds, a fact.

If at heart a man believes
And tells it to his friends,
He confirms that he is saved
And is God's until the end.

Call upon the name of Christ,
Jew or Gentile, all the same.
For whatever you need or want,
Just call upon His name.

But how can they ever ask
If they don't really believe?
And how can they do that, if
The word they won't receive?

How will anyone tell them
Unless first he's told to go.
How beautiful are those who
Tell, the Bible says it's so.

But not all who hear believe,
Isaiah said so well, "Lord,
Why do so few listen, when
I've such good news to tell?"

Faith will come to listeners;
What about the Jews? They
Have the written word; salva-
tion will be given others
If they still refuse.

CHAPTER 11

So has God deserted the Jews?
"Oh no, it is not so! He
Chose them in the beginning.
This the scriptures show."

When Elijah thought he was
The only believer left. "No
There are seven thousand more,"
God answered swift and deft.

Today shows no change; there
Are others still in the race.
They've come into the fold as
A result of God's good grace.

If they've come by grace,
It's not because of works.

So once again it was a gift
As per God's loving word.

Some have found His favor,
But others eyes are blind.
King David said it well, "Let
Their wealth become a bind."

Remember all you Gentiles,
God's promise is given to you,
Because you willingly believe,
Which the Jews refused to do.

So be not overbearing, taking
Credit unto your selves. But
Be humble, thankful followers,
For you've great news to tell.

Think, in time to come, when
His blessing includes Jews,
How much more his glory will
Be lavished upon you.

We've a special job to do, to
Make them jealous of your lot.
To hopefully speed them up
And turn their lives to God.

There will be a future day
When all Jewry will be saved.
Their fathers were promised,
And thus the road was paved.

Some fall along the way, but
As all Gentiles come who will,
The Jews will return to God,
And promises He'll fulfill.

God gave up the Jews, so as
To take the Gentiles in. So
He shows His mercies to you,
While others continue to sin.

His knowledge and His wisdom
Show what a great God we love.

Who could possibly counsel or
Guide this knowing God above?

CHAPTER 12

Let your body be a sacrifice,
One that God can use. Let the
Words and actions be honest,
As godly men would choose.

Don't be proud or arrogant,
Only show strength and faith.
Let each man do what's best;
Show love to the human race.

No matter what you do, do it
Well without show or bluster.
Preacher, teacher, common man,
The best that you can muster.

Be glad for what you have,
And help the sick and weak.
If any would treat you mean,
Just turn the other cheek.

Show everyone godliness,
Kill enemies with kindness.
Those who return bad for evil
Only show their blindness.

CHAPTER 13

Obey the laws of government,
Through God's will it rules.
Even though it often seems
We're being ruled by fools.

Law is not a fearsome thing,
If you work within its sphere.
Only if you break the rules
Is authority a thing to fear.

Follow the laws of the land,
Do only things that are good.
For it can save you trouble,
And you know you should.

Respect those in authority,
And pay your taxes too. Love
Your neighbor as yourself,
Be there with friendship too.

Avoid lust, cruelty, jealousy,
For this is the golden rule.
Love answers to everything,
Will keep all problems cool.

CHAPTER 14

If in your heart you think
Your brother's faith is weak,
Don't cause him consternation,
Or his discomfiture seek.

For instance if he believes
To eat certain meat is wrong,
Do not do so in front of him
Even if your faith is strong.

For if you believe it's Okay,
It isn't wrong for you. But
His faith is not as yours,
So it's wrong for him to do.

Don't find fault with anyone,
No matter what you believe.
For each will have his turn
Before God's judgement seat.

Some believe Jewish holidays
Are the ones we should honor.
Others say that every day
Is special to our Father.

Living or dying, we follow
God, forever His we'll be.
He died to be our Lord and
From sin to set us free.

"For as I live," God has said,
"Each knee will bend, tongue
Confess." Don't criticize
Others, live together instead.

Whatever a man believes,
For him it's the way to go.
And if you try to change his
Mind, that doesn't make it so.

CHAPTER 15

Do unto others to please them,
Don't just satisfy yourselves.
All Christ did for mankind,
They never treated Him well.

Long ago much was written, to
Teach courage and patience.
So He conquered sin and death,
Which will be our salvation.

So treat each other well,
For thus God meant it to be.
That between Jew and Gentile
There should be eternal peace.

So praise the Lord in harmony
For Christ, the Gentile King.
I know my people, you're wise
And will teach these things.

These things I've emphasized
And now make bold to say, I'm
Proud of what He's done by me,
The Spirit's power and grace.

I've preached to many, but
Many Gentiles still haven't
Heard. My hope is to travel
More and bring many the word.

I'm ready to travel at last,
For my work here now is done.
So I will stop at Jerusalem,
As I'm on my Spain-ward run.

I would deliver a gift to
The Christians who there live.
For those in Macedonia and
Achaia have very much to give.

Word was brought to them, by
Those who sent a gift. Life
In Jerusalem is difficult;
This should give a lift.

So as I journey onward, for a
Time I'll visit your homes.
The Lord of peace be with you,
When I travel on to Rome.

CHAPTER 16

Meet Phoebe a Christian woman,
Who is coming to see you
Soon. She's an honored sister,
To the church a welcome boon.

Deserving loving appreciation,
She's helped others and me.

And there are many more who
Have followed God's decree.

To note the numbers, there
Must be two dozen there. Each
Is immersed in God's work
Doing more than just a share.

Our Lord's grace be upon you,
For this was His secret plan.
To give Gentiles His bless-
ing since the world began.

As scriptures told of yore,
His message goes round the
World. So to Him who is wise,
May the Christian flag unfurl.

END OF ROMANS

1ST. CORINTHIANS

CHAPTER 1

To the Christians of Corinth,
Whom God so richly blessed.
May He give you blessings,
And may you offer your best.

I, Paul and brother Sosthenes,
Will be praying every day.
So God our Father and Christ
Will uphold you in every way.

I was chosen as His messenger;
I told you how it would be.
But dear brothers in Christ
May you always be at peace.

I've heard some of you claim
That you follow Paul;
Others say Apollos or Peter,
And that's not true at all.

None of us died for your sins
Or baptize you in our name.
Christianity is very serious;
It is not a one upman's game.

I preach the message of the
Cross in words of truth and
Power, The secret of reaching
People any day or hour.

The world ignores the message;
They'll find heaven by them-
selves. But God confounds
Sharp minds; His plan excells.

It seems foolish to the Jews,
From heaven they want a sign.
Gentile belief doesn't agree
So crowd it from their minds.

We preach that Jesus died to
Save ourselves and friends.

The Jews are quickly offended,
To Gentiles it makes no sense.

God has chosen some of each
To show His wondrous love.
Christ is the center post
Of the plan from God above.

God in His weakest moment, is
Stronger than others. Notice
That none who follow Christ
"Lord it" over their brothers.

God has used simple things
To bring the mighty low.
Our salvation through Jesus
Christ is due to Him alone.

So if one would boast, let it
Be of what God has done. He
Made us worthy of salvation,
Through giving us His son.

CHAPTER 2

Timid, trembling, I came, dear
Ones, words simple and plain.
I spoke of his death on the
Cross, of His love and pain.

The Spirit's power was there
Proving I spoke God's word. I
Want to plant faith in God
With the greatest story heard.

Among real Christians I speak
With great wisdom to all. But
It is foolishness to worldly
Men, who are doomed to fall.

This wisdom is of God, not
Understood by the wisest men.
But the plan has been there
Ever since the world began.

If men had understood, they'd
Never have crucified His Son.

So the scriptures mean, when
They proclaim to everyone-

His Spirit tells us also, the
Wonder and glory of it all,
And the unbelievable rewards
For those who answer His call.

We know these things through
The Holy Spirit's efforts.
God blends our thoughts with
His; He grants us His reports.

CHAPTER 3

I speak to you as babes, till
Your Christianity gets strong.
For some of the things you do,
Brothers, is definitely wrong.

For you resort to jealousy,
Divide into opposing factions.
I'm no better than Apollos;
Those are un-godly actions.

In you I planted Christian
Seeds; Apollos watered the
Same. God made it grow and
Glorious is His name.

We are partners in God's work;
Only He can make it thrive.
The only real foundation we
Have is our Lord The Christ.

We build with many things, of
The finest materials seen.
Gold, silver, jewels, or even
Straw, or what we glean.

A day of Judgment will come
These things will be tested.
What will burn in the fire,
It's usefulness is arrested.

The worker will be saved, but
His future prospects dulled.

If he defiles God's home,
From there he'll be culled.

Your body is His Temple; here
His Holy Spirit dwells. So
Think not you are brilliant,
For thus you condemn yourself.

Worldly wisdom is foolishness
As it says in the book of Job.
Man will fail in knowledge
And rocky will be his road.

So much He has given you,
Of the present and the future,
With Paul, Peter and Apollos
As helpers and as tutors.

All these and more is yours
And you belong to Christ. He
Belongs to our Father God,
So what can be more right?

CHAPTER 4

Think of Apollos and myself;
We came to serve our Master.
And so you see, we
Serve only as your pastors.

Remember that a servant does
As his master tells him to. I
Judge not whether good or bad;
That's a thing for God to do.

He will give the praise,
If it really has been earned.
But do not favor some,
While others you have spurned.

Why be proud and arrogant and
Think you've accomplished so
Much? God gave what you have,
Not your greatness or luck.

I often think, Apollos and I,
Are just put here on parade,

For people to point and stare
And watch for our mistakes.

Religion makes us foolish, as
In your wisdom you speak. You
Are so wise and contented,
And we are oh so weak.

People smile and fawn at you;
Looking at us, they laugh.
We've gone cold and hungry,
Supporting ourselves by hand.

We softly answer evil comment,
To those who laugh and curse.
Being patient with detractors,
Yet we're treated like dirt.

I wish not to shame you, but
As beloved ones, I counsel.
You may have many teachers;
Consider me a father as well.

It was I who brought you to
Christ; I preached the Gospel
To you. I beg you to listen,
Follow His example as I do.

I'll send Timothy to help; he
Will remind you of what I've
Said. I won him to Christ;
The word he's prone to spread.

Soon I shall come, and I'll
See how well you've done. To
See if you're just talkers,
Or if other souls you've won.

The Kingdom of God is power,
In every walk of life. I'll
Come with gentleness and love,
Not with scolding or strife.

CHAPTER 5

Many people are talking of
Sinful things you condone.

There are some in the church
That you should leave alone.

One who lives with a father's
Wife should be banished from
Your midst. Death must be his
Penalty; after resurrection
He may live.

There are other things too of
Which you should be ashamed.
Greed, drunkards, idolaters,
Lust, have all been named.

You boast about purity, yet
These things go on. So weed
Them out, cleanse yourselves,
Be deserving of God's son.

Jesus is He who was slain for
Us. So let us feast in Him
And grow, leaving behind this
Cancerous growth of sin.

Practice honor and sincerity
With all we meet and know.
Do not try to judge others,
For it has always been so.

There are within your church
Fakes, as Christian brothers,
Sexual sinners, greedy, drunk-
enness, wife beaters or other.

We're not to judge outsiders;
Those in the church are ours.
Take sinners from membership
Or fail in your great hour.

CHAPTER 6

Why accuse Christian brothers
In a court that's "Of the law?"
Asking outsiders to settle a
Dispute seems a last straw!

One day Christians will judge
The world. Why ignorant now?
Why not we in loving concern
Settle our own occasional row?

Why leave our Christian camp
For every problem we can name?
Please take note my friends,
I'm putting you to shame.

Why have lawsuits anyway,
By the unbelieving heathen?
You might better be cheated,
Than always try to get even.

You often cheat and lie and
Even treat brothers the same.
Heaven has no room for these,
So hang your head in shame.

Do not think for a moment
Immortality to us will cling,
Nor drunkards, slanderers or
Robbers, appeal to our King.

You can believe these facts,
For once upon a time long ago,
Ere He washed your sins away,
You followed the ebb and flow.

But now God has set you free,
Because of what Jesus did.
There is much that you can do,
Many sins of which you're rid.

But anything you do should
Be done wisely and with care.
Even over eating is a habit
That causes problems to spare.

Eating isn't so important;
It shouldn't matter anyway.
Because we won't need food,
In the promised land one day.

We were made for the Lord,
Not for our sexual diversion.
To join with a prostitute is
To give bodies to subversion.

Give to the Lord of yourself;
Make of your body His home.
At great cost He bought it,
Give willingly what He owns.

CHAPTER 7

Now you asked for my remarks,
Concerning the marriage scene.
To be married can be good,
If His work you don't demean.

A loving husband and wife
Can work together in harmony.
With much less chance of sin,
Fulfilling each other's needs.

If they make marriage vows,
Their bodies are each others.
Except when doing God's Work,
Your love life do not smother.

If woman and man would marry,
No reason it shouldn't be. Of
Course it might be easier for
Them to stay single like me.

Because we know complications
Often rear their ugly heads,
Especially as a family grows
And we have to add more beds.

So stay single if you can,
But if your body burns with
Lust, then marry a good
Woman, if you think you must.

The Lord would have you stand
By each other and do no wrong.
By giving strength to each
Other, lives can be a song.

No wife must leave a husband,
If she should perchance, then
Let her return, or live alone,
Give no other man a glance.

He must not divorce her
While she's been gone away.
Nor must he throw her out
If she wants to stay.

If either, not a Christian,
Still wants to stick around,
May the other make it work;
This seems to me quite sound.

As time goes on, who knows,
Both may become Christian.
The family may become united,
According to God's plan.

If a non-Christian cannot be
Happy, let that one go away.
For they might not be con-
verted, even though they stay.

So live as God intended no
Matter what you do. Whether
You marry or stay single,
Try to do as He'd approve.

Don't fret Jewish customs; it
Makes no difference at all.
It's important to please God,
As a Christian it's your call.

Whatever your line of work,
Whether as free or slave.
Remember, God has rescued
  you;
From evil you've been saved.

Christ has paid the price
And we all belong to Him. So
Continue the favored work,
For He washed away our sins.

Bad times we Christians face;
A single person can manage
Better. If one stays unwed,
The path may be unfettered.

There are many opportunities
To minister our Lord's work.
Happiness, sadness, or pov-
erty are really only words.

So single or married, do your
Bit; use your assets for our God.
We have much work ahead,
So labor sincerely at the job.

CHAPTER 8

The question of eating meat
That was offered in sacrifice.
Answers are many, of course,
And each thinks he's right.

Let's not show our ignorance,
But may we show compassion.
Remember that their thoughts
May run in different fashion.

Some folks believe many gods,
And before them all set meat.
Though new to Christianity,
A conscience silently speaks.

It seems sinful even now, for
Them to eat the hallowed food.
I won't eat that kind of meat,
Or cause them to come unglued.

Now we know God doesn't care
Whether we eat it or not. We
Can follow our brother's lead
And greatly improve his lot.

As my actions could cause my
Brother to feel he'd sinned,
I refrain from causing pain,
And I will not ridicule him.

CHAPTER 9

I'm an apostle of Jesus; I've
Seen Him with my own eyes.
So this is my ready answer,
To any who question my rights.

Your lives, through me were
Changed because of how I do.
I've taken on those habits
That most appealed to you.

I have earned my own living
While the word of God I teach.
Thus I hold your attention
Much better when I preach.

Barnabas and I do this, for
It befits our style. Yet you
Plan to clothe and feed the
Others of our rank and file.

There's no wrong in this, for
A man is worth his pay. It's
Always been the way of things,
For so the scriptures say.

It's well and quite all right,
To pay your minister's fees.
My own conscience says it
Just won't work for me.

CHAPTER 10

Remember our people's journey
As they wandered so long ago?
Guided by God's fire at night
And by day a column of smoke?

Safely He led between waters,
As they crossed the Red Sea.
By miracles he fed them, and
Yet they were displeased.

They grumbled and
    complained,
After idols prone to follow.

Sincerity always in question,
Promises empty and hollow.

With good water in the desert,
God was always their rock.
So be warned by their lessons,
Slow down and take stock.

Due to faithless complaining,
Idolatry and wicked ways, God
Let them use up their lives,
So saw not Caanan those days.

They became such heathen, as
With others wives they sinned.
Twenty-three thousand died,
All in one day done in.

Remember so many were bitten,
And died from venom of snakes?
Take warning of those things,
And in all actions be awake!

You're not above temptation,
Not only others do wrong. For
We need the help of our Lord,
To be upright and strong.

We've had examples before us,
To remind us of what is right.
Trust our God for strength,
So we can wage the good fight.

Idol worship avoid no matter
What form it may take. Think
Of the blessings of Christ
And His body, make no mistake.

No matter how many there are,
His love is adequate for all.
We drink and eat at communion,
All men invited to His call.

We are free to eat and drink
Of His blessings if we choose.

Do nothing before another;
His ego or faith may bruise.

Do not belittle a brother;
Help his pathway to be paved.
It's not what's best for me;
The effort may get him saved.

CHAPTER 11

Now I'm thankful you copy me,
For I follow Christ's path.
Keep a wife's responsibility,
Never incur a husband's wrath.

You are responsible to him
Just as much as he is to you.
Even as he is to Christ
In all that he thinks to do.

Men, remove your hat, while
Preaching or praying to Him.
A woman should cover her
   head,
This for her is no sin.

Man, made in God's image,
Is a glory that God designed.
Woman is the glory of man, to
Love with his heart and mind.

Remember, Adam was made
   first,
And that Eve came out of him.
But it has been reversed in
Sequence ever since.

However the start or finish,
God brought us to this life.
Let every one honor Him; do
Not feed bickering and strife.

If the Lord's communion supper
You are attending with others,
Don't push or crowd the poor;
Treat them as your brothers.

The bread you eat is Christ's
Body given for you. The wine
You drink is His blood. Not
To be imbibed like home brew.

I've heard you often overeat,
Crowding or grabbing for more.
Some may become quite obese,
Not leave enough for the poor.

Think on this my friends, it
Is a custom based on faith.
Partaking in manner unworthy,
Your soul could be at stake.

CHAPTER 12

Brothers please remember back
To those heathen days gone by.
You worshipped from idol to
Idol, may have wondered why.

No word can any idol speak,
Yet you often say, you get
Messages from the Holy Spirit
Who gives wisdom every day.

But whom can we trust, who
Makes brash claims so often.
Now here is a simple rule
To help your efforts soften.

None can curse our Lord if
Within the holy Spirit's power,
Or say that God is dead and
Make sense any day or hour.

The Holy Spirit is from God;
He comes in different forms.
He gives us help in many ways
To withstand life's storms.

Your hand, your foot, or eye,
Is an important part of you.
Every talent from the Spirit
Belongs to Jesus too.

If you heal or speak in tong-
ues, understand one who can -
You can greatly honor God,
And can be a boon to man.

If you live upright, love
Honor, and Christ obey, or
Enjoy the work you do, is
To brighten someone's day.

Thus it is with God's church,
Each job will be done. So do
Not hinder any, for the
Christian battle must be won.

CHAPTER 13

If I spoke many languages,
But still had no love for man,
Or could forecast the future,
As the past we all can scan-

If I had no love for others,
But had a mountain of faith,
Gave my wealth to the poor,
My soul I could not save.

Were I such a preacher that
For faith I were burned, if I
Still cared not for others,
His face from me'd be turned.

Love is patient, forgiving,
Gentle, soft spoken and kind.
It never bullies its way by
Lying to sway another's mind.

Everyone is love's friend, not
Dwelling on others' mistakes.
Stands for justice and truth
With all the friends it makes.

Some day gifts will disappear,
When God makes us perfect
    men.

We'll see with more clarity,
With our ignorance at an end.

In time we'll see his face,
In that promised land above.
For evermore have faith,
Hope, and above all, love.

CHAPTER 14

May love be our guiding light,
And in his gifts let us glory.
Let each practice Christianity
As we tell a wonderful story.

As tongues we speak or pray,
May blessing return to us. To
Preach and teach or prophesy,
Can bring others good luck.

Foreign language means little
Unless you can explain all.
To love, teach, or prophesy,
Are all God's greatest calls.

I glory in ability to speak
To God in languages unknown.
Little words of love can help
Another claim God for his own.

The scriptures of years ago,
Say God sent prophets afar,
To bring wisdom to His people,
So they might follow His Star.

Man is skeptical of truth, a
Stranger he'll hardly believe.
Words of loving admonition,
He is more likely to receive.

So don't talk all at once,
Keep meetings quite concise.
God loves everything in order,
We know His thoughts are wise.

Scriptures state some things,
Women be subservient to men.

If they have questions to ask,
When at home, do it then.

Today we have what's known
As women's lib. If we insist
On their silence, they'll
Have more than just a rib.

CHAPTER 15

Remember what the gospel is,
For it has never changed. It
Is still the truth it always
Was, with salvation its aim.

But if you never believed,
Then the good news is not for
You, I told it as it was,
And it is totally true.

Christ died for your sins,
And in three days He arose.
All according to Scripture
As the prophets foretold.

By the apostles He was seen,
Then by five hundred brothers.
Soon James saw Him too,
And then by all the others.

I finally saw Him too, but I
Hardly can see why. For I was
Born too late and caused
Many Christians to die.

For what I am now, I have
Only God to thank, for He
Lifted me from the ditch
And set me upon the bank.

Still I labor very hard,
Yet it's mostly God in me.
So why do you not hear
The truth of what I preach?

Some of you've been saying
This life is all there is.

So are we apostles all liars
And is salvation at risk?

If that be so, our preaching
Is all for naught. The truth
Is, Christ lives, with His
Death, our souls He bought.

Because of Adam's sin, death
Came upon this earth. But
When Jesus was born to man,
Eternal life came with birth.

So because of Adam
We all must die.
But because of Christ
We can still have life.

The time will come when
Christ will rule on earth.
And He will battle valiantly
To put the righteous first.

When He's won the war, He
Will return to His Father's
Rule. God will reign supreme,
So do not play the fool.

Some were never Christians
And never believed God's love.
Change your ways and allegi-
ance, prepare for home above.

The seed must die before it
Grows to grain, your earthly
Body must be exchanged for a
Spiritual, on a higher plain.

Our bodies are weak, often
Knowing sickness or disease.
The ones we'll have up there
From ailment will be free.

Death will be lost in victory;
Its sting will be no more.

Thank God for this, who gives
Strength through our Lord.

There's certain victory. Know
Your work is not for naught.
Your future is secure, since
Christ your future bought.

CHAPTER 16

These are some instructions
To handle Sabbath collections.
I gave the Galatians the same,
Hope they'll stand inspection.

Each Sabbath day, put aside
A portion of God's blessings.
Don't wait until I get there,
A point that I am stressing.

When I arrive we'll send, by
Messengers tried and true,
I'll go along to Jerusalem
If that seems good to you.

We'll take it to Christians
There, who've troubled times.
For we should stick together,
Through every land and clime.

I am coming to visit you and
I'd like to stay much longer.
I'll stop at Macedonia first,
Encourage them to be stronger.

At Ephesus I shall stay
Until Pentecost is past.
For here there's much to do,
And many enemies, alas!

Timothy is young of course,
Please make Him feel at home.
For he wants to come your way,
And nowhere else to roam.

I begged Apollos to visit you,
But He does not feel free.

For God's work must be done,
To labor on he felt the need.

So watch for any danger, and
Be God's men strong and true.
Whatever deed must be done,
May his love show through you.

Remember Stephanas and
  family,
Early Christians in Greece.
Please follow their direction,
Aid them in Christian deeds.

Also Fortunatus and Achaicus,
They've helped me while here.

Doing things you'd have done
To bring relief, and cheer.

I'm sure they helped you too,
You appreciate men like these.
Asian churches send love and
Greetings, may God you please.

Aquila and Priscilla love you,
Help me much, visiting too.
With my own hand I'll write
These last few lines to you.

END OF IST.CORINTHIANS

2ND CORINTHIANS

CHAPTER 1

As sure as my name is Paul,
Brother Timothy, a friend, we
Write Christians in Corinth
And Greece unto land's end.

May God the Father and Jesus
Bless and give you peace. He
Stands by us in our troubles;
He gives us strength to teach.

If we get in difficulty for
Bringing the world His story,
He still sustains our lives
And insures our future glory.

Dear friends rest assured,
He'll stand by you too. We've
Been pressed and tried, in
Asia we thought doomed.

But we left it in His hands,
He whom the dead can raise
Saved our very lives again!
May His Holy name be praised.

We expect He'll do so again;
Please pray for our continued
Care. And always remember my
Letters, truthful and sincere.

The reason we don't come, our
Visit might cause you pain.
I want to give you happiness,
To be welcome back again.

CHAPTER 2

I stayed away for a time, for
The timing was all wrong. I
Will come when things improve;
We'll make each other strong.

The man who caused trouble,
Caused less pain than you.
He's been adequately punished
By disfavor he's been through.

It's time to heal his wounds,
Time to love and comfort him.
Return him to our fellowship,
Save him from a life of sin.

For anyone that you forgive,
I'll gladly forgive him too.
As Christ would forgive, so
Do I, it's for our good I do.

I reached Troas, to preach
The Gospel I was compelled.
I couldn't find brother Titus;
I searched for quite a spell.

God through Christ has won
To Him our hearts and souls.
There's beauty in our lives,
Because of Christian goals.

It's up to men of integrity
To do Christ's cherished work.
Not skim the cream like some
As Christian work they shirk.

CHAPTER 3

Why need we recommendations
If we have each others trust?
Changes that God has wrought
Show our lives are just.

We trust God through Christ
Who keeps us in His design.
We teach not of commandments,
But the Holy Spirit divine.

Old ways lead to death, yet
Moses' face was aglow, when
From the Lord he brought laws
In the old days long ago.

So how much greater the glory
Of this eternal life we claim,
And unlike Moses' glory,
It will not fade away.

The old system seemed to veil
The truth from Israeli minds.
But the wonder of our Lord
Is the blessing of mankind.

CHAPTER 4

God has truly blessed us with
Work we're constrained to do.
We're in His presence always,
With faith we tell the truth.

If this news is hidden, it is
From those in Satan's clutch.
But those who believe in
Christ will gain very much.

For He who made the light
Has made us understand,
That Jesus' power and glory,
Will shine across the land.

We know His precious treasure
Shines within us too. But our
Bodies, weak and perishable,
Are prone to break and bruise.

It's obvious to everyone with
Christ's help only we stand.
We get bruised and battered
For preaching the news to man.

Even though we suffer, we can
Show our strength in Christ.
We're bringing more to God,
Preaching and paying a price.

So we suffer willingly as we
Toil in the work of our Lord.
We know through all eternity
We will reap a great reward.

CHAPTER 5

We know that these old bodies
Will be traded for better.
For those we live in now,
Are made of temporary matter.

Our God has promised us, that
When our lives continue there,

We'll see no pain or aging in
A heaven where all is fair.

We hurt in these we have,
Prone to aches and pains.
Death will give up to life,
As heaven's portals we gain.

This we sincerely believe,
So death now holds no fear.
We aim to please God always,
And continue our trials here.

It may seem we are bragging,
You must know that's not true.
We know there's a reward
For work and suffering we do.

Jesus died for us all, and it
Greatly changed our lives. So
God forgave men's sins, and
We are ambassadors for Christ.

Our sins absorbed by Jesus,
His goodness was given to us.
So listen to His call
And give Him all your trust.

CHAPTER 6

We beg you, listen to God,
He hears your questing cry.
The doors are opened wide
At this most favorable time.

We try to live in such a way,
None can ere complain, that
We ever caused any to stumble,
That many lives should gain.

Hardships we often suffer,
And problems of every kind.
Exhausted, but awake at night,
Troubles that boggle the mind.

We've proven to be ministers
And to be just what we claim.

Earth despises, criticizes,
Tries to distort our aim.

We suffer for your souls but
Smile when you see the light.
We are poor in worldly goods,
But spiritual gifts give life.

My dear Corinthian friends,
I hide not my love from you.
You are like my own children,
And my words to you are true.

Do no business with sinners;
Do not approve of evil ways.
There is no light in darkness,
So conform to brighter days.

God says, "You are my Temple,
And among you I shall walk."
So go with godly deeds,
And avoid much idle talk.

Separate yourselves from sin
And avoid all filthy things.
You're my sons and daughters
And also, you'll be kings.

CHAPTER 7

With these wonderful promises
Let us turn away from wrong.
So please open up your hearts
And welcome us with song.

Never have we harmed you,
Nor were any led astray. I
Have confidence in your word
And my pride in you is great.

Great has been my pleasure,
Because you are my friends.
When we arrived in Macedonia,
It seemed we'd met our end.

God had Titus encourage us;
He brought good word from
   you.
Proof of unfailing friendship,
Was the best of all good news.

I'm sorry you were hurt, if
It turned you to God I'm glad.
Sometimes He uses sorrow to
Turn us from the bad.

And for you it did the job;
In your concern you did well.
Got to the facts of trouble
And from the gates of hell.

After I'd boasted to Titus, you
Set my mind at ease. When
He told of your befriending
Him, it made me very pleased.

So once again we're brothers
In a wonderful quest of life.
We are one in perfect confid-
ence and no sign of strife.

CHAPTER 8

The churches in Macedonia
Did much in troubled times.
They accepted God, their
Actions were nearly sublime.

Of their substance they gave
More than I felt they could.
You are leaders in many ways;
I'm sure you'll give good.

I brag about you, telling,
How wonderful you are. So if
You give whatever you can,
You'll reach toward the stars.

You always wanted to help so
This will make good your plan.
You will prove to everyone,
You have great love for man.

Now I mean not to give them
Ease or cause destitution.
But only what you can afford
Is the wisest, best solution.

I'll send Titus and others,
Known as honest Christian men.
So the money'll be ready
When I get there again.

Please show them you love me;
Do that of which I've bragged.
Your gifts of love will help
Show Christian love unflagged.

CHAPTER 9

I know you need no urging;
Your hearts are made of gold.
To our friends in Macedonia,
That was what I told.

I'm taking these precautions,
To be sure my boast is true.
Remember the more you give,
Much more comes back to you.

God loves a cheerful giver,
And He'll fill all your needs.
The more you give cheerfully,
The more honorable your deeds.

Those you help will bless you;
God will bless you even more.
We pray for you fervently
For you've helped the poor.

You have shown the grace of
God; much for man you've won.
Thank God for His great gift,
The advent of His Holy Son.

CHAPTER 10

Gently friends, I speak to
Bring you into the fold. Some

Claim only when Paul is away
Are His letters really bold.

I wish not to be harsh, my
Friends, I hope not to be.
With God's help I'll win but
As a mere human I am weak.

With God's weapons, I'll
Break down the devil's castle
And bring back those rebels
Who are giving me a hassle.

Some claim that I'm all noise
And am only a timid man. But
With God's help and presence,
I'll work within His plan.

To claim authority over you
Is not boasting on our part.
Because we were the first
To put Christ in your hearts.

We pray your faith will grow,
Our work to be enlarged. So
We can move on again, to help
Others as we're charged.

If we'd boast it would be,
"See what God has done," for
What we accomplish on our
    own
With His help is really fun.

CHAPTER 11

Please be patient friends,
While I bare my heart.
My anxiety for you
Nearly tears me apart.

You seem so gullible, I fear
You may be led astray. These
False teachers are at work
Who would lead in wicked
    ways.

They will take your offerings
Where I have paid my costs,
They'll lead on false trails,
Until you're hopelessly lost.

The churches of Macedonia
Have so far paid my bills.
I have charged you nothing,
And I swear I never will.

I wish to bring salvation
To all my beloved friends.
Others will reap punishment
And will meet a bitter end.

God didn't tell me to brag;
I talk like a witless fool.
But those other men I'm sure,
Are only Satan's tools.

What they brag about I can
Too. Hebrews, Israelites
Or Abraham's descendants,
I can also claim I'm Jew.

I've served God longer, been
Jailed, whipped, and faced
Death, been robbed, stoned,
And at sea was wrecked.

Trudged through desert storm
Beaten by Gentile and Jew,
Crossed over flooded rivers,
A slave of God, spreading news.

Often hungry and weary, yet
Pushing through wind and rain.
The victim of angry mobs, in
Constant worry and pain.

I also fret the churches,
And any who step out of line.
Or those who hurt another,
Feeling pain for him is mine.

I should brag of weakness;
God knows I tell the truth.
Because He has spared my life
Ever since my errant youth.

Once when at Damascus, they
Set a trap at the city gate.
I was let down by rope and
Basket, over a wall to escape.

CHAPTER 12

Boasting is foolish, but hear
Me a moment longer. Fourteen
Years ago I had an experience,
That made my faith stronger.

I know not if body or spirit,
Or if both were taken there.
But I was up to paradise, a
Thing I'm forbidden to share.

It was more glorious than
Words can ever describe. If I
Boasted this, it would bring
More attention to my life.

But God gave me a problem
Which causes me bodily pain.
It keeps me weak and helpless,
Lest I should get too vain.

Thrice I prayed for relief,
God said "No," to me. "Better
A weak and humble apostle,
Than a bragging preacher you
Should be."

He also told me plainly, I'd
Be able to withstand the pain.
For He would stand by me, so
You see, I've much to gain.

So in my weakness is my glory,
For with His help I'm strong.

And with Him always present,
How can I ever go wrong?

Remember all those stories
False preachers tell to you;
There's nothing that with
God's help I cannot do.

I've never taken your money,
Nor asked for a place to stay.
You're like my own children,
And this is a parent's way.

Some of you wonder, if there
Isn't a hidden cost. But not
Even those brothers I sent
Ever caused you loss.

If you think I'm ingratiating
Myself into your lives,
That's not true at all, it's
Only for your good I strive.

I hope to find you loving
And kind to one another. Any
Disunity you may be suffering,
I'd like to have you smother.

I'd be humbled, sad indeed,
To find you leading corrupted
Lives. Such as living immora-
lly with other men's wives

CHAPTER 13

Three times I've visited you,
Each time you've been told.
But now I'm ready to punish,
I'm not just talking bold.

I'll give you proof that
Christ speaks through me.
And though He died upon the
Cross, He is no longer weak.

So take stock of what you are,
Do you really pass the test?

I hope you will agree
That I have done my best.

I pray you'll be responsible
And live good Christian lives.
I hope I can skip punishment
And make you strong in Christ.

In closing may I say, live in
Peace and happy with Christ.
Greet each other as friends,
And strive to do what's right.

**END OF 2ND.
CORINTHIANS**

GALATIANS

CHAPTER 1

To the churches of Galatia,
From Corinth I write to you.
It isn't the wish of man, but
Jesus' will we'd have you do.

From all the Christians here
We wish you all the best. My
Call is from God the Father;
He raised Jesus from the dead.

That you did turn away
From His will as I showed,
Is hard for me to believe,
For it's not the way to go.

You are being fooled by those
Who'd change things around.
There's no other way to heav-
en, than the one I told about.

Even an angel would be cursed,
If he changed the great story.
For it was told by Jesus, as
He shared with me God's glory.

You know what I was like, how
Christianity I would subdue.
But then I saw the light and
Declared it to folks like you.

I didn't consult the apostles
Or any man on earth. For

I was shown by our Lord
Of Jesus' wonderful birth.

Everything I've told you
Is within our Lord's presence.
So what you've heard from me
Is of Christianity's essence.

Yet the people knew me not,
Except as their former enemy.
Preaching the faith I'd tried
To wreck, they praised God
Because of me.

CHAPTER 2

Fourteen years I taught, be-
fore going to Jerusalem again,
Always taught the will of God,
Ignoring the threats of man.

I conferred with the brothers
As to the methods I had used.
My word to the Gentiles, they
Agreed was good and true.

I did not ask for circumcision,
For Titus my Gentile friend.
But some so called "Christ-
ians" made sorrow in the end.

None would listen to them, so
Harassment came to naught.

We believed that Christianity
Wasn't subject to Jewish laws.

The greatest leaders there
Told me go on just as before.
And Peter also who brought
Many a Jew to the Lord.

God gave us gifts to use in
A special way. To preach and
Help the poor for whom I've
Always worked and prayed.

Peter came to Antioch, I felt
I must speak my mind. For he
Catered to the Jews, and also
To the Gentiles, I'd find.

"We were born Jews," I said,
Long ago gave up their ways.
Why follow their customs, or
Of the Jews are you afraid?

Why practice deception
Just to please the Jews?
When only our trust in Jesus,
Is the all important news?

If we keep Jewish law, then
Why should Christ have died?
Grace then has no meaning,
Your acts you should decide.

CHAPTER 3

Oh foolish Galations, what-
ever made you change? You
Used to believe in Christ's
Death, now you seem deranged.

You were not saved by the law,
So why do you change about?
For once you've trusted Jesus,
Jewish law's lost its clout.

Remember the story of
Abraham?

He trusted God day and night.
And because of all his trust,
God made his future bright.

He also told Abraham, "I'll
Save all who trust as you do."
That also meant the Gentiles,
Just as surely as the Jews.

The scriptures say you're
Cursed if the law you break.
As the prophet Habakuk says,
"Listen, there's no mistake.

Only through trusting God
Will a man ever find His life.
And how true that saying is
When he believes in Christ."

Under the curse of law sooner
Or later a man will fall. But
Jesus wiped out our errors;
Now faith will save us all.

The promises made to Abraham
Were written down and signed.
They were meant as well for
That future son named Christ.

Four hundred thirty years
And the Ten commandments
    came,
Not to cancel Jewish laws,
That was not the game.

Jewish law was given Abraham,
A guide till Jesus came along.
To show that in following law,
Men could still go wrong.

Now with Christ to lead us,
Faith will bring us home, and
Once we are baptized in Jesus,
Our spirits no longer roam.

No longer are we Gentile, or
Free men, Greeks, or Jews. We
Are Abraham's descendants, so
God's promises are good news.

CHAPTER 4

Man may die leaving wealth
Which now belongs to his son.
But he is bound by guardians,
To do as told while young.

Such was the case with us
Until Christ came along.
Those Jewish laws were meant
To keep us from going wrong.

So as slaves we lived, to the
Laws which lined our paths.
Then Jesus came and showed us
This better way we have.

For no longer are we slaves;
God's own sons we are. Now
We've inherited life from Him
Who's brought us fast and far.

Why've you Gentiles returned
To the ways of Jewish law?
A hopeless way to go, your
Efforts will come to naught.

Those teachers tempting you,
Pervert your hearts and minds.
Once you accepted me with
Treatment loving and kind.

Being so far away, it is
Difficult to reason with you,
I'm afraid I must confess,
I don't know what to do.

Through those laws you'll not
Find the Lord whom you seek.
You'll be slaves to unknown
Gods, impotent and weak.

Brothers, we're not slaves;
We come through Israel from
Abraham's blood, whom God
promised bessings in floods.

CHAPTER 5

And so, my Gentile brothers,
You should readily see, you
Are not slaves to the law,
For Christ has set you free.

Whoever perverted you, will
Answer to God for sure. The
Death of Christ on our behalf
Is the only certain cure.

Some say that even I, preach
The circumcision rites. Now
If that were really true,
I would have an easier life.

Then the Jews would smile on
Me, not try to block my way.
But I'll still be persecuted;
I teach salvation by faith.

I wish these teachers would
Leave, so you could live in
Peace. Not to do what's wrong,
To do what's right, be free.

Love each other always, even
As the Scriptures say. Listen
To the Holy Spirit, and He'll
Lead you in the perfect way.

If you follow your desires,
You'll turn to envy and greed.
Anger, jealousy, hatred will
Let Satan plant wicked seed.

Let the Holy Spirit lead you
To peace, love, self control.
There's no conflict with Laws,
The way to save your souls.

So follow the Spirit's lead,
Let honor and fame go its
Way. Avoid anger or jealousy,
It would haunt us every day.

CHAPTER 6

In all things help others;
Even Christians can slip. So
Help that Christian lovingly,
For next time you may trip.

If he thinks himself too good,
To stoop and help another,
Is only fooling himself, and
His own hope he smothers.

For we will reap the harvest
Of all those seeds we sow.
So never weary of good works
Life, love and peace bestow.

Remember those other teachers
Only seek prosperity and fame.
Greed or jealousy guide their
Actions, and you're fair game.

Christ's enemies marks are on
Me, they mark me as his slave.
So may his grace rest upon us,
And help us to behave.

END OF GALATIANS

EPHESIANS

CHAPTER 1

To my dear Ephesian friends,
I'm Paul, whom God has chosen.
From this place in time, we
Thank Him we're His tokens.

Through the efforts of Christ,
God has made us His very own.
That spotless in His presence,
We'll stand before his throne.

To everlasting glory through
Christ His Son, we're near.
Praising our loving God,
Should be our goal most dear.

May the Holy Spirit guide you,
Show Christ's loving grace.
He has done so much for you,
You'll long to see His face.

It's by God's power that
Christ, from dead was raised.
He's King of everything, may
His glorious name be praised.

CHAPTER 2

Though we started as sinners,
As all who walk Satan's path,
He gained us by Jesus' blood
And saved us from His wrath.

For God is rich in mercy, and
He gave us a spirit of trust.
We can live by His guidelines,
Being loving, peaceful, just.

Thank God who made us thus,
We were heathens and bad news,
By those also unclean, who
Thought themselves good Jews.

In those days you were lost
There seemed no way to cope,
But now you belong to Christ
And at last there's hope.

For by Christ's death He made
Peace between Gentile and Jew.
He annulled Jewish laws and
Brought us all good news.

No longer strangers to heaven,
Nor to God are we estranged.
Jew and Gentile work together,
All for good has changed.

With apostles and prophets on
The very foundation you stand.
Joined by Christ's Spirit,
Dwelling in the promised land.

CHAPTER 3

As I sit in this jail today,
On you Gentiles I ponder, all
The things He's shown to me
Of his glories and wonders.

His plan is older than the
Mountains, deeper than a sea,
Bonding your Gentile futures
Into fellowship with me.

He has given me the power to
Do His word with finess.
For a nothing Jew like me,
It means I'm doubly blessed.

Please share the news I bring;
God has planned it since days
Of yore. To believe in Christ
Gives us wings and much more.

Do not worry that I suffer,
Feel honored it is for you.
On my knees in thanks I pray;
His Holy Spirit seeks you too.

May his glory work within us,
To do more than we can dream.
And through all future ages
May His wonders beam.

CHAPTER 4

Be patient with each other,
Worthy of things like these.

Be humble and patient, and
With one another be at peace.

Though I'm only Paul, and a
Prisoner doing His work, I'd
Have you serve God the Father,
Your Christian duty not shirk.

To the same glorious future,
Each of us has been called.
With the Holy Spirit's help,
We never will be stalled.

Special talents and abilities
Are gifts that God has given.
The Psalmist knew, and said
Jesus triumphed to heaven.

He'd won a victory over Satan,
He gave generous gifts to men.
From deep within earth, up to
Highest heaven He has been.

He has saturated everything
With the essence of His love.
Those abilities He gave to
Men, gifts from heaven above.

So men will be able to build
God's church, true and strong.
Until it's filled with Christ,
And will triumph over wrong.

Be not like men of darkness;
They have given in to evil.
Going with lust and distrust,
And their leader is the devil.

Forget your sinful past, and
Seek a higher plain. Tell the
Truth and love each other;
The other way leads to pain.

Cause no one grief by the
Wicked way you live. Use your

Mind and hands for others;
It is blessed that you give.

CHAPTER 5

Be full of love for others
In everything you do.
Follow Christ's example,
Who gave His life for you.

Let there be no sin among you,
Dirty stories or foul talk.
Show only God's goodness
And practice the perfect walk.

The bliss we hope for caters
Not to the greedy or impure.
God's wrath will fall on them,
Of that you can be sure.

Your heart was in darkness;
Now it's lighted from above.
So do only good deeds;
Show the world your love.

Don't condone or ignore wrong;
Champion only good. Exposure
May teach them right, we
All know something should.

Take care in all your conduct;
Spread His love and light.
Awake him who to God was
   dead,
And with God he may get right.

Wives should honor husbands,
And obey all that is right.
Even as the Holy church
Obeys the will of Christ.

You husbands love your wives,
And keep them safe from harm.
For you two are really one,
As of the church we're part.

We are also part of Christ,
And He is part of us.
We must always treat Him
With due respect and trust.

CHAPTER 6

Children, obey your parents
And this is promised to you.
A life full of blessings
Will be your certain due.

Parents, don't nag children;
They'll resent pushy ways.
Show them loving discipline;
Enjoy each other every day.

Slaves, obey your masters,
Give only your very best. If
Your work is truly deserving,
All effort will be blessed.

To you who own the slaves,
Be sure to treat them right.
Remember you are also slaves;
Your master is our Christ.

So put on the armor of God to
Withstand old Satan's wiles.
He will stop at nothing, nor
Will his hordes most vile.

They are of the spirit world,
An evil unseen, but strong.
Wear the shield of God's O.K.
And battle all that's wrong.

Wear the helmet of salvation,
The Sword of the Spirit too.
To stop Satan's fiery arrows
Wear God's belt of truth.

Pray to God without ceasing,
Remind Him of your needs.
So Christians everywhere will
Strongly state their creed.

Then also pray for me, that
I might boldly explain, that
Salvation is for Gentiles too,
Although I'm now in chains.

I send Tychicus to explain
How we are getting along. God

Give you peace my brothers;
May Christian grace be strong.

END OF EPHESIANS

PHILIPPIANS

CHAPTER 1

To the pastors and deacons,
And Christians in Philippi:
This letter is from Paul and
Timothy, the slaves of Christ.

My heart is full of joy, I know
His blessings are yours.
His work you'll carry on, by
His help you'll go the course.

He'll help you grow in grace
Until His return. I would
Have you be true and strong;
The hope within me burns.

Actually my being in jail for
Christ is proving a boost.
Even the soldiers know, it's
Because I preach His truth.

Some Christians here have no
Fear of prison because of me.
Some may preach from jealousy;
I'm glad it's Him they teach.

I often think when He calls,
I'll be glad when life is done. I

Know if I stick around, there
Are still souls to be won.

Whatever happens to me, carry
On as Christians should. By
Hearing good reports of you,
I'll know your faith is good.

CHAPTER 2

So please do not be selfish
I beg of you my brothers;
Don't be mean in any way, but
Love and help one another.

For Christ though He was God
Humbled Himself as lowly man.
Laid aside His mighty power,
Nor did He cry or yet demand.

To death on the cross, He was
Led to slaughter like a sheep.
God raised him up to heaven,
Because He was good, yet meek.

So at the name of Jesus, each
Head and knee should bow.
The fact that He is Lord is
Most obvious to men by now.

Live your lives as Christians
With no gripes or claims. In
This world of wicked darkness,
Let God's light be your aim.

If it should be that I die;
Please make me proud of you.
As He comes back let Him find,
You're Christians true blue.

If the Lord is willing, I'll
Send Timothy to see you soon.
Some think only of themselves,
But he's a Christian's boon.

You all know and love him;
He is like a son to me. Good
And willing help he's been
In helping me to preach.

Now I'll send Epaphroditus;
He's anxious to return to you.
He is like a brother to me;
He'll bring you all the news.

So treat him like a brother,
For he has been so true. He's
Been ill but is well again;
Has done much for you.

CHAPTER 3

And now dear friends
I'm telling you,
Be glad in the Lord
Whatever you do.

Beware of these men who
Preach Jewish law, for by
Preaching circumcision,
They grasp at straws.

Remember we are helpless
To attain glory by ourselves.
Yet if they really were right,
I'd have a good chance myself.

For I was born as a Jew, was
Circumcised at eight days,
Was a member of the Pharisees
Followed the law always.

So sure of its purity that
I persecuted God's church,
I Herded His people into prison,
And many were hurt.

But all of those things that
I thought legal and right,
Lost most of their value
On the day I met Christ.

Now I am certain that
Whatever I do,
That if I only believe,
He will pass me through

The portals of heaven
That for me he's opened wide.
And then forever up there,
With Him I'll abide.

Now I know my dear brothers,
I'm not good enough, but I
Will strain to do better, and
He will help where it's rough.

So pattern your lives,
And follow my lead,
And beware of those others
Whose God is their greed.

Our homeland is heaven
Where our Savior does dwell.
He'll give us new bodies with
Power that conquers all else.

CHAPTER 4

Dear Christians of Philippi,
You are my reward and my joy.
So stay true to the Lord,
Your best behavior employ.

Euodias and Syntyche, fine
Women, again be good friends.
They worked by my side with
Clement for betterment of men.

The rest of my fellow workers
Shared our labor and strife.
Their names will be written
In that great book of life.

Always be considerate and
Unselfish in what you do.
Worry about nothing but pray
The good Lord will come soon.

Then the peace will be yours
That passes all understanding,
If you are thankful to God
And not pushy or demanding.

Now as this letter I close,
Dwell on the better things.

Love your God and fellow men,
God's peace gives you wings.

Though I never was in need,
You've sent gifts and aid.
I have learned to get along;
With Him I'm not afraid.

So hungry or well fed, with
Heat of fever or with cold.
With Christ who's at my side,
The love of God will enfold.

Now thank you for your gifts,
I know you deserve the reward.
Many blessings be upon you as
Heaven you toil toward.

END OF PHILIPPIANS

COLOSSIANS

CHAPTER 1

Again this is Paul, Christ's
Slave and brother Timothy,
To our Christian brothers,
May you be filled with peace.

City of Colosse, we bring
Christ's great message to you.
We know you trust the Lord;
Keep the faith that's true.

Faith that Epaphras brought
Is changing the world today.
Our beloved fellowworker
Is here to help this place.

So let us all be thankful to
Our God who wants us fit, to

Share His kingdom of light,
And escape from Satan's pit.

Jesus bought our freedom, His
Blood washed our sins away.
He existed long ago, and
His power still holds sway.

The God of living Christians
And also of the dead, He
Is the head of His church,
And we shall know no dread.

Though you were His enemies,
He bought you back as friends.
Upon the cross He saved you,
A hopeless eternity to end.

If you believe the truth,
Stand steadfast and strong.

News is spreading over the
World, in God, none go wrong.

I, Paul, tell the news to all,
For it brings me great joy,
To've been sent to help His
Church and be God's envoy.

After centuries he's saying
Christ is your hope of glory.
So Jew and Gentile may share
The news of this great story.

We want to present each one
Of you in glory of perfection.
And we can only do so because
Of Christ's protection.

CHAPTER 2

If you knew the struggles I
Endured for you, my friends.
I pray to God to help you
Stop all your worldly trends.

Knit strong ties of love and
Knowledge of His secret plan.
Here is wisdom and hope that
He's offered free to man.

Some of those claim to know,
God's ways and philosophise,
With answers all their own,
But not truly knowing Christ.

For though I'm far from you,
My spirit is with you every
Day. I glory in knowledge too,
Of your unfailing faith.

Let Christ guide as you go;
Take His strength for every
Task. He has power over all,
If for your needs you'll ask.

Everything is yours in truth,
In Christ, whom you believe.

Your evil desires were lost,
And all your good retrieved.

So your sins all died on the
Cross with His beloved Son.
Satan lost his power over you,
So you've not lost, but won.

CHAPTER 3

Let heaven fill your thoughts
Since Jesus paid the price.
On rich treasures up there,
We should keep our sights.

Don't spend time aworrying,
About the things down here.
Drop all those worldly things;
Consider the heavenly sphere.

Remember you often angered,
And the trouble it caused.
Now all that is over; let's
Leave it on permanent pause.

Nationality, race, education,
Or social status cuts no ice.
For you've been chosen by God,
Who gave you this new life.

So practice the things of God,
And comfort to others give.
Let peace be your gift, as
You show men how to live.

Remember how Christ taught
Those loving words to us.
So teach them now to others,
And in your dealings be just.

Husbands and wives, love each
Other; be not harsh or coarse.
Children, honor your parents;
That's the wish of the Lord.

Slaves should serve masters
And give your very best.

It's really God who pays you,
When He calls you up to rest.

CHAPTER 4

Again I repeat, if you own
Slaves be just and fair.
Remember God is your master,
Whom you'll face up there.

Do not fail in prayers for
Any man or for your friends.
I know I'm in jail to preach
Jesus; this is not my end.

Pray that I'll be bold and
Tell it straight and true.
Be sure to use good judgment,
When the word is told by you.

Tychicus, our beloved brother,
I'm sending with the news.
Onesimus, one of our own,
Will come to cheer you too.

Aristarchus, a prisoner here,
Sends his love along, and
Mark, a relative of Barnabas,
Let him feel that he belongs.

Jesus, known as Justus, his
Love he also sends. And
Epaphras of your city, still
Prays and intercedes for men.

He's been an untiring worker,
Prays that you'll be strong,
For Christians in Laodicia
And Hierapolis, we pray long.

Doctor Luke also sends love,
As does Demas too I know. My
Greeting to those at Laodicia,
And to Nymphas, preaching in
His home.

Send this to the Laodicians,
And read my letter to them.
Urge Archippus to be sure,
To carry God's word to men.

Now in my own handwriting, I
Send my greetings to you all.
Pray for me here in jail,
And my greetings to you, Paul.

END OF COLOSSIANS

1ST. THESSALONIANS

CHAPTER 1

To the church at Thessalonica,
Peaceful blessing be your lot.
For you we pray constantly,
As we remember you to our
   God.

This letter from Paul, Silas and
Timothy, about A.D. 54, tells
The Christian church to keep
Their eyes upon the Lord.

"We give thanks," says Paul,
"For Christians like you. You
Listened carefully to begin,
The Holy Spirit led you true.

With the trials it brought,
You lead Christians in Greece;
You've spread the word abroad
Of God's great love and peace.

Everywhere we go, it seems,
We hear of your great faith.

How once you worshipped
  idols,
But to Christ you turned away.

Now the Living God is master
Of all our Christian lives.
Looking toward His return, to
Perfection we shall strive."

CHAPTER 2

Now dear brothers you know,
Our visit was worthwhile.
We'd just come from Philippi,
Where treatment was most vile.

God gave us courage to repeat
Truth for which we'd paid. So
With His help we spoke truth
And of men were not afraid.

We sought not to flatter you
And worked both day and night,
Brought God's word among you
And proved to be quite right.

Pleaded, wheedled, demanded
His excellence in the way you
Lived. It changed your lives.
You turned and honored Him.

Then others turned against us
Just as they had the Jews.
Persecuted and drove us out,
Because we spread God's news.

Killed their own prophets,
And they executed Christ. But
God's anger will reach them,
And they will pay the price.

We tried later to return,
And I tried several times.
But Satan held the reins
And we paid for his crimes.

But this is what we live for,
When a roll is called for men;
That we might stand together
When Christ comes back again.

CHAPTER 3

Finally then I worried until
It became too much to bear.
So I sent Timothy from Athens,
And I stayed alone back there.

He'd encourage and help you,
In trouble see you through.
We warned of that ahead of
Time, and it all came true.

Now he has just returned, and
His news is good indeed. For
Your faith is strong and sure;
From Satan you are freed.

We can stand our trials so
Long as you stand strong. We
Would like to see you too,
For it has been too long.

Our constant prayers are for
You; may your love overflow.
So stand before Him guiltless,
As toward that day we grow.

CHAPTER 4

You know dear brothers, how
To live godly lives each day.
Work closely to that ideal;
It is the only Christian way.

Lust not for another's wife,
God called us not for this.
You cannot ignore His rules
And as a Christian live.

So listen to the Holy Spirit,
God sent Him for a guide. May

Love show more and more,
A blessing you cannot hide.

So mind your own business,
And live with no regrets.
Those who are not Christian
Will accord you great respect.

Thus you'll find your income
Will be no problem to you.
For you'll have the help of
Heaven in everything you do.

Sorrow not for the dead, God
Will bring Christians back.
He'll be here before the
Living and the final act.

He'll come down from heaven
With a mighty trumpet shout.
The dead in Him shall rise;
We'll all be gathered about.

In the air we'll meet Him
And forever with Him remain.
What a glorious day when the
Promised land we've gained.

CHAPTER 5

When everything is peaceful,
And safety seems guaranteed;
Destruction will come to them,
Like a silent, waiting thief.

You are children of the day
Who do your work in the light.
So let us be awake watching,
Not asleep or drunk at night.

So put on the armor of hope,
Of love, forgiveness, peace.
Love and honor every man;
Pray unceasingly for each.

Do not belittle the Spirit,
Prophecies never ignore,
Check out what seems good;
All evil appearance abhor.

May the very God of Peace
Preserve you body and soul;
So at the coming of our Lord,
You meet Him well, and whole.

He will do just as He says,
For that is the way He is.
So greet your Christian
Brothers with a Holy kiss.

Now I'd like for you to
Pass this letter around.
And may the grace of Jesus
Christ with you all abound.

**END OF
1ST. THESSALONIANS**

2ND. THESSALONIANS

CHAPTER 1

Greetings to the church at
Thessalonica, safe in God and
Christ. May God bless you
With peace of heart and mind.

"I Paul, Silas and Timothy,
Give thanks for good you do.
All churches we'll tell of
Trials you're going through.

God is using your problems to
Prepare you for future life.
You'll be unworthy of heaven,
If too weak for this strife.

Do not decry your suffering,
In time you'll see His aim.
Fire that sets your temper is
An enemy's judgement flame."

CHAPTER 2

Ignore Satan's alarm, "The
Day of the Lord has begun."
For men of Satan will appear,
Long before the time has come.

With feats and miracles
To imitate our Holy King,
Many will most surely believe
And thereby lose everything.

Stand you firm upon the word,
Trusting only in truth. May
Jesus Christ, our Lord, do
Good things for you.

CHAPTER 3

Pray the Lord will save us
From Satan's every attack.
That we may trust God fully,
In our every speech and act.

Christ would have you earn
Every good thing you gain.
Nothing is worth while owning,
Unless it's bought with pain.

For he who will not work,
Does not deserve to eat.
Shun him in his laziness, so
He'll stand on his own feet.

We have set the example, for
We worked to earn our bread.
Our command would be to
   work
And earn it like the rest.

Don't treat him as an enemy,
As brother let him feel shame.
May you yourself know peace,
We ask in Jesus' name.

This is my handwriting, like
The writing on the wall. May
The Lord's wondrous blessing,
Be upon you, sincerely, Paul.

**END OF 2ND.
THESSALONIANS**

1ST. TIMOTHY

CHAPTER 1

Timothy, you're much like a
Son, whom God sent as envoy.
May He show you kindness,
And may you serve with joy.

When I left for Macedonia
I prayed that you would stay
And stop those false teachers
Corrupting the Christian way.

God gave me an important
  work
I entrusted to you, my friend.
And it's very important you
Bring their fables to an end.

Jewish laws cannot save, nor
Angels to God in long chains.
They are ignorant teachers
Who think to gain much fame.

Those laws were for murderers,
Sinners with rebellious hearts.
How thankful I am that God
Gave me His message to impart.

Though in the past I sinned,
And people I did persecute,
Wonderful things he showed
Me I could no longer refute.

He showed me how to trust
  Him;
My faith grows stronger every
Day. He is King of the ages,
And goes with me all the way.

Fight the battle my friend
And win with love and prayer.
When the war is over,
We'll all meet over there.

Always follow your conscience,
Where the Holy Spirit dwells.
And if you heed His prompting,
You'll know that all is well.

Some ignored their conscience;
Soon they lost their faith.
If that's laid aside, friend,
You've also lost your way.

CHAPTER 2

Pray for men where they are,
Give thanks in all you do.
For kings, queens, rulers, for
The poor and homeless too.

Remember those in authority
And wish them lives of ease.
So we can live in quietness
And do our work in peace.

God longs to see men saved,
So they'll know in fact,
That Jesus is our go-between
By His unselfish act.

God gave the world a message
Just when the time was right.
I was chosen his missionary,
To carry on a faithful fight.

The Gentiles must be told of
God's salvation plan to save.
I hope men everywhere will
Lift up Holy hands and pray.

Hold no anger or grudges, men;
May wives support your work,
Being not noisy or vivacious,
Above all, not painted flirts.

Paul gets quite serious in
The letter he writes, to say;

Woman was the first to sin,
And thus led man astray.

God sent them great travail,
Whenever a child is born.
But they can still be saved,
If to Christ they'll reform.

If man would say those things
On the earth these days,
The emancipated woman would
Practically blow him away.

CHAPTER 3

Now a man who'd be a bishop
Must be gentle, kind and wise,
Not quarrelsome or boasting,
Definitely not given to lies.

Never be arrogant or haughty,
Being a good teacher of faith.
Standing up to Satan and the
World, full of wisdom, grace.

With a wife kindly and gentle,
A family that's doing as told,
All standing for good, for
Christianity always is bold.

He may have only one wife, be
Sober hard working and loyal,
One who doesn't love money,
Cannot be drawn into quarrels.

As for bishops of the church,
Also for pastors and deacons.
God's church is duty bound to
Be Christianity's beacon.

Godliness is difficult, the
Example before us is Christ,
Who is our arbiter with God,
Serves as our guiding light.

CHAPTER 4

The Holy Spirit has spoken of
What will be in later times.
Followers of the devil will
Cause trouble and many crimes.

They'll tell lies and smile,
Claim it's sinful to eat meat.
Marriages they'll destroy,
Where possible they'll cheat.

But remember marriage is holy,
And everything is God's gift.
For everything God has made,
And a blessing of food is fit.

So be a better Christian; do
Not argue over foolish things.
To exercise the body is Okay,
Exercising Spirit gives wings.

We'll work and suffer much,
For the teaching of the word.
To be a pattern for men is
Glory to which we're spurred.

So preach scripture in church;
Use abilities God gave you.
Control your acts or thoughts;
To what is right be true.

CHAPTER 5

As paths of earth you tread,
Older men as fathers treat.
And to those younger ones, as
To beloved brothers speak.

Young girls consider always
As pure sisters in your minds.
Treat all older women as
Mothers and always be kind.

Now if a husband dies, and
His wife is left alone,

If she lives a saintly life,
The church should be her home.

Of course if she has children
Who are able to provide, then
Charity starts at home, it
Should be everyone's pride.

A Church must deal with care.
For a widow who's gossipy or
Flirty, may give members
The connotation of dirty.

If a widow can't find shelter
In shade of her family tree,
Her relatives are worse than
Heathen; that is plain to see.

If she be a church worker, at
Least sixty, she should be.
A record of good behavior and
In the community be at peace.

For young widows it's diffic-
ult to think only of other's
Needs. Better marry again
And guide a family's deeds.

If you have a minister, who
Preaches well and teaches too,
Earns all that you pay him,
Then pay him his just dues.

Do not condemn your pastor,
Unless two or more together.
To keep hot tempers under
Control is so much better.

Always live good clean lives,
Choose a pastor with care.
Some are not what they seem,
So make no mistakes there.

Drink some wine occasionally,
Only for a medicinal reason.

And remember some men's sins
Are only hidden for a season.

CHAPTER 6

Now slaves be not slackers,
Don't let God's teaching down.
Basics for Christian living
Are all wholesome and sound.

Anyone who argues this is
Really stupid and a fool.
If riches are too important,
The news is just a tool.

Would you be truly rich, if
Happy and good you are?
Bare and broke you came this
Way, so that is really par.

If food and clothes we have,
We really need little else.
But lusting for great riches,
Leads sooner or later to hell.

Some have forsaken their God
In search of quicker riches.
Timothy, you are God's man;
Beware those wayside ditches.

Work while the sun is shining;
Fight the battle for Christ.
Be patient and gentle always
Preparing for eternal life.

Do what Christ tells you to,
Until the day He shall return.
When Heaven reveals Him to
The Kingdom faithfully earned.

For God will reveal Him, the
Great King of the blinding
Light. He who can never die,
That Holy Father of Christ.

Tell the rich to use their
Money to help those in need.

It will store up treasures in
Heaven, count more than greed.

Timothy, my son, labor on at
Work God entrusted to you. Do

Not argue with any who claim
To know God's mercy on you.

END OF 1ST. TIMOTHY

2ND. TIMOTHY

CHAPTER 1

My dear son Timothy, this
Letter is from Paul,
A missionary for Christ
Ever since I got the call.

How I thank God for you, I
Thank Him both day and night.
I pray He'll keep you safe
And make your pathway bright.

He is my Father's God,
To whom my very life I owe.
And I know you love Him too,
For in many ways it shows.

Your mother Eunice loved Him,
Your grandmother Lois, too.
Stir yourself to strength and
Boldness that God gave you.

Fear will never faze you, or
Cause faith to waver. Strong,
You'll stand for Christ,
And God will show His favor.

God has shown His plan; He
Sent Christ to show the earth.
Even in jail I'm unashamed,
While awaiting His return.

Hold tight the eternal hope
And faith Christ offers you.
Guard well the Holy Spirit
Which lives within you too.

The Christians of Asia are
On a path that seems wrong.
Phygellus and Hermogenes
Deserted; Onesiphorus is strong.

God bless him and his family,
For in Rome then here again;
He visited me often in jail,
Brave in his Christian stand.

CHAPTER 2

Now my son be strong, with
Faith that comes from Christ.
Teach others what I've taught;
The time to believe is right.

Show truth to trustworthy men,
Who'll pass it on to others.
Be a soldier of Jesus Christ,
Be ready to stand and suffer.

Don't be involved in sin;
Be Christian tried and true.
No man can win the prize,
Unless he follows the rules.

Now Christ was born a man,
A descendant of David's line.
That he was God He proved,
He arose in three days time.

I've preached these truths;
It's why I'm in trouble here.
God's word is not in chains;
I'll preach it without fear.

I suffer to bring a good life
To those whom God has chosen.
I know He will never fail me,
Though I'm weak and broken.

Though our time on earth
Is filled with fear and care,
We'll live by His side, when
The roll is called up there.

Remember these great truths
And tell the wondrous story.
Bid them keep the peace,
As you lead them on to glory.

Be an honest worker so He'll
Say, "Well done, faithful one;
You have a place in heaven
And won the race you've run."

Teach people not to argue,
For heated words cut deep.
Such things cause heartache
And nights of lost sleep.

Hymenaeus and Philetus' argu-
ments caused doubt. They said
Resurrection had occurred
Caused some to fall out.

Like mountains, truth is firm.
Like a signpost proclaims, He
Knows those who belong to
  Him,
Can call each one by name.

In homes are many vessels, of
Gold, silver, wood and clay.
You can be like those of gold,
If from sin you stay away.

So avoid all evil thoughts,
You'll have a heart of gold.
Honor God with pure heart,
He'll gather you to His fold.

Preach courteous behavior;
Speak meekly and with truth.
So they escape Satan's clutch,
And seek eternal youth.

CHAPTER 3

This you should know my son,
Of trouble in the last days.
Of loving selves and money,
Proud, boasting of their ways.

Loving wicked pleasures,
Taking much but never giving.
Leading many to sin or sorrow,
And slothful in their living.

They'll claim to be religious,
But that's only for effect.
Leading foolish women astray,
And many lives they'll wreck.

They will always be learning,
But never know the truth. As
Jannes and Jambres resisted
Moses, so will these men do.

Remember the persecutions at
Antioc, Iconium, and Lystra I
Endured? God delivered me, He
Always led me safe and sure.

As a child you knew His word,
It made you wise and strong.
Truly follow Jesus' teaching
To be respected by the throng.

God inspired all scripture,
The righteous guide you need,
A shield from a wicked world,
Murder, mayhem, sin or greed.

CHAPTER 4

Now I solemnly urge you to
Preach the living word.
If convenient or not, from
Your lips it should be heard.

Stand firm, steady for Jesus,
And bring others to Him too.
Try to leave nothing undone
That you'd ought to do.

A time is coming soon, when
I'll be no longer near. But I
Have fought the honest battle;
So for Paul, have no fear.

In my Lord I'll soon know
That heavenly place of rest.
And there will be a starry
Crown, for I've done my best.

And I'll not be alone, but
In the company of many more,
Who've fought the good fight
To bring others to the Lord.

Please come visit me; come
As soon as you can. Demas
Has deserted me, I feel
I've been failed by man.

Only Luke is still with me,
Crescens has gone to Galatia.

Tychicus has gone too, and
Titus has left for Dalmatia.

Please bring a cloak I left
At Troas, with Carpus too.
Books are important also, but
The parchment I'd choose.

Beware of Alexander the metal-
smith; he is harmful to our
Cause. Nearly everything we
Did, he fought without pause.

When I came before the judge,
I found myself alone. All
Those I'd counted as friends
Had quite suddenly flown.

The good Lord stood beside me
And even helped me preach a
Sermon for the world to hear,
Kept me from the lion's teeth.

He will deliver me from evil,
Bring me to the promised land.
May the glory be His forever,
The greatest friend to man.

Say "Hello," to Priscilla,
Aquila, and Onesiphorus.
Erastus stayed at Corinth
Sick, and I left Trophimus.

Try to come before winter.
Greetings from your friends
And all. And now Farewell
From a loving brother, Paul.

END OF 2ND. TIMOTHY

TITUS

CHAPTER 1

I am Paul, the slave of God,
And the messenger of Christ.
Sent by God to preach to man,
So men may have eternal life.

He promised before the world,
And He always tells the truth.
So in his own good time, He
Chose me to reveal His proof.

So I write this letter, Titus
For you are like a son to me.
May you receive all of God's
Blessings and lasting peace.

Back on Crete I left you to
Do whatever was needed.
Appoint bishops and elders to
The church, make sure God's
Word is heeded.

Be sure to appoint family men
Who live above reproach. Who
Live their lives as godly men
And never break their oath.

Good, steady men of wisdom,
Who'll reason but condone no
Wrong. Who'll teach others,
Lead them in truth and song.

There are those who believe
Old Jewish laws must rule.
Only a strong and righteous
One, old fallacies can cool.

A person who's pure of heart
Sees good in everything. A
Rebellious and disobedient,
May to dishonor sink.

CHAPTER 2

As for you, Titus, be sure to
Speak up for all that's true.
Teach elders to be sensible,
To use love and patience too.

Teach older women the same,
Show no ill to others or im-
bibe. Help the younger ones
And thus improve the tribe.

Teach young men to behave,
And bring honor to their kind.
You'll be an example here to
Capture the growing minds.

Urge slaves to serve masters
With honor and no back talk.
Be trustworthy in all things;
Practice the Christian walk.

Eternal salvation is ours
Now, and it is ours for free.
But we must also realize
That we should sinless be.

For if we've won the prize,
And if eternal life is ours,
We must live godly lives, to
Deserve blessings showers.

Jesus died so this might be
Encumbent on us for sure. So
We live as God's own people
With our hearts most pure.

Teach your people with
Love for what's just. You
Have every right to correct
Them, if you feel you must.

CHAPTER 3

Remind the people, government
Should be honored and obeyed.
Always work an honest day
So you'll deserve your pay.

When the time was right,
God, our Savior, did appear.
Washed away our sinfulness
With His love and tears.

We didn't deserve it, but the
Holy Spirit was His gift. And
Because of His wonderful love,
We all got this great lift.

He who causes trouble should
Be told a couple of times.
Then ignore him completely;
This makes it his own crime.

Don't get involved in discus-
sions of Jewish laws or rules.
Theories are not worth it,
Are only the work of fools.

Everyone here sends the best;
May His blessings be with you
All. You have passed the test,
I sincerely sign this, Paul.

END OF TITUS

PHILEMON

CHAPTER 1

From Paul the jail bird, who
Preaches for Jesus Christ.
And from brother Timothy, to
Philemon, of our pride.

To the church at Apphia, our
Sister and Archippus a Chris-
tian too. I thank God, dear
Philemon, when I think of you.

I know your faith is strong;
It shows in the way you live.
As great strength and courage
To God's people you give.

Now I'd like to ask a favor,
I suppose I could demand, for
Onesimus, a runaway slave to
You, but to me, God's man.

He is like a son to me since
I owe him to the Lord. His
Loss to either of us is
Something we can ill afford.

His name means "He is useful,"
So I'll send him back to you.
I'd really like to keep him,
To help me preach good news.

Please think of his leaving
You, as for a limited time.
Now that he's returned, that
He's wiped out earlier crime.

That he is no longer a slave,
But a beloved brother to you.
If in any way he's harmed you,
I will gladly pay his dues.

Remember I brought you faith,
And thus you owe me your soul.
But that you do so lovingly
Is really my whole goal.

Please save a room and bed;
I pray to come visiting soon.
Epaphras sends his greetings,
A fellow prisoner and my boon.

Mark, Aristarchus, Demas and
Luke, who have answered God's
Call, pray the blessings of

Jesus Christ be upon your
Spirit. Paul.

END OF PHILEMON

HEBREWS

CHAPTER 1

In visions and in dreams
Often face to face,
God tried to tell our fathers
About His saving grace.

Through His Son He has spoken,
So we know more of His plans.
The fact that Christ is God
Leaves nothing now to chance.

He regulates the universe;
The sun and moon are His.
He shines with godly glory
And died for all our sins.

Beside the God of heaven, in
Great honor and glory He sat,
Becoming greater than angels,
And that is a proven fact.

He was called the Son of God,
By the God of everything. His
Firstborn came to earth, and
He said, "Let the angels sing."

The scriptures tell of angels,
Messengers swift as the wind.
Servants who are made of fire,
They were told to worship Him.

To His Holy Son God says,
"Forever will your kingdom

Last. You will be, though
Heaven and earth shall pass."

Never said He to an angel,
"Sit here by my side, while I
Put your enemies at your feet,"
That is what He told Christ.

He didn't say it to an angel;
They are only spirits that He
Sends to protect and guide
Those whom He's chosen of
men.

CHAPTER 2

We must listen carefully to
The truth that we have heard.
For the angels tell no lies,
They speak His Holy word.

There's no chance for escape,
If we shun the pearl of price.
We've been offered salvation
Paid for by our Christ.

Promises we've been given are
Backed by signs and wonders.
We'll be higher than angels
In a wonderful home up yonder.

In Psalms David asked, "Why
Is mere man your concern? Or

Son of man to have your honor,
By which the scriptures burn?"

He was lower than the angels
For a little while. But then
Crowned with glory and honor,
And basks now in your smile.

Though this is in the future,
We've seen Jesus on the cross.
And though He suffered there
For us, it was to Him no loss.

He suffered to be the leader,
Perfect to bring life our way.
We share His Father with Him,
And to call us brothers,
He's not ashamed.

According to God's scriptures
We'll be under Jesus' command.
He could only break Satan's
Power by being the Son of man.

So He can be faithful to God
And still show us mercy too.
He suffered by temptation,
A priest who knows what to do.

CHAPTER 3

By heaven you were chosen
Brothers; count Christ a high
Priest. He was faithful as
Moses by whom God was
   pleased.

Jesus' glory is greater than
Moses'; He's a faithful son.
He was there in the beginning
When this planning was begun.

Christ is in charge of God's
House; in us He is at home,
If we are true to Him and

Don't let our conscience roam.

Keep courage and trust Him,
Not as the Israelites did.
They cried for comfort, while
Actions cancelled their bid.

Forty years they complained
While with patience He pled.
They lost title to Caanan
Wandering wilderness instead.

So the Holy Spirit bids us
Listen carefully to Christ.
Be not as those children were,
Who paid a terrible price.

Be careful of your hearts too,
Follow not the glamor of sin.
Trust Him as your brother;
Live by Christ who is within.

Today is the time to listen,
And always trust in His name.
Christianity is a full vocat-
ion, never a careless game.

Remember those of Exodus, how
Their doubts led them astray.
Forty years of confusion, and
To idols they often prayed.

Many missed a land of promise,
Because of lust and distrust.
When Moses lead in circles,
They ate their own dust.

CHAPTER 4

God's promise still is good,
He offered us a place of rest.
But we should tremble in fear
Lest we fail the test.

Because, just like others
Who failed so long ago, any

Serious doubts or failures,
And we our hopes may blow.

Although we know He's
waiting
And offers a place of rest,
We must qualify by faith
And still live at His behest.

Joshua led the Children's
Children into Caanan's land.
It wasn't the place God meant,
Speaking by David back then.

Today when you hear Him call,
Answer with an open heart. He
Can see the man within and
Knows what we really are.

Jesus, our high priest under-
Stands, will mediate for His
Own. Let us live as He would,
To boldly approach His throne.

We hope to receive His mercy,
Pursuing good lives and deeds.
In love with perfection with
Grace in times of need.

CHAPTER 5

A Jewish high priest is only
A go-between for us and God.
Presenting sacrifices for sin;
It's all a part of his job.

Temptations and weakness of
Men are problems he knows.
He is elected of God; it's
Not just a vocation he chose.

Christ did not elect Himself,
As high priest of all men. He
Was chosen so by His Father,
It happened away back when-

God said, "Like Melchizedek
That Great king, you'll be a
Priest." But in Gethsemane He
Prayed to God He'd please.

Even God's Son had to learn
What it is to love and obey.
Proving through experience
Can lead us to better days.

I'd like to teach you more,
But you've a short attention
Span. Perhaps I'm a bore, but
Remember, I'm only a man.

Long you've been Christians;
By now should be strong. But
You're back where you started
Don't see right from wrong.

CHAPTER 6

Some things you well know, so
Let us move to others. You
Know of His teachings; you've
Tasted good news my brothers.

It's impossible to have known
All blessings of His glory,
Only to slip in the Christian
Duty, lest a change in story.

If you renounce Him in public,
Causing much stress and pain,
How do you repent sincerely,
Get in His good graces again?

If land produces for years,
Then grows thistles and weeds,
A farmer forgets good seasons
And good return on his seed,

Thinks of thistles and thorns,
Of how little profit it earns.
So condemns it to the flame,
And sets it afire to burn.

I'm sure, my friends you are
Producers; God will remember
Efforts past. Love and help
Others as long as life lasts.

Knowing the effort we made,
The wonderful life in store,
Look eagerly to God's promise
And wonderful time of reward.

Remember His word to
  Abraham
When He swore by His own
  name.
Abraham patiently waited, and
Thus gained considerable fame.

The oath of God is immutable,
We know our Lord cannot lie.
Accept His offer for eternity
And know we never will die.

We know our hope is assured,
Our souls locked in His love.
Christ, our Melchizedek, will
Assure our arrival above.

CHAPTER 7

Melchizedek was a mighty king,
And he was also a priest. He
Was King of the City of Salem,
The meaning of which is peace.

Melchizedek's name is justice,
He blessed Abraham one day.
And Abe gave him one tenth of
All the booty he had gained.

Fresh from battle was Abe,
Over many kings he had won.
Melchizedek never died or was
Born, like unto God's son.

That he was a great priest is
More than first you'd believe.

He is greater who blesses,
Than he who receives.

Melchizedek was greater than
Those priests of Aaron's day,
Who by law received tithes,
One tenth of everyone's pay.

Aaron's priests have passed,
But Melchizedek lives forever.
The Priesthood of Christ,
None can reduce or sever.

Why should God send His Son,
Who wasn't a Levite by birth?
Because rules must be changed
To save people of this earth.

The priests, called Levites
Of God, by Moses ordained,
Obviously couldn't save men,
And the Devil must be shamed.

So Jesus came down, risking
Eternal life for you and me.
He lives as a priest forever;
He's the kind that we need.

The priests of earlier times
Were weak, sinful as we are.
Jesus is sinless and eternal,
Able to lead us to the stars.

CHAPTER 8

What we have just said, is
Christ, the greatest priest,
With power of life or death,
Is here now for you and me.

The Temple of Heaven was
Built to His Father's demands.
Priests must offer sacrifice,
So Christ patterned after man.

He's much greater than they,

But here He could not serve.
They offer sacrifices here
As priests on earth.

It is a copy of that other,
When God told Moses long ago,
To copy the one in heaven, as
On the mountain he was shown.

Christ is important, for He
Passes God's promises to us.
He was unhappy with us,
Like metal riddled with rust-

The old covenant never worked,
So He said, "I'll make an-
other, and it will make
Them act more like brothers.

In their minds my laws I'll
Inscribe. At heart they shall
Know that they are my people,
If they'll so decide.

Forgiving, when they slip,
Sins, I will remember no more.
The old covenant is outdated;
A much better life is in store."

CHAPTER 9

That covenant with his people
Was kept in a beautiful tent.
In that tent was another room,
Here only a high priest went,

Called the tabernacle tent,
Made of many animal skins.
Here was the golden sensor,
And many other things within.

The golden pot of manna, and
Aaron's rod that budded. The
Tables of the covenant, and
The Ark that was gold studded.

And over it the cherubim, it
Shadowed the mercy seat. Once
A year they sacrificed, the
Duty of the great high priest.

A time of offerings for the
Priest and people too, to
Atone to God for sins, and
It seems, to pay their dues.

You see, the old system was
One of gifts and sacrifice.
What we have today is better,
And Jesus paid the price.

He was the priest who entered
Heaven's Tabernacle for us.
His blood He sprinkled there,
Upon the mercy seat, in trust.

Thus He secured our future
In that heavenly realm above.
Freed of the penalty we de-
serve, by Jesus and His love.

He was pure and without sin,
A sacrifice for anything. So
He died that we might live,
He gave us hope and wings.

Moses sprinkled the blood of
Animals on things he blessed.
Jesus' blood served for us,
As He passed a critical test.

It's destined for men to die,
And then face judgment day.
But Jesus only died that once
When for our sins He paid.

And He will come again to
Bring salvation to His own.
To all who waited patiently
With faith before His throne.

CHAPTER 10

Many times they sacrificed
In those days gone by. But
Never washed away the guilt,
Though every year they tried.

That was the price they paid,
For living under Mosaic rule.
The blood of animals cannot
Save; to us it seems cruel.

Jesus did the ultimate deed
When he put His life on line.
Did away with useless things
And gave us hope for all time.

We know the peaceful hearts
That His action brought to us.
The Holy Spirit brings proof
Of Christ's undying love.

He eliminated useless ritual
As practiced in days of yore.
As clean as driven snow, He
Remembers our sins no more.

Let us walk in the presence
Of the mighty God of creation.
Christ is there to light the
Way for men, tribes, nations.

In Moses' day the sinner met
Quick and fatal retribution.
Christ died on the cross, but
For deliberate sin, there is
No restitution.

Yes, if we've known His love
And still reject our Lord,
Then Justice will be swift,
And more than we can afford.

Many times you've suffered,
Sympathized with suffering
Friends, but at heart smiled,
Because you knew it would end.

Those who trust in God,
Must live by faith alone.
For that is the very trust
That assures our souls a home.

CHAPTER 11

Faith is a thing you know,
Although it may not be seen.
To those who do not believe,
It seems a worthless dream.

But to we who have the faith,
It's as sure as life itself.
A haven in times of trouble,
A sure and certain help.

By faith in olden days, the
Patriarch's did great things.
Wrote a history of God's love
And heard the angels sing.

By faith, Abel brought an
Offering surpassing Cain's.
Though Abel is long dead, by
That faith he gained fame.

Enoch also trusted God, and
By faith, death escaped. God
Was pleased he believed, from
Earthly cares took Enoch away.

Noah heard a weather warning,
Right from the very start. He
Saved man for modern times,
For he had a believing heart.

Abraham heard God's promise,
Followed the Master's plan.
Travelled far, faith his star,
He saw the promised land.

Isaac, and his brother Jacob,
Like Abraham lived in tents.
God was there in their hearts,
Wherever they lived or went.

Confidently they waited to
See a golden city of promise.
There was no room in their
Lives for a doubting Thomas.

Abraham fathered a nation,
Long after he was too old.
And Sarah by faith conceived,
Mother of millions, untold.

The folks I've mentioned
Never reaped a full reward,
But their home was heaven,
And the leader was the Lord.

Now to be called their God,
Our Lord is not ashamed. For
They have a home in heaven,
"The Holy City", is its name.

Abraham trusted God, as he
Built the Altar of sacrifice.
Here his son was to die, yet
Determined to pay the price.

He was sure God would save
This son he loved so much.
Ere the knife descended, his
Faith proved more than luck.

Again Israel's fate, hung by
Little more than a thread.
Abraham must have felt Isaac
Had returned from the dead.

By faith Isaac knew God
Would bless his beloved sons.
His blessings followed both,
Even as Jacob was on the run.

By faith Jacob blest Joseph's
Sons; few had faith as Joseph
Did. Moses' parents too, and
Their son from death was hid.

By faith, Moses left royalty,
Led Israel from its masters;
Through sea and wilderness
Trying for greener pastures.

Without faith, those Jews
Would've drowned in the Sea.
Without that faith of course,
They'd never've tried to flee.

And it was faith that brought
The walls of Jericho down. And
That was why they marched a
Week, circling the town.

Since she trusted God, and
Had faith in His great power,
She helped the spies, didn't
Die, nor did Rahab cower.

Now what more can I say, but
Think of those gone before.
They escaped lions and fire,
And by faith the deadly sword.

Some have won great battles,
While others ran away.
Others died by evil hands,
Rather than fail their faith.

Many were chained in
  dungeons,
In dens and caves others hid.
Deserts and plains they wan-
dered, as for glory they bid.

Often sick, hungry, wounded,
And ill treated too. They
Roamed the earth as aliens,
While Satan stirred his brew.

Too good for this world,
Those faithful men of old.
God saved their great reward,
That beautiful City of Gold.

CHAPTER 12

Now we have many witnesses,
Those of faith and of trust.
Let us avoid all wickedness,
Envy, lies, hatefulness, lust.

Let nothing slow our progress,
Or entangle in our feet. Run
The race that God has set us,
In our living be discreet,

And keep our eyes on Jesus,
He gave all, so we might live.
Consider His care for those
Wicked men who murdered
  Him.

Imagine His struggle and His
Sweating drops of blood. When
You think He's punishing you,
Then do not forget His love.

If He didn't love you, He'd
Let you go your errant way.
Keep yourselves from trouble,
Help to shape a better day.

Brook no bitterness among you,
Or ignore God as Esau did. He
Gave a birthright for food,
Too late made another bid.

Never have you had to stand,
Cold terror in your heart.
Flaming fire, gloom, darkness,
Blowing your mind apart.

On Mt. Sinai the Israelis did,
When God gave them His laws.
Staggered under God's
  command,
More scared folks you never saw.

Even Moses knew great fear
And was badly shaken that day.

But you've climbed a mountain,
And have come a greater way.

Honor God and obey Him well,
Our future is in His hands.
People did not escape when
Ignoring Moses, God's man.

"Next", He says, "I'll shake
The earth and heavens too."
Make sure your foundation is
Solid, or He'll shake you.

So let us please the Lord, and
Do nothing to raise His ire.
Serve Him with happy hearts,
For God is a consuming fire.

CHAPTER 13

Let all love continue, str-
angers help and plenty share.
Many have entertained angels
While they were unaware.

Do not forget the bondsmen,
Who spend their lives in jail.
If `twere you instead of them,
You'd feel weak and frail.

Marriage, an honorable estate,
Where there's no sin in bed.
But adulterers, whoremongers
Might be better off dead.

He said He'd never leave us;
That never will we be alone.
So as the Lord is my helper,
There is no fear in my home.

Never covet those things we
Like but cannot afford. Think
Of your Christian teachers,
Follow their ways with accord.

Remember Christ is forever,
Today, tomorrow He's the same.

So don't be swayed by riches
Or follow doctrines of shame.

Be willing to go beyond the
Calls of this world.
Our glorious home in heaven
Is of far greater worth.

So always stand upright, pray
For those who preach to you,
So they don't fail the Lord,
Or you'll be sorry too.

Pray that consciences will be
Clear and will stay that way.

May God's peace be upon you
Forever and a day.

May our Lord lead you, who
Gave his blood to bring us
Home. To Him be glory now and
Forever; may we never roam.

Brother Timothy from jail was
Released, so we'll visit you.
God's grace be with you, and
The Christians send love too.
Paul.

END OF HEBREWS

JAMES

CHAPTER 1

This was for the Christians
Over the world scattered, who
By dispersion were harried,
And many were badly battered.

James was a known pillar in
The Christian Church. This is
The first epistle, to keep
Them out of the lurch.

"Count it as joy," He said,
"If temptations try you sore,
Withstanding these problems,
Strengthens you much more.

Ask God for help when needed
And know it will be given.
You can be sure ere you ask,
You'll get help from heaven.

If you cannot ask in faith,
Knowing wisdom will come,
Then God cannot give help,
Your mind will be quite numb.

Though you may feel lonely,
Judged by this earth's rules,
Rejoice in being a Christian,
Not a member of Satan's school.

The rich man in his lust for
Wealth will pass away. For
As the flower in heat of sun,
He may not last the day.

He who resists temptation
Will receive a crown of life.
Never say God tempted you, He
Will not increase your strife.

Every man is sorely tempted
By his own lust and enticed.
If he stoops to active sin,
In death he'll pay the price.

Do not err my beloved ones,
Every gift comes from above.
We're the most honored of His
Creatures, proven by His love.

So be quick to listen
And be slow to speak.

Anger is a terrible thing,
And it makes a Christian weak.

So avoid all heated arguments,
And be ye not brash or bold;
Meekness and the love of God
Can surely save your soul.

Be doers of His word,
And be not listeners only. He
Who forgets a Christian duty
Will know a life most lonely.

If one claims religion, but
His tongue does not control,
His religion is in vain,
And he'll be out in the cold.

Religion in its glory, means
You'll help, and errands run,
Aid the poor and widows,
Guide true the widow's son.

Always maintain honesty and
Honor in everything you do,
Keeping clear of worldly vice,
And to your God be true.

CHAPTER 2

Faith is incomplete, if you
Favor the rich over the poor.
Your acts negate your faith,
It wrecks your hopes for sure.

The rich often ridicule and
Discount Jesus' name. They
Expect that all their riches
Will bring them lasting fame.

Love thy neighbor as thyself,
Be ye rich or poor. Helping
Him when help he needs, is
Your path to heaven's door.

To regard one and not another,
God's law you've transgressed.

With faith but no real love,
You've missed a crucial test.

If all God's laws you keep,
Yet slip in only one, it's
As bad as flaunting them all,
Your problems have just begun.

Though you do good works,
And still you have no faith,
One is zero without the other,
And you'll have lost the race.

Remember Ahab and Abraham?
Faith was joined with action.
That is the only way to God
And a life of satisfaction.

CHAPTER 3

Remember, my dear brothers,
Faith will control the tongue.
A source of pleasure, or from
Careless wagging, evil sprung.

A small bit in a horse's mouth
Will steer him where you wish.
A tiny rudder on a ship, will
Control its roll and swish.

The tongue is also small, but
Enormous damage it can do.
A tongue is like a flame of
Fire, unless managed by you.

We can train most animals
And also birds and fish,
So they will do our bidding,
Whenever we should wish.

But it seems no man, his
Tongue has really tamed. It
Often praises, then curses,
Bringing its owner shame.

Now you well know my friends,
This should never be; you can

Not get figs from a grapevine,
Or olives from a fig tree.

If you're really wise only
Good deeds come forth. If
You don't brag about them,
Goodness and wisdom are
    yours.

If jealousy or bitterness you
Exude, these are like lies,
Caused by Satan's treachery,
Making good intentions die.

Inasmuch as we are teachers,
We must not see others' faults.
Our sin would be greater, so
Let's cause tongues to halt.

Remember that all kindness
Is honest and sincere. Making
Peace and forgiving others
Must all start right here.

CHAPTER 4

Why quarrel, argue, and envy?
Why should you rob and kill?
The real reason you do is
You do not honor God's will.

Worldly pleasures are evil;
To God, are enemies most vile.
So now you are enemies of His,
If this has become your style.

The Holy Spirit is within us,
Warning against evil thoughts.
So give yourselves now to God;
Don't be angry or distraught,

Resist the devil; he'll flee,
He cannot withstand good.
Think oft' of the Holy Spirit;
He'll be where Satan stood.

Be ye humble before the Lord;
He will lift you up. Speak
Only good of one another,
And God will fill your cup.

You should love your brother
Is the message of God's law.
Make no plans without Jesus;
That would be the last straw.

Include Him in your plans,
In all you think or do.
Remember not doing
Right can be very sinful too.

CHAPTER 5

Look you rich men, who've
Ground poor men under heel,
Your wealth is false promise;
Great sorrow you shall feel.

Servants' cries fill the air
For you cheated in the past.
You only thought of pleasure;
This behavior must not last.

As for you dear brothers, who
Wait patiently for the Lord's
Return, do not be too anxious;
He comes closer as you learn.

Don't gripe about each other,
For remember no one is pure.
Let the good Lord judge; it
Is not our job that's sure.

Remember those old prophets,
All trustworthy and true. In
Spite of persecution and pain,
A perfect example to you.

Above all, dear brothers, I beg
You don't curse or complain.
By saying a simple yes or no,
You'll have much to gain.

If you are sick or hurting,
Approach the Lord in prayer.
For he is always waiting,
And He will meet you there.

The church should pray sin-
cerely, for those in troubled
Times. God will heal illness
And even forgive their crimes.

Remember the prophet Elijah?
How hard for drouth he prayed!
It was three and a half years,
Before again it rained.

Sincerely again he prayed,
That the rains now would come.
And again as he had asked,
It was truly done.

Now if anyone has slipped,
And you should lead him back,
You have saved a precious
Soul, by getting him on track.

END OF JAMES

1ST. PETER

CHAPTER 1

I'm a missionary of Christ;
This is Peter writing to you.
Good people driven from Jeru-
salem, dispersed former Jews.

It's a matter of destiny, my
Friends, He decided long ago.
He knew you'd be His, so sent
The Holy Spirit to bestow

The blessings of our God, so
Peace and grace multiplied,
For we were decreed by God
To be the family of Christ.

By His mighty power he will
Give eternal life to you.
Then by testing and by trials
Prove your spirit's true.

So now you are happy with joy
The prophets never understood.
Joy that comes from heaven
And can only make things good.

Much of what they prophesied,
Was to them so much Greek.
For often the Holy Spirit
Controlled their speech.

Wondered at the marvels they
Found themselves proclaiming.
Told they'd never see it but
Were never heard complaining.

The Holy Spirit told them the
Story way back then. The same
Spirit tells us now, and
This still is not the end.

You'll be more receptive to
Kindness when Christ returns.
Remember you're His children;
Our heritage He has earned.

God has no favorites, so you
Will be judged by what you do.
With faith and hope in Him
You'll know life is renewed.

This life we know is fleeting,
But our new home is forever.

Our happiness beyond this one,
Nothing can possibly sever.

CHAPTER 2

So get rid of all hatreds; do
Not pretend to be good. Be
Not dishonest or jealous;
Behave as Christians should.

Give up your old bad habits,
Try for full salvation. Come
To Christ, the living rock,
Our true Christian foundation.

You are now building stones,
So keep God's house together.
He sent His Son for a corner-
stone, to hold a bond forever.

To believers He is precious,
Because of Him some will fall.
If they'd listen to His word,
There'd be no trouble at all.

Your lives are full of beauty,
Since hearing His clear voice.
And remember you were called,
Through God's Royal choice.

You know you are God's own,
But you never knew Him before.
He's changed you for better;
Let's sing His praises more.

Now your real home is heaven,
But there are many evils here.
Avoid those wicked pleasures,
Save your souls from fear.

Let your lives be examples,
Of the good and perfect man.
Obey all laws explicitly,
According to God's plan.

Let the doubters ridicule;
Be convinced by how you live;

They too should serve our God,
And human failings forgive.

So respect your fellowman,
Love Christians everywhere.
Fear God, honor government,
And all your blessings share.

Of course you get no credit,
If guilty as charged. But if
You're beaten when innocent,
The reward will be enlarged.

He gave His life, suffering
As a way to treat our souls.
For lives of ease and comfort,
Are not the Christian role.

Christ bore our sins! Took
All those jibes and sneers.
In His body He took wounds
That you and I would fear.

Like sheep we wandered away,
But our savior kept us whole.
Returned us to our maker and
Is the guardian of our souls.

CHAPTER 3

You wives should try to fit
Into your husbands' plans.
To save his immortal soul,
Be responsible for your man.

A good life is better than
Beautiful hair or pearls.
Like the saintly women of old,
Let the banner of love unfurl.

Follow Sarah's example, who's
Husband Abraham's dream was
Hers. Husband, love your wife,
And never cause her hurt.

This thought I offer you, one
Loving family you must be. So

Prayers will be answered,
Doubts and terrors flee.

Repay good for evil; answer
Unkind words with respect. Be
Kind and thoughtful to others;
And God, your lives will bless.

If you want a happy life, keep
Peace with a pleasant tongue.
For therein lies your future
With songs of happiness sung.

In Christ, find kindness,
If harsh words come your way.
Just as His spirit visited
The prisoners, who were
Spirits from another day.

Baptism is not just a bath;
It shows we have asked for
Him to cleanse our hearts,
For us an impossible task.

Christ, we know is in heaven,
In glory at God's right hand.
He is our great intercessor,
The heavenly hope of man.

CHAPTER 4

A time will come when you'll
Suffer, as He did. But as
The body suffers, of sinful
Acts you're more easily rid.

All wild desires, which
Only lead your heart astray,
Will fade in importance as
You face a brighter day.

Your former friends will won-
der and may laugh with scorn.
But they must face judgment,
As you see a brighter morn.

It's why good news was given,
To those who died by flood.
So they might live in spirit,
If not in flesh and blood.

Love others as yourselves;
Be first to offer a hand. For
Time is short upon the earth,
For useful work by mortal man.

Things at which you're good,
No matter what it be, each
One has a special trait, and
Excels in some ability-

Preach and teach in Jesus'
Name, give God all the glory.
Be sure you give Him fame by
Telling the grand old story.

Be happy for all your trials
And be partners with Christ.
You can share in His glory,
Unattainable at any price.

Be happy to be a Christian,
To be called by His name. For
A time has come for judgment,
And we shall not be ashamed.

If we face judgment, what of
Those who never believed?
Trust Him who made you, so
You'll be relieved.

CHAPTER 5

Now I, who am an elder, exhort
You who are elders too;
Lead well the flock of God,
Which was entrusted to you.

Not doing so for money,
But with happy, healthy minds.
And you younger elders submit,
To the more aged of your kind.

Serve each other humbly and
Serve our God the same. For
He watches and preserves
You, that's better than fame.

Beware of attacks from Satan,
Who like a hungry lion prowls.
Stand firm before onslaughts
And never throw in the towel.

Christians around the world,
All go through sufferings too.
If you stand firmly at the
Trials, God will come for you.

Firmly He will make you
Stronger than you were before.

And to Him will be the glory
And great power forever more.

Now by Sylvanus I send this
Note; he is tried and true.
It should bring encouragement
To every one of you.

Your sister church in Rome
Sends all our love your way.
So as Christians, treat each
Other for many wonderful days.

END OF 1ST. PETER

2ND. PETER

CHAPTER 1

Now I, Simon Peter, proclaim
To all people of our faith,
God promises us all things,
From sin and lust will save.

But you must sincerely work,
And put other things aside.
By letting Him have His way
With you He will abide.

Dear brothers work to prove
Your fealty to our Lord today.
That you may never stumble
Or ever fall away.

The Lord has let me know
I'll not be here long. So I
Will keep reminding you while
Here of Christianity's song.

We tell no fairy tales; my
Eyes have seen His glory. In

Our hearts Christ the morning
Star lights up His story.

The Holy Spirit told the
Prophets what to say. For
Those prophecies came not by
Man, even on man's best day.

CHAPTER 2

There were false prophets too,
Who taught what was not so.
They caused trouble for God,
Were condemned long ago.

Even those fallen angels
Were condemned for sin.
So how could mere men
Ever get the better of Him?

Many of those of ancient time,
For greed or lust He drowned.
For a time, Noah's family
Were the only ones around.

From the city of Sodom, God
Rescued Lot, a godly man. It
Seems there were so few of
Them since the world began.

For he did not participate
In the orgies of that time.
But stood four square for God,
Steadfastly resisted crime.

The Lord can rescue you and
Me until that judgment day.
And punish those who need it
In His own inimitable way.

Some are willful and scoff
At those glorious ones of old.
But they'll pay a big price,
For being so wickedly bold.

Even the angels of heaven
Speak not with disrespect.
So these same evil teachers
Will learn to deeply regret.

They know so little about
The world they spurn, that
With the demons of hell, in
Eternal fire they'll burn.

They practice greed and the
Human family disgrace. They
Are like Balaam, whose beast
Of burden set him straight.

They are destitute of Spirit;
Their words are learned lies,
Preach a theory of liberty, but
Pollute the word of Christ.

Those who follow are misled,
For once they believed the
Lord, but now doubt; they've
More trouble than before.

CHAPTER 3

Many will be who scoff and
Claim nothing will change.
And life will never end, for
Their wits are quite deranged.

They forget that God made the
World. Floods are at His com-
mand. It's only by His loving
Will that the earth still stands.

But remember my dear friends
That a thousand years to Him
Is like a day of time to us
In this old world of sin.

Now He is surely coming, of
That you can be certain. And
No doubter can ever hope to
Hide behind a curtain.

As a fiery flash of finish
Is visited upon this world,
Those will be survivors who
Have God's flag unfurled.

So bring more souls to heaven,
In the time you have left.
Grow in Christian stature to-
ward the day of wondrous rest.

END OF 2ND. PETER

1ST. JOHN

CHAPTER 1

As the world began, He was
Here, God's message of life!
I've touched and spoken to
Him, the one we call Christ.

First He was with the Father,
And then He was shown to us.
This we've actually seen, and
It's not a matter of luck.

If you do as per this letter,
You can share in joys we know.
For our God is total light,
And we'll bask in its glow.

But if we say we have no sin,
We only fool ourselves.
Yet by confessing all to Him,
He is an ever-present help.

Christ shed His blood for us;
He'll cleanse us from wrong.
God says we all have sinned;
We're coming on too strong.

CHAPTER 2

And now my little children
From all sin steer clear. But
If you do accidentally slip,
Christ is our advocate here.

If we keep His commandments,
He'll be our go-between for
Sure. He will abide with us
And help to keep us pure.

He who claims to be Christian
But avoids the Christian way,
Is a liar and is last and
Will have the devil to pay.

I write no new laws; here is
One from an early time. Be
Sure you love your brother
And be safe from crime.

If you hate your brother, in
Eternal darkness you'll plod;
And stumbling blindly through
Life, you'll be far from God.

My children, young and old,
Because you have overcome,
The word of God abides in you;
Do not fear the wicked one.

Trust not in worldly things,
For this shall all pass away.
For those who love our God,
There is forever and a day.

You've heard of "Anti christ,"
And I say there are many now,
Who will pay Satan's price,
For they're liars, and proud.

They have left our ranks and
Against our Lord they preach.
So as far as we're concerned,
They are the devil's freaks.

But if you believe in Jesus,
Then you have the Father too.
Believe what you were taught;
That's the best you can do.

So my friends be sure to keep
The spirit within your heart.
If you listen to His truth,
Christ's love will not depart.

CHAPTER 3

How lucky can we be that
God should call us sons?

But the world accepts us not,
For they are doubting ones.

This great hope lives in us,
Because we know He's pure
Will return to take us home
For His word is sure.

If you abide in Christ, it
Is obvious to all about. But
He who hates a godly brother
Is following the devil's route.

For this reason Jesus came
To destroy old Satan's works.
And if you love as Jesus does,
You are children of the Lord.

So do not be like Cain, who
Killed his brother Abel. He
Was a follower of the devil,
Weak of character, unstable.

Be not amazed dear friends,
If the world despises you.
Because it goes the devil's
Way, honors not the truth.

Follow the loving example
Of He who died for us.
Keep your conscience clear
And live in perfect trust.

CHAPTER 4

My beloved friends, don't
Believe all you hear. There
Are many teachers around
Who aren't what they appear.

If you trust in Jesus Christ,
And agree He came as man,
You've been children of God
Ever since the world began.

But if you're against Him, we
Know you're on the devil's
Side. Have no love for God or
Man but serve Anti-christ.

They are of this world, and
Homage the world pays. But
We have come from God, and
The godly follow His ways.

A loving and thoughtful one,
We know that God loves Him.
For He sent His only Son
To save you and me from sin.

In the face of such love,
How can we ignorantly rest?
For our God has done much to
Make our lives well blessed.

Let us live in harmony with
The Holy Spirit in our lives.
With Him in us and we in Him,
Christian love will thrive.

If we live in Christ, days on
Earth will be complete. Those
Who scoff and know not love,
Or follow Satan can't compete.

We have no reason to fear
For God is on our side. And
When love like His surrounds
Us, only peace can abide.

If a man says "I love God,"
But doesn't love all others,
He doesn't love our God, and
He lies and serves another.

God has said we should love,
Not only Him but others too.
This is Christianity's way
And nothing less will do.

CHAPTER 5

Whosoever believes our God
Who calls Christ His Son,
Believes also the Holy Spirit,
And eternal life has won.

Whoever is born of God, he
Finds it an easy task to obey.
And these bear witness to men,
To follow Jesus is the way.

We know He is God's Son, as
Witness these voices. Three
Times by God, by the word,
And when our Heart rejoices.

If any man believes in Christ,
He believes what God declares.
Jesus is His Son, whose will
Leads to that home most fair.

I write this letter sincerely
To you who believe in Christ.
So you may know for sure, He
Is the way of eternal life.

He will listen for our call,
If we ask in good will for
Forgiveness for our friends,
Their lives He will fulfill.

We are all God's children
And he will keep us secure.
Because we also are Christ's,
His promise of life is sure.

So keep away from the devil,
Christianity's armor put on.
Hold His place in your heart,
I remain, sincerely, John.

END OF 1ST. JOHN

2ND. JOHN

CHAPTER 1

From John, the old church el-
der, to Syria, the lady that
I love, in Christianity and
Truth like that above.

And now, dear lady, I beseech
As if I'd sent a law unto you.
Listen to the Holy Spirit
And honor God in all you do.

I found you walking straight
Following the Lord's command.
This is the law of liberty
To take a Christian stand.

For many would deceive you,
Claiming Christ is a myth.

But we have the Holy Spirit,
Who is God's living gift.

Don't listen to the doctrine
Of Antichrist who beckons.
Do not help him in any way,
Or with our God you'll reckon.

Having many things to write,
I'd prefer this to your face.
And we'd have a joyous visit
On the wonders of His grace.

Sincerely,

John

END Of 2ND. JOHN

3RD. JOHN

CHAPTER 1

My dear friend Gaius, I'm so
Pleased with reports of you.
Of good you bring Christians
And all fine things you do.

Of how you help travelers, of
Friendship and good deeds,
How you help the missionaries,
Ministering to their needs.

You are working for the Lord;
Take no food or help from
Others. The duty is ours to
Truly be their brothers.

I sent a letter to the church
Praising your Christian ways.
Diotrephes, who leads them,
A stumbling block portrays.

When I arrive we'll discuss
It. Meantime do your best to
Aid and abet God's children
And pass the Christian test.

And so I'll say goodbye for
Now but hope to see you soon.
We send our love to you, and
May our Lord be your boon.

END OF 3RD. JOHN

JUDE

CHAPTER 1

This word from Jude, servant
Of Christ, brother of James.
To Christians everywhere, lo-
ved of God, chosen by name.

Dear brothers, I would speak
Peace and love but write in-
Stead. Love and righteousness
To defend for which He bled.

Some who teach among you say
You can do what you please
After accepting Christianity,
But Anti-christs are these.

Long their fates were written;
They've turned from Christ.
Think! God saved Israel, but
Many rebelled and they died.

Also, there were angels with
Good and loving ways. They

Turned to lives of sin, wait
In chains till judgment day.

Think of Sodom and Gomorrah,
Those lusting, sinful towns.
Of men who sought other men,
Their cities God burned down.

This should be warning enough
That there is a hell indeed.
Fallen Christians can get
There with astonishing speed.

These false teachers go on
Blithely in immorality.
Scoffing at the glorious ones
And laughing at authority.

Even the mightiest of angels
Rebuked not Satan over Moses'
Remains. He said, "The Lord
Rebuke you," for he Had
Nothing to gain.

These men mock and curse at
Things they don't understand,
Behaving worse than animals
Bear not the behavior of man.

Like the murderer Cain or
Balaam thinking of his purse.
Like Korah, they'll hear God
And die beneath His curse.

These are evil sinners who
Care not for others, leaving
Shame and disgrace behind,
Smear the name of brothers.

Seven generations after Adam,
Enoch said, "These men are
Malcontents, loud of mouth,
Foul of thought, evil bent."

You, dear friends, must build
Lives strong on faith. Then

Sure in the power of prayer,
For eternal life we'll wait.

Be merciful to the doubters;
Save them from the flames of
Hell. Be kind, save the souls;
Do not fall to their spell.

Hate their every sinful act;
Help them change their ways.
May God's glory shine on you
All your remaining days.

Now to our glorious Lord, may
All splendor and majesty be.
May He keep you in His care,
From your presence never flee.

END OF JUDE

REVELATION

CHAPTER 1

This is the book of Revelat-
ion of Jesus Christ, God's
Son. `Tis of the time which
Was, is now, and is to come.

To His servant John, God sent
His angel to prepare testi-
mony of Jesus Christ, and
God's word to us He'd bare.

Blessed is the listener who
Takes these things to heart.
This is not a time to doubt
Or pick His words apart.

To the seven churches in Asia,
May grace and peace be to you.

From God who was, is and will
Be, may great things accrue.

From the seven spirits, who
Are before His throne, from
Christ who made Christianity
The main theme of our homes.

He served faithfully and died,
That we might know God's love.
He made us priests unto God
And washed our sins in blood.

May every eye behold Him
  when
In clouds of glory He returns.
Then every man on earth
Will have a great concern.

For He is Alpha and Omega,
The beginning and the end,
And all the nations of the
Earth to His will shall bend.

I, John your brother, on the
Isle of Patmos had a vision.
And the one who lives forever
Gave me this writing mission;

To tell things to the seven
Churches of my time. I saw
Seven stars and candlesticks,
These dazzled eyes of mine!

The seven stars lead the
Churches of seven lands. The
Candlesticks depict churches
For the service of man.

CHAPTER 2

"Write to the churches," He
Said, "To the leaders say, I
Watched the work you did and
You earned my blessing today.

Yet there's something lacking,
For you love me not as before.
You work not as you once did."
By the Spirit spoke the Lord.

So let this message through
And take God's word to heart,
Or your church will lose its
Standing and be torn apart.

But those who are victorious
Eat from the tree of life.
Now to the church in Smyrna
I'm constrained to write,

The word from Him they killed,
But who lives to rule again,
I know of your poverty and
Slander you suffer from men.

They claim to be God's child-
ren, they masquerade as Jews.
But they often work for Satan
And in general are bad news.

Do not fear to suffer, Satan
Will try you soon. Stand str-
aight before your tormentors
And do not weaken or swoon.

He who is victorious need not
Fear the second death. So let
Everyone who can hear listen
With baited breath.

Now to the church at Pergamos,
To the leaders there I write,
You live in Satan's lair, but
The future still looks bright.

I won't ignore the practice
Of allowing Balaam's ways
To be ignored by your church,
In these enlightened days.

Your loyalty will mean little,
If your people still indulge
In sexual sin and idol feasts
As practiced by Satan's cult.

Let everyone who can hear
Heed the Spirit's advice; and
He'll eat the hidden manna
Of value greater than price.

Write this to Thyratira, to
The church leaders there. So
Says the Son of God, "Of
Your good deeds I'm aware.

I know how you love and serve
And strive to help the poor.
I know of your improvement
And how you try to do more.

But you're allowing Jezebel
To lead my servants astray.
Sexual sin is harmless, she
Says, as she leads them away.

I gave her time to change, but
She plays her dangerous game.
So I'll lay affliction on her:
Her followers will be shamed.

Unless they all repent, I'll
Strike her children dead. And
Each of you as deserved will
Reap your reward in dread.

But those who keep my tenets
Will be kings with an iron
Hand. Heed the Spirit's call,
You churches of the land."

CHAPTER 3

To Sardis churches I write
And to the leader declare, a
Message from the Son of God
And the seven Spirits there.

I know your reputation, as a
Church you are almost dead.
Strengthen what remains, for
You are at the point of death.

Once you actually listened;
You must turn to me again, or
I shall bring retribution on
You to be costly in the end.

There are some among you who
Tried hard to do what's right;
So they will walk with me
And will be clothed in white.

I'll name Him to the angels
And to my heavenly Father, too.
Listen to the Holy Spirit; it
Is what you churches can do.

Now to the church which is in
Philadelphia write; I've left
Before you an open door, and
No man can close it tight.

For you have kept your vows
And not denied my name.
But those who've joined the
World play a losing game.

I'll come unexpectedly so
Hold on to your crown. You'll
Inhabit the City of God;
Others in tears will drown.

To the church at Laodicea,
The leaders should hear this:
A Message from He who stands
Firm, the faithful witness.

I know you are not serious;
You think you've got it made.
You have things of comfort
And now can sit in shade.

But you are spiritually poor,
Miserably naked and blind.
My advice is to buy my gold,
Which was in the fire refined.

By your sinlessness, purchase
Snow white garments from me.
I only chastise those I love,
So open your eyes and be free.

I stand at the door and knock,
And if any man will open wide,
He'll join me in heaven and
From Satan never need hide.

The Spirit of churches says
Open your ears and hear. He
Who does as the Spirit says
Will have nothing to fear.

CHAPTER 4

I saw through an open door, a
Voice like thunder I'd heard
Before, said, "Come, I'll tell
You of the future and more."

Then the Spirit propelled me,
And I now sat in His presence.
He glowed like a diamond, en-
circled by a rainbow's essence.

In fact much like an emerald,
The glow encircled His throne.
And two dozen smaller thrones
Surrounded that of His own.

Twenty-four elders sat there;
Each was clothed in white.
Thunder came from His throne
Along with flashes of light.

Before Him were seven lighted
Lamps, as on a crystal sea.
Four beings stood about with
Eyes fore and aft, it was
Obvious to me.

One appeared like a lion, and
Another an eagle in flight.
One looked like an ox, and
A man, a very imposing sight.

Each had six wings with many
Eyes that seldom came to rest.
And they praised almighty God,
Who is the King they blessed.

Then those twenty-four elders
Fell down before His throne.
They cast their crowns, before
Him; they've claimed their own.

CHAPTER 5

In the hand of God I saw a
Scroll written on both sides.

And a mighty angel shouted;
His message I'll describe.

"Who's worthy," he asked, "to
Open the seven seals? None
In all creation could, and
Then I cried for real."

But one of the elders said,
"Stop weeping now and look,
The Lion of Judah prevailed,
And He can open the book."

So I looked and sure enough,
There was a Lamb on the floor.
He was before the beings and
The Elders, all twenty-four.

His wounds once caused death.
With seven horns, seven eyes;
To represent Spirits of God
We know have earthly ties.

Then He took the scroll from
The great one on the throne.
All creatures bowed to Him
And claimed Him as their own.

The four and twenty Elders
With harps and golden vials,
Incense of people's prayers,
Sang of His earthly trials,

Songs of tribulations, His
Blood bought their salvation.
He'd made them priests of God;
He'd rescued from all nations.

I heard all those in heaven,
In earth and sea below, gave
Him the praise and glory it
Was their pleasure to show.

CHAPTER 6

As I watched I heard thunder,
As a first seal He broke. And

As He unrolled the scroll,
A living being spoke.

He showed me a white horse,
Whose rider held a bow. A
Crown was on his head and
Off to battle he rode.

Another beast now bade me look,
The second seal he broke. The
Rider with a sword to banish
Peace a red horse he rode.

Anarchy, war, killing broke
Out everywhere upon the earth.
The third beast said, "Come,
This seal is the third."

He rode a black horse with
Balances in his hand. He pre-
dicted high prices for food;
Famine would cover the land.

The fourth seal was broken,
Its riders name was death.
His steed was very pale, and
Yet another horse was left.

The rider's name was Hell, a
Fourth of earth would control.
With war, famine, and disease,
They would take their toll.

The fifth seal was broken,
I saw an altar there. With
The souls of martyrs, truth
Of God on earth had shared.

"Sovereign Lord," they called,
"Thou who art holy and true,
When will you judge the earth
For what they put us through?"

CHAPTER 7

Calm were the winds with a
Great hush upon the land. Not

A rustle of the leaves and
The sea was smooth as glass.

Four angels stood upon earth,
Kept the winds in abeyance.
Another came from eastward
Calling them to forbearance.

"Wait," he cried, "do no dam-
age yet, harm not earth, seas,
Or trees, until God's people
Are marked by he who carries
His living Seal."

On people's foreheads they put
The mark that would tell, a
Hundred forty-four thousand
Of twelve tribes of Israel.

From the tribes they came,
Twelve times twelve thousand
Strong. From all over earth
Came a much greater throng.

Before the throne of God they
Stood thus, before the Lamb.
Crying thanks for salvation,
Palm branches in their hands.

About the throne and beings,
Those angels crowded round,
Calling, "Blessings, power,
Love to God," a happy sound.

"Who do you think the angels
Are?" an Elder asked of me.
"I've no idea," I said, "but
Please tell who they be?"

"They're of the tribulation,"
He said, "to serve God night
Or day. Jesus' blood washed
Them, will keep them safe.

Free from cold or heat, and
He'll wipe away their tears.

His manna they'll eat for-
getting terrors and fears.

CHAPTER 8

The Lamb broke the seventh
Seal; silence ruled in heaven.
Angels standing before God
With trumpets totaled seven.

An angel with a golden censor
Stood at the altar there. He
Was given a lot of incense to
Mix with His people's prayers.

Smell of prayers and incense
From altar to God ascended.
With the altar's fire in the
Censor to earth he descended.

Threw it on earth where like
Thunder it crashed. There it
Caused a mighty earthquake,
A storm of lightning flashed.

Now the seven angels prepared
Their mighty trumpets to blow.
And the first to peal a blast
Sent fire and blood below.

One third of all the earth
Burned to a hopeless crisp.
Grass was cooked and water
Boiled. I never saw a sight
Like this.

The second angel blew, a
Burning mountain fell in the
Sea. Much of the ocean turned
To blood, many fish deceased.

It sank a third of the ships
And made a chaos of the deep.
It made a hell upon the earth,
As God's wrath it reaped.

The third angel trumpeted;
A great flaming star fell,
Poisoned much water caus-
ing death to many as well.

Number four blew his trumpet,
A third of the sun blighted;
Moon and sun were darkened;
Nothing was easily sighted.

And I saw a lonely eagle, as
Through the heavens he flew.
Loudly he was crying, "Woe to
People of earth real soon."

CHAPTER 9

A fifth one blew his trumpet
And I saw a star that fell;
He was given the key to
The bottomless pit of hell.

He opened the doors thereof,
A great pall of smoke arose.
Sun and air were darkened
By reason of all the smoke.

To scourge the men of earth,
From the smoke big clouds of
Locusts came. Not to damage
Trees or plants, but ungodly
Men they cause great pain.

The tails are scorpion stings,
And men will seek to die. But
Death will give no release,
Although many will surely try.

As steeds of battle they came,
The heads wore crowns of gold.
Their faces like unto men's,
And these other facts unfold.

Hair like that of women with
Teeth like fangs of lions,

Noises like a great battle,
With breastplates of iron.

They'll sting like scorpions,
Hurt men a hundred fifty days.
Their king is of the bottom-
less pit and different names.

In Hebrew Abaddon, in English,
Destroyer of men. In Greek it
Is Appolyon. There are two
More terrors when this ends.

The sixth angel blew, a voice
From where an altar stands,
Before God, sent four demons
To wreck havoc upon the land.

Two hundred million men, I
Heard announced. The horses'
Heads were like lions and
Fire came from their mouths.

Tails like heads of serpents
Could bite, cause death and
Pain. A third of men died of
Sulphurous smoke and flames.

The people of earth erred,
And all their sins persisted.
Worshipping brass, gold and
Idols who never existed.

CHAPTER 10

Now another mighty angel
    came
Clothed in rainbow and cloud.
A shining face like the sun,
He cried with voice so loud.

Like flashes of fire his feet
Planted on shore and on sea.
Seven thunders answered his
Voice, it seemed to signal me.

As I was about to write, a
Heavenly voice bade me desist.
"Write not," Thunder said,
And an angel spoke like this.

His hand toward heaven, he
Swore by God of all things.
This shall be the end of time,
The seventh trumpet brings.

God's mystery so long withheld,
Will be shown to you and me.
Truth that the prophets told
Will now be plain to see.

Now the voice I'd heard from
Heaven spoke plainly again.
"Go get the book," it said,
"He holds within his hand."

So I went to the angel with
A foot on land and on sea,
When I took the little book,
He said this to me.

"Take, eat, and chew it well;
Taste bitterness in the belly.
It's like honey in your mouth
And will be as sweet as jelly."

And so I found it true, as
He bade me more to prophesy,
To speak to many people, to
Kings, nations and tribes.

CHAPTER 11

I was given a measuring stick,
The Temple was told to do.
Including where the altar was,
The number of worshippers, too.

"Not the outer court," they said,
"It'll be taken by the nations.
Forty-two months to trample,

But for my two witnesses I'll
Improve their stations.

Candlesticks and olive trees
Standing before the God of
All, are really two witnesses
Who will rally to my call.

Anyone who would hurt them
Will die by a flaming breath.
With power of rain or drought,
They can deal life or death.

When testimony is complete,
Satan will from hell ascend.
He will cause their deaths,
And it will seem the end.

Three and a half days, their
Bodies will lie on the street.
Men of many nations will gaze,
Comment on Satan's cruel feat.

But when the time has come,
The two shall rise and stand.
A great fear will grip the
People across the sinful land."

A voice from heaven will say,
"Come on up here and dwell."
While enemies watch in terror
But cannot break the spell.

From a great earthquake then
A tenth of the city will fall.
Seven thousand die that day;
Now men will heed God's call.

So the second trial is past;
There is yet another to go.
As the seventh trumpet sounds,
There'll be still another woe.

Great voices came from heaven,
Thanking God for things done.

In his battle with the devil,
He had undoubtedly won.

The four and twenty Elders
Bowed before Him and said.
"Thanks be you defeated Satan,
And you shall rule instead."

You are God almighty who was,
Is and always will be. It is
Time to judge nations and
Reward who've honored thee.

God's Temple in heaven opened;
The ark of His covenant I saw.
Voices, hail and lightning
I'll remember to the last
Breath I draw.

CHAPTER 12

A pageant appeared in heaven;
I saw a beautiful woman up
There. With clothing like the
Sun and stars in her hair.

She stood upon the moon
Giving birth in great travail.
Then appeared a great dragon,
A third of the stars captive
To his tail.

Seven heads he had, and ten
Horns, each head with a crown
Adorned. Ready to devour her
Child as soon as it was born.

A man child she bore, which
Was caught up to God's throne.
The woman fled to the wilder-
ness, but she was not alone.

Safety, assured by God for
Twelve hundred sixty days,
Where in safety and plenty
She had a place to stay.

In heaven there was war, and
Michael and his angels, fought
Against Satan and his angels,
Who battled there for naught.

They were cast upon the earth;
A heavenly voice proclaimed,
Gods power is great, and His
Servants all evil overcame.

So rejoice all ye heavens
And all you who dwell therein.
Woe to dwellers on the earth;
Wrathful Satan cannot win.

He knows his time is short;
His anger is a terrible thing.
He'd follow and persecute the
Woman, but God gave her
    wings

So she can fly away to safety,
And retire to her retreat.
So she'll be safe from Satan,
Those hundred eighty weeks.

Then the fiery serpent Satan
Did his best to put her down.
He flushed a great flow of wa-
ter toward her from his mouth.

But earth soaked it all up,
And the danger thus allayed.
The dragon then attacked her
Children who sincerely prayed.

CHAPTER 13

Seaward, a great beast arose
As my vision changed. With
Seven heads and ten crowns on
Its horns with wicked names.

Leopard like, with feet like
A bear's, and a lion's mouth.

The dragon gave authority to
Him and such brutal power!

One head had suffered a wound
Fatal to anyone else. But the
Wound had healed perfectly;
The beast was completely well.

Now all of the world marveled
And followed the beast in awe,
Because of all the miracles
By a creature they often saw.

Two and a half years he swore
And ridiculed God's name.
All the world he controlled,
As he ruled in imperious fame.

Those people of the evil one
Followed all his demands, for
Their names were not written
In the book of life or Lamb.

Now everyone listen! God's
People may be in prison or
Killed. This is a chance to
Overcome; let fear be stilled.

Then another beast I beheld,
As up from earth he reared,
With speech of a dragon and
Horns of a ram, he appeared.

All power of the first beast
Was his to use as he pleased.
So he made the world worship
At the first beast's feet.

Miracles he performed making
Flames to lance from the sky,
Deceiving men with his magic,
As the first beast stood by.

He made the people of earth
Make a statue of beast number

One. He gave it life and a
Voice which none could shun.

He caused all to be marked,
Rich and poor, slave or free,
On the right hand or the
Forehead, for all men to see.

Jobs were not to be had,
Nor could food be obtained
Unless stamped by his code
Or the number of his name.

Here is the value of his
Code when affixed. The
Numbers of his name equal
To six hundred sixty-six.

CHAPTER 14

Now I saw a Lamb standing
On Jerusalem's Holy mount,
A hundred forty-four thou-
sand more, the Bible count.

In heaven I heard singing
Like a beautiful waterfall.
Those who made up the choir
Had heard the glory call.

At God's throne they sang,
As pure as the driven snow.
They are undefiled, follow
The Lamb wherever he goes.

From the men of earth they
Came minus blemish or spot.
An offering to the Lamb
Consecrated to their God.

Through heaven I saw an-
other angel fly. Favor
God, extol His greatness,
I then heard him cry.

Worship He who made earth,
The heavens and sea. All

The wonders of His crea-
tions are obvious to me.

Another followed, shouting,
"Babylon is fallen, is down.
For she seduced the nations
And spread impurity around."

Now a third angel followed
In heaven's flawless skies
Crying, "Worship the creature
From the sea and surely die.

If you're marked by the beast
On forehead or hand, you'll
Be burned in sulphurous fire
In the presence of the Lamb.

Forever you'll suffer with
No relief day or night. By
Worshipping the awful beast,
You did not what was right.

So encourage God's people to
Behave themselves like saints.
Remain firm in trusting Jesus,
Have no qualms or complaints."

Now I heard a voice in heaven
Saying, "Write this all down.
God's martyrs are bound for
Heaven for reward and
  renown."

Then upon a white cloud I saw,
One sitting, called "Son of
Man", a crown of solid gold
And sharp sickle in His hand.

Then an angel from the Temple
Called out to Him, "It's time
To use the sickle; earth's
Harvest should now begin."

Over earth He swung a sickle,
The harvest was gathered in.

Then another angel from the
Temple joined work with Him.

The angel with power of fire
Cried, "Cut the grapes of
Earth. They are ripe to pick
And time to judge their worth."

In a winepress of God's wrath,
Grapes of earth they trod.
Blood flowing like a river
From the winepress of God.

CHAPTER 15

I saw great signs in heaven
Of wondrous things to come.
There'll be seven plagues by
Angels, ere His wrath is done.

It appeared an ocean of fire
Reflected on another of glass.
As I watched, victorious ones
Before me appeared to pass.

All were holding harps and
Singing as they moved along.
They were singing of the lamb;
This was also Moses' song.

"God's works are marvelous;
Thy works are just and true.
Thy judgments are manifest;
All nations will worship you."

Heaven's Tabernacle was
   opened;
Seven angels came from there.
Breasts with gold were girded,
Clothes white, pure and fair.

Each one got a vial of wrath
By one of those four beings.
The Temple filled with smoke;
God's glory was worth seeing.

CHAPTER 16

A mighty voice in heaven now,
To the seven angels called.
"Empty the deadly vials, God's
Wrath is no longer stalled."

An angel left the Temple; he
Poured his flask on earth.
All men broke out with sores,
Who had not put God first.

The second poured his flask
Upon the ocean's waves, and
Nothing within the sea from
A bloody froth was saved.

Rivers and seas turned bloody;
The third angel did his thing.
And I heard him declare, "Oh
Lord, it's justice you bring."

I heard the altar angel say,
"Lord your justice is true."
Number four poured his flask
Upon the sun, and fire
Scorched the earth anew.

The fifth poured his vial on
The ocean creature's throne,
Put his kingdom in darkness,
His subjects in agony groaned.

In the great Euphrates River,
No. six poured his flask. It
Dried up that wonderful water
So eastern kings could pass.

They marched armies westward
To fight the legions of God.
Now three wicked spirits from
The dragon in forms of frogs--

Spirits of the devils, who'll
Lead earth's kings that day,

Against those of almighty God
Are readying for the fray.

Take note, says God, "I will
Come quite unannounced, for
All who wait in godliness,
Joy will be pronounced.

For those who bring me honor,
Help bring glory to my name,
Will never live in nakedness,
Or will they ever be ashamed."

Earth's armies gathered at
That place called Armageddon.
Angel seven poured his flask;
A shout went up from heaven.

"It's finished," a voice said.
Earthquakes hit, lightning
Flashed, earth trembled and
Hail fell, thunder crashed.

Babylon split into thirds,
Heaps of rubble cities became.
The fierceness of God's anger
Made them all fair game.

Great Islands fell away, and
The mountains were not found.
Men were struck by hailstones;
Some weighed a hundred
     pounds.

Men madly cursed the hail,
Blamed God for their grief.
For ages He'd warned them,
Was patient beyond belief.

CHAPTER 17

One of those angels who'd
Poured the plagues on earth
Came over and talked to me,
Then he brought me forth.

He showed me a noted prostit-
ute who'd led earth's kings
Astray. People had followed
The kings and lost their way.

Now I saw a woman sitting on
A scarlet beast, with
Seven heads and ten horns,
Strange to say the least.

She wore bright clothing,
Gold jewelry, precious stones.
In hand a cup of obscenities
And not that alone.

On her forehead was written
"Babylon, mother of wicked-
ness," I stared in horror, for
She was total drunkenness.

She was drunk on the blood of
The Christians she had killed.
"Why are you surprised?" He
Asked, "there is more still.

She's a symbol of the city
That rules the kings of earth.
The beast she rides was alive,
From hell will know rebirth.

He'll rise from the pit to
Be banished to eternal hell.
Those who wouldn't believe
Will be too shocked to tell.

Seven heads are mountains on
Which the woman sits. So can
You understand this mystery?
For it will test your wits.

There are seven kings, five
Fallen, but one is yet about.
The other's time has not come,
But soon he'll quickly rout.

The beast that is and yet is
Not is the one she's astride.
He's number eight of seven,
And to perdition goes his
Power and pride.

The scarlet animal that died;
The eighth king is he. Having
Reigned before as one of the
Seven, doom is his to be.

Now those ten horns represent
Ten kings who come to power.
They'll rule with the beast
For a time that seems an hour.

They hate this wicked woman,
Will cause her desolate places.
Land and waters where she sat,
Are the people of all races."

CHAPTER 18

An angel came from heaven by
The light and power of glory.
"Babylon is fallen, is gone,"
He cried, telling this story,

All nations shared her filth,
Commerce profits by her greed.
A voice called from heaven,
"Come, people, or be deceived.

Her sins reach to heaven; God
Will repay her in kind. She
Brews trouble for many with
Problems that boggle the mind.

Reward her as she deserves;
Avoid her sins like a plague.
Retribution will overtake her;
`Twill be the news of the age.

Merchants and kings sorrow
Through the smoke of her fall.

She's fallen to the misery of
Failure as belle of the ball.

All those things of luxury;
Frankincense, ointments, wine,
Horses, chariots, slaves of
Imaginations throughout time.

Fruits of a lustful queen
Suddenly a thing of the past,
Those made rich by her folly
Will cry,"Alas, alas."

Her hauteur is no more; it
Is very low. They'll weep,
And wail in sorrow, for her
Past beauty doesn't show.

Rejoice, oh heaven this hour,
She got what she deserved.
Christians, prophets, apost-
les, justice has been served.

An angel threw a large rock,
And it splashed in the sea.
He shouted, "Like that rock,
Babylon will no longer be.

Never to make beautiful music,
Nor kill prophets and saints.
She deceived all the nations,
Ignoring people's complaints."

CHAPTER 19

I heard a multitude in heaven
Say, "Salvation, honor, glory
Belong to our Lord and God,
A just ending to this story.

Righteous is His judgment;
She was punished by His hand."
Then they cried "Hallelujah,"
As smoke rose from the land.

The twenty-four Elders and
Four beings knelt before the

Throne, crying "Amen, Lord in
Heaven, never leave us alone."

A voice from the throne said,
"Hallelujah, praise God great
And small. The Lord reigns
And decrees justice for all.

Let us be glad and rejoice
And give honor to Him. The
Lamb's bride is made ready,
Will be wearing fine linen.

These are ethics of saints;
The blessed are invited, to eat
With the Lamb and His bride
As in wedlock they're united."

I'd have worshipped him, but
He said, "I'm a servant like
You. We've testimony of Jews,
Lore of prophecy, good news."

In heaven I saw a white horse,
Its rider was faithful and
True. Eyes like flames, many
Crowns on his head, a name on
His forehead only he knew.

His clothing dipped in blood,
God's armies on white horses
He Leads. All were clothed in
Linen, white, spotless, clean.

His name was the word of God,
A sharp sword in his teeth.
He'd take no insolence from
Nations who'd get no relief.

This is what was written on
His robe and on his thigh.
"King of Kings, Lord of Lords."
An angel, in the sun stood by.

To birds he shouted loudly,
"Attend our God's great feast.

Feed upon the flesh of men
Of the greatest to the least."

I saw the evil beast aligning
The governments of the earth.
The angel on the white horse
And his armies came out first.

The evil one was captured;
His false prophet too, and
Cast into a fire of brimstone,
Where no harm could they do.

Then he upon the white horse
Killed those who were left.
And all the birds of heaven
Gorged themselves on flesh.

CHAPTER 20

An angel brought a key and
Locked the devil in the pit,
Bound him with a heavy chain,
A thousand years this was it.

A thousand years he'd be
Where he could do no harm.
Then for a little time again
He would ply his fatal charm.

I saw thrones of judgment
With souls of martyrs there,
Who'd not adored a beast, or
Had a mark on foreheads fair.

A thousand years they'd reign,
While all others would sleep.
Blessed of resurrection, which
Is the first one that's to be.

They'll be known as priests,
Serve Christ a thousand years.
And Satan will be loosed to
Cause more trouble and tears.

He will organize the sinners,
Numerous as sands of the sea.

They'll encircle God's people,
So they barely have a plea.

But God sent fire from heaven
And devoured Satan's legions.
Then he who had deceived
  them
Was cast into a fiery region.

The lake of brimstone where
The beast and sinners are.
Ever tormented they'll be, as
If banished to a blazing star.

Then I saw the judgment day,
As they stood great or small.
Everyone must answer God and
No chance to hem or stall.

From floors of seas they came,
From death or hell arose.
Every waiting soul was judged,
According to his earthly role.

Both hell and death were
Cast into the Lake of Fire.
This is the second death
From which no one can retire.

CHAPTER 21

Now I, John, saw an oceanless
Earth and new sky. The old
One had disappeared, and from
God came a beautiful sight.

The earth now was new, with
New skies, but no seas. The
City was New Jerusalem,
Too glorious to believe.

And then I heard the cry,
"God's throne's now among
  men.
He will wipe away their tears
And live in peace with them.

Yes, He will be their Father;
His children they will be.
He will end death and sorrow,
And from pain they'll be free.

Then He upon the throne said,
"I'm making all things new.
Now write everything down,
For I'm telling you the truth.

For I am `A,' and I am `Z.'
The beginning and the end.
And I will give eternal life
To those who are my friends.

Any who turn from me who
Worship Satan are liars. Mur-
derers will suffer eternally
In the brimstone lake of fire.

This is the second death
For those who died in sin."
Then one of the seven angels
Showed me heaven; I looked in.

As stones of precious metals
Were jewelled gates and walls
With names of His apostles,
All twelve of them in all.

North, south, east and west,
Stood three gates to a side.
The city as wide as long, the
Foundation with all twelve
Tribe's names inscribed.

Each side was the same,
Equal to fifteen hundred miles.
An angel held a golden measure
And did the job with style.

The dimensions were of a cube,
As wide and high as long. The
Thickness of the walls were
Two hundred sixteen ft. across.

The walls were of jasper in-
Laid with gems emerald green,
And many other precious stones,
More than I have ever seen.

Each gate was made of a single
Pearl, the main street of pure
Gold. Its glow will light the
Nations, so I was told.

There was no Temple to be seen,
For the Lord and Lamb are
There. In this glorious city,
They are worshipped
   everywhere.

Nations of earth will bring
Glory; its gates will never
Close. Night will never settle
There; it need fear no foes.

No evil is permitted there,
No abominations and no lies.
Only those with names written
In God's great book of life.

CHAPTER 22

Down the middle of main street
Coursed the River of Life. A
Dozen different kinds of fruit,
Lined the banks on each side.

Each month they grow a crop,
Medicinal leaves to heal nations.
With no evil in that city,
None there without salvation.

Before His throne they serve
Him, shall also serve the lamb.
There'll be no dark of night,
For the chosen of God's plan.

They'll look upon His smiling
Face; forever they shall reign.

Stamped upon their memories
Will be His holy name.

Then the angel said to me,
These words are sure and true.
God told His prophets of the
Future, and He is coming soon.

Blessed are whoever believe it
And all written in the scroll.
I'd have worshipped the angel
Whom to me all this had told.

"Nay," he said, "I'm only Jesus'
Servant, as you or prophets
Are, as are those who heed the
Truth and worship from afar.

Do not seal this writing," he
Said, "the time of fulfillment
Is near. When we will love Him
More, others will be in fear."

Wash your robes in holiness,
So you may enter the gates of
Life. For those outside have
Rejected God, are bound for
Eternal strife.

Jesus has sent His angel to
Tell the churches these things.
Jesus is David's descendant who
Will give His people wings.

Yes, He's promised faithfully,
That He is coming soon. May
The grace of our Lord Jesus
Be your certain boon.

Amen.

END OF REVELATION

About the Author

Always an avid reader of practically everything available, George Haveman says, "Poetry has been a favorite ever since my earliest recollection. It is something I always enjoy."

In 1977 he wrote and published "THE BEGINNING" a small booklet based on the book of Genesis. It was an instant favorite by many of his friends and acquaintances. So with general encouragement, the most natural move was to do the rest of the Holy BIBLE in verse.

After eighteen years spare time and a great deal of effort, "THE BALLAD OF THE BIBLE," was done. A take-off on the "LIVING BIBLE". All sixty-one books in the, verbiage of today, with parallel books and chapters for easy cross reference when curiosity demands.

"Once I got the idea," he says, "I felt compelled to push on to the best of my ability. I truly must believe, it was God's will to get the job done, because whenever I got stuck, a few seconds prayer always brought help from somewhere. I'm just not that sharp on my own. It became an obsession, and took up most evenings and holidays when I could get away from my work. My wife occasionally helped, and soon was as deeply involved as I was."

George and Lois operate a small commercial, airport which he built in 1946, in Michigan's lower peninsula.

At seventy four, still active as a flight instructor and mechanic, he says, "Airplanes were my first love. Who wants to give up at any age, when they're enjoying what they do? And writing this has been one of the greatest blessings I have ever known."